AF378715

BRUEGEL

Studio Vista London

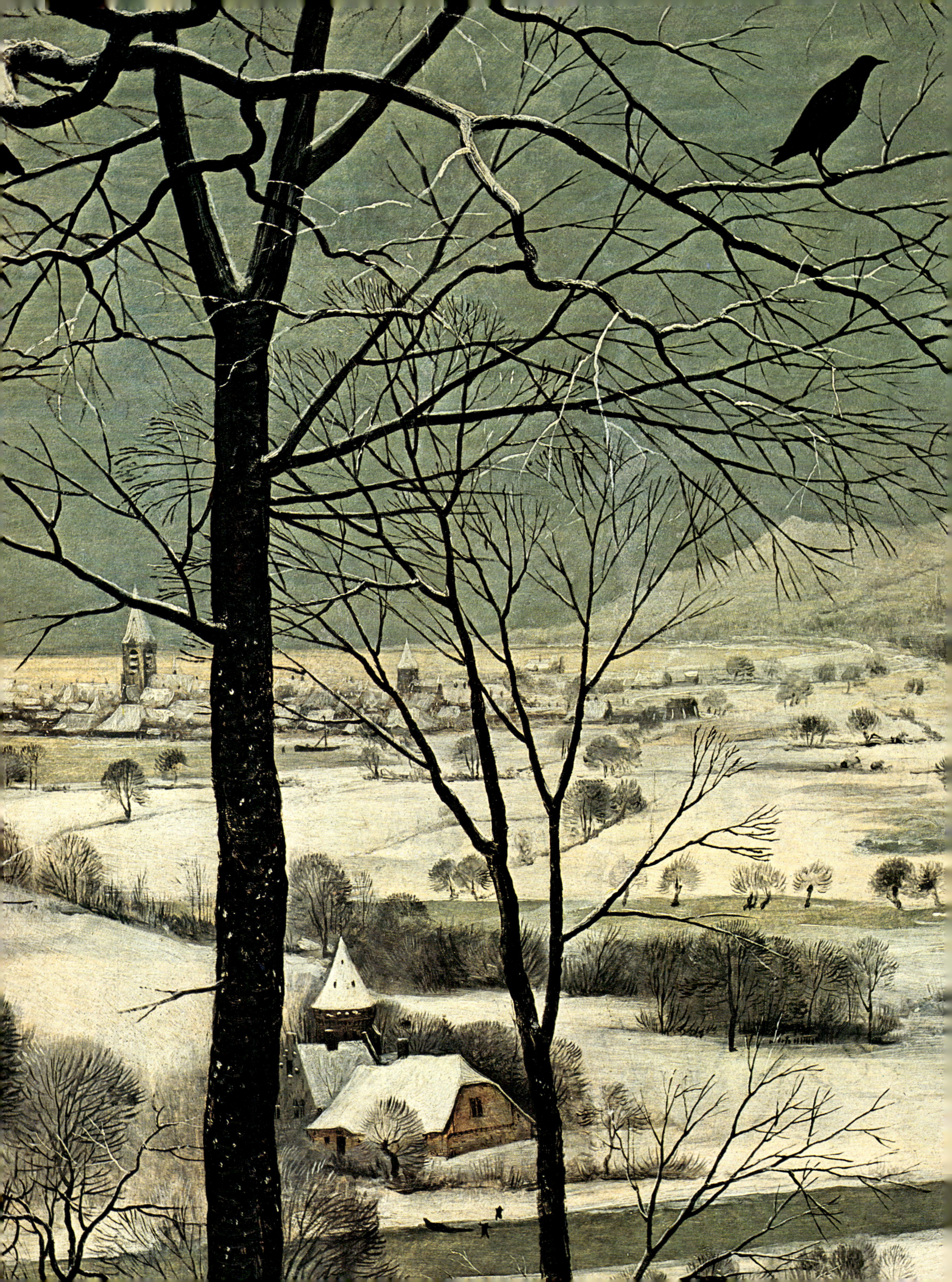

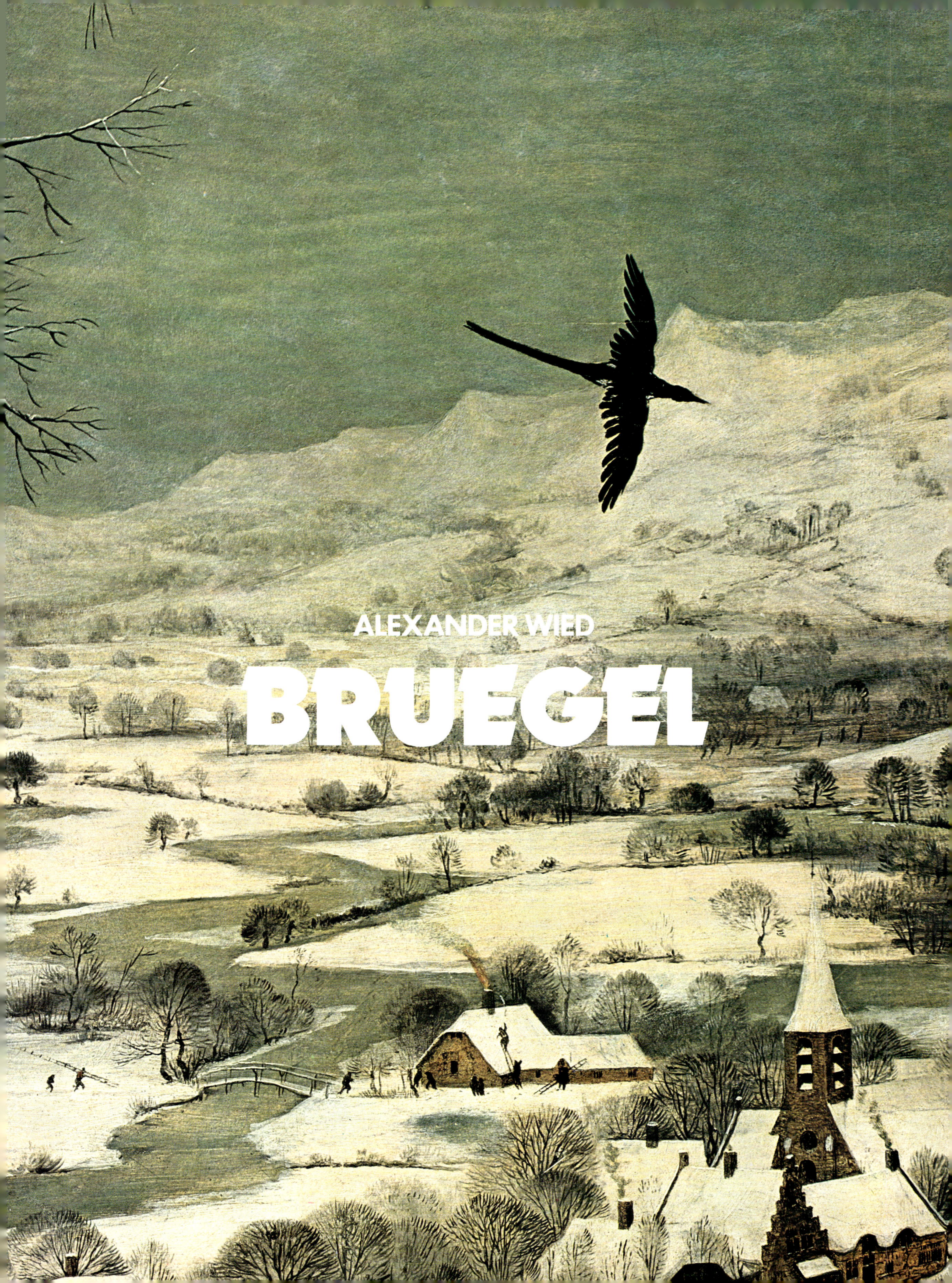

ALEXANDER WIED
BRUEGEL

Overleaf
HUNTERS IN THE SNOW
(detail)
Oil on panel; 117 x 162cm (40 x 63in)
Signed and dated: 'BRUEGEL M.D.LXV'
Vienna, Kunsthistorisches Museum,
Gemäldegalerie
See page 121

BRUEGEL

Text
ALEXANDER WIED

Translation
ANTHONY LLOYD

A Studio Vista book published by Cassell Ltd.
35 Red Lion Square, London WC1R 4SG
and at Sydney, Auckland, Toronto, Johannesburg,
an affiliate of
Macmillan Publishing Co. Inc.,
New York

© 1979 Arnoldo Mondadori Editore S.p.A., Milan
1st Italian edition: October 1979
Libri Illustrati Mondadori

First English language publication 1980

ISBN 0 289 70974 1

Printed in Italy by Officine Grafiche di
Arnoldo Mondadori Editore, Verona

Contents

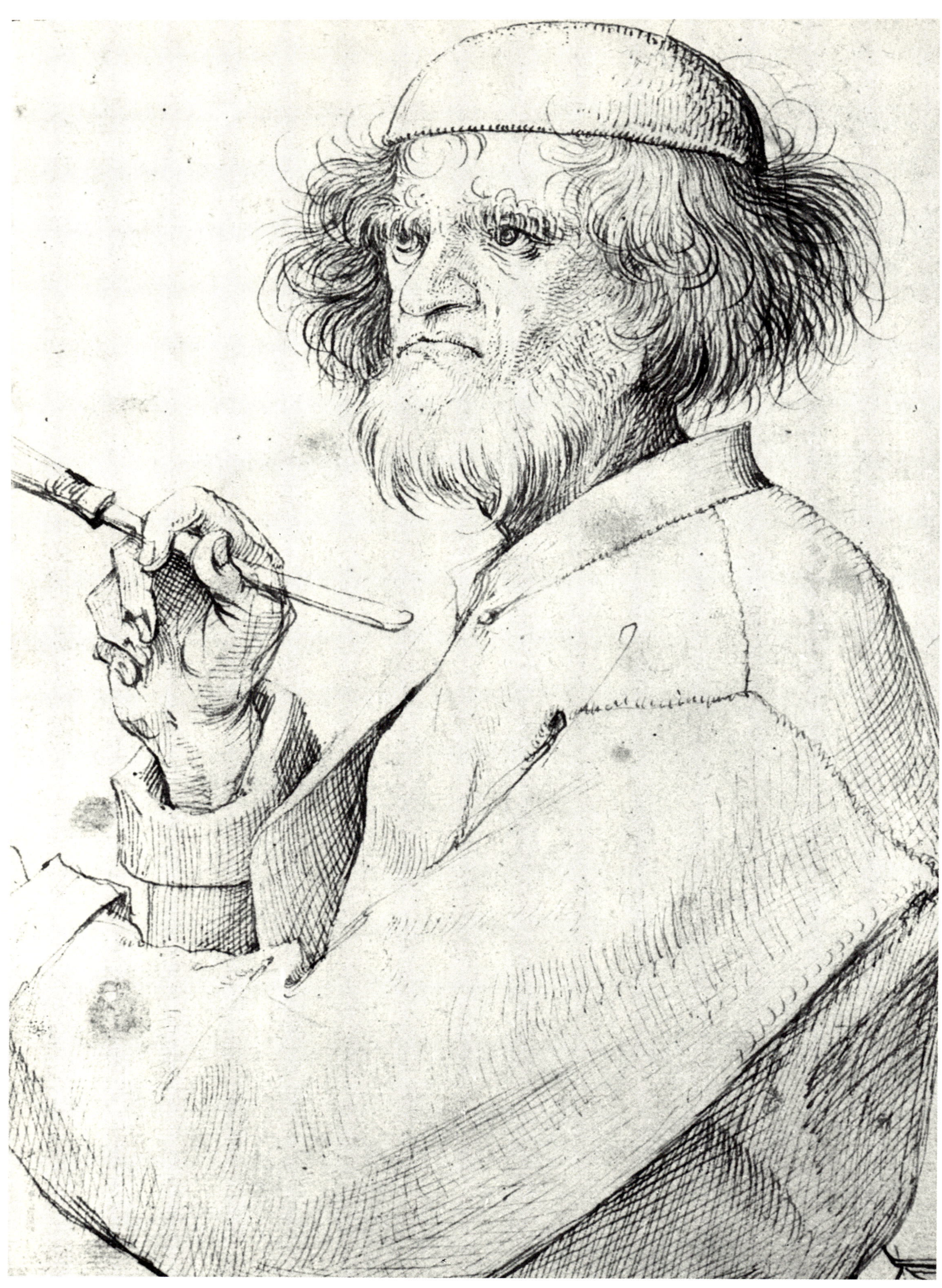

Foreword

It is only in the last eighty years that the art of Bruegel has been fully appreciated. Such discussion of his work as took place in the nineteenth century tended to dismiss the artist as second-rate and uninventive: 'He limits himself', according to Hymans, writing in 1890, 'to the more obvious things in life.' A century that based its appreciation of art on classical conceptions of formal beauty would not react well to Bruegel's scenes of peasant life. Furthermore misreading of a remark in van Mander's account of Bruegel gave the impression that the artist himself was a peasant, so his work was considered naïve in the simple tradition of native Flemish artists. In fact Bruegel was a talented and professional artist, whose work springs from a powerful and intelligent approach to his subject. Ironically, his art was also opposed to the Italian ideas of beauty current in his own day, and, since many of his pictures were for years in inaccessible private collections, it has taken a long time for the artist to have justice done him by his critics. Appropriately, it is in the 'century of the common man' that this essentially human artist has come into his own at last.

That Bruegel's art speaks to our own age is clear from the considerable number of books and innumerable articles that ave been published about him in this century, and the several important exhibitions, of which the most recent was *Pieter Bruegel der Altere als Zeichner* (Peter Bruegel the elder as a draughtsman) held in Berlin in 1975. As the study of Bruegel's art has increased, so has the discussion concerning its meaning and the artist's intentions, as revealed both in his paintings and, more especially, in his drawings and prints. The lack of almost any contemporary documents about the artist's life has meant that there is considerable disagreement on some questions of interpretation, and if we refer here quite often to the opinions of other writers, this is not so as to belittle the artist's achievement but to illustrate the relevance and interest his work can still generate. Charles de Tolnay, for example, has written at length on both the paintings and the drawings, and Professor F. Grossmann's ife work has been the compilation of a catalogue of the paintings. Other art historians, in particular Stridbeck, Stechow, Menzel, Auner and Friedlander, have joined in the debate, and their views will be discussed again in this volume.

While, as we have said, the interest in Bruegel's art is very much a twentieth century phenomenon, to which the considerable number of books on the artist bear witness, this can have its drawbacks. For no book can replace the original work of art, and it may be that the very availability – through books, reproductions, film and television – of images of original works of art can rob those works of their freshness. They can become too familiar, can cease to be unique. Similarly, the concentration needed for the real appreciation of works of art can sometimes be difficult to find amid the visual abundance of the modern world. All that a book can hope to do is to explain the beginnings of appreciation, and to pave the way for understanding the original.

ARTIST AND 'CRITIC'
Detail
Pen drawing in maroon on paper;
250 x 216 mm (9¾ x 8½ in)
c. 1565
Signed at bottom left, in lighter ink:
'BRVEGEL'
Vienna, Graphische Sammlung Albertina
See complete drawing on p. 127

Burgundy

A work of art may often be directly related to an event in history, even though history itself may only provide a partial explanation of a work of art. However, history is more than the backdrop to the work or performance of the artist: the interrelation of art and history is real, though complex, even if it must be admitted that for a long time historians were content to regard the fine arts as the surface decoration of the period they were studying. The history of the 15th and 16th centuries has ben particularly developed through the insights gained from studying art. One of the most important and influential historians in this field was Johan Huizinga, whose book *The Waning of the Middle Ages* studied in detail the courtly and social life of northern Europe, particularly the Dukedom of Burgundy. He made it clear that many of the ideas of thought and action that had for a long time been considered 'medieval' in fact survived well into the 15th and 16th centuries, in particular the notions of chivalry, honour and personal service. The late middle ages (or early renaissance, as you will) were turbulent, passionate and dramatic times. The growing conflict between the townships and the nobility was mirrored in the religious troubles of the time, and the growth of protestantism went hand in hand with the rise of the urban bourgeoisie. Nowhere was this change more evident, nor more vivid, than in the north of Europe, and Pieter Breughel's paintings survive as a tribute to the vitality and vigour of the period. But to understand his art it is necessary to look back a little at the history of his times.

The Dukedom of Burgundy had no more than four rulers during the years from 1363 to 1477, a period of just over a century, and those four generations saw the meteoric rise to power of the dukedom, and, in the end, its independence catastrophically crushed. At its height, no princely court in all Europe, not even the court of the King of France, could surpass the Burgundian court at Dijon in brilliance, in refinement – or, indeed, in lascivious excess – or in its bloodthirsty lust for power, that harked back to an earlier and crueller age.

When the last of the Capetians died in 1363, the Dukedom of Burgundy had reverted by feudal tenure to the French crown. John II of France (known as John the Good) gave it in fief to his youngest son Philip, who during his own lifetime became known as 'the Bold' – as did Charles, the last Duke of Burgundy. The next hundred years were marked by bloodthirsty rivalry between the Dukes and the French king and his vassals, ruthless expansion, brilliant successes and an alliance with England against France. The politics underlying these conflicts had a direct, personal character which we now find hard to imagine, for almost all those involved were in some degree related. One has the impression of an incessant family dispute over an inheritance.

Flanders, Artois and the free County of Burgundy with its capital Besançon went to the Duke by marriage in 1369. But the most important territorial gain in our present context was the acquisition not only of the northern counties of Hainault, Holland and Seeland in 1428 but also of the Duchy of Brabant and Limburg in 1430. In the same year Philip the Good of Burgundy married his third wife, Isabella of Portugal, and marked the occasion by founding the Order of the Golden Fleece, which after Burgundy's demise was to become the noblest order of the House of Habsburg. Thus the lush pastures and vineyards of the south joined the economically powerful industrial cities of the north, which were the main buyers of English wool for their costly fabrics: Ghent and Bruges in Flanders, Brussels and Antwerp in Brabant. The only task left now was to connect the two divided parts of the Duchy, Burgundy and the Netherlands, by acquiring either Champagne or Lorraine, thereby re-establishing the old Middle Kingdom of Lorraine. By 1435 Burgundy had become *de jure* what it had already been *de facto*: released from French feudal ties, it was an independent kingdom. The year 1447 saw Philip the Good negotiating with the German King Frederick (from 1452 the Emperor Frederick III) about Burgundy's elevation to the status of a kingdom. Charles the Bold was finally undone by his ruthless wars of aggression on the one hand, and the diplomatic cunning of his opponent Louis XI on the other. His overthrow at the Battle of Nancy in 1477 resulted in the disintegration of his kingdom. The French king took possession of Burgundy, Artois, Picardy and Hainault, while only the Netherlands went to the House of Habsburg by the marriage of the Burgundian heiress Mary to Maximilian of Austria. The Habsburgs' renowned matrimonial policy was continued with the marriage of Maximilian's son Philip the Fair to Joan (later 'the Mad'), the daughter of King Ferdinand of Aragon and Isabella of Castille. Though Philip the Fair predeceased his father the Emperor Maximilian, he left a successor to the throne in Charles, later the Emperor Charles V, who on Maximilian's death in 1519 became heir to the whole of the Spanish and Habsburg empires. The ruler with a Burgundian

Dominicus Lampsonius
PORTRAIT OF PIETER BRUEGEL
Copper engraving from *Pictorum aliquot celebrium Germaniae inferioris effigies.* Antwerp 1572.

RIVER VALLEY WITH MOUNTAIN IN
BACKGROUND
Pen drawing in maroon on greyish-blue
paper; 175 x 265 mm (6⅞ x 10½ in)
Dated bottom centre: '1.5.5.2'
Paris, Louvre
Slightly damaged, this is regarded as the first
of the three drawings of 1552 and therefore
the very first evidence we have of the master's
art. Above right is an unauthentic signature,
'*Bruegel fecit*', at bottom centre the date:
'1.5.5.2.'. The low focal point and natural
perspective indicate clearly that this is a
drawing from nature.

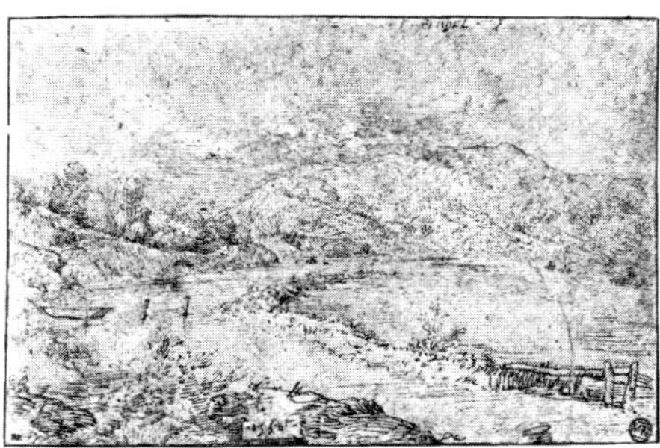

LANDSCAPE WITH SAILING SHIPS
AND A BURNING TOWN
Oil on panel; 24.4 x 34.8 cm (9 x 13 in)
c. 1552–1553
Dortmund, Becker Collection
This small painting was first attributed to
Bruegel by Grossmann in 1955. Although
the style is not yet completely mature, the
subject and its interpretation conform with
what could have expected from Bruegel
during the period with Clovio in Rome. The
later discovery of a second version of this
picture resolved the problem of its attribution to Bruegel. The composition is very
close to the landscape tradition of Patinir and
its subject is most probably the destruction of
Sodom, a very common theme at that time.
In this case the figures on the right would be
Lot, his wife and daughter. All his life
Bruegel loved depicting ships; it is not by
chance, therefore, that the first of his
paintings and also the one presumed to be his
last, the *Storm at Sea* (p.183), are seascapes.
The difference between these two works is
ample evidence of Bruegel's greatness.

grandmother, Spanish mother and German father had grown up as a Flemish prince
who was loved by his subjects and spoke their language, though at this time the
Netherlands were governed by his sister, Mary of Hungary. Unfortunately this feeling
for the people was not inherited by his son Philip II, who had been brought up in Spain
and aroused dislike on his first public appearance, a journey through the Netherlands
and Germany in 1549–1551. Unable to speak Dutch, he was considered 'arrogant and
aoof', as reported in a letter by Antoine Perrenot de Granvella, Bishop of Arras and later
minister to Margaret of Parma.

Antwerp

Antwerp's rapid rise to a city of world rank took place in the first half of the 16th century
at the time of the decline of Bruges. In 1487 this proud city had taken the Archduke
Maximilian prisoner and had several of his ministers executed. Frederick III moved
against Bruges with his army and both Antwerp and Amsterdam gave him support out
of economic envy. The port of Sluis was blockaded for ten years. 'The Italians began to
bring their own silks to Antwerp to sell them there and the Flemish weavers who had
settled in England also sent their goods there, so that the city of Bruges lost two important trading partners,' as Schiller said: 'Its haughty pride had long since offended

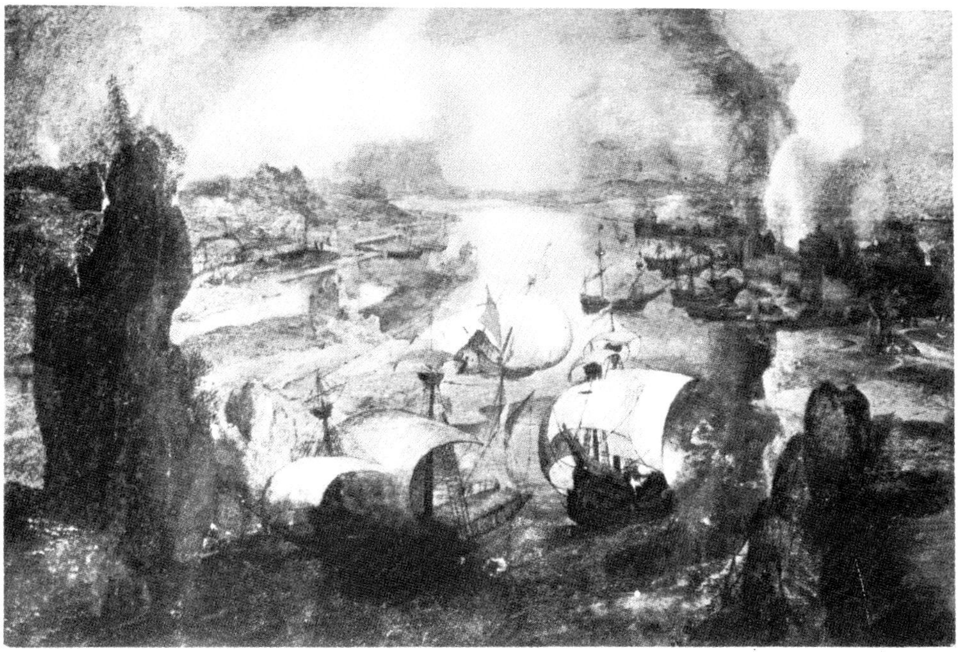

the Hanseatic League, which now also abandoned it and moved its depot to Antwerp. In
1516 all the foreign merchants left and only a few Spaniards remained.' But the crucial
factor in Antwerp's favour was the possession of a sufficiently deep and spacious harbour
at the mouth of the Schelde, for overseas trade was flourishing after the discovery of
America and the sea route to India via Lisbon and Africa. For example, 1503 saw the
arrival of the first spice ship to enter Antwerp's harbour. European princes established
factories, new branches were opened by merchant families such as the Fuggers and the
Welsers from Augsburg; the Spinolis came from Genoa, the Gualterottis from Florence,
the Bonuisis from Lucca. By 1550 Antwerp was already being called the 'diamond in the
world's ring'. At the same period a Venetian envoy, Marino Cavalli, declared: 'I mourn,
for I have seen Venice outstripped by Antwerp'. The brilliant and prolific administrator,
builder and townplanner Gilbert van Schoonbeke had a decisive influence on the city's
appearance. An invaluable source on this, as on so much else, is Ludovico Guicciardini's
topographical work *Descrittione di tutti i Paesi Bassi (A description of the Low
Countries*) which appeared in Antwerp in 1567 followed by a French edition in 1568.
He tells us that the city spent a million gold crowns on the external walls and moats.

Eight waterways led from the Schelde to the city centre. Seventy-four large and small bridges spanned the canals and over one hundred vessels could moor along the biggest of these without obstructing one another. The city contained two hundred and twelve streets and twenty-two squares, thirteen thousand houses, five city gates, and forty-two churches, monasteries, hospitals and other religious buildings. The main church of Notre Dame had a bell tower with thirty-three bells, the largest of which, called 'Carolus' after Charles V, was only rung on rare occasions. 1531 saw the foundation of Antwerp's famous stock exchange, the world's first international financial institution. Guicciardini also gives a detailed account of the city's system of government. He tells us that, properly run, it differed only slightly from the one attributed by Polybius to a 'true, genuine and happy republic', being a mixture of three orders, namely monarchy, aristocracy and democracy. This was to ensure that 'the prince retained his lands, persons of distinction their authority and the common people their power and weapons'. Apart from the various fairs which enjoyed their own special privileges there were also two horse fairs a year, combined with a skin market. Big businesses were actively encouraged. The printer Christophe Plantin from Tours, of whom we shall have more to say, settled in the city; Piccolo Passo of Urbino set up a majolica factory, merchants from Cremona built glassworks along the lines of those at Murano; Arnold van Ort started glass-painting workshops. There were thirty printing works, a public library in the town hall and a local gazette, *La Courante*, one of Europe's oldest newspapers. Almost every street had its theatre and the farces and allegorical plays of the *rederijker kamers* or chambers of rhetoric were in great demand. Over three hundred and fifty painters and sculptors were living in Antwerp in 1560. A poem in praise of the city dated 1561 says: 'Some one hundred years ago the cloth trade was all we knew about, but now they come to us from Italy and even India'. Or again: 'By virtue of its prudence and diligence Antwerp has become so mighty that neither Cairo in Egypt, nor Alexandria, nor any other city in Asia, Africa or Asia Minor, nor Venice in Italy, nor Lyons in France, nor Paris, nor London in England can be compared with it'.

Around the middle of the century it was claimed that not a single person lived in Antwerp who was not prosperous in his particular station. But this must have been something of an exaggeration, as we can see from one of Charles V's prohibitions: the poor were forbidden to beg in the costume prescribed for lepers, who for their part, according to Jedlicka, enjoyed the privilege of burying corpses rotting on the gallows.

Yet at the same time future events were already beginning to cast their shadow over Antwerp as it revelled in its luxury, and indeed over the whole of the wealthy Netherlands. For the people's innate urge for freedom was becoming enmeshed with the difficulties thrown up by the new religion. Protestant doctrines of every kind (Lutheranism, Calvinism, Anabaptists and others) had spread abroad, but were not going to be tolerated by the Catholic emperor. Charles V issued several edicts, the known and detested bills, or 'plakkaten', which provided for organized persecution of heretics. An edict of 1550 specified the death penalty for all heretics described as *'seditieuse personen ende perturbateurs van onsen staet ende der gemeyne ruste'*, ('seditious persons and disturbers of our state and the general peace'). Men were to be put to death by the sword and women by being buried alive (only if they recanted, otherwise they were burnt at the stake).

Thus, undoubtedly, it was no easy inheritance which Philip II assumed in the Netherlands, but the situation was aggravated by his lack of involvement with country and people on the one hand and on the other by his Catholic obstinacy and fanaticism, which went beyond all the claims of political good sense. When Charles V solemnly handed over the government of the Netherlands to Philip in Brussels on 25 October 1555 the latter let Cardinal Granvella speak on his behalf, with the excuse that although he understood French he was unable to speak it ell enough. Having resided unwillingly in the Netherlands for four years, Philip took ship for Spain at Vlissingen in August 1559, never to return again. Fourteen days before deparing he ordered the Council of Brabant to implement the edicts with all necessary harshness. Yet the Reformation, and especially Calvinism, continued to spread. As a result Philip II's sister Margaret of Parma, who was governing on the king's behalf, came under criticism for being too indulgent. Charles V abdicated in 1556 and the division of the empire that followed gave Spain and its colonies of Naples, Milan, the free county of Burgundy and the Netherlands to Philip II (1556–1598), and on the ther hand the German patrimonial lands and the imperial title to Charles's brother Ferdinand I. Philip was one of the most powerful monarchs in the world. Yet it was this very monarch whom a small but resilient nation defied with the courage of despair and finally overcame. The political situation in the Netherlands was growing increasingly tense: not even the recall of the hated Car-

LANDSCAPE WITH CHRIST APPEARING TO THE APOSTLES AT THE SEA OF TIBERIAS
Oil on panel; 67 x 100 cm (26½ x 39½ in)
Signed and dated: 'P. BRVEGHEL 1553'
New York, private collection
This is the first signed and dated painting by Bruegel; it was attributed to him by Friedländer and published for the first time by Tolnay in 1935. The theme is taken from chapter 21 of the Gospel according to St. John. It was executed during the journey in Italy and, like the foregoing picture (p. 9), has a compositional scheme very close to that of Patinir – certainly more so than any other landscape of Bruegel's. The figures are probably by Maerten de Vos, Bruegel's putative travelling companion in Italy.

dinal Granvella on 13 March 1564 could do anything to improve matters. Antoine Perrenot de Granvella – born in Besançon in 1517, Bishop of Arras for twenty-three years, minister to Charles V in 1550 and later Viceroy of Naples, Archbishop of Mechela from 1560 – was appointed to the Council of State in Madrid in 1555 and died there in 1586. Friedrich Schiller wrote of him: 'A penetrating, comprehensive mind, a rare facility in great and intricate affairs, this man wonderfully combined extensive learning with enduring iligence and untiring patience, and the most adventurous genius with an altogether deliberate practicality. The State was his concern by night and by day; un-sleeping and sober, he would ponder matters great and small with equally conscientious attention to detail. He would not infrequently keep five secretaries busy at the same time and in different languages, of which he is said to have spoken seven. A critical sense of reason, matured slowly over the years, expressed itself with force and elegance when he spoke, and all around would listen spellbound as the truth was declared in a mighty

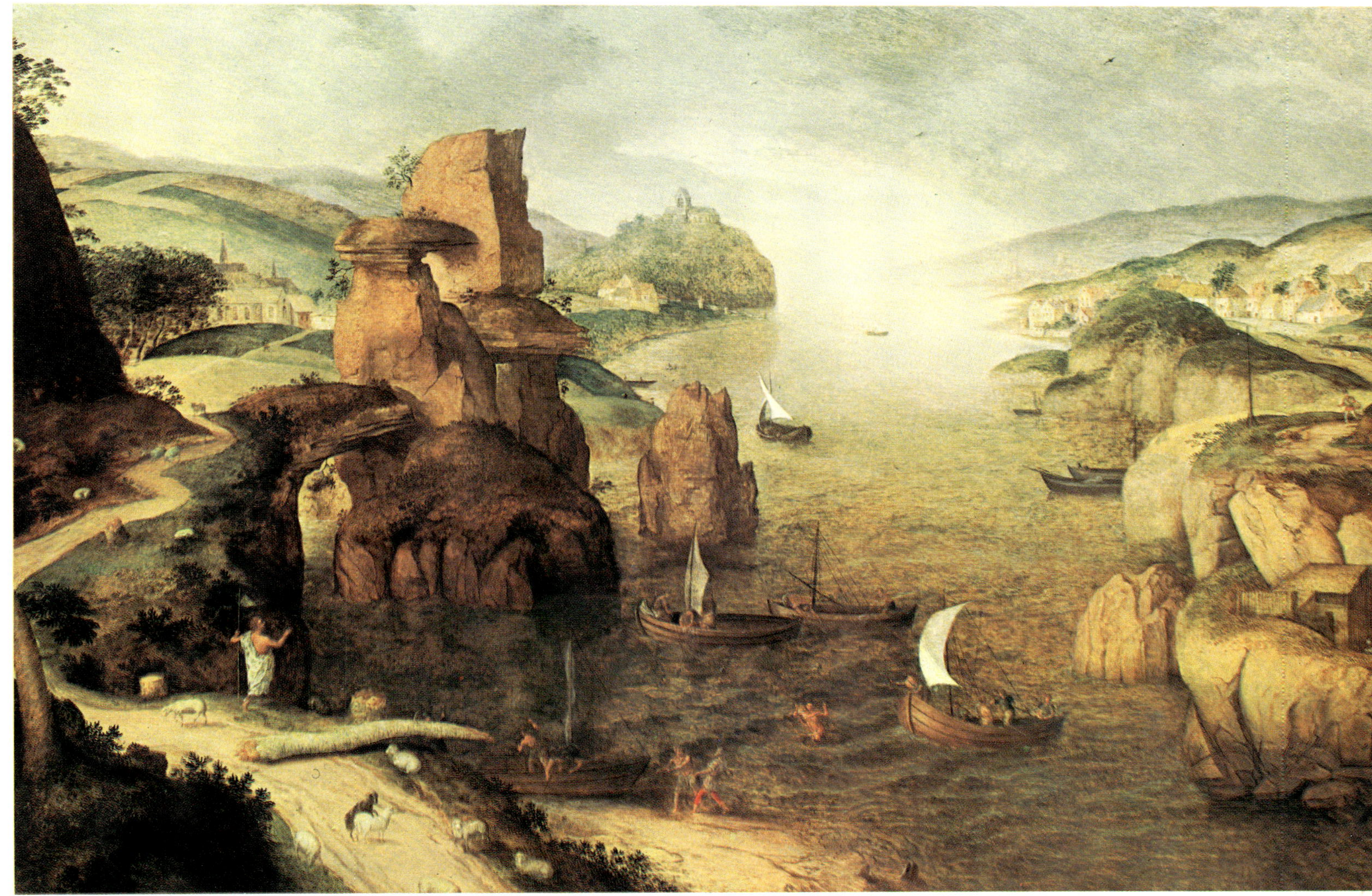

torrent of eloquence. His loyalty was incorruptible …' He was a considerable art collector and Bruegel gained his favour. Anthonis Mor and Titian painted portraits of him.

Count Egmont, who had travelled to Madrid to suggest administrative reforms to the king, returned therefrom thinking that he had won a major diplomatic victory. 'But in fact word had been passed around the Spanish court that everything must be done to win him over,' as Pirenne explains, 'As a result his stay there seemed like one long ecstatic celebration. Everything flattered his vanity. He found himself being received and treated both by His Majesty and by all the other lords and knights at the court with such overwhelming and attentive demonstrations of favour as had never before been enjoyed by any other private nobleman or retainer, however distinguished'. A sober examination of the papers brought home to the Netherlands revealed that they contained no concessions whatever. Anger and indignation rose beyond measure. The infamous missives drawn up by Philip II on 17 and 20 October 1565, in which he considered, among other things, whether it might not be more expedient to execute the adherents of the new doctrines in secret, stiffened the heretics' resolve still further. Even in Granvella's time there had been so many Calvinists in Antwerp that he wrote to the king telling him they were more numerous there than in Geneva. Charles V's daughter, Margaret of Parma, whose attitude as ruler was inclined towards tolerance, found herself in an exceedingly embarrassing position and declared she 'had better retire to her own domains since he [the king] was unable to set about anything properly'.

The people's discontent was brought to a climax by the sorry state of the nation's industry, critically affected by the emigration of workers but even more by the excessive price rises of 1566. Calvinist preachers added fuel to the fire of indignation until finally on 11 August 1566 the deeply exasperated masses broke out in open revolt to put an end at last to 'Roman idolatry' and destroy the 'idolaters' who were defiling the temple.

The flame of iconoclasm spread rapidly, beginning in the industrial districts of Mondschoote and Armentières. There were disturbances in Oudenarde on 18 August, Ant-

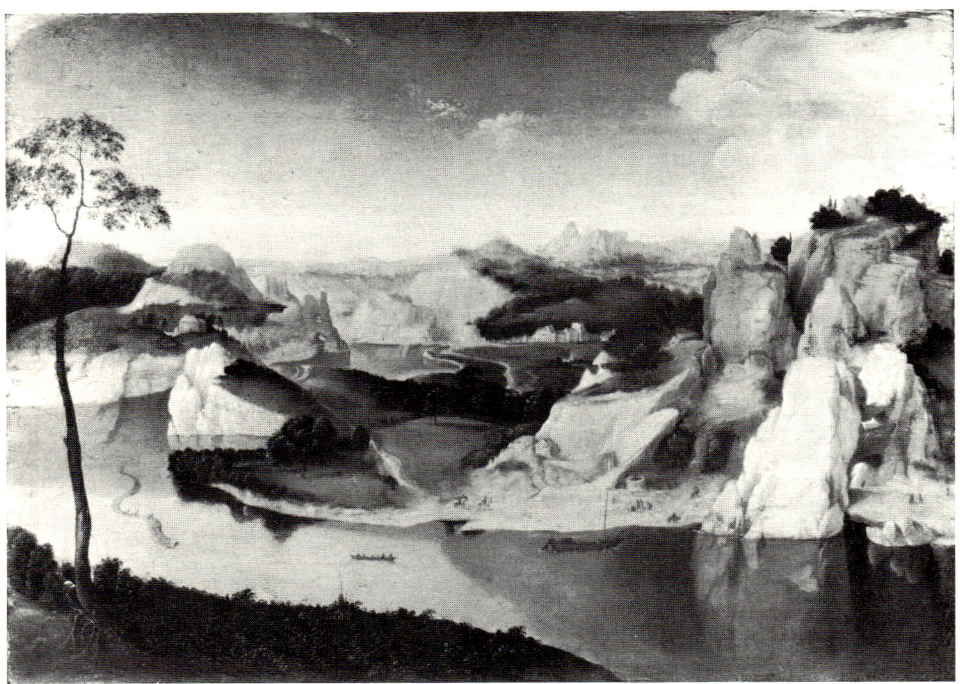

werp on the 20, Ghent on the 22, Tournai on the 23, Enghien on the 27 and then the trouble spread northwards to Zeeland, Holland and Friesland, and finally to Leeuwarden on 6 September. Löwen, Delft, Haarlem, Gouda and Rotterdam escaped the ravages thanks to the determination of their municipal authorities, while Count von Aremberg and Count von Meghem preserved Friesland and Geldern.

The most horrific excesses occurred in Antwerp, the damage done at St. Mary's church alone being put at 400,000 guilders. Brabant was not spared either. The churches at Malines, s'Hertogenbosch, Breda and Bergen op Zoom were despoiled of their treasures. Even the capital, Brussels, came under threat, and Margaret of Parma was already preparing to flee to Mons, kept in readiness for her by the Catholic Duke of Aerschot. Under pressure from the pillaging mob, concessions on religious observance had been wrested from Margaret which she was obliged to declare null and void once the situation had calmed down again.

The Calvinists thereupon recruited troops, as they had a war chest of three million guilders and asked the Prince of Orange, who had Antwerp under his control, to take command. William of Orange was hoping for support from German Lutheran princes and hesitated to join up with the Calvinists, who were now being harassed by government troops outside Antwerp. In the event he kept his troops inside the city, showing quite clearly that his motives were purely political rather than heroic. By 24 March 1567 the rebels' military situation had become hopeless. Counts Hoorn at Tournai and Hoogstraten at Malines now swore an oath of absolute obedience to Philip II, while Egmont had already come to terms with Margaret of Parma. But William of Orange refused to swear the oath and retired to Dillenburg, the town of his birth in the county of Nassau in Germany. According to Schiller: 'A few days later Margaret entered Antwerp in triumph and with all the pomp of the victor, accompanied by a thousand Walloon horsemen, all the knights of the Golden Fleece, all the governors and coun-

Netherlandish Master
RIVER LANDSCAPE WITH TWO ARTISTS DRAWING
Oil on panel; 51 x 68.5 cm (20 x 26 in) (fragment)
c. 1530–1540
London, National Gallery
This interesting picture, whose painter has not yet been established, is closely linked to an engraving of 1553 from a drawing by Bruegel showing a *River Landscape with Mercury and Psyche* (p. 19). Similarities exist in the figures of the two artists drawing, as well as in the landscape. Glück therefore thinks this painting could possibly be attributed to Bruegel.

Netherlandish Master
LANDSCAPE WITH THE BEHEADING OF SAINT CATHERINE
Oil on panel
Neither signed nor dated
Washington, National Gallery
The work made its appearance in Berlin in 1930, having previously belonged to the C. Benedict Collection as a work by Pieter Bruegel. It was published by Michel in Paris in 1931. After cleaning, various secondary figures which Glück and Friedländer had considered doubtful turned out to be unauthentic. Glück was inclined to regard it as a work of Bruegel's executed in Italy before 1553 in view of the original backing of poplar wood. The painting is now no longer considered to be a juvenile work by Bruegel but an interesting example of landscape art of the period immediately prior to his.

cillors, the whole of her own court and a large number of officials. She began by visiting the cathedral, which everywhere still bore the pitiful traces of the iconoclasts' fury, so that her prayers were mingled with the bitterest tears. Immediately afterwards four rebels who had been caught escaping were executed in the public market. Every child baptized in the Protestant way had to receive the sacrament again from a Catholic priest … By the end of April all the Catholic churches were bedecked even more splendidly than ever before … The common masses, generally prone to following fortune, now duly proved just as assiduous in hastening the downfall of the vanquished as they had been furiously behind their cause only a short while before. A fine church built by the Calvinists in Ghent vanished in less than an hour. Beams from the demolished building were used to make gallows for those who had laid hands on Catholic churches. Every place of execution overflowed with corpses, every prison with victims of reprisals, all the roads were jammed with refugees. No town was so small that it had not seen between

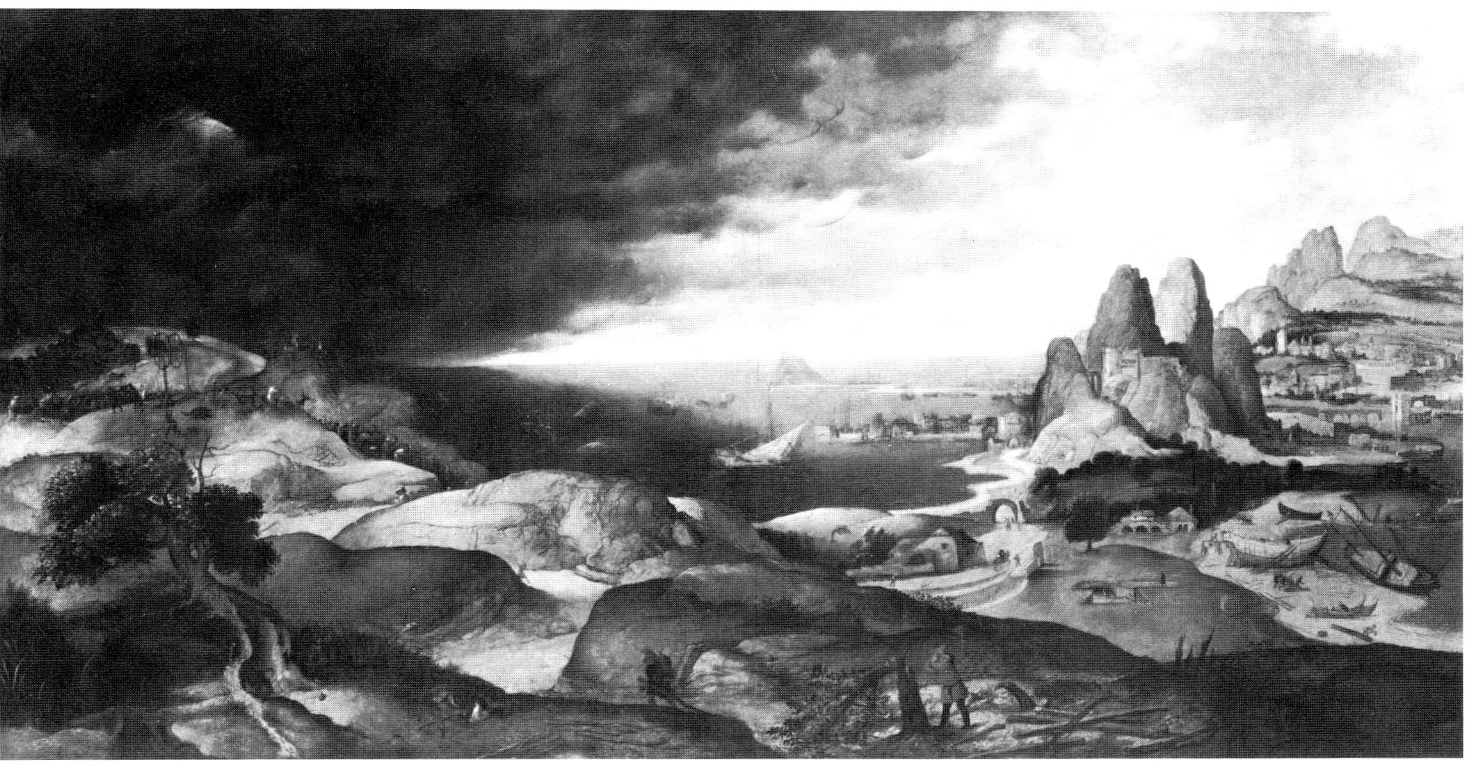

fifty and three hundred of its citizens led off to their deaths in this murderous year, not even counting those who fell into the hands of fanatics in the open country and were strung up straight away as common robbers without mercy or interrogation.'

On 30 December 1566 Duke Alba was ordered to take the Spanish regiments assembling in Lombardy to the seventeen provinces. The vanguard of Alba's troops entered Brussels on 9 August 1567. But his pitiless regency, intended as a punitive measure, came to nothing as a result of the provinces' indomitable striving for freedom and the bankruptcy of the Spanish State. The rebels had united in the League of the Gueux. 'Vive les Gueux!' 'Long live the beggars!' rang out the cry. But first came an appalling period of terror. Alba himself entered Brussels on 22 August 1567: Egmont and Hoorn were arrested immediately and beheaded on 5 June 1568. An infamous court-martial, the so-called *Bloedraad* (council of blood), was set up in which sentences of fanatical severity were passed. On 5 May 1571, for instance, the court announced to a number of convicted heretics that unless they were prepared to die as Catholics the tips of their tongues would be burnt off before their execution.

A resistance movement now began to form all over the Netherlands. But a new campaign led by Prince William of Orange in 1568 came to grief at the Battle of Heiligerlee and William fled to Picardy. In 1570 Philip II proclaimed a 'pardon', but this was recognized as no more than a farce and only caused further embitterment. The war went on until Philip's government became bankrupt in 1575, bringing a temporary respite. The seven northern provinces in the Union of Utrecht under William of Orange declared their definitive independence from Spain in 1579 (not recognized until 1648); and the secession of the southern provinces (later Belgium), which remained Spanish until 1714, took place in 1609.

To crown the misery of the age there was the permanent threat of hunger. Bad harvests would immediately have a catastrophic effect, for the corn merchants effectively controlled the market by charging exorbitant prices. Hunger was compounded by diseases like typhoid, scarlet fever, diphtheria, smallpox, leprosy, even the plague, and finally by syphilis, which had been the scourge of Europe since Columbus's return in 1493 and against which medicine was almost entirely helpless, as it was against many other diseases.

This then, was the milieu in which Bruegel passed his life. Politically and religiously a time of great troubles, with every man's physical well being at the mercy of crop failure, economic problems, civil strife or war. But history perhaps always paints the darker picture. It is clear that Antwerp, in Bruegel's lifetime, was a prosperous community that attracted artists, and offered to its residents a diverse intellectual life. Within the world

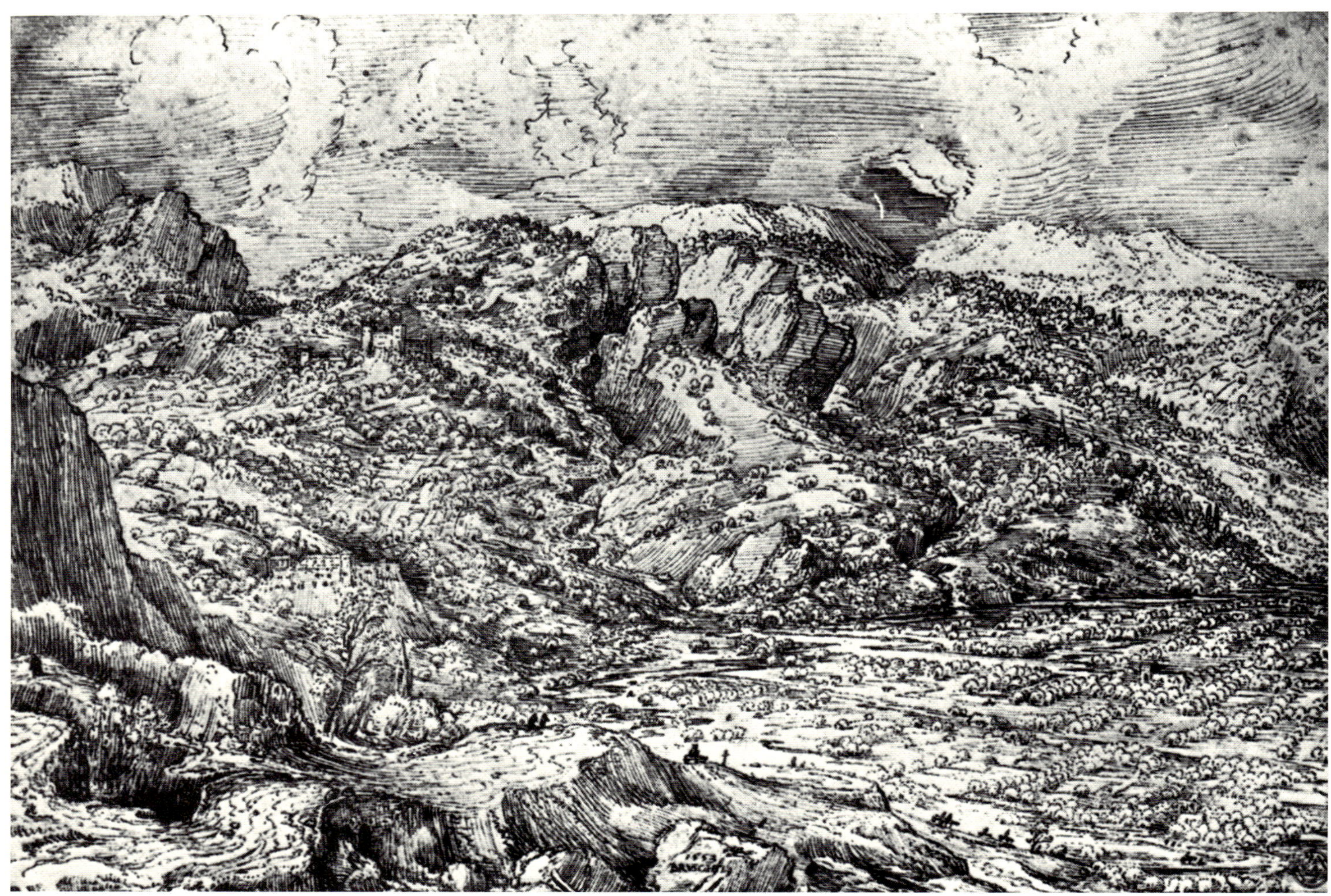

of painting, it is worth noting that there were two main schools. On the one hand artists were assimilating the ideas of the late Italian Renaissance, particularly as regards portrayal of the human figure. The chief exponents of this Italianate or Romanist school were Jan Gossaert, Pieter Cocke van Aelst, Frans Floris and Willem Key. On the other hand there were artists who were trying to develop the native traditions of late Gothic art, particularly Joachim Patinir. Artists such as Quinten Massys, Joos van Cleef, Jan van Amstel and Pieter Aertsen, formed part of this latter group, with a particular interest in landscape painting. Both these schools of art were to influence Pieter Bruegel.

The Life of Pieter Bruegel

Surprisingly, nothing is known about the life of one of the first great modern painters apart from the meagre and partially incorrect biography given by Carel van Mander, the 'Dutch Vasari', in his *Schilderboeck*, published in Haarlem in 1604. Even more astonishing is the fact that Bruegel himself left nothing in writing: no diary, letters, will, papers – none of the things we could have expected from a classically educated painter of this period and such as we have from Leonardo, Michelangelo or Dürer. The latest research has revealed that not even the handwriting of the colour specifications for the *'naar het leven'* studies, up to now regarded as Bruegel's 'flowing classical hand', is definitely attributable to him. So, apart from a few laconic entries in official documents, we are left with van Mander's biography and the works themselves as a basis for discussion. In view of this, the following reproduces the whole of van Mander's text, to

ALPINE LANDSCAPE
Pen drawing in maroon on white paper speckled with mould; 236 x 343 mm (9¼ x 13½ in)
Signed and dated at bottom centre: '1553 / BRVEGHEL'
Paris, Louvre
The authenticity of the signature is in doubt; there are also differing opinions about whether this is a drawing from nature or a studio composition. The work contains hints of Venetian landscape (Campagnola, Titian), it belonged to P. J. Mariette, one of the best-known collectors and publishers of 18th-century French art who mentions it in his *Primer* (published posthumously in Paris in 1851–1853). It is probably a preparatory drawing for an engraving.

LARGE RHINE LANDSCAPE
Pen drawing in maroon tones on white paper; 350 x 435 mm (13 x 17 in)
c. 1555–1560
Signed at bottom right: 'P. BRVEG..L'
New York, Pierpont Morgan Library
Not only the biggest but also the richest and most complete of Bruegel's landscape drawings. The work only came to light in 1952 and was sold by Christie's of London to the Pierpont Morgan Library. Benesch has identified this landscape as the Rhine valley between Trums and Ilanz, with the castle of Jorgensberg and the village of Ruis. However, this involves one or two problems. It would mean that on his return journey from Italy Bruegel chose the difficult route to the east via Chur and Innsbruck after crossing the St. Gotthard. This is beyond doubt a study from nature finished in the studio.

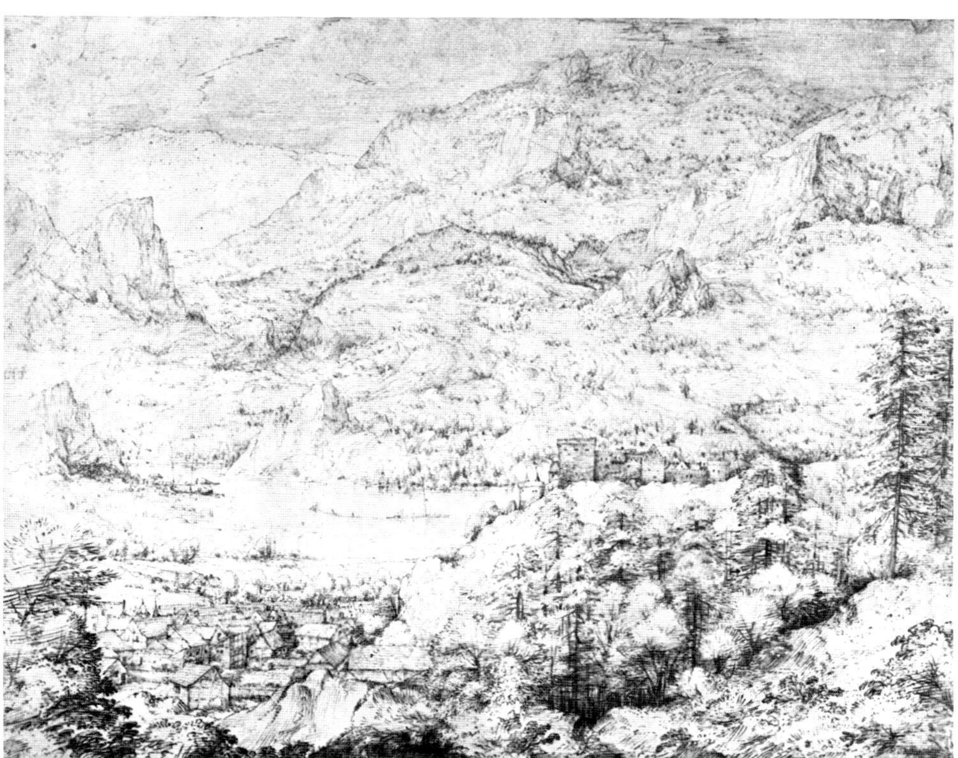

which reference is made in many of the later comments on Bruegel's life and works.

'Nature was wonderfully felicitous in her choice when, in an obscure peasant village in Brabant, she selected the gifted and witty Pieter Breughel to paint her and her peasants, and to contribute to the everlasting fame of painting in the Netherlands.

Pieter was born not far from Breda, in a village called Breughel, a name he took for himself and his descendants. He learned his craft from Pieter Koeck van Aelst, whose daughter he later married. He often carried her in his arms when she was little, and when he lived with Aelst. From Aelst he went to work with Jeroon Kock, and then he went to France and to Italy.

He practised a good deal in the manner of Jeroon van den Bosch, and made many similar weird scenes and drolleries. For this reason, he was often called Pier den Droll. Indeed, there are very few works from his hand that the beholder can look at seriously, without laughing. However stiff, serious and morose one may be, one cannot help laughing, or smiling.

Pieter painted many pictures from life as he travelled about, so that it was said of him, that while visiting the Alps, he had swallowed all the mountains and cliffs, and, upon coming home, he had spat them forth upon his canvases and panels; so remarkably was he able to follow these and other works of nature.

He settled down, selecting Antwerp as his residence, and there he entered the guild of the painters in 1551. Breughel did a great deal of work for a merchant by the name of Hans Franckert, a noble and worthy man who liked to chat with him, and saw him every day. With this Franckert, Breughel often went on trips among the peasants, to their weddings and fairs. The two dressed like peasants, brought presents like the other guests, and acted as if they belonged to the families or acquaintances of the bride or groom. Here Breughel delighted in observing the manners of the peasants in eating, drinking, dancing, jumping, making love, and engaging in various amusements, all of which he knew how to copy very comically and skillfully, and equally well with water-colour and oils; for he was exceptionally skilled in both processes. He knew well the characteristics of the peasant men and women of the Kampine and elsewhere. He knew how to dress them naturally and how to portray their rural, uncouth bearing while dancing, walking, standing, or moving in different ways. He was astonishingly sure of his composition and drew most ably and beautifully with the pen. He made many little sketches from nature.

As long as he remained in Antwerp, he lived with a servant girl whom indeed he would have married, had it not been for the unfortunate fact that she used to tell lies all the time, which was repugnant to his love of truth. He made a contract or agreement with

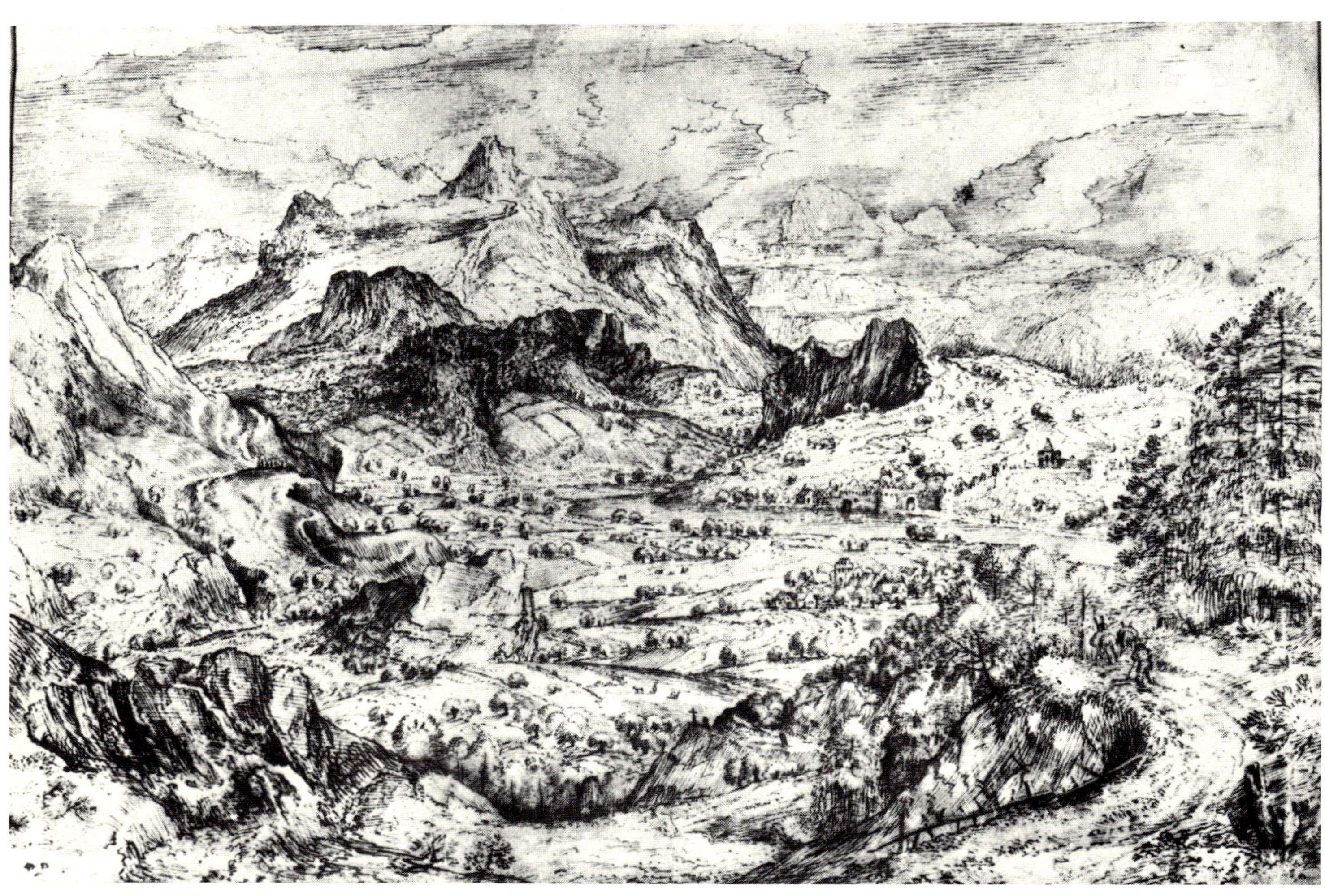

her that he would check off all her lies upon a stick. For this purpose he took a fairly long one, saying that if the stick became full of notches in the course of time, it would prevent the wedding. This happened before much time had elapsed.

At last, when Pieter Koeck's widow had finally settled in Brussels, Breughel fell in love with her daughter, whom, as we have said, he had often carried in his arms when she was a child, and he married her; but her mother requested that Breughel leave Antwerp, and make his residence in Brussels, in order that he might get his former mistress out of sight and out of mind. This also happened.

Breughel was a quiet and able man who did not talk much, but was jovial in company, and he loved to frighten people, often his own pupils, with all kinds of ghostly sounds and pranks that he played.

Some of Breughel's most significant works are at present in the possession of the Em-peror; for example, a great *Tower of Babel* with many beautiful details. One can look into it from above. Furthermore, there is a smaller representation of the same subject. There are, besides, two *Carrying of the Cross* paintings, very natural-looking, always with a few drolleries in them somewhere. Again, there is a *Massacre of the Innocents*, in

ALPINE LANDSCAPE WITH TWO MULES
Pen drawing in maroon tones on white paper; 294 x 425 mm (11¼ x 16 in)
c. 1555–1556
London, Courtauld Institute
(formerly in the collection of Count A. Seilern)
This large composition has certain similarities with the 'Large Landscape' engravings. The precision of the outlines suggests that it is a preparatory drawing for an engraving which was not executed. The date 1555–1556 has been established on the basis of the correspondence between the rocks at bottom left and those which appear in a *Landscape with Mountain Chain* dated 1556. This drawing possesses a greater degree of spatial unity along Italian lines, but without sacrificing any of Bruegel's own originality.

which there is much to see that is done true to life, of which I have spoken elsewhere – a whole family, for instance, begging for the life of a peasant child whom a murderous soldier has seized in order to kill it; the grief and the swooning of the mother and other events appear realistic.

Finally, there is a *Conversion of St. Paul*, also representing some very beautiful cliffs. It would be very hard to enumerate every thing Breughel did – fantasies, representations of hell, peasant scenes, and many other things.

He painted a *Temptation of Christ*, in which one looks down from above, as from the Alps, upon cities and country borne up by clouds, through the rents in which one looks out.

He made a *Dulle Griet*, who is stealing something to take to Hell, and who wears a vacant stare and is strangely dressed. I believe this and other pictures are also in the possession of the Emperor.

ALPINE LANDSCAPE
Pen drawing in maroon tones on white paper;
195 x 322 mm (7 x 12½ in)
c. 1555–1556
London Courtauld Institute
(formerly in the collection of Count A. Seilern)
A masterpiece of Bruegel's graphic art, executed on the basis of ideas gathered during the crossing of the Alps and then finished in the studio, as confirmed by the area in the foreground. Various motifs in this drawing appear, further elaborated, in the 'Large Landscape' series published by Hieronymus Cock: the large cliff on the right is found again in the engraving entitled *Paysage Alpestre* (Bastelaer 8).

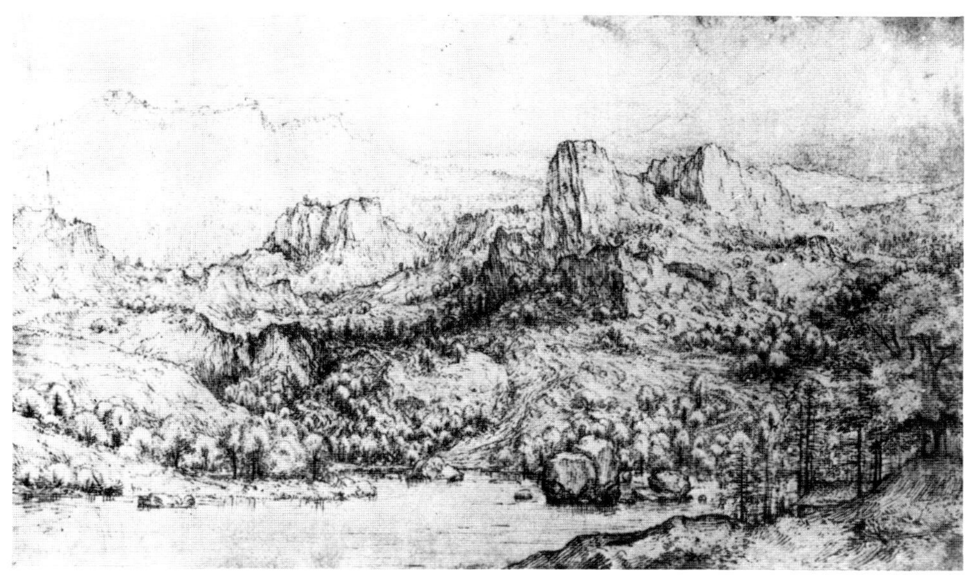

Sr. Herman Pilgrims, an art lover in Amsterdam, has a *Peasant Wedding* done in oils, which is very beautiful. The faces and bare limbs of the peasants in it are yellow and brown as if they were sunburned, and they show ugly skins, different from those of city dwellers.

He painted a picture in which *Lent* and *Carnival* are fighting; another, where all kinds of remedies are used against death; and one with all kinds of children at games; and innumerable other little, clever things.

Two canvases painted in water-colour can be seen in the home of Sr. Willem Jacobsz., who lives near the new church in Amsterdam. They represent a *Peasant Wedding*, where many amusing episodes together with the true character of the peasant may be seen. Among the group giving presents to the bride is an old peasant who has his little money bag hanging around his neck, and who is busy counting the gold into his hand. These are unusual paintings.

Shortly before his death, the townsmen of Brussels commanded Breughel to represent in pictures the digging of the canal from Brussels to Antwerp. These pictures were not completed because of his death.

Many of Breughel's strange compositions and comical subjects can be seen in his copper engravings. He made many skilful and beautiful drawings and he supplied them with inscriptions which, at the time, were too biting and too sharp, and which he had burned by his wife during his last illness, because of remorse, or fear that most disagreeable consequences might grow out of them. In his will he left his wife a picture of *A Magpie on a Gallows*: by the magpie, he meant the gossips whom he delivered to the gallows. In addition, he had painted a picture in which Truth triumphs. According to his own statement, this was the best thing painted by him.

He left behind him two sons who were able painters. One was called Pieter and studied with Gillis van Conincxloo and painted portraits from life; the other, Jan, learned water-colour painting from his grandmother, the mother of Pieter van Aelst. Jan studied the process of oil-painting with a certain Pieter Goetkindt, who had many beautiful things in his house. He went to Cologne and then to Italy, where he made a great name as a landscape painter; he also painted other subjects, very small in size, a type of work in

which he excelled. Lampsonius speaks of Pieter Breughel in the following lines, with the question:
Who may be this other Jeroon Bosch, who came in this world again, who pictures to us the fantastic conceptions of his own master again, who is most able with the brush, who is even surpassing his master?
Ye, Pieter, ye work in the artistic style of your old master. but you rise still higher: for reason that you select pleasant topics to laugh about. through these you deserve great merit and with your master you must be praised for being a great artist.'
Van Mander's claim that Bruegel came from the village of Breughel not far from Breda sounds at first quite unimpeachable, but in fact the situation is less clear than it seems, for there are three villages called Breughel and none of them is near Breda. One is in northern Brabant (now Holland) thirty-four miles to the east of Breda, while the others. Groote Brögel and Kleine Brögel, are situated close to each other in the Limburger

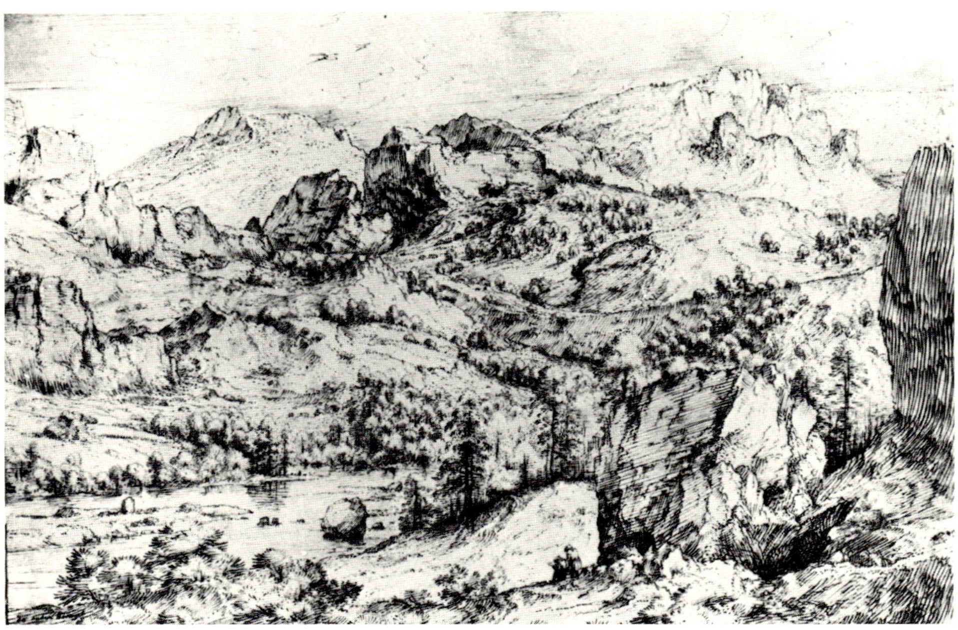

ALPINE LANDSCAPE WITH ARTIST DRAWING
Pen drawing in maroon tones on paper; preparatory drawing in black charcoal; 277 x 396 mm (11 x 15½ in)
c. 1555–1556
London, Courtauld Institute
(formerly in the collection of Count A. Seilern)
The affinity of this drawing with the preceding one (p. 17) places it in the same period: immediately after the return from Italy, when Cock was beginning to execute the 'Large Landscapes' (Bastelaer 3–17). The artists drawing in the foreground, a fairly frequent motif in those years, are derived from Italian art and are also present in another composition by Bruegel entitled *Landscape with Mercury and Psyche*, which survives only in the engraving by J. Hoefnagel (see opposite).

Kampine (now Belgium) which in Bruegel's day belonged to the diocese of Lüttich and was thus outside the Netherlandish provinces. The distance from Breda is even greater in this case (about forty-three miles), but it is not far at all – only three miles – to the little town of Brée. As Brée was called Breede or Brida, or in Latin Breda, in the sixteenth century, it has been asserted that van Mander confused the Breda (Brée) in Limburg with the Breda in Brabant and that, accordingly, Bruegel was born near Brée. But as Charles Terlinden and Fritz Grossmann have rightly pointed out, it is hard to imagine that a Netherlander living at the end of the 16th century would have confused the Lüttich area with Netherlandish territory. At any rate, van Mander's claim is inconsistent and probably no more than an intelligent guess (of the kind also made by Vasari, for example, in his biographies of Giotto and Leonardo). In other words he chose a peasant background on the basis of the peasant themes in Bruegel's paintings. Another point is that there were several Bruegels of high social standing in Antwerp and Brussels in the 16th and 17th centuries, whose relationship to the painter is unknown. One of them, a contemporary, even had the same Christian name: Maitre Pierre Brugelius, Professor of Medicine at Brussels. Nobody has claimed that any of the other Bruegels came from a village of the same name, but that does not rule out the possibility that all these families, including the painter's, derived their name from an ancestor's place of origin. Nor does the entry in the guild lists as 'Pieter Brueghels' support the village theory: as Friedländer and others have pointed out, the 's' at the end of Netherlandish names simply indicates a patronymic – 'Pieter the son of Brueghel', not 'Pieter from Brueghel'.
The older of the known sources, on the other hand, sounds more plausible and less problematic. Guicciardini stated in 1567 that Bruegel came from Breda: '*Pietro Brueghel di Breda grande imitatore della scienza, fantasie di Girolamo Bosco, onde n' ha anche acquistato ill sopranome di secondo Girolamo Bosco*' ('Pieter Bruegel of Breda, a great imitator of the art and phantasies of Hieronymus Bosch, for which reason he was nicknamed the second Hieronymus Bosch'). Although Guicciardini was a

foreigner, his words have a certain ring of truth in so far as his book was published in 1567 when Bruegel was still alive, whereas van Mander's *Schilderboeck* appeared only thirty-five years after Bruegel's death. Although Guicciardini does not expressly give Breda as the painter's birthplace, the obvious assumption is that it was – particularly as the mistaken view that Bruegel was a peasant's son has been finally disproved. Everything points to Bruegel having been a city-dweller and, indeed, a highly-educated one on friendly terms with the humanists of his time. His works demonstrate this constantly.

The town of Breda, which then had roughly 8,000 inhabitants, merits closer examination for a number of reasons. Auner in particular, for whom there can be no doubt that Bruegel was born at Breda, draws our attention to its importance in his commentary published in 1956. As he points out, Breda was the residence of the Netherlandish line of the counts of Nassau, who had settled there in the early 15th century and distinguished themselves by their emphatic allegiance to Charles the Bold.

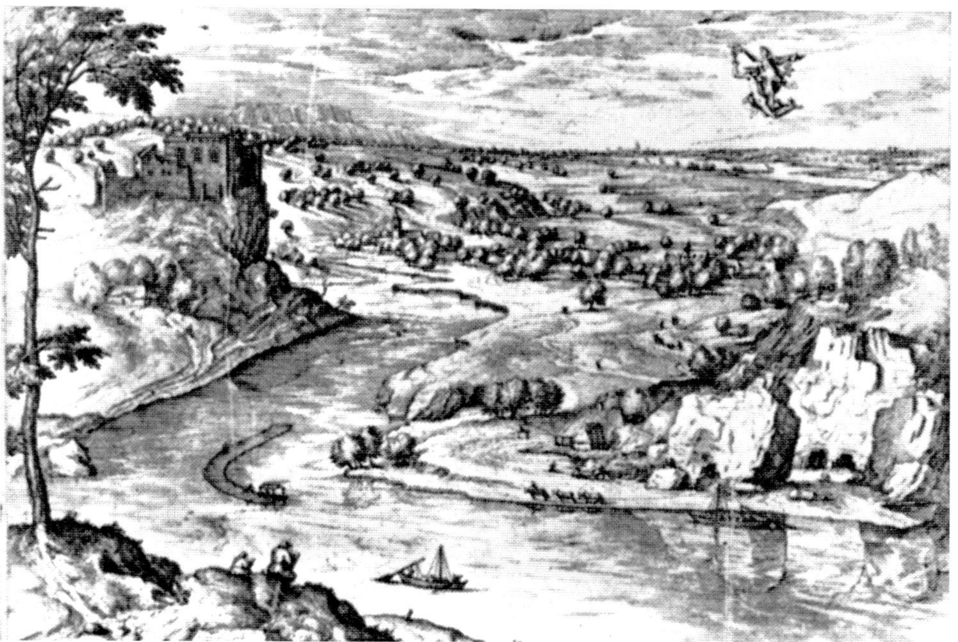

Count Engelbert II of Nassau was the only man of rank in the land to pass this loyalty on to his descendants – his daughter Mary, her husband Maximilian and their son Philip the Fair – thereby helping to establish the Habsburg dynasty in the Netherlands. It was he who bore the prime responsibility for Philip the Fair being educated as a Burgundian prince and not even made to learn German. A member of the Regency Council, he was appointed governor of all the Netherlands by Maximilian in 1501 when Philip the Fair went to Spain. His nephew and successor Henry IIIrd Count of Nassau educated Charles V and became famous as his military commander; after Philip's death, Henry was the most influential member of the Supreme Council under Philip's sister Margaret. From Spain Charles then entrusted him with the mission of ensuring his election as German Emperor. By about 1530 there were almost no limits to the esteem in which Charles held him, nor to the influence which Henry exerted over his master. Henry spent the last years of his life almost entirely in Breda, where in 1534 work began on building the enormous fortifications and two years later on the construction of a new castle. Henry's name is closely bound up with the acceptance of Renaissance culture and humanism in the Netherlands. He was on friendly terms with Erasmus of Rotterdam: Jan van Scorel and Barend van Orley, to whom Pieter Coecke was apprenticed (Coecke in his turn teaching Pieter Bruegel), often visited his court. When Henry died in 1538, his son René, who in 1530 had inherited the title of Prince of Orange from a maternal uncle, was the most highly respected of the princes of the Netherlands. Following his early death from a wound in 1544, both his title and the possessions of the Barony of Breda went to his young German cousin, William of Nassau, who was being educated, on Charles V's instructions, in Brussels by a younger brother of Cardinal Granvella. William of Orange then took up residence in his magnificent castle at Breda which, according to a contemporary, was the finest and strongest fortress he had ever seen in the whole of Germany. Auner tells us: 'William of Orange was one of the last to uphold that closed style of life which had evolved at the Burgundian court at the end of the

Middle Ages and which for a short while set a pattern with its revival of chivalrous ideals. The degree to which he felt himself a Burgundian can be judged from the fact that, although his mother tongue was German and he spoke seven languages, all the letters he wrote in his own hand are in French, i.e. the official language of the Brussels government and the colloquial speech of the Netherlandish high nobility'. In conclusion Auner refers to the chivalrous Burgundian concept of the world and a society dedicated to a noble way of life; to events which may have impressed Bruegel in his childhood, the great fire of Breda in 1534 and the building of the fortifications and Henry III's castle; and finally to Bruegel's knowledge of country life. In later life, it seems, he no longer saw peasants through the eyes of a townsman, like Pieter Aertsen for example, nor in literary terms, but rather as a country squire, who, whilst not one of them, had nonetheless been familiar from childhood with their way of life. Auner also thinks it probable that Bruegel had already been given painting lessons in Breda by a watercolour

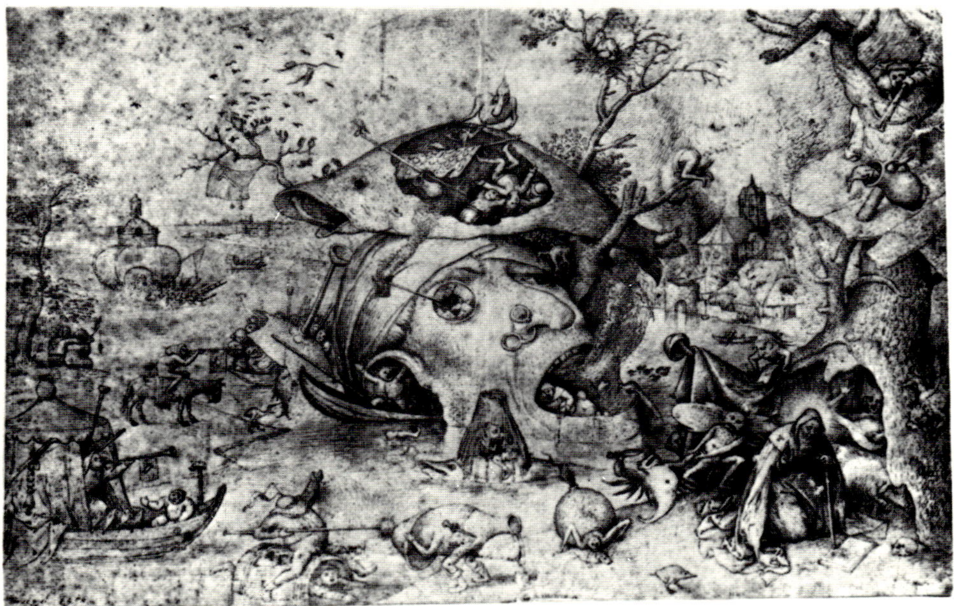

THE TEMPTATION OF ST. ANTHONY
Pen and brush drawing in maroon on brown paper; 216 x 238 mm (8 x 9¼ in)
Signed and dated at bottom left: 'Brueghel 1556' (of doubtful authenticity, may be later reproduction of authentic signature)
Oxford, Ashmolean Museum
Preparatory drawing for an engraving, not inverted (Bastelaer 119). The fact that the drawing faces the same way as the engraving, the apocryphal signature and the use of a brush, which is unusual with Bruegel (see *The Resurrection*, p. 77), have occasionally given rise to doubts about who executed this work, which is in fact most certainly authentic. The composition, which has affinities with Bosch, is together with the 'Large Landscapes' one of the first works attested by Hieronymus Cock's records.

painter who was presumably in the service of Henry III and that he then went to Antwerp where Pieter Coecke was able to put his talents to good use in his cartoon workshop.

The year of Bruegel's birth is still uncertain but the likelihood is that he was born between 1525 and 1530. This derives from the fact that in 1551, or more precisely between October 1551 and October 1552, as Monballieu stresses, he entered the Guild of St. Luke in Antwerp as a master – at the same time as Giorgio Ghisi of Mantua. This presupposes, of course, that he served the normal apprenticeship and had not already become master in another town, for example Breda, before going to Antwerp. A further hypothesis, proposed by Bedaux in 1974, restricts the year of birth to 1527 or 1528. This theory rests on an engraved portrait dated 1606 by Agidius Sadeler which shows the elder Bruegel with his son Pieter in a kind of ideal union. Since Pieter Bruegel the Younger was forty-one or forty-two in 1606, Bedaux arrived at 1527 or 1528 on the basis of a caption on the engraving. This is the result if 41 or 42 years are subtracted from 1569, the year in which Pieter Bruegel the Elder died. However, the hypothesis cannot be proved and has been rejected verbally, for example, by Grossmann.

According to van Mander, Bruegel 'learnt his art with Pieter Koeck van Aelst, whose daughter he later married'. This, too, has occasionally been questioned because Bruegel's art betrays no common ground whatever with the work of the Romanist Coecke. It has even been suggested that van Mander simply assumed the existence of such common ground because he knew of the marriage with Coecke's daughter Mayken. Strange though it may seem that Bruegel should have had a master whose artistic notions were diametrically opposed to his own, there can be no doubt in this particular case about the accuracy of van Mander's report. In his time Pieter Coecke was one of the most respected painters in the country. Born in Aelst in 1502, he was a pupil of Barend van Orley in Brussels and became a free master in Antwerp in 1527. He was court painter to Charles V and in 1533 travelled to Constantinople for van der Moeyen, the Brussels carpet makers. Although the Islamic ban on pictures prevented the Sultan from ordering any carpets, he did have his portrait painted by Coecke. The latter learnt Turkish and after about a year's stay returned to Antwerp crowned with honours to become Dean of the Guild of St. Luke in 1537. In 1539 he published his translation of Vitruvius and in that year he began an edition of the writings of Berlio which his wife continued after his death until 1553. 1549 saw Coecke working with others on festive decorations for the entry of Philip and Charles V into Antwerp. His second marriage was to the miniaturist and watercolour painter Mayken Verhulst. She bore him three children of whom the youngest, Mary or Mayken, became Pieter Bruegel's wife. A panel attributed to Coecke in the Kunsthaus in Zurich shows the artist himself with his wife and children. It is not known exactly what Bruegel did in Coecke's successful studio, which must have been of some considerable size. Perhaps, as Grossman suspects, he was engaged – more or less enthusiastically – on the elder artist's big decorative commissions, the sketches for tapestries. Again according to Grossman, he may in the course

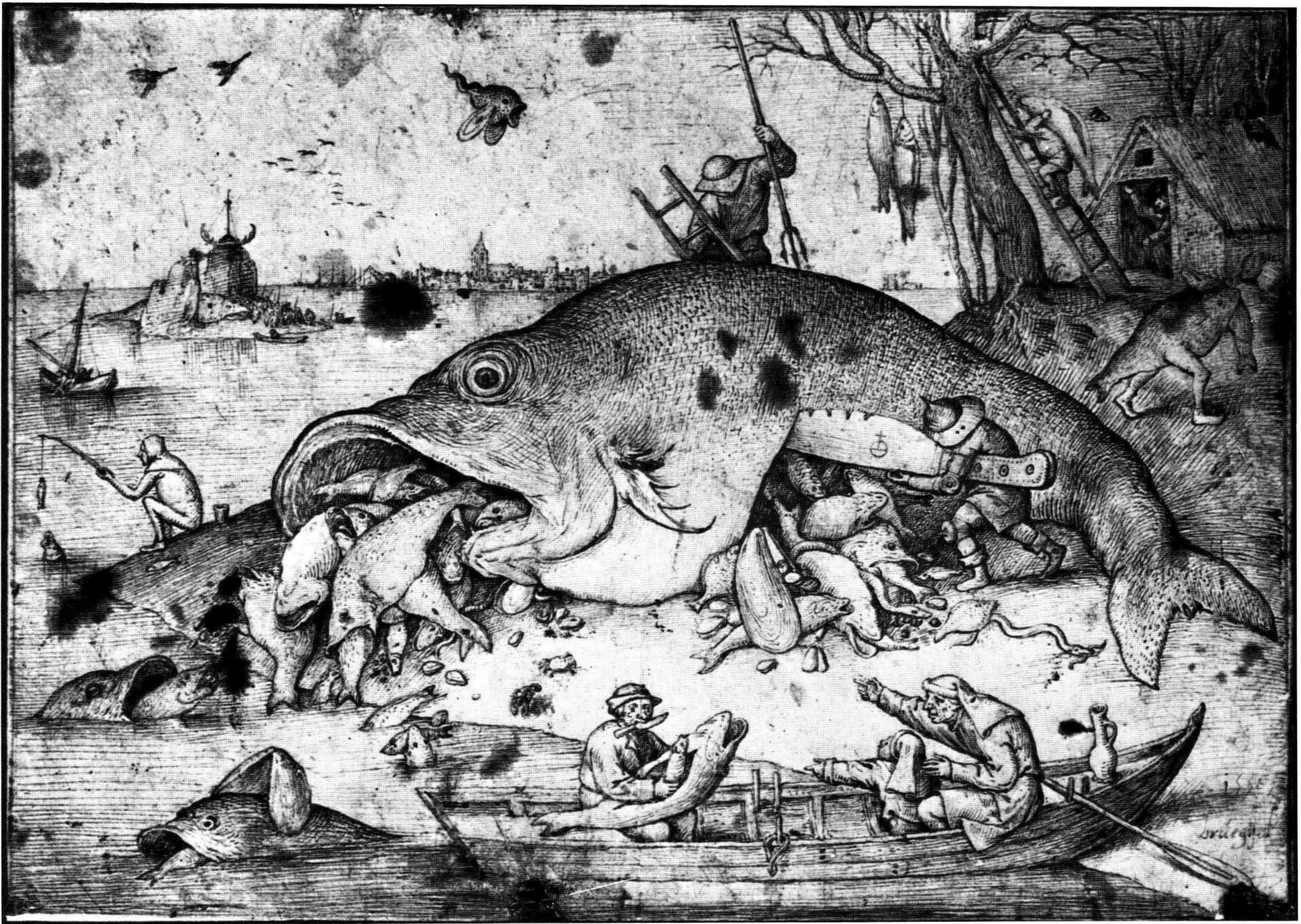

BIG FISH EAT LITTLE FISH
Pen drawing in dark grey on paper, blemished; 216 x 302 mm (8½ x 11 in)
Signed and dated at bottom right: '1556 / brueghel'
Vienna, Graphische Sammlung Albertina
Preparatory drawing for the engraving by Pieter van der Heyden published by Cock (Bastelaer 139); in the first edition the name of H. Bosch appears as *the inventor*. This indicates that the drawing, without any doubt by Bruegel, is an elaboration of motifs from Bosch. But the work's overall conception is typical of Bruegel and his ability to translate metaphorical language into images.

of this work have come into contact with Jan Vermeyen, whose cartoons of Charles V's Tunis campaign in the Künthistorisches Museum in Vienna contain ideas for Bruegel's *View of the Bay of Naples* (page 26).

Tolnay, Stridbeck, Lugt, Grossmann and others maintain that scholars have repeatedly tried to prove a link between Bruegel and Italian art, either indirectly through Coecke's studio, the Romanists of Antwerp and Brussels, and Bruegel's work in Hieronymus Cock's publishing house at Antwerp, or directly through Bruegel's journey to Italy. There was an unwillingness to believe that Bruegel could have succeeded in swimming against the contemporary tide and arriving at his own superlative approach to art without any help from Italy. Was it really possible to remain insulated from the continual influences, particularly of the engravings in Cock's publishing house? Apart from the insoluble problems surrounding Breugel's iconography, this is one of the trickiest questions facing researchers and no definitive assessment can be attempted here. Suffice it to say that Italian motifs, and specifically Venetian ones, appear at an early stage in the landscapes and later in his human figures too, but in neither case is there any evidence of direct borrowing. Examples adduced in an attempt to prove the contrary have so far been unconvincing. At most we may be dealing with virtually undetectable metamorphoses of compositional ideas.

It would be interesting, too, to know more about Coecke's wife, Mayken Verhulst Bessemers, who later became Bruegel's mother-in-law and of whom we learn from van Mander that she taught her grandson Jan Brueghel the Elder how to paint in water-colour. Bergman's attempt to identify the Brunswick Monogrammist with Mayken Verhulst having proved a failure, she remains, as a painter, shrouded in uncertainty; no painting has been proved to be her work, although Guicciardini mentions her as one of the four main painters of the Netherlands. Nonetheless, Bruegel does seem to have been in touch with the Brunswick Monogrammist, probably early on, through the Coecke

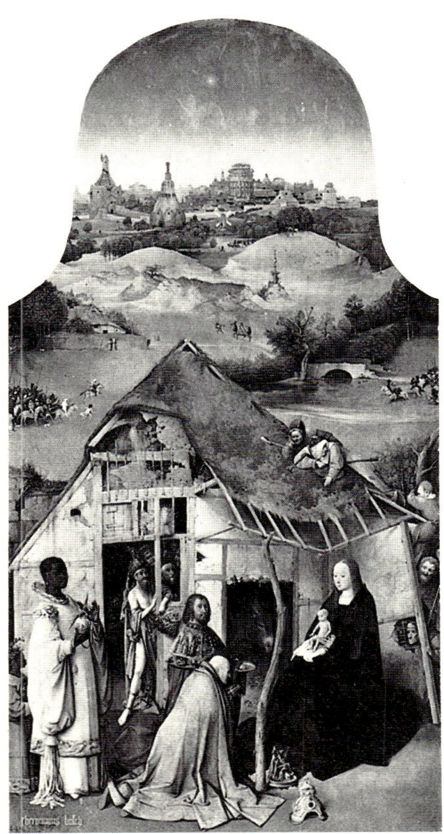

Hieronymus Bosch
ADORATION OF THE MAGI
(central portion of the *Epiphany Triptych*)
Oil on panel; 138 x 72 cm (54 x 28 in)
1510
Madrid, Prado
The central panel of the famous Triptych in the Prado reveals the importance to Bruegel of the local late gothic tradition.

ADORATION OF THE MAGI
Tempera on canvas; 115.5 x 163 cm (45½ x 64 in)
c. 1556
Brussels, Musées Royaux des Beaux-Arts
This painting was acquired from the Fétis Collection and donated to the Brussels museum. Its poor state of preservation is due in part to the very liquid tempera technique, used for the fabrics which replaced tapestries. The work contains similarities, particularly in the tumbledown building, with the central panel of the *Epiphany Triptych* by Bosch (at left). With its wealth of figures the composition is an early example of Bruegel's ability to create crowd scenes. Unfortunately his masterpiece from his point of view, the *Feast of St. Martin*, is lost and is only preserved in a copy (p. 24).

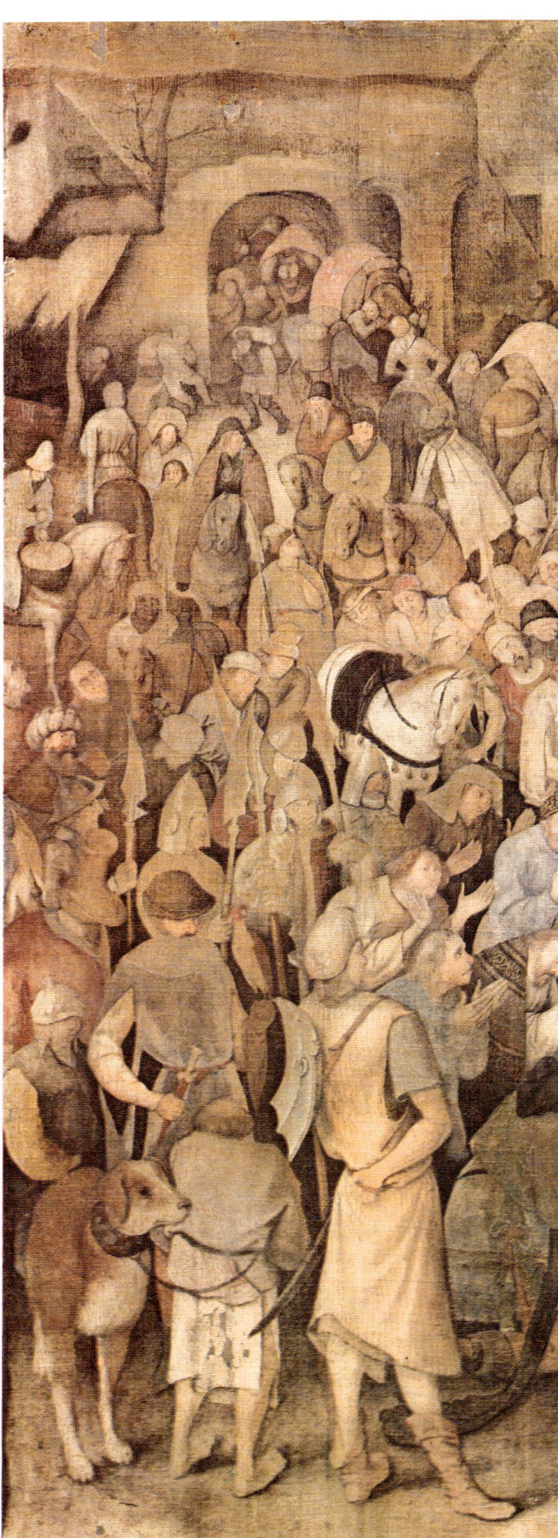

family, since the Monogrammist has now been reliably identified with Jan van Amstel. The most recent credible argument, put foward by Friedrich Schubert in 1970, confirms the theses of Glück, Genaille, Hoogewerff, Faggin and others.

Jan van Amstel is of unusual interest because he not only introduced innovations into landscape art which go beyond Patinir's achievements but also evolved a style for the human figure which, like the landscapes, has a direct association with the development of Bruegel's style. The scenes showing a mass of small figures set in a landscape are specially important as a stepping-stone to Bruegel's art, as we can see from one of Jan van Amstel's depictions of Christ bearing the cross, now in Amsterdam (page 90). The neat round forms of his figures, blown out like balloons, highlighted here and there and often shown from the back, are stylistic features which point to Bruegel and are particularly evident in van Amstel's most important work, the *Feeding of the Poor* in the Herzog-Anton-Ulrich Museum in Brunswick. Of special interest is his technique, noted by van Mander, of using the priming coat in the actual picture, a peculiarity which, together with the light brushwork, is found in none of van Amstel's contemporaries and only emerges again with Pieter Bruegel.

Born in about 1500, Jan van Amstel came from Amsterdam and was the elder brother of Pieter Aertsen. He became a free master in Antwerp in 1528, and so belongs to the generation immediately preceding Bruegel's. In 1536 he became a citizen of Antwerp as 'Jan van Amstel Aertssone'. As Pieter Coecke's brother-in-law, he had family ties with him in addition to the artistic associations revealed by Schubert on the basis of various figure compositions which van Amstel evidently borrowed from Coecke. In two par-

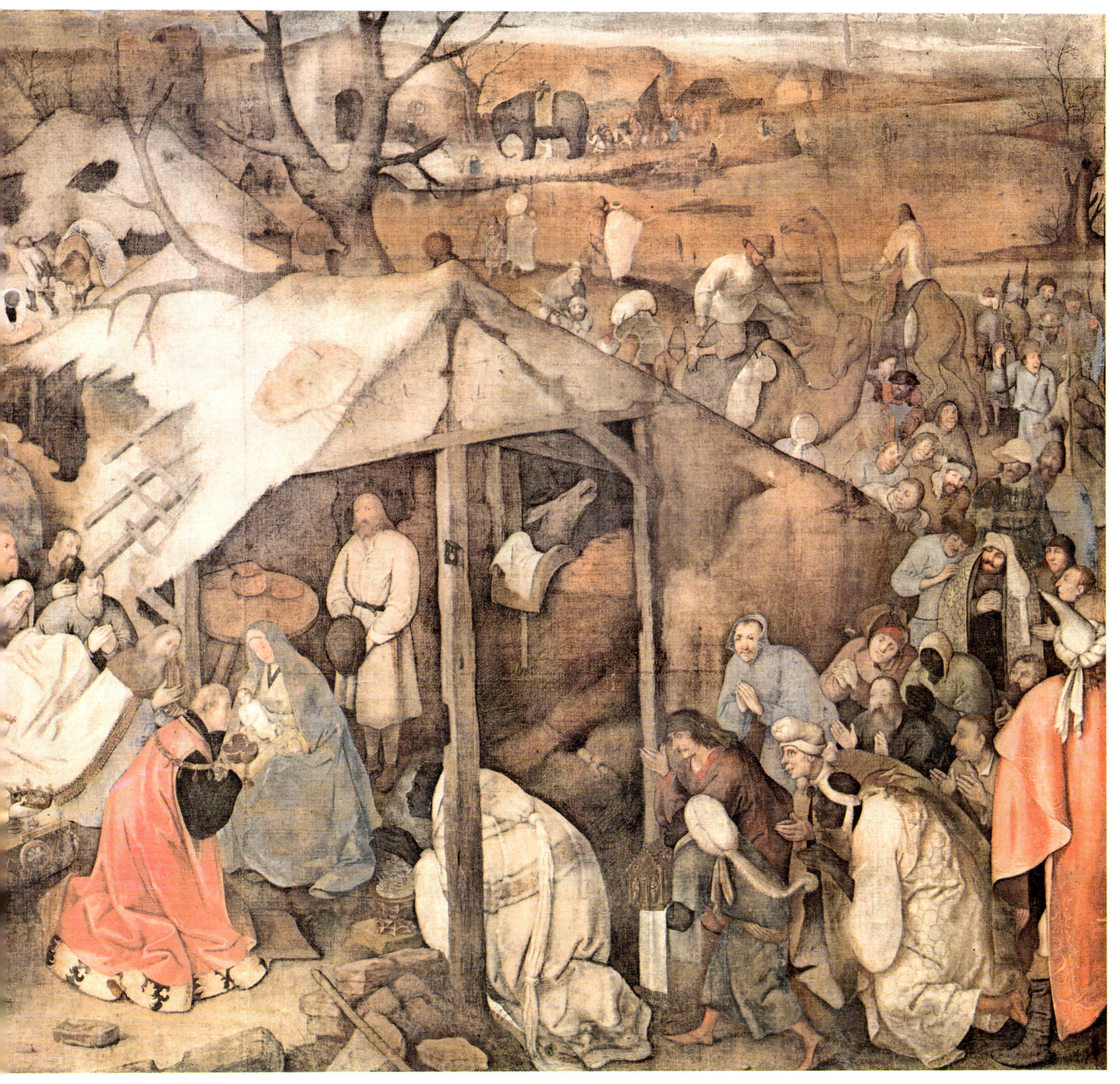

ticular cases they even worked together on the same painting, van Amstel executing the landscape background. Jan van Amstel must have died in about 1542 in view of the fact that his widow, by her second marriage to Gillis van Conincxloo I, gave birth to a son Gillis (later to become the famous landscape painter), on 24 January 1544.

Brugel's departure from Coecke's studio is surrounded by as much uncertainty as his arrival. According to Grossman, Coecke 'apparently spent the last few years of his life in Brussels', where he died on 6 December 1550. Jedlicka says Coeke moved to Brussels as early as 1544 and Auner also assumes this happened soon after 1544 in the light of an edict issued in that year by Charles V in an endeavour to stop the faking of Brussels carpets by manufacturers in Antwerp. But this would raise the question of when Bruegel could have been apprenticed to Coecke in Antwerp. The latest supposition is that Coecke moved to Brussels in 1549. Bruegel too seems to have left Antwerp – either at this time or possibly not until after Coecke's death in about 1550 – for we find him from

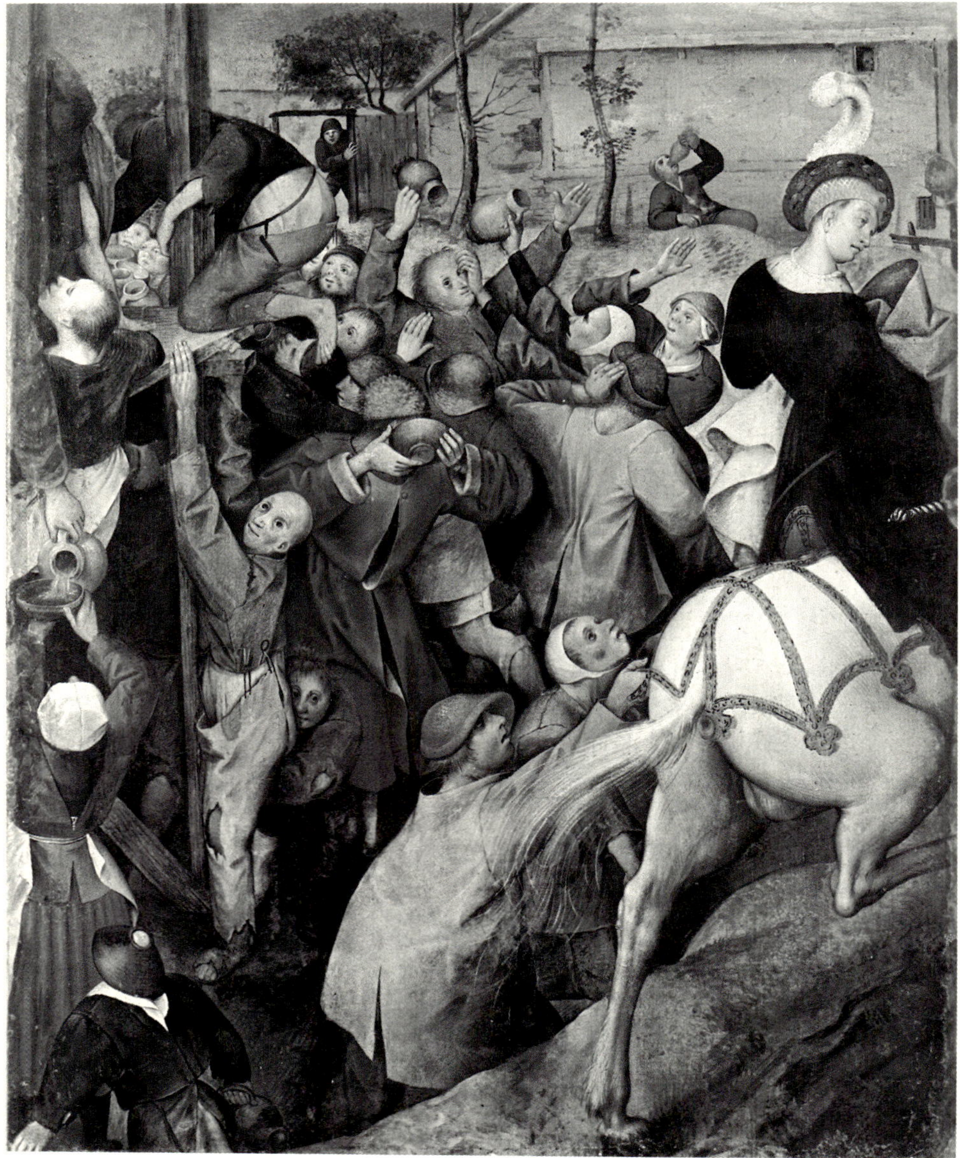

THE FEAST OF ST. MARTIN
*Tempera and oil on canvas; 92.5 x 73.5 cm
(36¼ x 28 in) (fragment)*
Neither signed nor dated
Vienna, Kunsthistorisches Museum
Still complete when in the collection of Leopoldo Guglielmo, Archduke of Austria, in 1659. This is a fragment of a good copy of an important composition dating from Bruegel's early years known only through a copy in the antiquarian market (Bastelaer – de Loo, p. 314 with plate) and from an engraving by N. Guerard. There are two versions of the composition by Pieter Balten. The fragment is now generally regarded as a copy, but this dispute will no doubt go on for a long time. In spite of everything, Bruegel's authorship cannot be ruled out so unequivocally if it is remembered that the work is executed on canvas, exactly like the *Adoration of the Magi* in Brussels (pp. 22–23), which is definitely authentic and of the same period, and that it seems to have been badly restored at an early stage in an attempt to stop the easy deterioration of the tempera.

September 1550 to October 1551 at Malines, in the studio of a certain Claude Dorizi, working with Pieter Baltens on an altar for the local glovers' guild. This is revealed in a legal document dated 1608 and published by Monballieu in 1964. We know precisely what conditions governed the allocation of the work and in particular that the elder of the two, Pieter Baltens, a member of the Antwerp painters' guild since 1540, executed the central panel, while Bruegel was only responsible for painting the outer wings in grisaille. Unfortunately this first attested work of Bruegel's is lost. However, the document confirms Gustav Glück's old theory of Bruegel's connection with Malines, where at that time there were 150 studios specializing in watercolours on canvas. Bruegel himself used this technique in several pictures, for example in the *Adoration of the Magi* in Brussels (page 23), the *Parable of the Blind* (page 159), and the so-called *Misanthrope* (page 161) in Naples. Watercolour painting at Malines was used primarily for wall hangings and involved painting on cloths of standard format as a substitute for the very much more expensive Gobelin tabestries.

Van Mander had a poor opinion of the Malines technique and mentions in his biography of Hans Bol, a native of the town, that he served his apprenticeship *'by een van die gemeen slechte Meesters'* ('with one of the thoroughly bad masters'). And with justification, for these painted cloths were common, mass-produced articles turned out by the shipload for export, mainly to Portugal, Spain and Italy. The important thing was not the quality or the signature of a famous artist but quite simply the subject. In 1535, for example, Federigo Gonzaga was offered three hundred Netherlandish paintings, apparently by a dealer with business connections in Antwerp: the Duke bought a hundred and twenty, including twenty depictions of fires, according to Auner. But items of this kind were going to Italy even earlier. According to Glück (1910), the 15th century inventories of the Medici palaces in Florence and also of the Villa Careggi feature painted wall hangings as decorations over doors and fireplaces, including an allegorical representation of Lent being mocked by revellers eating and drinking.

Glück put forward the theory in 1910 that Bruegel had started as a watercolour painter. He recalls the absence of the 'chiaroscuro' and the 'values' that had been current since Leonardo. The plane quality of Bruegel's figures derived from the same quality in wall hangings, and the stereotyped wide format of his wood panels matched that of the cloths supplied in certain standard sizes to painters specializing in such hangings: about 120 x 170 cm for a *dobbel-doec*, roughly the measurements favoured by Bruegel for his large-scale pictures. Like Huizinga after him, Glück stresses the 15th-century Burgundian tradition which continued to exercise an influence on certain thematic fields right into the 16th century. Jan van Eyck also painted on canvas – an otter hunt, for example; Roger van der Weyden painted whole rooms full of hangings in Bruges; Patinir, Lucas van Leiden and Jan Scorel produced paintings on canvas, and some by Bosch are mentioned in Philip II's inventories. All we know is that after Coecke's death and the intermezzo in Malines – which, of course, also raises questions about Baltens' influence on Bruegel – Baltens subsequently got involved in Bruegel's world and became dependent upon him. We may recall in this connection that Bruegel became master in Antwerp in 1551. Certainly, fate seems to have been at work when the names of Bruegel, Giorgio Ghisi and Hieronymus Cock were entered together in the guild's list, for Bruegel was to be associated with Cock 'professionally' for almost the whole of his life.

Hieronymus Cock (c. 1550–1570) was a new and modern phenomenon for Antwerp. He was a born administrator: having begun as an artist himself he went on to become publisher, printer and art dealer, spurred on by the example of Roman publishers specializing in engravings. He had an unerring nose for novelty; the laws of supply and demand were at his finger-tips. He must have travelled to Rome sometime between 1546–1548 because the year 1548 saw the appearance of the first engraving in his art publishing house at Antwerp, 'Aux quatre vents' or 'In de vier winden'. The firm's name was appropriate, for artists and new artistic trends from all quarters of the globe were soon to be found there. His activities as an art dealer and publisher were extremely varied and very successful: *'laet de kock koken on't volcks wille'* ('let the cook get on with his cooking for the people's sake') was the sort of punning maxim he occasionally used on his own publications. People let him get on with it and he duly became rich. His role as intermediary for Italian art, in particular, cannot be over-emphasized. He published engravings after Raphael, Bronzino, Sarto, Giulio Romano, Michelangelo and Titian, and did business with the main representatives of the Netherlandish Italianizers such as Franz Floris, M. Heemskerck, Lambert Lombard and Lambert Suavius. He brought the well-known Mantuan engraver Giorgio Ghisi to Antwerp to develop the art of copper engraving there, all the engravings executed by Ghisi between

1550 and 1555 being published by Cock. At the same time he promoted the native
traditions of landscape painting and of moralizing allegories and depictions of everyday
life whose main representative was Pieter Bruegel. He supported the new ornamental
tendencies and the new architectural art of Cornelis Floris and Vredemann de Vries. He
also published maps, plans and views of cities and collaborated closely with the
geographer Christophe Plantin, who at that time was becoming one of Europe's
foremost book publishers. After Ghisi he successively employed many of the most
important engravers in his workshop, including Pieter van der Heyden, Philip Galle,
Cornelis Cort, Hans Collaert and Hieronymus Wierix. Finally, Cock must have been,
like Bruegel, an admirer of Hieronymus Bosch. Whether on his own initiative or on that
of Cock, Bruegel modified works by Bosch for copper engraving and produced similar
drawings himself for Cock's publishing house. These and the drawings in the Large
Landscape series, composed after drawings and sketches made on the Italian journey,

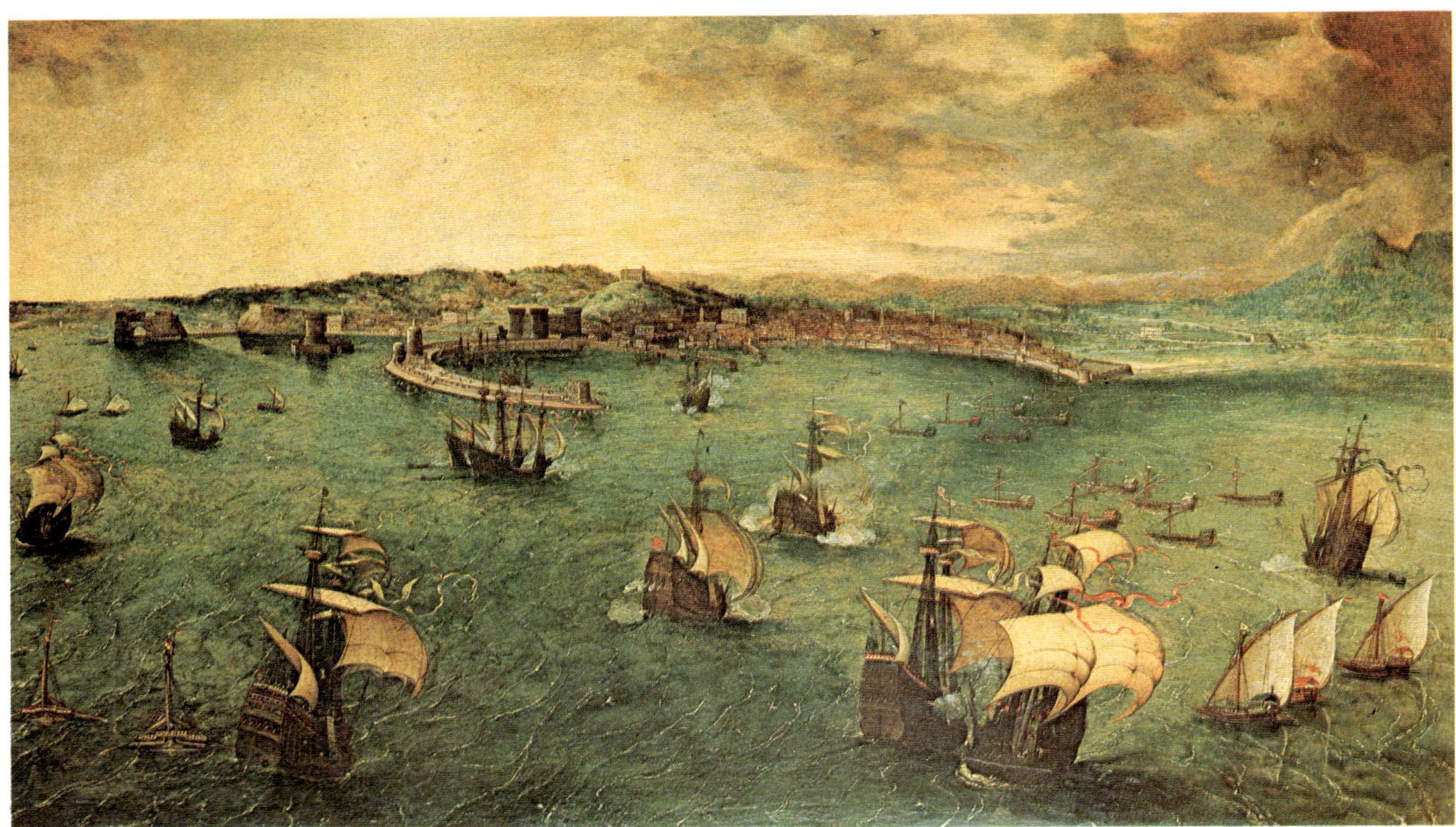

were the first work done for Cock.
Although we have no reason to doubt van Mander's statement that Bruegel went to
work with Hieronymus Cock after learning his art under Coecke, there is no clear
evidence of Bruegel's collaboration with Cock until 1555. A drawing with a mountain
gorge (now in the Louvre), used in an engraving in the 'Large Landscape' series
published by Cock, is dated 1555, and none of the figure compositions engraved after
Bruegel is dated earlier than 1556. But Bruegel had travelled to Italy between 1551 and
1555, staying there during 1552 and 1553 or possibly even longer.
Opinions differ about the immediate reason for this trip. Grossmann is at best doubtful
about the possibility that Cock commissioned Bruegel to go to Italy and execute landscapes for engravings, even though Cock later published such engravings: for
Grossmann the reason was quite simply that it was customary at the time for northern
artists to make pilgrimages to Italy. Auner, on the other hand, suggests as a more
pressing and topical occasion for the journey the financial crisis which broke out in 1551.
This was provoked by the war between Charles V and Henry II over the possession of
Parma, when, no matter how high the interest rate, it became impossible to raise money
on Antwerp's Exchange. But Auner sees the immediate reason in the financial situation
of Mayken Verhulst Bessemers, Coecke's widow, who was entitled after her husband's
death only to his goods and chattels, and thus found herself in a precarious position. As
Coecke's studio went to his eldest son, there was no question of Bruegel entering the
business by marrying the widow. However, Auner claims that Mayken Verhulst pinned

The painting is mentioned for the first time in the inventories of the Galleria Doria of 1794 and was probably owned before that by Cardinal Granvella and Rubens. One of the rare landscapes by Bruegel which show a definite locality, it was painted at Antwerp on the basis of sketches made in Italy. It is generally regarded as a juvenile work and only Winkler and Grossmann date it later (1562–1563). Some of the buildings can still be identified today. According to Smekens it depicts a Turkish attack. The ship on the left in the foreground appears, inverted, in the series of engravings of sailing-ships dated 1560–1565. The pier was in fact of angular shape, but Bruegel made it round for artistic reasons. Detail on *pages 28–29*.

her hopes on Bruegel and suggested the trip to Rome to him, presumably trusting he would return from Italy as a fully-trained figure painter and elegant Romanist – a second Coecke – and could be found a secure job as a cartoonist through her connections with the Brussels carpet industry. Fortunately for posterity, this was not the way. Although Auner's theory cannot be proved, it is however, not entirely absurd when we recall that Bruegel's close association with Coecke's family lasted right through to his marriage to the daughter in 1563.

Bruegel apparently set out for Italy very soon after becoming master, for by 1552 he was already in the southernmost part of the country. It can also be assumed he did not travel alone, frequent highway robberies making journeys of that length a dangerous undertaking. He may have joined up with Netherlandish or Italian merchants, perhaps in Lyons. The suggestion has also been made that his closer entourage included the painter Maerten de Vos, who became famous as a Mannerist after returning to Antwerp. De Vos was certainly in Italy at the same time as Bruegel and both are mentioned in a Latin letter of 1561 written by the geographer Scipio Fabius of Bologna to Abraham Ortelius. In it Fabius complains that Ortelius had not told him about Martin Fuchs (de Vos), 'the most excellent painter, as dear to me as a brother. I should like to know how he and Petro Bruochl, whom I value equally, are faring. My brother Octavian and I hope very much that they are well and ask you to give them a brotherly kiss on our behalf' (Auner). It seems that the two painters were guests together at Fabius' house in Bologna. Auner rightly rejects the possibility put forward by Popham that 'Petro Bruochl' could have been the professor of medicine from Brussels. Maerten de Vos' friendship with Bruegel also gives grounds for speculation as to whether the staffage figures in Bruegel's painting of 1553 entitled *Christ on the Sea of Tiberias* (page 11) might be by Maerten de Vos. And perhaps the two artists drawing the landscape in Joris Hoefnagel's engraving with Mercury and Psyche (page 19), which bears the inscription *'Petrus Bruegel fecit Romae A° 1553'*, are more than a compositional convention and in fact refer specifically to the two painters Bruegel and de Vos? Surprisingly, Bruegel seems not to have been content with the usual destination of Rome but journeyed much further south; and on the return journey he seems to have travelled about in the neighbouring countries to the north of Italy, although opinions are at variance about this. That he spent some time in Calabria has been concluded from the drawing in Rotterdam which shows Reggio in flames. Unsigned and undated, the work was substantially altered and distorted by washing during the 17th century, but Frans Huys' engraving after Bruegel identifies it beyond any doubt as Reggio and the year 1552 is indicated by the fire resulting from a Turkish attack in that year. Bruegel must also have crossed over from Reggio to Messina, as we may infer from the same engraving which shows a *Naval Battle in the Straits of Messina* and in which both Reggio and Messina are depicted. Grossmann even suggests that the journey was continued at least to Palermo, in view of the echoes of the famous *Triumph of Death* fresco, in the Palazzo Selafani at Palermo (page 70), to be found in Bruegel's painting in the Prado (page 71). Further evidence of Bruegel's travels in southern Italy is provided by the *View of the Bay of Naples* (page 26). A drawing in Berlin, signed and dated 1552, shows a landscape with an unidentified Italian monastery, while the drawing dated 1552 in the Louvre is of the bank of a calm stretch of water in mountainous terrain (page 9). Both works – the earliest ones with a date – were presumably executed in southern Italy since we know for certain that Bruegel was back in Rome in 1553. Auner, however, says they originated in Burgundy or the south of France. Bruegel's stay in Rome is attested by two of Joris Hoefnagel's etchings with the inscription 'Petrus Breugel fecit Romae A° 1553' and by a drawing of Ripa Grande (at Chatsworth), although the latter is not unanimously recognized. Further evidence is provided however, by his meeting with the miniaturist Giulio Clovio, for an inventory of the latter's property drawn up after his death includes the following: *'Un quadretto di miniatura la metà fatto per mano sua et altera da M° Pietro Brugole'*. This points to collaboration between the unknown young Fleming and this respected painter, some thirty years older than Bruegel, who was held in high esteem by the greatest Italian art connoisseurs of the time and whom Vasari called *'un piccolo e nuovo Michelagnolo'*. The inventory also lists a small painting of the Tower of Babel on ivory, a miniature no doubt inspired by Clovio, and *Un quadro di Leon (Lyons) di Francia a guazzo di mano di M° Pietro Brugole'*, which confirms van Mander's contention that Bruegel travelled to Italy via France. Two landscapes and a study of a tree in gouache are mentioned as well. All these works have been lost, but Tolnay tried in 1965, and again later, to attribute to Bruegel a number of miniatures used to embellish works by Clovio. One of these, in the *Towneley Lectionary*, now in New York, shows a port with a large number of ships in a storm below the main register depicting the Last

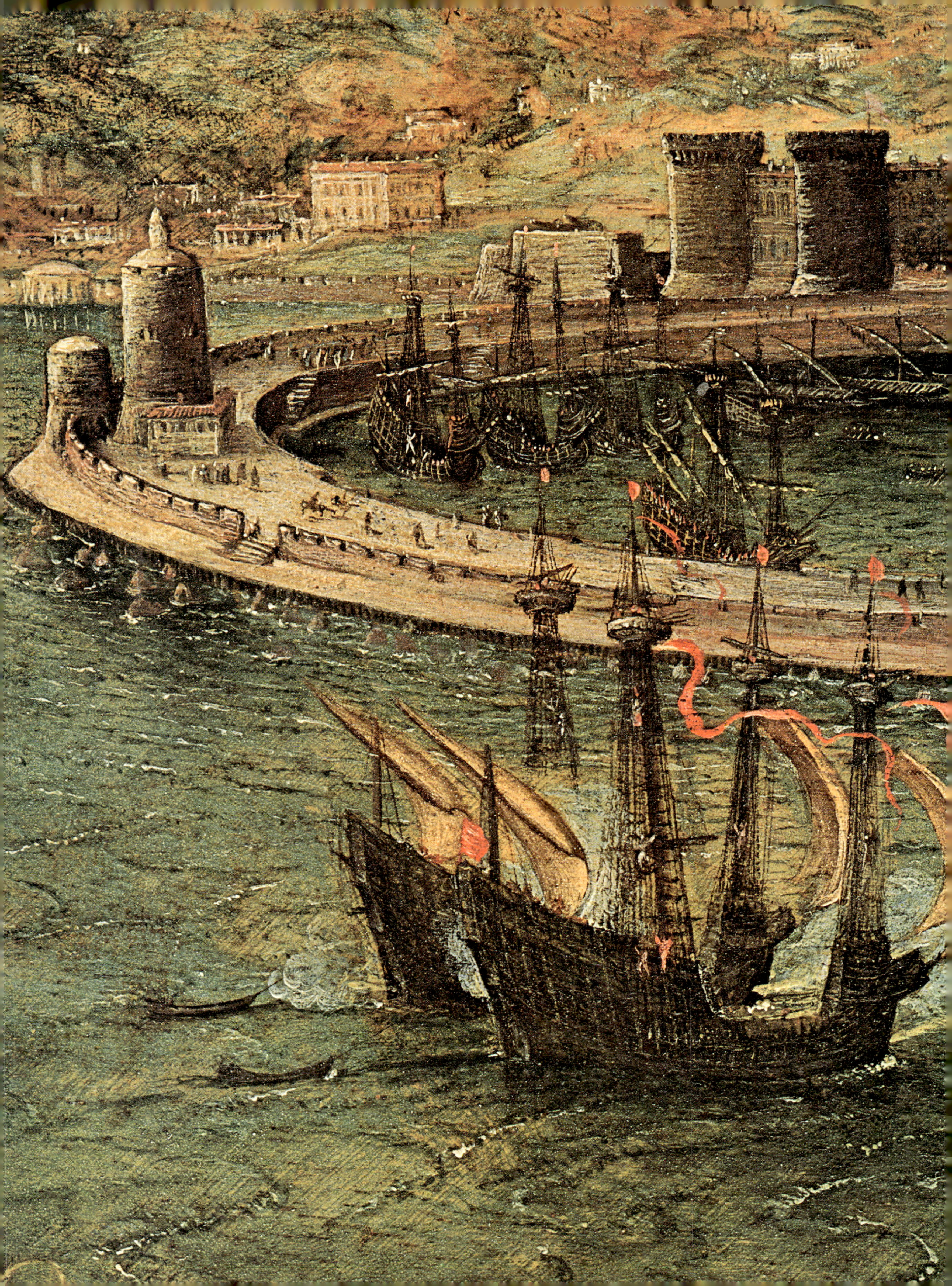

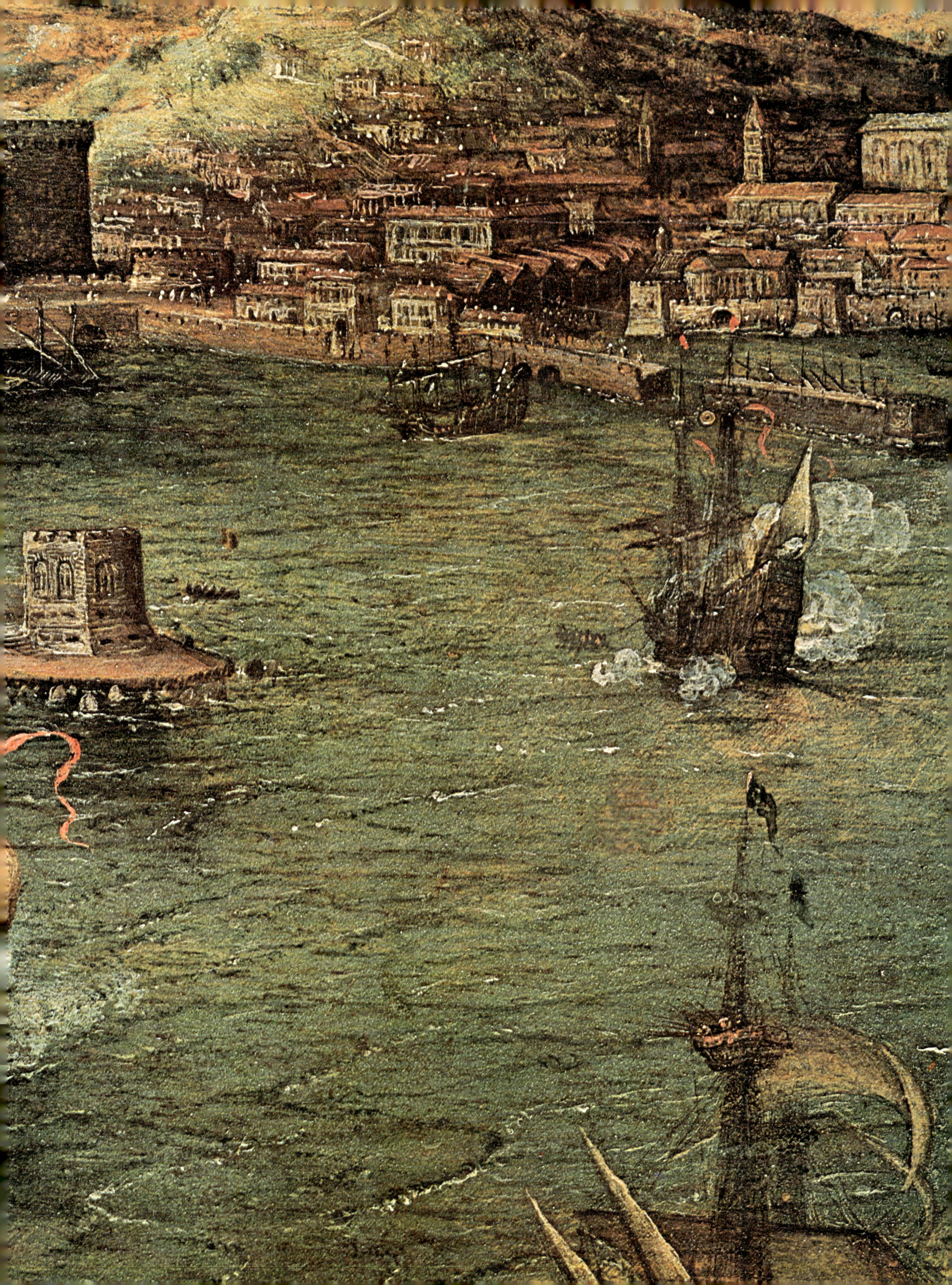

Judgement. The Lectionary is one of Clovio's finest works as a miniaturist. What does seem certain is that landscapes were what Clovio wanted from Bruegel when they worked together. But Auner goes rather too far when he claims that Bruegel was simply seeking work during his stay in Rome and met with a rude rebuff from Clovio when the latter tried his skill.

Be that as it may, Bruegel seems not to have found what he was looking for in Rome. According to Auner, who believes Bruegel to have been an Anabaptist, it was the burning of two heretics on the Campo dei Fiori in September 1553 at the instigation of the Inquisition which prompted him to leave and make his way to the autumn fair in Lyons that same year, but this is pure speculation. Grossmann describes the detours and 'remarkable zigzags' which Bruegel must have made on his homeward journey in order to satisfy his interest in the exotic world of mountain peaks and valleys. A drawing of the Ticino valley south of the St. Gotthard, a lost painting of the St. Gotthard which

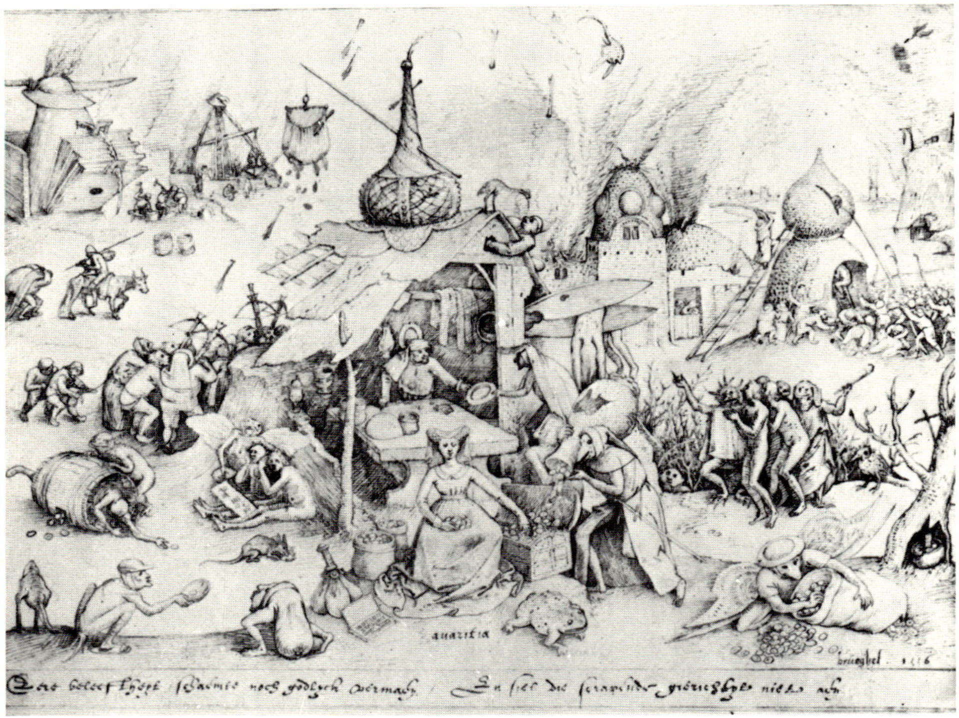

AVARITIA
Pen drawing in dark maroon on paper; 228 x 297 mm (9 x 11 in)
Signed and dated at bottom right: 'brueghel 1556'
London, British Museum, Printroom
Preparatory drawing for the engraving by Pieter van der Heyden (Bastelaer 128). The first of the series of *Deadly Sins* which, like almost all engravings from works by Bruegel, was published by Hieronymus Cock in Antwerp. It was to this series of allegorical fantasies that Bruegel owed his fame as a 'second Bosch'. However, Bruegel differs from Bosch in certain fundamental respects, especially in his rationalistic conception of sin. This is expressed stylistically in his ironical and humorous or thoroughly sarcastic treatment of figures and actions. The inscriptions on this and the other drawings in this series are not by the artist.

belonged to Rubens, a drawing inscribed 'Waltersspurg' (not in Bruegel's hand) which Benesch recognized in 1953 as Waltensburg on the Upper Rhine in the Canton of Grisons: all this would seem to suggest that instead of turning west in the Rhine Valley, Bruegel went east to the Tyrol, where he got at least as far as Innsbruck as we can see from a drawing of the Martinswand (now in Berlin). This work, however, is the subject of more controversy. Tolnay, who located it, regards it as a copy; Münz attributes it to Roland Savery and doubts whether it really is the Martinswand; while the Berlin exhibition catalogue of 1975 upholds both its authenticity and the identification of the locality. As it was customary to avoid, if possible, the dangerous route across the Alps in winter, Grossmann concludes that Bruegel only set off homewards in the spring of 1554, the majority of the landscape drawings being executed on the return journey. He would then have been back in Antwerp by 1555 at the latest because it was in that year that he began the series of Large Landscapes for Cock. But Auner, who gives a detailed description of the terrors of travelling in the Alps in those days, holds completely different views about the painter's Alpine wanderings: 'There can be no question of a foreign painter travelling here and there all over the Alps in the mid-16th century, so only two other possibilities remain: either the localities have been incorrectly identified or else the drawings are not by Bruegel but by a later imitator of his drawing technique. Until these questions have been cleared up it will be reasonable to assume that Bruegel returned home the way he had come, the way he already knew' – in other words via the Mont Cenis and Lyons. Grossmann's rejoinder is that Auner's arguments against the identifications proposed by Tolnay and Benesch are inadequate and that he disregards the important eastern route through the Alps and via Munich used by other Netherlandish artists such as Joris Hoefnagel and Hendrik Goltzius.

It was in Antwerp that Bruegel's potential reached its full fruition. Here was the ideal environment for the development of his creative genius, surrounded by friends and acquaintances who included the city's leading humanists – the celebrated cartographer and geographer Abraham Ortelius, for example, who like his friend the publisher Cristophe Plantin had become an adherent of the Anabaptist and antinomian doctrines of Heinrich Niklaas (Auner). Bruegel's modification of his name and signature in 1559, coinciding with his emergence as a prominent painter, may have been an outward sign of this humanist tendency. The change from Gothic minuscule to Renaissance capital in the signature and the dropping of the 'h' in his surname could mean he was considering latinizing his name to Brugelius or Bruegelius, forms actually used by Ortelius not long after (Auner). It might be worth mentioning at this point that the way we now spell the name of Pieter Bruegel the Elder reflects his own signature from 1560 onwards, while that of his descendants can be written 'Brueghel' with an 'h.'

Van Mander speaks of the merchant Hans Franckert, who was Bruegel's daily com-

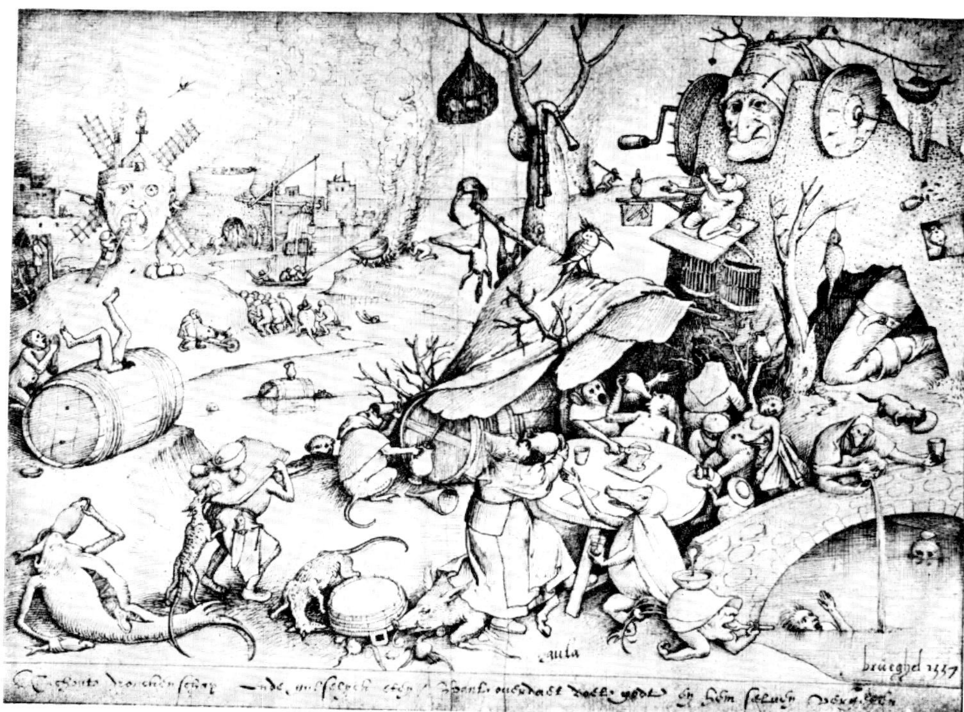

panion and with whom the painter went in disguise to a peasant wedding, bringing presents and pretending to be one of the relatives, as a 'noble and excellent man'. Franckert, a merchant from Nuremberg, entered the Guild of St. Luke in Antwerp in 1546, no doubt as a member of the chamber of rhetoric affiliated to it since 1480. Why, as Auner contends, should this Franckert have been no more than a miserable petty profiteer for whom Bruegel merely painted hangings which he then tried to sell to peasants? Nor does Auner believe van Mander's account of the visits in disguise to peasant weddings, seeing this as an anecdote to cover up the fact that Bruegel sold painted hangings to the peasants – the theory being that he would have wanted to keep such transactions secret because they might damage the reputation of a painter whose works had been acquired by the Emperor. Grossmann, too, regards these tales of disguise as a typical 16th century convention of the kind one might expect in biographies of artists to throw light on their faithful reflection of peasant life. Similar expedients would be Vasari's casting of Giotto in the role of a shepherd or Lomazzo's story (in his *Trattato dell' arte de la Pittura* of 1584) that Leonardo once gave a feast for some peasants and got them to laugh by means of all sorts of tricks and jokes so he could study their expressions. The first scholar to draw attention to this was E. Gombrich. But who is to say that Bruegel was not himself a rich man, perhaps the son of well-to-do parents and in no way dependent on earning his keep by painting wall hangings or some similar occupation – rather like his contemporary, the nobleman Cornelis van Dalem? The question is deliberately provocative and serves as a reminder that little is known for certain about Bruegel's life. It is remarkable all the same that only a few works in oil have survived which predate the first painting, dated 1557, known definitely to be by Bruegel, (the *Parable of the Sower*, page 41.) This indicates that clients wanting paintings came forward only gradually after Bruegel had achieved a certain fame with engravings. Had he been financially independent he would probably not have held back for so long from painting, which was more costly. In the event his production of oil paintings suddenly burst out like a long pent-up stream, burgeoning in exuberant self-fulfilment in the last twelve years of his life. In other words, I believe Bruegel would have painted pictures even without commissions, however contrary that might have been to the practice of his time: pictures for himself or his best friends. And was this not, in fact, almost the case? Is it not striking that Bruegel's clientele consisted of a select circle of friends and connoisseurs – indeed, how could it have been otherwise with his particular type of art? Despite the timeless quality his works have acquired in the public world of art, they still retain the character of private communications: unthinkable in a church but entirely apposite in the rooms of the meditative, 'Mannerist' Emperor Rudolph II. The thinking behind them is so obviously independent that ecclesiastical

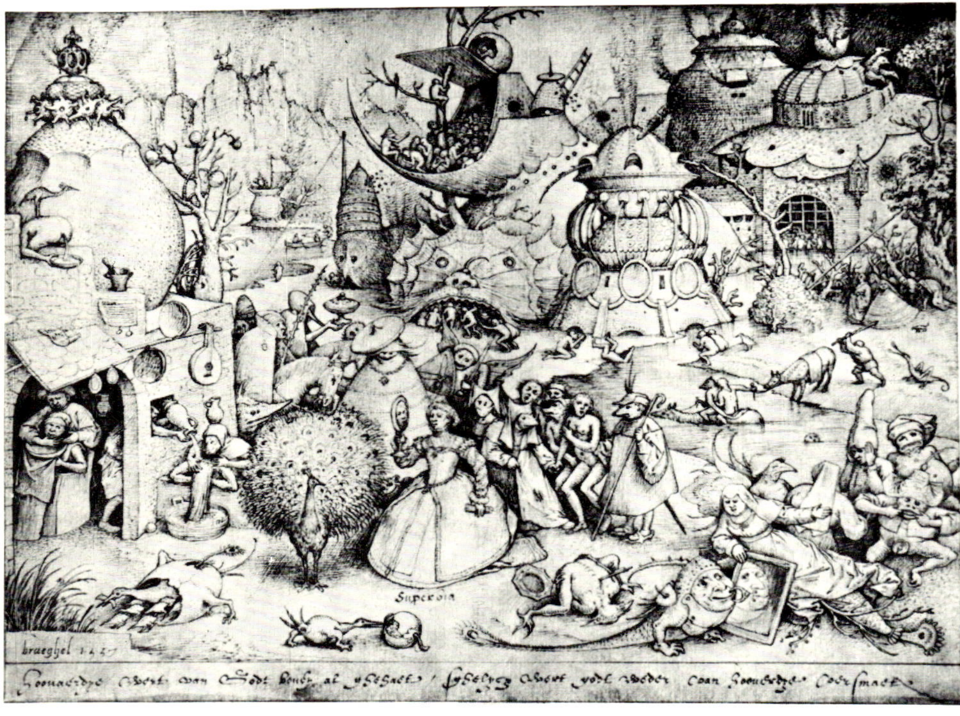

SUPERBIA
Pen drawing in maroon on paper; 230 x 300 mm (9 x 11 in)
Signed and dated at bottom left: 'brueghel 1557'
Paris, Institut Néerlandais
(formerly in the F. Lugt Collection)
Preparatory drawing for the engraving by Pieter van der Heyden (Bastelaer 127) in the series of *Deadly Sins*. Pride or arrogance is regarded as one of the worst sins because it leads to many others. The Netherlandish inscription (not by the artist) states: 'God hates pride above all things, just as God is distained by pride'.

commissions were out of the question from the start. At any rate, none are known. Bruegel's works seem intended precisely for the newly emerging type of discriminating, educated and cultivated collector.

One of the earliest collectors of note was the famous cardinal Antoine Perrenot de Granvella, Archbishop of Malines from 1560 and Chairman of the Netherlands Council of State up to 1564. Another was the rich and highly-respected art connoisseur Niclaes Jonghelinck.

Granvella, discussed in some detail earlier on, owned one of the major international art collections of his time, divided between his palaces in Brussels, Malines and Besançon. He clearly prized Bruegel's works unusually highly, because he gave separate instructions for the recovery of those paintings when the Archbishop's palace was plundered during the troubles of 1572. We do not know which or how many pictures Granvella possessed, except that the *Flight into Egypt* (page 82) can definitely be traced back to him. Granvella left the Netherlands in 1564, so we can assume he personally acquired the pictures before that date. Niclaes Jonghelinck owned no fewer than sixteen of Bruegel's paintings, including the scenes of the months (pages 102–103), the *Tower of Babel* (page 85), and *Christ Carrying the Cross* (pages 94–95), all of which are now in Vienna. They were used, together with a picture by Dürer and twenty-two works by Franz Floris, as security for 16,000 guilders. Niclaes Jonghelinck was the brother of the sculptor Jacques Jonghelinck, to whom he probably owed his connection with Granvella, the cardinal having a very high opinion of Jacques, who kept a studio in one of the ancillary buildings of the Brussels palace. Unfortunately, it is not known how many works were owned by Abraham Ortelius, but he certainly had the *Death of the Virgin* (page 100). This grisaille must have meant a great deal to him as he had it engraved in copper in order to give copies to his friends.

Taking up the thread of van Mander's account once again, we come to the story of the girl whose lies Brugel recorded with notches on a stick. This may be a fabrication, but at any rate nothing came of the relationship and at Easter 1563, in Brussels, Brugel married Mayken Verhulst, youngest daughter of the late Pieter Coecke and Mayken Verhulst Bessemers. The entry in the marriage register of the church of Notre-Dame de la Chapelle states briefly: 'Pieter Bruegel, Mayken Cocks ... solmt'. The latter word has always been interpreted as an abbreviation of 'solemniter', indicating a special ceremony, but Menzel rightly points out that it could also be read as 'solvit', i.e. 'paid'. However, on his marriage Bruegel had evidently moved to Brussels and we have to ask ourselves why – after all, the bride would normally have gone to her husband's home. However good-natured and compliant the painter may have been, it is hardly possible to imagine him leaving the place where he had so many professional contacts, clients, friends and acquaintances simply at the behest of a mistrustful mother-in-law: according

IRA
Pen drawing in maroon on paper; 230 x 300 mm (9 x 11 in)
Signed and dated at bottom left: 'brueghel 1557'
Florence, Uffizi
Preparatory drawing for the engraving by Pieter van der Heyden (Bastelaer 125) in the series of *Deadly Sins*. A painted copy exists in the museum at Rouen. Despite the coarseness of certain details the drawing is not without ironical features. The large figure in the centre sitting astride a barrel has similarities with the figure of 'Dulle Griet' in the painting at Antwerp (p. 69).

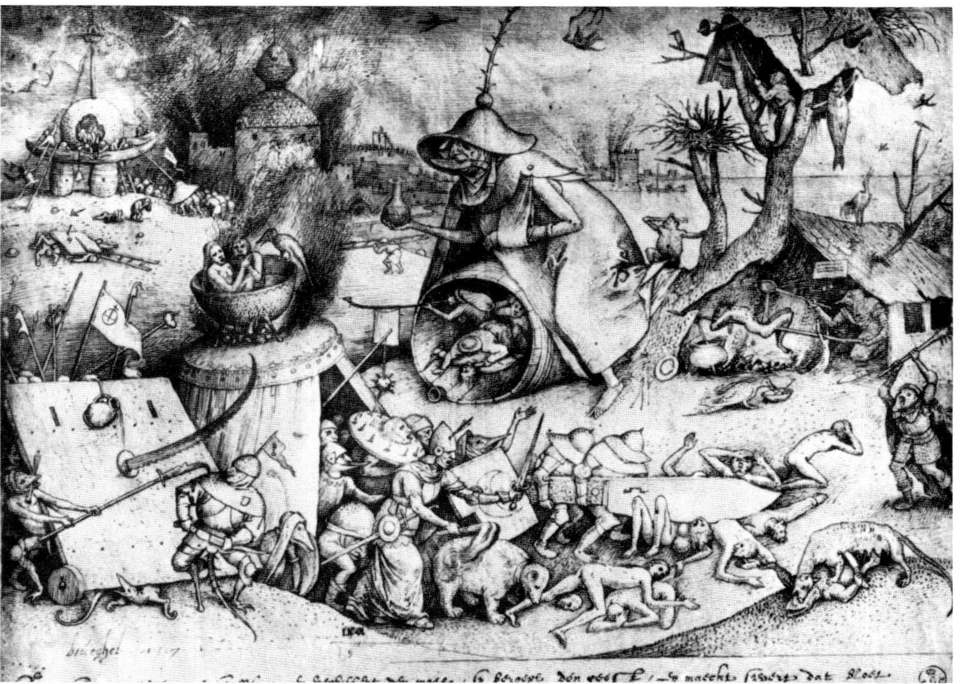

to van Mander she made it a condition of the marriage that Bruegel should move to Brussels 'so that he might forget the other girl'. While Auner sees the reasons for the move as mainly material (taking into account the economic crisis of 1562) and even considers a joint studio run by the painter and his mother-in-law to be a possibility, Jedlicka favours a religious explanation. According to his theory, Bruegel either sympathized with or was a member of Hendrik Niclaes' Schola Caritatis sect and no longer felt secure in Antwerp following the alleged flight of the printer Plantin. But why then, argue Auner and Grossmann, would he have gone to Brussels of all places, the seat of the government and its agencies, where a heretic would have been exposed to far greater dangers?

However that may be, Bruegel was away from Antwerp – before moving to Brussels – in the crisis year of 1562, when the beginning of the first Huguenot War in France, occasionally threatening to spill over into the Netherlands, caused many wealthy people to stop commissioning works of art. A number of drawings dated 1562 and showing the towers and gates of Amsterdam (page 73) reveal that this was where he went.

It was in Brussels that Bruegel spent the last six years of his life and reached that artistic maturity which marks the peak of his achievement. Here he produced his greatest and most famous works like the scenes of the months, the *Peasant Wedding Feast* (pages 164–165) the *Peasant Dance* (pages 168–169), the *Land of Cockaigne* (page 147), the *Sermon of St. John the Baptist* (pages 134–135), the *Parable of the Blind* (page 161) and many other mature works. Bruegel must have worked like one possessed, all his forty-eight surviving paintings, except for three early works, being produced in no more than twelve years (1557–1569).

Almost two-thirds of this output – some thirty masterpieces – were produced in the last six years in Brussels, and this figure does not include works which have been lost or are only preserved in copies. The volume of graphic work done for Hieronymus Cock naturally declined, though without drying up altogether. From 1565 onwards we find a number of engraved works appearing: a series of copper engravings with sailing-ships, the *Fall of Hermogenes*, the drawing for which survives (page 98), the *Parable of the Good Shepherd*, the *Walk to Emmaus, Spring* (page 26) *Summer* (page 152). Undoubtedly Bruegel was already very highly thought of in his own lifetime. Perhaps something of this was due to the interest shown in him by Granvella, who was not the most popular but certainly the most powerful man in the Netherlands.

This association also throws light, of course, on Bruegel's political stance, about which various conjectures have been made. All sorts of details in Bruegel's pictures have been seen as covert hostile allusions to the Habsburg regime – a point which will be taken up when we examine the pictures individually. But if such allusions were really present, they would unquestionably have been evident to Granvella, the Archduke Ernst and Rudolph II, who were particularly keen collectors of Bruegel's paintings. That Bruegel

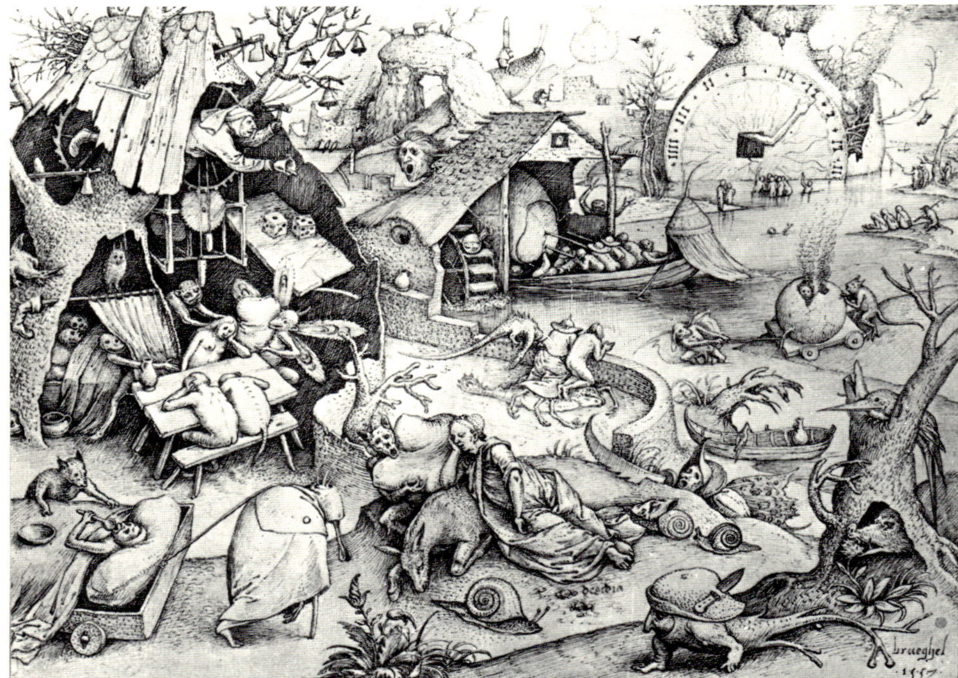

DESIDIA
Pen drawing in dark maroon on paper; 214 x 296 (8 x 11 in)
Signed and dated below right: 'brueghel / .I.5.5.7.'
Vienna, Graphische Sammlung Albertina
Preparatory drawing for the engraving by Pieter van der Heyden (Bastelaer 126) in the series of *Deadly Sins*. The Netherlandish inscription (not by the artist) has been cut off and stuck on the back. It says: 'Sloth deprives a man of strength and dulls his nerves, so that he is no longer capable of doing anything'.

was unhappy about Spain's control over his country since Philip II is clear, but it would have been senseless for him to compromise himself. Political innuendoes were hardly to be expected in a country in which one could be hanged for a thoughtless remark.

Bruegel's association with Hendrik Niclaes' non-reformed sect Schola Caritatis is also hypothetical, though certainly not improbable. The publisher Christophe Plantin, for example, belonged to it. But Niclaes' really important writings entitled *Speculum Justitiae: De Spegel der Gerechticheit, dorch den hilligen Geist der lieften Jesu Christi unde den vorgodeden Minsch* H.N. (1580, place of printing not given) did not appear until eleven years after Bruegel's death, although their message would undoubtedly have been current beforehand. The main burden of this doctrine was that the soul needed no earthly assistance for its redemption: it would be released through heavenly love alone. All religions were equally valid symbols of one fundamental truth, which even in Holy Scripture had only been represented in allegorical form.

Auner maintains that Bruegel belonged to the Baptist movement, but his arguments, though attractive, are inadequate. He ends by quoting the passage in van Mander which deals with Bruegel's contrition. It seems that before his death Bruegel asked his wife to burn some drawings 'because they were partly far too bitter or caustic', 'either out of contrition or from fear that his wife could get into trouble or have to answer for them in some other way'. But what, in the eyes of the Catholic van Mander, could Bruegel have needed to be contrite about if not his deviation from the doctrines of the Catholic Church? My own conviction is that as an individualist and humanist, Bruegel had close associations with neither a party nor a religious group, even if he was aware of such things. However familiar he may have been with humanist writing since Erasmus, my view is that Bruegel's intellectual independence must have been enormous, comparable to that of Michel de Montaigne, Rabelais or Shakespeare.

Van Mander tells us that the City Council of Brussels gave Bruegel an official commission to record the excavation of the Brussels-Antwerp canal, which was completed in 1565, in a number of '*stucken*' (meaning either paintings or else cartoons for tapestries), but Bruegel's death on 9 September 1569 prevented this work from being completed, or perhaps even begun. At any rate, nothing has survived. His children were born in Brussels: Pieter in 1564 or 1565, Jan in 1568 and a daughter, about whom nothing is known at all. Although much younger than Bruegel, Mayken outlived him by only nine years; on her death the two sons Pieter and Jan were taken in care by their grandmother Mayken Verhulst, who, as we have mentioned, taught Jan how to paint in watercolour. Pieter Brueghel the Younger (1564/65–1638) became well known as 'Hell Brueghel' and as a skilful copyist of his father's works. Jan Brueghel the Elder (1568–1625) earned for himself the epithet of 'Velvet Brueghel'. He later set above his parents tomb in the church of Notre Dame de la Chapelle in Brussels an epitaph, for which Rubens painted Peter being presented with the keys. David Teniers II, who married a granddaughter of the elder Bruegel, had the epitaph restored in 1676. A century later the church officials sold Rubens' painting and replaced it with a copy.

The Drawings

Bruegel's paintings are today far better known to the public at large than his drawings
are. This is partly due to the wide availability – and popularity – of his pictures in
reproductions, and partly to their accessibility in museums and other public collections.
During Bruegel's lifetime and for a short time afterwards, however, the situation was
precisely the reverse. His best paintings vanished from public view into the private
houses and collections such as the Habsburg collection; but the drawings, popularized
in engravings published by Hieronymus Cock, made Bruegel well-known and were used
as a criterion for assessments of his artistic achievement as a whole.
Bruegel's graphic art, of which the most important and representative examples are
shown in this volume, today ranks once again among his finest work. Chronologically
the drawings come at the beginning of the known opus and the two landscapes of 1552

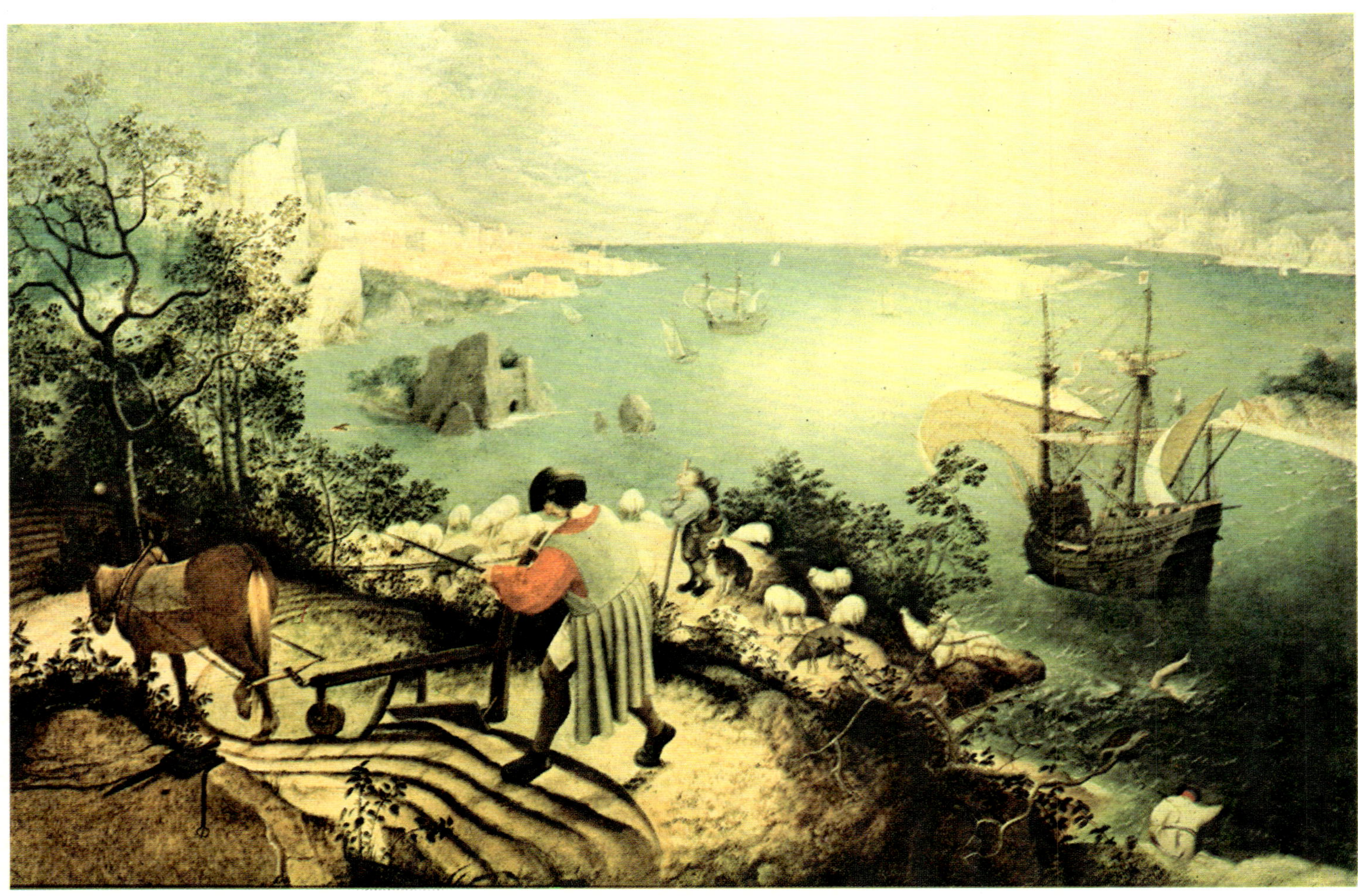

that can be dated to his Italian journey are the earliest surviving instances of Bruegel's
art. The pure landscape drawings already contain the materials that will allow nature to
be so magnificently depicted in later paintings. At the same time the graphic work with
its florid satirical and allegorical compositions makes us at once aware of the intellectual
climate of late humanism and the iconography of Burgundy and the Netherlands. This is
not the only basis for studying the drawings, but as they thereby form a natural in-
troduction to the paintings it seems best to consider them first.

THE FALL OF ICARUS
Oil on panel transferred to canvas; 73.5 x
112 cm (29 x 44 in)
Neither signed nor dated
Brussels, Musées Royaux des Beaux-Arts
Possibly from the Prague Imperial Collection
(1621); acquired by the Museum of Brussels
in 1912. As with the other *Fall of Icarus* in
the van Buuren collection (opposite page),
assessment is made difficult by the work's
poor state of preservation. Opinions differ as
to the artist: while Glück regards both works
as original, Jedlicka at the other extreme
considers both to be copies giving preference
to the smaller van Buuren version. Today
both paintings are generally thought to be
the only remaining copies of a lost original,
an important and highly poetic juvenile
work.

After a hundred years of exploratory development, landscape art came into its own as a distinct genre in the early 16th century: in the diary he kept during his journey to the Netherlands Albrecht Dürer mentions Joachim Patinir simply as 'the good landscape painter'. Dürer's brilliant watercolour landscapes would scarcely have been known in the Netherlands, although his work as a landscapist might have been known from the prints made after his drawings. Nor would artists in the Netherlands have seen many of the landscapes produced around 1520 by Albrecht Altdorfer, Wolf Huber and other members of the Danube School. Their successors Augustin Hirschvogel and Hans Lautensack, older contemporaries of Bruegel's, were also outside the mainstream of artistic influence, although links with Netherlandish achievements can be detected here and there. Initially, Bruegel's landscape art owes as much to native traditions as

THE FALL OF ICARUS
Oil on panel; 63 x 90 cm (24 x 35½ in)
Neither signed nor dated
New York and Brussels D. M. van Buuren Collection
Acquired in Paris from Mme J. Herbrand (cf. the version in the Brussels Museum, opposite page). This painting is generally preferred to the other, but the poor state of preservation of both works makes any comparison difficult. The encounter between Ovid and Bruegel, extraordinary in itself, produced an unusual and charming result in these two pictures.

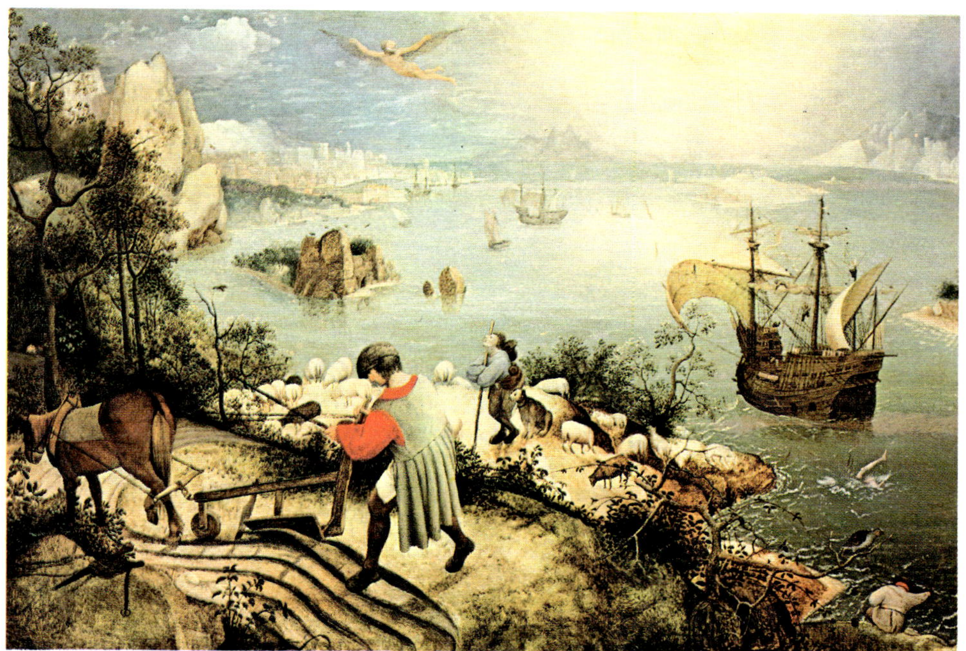

exemplified in Patinir and his successors Cornelis Massys, Matthijs Cock and Jan van Amstel as to Italian patterns of landscape drawing. Examples of the Italian achievement can be found in woodcuts by Ugo da Carpi and Campagnola in the style of Titian, in engravings by Cornelis Cort after Girolamo Muziano, and in Venetian landscape art. Bruegel's interest in such examples was in mastering spatial unity as the Italians had done, thus eliminating the structural complexities of Patinir's landscapes in favour of a logical and clearly visible relationship between foreground, middle distance and background, and representing spatial depth in a plausible manner. Münz draws attention to Maerten Heemskerck's role in assimilating and passing on Italian influences, particularly the achievements of Campagnola, whose sketchbooks of the mid-30s already contain 'those great, sweeping curves which connect the foreground with the rest of the picture'. Lugt was the first to point out that whereas Bruegel's invented landscapes clearly betray Venetian influence, his depictions of actual scenes in nature are 'pure' Bruegel from the very outset.

A fine example of early perfection here is the magnificent drawing of 1552, now in the Louvre (page 9), in which the low focal point chosen shows that the drawing is a study of nature for its own sake. Like the work of the same date in Berlin which has been slightly impaired by later watercolouring, it is generally thought to have been executed in Italy. Auner contends that they were done in France before Bruegel crossed the Alps.

It should be mentioned here that the catalogue of the 1975 Berlin exhibition entitled *Pieter Bruegel the Elder as Graphic Artist*, which is full of new information from recent research, presents a third drawing, previously published by Arndt in 1966, which can very probably be assigned to the same year, 1552, and is in the Biblioteca Ambrosiana in Milan. The subject of the drawing is an imaginary landscape in the manner of Titian: the composition in many ways suggests a lateral inversion of the etching entitled *Pagus Nemorosus* in the series of Large Landscapes printed by Cock. The catalogue also contains a number of studies of trees with twisted trunks and close-up views of woodlands, all betraying Italian influence, some of which only exist as copies and which up to now have not been regarded as Bruegel's work.

In 1552 Hieronymus Cock began to publish a series of twelve etchings showing imaginary landscapes (except for *Pagus Nemorosus*, which is of an idyllic Flemish village on the edge of a wood all the subjects are Alpine scenes). These Large Landscape compositions consist of real scenes from the Italian journey – partially rearranged – together with freely invented elements. Their exaggerated, dramatic character fulfilled a certain craving for sensation in a public which would hardly have been content with mere representations of actual landscapes, even though a modern taste might find strict representation more interesting. The drafts for this series of etchings have all been lost except for one (in the Louvre, dated 1555). Naturally enough, too, the etchings are without that subtle softness of mood peculiar to Bruegel's own direct creations and found in masterpieces such as the *Large Rhine Landscape* of 1555–60 in New York (page 15) or the *Alpine Landscapes* of 1555–1556 in London (pages 16 and 17).

All the scholars agree that the *Large Rhine Landscape*, one of the finest of all Bruegel's graphic works, is not a study made directly from nature but was executed in the studio on the basis of a sketch. Bruegel's technique was to add an invented but appropriate foreground to the original, real landscape, a method revealed by a number of drawings (in Dresden and elsewhere) in which the foreground has been left blank. Benesch attempted in 1953 to identify the locality depicted as the castle of Jörgenburg and the village of Ruis in the Upper Rhine Valley between Truns and Ilanz, but this has yet to be confirmed. What is certain is that the work was inspired by impressions gathered during the Italian journey. While Münz assumes the drawing was completed in 1553 or 1554 in the course of the journey, other scholars go for a later date between 1555 and 1560 – which may perhaps be more likely in view of the maturely controlled strokes and the superlative precision in the use of graphic techniques. The difference is made clear by a comparison with the *Alpine Landscape* dated 1553 in the Louvre (page 14). This may be an unused draft for an engraving, as is suggested by the unity of the composition and the careful elaboration of detail. A certain modification of the pen strokes, giving a rather three-dimensional appearance, reinforces this idea. That the artist had studied Venetian landscape drawings is demonstrated by the lively curves, the winding path in the foreground which seems to continue in the serpentine line of the torrent. The same can be said of the even more mature *Alpine Landscape with two Mules and Driver* in London, which can be dated about 1555–1556 (page 16). Here, too, the bolder strokes seem to be yearning for translation on to the copper plate. This expansive landscape forms a kind of enclosed basin stretching from the foreground to the undulating mountainous shapes of the middle distance and background. The play of shadows in the drawings intensifies the dramatic effect. A group of rocks in the foreground was also used in the engraving entitled *Insidiosus Auceps* in the 'Large Landscape' series. It might here be worthwhile recalling the 'expressionistic' interpretation of these and similar landscapes put forward by Tolnay. This interpretation suggests that Breughel took a pantheistic approach to nature, seeing nature as a source of mystical inspiration. This idea has been scorned by other writers, and it does seem that such a conception of nature would be well in advance of similar, later ideas such as those of Goethe. But even extreme interpretations of an artist's work can be of value if they throw the traditional view into relief and provoke new ideas.

Opinions differ as to whether this work is a study from nature or a studio composition, and the truth may well be that it contains elements of both. Of course, such considerations are merely a preliminary to the question of what these drawings mean to us today and how we can find the best emotional approach to them. For one thing is certain: our feeling for nature and our concept of landscape is quite different from that of the 16th century.

What is fundamentally new in Bruegel's landscape drawings is an immediate impression that everything is in its natural place; even the studio works look as though nature, not artifice, was the driving force behind their composition. This is the first impression obtained from Bruegel's landscape drawings, distinguishing them fundamentally from all the drawings of his predecessors, which by comparison seem like mere empty stage sets. Van Mander tries to reproduce this impression metaphorically when he says Bruegel's mountain landscapes are as natural as if he had swallowed the mountains during his journey and spat them out again later on to canvases and panels.

In the *Alpine Landscape* in the Courtauld Institute, London (page 17) Bruegel uses exclusively graphic techniques with no brushwork or washes to conjure up the effects of light and air, indeed the whole mood, of an Alpine lake as no-one before him had ever done. His method of representing trees in sunlight by no more than a white circle

LANDSCAPE WITH THE TEMPTATION OF ST. ANTHONY
Oil on panel; 58.4 x 85.7 cm (23 x 33 in)
Neither signed nor dated
Washington, National Gallery. Kress Collection
This interesting work is regarded as authentic by Friedländer, Glück, Delevoy and Puyvelde and dated around 1557; although other writers such as Tolnay and Jedlicka reject this, considering it to be a juvenile work by Jan Brueghel the Elder. The later view is more realistic: despite the high quality of the execution the work has a heterogeneous character incorporating elements of Bruegel, Bosch and Patinir. Grossmann does not register the work at all; the problem of its authenticity was aired again during the Brussels exhibition of 1969.

framed by a series of fine little strokes has often been imitated, but no-one has ever equalled Bruegel in his ability to suggest the rounded, three-dimensional quality of real trees. Not a line of shadowing is accidental, not a stroke out of place, not one square millimetre uncontrolled: every little detail is right. The same applies to this landscape as a whole: calm, natural, solid and organically sound, untouched by man, yet ennobled by the artist.

To all of which we have to add the impression of lightness: a lightness of touch which never overflows into mere virtuosity but seems dictated by the timeless discipline of Nature herself. This sort of perfection is found in Michelangelo's drawings or the music of Bach.

The treatment of the foreground reveals beyond any doubt that this magnificent drawing, too, was finished in the studio after the Italian journey. Tolnay points out that some of the rock formations were used in the 'Large Landscape' engravings. The same

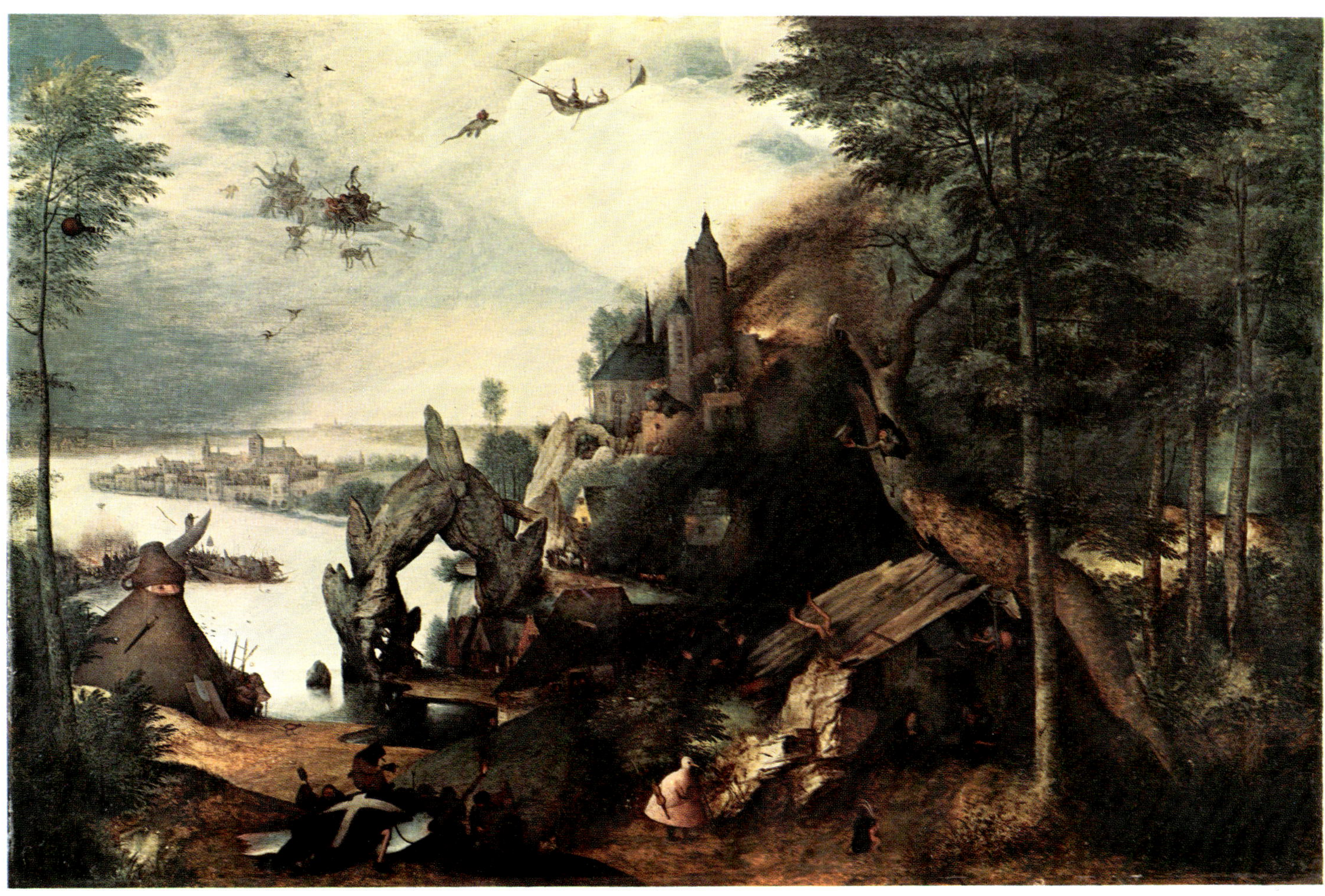

applies to the stupendous *Alpine Landscape with Artist Drawing* (page 18), which is closely related to it and was presumably executed at the same time. The motifs are certainly strikingly similar. Moreover the mass of scree reaching down into the water occurs again, adding a touch of wild ruggedness, in the *Paysage Alpestre* belonging to the series of etchings. There is also a resemblance in the mood created by the copious play of light. And a special nuance is added by the artist drawing in the foreground with a friend looking at the sketch-book over his shoulder. This motif occurs for the first time in Northern European art in an anonymous river landscape in London (page 12) which has links with an etching (page 19) called *Mercury & Psyche* and made in 1553 by Hoefnagel after Bruegel. Gudlaugsson notes that the same motif is present in a woodcut with a view of Florence dated 1482 and attributed to Lucantonio degli Uberti, and adds that the motif could have been introduced into Netherlandish painting by Matthijs Cock. We can imagine Bruegel's travelling companion, supposedly the painter Maerten de Vos, looking at Bruegel's sketch-book over his friend's shoulder.

In 1559 Hieronymus Cock published a series of fourteen etchings entitled *Multifiarium casularum*, followed in 1561 by a further thirty, called *Praediorum Villarum*, both unsigned. A third edition by T. Galle in 1601 names Cornelis Cort as the artist, but

C. J. Visscher of Amsterdam, who published copies of this landscape series in 1612, says Pieter Bruegel was the originator. 'The special importance of these village scenes', says the catalogue of the Berlin exhibition, 'lies in their brilliantly unconventional treatment which seems to anticipate Dutch landscape art of the 17th century – something which it was long thought only Bruegel could have been capable of.' Friedländer, too, made these landscapes the central theme of a book on Bruegel published in 1921, but even before this scholars such as Burchard and Baldass were inclined to favour Cornelis Cort. Hans Bol, Cornelis van Dalem and Hieronymus Cock himself have also been put forward as the originating artist. At any rate, no doubt now exists that Bruegel cannot be regarded as the originator of this series. The most recent attempt to identify the master of the 'Small Landscapes' was made during a discussion following the 1975 Berlin exhibition by E. Haverkamp-Begemann, who proposed Joos van Liere.

The large landscapes directly associated with the Alpine trip during the Italian journey and with the 'Large Landscape' series of engravings may be contrasted with a group of rather different, intimate landscape studies of smaller format and smaller visual scope. Executed in 1559–1561, that is, after the large compositions, most of them show castles or ruined castles perched on precipitous cliffs above river valleys, or steep mountain paths leading up to castle gates. Then there are intimate village scenes which far surpass the series of 'Small Landscapes' in artistic achievement. A modification of technique can also be detected in this group, from which we have selected the *Mountainous Landscape with Narrow Path between Rocks* of 1560, now in Berlin (page 62). Their lightness, avoiding heavy contours, already looks forward to the dot technique which later the artist was to use widely. The drawings were not intended for reproduction by printing nor are they from a sketch-book, because their formats vary and most of them are signed and dated separately, which would not have been necessary in a sketch-book. They should rather be considered as independent works, which is how Bruegel thought of them – as suggested for one thing by the careful signatures, mostly in the 'humanist' style with capitals: 'BRUEGEL'.

We should also mention here the only etching known with certainty to have been made by Bruegel, the *Rabbit Hunt* of 1560 (page 63). Published by Hieronymus Cock, it has the signature 'BRUEGEL' at bottom left and next to it the date '1560', which up to now has been wrongly read as '1566'. Stylistic considerations point to an earlier date, and this is borne out by a (laterally inverted) copy of the lost draft for the etching in the Institute Néerlandais in Paris (Coll. F. Lugt), which is dated 1560. The composition recalls both the 'Large Landscape' series of engravings and also the group of 'Small Landscapes' of 1559–1561. P. Fehl (quoted in the 1975 Berlin catalogue) makes a comment on the etching's iconography which, though interesting, needs to be treated with circumspection: for the hunter is aiming at two rabbits simultaneously and will not in fact hit either of them. The drawing in Paris (not the etching) shows a third rabbit in the foreground, no doubt to show that the hunter could hit it more easily than the two further away if he would only be content with one. Fehl then cites a proverb from Erasmus of Rotterdam: 'Duos Insequens Lepores Neutrum Capit' (He who chases two hares catches neither). The man with a spear he regards as a marauding soldier about to threaten the hunter, who would then himself become the hunted. The action and the contrast with the idyllic calm of the natural landscape would be characteristic of Bruegel's irony and pessimism; and with this is coupled the cunningly contrived formalization of the proverbial scene, whose significance would be clear to the initiated.

Two other masterly drawings which do not belong to the group just mentioned but come next to it chronologically display interesting variations of style and content. These are the *Rocky Landscape with Castle at Left* in Munich, signed and dated 'bruegel 1562', and the *Village Landscape* in Brunswick, also signed and dated 1562. The first of these (page 72) clearly harks back to the 'panoramic landscape' genre, a type of landscape composition produced in the late 15th and early 16th centuries which gives a bird's-eye view of the landscape from an elevated vantage point, depicting it as a complete compendium of creation. It shows a river valley, dotted with a multitude of islands, with a steep triangular wedge of land in the foreground. A path leads down to the river and over two footbridges to the gates of a castle, behind which rise steep cliffs marking the edge of the composition. The valley recedes into the far distance. The drawing is executed with extreme delicacy, its pictorial structure recalling the richness of already existing paintings like *The Flight into Egypt* of 1563 now in London (page 82). The *Village Landscape* (page 73), on the other hand, shows a group of thatched houses on a stream in more 'natural' perspective, its motifs closely related to the village scenes of the 'Small Landscape' series of 1561. Bruegel seems here to have been experimenting with his style, or rather his technique, for by leaving the roofs white he has instilled into

LANDSCAPE WITH THE PARABLE OF THE SOWER
Oil on panel; 74 x 102 cm (29¼ x 40¼ in)
Signed and dated: '. . VEGHEL 1557'
San Diego (California), Timken Art Gallery
Mentioned for the first time by Friedländer in 1931, this painting was acquired by the Timken Art Gallery in 1965 from the Stuyck de Bruyère Collection of Antwerp. The scene comes from the Gospel according to St. Matthew (13: 3–8). Developed from the so-called 'panoramic landscape', this composition brings to fruition Bruegel's long study of nature as exemplified in the landscape drawings.

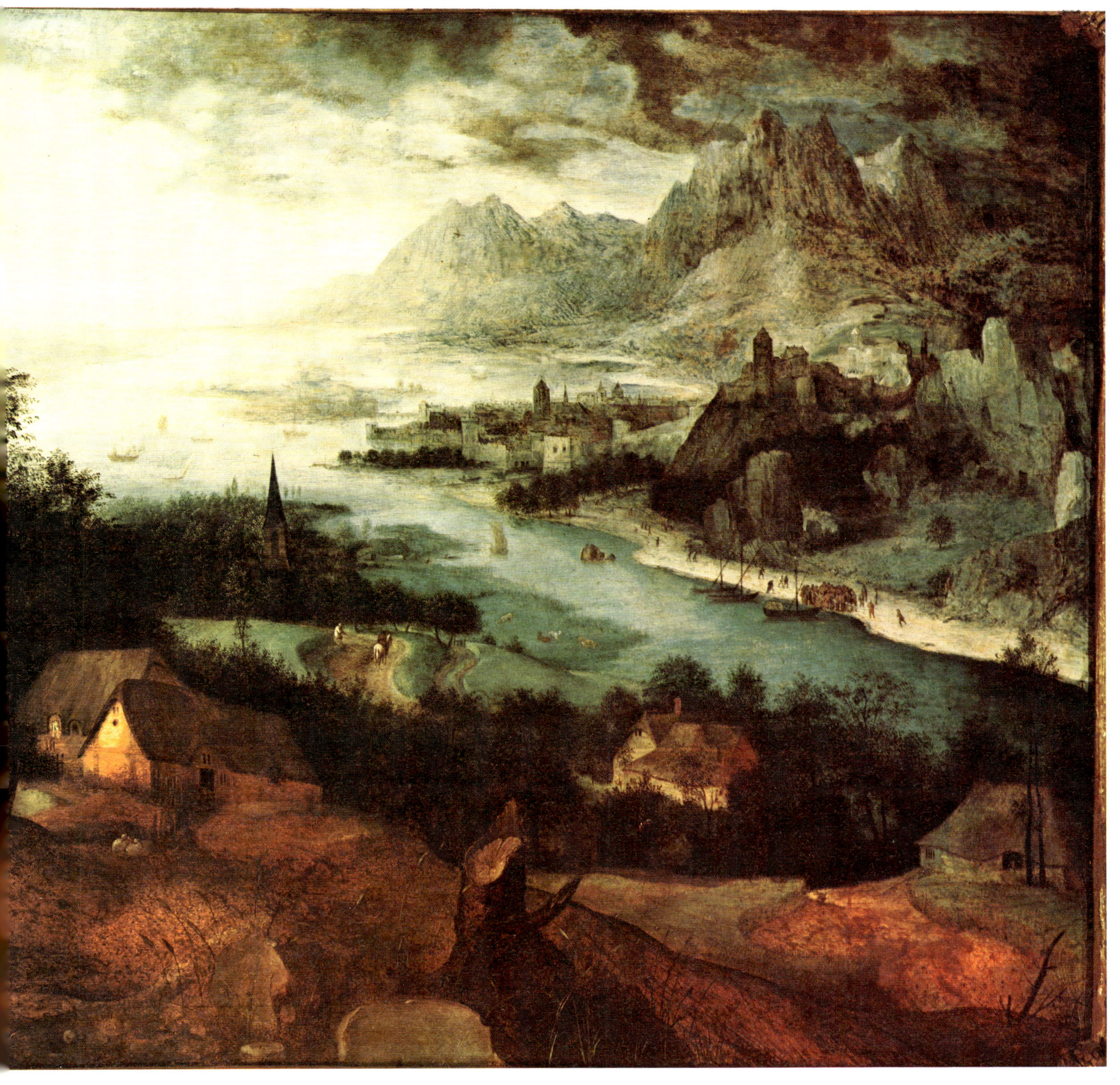

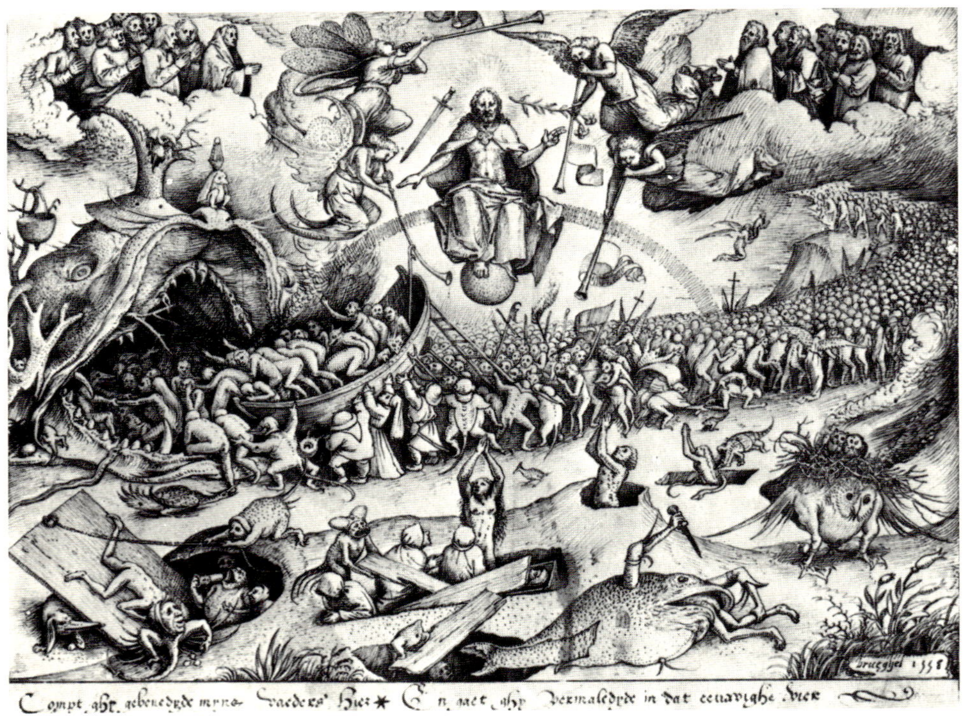

THE LAST JUDGEMENT
Pen drawing in dark maroon on paper; 230 x 299 mm (9 x 11 in)
Signed and dated at bottom right: 'brueghel 1558'
Vienna, Graphische Sammlung Albertina
Preparatory drawing for the engraving by Pieter van der Heyden (Bastelaer 121). This representation of the *Last Judgement* is traditionally associated with the *Vices* (as in the cycle of vices by Bosch in the Prado) and in a certain sense concludes the series. The text accompanying the drawing (not by the artist) says: 'Come to me, you who are blessed by my father; and you who are damned, sink down into the eternal fire'. Another *Last Judgement* taken from a drawing M. van Heemskerck was published by H. Cock in 1564; this confirms the 'stylistic pluralism' which characterized Cock's attitude to art.

the drawing a soft, veiled quality as though the houses had grown out of the ground and been topped with a crust. Here Bruegel has gone further than elsewhere in modelling the forms out of the whiteness of the paper: there are scarcely any contours and the white is delimited not by lines but by the darker adjoining areas. Despite this 'pictorial' approach Bruegel uses no shading and achieves his effect by exclusively graphic means. It has been suggested that the white areas in the foreground were left for the later addition of figures which would have given the drawing some special significance. But this is contradicted by the complete signature and the signs of tracing (similar to those on the drawing of the blind man, now in Berlin, page 160) which must have been connected with a preparatory phase prior to the engraving process. However, it is the case that no engravings of either of these drawings are known. In all its refinement the *Village Landscape* seems vaguely unquiet, artificial and affected compared with the views of Amsterdam of the same year, which are sober and static, as for example can be seen in the *Gates and Towers of Amsterdam* (page 73). In these drawings Bruegel perfected his pointillist technique, modelling his bodies with fine strokes, marks and dots – a technique characteristic of his drawings towards 1570 like *Spring* (page 126), *Summer* (page 152) and the *Beekeepers* (page 153) and imitated by several artists such as

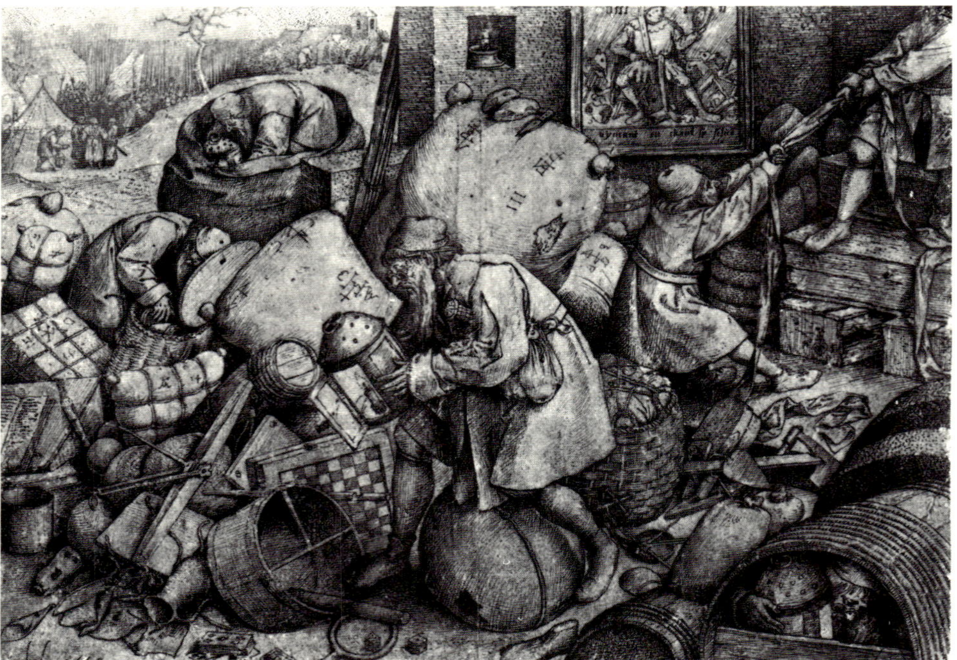

'ELCK' or EVERYMAN
Pen drawing in maroon on white filigreed paper with reddish discolouring;
210 x 293 mm (8¼ x 11½ in) (trimmed on one side)
Signed and dated at bottom left: 'brueghel. 1.5.5.8'
London, British Museum, Printroom
Preparatory drawing for the engraving by Pieter van der Heyden (Bastelaer 152). 'Elck' (Everyman) is one of the most fascinating figures of the first period in Bruegel's graphic art. The various attempts at interpretation have revealed this drawing's great thematic richness, its condemnation of egoism, unbridled greed and aimless bustling, and its capacity to translate the concept of vanity into images.

Fabriczy, the Savery brothers and Pieter Brueghel the Younger. It is perhaps significant that apparently no more pure landscape drawings were produced after 1562 – at least, none have survived. The *Spring* and *Summer* drawings of 1568 cannot be considered as pure landscapes because they are dominated by human figures.

One of the achievements of the Berlin exhibition of 1975 was to put together the results of recent research. Among other things this research had led to the elimination from Bruegel's *oeuvre* of a group of drawings known as the *'naer het leven* studies and regarded until recently as an unquestionable and important part of his graphic output. The studies consist of about eighty drawings now in various galleries, and mostly of human subjects, such as rustic types, carters, servants, beggars, cripples, peasant women, market women and the occasional animal, all clearly sketched *naer het leven* or straight from life. Most of the drawings have detailed inscriptions giving the colours of the various items of clothing, which are represented with great accuracy, and at the very

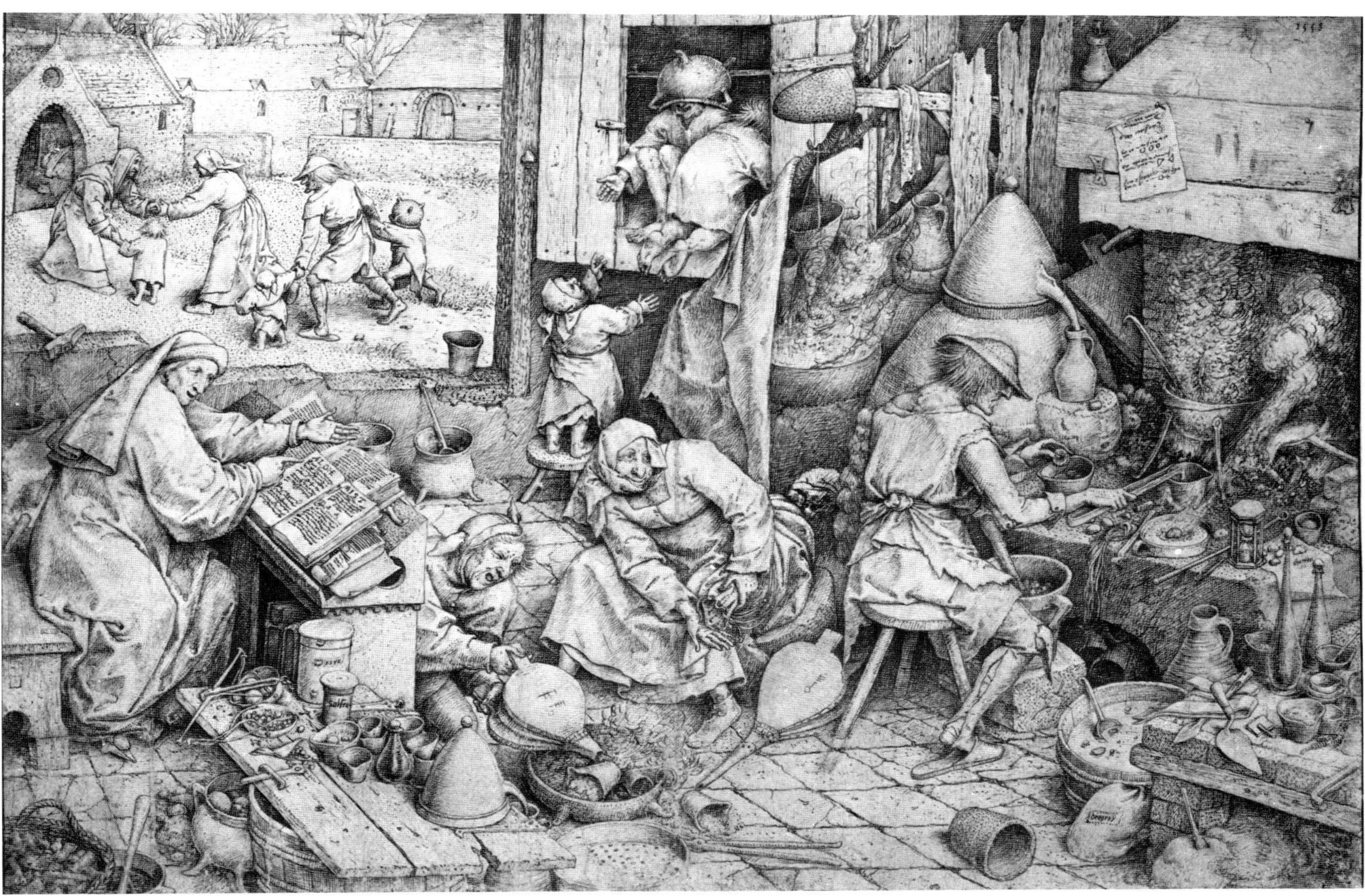

THE ALCHEMIST
Pen drawing in maroon on paper; 308 x 453 mm (12¼ x 17¾ in)
Signed and dated at top right: 'BRVEGHEL / 1558'
Berlin, Kupferstichkabinett (Crozat Collection)
Preparatory drawing for the engraving by Philip Galle (Bastelaer 197) published in several different editions by H. Cock. This is one of the best and most widely discussed works of Bruegel's early period. There is in fact no evidence in this work of a general aversion to alchemy; however it is clear that Bruegel, in accordance with the satirical tradition of the Renaissance initiated by S. Brant's *Ship of Fools*, wishes to give an ironical warning about the undesirable consequences of charlatanry.

bottom carry the words *'naer het leven'* from which the series took its name.

Research by F. V. Leeuven and J. A. Spicer has now finally eliminated Bruegel from the list of possible artists. The types of paper used and the clothing shown – in so far as these can be localized at all – give the origin of the drawings as the south of the German Empire, Bohemia in about the year 1600. Most probably the studies were executed by Roelant Savery. The fact that the team of horses (in the Vienna Albertina) appears in a signed picture by Savery dated 1600 in the Hermitage in Leningrad gives a clue for the dating of the series, which was probably produced in a short time in the form of a sketch-book. The marked variations of quality which suggested, to Tolnay particularly, the involvement of artists besides Bruegel are satisfactorily explained by attributing these drawings to Savery, and a further reason for the attribution is the fact that the *'naer het leven'* studies are not used at all in Bruegel's paintings. Of course, mystery still surrounds the fate of the sketches and drawings Bruegel made for his paintings, for such sketches must have existed. From among this group of works now to be eliminated from Bruegel's oeuvre Tolnay has pinpointed three important drawings which are in fact by Bruegel: *Four Men in Conversation* in the Louvre, *The Shepherd* in Dresden (page 75) and *Artist and 'Critic'* in Vienna (page 127). These obviously do not belong in the *'naer het leven'* series as they have no colour data and, except for the *Four Men in Conversation*, could hardly have been drawn from life.

The carefully contrived balance of the figure in *The Shepherd* immediately suggests a studio composition rather than a drawing from nature. This is indeed a final draft and not just a sketch made on the spot, for the shepherd appears in the middle of a flock of geese on several circular panels illustrating proverbs which were produced by Bruegel's followers. As Marlier and others point out, Jan Brueghel the Elder also used this invention of his father's, which appears in two paintings entitled *The Adoration of the Magi* in Vienna and London. The Albertina in Vienna has a very faithful copy of the original drawing in Dresden, which Tolnay dates 1559–1560 and Münz 1560–1563.

Allegorical and satirical compositions

Artist and 'Critic' (page 127) must also be regarded not as a study from life but as a studio composition. The subject matter of the drawing also raises the question, central to the appreciation and interpretation of Bruegel's art, of the relationship between the literal and the allegorical in his pictures.

Soon after returning from Italy Bruegel began working on his first large allegorical compositions as well as on the 'Large Landscape' series for Hieronymus Cock, thus leading a kind of artistic double life. The year 1556 saw the execution of the drafts for engravings which were published by Cock and laid the foundations for Bruegel's reputation as a second Hieronymus Bosch: these were the *Temptation of St. Anthony* (page 20), *Big Fish Eat Little Fish* (page 21), the *Ass in School*, the allegories of the Seven Deadly Sins (pages 30–34) and the *Last Judgement* (page 42), *Elck* (page 42), *The Alchemist* (page 43), the Seven Virtues (pages 56–57), *Christ in Limbo* (page 65), the *Fall of Hermogenes* (page 98) and others. It is not clear whether *Artist and 'Critic'* was also meant to be engraved; Grossman and Benesch suspect this is an independent work of art which has to be seen neither as a study for a painting nor as a draft for an engraving. The drawing must have won fame rapidly, because four copies exist (by Jacques Savery, Joris Hoefnagel and two unknown artists). The paint-brush identifies the main figure in his 'medieval' smock as a 'painter'. He is standing in front of an easel, which is omitted in the drawing, his eyes gazing out into the distance from under shaggy eyebrows 'as though he is watching some far-off object' as Stridbeck puts it. His tousled greying hair sticks out wildly from under his painter's cap and the white beard is dishevelled too. His features, with the corners of the mouth turned down, express heroic gravity and saturnine gloom mingled with a trace of revulsion and contempt for the world in general. A stark contrast is offered by the 'critic' with his relaxed and artful expression, the nose giving his face a rather bird-like look. The whole effect of the composition relies on this contrast of physiognomies. The 'critic' is looking somewhat wryly through his glasses over the painter's shoulder at the imaginary picture, his right hand delving into a purse. He, too, is dressed in medieval clothes. Backing up his interpretation of the piece as an allegory of painting, Stridbeck says in this connection that in the rhetorical dramas of the 16th century which were an important source of inspiration for Bruegel, 'the allegorical figures would appear in 15th century costume whose old-fashioned and therefore neutral character stressed their universal, timeless quality'.

Scholars have shown particular interest in whether the 'artist' is a self-portrait, though no conclusive evidence has ever been put forward. In fact the refined features of Bruegel's face in the copper engraving from Dominicus Lampsonius' *Pictorum aliquot celebrium Germaniae inferioris effigies* of 1572 (page 8) bear no resemblance to the 'painter' – neither does the supposed self-portrait in the crowd in *Christ Carrying the Cross* in Vienna (page 93). Tolnay regards the 'artist' as a portrait of Hieronymus Bosch, while Benesch sees in it an idealized portrait of Bosch, but neither view can be proved.

Astonishment and admiration, but also cunning and curiosity, have been detected in the expression of the 'critic', or 'connoisseur' as he has also traditionally been called. It has been pointed out frequently that the 'connoisseur' has links with Bosch's painting *The Juggler*, and indeed there is a certain similarity with the spectator in that work – also bespectacled – whose purse is being cut open. (It was on this resemblance that Tolnay and Stridbeck based their interpretations.) F. Gils thinks Bruegel may have portrayed himself with the English poet John Heywood. But however varied the interpretations may be, there is general agreement that the drawing reflects a fairly poor relationship between artist and layman. If this is true then the traditional titles *Artist and Con-*

THE TWELVE PROVERBS
Oil on panel; 74.5 x 98.4 cm (29⅜ x 38¾ in)
(diameter of each medallion 21 cm (8¼ in))
The twelfth proverb has a signature and the remains of a date: 'BRVEGEL....8'
Antwerp, Museum Mayer van den Bergh
Opinions about this work differ, too. The individual plates were only later combined to form a single picture and all of them are closely linked to the *Proverbs* in Berlin (p. 47). While some scholars agree in regarding these individual tondi as authentic

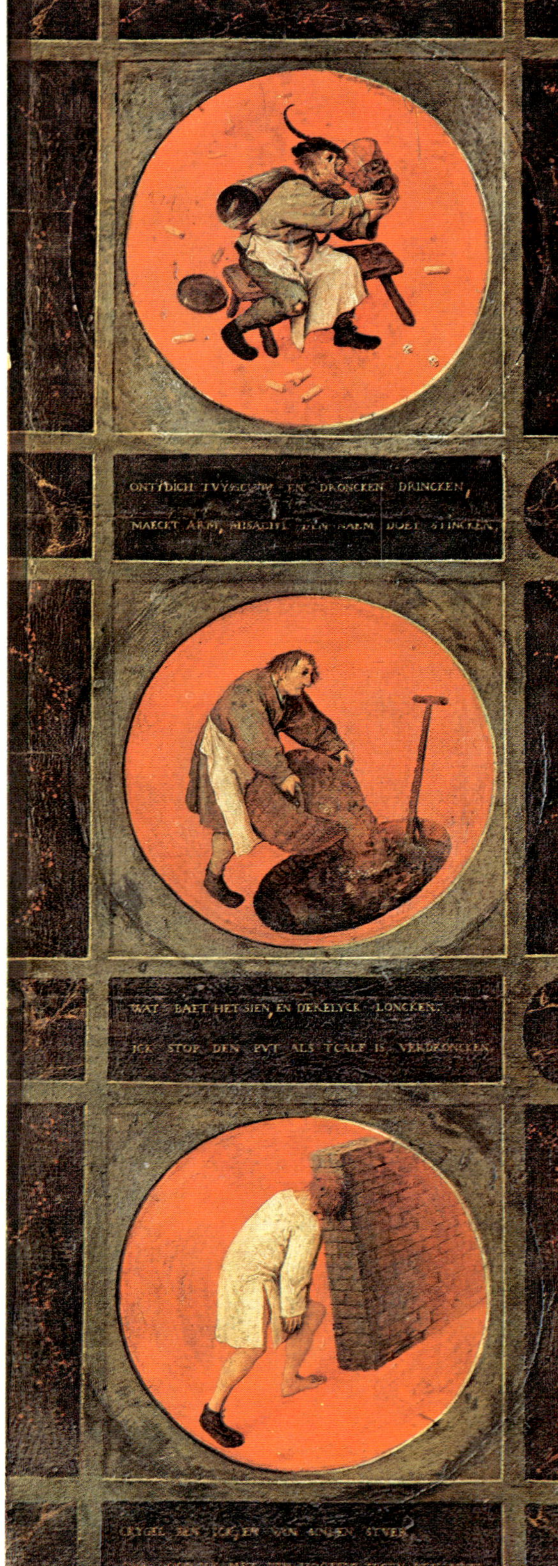

studies and more precisely as preparatory
studies for the large composition in Berlin,
other critics, especially Grossmann, reject this
with the contention that they are copies by
Pieter Brueghel the Younger. Recent attempts
have been made to resolve the question once
and for all by means of X-ray examinations.

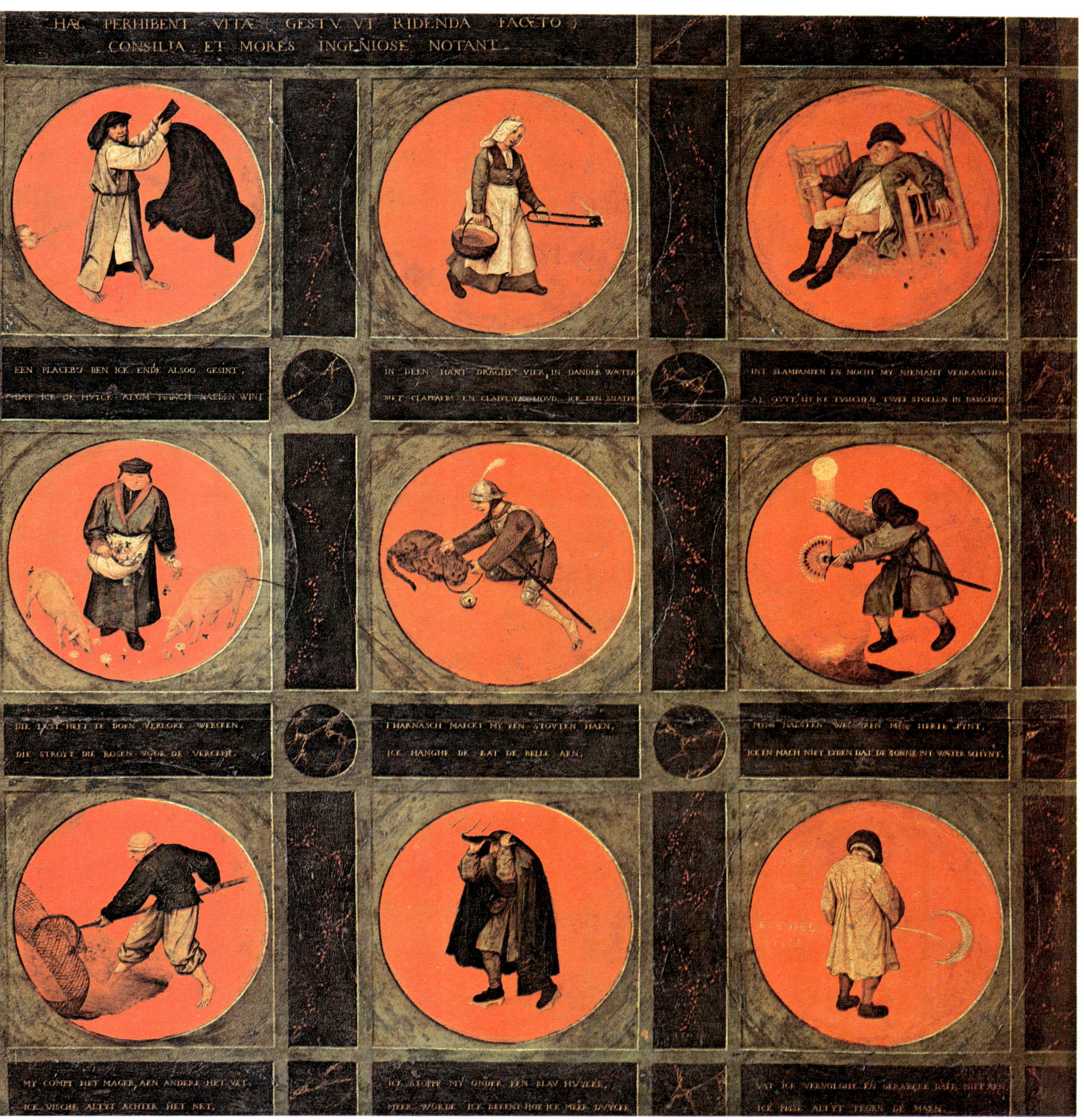

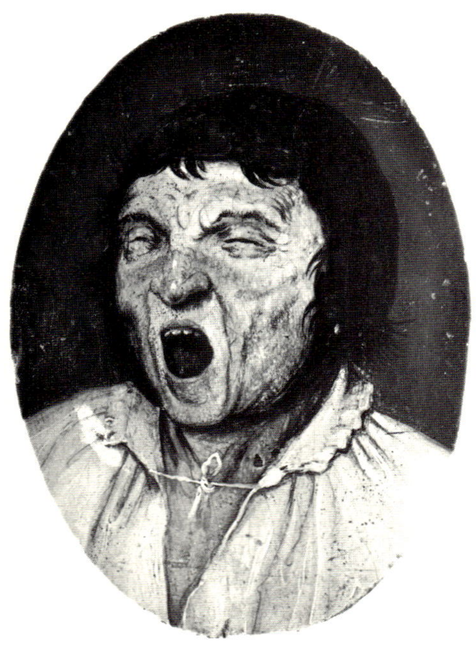

YAWNING MAN
Oil on oval panel; 12.6 x 9.2 cm (4 x 3 in)
Monogrammed: P.
Brussels, Musées Royaux Des Beaux-Arts
In the M. S. Scheikevich Collection in
Moscow in 1907; acquired by the Brussels
Museum in 1949. Thought at first to be by
Hulin de Loo and Michel, this little painting
is now regarded by scholars as the work of
Pieter Brueghel the Younger or else of an
unknown artist. It may originally have been
part of a series of heads showing the seven
mortal sins and would have represented
Sloth. Lucas Vorsterman engraved it as a
character study. An identical picture is
mentioned in the Rubens inventory of 1640.
The catalogue of the 1969 Brussels Exhibition
quotes this work as being of dubious
authenticity and dates it before the *Twelve
Proverbs*.

noisseur and *Artist and Critic* are misleading unless 'connoisseur' and 'critic' are put in
apostrophes to indicate irony. For, it seems, despite his careful scrutiny the 'connoisseur'
cannot see the meaning of the picture or understand the painter's *raison d'être*. The
painter's bag (almost obliterated by the trimming of the Vienna original, but seen in
the copies) is thought to be a purse, which would mean a picture is about to be bought.
The austere, heroic artist must needs sell his works even to a philistine, who will most
likely be mean as well to judge by the way his hand is thrust into the purse – a
traditional sign of avarice. In view of this the catalogue of the Berlin exhibition renamed
the work *Painter and Customer*. In the same catalogue F. Angelewsky draws attention to
two Dutch proverbs which among other things suggest that Brueghel's drawing could
have the additional significance of a *momento mori*. I tend to think that the two utterly
different idealized types represent the contrast between two worlds or two modes of
existence: on the one hand the artist engaged in his struggle, on the other the fussy,
petty-minded bourgeois. Here the visonary, here his opposite, a contrasting pair like
Faust and Wagner in Goethe's *Faust*. The stroke of genius seems to me to reside in the
idea of evolving a picture from no more than the physical dissimilarity of two faces.
From this derives the drawing's curiously powerful intensity, which leaves a lasting
impression on anyone who sees it. Despite their great accuracy, the copies fail to
reproduce entirely faithfully the details of the two facial expressions in the original.

Reducing the composition to only a few figures – half-figures in this case, the only
instance of it in Bruegel's oeuvre – is a typical feature of the late phase in Bruegel's art,
which makes the generally accepted dating of around 1565 clearly preferable to Tolnay's
date of 1560 or 1561. Stridbeck further points to the Italian influence in the 'accentuated *contrapposto*' and in the 'illusion of space and volume created by the bent
left arm', recalling Raphael's Castiglione portrait in the Louvre; there is scarcely any
evidence of Italian influence in Bruegel's work before the last few years of his life. The
original signature must have been lost when the drawing was cut: the present one is in a
lighter ink and of later date.

The Temptation of St. Anthony (page 20) and all the remaining drawings are drafts for
engravings which Bruegel executed for Hieronymus Cock's publishing house. The
Temptation of St. Anthony is generally regarded as the earliest surviving work for Cock.
Like *Big Fish Eat Little Fish* and the *Ass in School*, it is dated 1556. But the date and the
signature have long been 'considered of doubtful authenticity, particularly since the
drawing is not laterally inverted in relation to the engraving. Yet Tolnay and above all
Grossmann have produced convincing evidence in support of Bruegel as the artist. The
somewhat singular impression made by the drawing stems from the combination –
unusual in Bruegel – of pen and brush technique, which is otherwise found only in the
Resurrection in Rotterdam (page 77).

The subject of temptation must have accorded with the mood of the age. Grunewald's
main work, for example, is an altarpiece on the theme of St. Anthony, and Bosch had a
special preference for the subject. It is clear that, because of his work with Cock, Bruegel
would have played a part in the revival of interest in Bosch's work which took place in
the middle of the century. Thus it is not surprising that the first of the allegorical works
is a St. Anthony: a Bosch subject treated in a similar manner.

The drawing's message is expressed in the Latin text on the engraving, a quotation from
Psalm 34: 'Many are the afflictions of the righteous: but the Lord delivereth him out of
them all'. The focal point is the gigantic floating head which Tolnay interprets as
'Peter's head' (i.e. Peter the hot-blooded). He sees it as derived from works by Thomas
Murner and Johann Fischert, identifying it as a symbol of the corrupt Church, though
there is no unequivocal evidence for this. Tolnay has associated the head and various
details with Netherlandish proverbs such as *'Zijn hoofd is zoo hol als een ledige
eijerdop'* (His head is as hollow as an empty egg-shell') or 'If the head is full of smoke,
no light can shine in'. The head is wearing spectacles, but instead of resting on the nose
they are stuck through one side of it, reflecting the proverb *'Het is geen neus om een
bril te dragen'* ('That is no nose for wearing spectacles', in other words, not the nose of a
wise man). The fish on the head would refer to the proverb *'Laat de haring met over je
hoofd heen zwemmen'* ('Don't let the herring swim over your head'). The herring
symbolizes the Papacy ruling the world, the document on the tree being a Papal Bull. A
different explanation is offered by the 1975 Berlin catalogue, which relates the window-
eyed head to Bosch himself. The latter uses it in his portrayal of the dream of Tondalus,
a 12th-century Irish knight who saw Heaven, Hell and Purgatory in a vision and
abandoned a life of sin to become a monk. In *The Vision of Tondalus* Hell is
represented as seven valleys in which the seven deadly sins are punished. In Bruegel's
picture, however, we cannot pinpoint the deadly sins individually. Parts of the com-

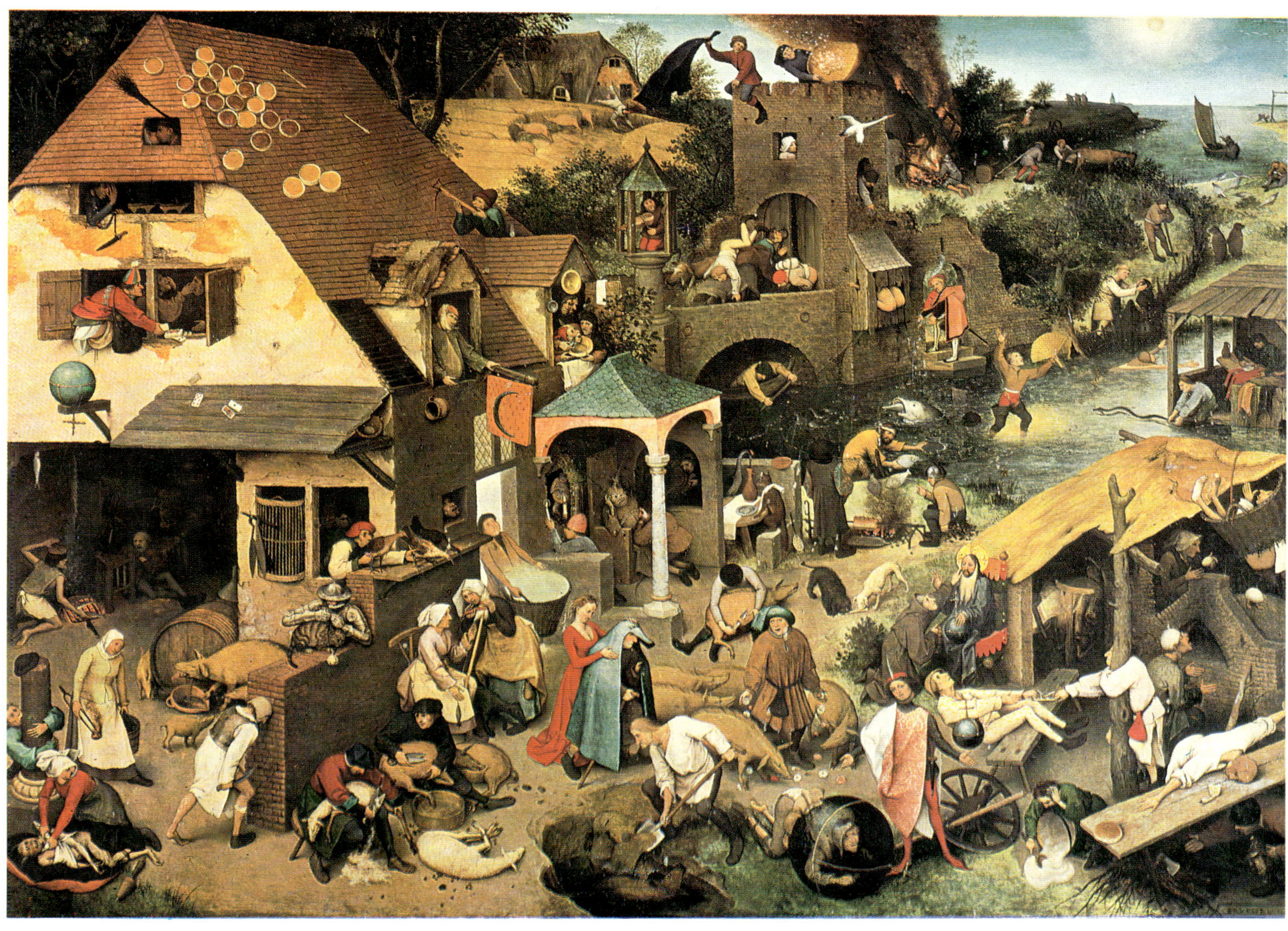

NETHERLANDISH PROVERBS
Oil on panel; 117 x 163 cm (46 x 64 in)
Signed and dated: 'BRVEGEL 1559'
Berlin, Staatliche Museen, Preussischer
Kulturbesitz, Gemäldegalerie
Mentioned for the first time in the inventory
of Pieter Stevens (1668), this is the first of
Bruegel's large pictures in which we find the
characteristics of his mature style.
Illustrations of proverbs appeared frequently
before Bruegel's time, but the idea of com-
bining a variety of scenes in a kind of
'landscape of proverbs' is entirely new.
Bruegel weaves this ensemble of absurd
activities into an image of a mad, topsy-turvy
world as symbolized in the inverted blue
globe on the left.

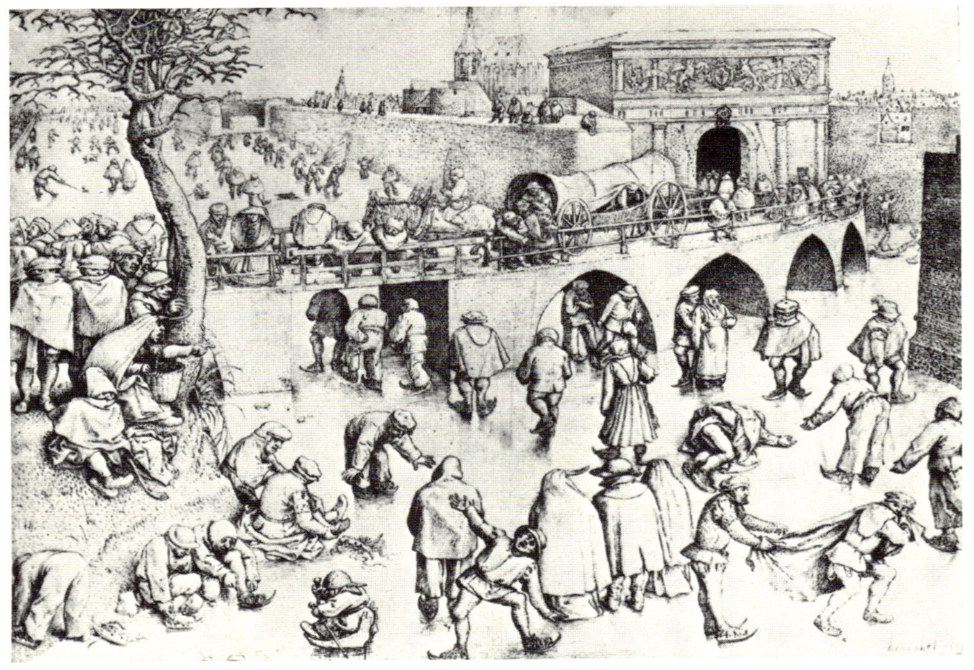

SKATERS AT THE GATE OF ST. GEORGE
Pen drawing in maroon on paper; 213 x 298 mm (8⅜ x 11¾ in)
Signed and dated at bottom right: 'brueghel/ 1558'
Private American collection
Preparatory drawing for the engraving by Frans Huys published by H. Cock (Bastelaer 205). The second version of the engraving does not bear the name of Cock and is erroneously dated 1553; this gave rise to the mistaken view that Bruegel had already returned to Antwerp from Italy in 1553. A later version of the engraving, showing the scene in entirely new and extraordinarily realistic terms, carries a text with an allegorical and moralizing interpretation of the drawing as a metaphor of the instability of human life.

position appear in a *Temptation of St. Anthony* of the Bosch School in the Galeria Colonna in Rome and the saint himself occurs in a number of drawings by Bosch. The figure enclosed behind rails and riding on the smaller fish in the foreground is presumably an allusion to those who are the prisoners of their carnal urges, the fish being a symbol of male sexuality. The grotesque group fighting like jousters in the foreground vaguely recalls a similar scene in the *Battle Between Carnival and Lent* (pages 50–51), but, to quote the Berlin catalogue 'whereas in the latter we have two clearly distinguishable sides locked in combat, the battle here has reached chaotic proportions, signifying the senseless struggle of everyone against everyone else in the world at large'. The only figure not attacked by the horde of devils is the saint, who turns his back on the nightmarish vision.

Big Fish Eat Little Fish (page 21), the famous illustration of the proverb, was published by Cock as the work of Hieronymus Bosch. However, the Albertina Museum Collection contains Bruegel's preparatory drawing, impeccably signed and dated 1556, so it has been assumed that Cock put the more celebrated name of Bosch on the engraving for commercial reasons, ruthlessly passing Bruegel over. But Grossmann and Münz see Cock's intention in a less critical light, suggesting that Bruegel may actually have used a work by Bosch or at least modified certain of Bosch's ideas for his own composition. This would justify the use of Bosch's name as 'inventor'. In Grossman's view Bruegel had been preoccupied with Bosch before his association with Hieronymus Cock, which

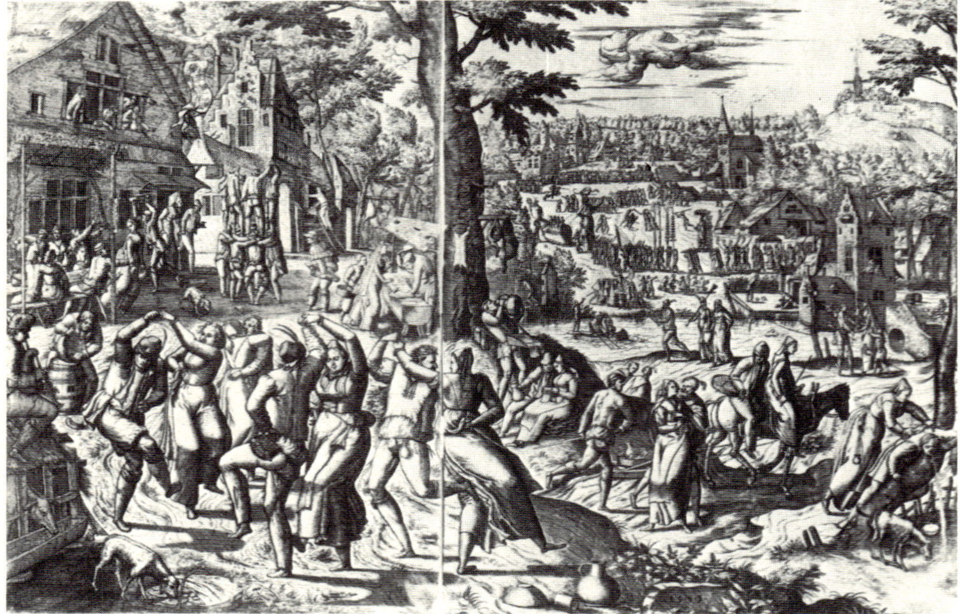

Pieter van-der Borcht
THE FEAST OF ST. GEORGE
Etching; 309 x 592 mm (16⅜ x 23¼ in)
Dated: '.1.5.5.3.'
Vienna, Graphische Sammlung Albertina
This work pre-dates Bruegel's *Feast of St. George* of 1559 (preserved only in the engraving) by only a few years and seems to have had a strong influence on Bruegel's scenes of peasant life (see drawing on opposite page). This etching is a typical example of the kind of local art which inspired Bruegel at the beginning of his career.

would not be surprising in view of the general revival of interest in Bosch and his many imitators like Jan Mandyn and Pieter Huys. Even the Romanist Pieter Coecke was impressed by Bosch. On the other hand Grossman gives Bruegel's name to several important drawings which had initially been attributed to Bruegel but then to Bosch (including the one of cripples and beggars in the Albertina, (page 154). Personally I tend to think this drawing is entirely Bruegel's work. Certainly, the big knife being used to slit open the fish's belly appears in other contexts in Bosch's paintings; but the humanistic, moralizing rationality and drastic immediacy of this visual expression of proverbial wisdom could only have come from Bruegel's hand. The striking arch of the fish's back seems to gather all the details into a coherent whole. The large, jagged knife wielded by the soldier bears the symbol of the world, an orb with a cross. In this world the big 'fish' gobble up the little ones; this is the message of the caption put in the mouth of the father sitting in the boat. Next to his outstretched hand we find the word

THE KERMIS AT HOBOKEN
Pen drawing in maroon on paper; 265 x 394 mm (10⅜ x 15½ in)
Signed and dated at bottom left: '1559 / BRVEGEL'
London, Courtauld Institute, Lee Collection
Preparatory drawing for the engraving by Frans Hogenberg published by Bart. de Momper (Bastelaer 208). The drawing's poor state once gave rise to doubts about its authenticity, which has now been confirmed. This is Bruegel's first depiction of a *kermis* and is of the same date as the *Feast of St. George* of 1559 which has only come down to us in the engraving by Lucas (?) Duetecum. Pieter van der Borcht's *Feast of St. George* of 1559 (opposite page) could have inspired this composition.

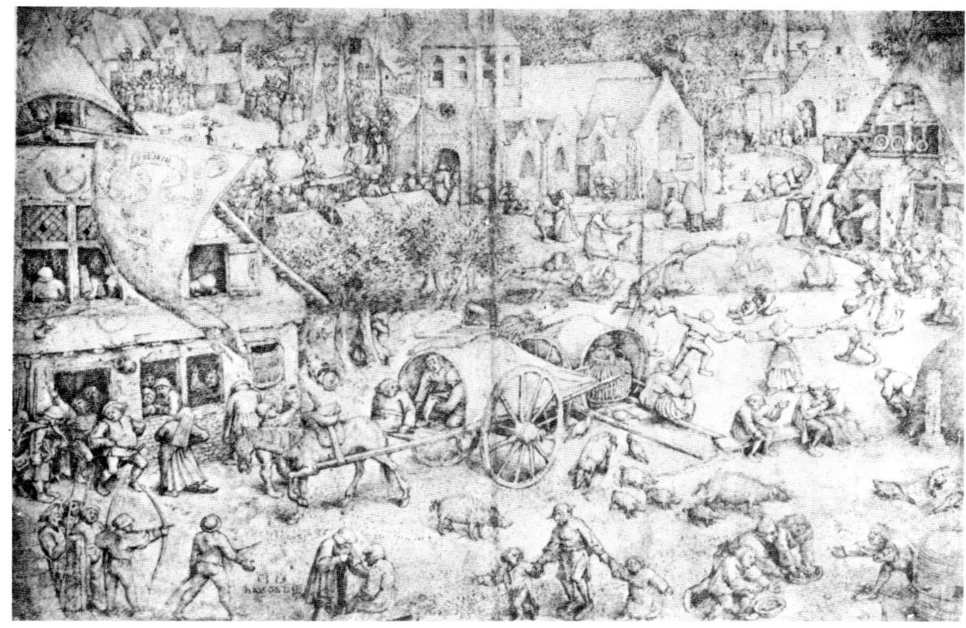

'ECCE', or 'look': he is showing his young son what life is about. The engraving's content of social commentary is developed in a later etching which uses a variety of typical Bruegel motifs. Here the details are explained in the background on the right: while the small fish are hanged, the big ones are allowed to go on swimming because otherwise the wooden gallows would break. Furthermore the angler on the left in the background trying to catch a bigger fish with a minnow hints at the fact that fish are caught with fish; in other words that man's greed and weakness will always be present. In the general mêlée of fish devouring and being devoured, a strange note is struck by the two large mussels attempting to get their share. This may well be a sexual allusion, for if the fish has traditionally been seen as a symbol of male sexuality, the mussel has been its female counterpart. The two symbols are united with unsurpassable clarity on the far right of the *Fall of the Rebel Angels* (page 66–67), where a green fish with whipping tail lies in a wide-open mussel.

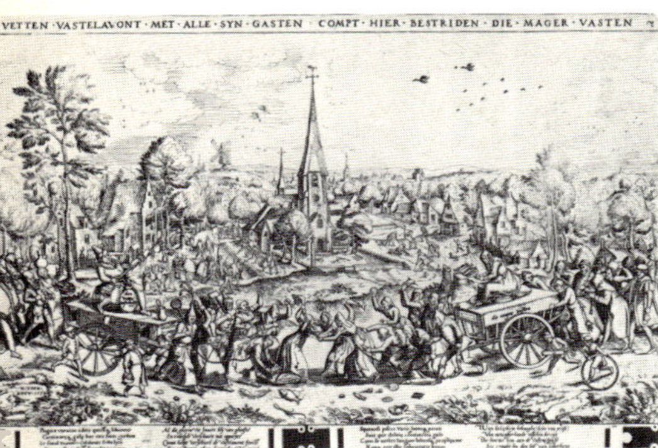

Frans Hogenberg
FIGHT BETWEEN CARNIVAL
AND LENT
Etching; 326 x 516 mm (12⅞ x
20¼ in)
Inscription on the band at
bottom: 'H. COCK EXCU. 1558.
Frans hoechghenberghe'
Vienna, Graphische Sammlung
Albertina
The theme is depicted in a
painting by Bosch known to us
only through a copy. Hogenberg's
etching, executed only one year
before Bruegel's painting, could
have inspired his choice of
subject. A comparison of this
work with the painting reveals
Bruegel's great skill in transforming and elaborating the
iconographical tradition of his
time.

BATTLE BETWEEN CAR-
NIVAL AND LENT
Oil on panel; 118 x 164.5 cm
(46½ x 64 in)
Signed and dated: 'BRVEGEL 1559'
Vienna, Kunsthistorisches
Museum
Mentioned for the first time by
van Mander in 1604, this com-
pilation of folkloristic scenes
offers us a vast and extraordinary
panorama of the life of Bruegel's
contemporaries. This ancient
Burgundian theme was treated by
Bosch and, shortly before
Bruegel, by Frans Hogenberg
(above). The two antagonists,
corpulent Carnival and skinny
Lent, confront each other in a
kind of joust. They were seen as
allegories of Lutheranism and the
Catholic Church respectively.
Details on *pages 52–53*

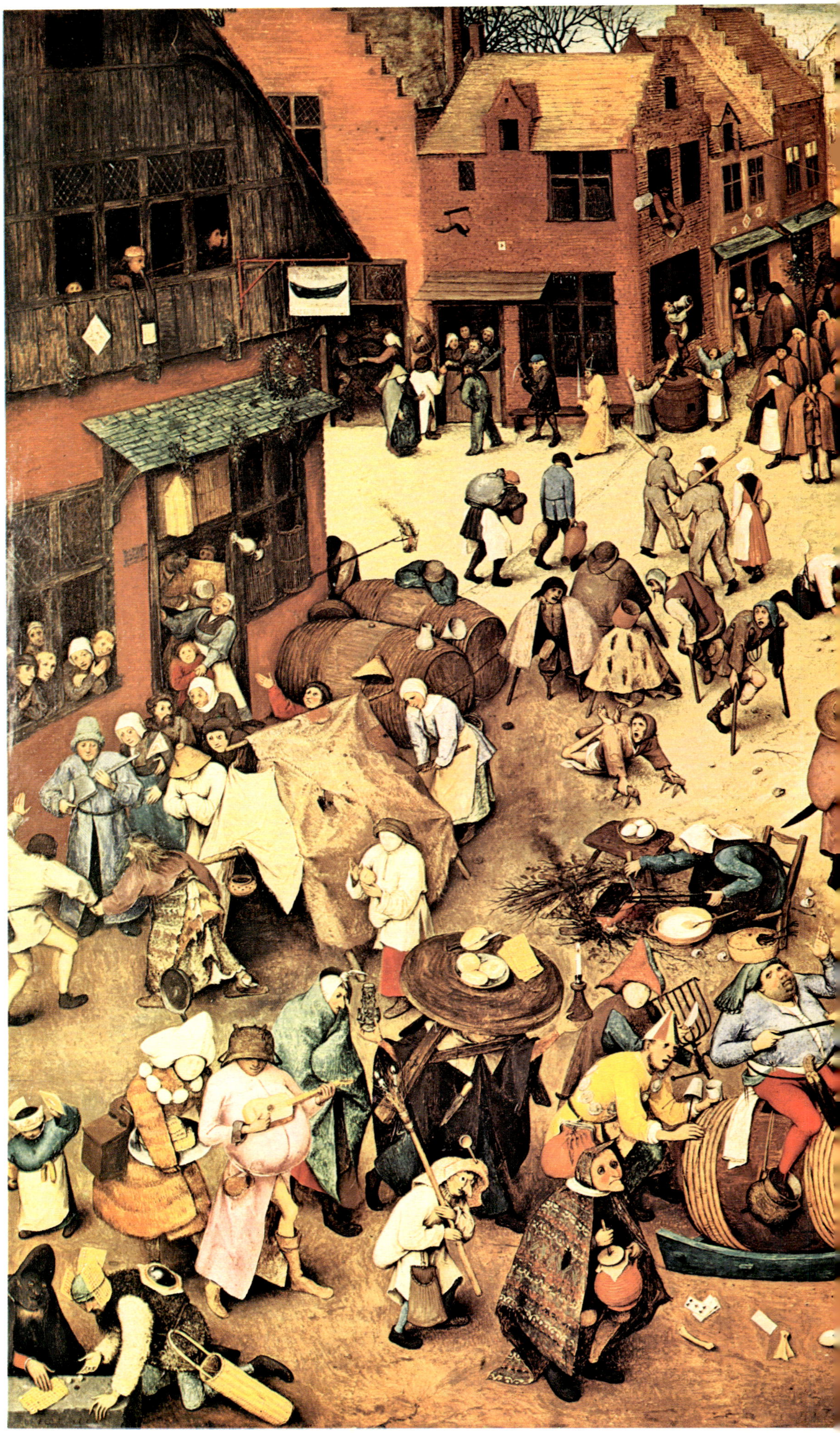

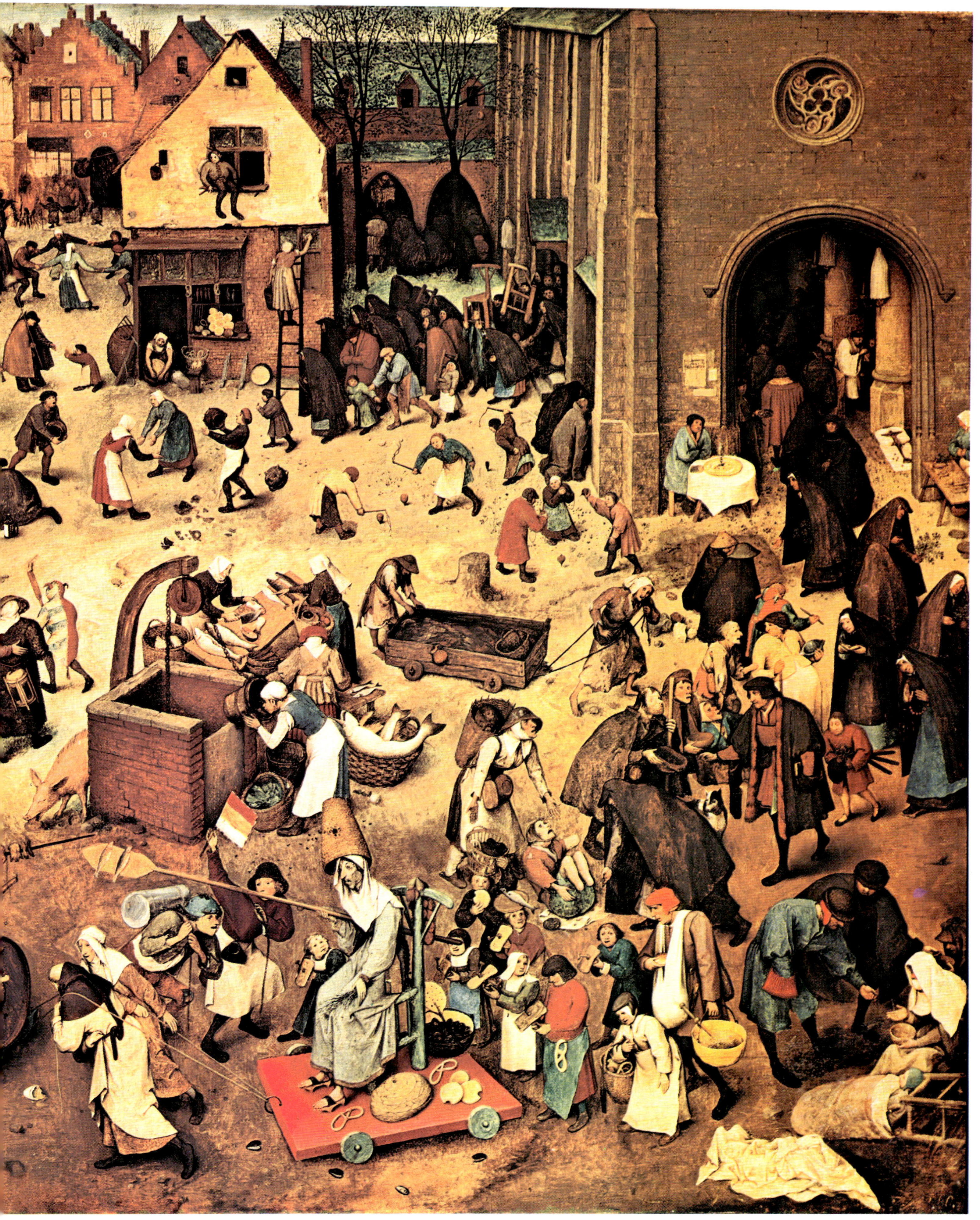

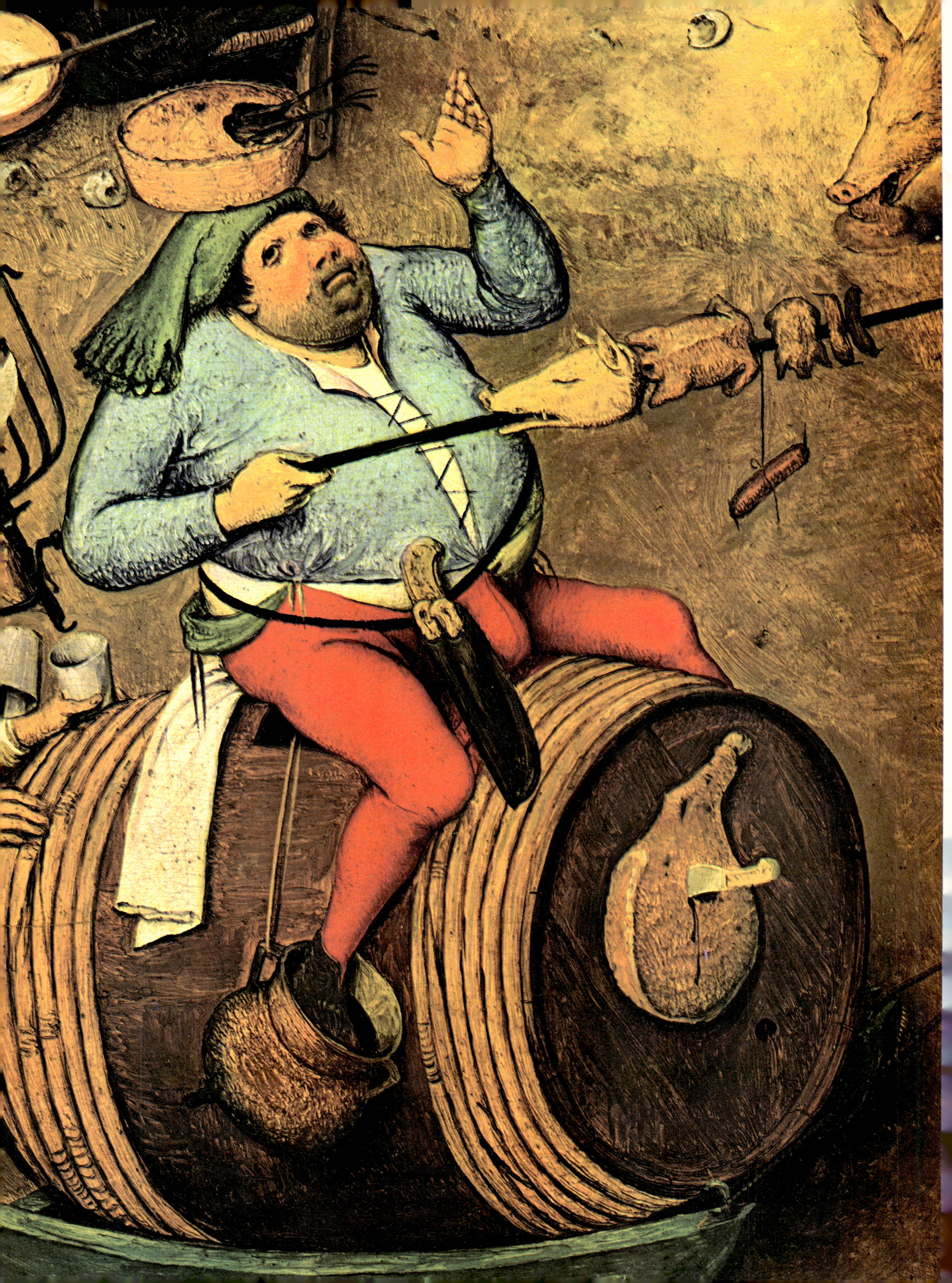

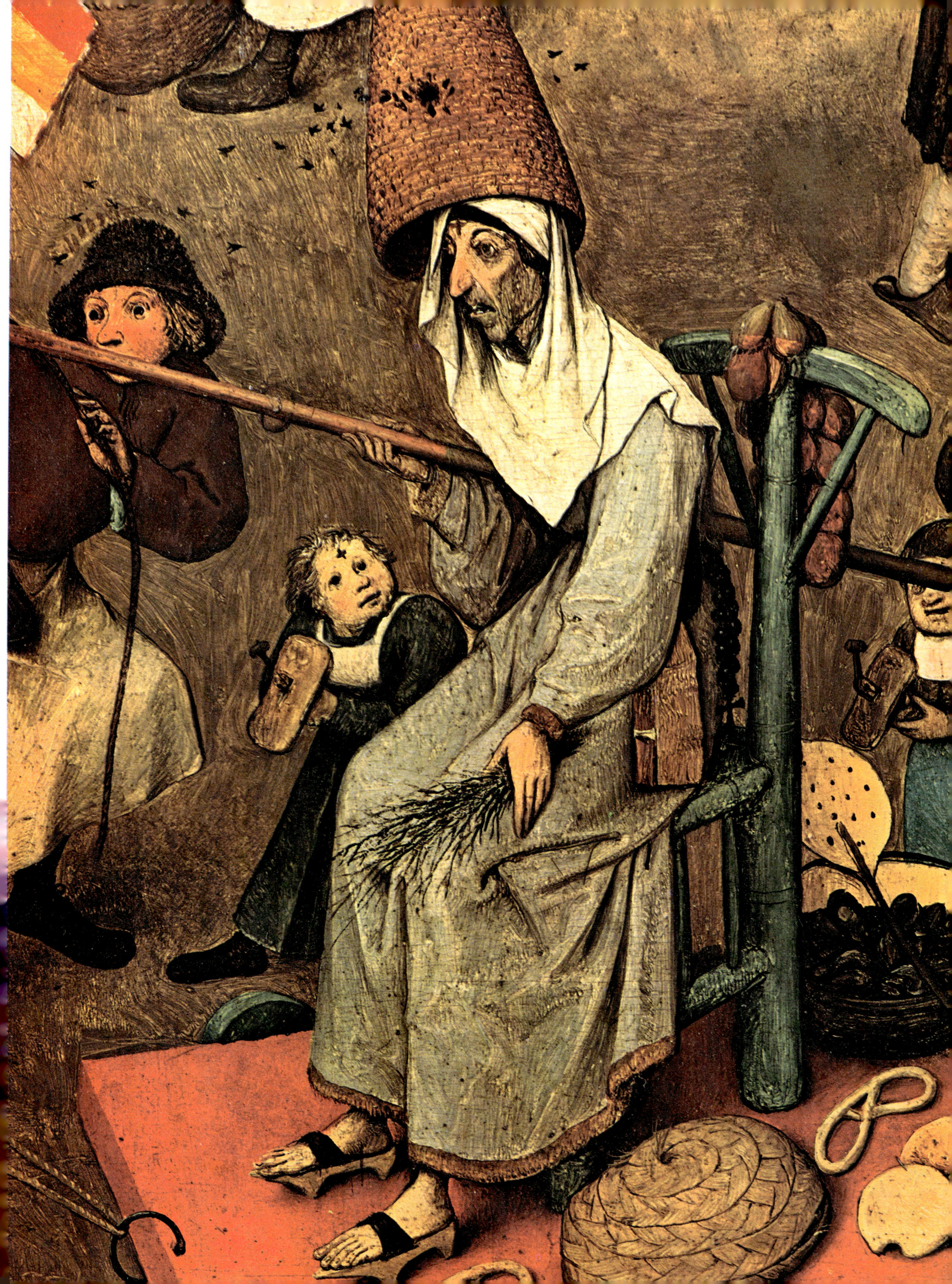

Bruegel must have been familiar with this subject from his earliest youth, for it was an integral part of medieval Catholic culture, spread abroad among the people in writings and sermons. The seven deadly sins are *Superbia* (pride), *Avaritia* (avarice), *Invidia* (envy), *Ira* (wrath), *Luxuria* (lust), *Gula* (intemperance) and *Desidia* (sloth). The seven virtues appeared as a counterpart to this series two years later, in 1559–1560: *Fides* (faith), *Caritas* (charity), *Spes* (hope), *Prudentia* (prudence), *Fortitudo* (fortitude), *Justitia* (justice) and *Temperantia* (temperance). During the Middle Ages, vices and virtues were increasingly represented as allegorical female figures, though animal attributes and activities or objects were also used for the vices. By the 15th century artists were dispensing with animal attributes, such as the ass for sloth, the pig for intemperance or the peacock for pride, and simply showing characteristic activities, as in

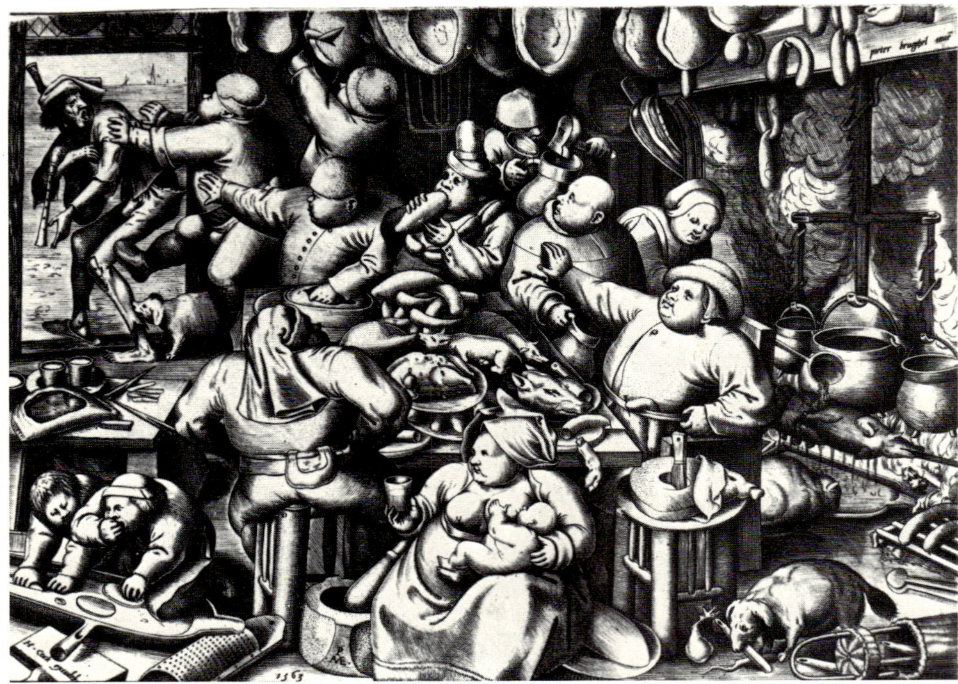

Pieter van der Heyden after Pieter Brueghel the Elder
THE FAT KITCHEN
Copper engraving; 224 x 290 mm (8 x 11 in)
Inscription and date on plate: 'pieter brueghel inve. H. Cock excudeb 1563 P AME'
Inscriptions in French and Netherlandish
Vienna, Graphische Sammlung Albertina
Companion to the *Thin Kitchen*. Bruegel's drawings for the two engravings, which appeared in several editions (Bastelaer 154–163), have not survived. From the thematic point of view the two works are linked to the *Battle Between Carnival and Lent* (pp. 50–51), which prompted the German poet J. Fischart (1546–1590) to formulate a number of critical reflections on the society of the time.

the series of vices by Hieronymus Bosch on the Prado Museum tabletop. A striking feature of this painting is that Bosch does without devils and demons, depicting the allegories in everyday scenes, while Bruegel sets his cycle in a world dominated by infernal creatures as well as reviving the old technique of using animal attributes. The presence of demonic beings or the devil himself is also a product of native late-medieval tradition, though combined here with the new, rationalistic view of sin to give something entirely new.

Interpreting the series is an intricate task which has been undertaken in the greatest detail by Gelder and Borms and C. G. Stridbeck. It will be sufficient here to examine one or two important examples.

Avarice (page 30) is represented by a young middle-class wife in 15th century costume delving into a chest full of money and holding a pile of coins in her lap. Further sacks of coins fill out the traditional picture of avarice, of which Coornhert writes: 'The vile preoccupation of the miser generally manifests itself in unjustified acquisition, thrift and shameful hoarding'. This gives rise to a variety of rather sinful activities such as deceipt, falsehood, strife, enmity, and war, so that avarice plays a key role among the deadly sins in general. At the feet of Avaritia we see her animal attribute the toad, over which a monster and a second toad are busy filling Avaritia's money-chest from a broken pitcher. A winged demon with a sack of money in the bottom right-hand corner symbolizes perennial greed. On the opposite side is a group of two figures: a body composed of a money-bag and a squatting beggar who obviously is not going to get anything from this personification of miserliness. These corner figures form a 'classic' triangular composition together with Avaritia in the middle and the roof's ridge at the top. The central figure is the usurious pawnbroker in his dilapidated hut. An enormous pair of scissors projecting from the hut and cutting a human figure in two shows what happens to those who have to employ the services of a usurer. Gelder and Borms showed that this image illustrates the old proverb '*Dáer hangt de schaar uit*' ('The scissors are hanging out'), meaning some unfortunate person is being robbed of his money. Like the knife in *Big Fish Eat Little Fish*, the scissors are marked with an orb and cross, the symbol of the world; and also, as Stridbeck points out, with the sign for the element 'earth', an allusion to Pluto, the god of earthly riches. To the right of the scissors, two new, naked victims are being driven by the demons of avarice. On the usurer's left we see a naked elderly couple busy with some sort of calculation, perhaps a list of debts, surveyed by a winged toad. In front of them another toad-like monster rolls a naked sinner in a nail-studded barrel from which money is flowing, the victim making a desperate attempt to grab any coin. Behind the hut a crowd shoots arrows at a bag full of money while one of the spectators, fascinated by the flowing coins, has his own money stolen. In the background on the right, an armed horde storms a money box in the form of a strange domed building. The scene in the top left-hand corner is more difficult to

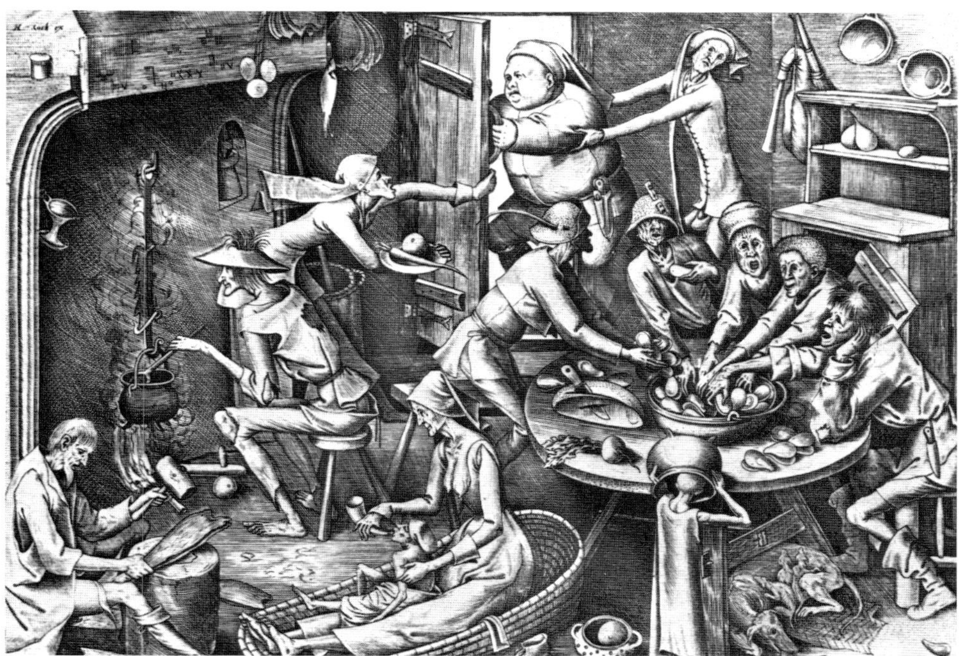

make out. Bax thinks the rider sitting back-to-front on a bull is a thief who has stolen a chalice. Bosch's haywain triptych has a similar figure riding a bull on the way to Hell, also with goblet and pan. As for the conical structure with bellows, smoking hat and knife, Stridbeck sees these as a kind of furnace or mint in which coins are being struck. At any rate, the man with hammers could be interpreted in this way. The scales of righteousness in the far background recall the Last Judgement, but the significance of the cap on top of them is unclear. In common with all the other captions, the one beneath this drawing is not by Bruegel, but presumably by a calligrapher in Cock's workshop. It reads: '*Eere, beleeftheit, schaemte noch godlyck vermaen / En siet die scrapende ghierigheyt niet aen*' ('Rapacious greed takes heed neither of honour, decency, shame, nor godly admonition').

In *Gula* (page 31), interperence, or lack of moderation in eating and drinking, is symbolized by a fat bourgeoise sitting on a pig, the animal attribute of intemperance, and drinking from a jug of wine. A pot-bellied demon with a pig's face and a drinking vessel in its hand is pointing at her. Two naked women, obviously drunk, belong to the same company around the table, who seem to be simultaneously guarded and served by demons. Bruegel evidently regards the main evil exemplified in Gula as weakness for the bottle, as we can see from the central location of the wine cask. In the left foreground is a head walking about and eating, with a spoon in a bowl on top of its cap. This is an illustration of the proverb '*Boven op zijn hoed staat de lepel in den pappot*' ('He has a spoon in a porridge-bowl on his head'), which alludes to spendthrifts and gluttons. The man vomiting belongs to traditional Gula iconography. The pig carrying Gula tucks into the contents of the overturned tub; a dog-like animal tries to get something too, while a second steals a pie from a demon-waiter with a pointed beak; and on the far right a fish-like creature gobbles up a fish, although its own belly has already burst open. Behind all this a naked man shut up in a wine cask waves his protruding legs in the air. The cask is set on the edge of a steep drop – 'a drastic illustration of the

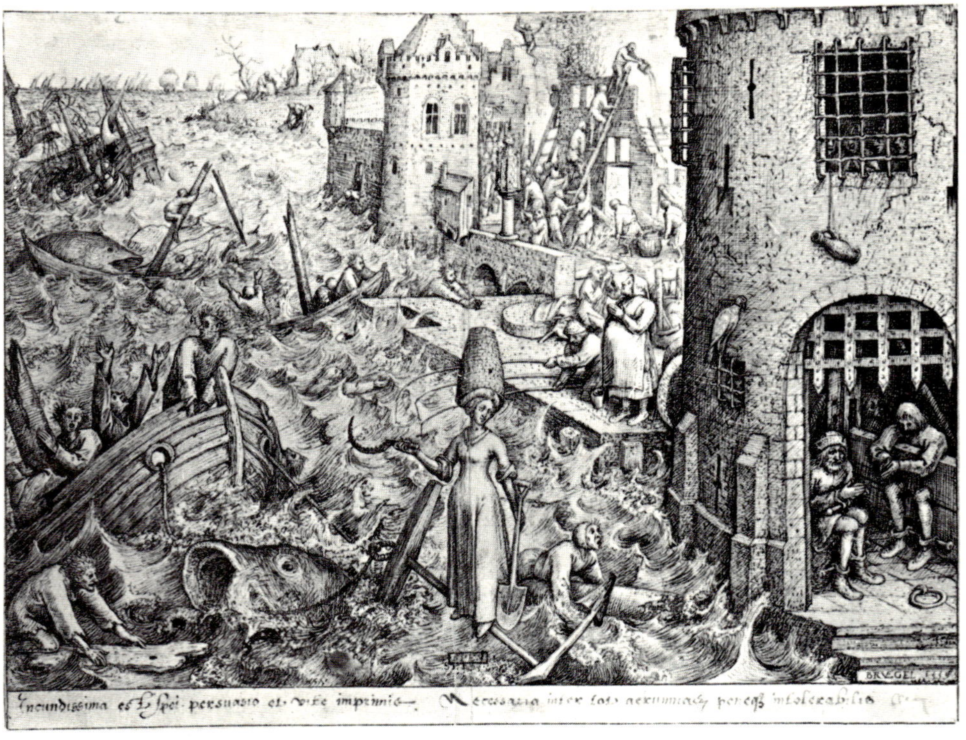

SPES
Pen drawing in greyish brown on paper; 224 x 295 mm (8¾ x 11⅝ in)
Signed and dated at bottom right: 'BRVEGEL 1559'
Berlin, Kupferstichkabinett
Preparatory drawing for the engraving by Philip Galle (Bastelaer 133) in the series of *Virtues*. The seven engravings were published by H. Cock from 1559 onwards (not dated) as companions to the series of *Deadly Sins* of 1556–1557. Bruegel has set the *Virtues* in more realistic surroundings than the *Deadly Sins*; moreover these drawings contain a degree of exaggeration and ironical invention which transforms the whole significance of virtue into its contrary.

precarious situation of the drinker', according to Stridbeck. In the background is a gigantic, voracious head with windmill wings whose open mouth is being filled with sacks of flour, according to Bax a symbol of gluttony. The pot-bellied figure who has to carry his paunch in front of him on a wheelbarrow speaks for itself. In the far background, people are being cooked in an enormous pot. There is not an easy explanation, though, of the colossal kneeling figure at top left. Tolnay recognizes in it the proverb '*Hij heeft zooveel wind, dat een molen ervan zou omgaan*' ('He has enough wind to turn a mill'). The vapours produced are pouring out of openings at the back, enabling a fish to be smoked. Stridbeck interprets the monkey on the right looking out of the window as an emblem of servitude and the captive giant as a symbol of the gourmand enslaved by his vice, intemperance, but neither hypothesis is entirely satisfactory.

Superbia (page 32) or pride is considered the worst of all the deadly sins, the root of all evil. *Des Coninx Summe*, an early 15th-century document, states among other things that pride is against God and God against pride. The inscription below the drawing says

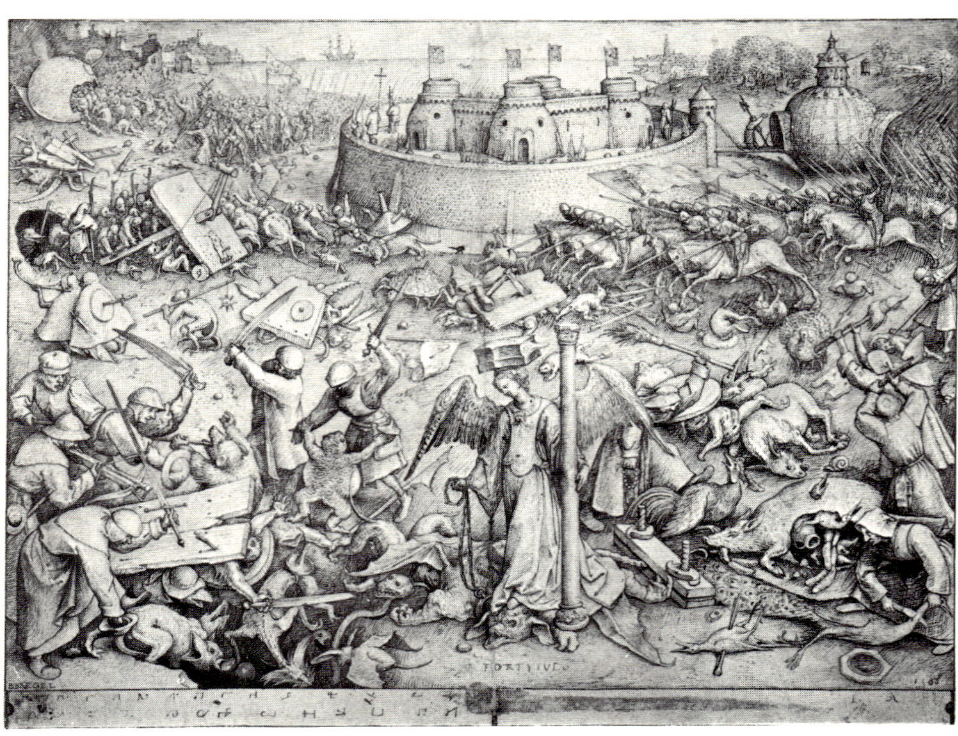

FORTITUDO
Pen drawing in maroon and violet on filigreed paper; 224 x 293 mm (8¾ x 11⅝ in)
Signed at bottom left: 'BRVEGEL'; dated at bottom right: '1560'
Rotterdam, Museum Boymans-Van Beumingen
Preparatory drawing for the engraving by Philip Galle (Bastelaer 137) in the series of *Virtues*. As the apparently authentic inscription shows, FORTYTUDO seems to be more distant than any of the other subjects from the strictly theological concept by virtue of the irony with which it is treated.

the same: God hates pride above all things, just as pride holds God in derision. In a
similar tone, the most abominable of all terrible curses was held in Burgundy to be '*Je
renie Dieu*' ('I deny God'). Unlike the other allegories in the series, Superbia is
fashionably clad in contemporary costume and identified by the peacock, her animal
attribute, and looking-glass, with demons on foot and on horseback all around. Behind
her a devil displays a sign with a pair of scissors painted on it – possibly an allusion to the
tailor's trade, although Stridbeck regards it as an emblem of avarice. On the right we
can see into a barber's shop: both trades, the tailor's and the barber's, are associated
with vanity. To the left behind Superbia some demons are bringing up a naked woman,
a detail that has been variously interpreted as representing shame consequent upon
pride, a sinner in the hands of procurers, man in the power of demons and Superbia's
close relation Luxuria or lust. The last of these would fit in with the explanation by
Stridbeck, who sees the figures standing behind Superbia as further deadly sins

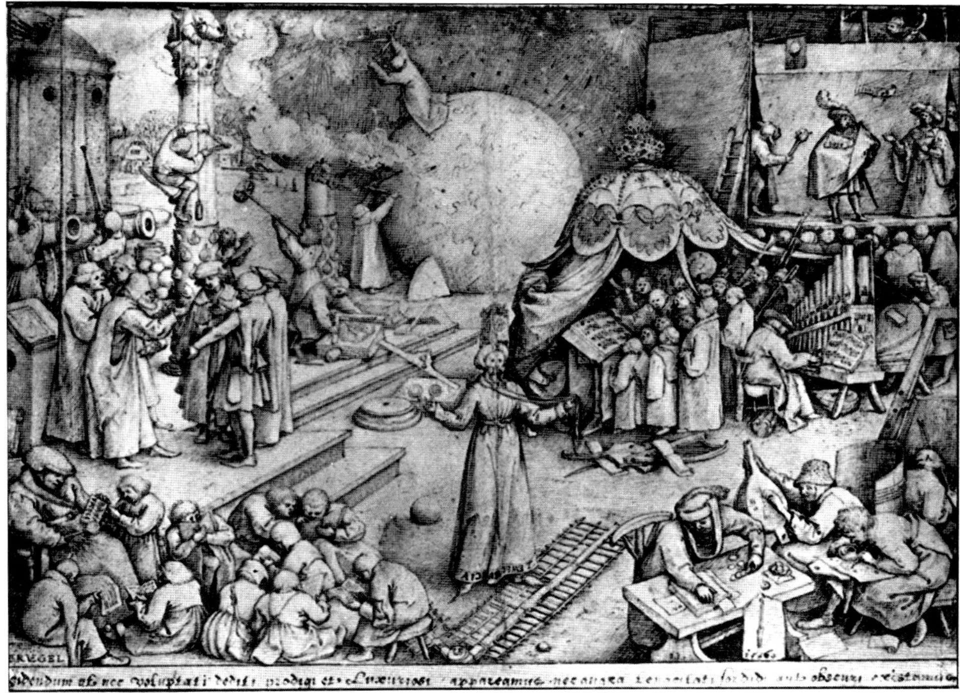

TEMPERANTIA
Pen drawing in greyish-maroon on filigreed
paper; 220 x 295 mm (8⅝ x 11¼ in)
Signed at bottom left: 'BRVEGEL'; dated at
bottom right: '15.60'
Rotterdam, Museum Boymans-van Beuningen
Preparatory drawing for the engraving by
Philip Galle (Bastelaer 138) in the series of
Virtues. The association of the allegory of
temperance with the seven liberal arts is a
novelty. The drawing bears a Latin text in
another hand: 'We should try not to live a
life of futile pleasure dissipation and vice,
but also endeavouring not to live in greed,
ignorance and misery'.

belonging to her retinue, for example Ira (wrath), Invidia (envy) and Avaritia (avarice).
The group in the foreground on the left probably symbolize gossip and slander. The
background is taken up with fantastic buildings, a diabolical architectural landscape
reminiscent of Bosch. Tolnay reocgnizes a proverb in this 'anthropomorphous and
zoomorphous' architecture with its weird shapes recalling pots and pans: '*De Ketel gekt
met den pot*' ('The pot makes fun of the pan', in other words the one is no better than
the other). In the middle the jaws of hell are swallowing up naked sinners. This drawing
in particular contains many details which remain unexplained.
Ira (page 33), or anger, illustrates an incredible variety of forms of human nastiness
breaking out in active aggression. In fact it illustrates aggressiveness itself, for the mêlée
of conflicts is without any meaning or logical coherence; the spectator is confronted with
blind rage, quite lacking in direction, suddenly bursting forth from the battle tent. The
theologian Coornhert speaks of the anger that flares up and quashes reason, of the
blindness induced by rage, which transforms a man into a wild animal beyond the reach
of common sense, of anger as a form of madness. The text belonging to the drawing
says: 'Anger exaggerates speech, embitters the mind, deranges reason and darkens the
blood!' Ira is at the head of a band of armed soldiers, and she herself is heavily armed
and clad in helmet and armour. In one hand she carries a sword, in the other a torch,
both emblems of war, and the arrow of anger is stuck in her helmet. She is preceded by a
bear – the traditional animal attribute – biting a naked man in the calf, and by two
grotesque squires absurdly armed with an outsize kitchen knife with which they cut into
people like a pile of worms. One of them seems to have escaped the knife but finds
himself confronted by a warrior with a gaping, grimacing mouth who is about to deal a
mighty blow with a mace. In the right foreground a she-wolf bites through the throat of
a toad-like monster which in turn is ramming a knife into the other animal's belly. To
the left a crippled soldier has come to do battle with the 'world' (identified by the

symbol on the flag), which is entrenched behind a big, wheeled battering-ram with a saw-blade. He is already being attacked by devil carrying an arrow in its mouth. Stridbeck, probably wrongly, identifies the key on the knight's helmet streamer as a symbol of power, whereas Tolnay sees it as the key of St. Peter. But the Church's champion has a wooden leg: the other is a cock's foot, and he has a devil's tail as well. Clearly Bruegel's sympathy lies with none of the protagonists. In fact the group has a certain bizarrely comic quality.

The middle of the drawing is dominated by a gigantic figure carrying in its mouth a knife, the symbol of Ira. Although wounded (one arm is in a sling) – or precisely because of that – it seems intent on killing. Bastelaer and Tolnay interpret the contents of the bottle it carries by reference to the proverb about self-destruction: 'He's drinking his own blood', or again 'The fool cuts himself with his own knife and gets drunk with his own bottle'. But I find this just as unconvincing as Tolnay's other attempts to explain details of this drawing by reference to proverbs. Yet the bottle could quite simply contain poison. Underneath its cloak the figure has a wine cask – deliberately put at the very centre of the drawing, at the intersection of its diagonals. This could mean the various events depicted are consequences of drunkenness: murder, despair (the figure tearing its hair), war (the trumpeter).

Next to the tree in front of the hut, a figure is being roasted on a spit and basted by the demon of rage, whose knife lies close by. Stridbeck here picks up Coornhert's notion of the sinner's self-punishment through sin. The couple in the boiling pot could be seen in the same way.

The background offers a panorama of destruction resulting from anger: battle scenes, burning buildings and an execution on the gallows. The ship on two wine casks is commonly associated with the 'Ship of Fools', and also the '*blauwe schuyt*' or ship of doom (compare the imagery of the *Last Judgement* and the *Battle Between Carnival and Lent*). However, it may have a different significance.

Desidia (page 34), or Sloth sleeps on an ass, its emblem, while the devil obliges with a cushion. Snails, symbols of slowness, crawl all around. In the foreground a man spoons up gruel while a demon of idleness pulls him along in a travelling bed. As Romdahl has pointed out, this demon with the spoon-shaped beak appears (laterally inverted) on the left wing of Hieronymus Bosch's *St. Anthony* triptych in Lisbon. Another group of naked idlers sits sleepily at a table. A demon with insect's wings is passing the woman a cushion while two others smirk from behind a bed hanging, apparently sure of their victim. The devils with the cushion are derived from the proverb 'Idleness is the devil's pillow' and this motif can also be found in Bosch's series of vices in Madrid, and elsewhere. In other words, indolence is the root of all evil: 'for Satan finds some mischief still for idle hands to do.'

The couple in bed is clearly an allusion to Luxuria: idleness is chosen by those who want to earn their money at play instead of work. Jugs placed at various points are probably associated with drunkenness. Despite many attempts, a number of details have never been satisfactorily explained – for example the clockwork mechanisms, bells, the sundial and people bathing. They may be to remind the slothful to heed the fleeting nature of time.

The giant in the mill – which won't work because of the water's sloth – apparently suffers from sluggishness of the bowels, so that a whole boat's crew has to help him answer the call of nature! But is this really what the scene means? According to Stridbeck the presence of the figure and the fact of its being enclosed in this way, which have parallels in other scenes in the series, represent a form of mental captivity.

The *Last Judgement*, signed and dated 'bruegel 1558' (page 42), to some extent rounds off the series of deadly sins and provides a link with the seven virtues. Depictions of the Last Judgement are traditionally associated with the deadly sins, as is the case with Bosch's cycle of vices in the Prado. With regard to composition, too, Bruegel sticks to established schemes – compare Allaert du Hameel's engraving after Bosch, or even earlier Netherlandish paintings of the 15th century such as the works of Memling.

THREE HEADS
Oil on panel; 24.7 x 33.6 cm (9 x 12¼ in)
Neither signed nor dated
c. 1560(?)
Copenhagen, Statens Museum For Kunst
This fanciful composition to which scholars have so far paid little attention is shown here because its indisputably Bruegelian qualities would seem to merit further analysis. Thematically it is related to the *Fat Kitchen* and *Thin Kitchen* (pp. 54, 55) and to the *Battle Between Carnival and Lent* (pp. 50–51)

The seven vices are matched, rather more positively, by the seven virtues. Cock began publishing the series as engravings in 1559 and Bruegel executed the drawings in 1559 and 1560, about two years after the *Deadly Sins*. While the later were set in an imaginary, pandemonian landscape, the *Virtues* (except for *Fortitude*) are placed squarely in the context of the contemporary bourgeois world. But even here Bruegel uses the same representational scheme, surrounding a central female allegory with appropriate scenes. The captions in this series are not in Flemish but in the more 'distinguished' Latin.

Spes (Hope) (page 56) is one of the three theological virtues: faith, hope and charity. Here, she stands on her emblem, an anchor, amid roaring waves. She is holding a sickle and spade and on her head is a bee-hive, medieval symbols of hope that were already

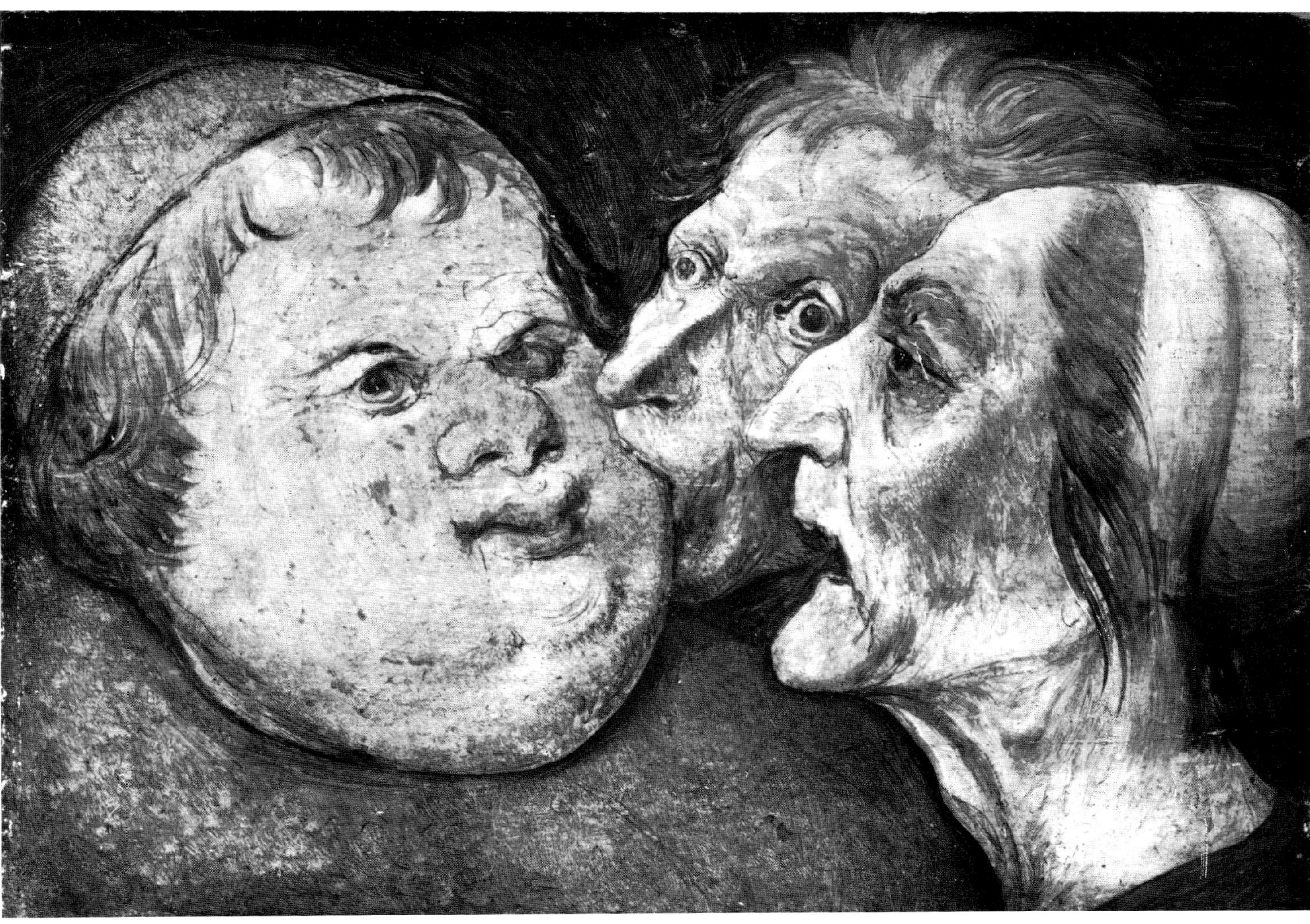

falling out of use in Bruegel's time. Being agricultural articles they were associated with the peasants' hope of a good harvest. Bergström has shown that almost all Bruegel's scenes derive from a literary and pictorial tradition which had developed some time before: some of the motifs feature in a woodcut of 1545 by Hans Vogtherr. The Latin inscription underlines the need for hope: 'The conviction given us by hope is exceedingly pleasant and a necessity in a life with so many almost intolerable afflictions'. The widely differing scenes compressed into one narrow space show those who are in need of hope: the shipwrecked souls threatened by the sea, the imprisoned, those who fight fires, those who pray, and finally a fisherman who has put out three rods despite the storm. Considering the mortal danger in which the castaways find themselves, the fisherman's activity seems rather perverse. And indeed Stridbeck notes – echoing Coornhert – that hope is not always entirely laudable; for instance when directed towards vain, wordly desires. There is, therefore, a grain of truth in Tolnay's interpretation of the series as depicting follies in a foolish world. One has the impression, at any rate, that Bruegel was not over keen to portray the virtues in the clerical sense.

Nor has he shown them in an entirely flattering light: the central motif in *Prudentia*, for example, is the hoarding of winter supplies. His approach to his subject, in fact, seems rather cool and objective. We can hardly suppose, to take another instance, that Bruegel identified himself with the horrific punishment and methods of torture depicted in *Justitia* or regarded them as acts of virtue; nor, however, can the drawing be seen as an attack on contemporary Justice. The artist's attitude remains cold and distanced.

The grotesque study entitled *Fortitude* (page 56), on the other hand, seems to me to contain obvious traces of irony and satire which enable us to impute to the artist a certain aloofness from the theological content. *Fortitude* is about strength and courage, symbolized in a figure with angel's wings and a breastplate featuring a lion's mask. Most of the attributes are traditional: the anvil as a symbol of strength, the press for the soul's triumph over itself, the dragon trying to penetrate the conscience but overcome by superior force. The pillar is a traditional emblem of strength, being a structural element which has the function of supporting others. The caption also expresses man's struggle with himself: real strength means mastering oneself, conquering anger and other vices. The seven vices in the form of their animal attributes are accordingly disposed of in no uncertain fashion: a peasant woman slaughters the peacock (Superbia), a young lad kills the pig (Gula) with a hatchet, a girl thrashes the ass (Desidia) with a distaff while the turkey (Invidia) looks on dumbfounded. Another girl beats the cock (Ira) to death with a broom. The left side of the picture has some more amusing details: a large toad (Avaritia) tries to rob a knight who is just about to strike it with his sword, while a cross-bowman misses his mark at point-blank range and hits a board.

Here again we have the medieval motif of the conflict between virtue and vice represented as a battle or tournament. But far from indicating artistic conservatism, this use of an old-fashioned technique is typical of Bruegel's thoroughly modern approach; the 'quotation' receives an injection of irony from the manner of its presentation. Bruegel is playing with tradition. The peasant woman slaughters the peacock as though it were a goose in her kitchen, thus vanquishing Superbia. The genre realism of the weapons such as the broom, kitchen knife or distaff in association with the allegorical content make the scene ambivalent. It adds a new dimension: of humour, of the absurd.

The castle in the background is guarded by the twelve apostles (their haloes can be seen behind the wall) and the four flags show the emblems of the four evangelists. A Christian army (with Christ crucified on their banner) has just made a sortie, driving the infernal horde towards the jaws of Hell with lances poised. Tolnay notes the anthropomorphism of the fortress: gates like mouths, windows like eyes, heads of Leviathan symbolizing vice.

The strip below the picture has a peculiarity: unlike the ones on the other drawings it has no inscription by the calligrapher, but instead an illegible scrawl on the left in the same ink as the drawing. This means it was probably done by Bruegel himself, like the mis-spelt word 'FORTYTUDO' which reveals that, unlike his humanist friends, the artist was not a master of the Latin language. The word 'TEMPERANCIA' laterally inverted on the hem of Temperantia's dress (page 57) is also wrongly spelt.

Temperance (page 57) is the last of the four cardinal virtues (Prudentia, Fortitudo, Justitia and Temperantia). Standing on the sail of a windmill, she has a clock on her head, a bridle around her mouth, spectacles in her hand, a snake as a belt around her waist and spurs on her feet. The clock symbolizes uniform rhythm, the bridle alludes to self-control and the spurs are to prevent sloth. Various conflicting interpretations have been put forward of the snake, windmill sail and spectacles. What is completely new in this drawing is the association of Temperantia with the seven liberal arts (*artes liberales*). Otherwise, these are assigned to the planet Mercury within the planetary cycle or possibly linked with the virtues in general, but never with a single one alone. The Latin inscription fails to elucidate the connection, simply recommending moderation in sensual pleasures and warning against wantonness and avarice.

Below left we find Grammar represented by a village school and behind it Dialectics in the guise of five men in discussion. Geometry is symbolized by two men measuring a column, a sculptor working in relief and a figure apparently denoting the art of war; in the background a surveyor can be seen. A remarkable feature of the representation of Astronomy is that Bruegel takes account of the tilt of the earth's axis, although Copernicus' *De revolutionibus orbium coelestium libri sex* had appeared only seventeen years earlier in 1543. Stridbeck thinks Bruegel is poking fun at the geocentric conception of the universe by juxtaposing an enormous globe and tiny stars. Tolnay regards 'Music' as a respresentation of its very opposite, in other words of dissonance, with secular music of the lute and bagpipe and church music mixed in harmonious confusion. He takes this

CHILDREN's GAMES
Oil on panel; 118 x 161 cm (46¼ x 63⅜ in)
Signed and dated 'BRVEGEL 1560'
Vienna, Kunsthistorisches Museum
Acquired from the Archduke Ernest in 1594. Children's games, like proverbs, had already been depicted before Bruegel, especially as book illustrations; but here again, as in the *Netherlandish Proverbs*, Bruegel treats an apparently quite straightforward subject in a completely new way. Far from simply giving us an encyclopaedic vision of all known children's games, Bruegel is illustrating the mechanical and senseless behaviour of men in general. It has been pointed out more than once that the characters in this picture have the appearance and particularly the faces of adults rather than of children . This confusion of roles helps once again to create the impression of a topsy-turvy world.

as evidence that a topsy-turvy world is represented in the whole of the 'Virtue' series, as in the school scene where a pupil teaches the moronic-looking schoolmaster while the other children imitate the pompous behaviour of grown-ups. Gelder and Borms, too, have drawn attention to the satirical character of the music scene, which could almost qualify as an illustration for the passage on theologians in Erasmus' *Praise of Folly*: 'They believe they are offering up the most wonderful feast to the ears of the saints when they bawl out their carefully counted but uncomprehended psalm verses with their asses' voices in the church'. Rhetoric is depicted in the theatre scene, where the actor has the word 'hope' on his cloak, but the rest of the writing cannot be deciphered with any certainty. Finally, at bottom right, we find Arithmetic represented by a money changer, with two secondary figures whose significance is unclear. Surprisingly, in this context, there is also a painter at his easel on the far right of the picture. Tolnay's view is that he is painting a Madonna; but Stridbeck regards it as a portrait, his theory being

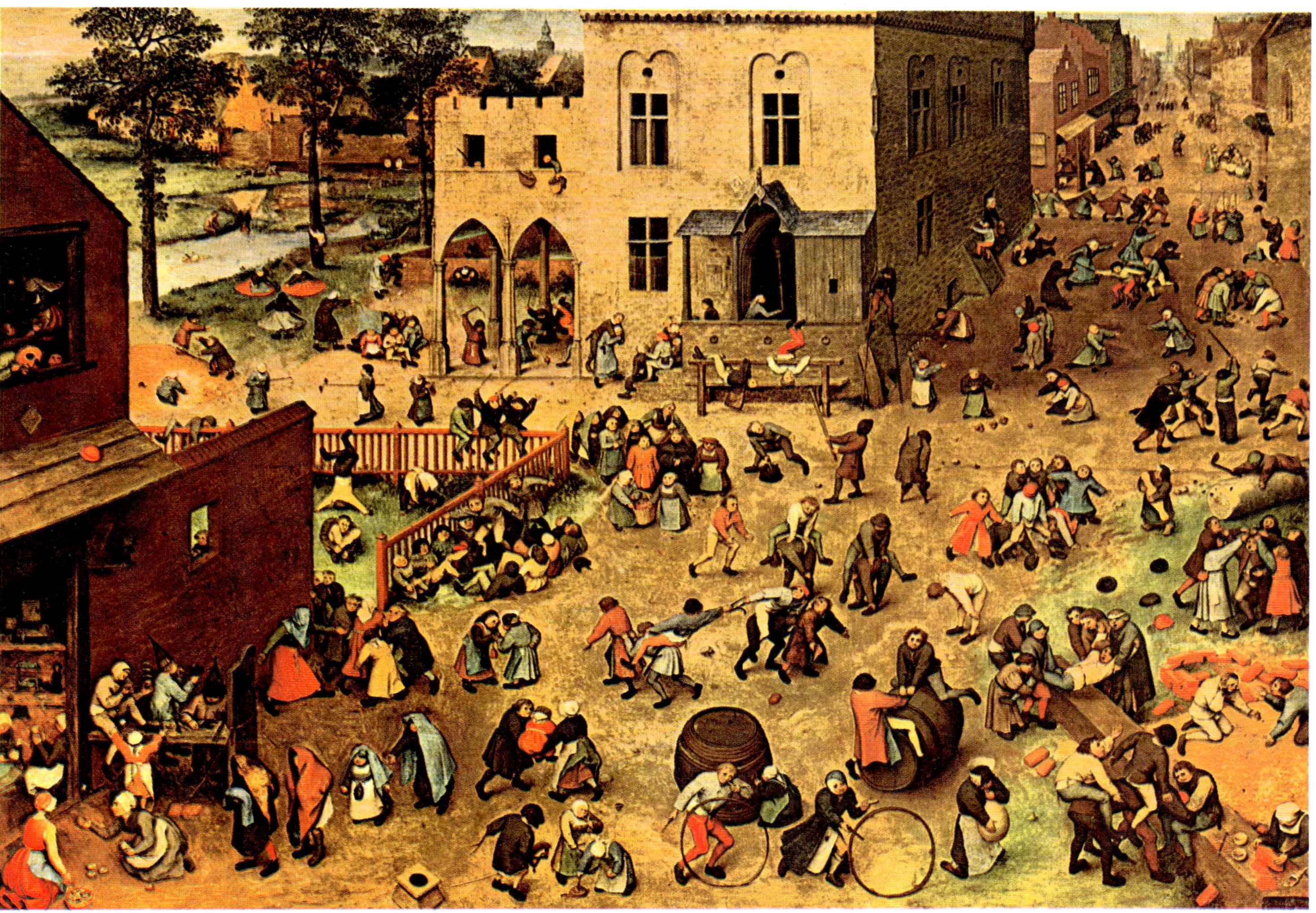

that portrait painting, which van Mander in his didactic poem describes as a perversion of art, was only justified as an artist's source of income. This would provide a link with the money changer. Auner sees the painter working on his own at a distance from the others as Bruegel's ironical way of alluding to the insignificance of painting.
These few examples of Bruegel's graphic art show how many different and sometimes contradictory interpretations it inspires, despite the help offered by titles, mottoes and a fairly clear iconographical programme.
The ambiguity used as a deliberate ploy in many of Bruegel's pictures will become increasingly evident as we proceed. But first let us return to some important secular drawings or drafts for engravings produced in 1558–1559 between the series of Vices and Virtues.

Elck (Everyman, page 42) is one of Bruegel's allegories belonging not to the theological but to the contemporary lay ethical sphere. Erasmus' *Praise of Folly* crops up constantly in this connection, as do the names of Coornhert and Franck. If we begin by looking at the drawing without trying to interpret its content, our first general impression is one of restlessness, of a sinister, feverish searching. The mere appearance of Bruegel's great allegories conveys their essential mood which can then be explained by reference to their content.

The central character is Elck, or Everyman, a wiry greybeard who in some ways anticipates Shylock. Bent slightly forward with lantern in hand (although it is broad daylight), the bespectacled figure searches around in a jumbled pile of bundles tied up with string and a confused miscellany of other objects. Closer examination reveals that

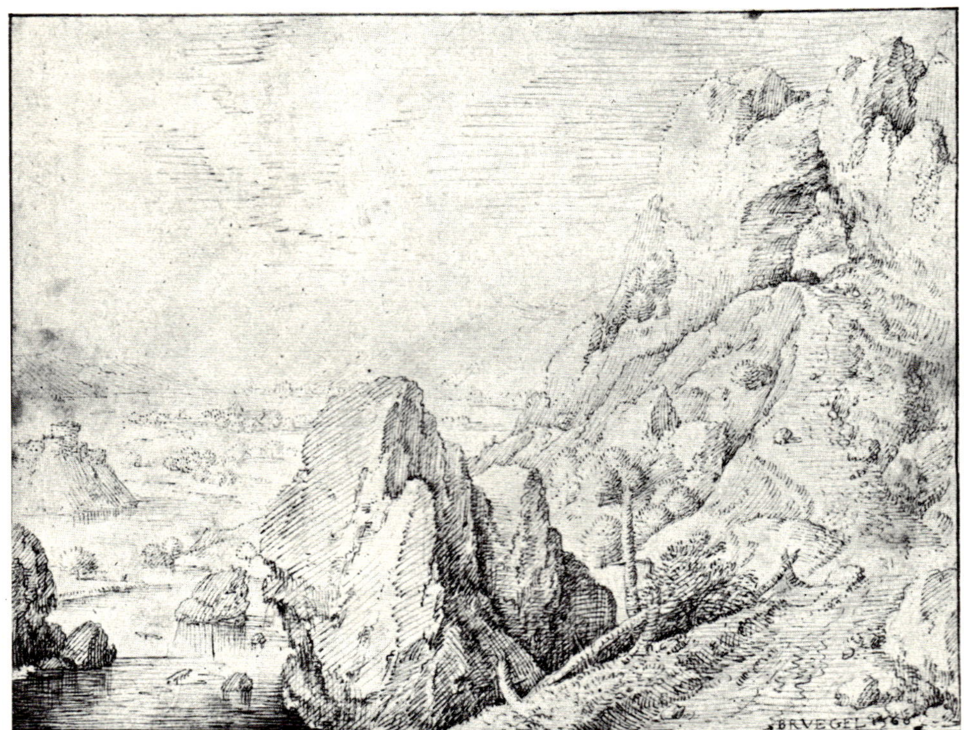

MOUNTAINOUS LANDSCAPE WITH NARROW PATH BETWEEN ROCKS
Pen drawing in yellowish ink on white paper; 144 x 189 mm (5¾ x 7⅜ in)
Signed and dated at bottom right: 'BRVEGEL 1560'
Berlin, Kupferstichkabinett
This curious mountain landscape belongs to a series of small compositions executed in 1559–1561, but not from the same album, as demonstrated by the precise signing and dating of the individual sheets. In this drawing Bruegel anticipates the pointillist technique of later works. The path motif is taken up again in the *Conversion of Saul* (p. 142), while the natural arch is a throwback to the earlier landscape motifs of Patinir and his followers.

Elck in fact appears in the picture no less than eight times. He is also seen searching in a barrel, in a basket and in a sack, while two Elcks are tugging at a length of material, and in the background he is again searching near some soldiers and, finally, by the church. On the wall of the house hangs a picture of a fool in the midst of a desolate collection of junk, looking at himself in a mirror. Underneath it says *'nymant en ckent sy selve'* (nobody recognizes himself) and the word *'nemo'* (nobody) appears, mirror-inverted, in the picture itself. The drawing was engraved twice in Cock's establishment by Pieter van der Heyden and Johannes Galle and provided with slightly varying explanatory texts in Latin, French and Flemish, the Flemish one on van der Heyden's engraving being the most informative. It says: 'Every man searches for himself in everything: in all the world, whithersoever he flees. How then can anyone escape when everyone only ever searches for himself? Every man tries to get the longest end, and is shown here, one pulling from above, another from below. Scarcely anyone knows himself. Those who understand this behold a remarkable spectacle'.

In the light of these texts the drawing has been interpreted as an allegory of human egoism, the most detailed analyses being those by Grauls and Stridbeck. Grauls was the first to notice that the text contains three different proverbs or sayings: 'Every man searches for himself', 'Every man tries to get the longest end' and 'Nobody knows himself'. The first two refer to human egoism; the last, which occurs in Villon, was used so frequently in 16th-century morality plays and farces as to be considered a commonplace. Fools and jesters, in particular, were apparently always quoting it. Stridbeck sees in it a reversal of the Delphic oracle's motto 'Know thyself', as an admonition to greater self-knowledge and a remedy against selfishness. So in the first place Elck represents the insatiable searcher enmeshed by greed: the bulging purse at his belt is a symbol of avarice. The picture's diagonals intersect in the main figure which is emphasized by the whole composition. The diagonal from top right to bottom left is brought out by the cloth-tugging scene, Elck's forearm and the edges of the chess-board and scale beam; the other, much less accentuated, by Elck's stooping posture.

A *rederijker* pageant held in 1563 expressed ideas strikingly similar to these suggested in *Elck*: 'How would it be if Elck wasn't always looking for himself, and rejected greed and egoism? ... Then Elck would at last enjoy a quiet and peaceful existence'. Clearly the moral injunction refers to an exaggerated regard for material things to the neglect of spiritual values. This fits in with the vain, wordly nature of the jumbled pile of objects including a chessboard, dice, playing cards, mirror, drum, scales, desk, money-bags, trowel, axe, and so on. The overturned, broken globe over which Elck is stepping acts as an all-embracing symbol of everything transitory, uncertain, wicked and false. Yet Elck is not entirely reprehensible; his tireless searching reveals him not only as an agent but

LANDSCAPE WITH RABBIT HUNT
Etching; 213 x 284 mm ($8\frac{3}{8}$ x $11\frac{1}{4}$ in)
Signed and dated at bottom left in the ornamental scroll: 'BRVEGEL 1506'; the publisher's name appears at top right in another hand: '*H. Cock excu*'
Vienna, Graphische Sammlung Albertina
Bruegel's only signed etching, published by H. Cock. It has been established on the basis of a dated copy of the preparatory drawing, now lost, that the date 1506, read until recently as 1560, should in fact be corrected to 1566. The composition recalls other drawings of the same period. Bruegel uses swift, spontaneous strokes of the etching-needle in an attempt to capture the lightness of his brilliant landscape drawings; however, it seems that this interesting experiment was not repeated.

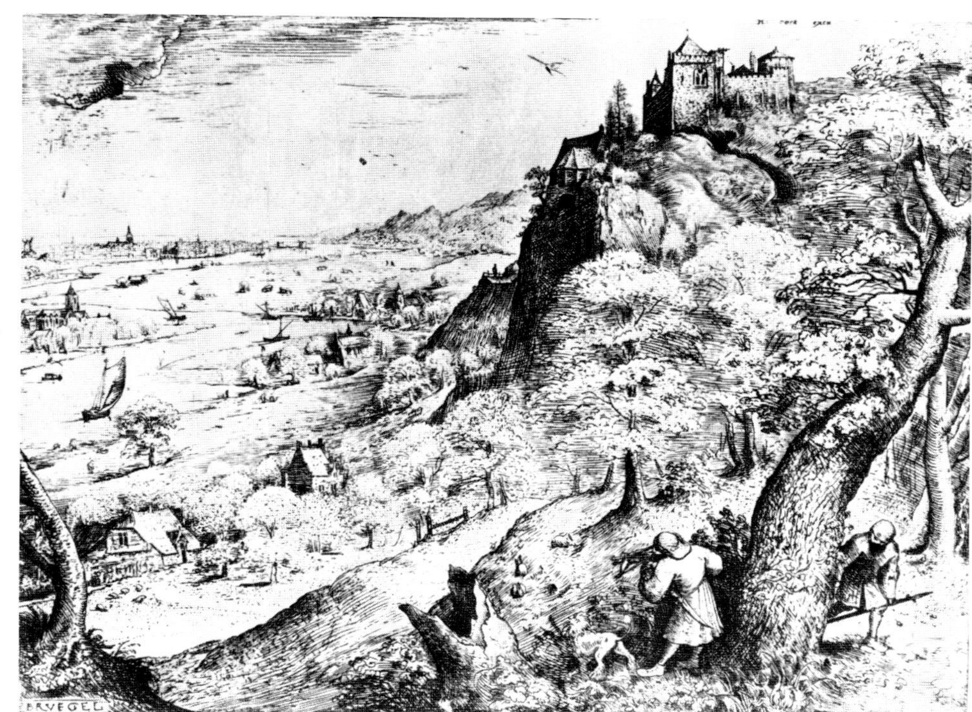

also as a victim. Moreover the explanatory text on the engraving with its reference to self-knowledge puts the whole subject in a milder light. Elck is certainly searching, but in the wrong place or in the wrong way. The significance of the background scenes is unclear. According to Stridbeck, the Elck near the soldiers refers to man's greed leading to war and dissension, while Elck on the way to the church implies that Church and clergy are full of covetousness and rapacity. But the message could also be that even there Elck will not find what he is looking for, namely himself. Tolnay has identified the fool in the picture, with the legend '*nemo*', as the antithesis of Elck; in a topsy-turvy world the 'happy' man is the carefree fool who has the time and leisure to look at himself in the glass amid a pile of worthless trash. Stridbeck may be wrong in disputing this, claiming the fool could never fulfil a positive role because he was simply the traditional symbol of stupidity: compare, for example, Shakespeare's fools only twenty years later. Finally, Barnouw stresses the truth of the observation that nobody knows himself in this selfish world – which is why the man is astonished to see a fool in the looking-glass. This strongly implied critique of vanity and a certain mysteriousness of mood put the drawing on a par with Dürer's *Melancholy*.

The famous drawing, *The Alchemist* (page 43) also published by Cock and probably engraved by Philipp Galle, is signed and dated 'Brueghel 1558'. The signature's authenticity has been queried because of the unusual ligature of *h* and *e* and the slanting of the letters, but this may be unjustified. After all, it was precisely at this period that Bruegel modified his signature from gothic minuscules to Latin capitals. The *Alchemist* is one of the most widely discussed of Bruegel's works, but examination here will be limited to a few fundamental issues. The engraving soon made it very well-known, for Vasari mentions it in 1568 in the second volume of his *Lives*. It is the first of

Cock's engravings to be described in the account of Marcantonio Raimondi, although Vasari does not give Bruegel's name: '… and in another is an alchemist, racking his brains as he dissipates all that he possesses, until finally he leaves for the poorhouse with his wife and children. This picture was drawn by a painter …'

In a rather desolate room resembling a kitchen we see a man with shaggy hair and tattered clothes sitting at the hearth in front of a variety of simmering vessels and other utensils. A scholarly man in late 15th-century costume sits at the reading-desk, gesturing with one hand towards the scene before him and pointing with the other at the open book. Here we can read the words 'ALGHE MIST', a pun on the Flemish '*al ghemist*' meaning 'all is lost'. While a grimacing fool with ass's ears kneels at a charcoal brazier in front of the desk pumping madly with a pair of bellows, the alchemist's wife displays her empty purse to show that all the money is gone. Behind her three children are playing by an empty cupboard, one with an empty cooking pot on his head to illustrate the absence of food. Outside, in the background, the shaggy man with wife and children appear again on their way to the poorhouse. A woman has come out to take them in. Clearly, then, the drawing's message is that alchemy leads to the poorhouse, and research has been directed towards determining Bruegel's exact attitude towards alchemy. Everything suggests he disapproved, although the opposite view has been put forward on the basis of an incorrect translation of the engraving's Latin text. At the same time it has to be said that Bruegel's intention was not to condemn alchemy outright but simply to attack certain of its excesses, in particular, the charlatans and senseless bankruptcies it entailed. That the 'bad' alchemist here is also seeking the philosophers' stone is revealed by the Latin caption which seems to me to acquire a tinge of irony from its onomatopoeic imitation of the abracadabras of witches's parlours. It says: 'The ignorant must endure their lot, living by the sweat of their brow. The power of the highly esteemed stone – which costs little but is rare – is the only thing that is certain, quite worthless, but universally known [ironical ambiguity: the only certain thing, *unica res certa*, is that one ends up in the poorhouse]; incorporated with its four natures in the saturated cloud of misfortune, it is not a mineral object to be found at some particular spot at some specific time, but by virtue of its peculiar properties is located everywhere'. Only a few of the notes written here and there are legible, and are of no significance. The same can be said of the alchemistic signs on the piece of paper above the fireplace, which do not give any sort of coherent alchemistic recipe.

In the catalogue of the 1975 Berlin exhibition, M. Winner identifies three possible sources which could have inspired Bruegel's drawing: an illustration in 'Alchemy' entitled *Ship of Fools*, which can be traced back to Dürer and was definitely known in Antwerp; secondly, one of a series of woodcuts executed by Cornelis Anthonisz of Amsterdam and dated 1541 whose subject is the allegorical figure Sorgheloos declining into abject poverty; and thirdly a passage in Petrarch in which the poet is critical of alchemy, accompanied by a woodcut of the master with adept and assistant. Further censorious assessments of alchemy are found in Erasmus and in a work by Barthal Beham dated about 1524. Contemporary artists also dealt with the subject of alchemy independently of Bruegel; these included Maerten de Vos, Jan Verbeeck and Marcus Gheeraerts.

Winner has shown that Bruegel followed the original scheme of portraying an adept (the alchemist/scholar) and an assistant (the worker at the hearth). However, it seems to me that Bruegel has slightly modified the significance of the two figures. For otherwise there is no obvious reason why the 'scholar', as the bankrupt owner of the enterprise, should not go to the poorhouse as well, instead of just the 'assistant' with his wife and children. In my view the scene contains a mixture of real and allegorical figures. The actual alchemist and owner of the laboratory is surely identified through his starving family: he is the only one who goes with them to the poorhouse. The 'scholar' and his caricature the fool – removed from contemporary reality by their costume – are not real participants in the action but an allegory of alchemy split up into two individuals. This is underlined by their physical similarity. This allegory is an illustration of the alchemist's obsession, the 'scholar' personifying this theoretically with his obscure books, the fool in practice with his idiotically compulsive, unsuccessful efforts with the bellows. This explanation is in no way contradicted by the French text accompanying some of the prints. So Bruegel has apparently elaborated his subject at two different levels: in a genre scene with allegorical overtones (alchemist and family) and an allegorical one with genre detail ('scholar' and 'fool'). Finally, we should also mention Menzel's view that the 'scholar' *is* the alchemist and also the bed-ridden figure who can be seen through the open door of the poorhouse. But one way or another the *Alchemist* is indisputably one of Bruegel's most rewarding drawings. The splendid delicacy of the lines, the care and the precision with which apparently quite insignificant objects are represented, reveal Bruegel at the height of his artistic powers. A year later, in 1559, he was to begin work on his first three great panel paintings: the *Proverbs*, the *Battle Between Carnival and Lent* and the *Children's Games*.

Both *Skaters at St. George's Gate* and *Kermis at Hoboken* are of the greatest interest because they usher in two new games which apart from being developed by Bruegel himself persisted well into the 17th century in Dutch and Flemish painting: the winter landscape and the *kermis*, or fair.

The *Skaters at St. George's Gate* (page 48) shows a crowd of people on the frozen moat outside St. George's Gate at Antwerp. The different degrees of uncertainty with which people are moving on the slippery ice are beautifully depicted and testify to Bruegel's acute powers of observation, enabling him to pick out and reproduce the significant and characteristic aspects of a particular movement or posture. The scene contains a wealth of

CHRIST IN LIMBO
Pen drawing in dark maroon on paper; 224 x 292 mm (8¾ x 11½ in)
Signed and dated at bottom left: 'BRVEGEL / 1561'
Vienna, Graphische Sammlung Albertina
Preparatory drawing for the engraving by Pieter van der Heyden (Bastelaer 115). Once regarded as forming the conclusion of the series of *Virtues*, this work contains an abundance of demonic creatures which strongly recalls Bosch. The precision of the lines reveals the artist's intention of facilitating the engraver's task in order to improve the quality of the final result. Interpretations of the scene have been many and various. The drawing bears a Latin inscription in another hand.

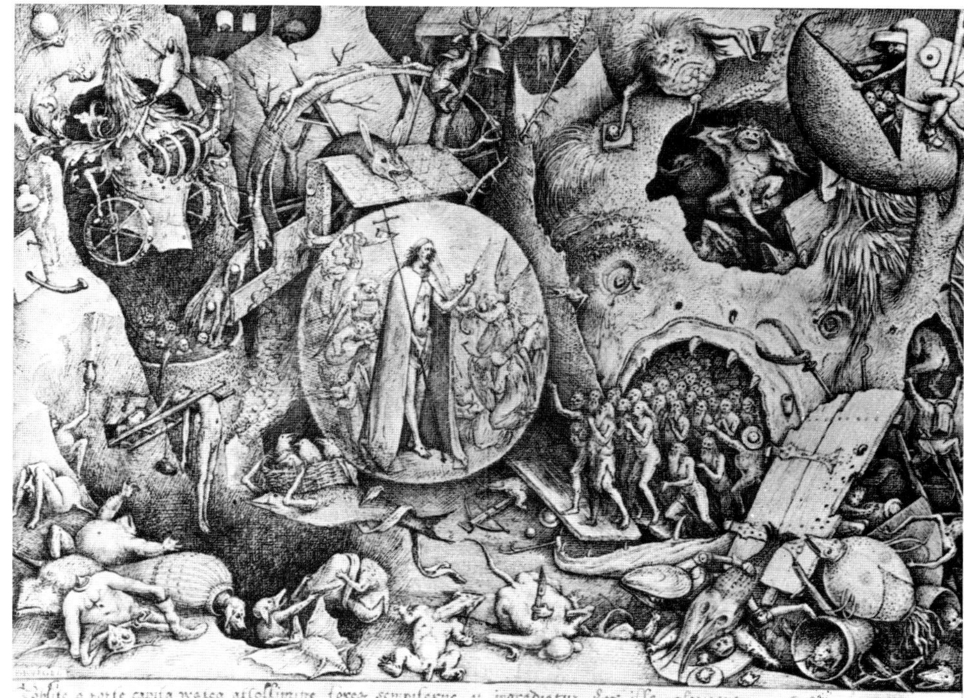

genre detail like the child on a sledge made with animal's bones. Now in a private collection in America, the drawing was engraved for Hieronymus Cock by Franz Huys and the second version published after 1600 erroneously bears the date 1553, from which it has been concluded that Bruegel must already have returned from Italy by 1553. But the rediscovered draft is dated 1558, and Auner's reservations about this – particularly his claim that '3' was changed into '8' – are rejected by Grossmann and Münz. As a purely narrative representation of people in a real landscape the drawing is a complete novelty, though it was no more than a year later, in 1559, that Pieter van der Borcht's great etching entitled *Skating Outside Malines* appeared. This, by contrast with Bruegel's work, shows men and women of the upper classes on the ice. The second, modified version of Bruegel's engraving has the rather trivial, humanistic legend '*Lubricitas vitae humanae*', suggesting a comparison between the ice-rink and the slippery path along which we progress through life. This approach clearly indicates the public's need to draw a moral from works of art or at least to participate in the solution of a pictorial puzzle. According to the Mannerist theory, any pictures which can be understood without an explanatory text are trivial. Paolo Giovio thinks that, while a picture should not be too obscure, its meaning ought not to be so obvious that any plebeian can understand it. So it was typical of the prevalent aesthetic approach to suspect a hidden meaning. If there was one, an educated contemporary would generally be able to understand it without difficulty. Looking at works of art in two different ways was in any case a matter of habit in those days. In the absence of any obviously allegorical meaning, the necessary addition was made subsequently, as in the present case with the skaters. This is why many of Bruegel's pictures can be considered equally well as genre compositions or as allegories, and why it is often hard to decide whether one approach is better than the other.

THE FALL OF THE REBEL
ANGELS
Oil on panel; 117 x 162 cm
(46 x 63¾ in)
Signed and dated: 'M. D. LXII
BRVEGEL'
Brussels, Musées Royaux Des
Beaux-Arts
Sin, Hell and Death were
central themes in Bruegel's
work in the course of 1652.
This and two other paintings,
Dulle Griet and *The Triumph
of Death,* were probably produced for the same client who
wanted Bruegel to paint
pictures in the manner of
Bosch. The Fall of the Angels
is a theme which also appears
in the work of Bosch, but only
as a secondary scene in some of
his depictions of paradise.
Bosch originated the idea that
the angels were transformed
into infernal monsters during
their fall. Bruegel has ex-
panded the scene into a
tumultuous confusion of inter-
twined figures. The Archangel
Michael, at the centre in a
golden suit of armour, and his
helpers are defeating the
hordes of rebels, driving them
for ever into the chaos of Hell.

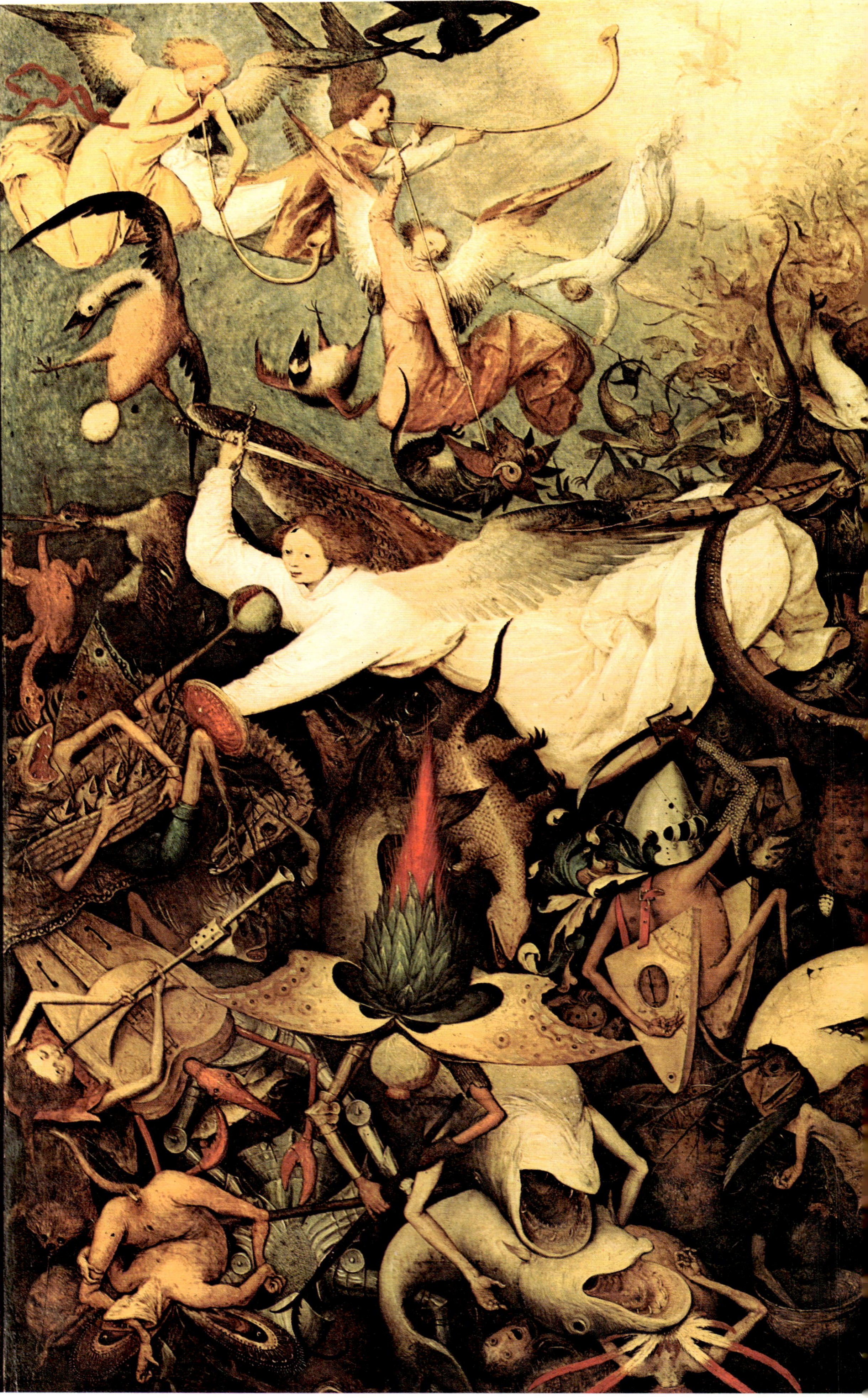

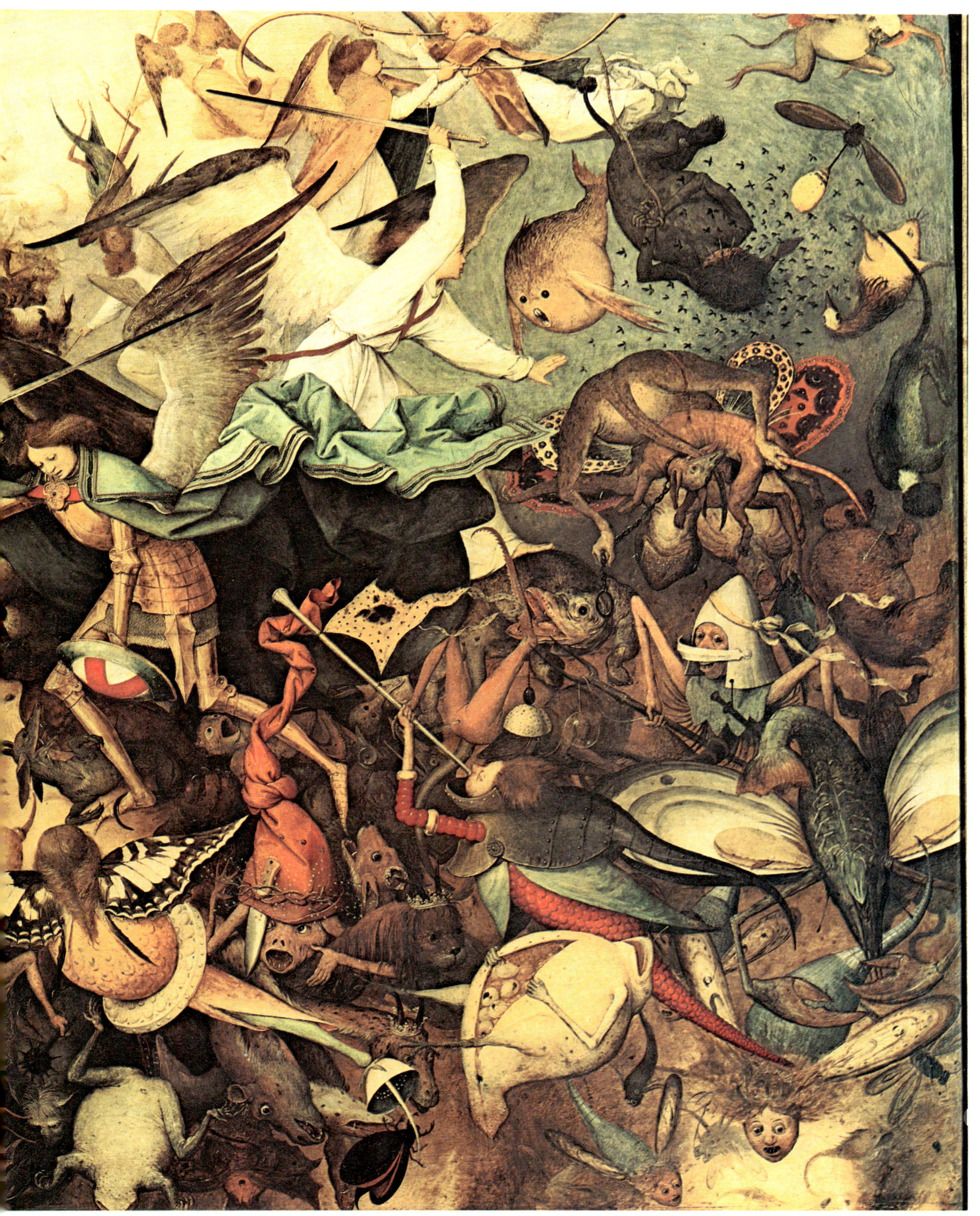

The same applies to the *Kermis at Hoboken* of 1559 (page 49) which Frans Hogenberg engraved without indicating the date, but changing two details in the draft. This may have been due to the fact that the publisher, Bartholomäus de Momper, did not keep such a close eye on his engraver as Cock. In the same year Pieter van der Borcht executed a drawing on the same subject called the *Feast of St. George*, (page 48) which although produced independently of Bruegel's may have suggested certain ideas to him. Despite its grandiose spatial quality, van der Borcht's work is more old-fashioned, less relaxed in its treatment of the human figure, and differs in the distribution of groups of figures both from Bruegel's undated composition of the same name, the *Feast of St. George*, of which only engravings have survived, and from the *Kermis at Hoboken* of 1559. Hoboken is a village near Antwerp where, it seems, the townspeople liked to go drinking because the beer there was cheaper than in the town. In 1559, the year when the drawing was done, Melchior Schetz bought the village from William of Orange. This may have been the occasion for the drawing's execution: a plea to the new owner not to be too strict with the laws against excess during the festivities of the fair.

A *kermis* was originally a religious celebration on the anniversary of the consecration of a church. But by Bruegel's time the religious purpose had been largely swamped by fairs and money-making and the *kermis* was always an occasion for alcoholic excesses. For this reason the drawing was suspected of having a double meaning and of incorporating an allusion to '*gula*' or intemperance. The numerous pigs and beer-mugs could certainly be seen as symbols of '*gula*' and the caption is quoted in support of this view: 'The peasants make merry at these festivities, dancing and capering and getting swinishly drunk. They have to hold their kermis even if they carouse themselves to poverty and die of it'. Nevertheless, we find nothing anywhere in the drawing that cannot be explained by the context nor is there any special motif to justify the assumption of an allegorical meaning. The flag and the archer in the foreground can be taken to show the picture is one of the three special *kermis* celebrations held annually at Hoboken, namely the archers' guild festival on the second day of Pentecost.

Apart from these folkloristic productions Bruegel went on working right into the 1560s, though less frequently, on religious subjects for engravings, some of them demon-ological in character. They include *Christ in Limbo*, 1561, (page 65), the two drawings with St. James and the magician, 1564, (page 98), one of which only survives as an engraving, and *The Resurrection* 1561–1562, (page 77), which, although presumably not intended for it, was in fact engraved.

In the first drawing Christ has descended into Limbo, surrounded by angels playing musical instruments, to free the forefathers of mankind. In the abundant demonic motifs, as in the scenes with the magician, Bruegel harks back to Bosch. Tolnay and Münz regard this drawing as completing the *Virtue* series, but more recent research has refuted this notion. The doors of the jaws of Hell have fallen away and the first of the liberated souls are already stepping over one of them, worshipping Christ with gestures of faith. Behind the other door, devils can be seen in a state of confused agitation while others in the foreground suffer paroxysms of exasperation and rage because of Christ's arrival. The Prince of Darkness sits with an enigmatic expression on his face in the burst cranium of the infernal head. Here again Tolnay offers the most original but scarcely acceptable theory that this expression reflects the fact of his being beyond salvation. For the host of the faithful hardly expected redemption: they came here, where the wheel of Hell continually turns, to be cast into the everlasting fire to the accompaniment of satanic screems of glee. 'Thus humanity passes from Limbo into Hell itself'.

The *Fall of Hermogenes* (page 98) is very much harder to interpret. Its subject-matter comes from *Legenda Aurea* of Jacobus de Voragine, which tells of the struggle between the apostle James the Elder and the magician Hermogenes. James has entered the wizard's sphere of influence and is teaching his followers. Hermogenes threatens him with death if he continues preaching, but the magician's 'apostle' Philetus, who brings the message, is converted by James. On returning to his master Philetus is punished for his apostasy by being fixed to the spot. At the height of the struggle Hermogenes sends two of his vassal spirits to James to fetch him. James overcomes them with the help of an angel and makes them bring Hermogenes to him, breaking the magician's power. Now he, too, receives instruction and is obliged to recant his heresy in public. To protect Hermogenes from the demons which continue to menace him, James gives him his miraculous pilgrim's staff.

Bruegel depicts the legend in two separate parts, the first of which has only survived in its engraved form. This shows the demons who have returned from their unsuccessful mission, the spell-bound Philetus, and James giving a blessing as he makes a spirit burst in the air. The drawing shown here, now in Amsterdam, is dated 1564 (Bruegel wrote

DULLE GRIET (MAD MEG)
Oil on panel; 115 x 161 cm (45¼ x 63⅜ in)
The signature and part of the date have dis-appeared, leaving only: '…MDLXI'
1562
Antwerp, Museum Mayer van der Bergh
Mentioned by van Mander in 1604 as belonging to the collection of Rudolph II. The full date most likely read 1562. This is one of Bruegel's most complex works and a vast amount has been written about it. The central figure, derived from Netherlandish folklore, has arrived at the gate of Hell, and this has suggested an association with the proverb 'The best woman found in the world was the one who tied the Devil to a cushion'. Of the extremely numerous interpretations of *Dulle Griet*, the one proposed by Grossmann is the most straightforward. He sees the picture as an allegory of avarice and greed.

MDXLIIII or 1544 by mistake, transposing the L and the X) and was published as an engraving by Hieronymus Cock in 1565, as was its companion piece. It contains the scene in which the demons bring Hermogenes to James, but differs from the legend in having not just two of them but a whole horde. These have adopted rather drastic tactics, casting the magician together with his chair and book at the feet of the waiting James, behind whom a crowd of the converted throngs through the church door to watch. Hieronymus Bosch or one of his school also treated this theme in the wing of an altarpiece in Valenciennes whose companion with the second scene has disappeared without trace. The compositional treatment bears no relation to Bruegel's drawings, which are far richer in this respect than Bosch's picture, but the latter may have provided a thematic suggestion.

In a complicated analysis of Bosch's *Marriage at Cana* and the *Conjuror*, W. Fraenger finds in both of Bruegel's drawings hidden interconnections and pointers to an arcane

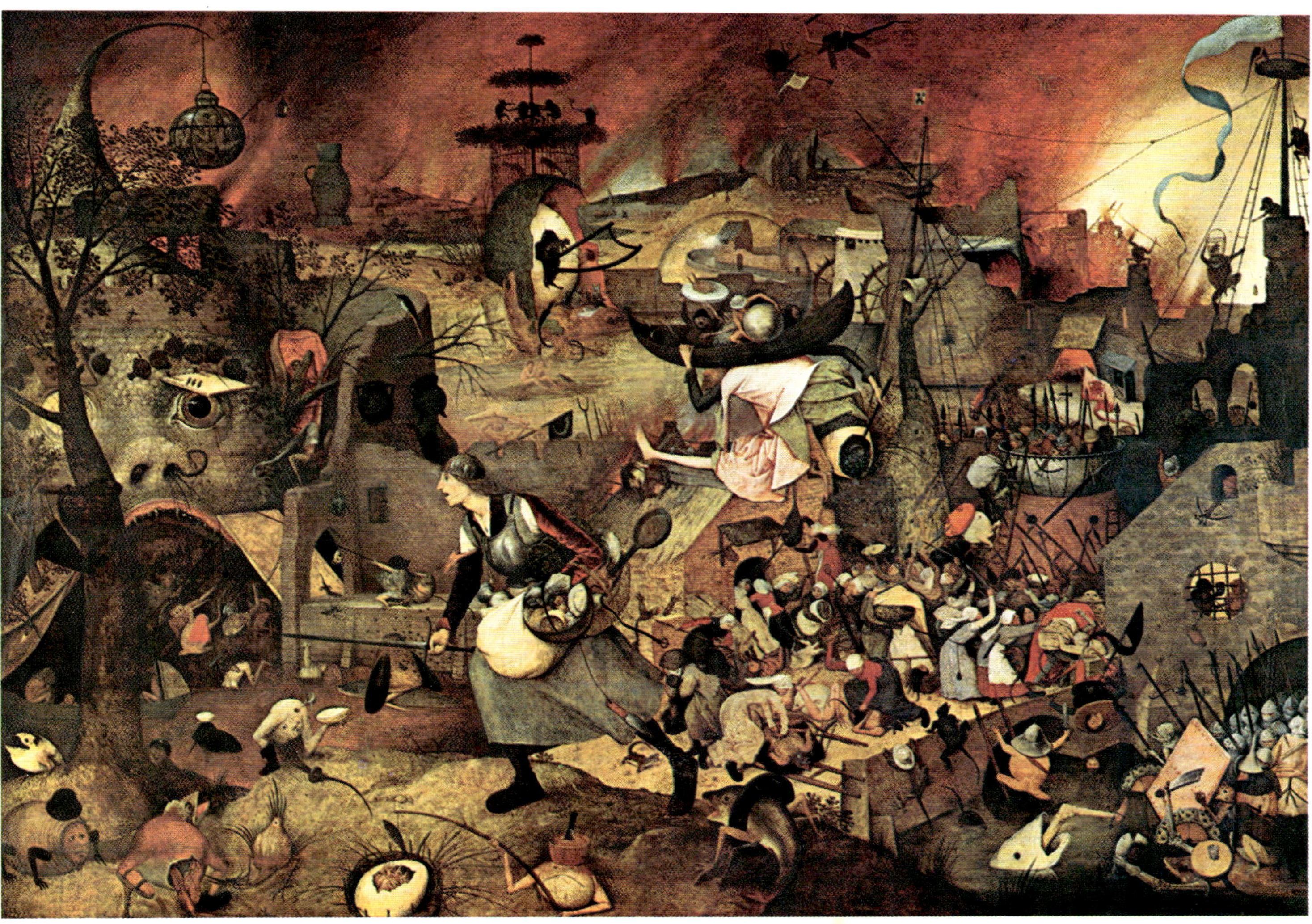

mystery of Semitic *gnosis*, a kind of castration ritual. And indeed, the same game which constitutes the main motif in Bosch's *Conjuror* appears in Bruegel's drawing at bottom left and on the table below the tightrope walkers. Bosch includes a frog in this 'game', while Bruegel has a frog-like creature with two hands and a lock on its mouth. Clearly there is a connection, but the details of Bruegel's Hermogenes engravings remain obscure for those unwilling to go along with Fraenger's controversial theory, which explains Bosch's work by his membership of an 'Adamitic, heretical community with Jewish and Gnostic associations'. But to assume that Bruegel intended the apostle James to symbolize the victory of the true Catholic faith over superstition and heresy would be to jump to an equally extreme conclusion about Bruegel's religious sympathies. On the contrary, Tolnay sees in the images an attack on the brutality of the Catholic church, with James embodying the vengeful Inquisition mercilessly slaying heretics. But perhaps it may be nearer the truth to suggest that purely denominational questions were largely a matter of indifference to Bruegel – as they were to his friend Ortelius, who once spoke of 'Catholic sickness, Gueux fever and Huguenot dysentery'. It may be that Bruegel merely wanted to point out in a faintly moralizing tone what could become of a black magician, of whom there were plenty in the 16th century, who was overthrown by his own spirits. Bruegel certainly had a special and lasting interest in the subject of over-throwal, as we can see from the *Fall of Icarus*, the *Fall of the Rebel Angels*, the fall in the *Conversion of Saul* and the *Parable of the Blind*.

The last drawings

Since its first publication in 1924, the authenticity of *The Resurrection* (page 77) in many ways an unusual drawing, has been doubted only by Tolnay and Münz. It is now generally accepted as genuine, not least as a result of Grossmann's convincing analysis. The composition betrays the influence of Old Netherlandish painting of the 15th century – with strong echoes of Memling, who in his turn had taken ideas from the circle

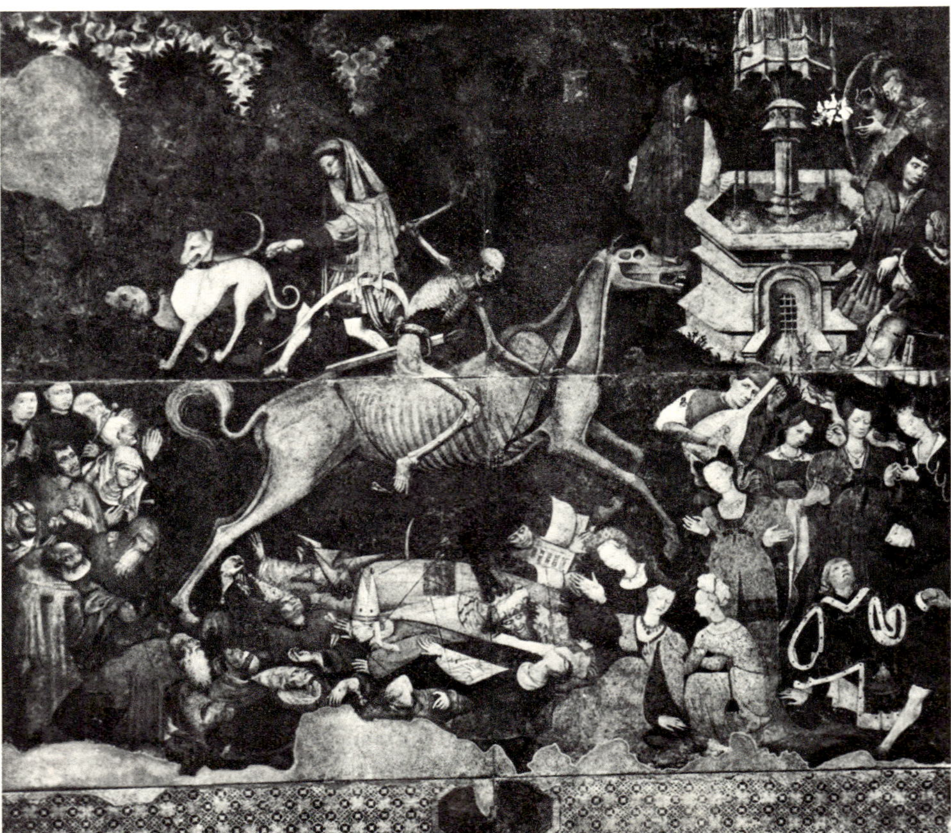

of van Eyck and Rogier van der Weyden – and also of other, older pictorial traditions. Bruegel's composition, which synthesizes the descriptions of the Resurrection in the Gospels of St. Mark (Ch. 16, v. 1–7) and St. Matthew (Ch. 28, v. 1–8), furthermore chooses a different moment in the story from that of his predecessors, enabling him to show the woman at the tomb and the angel sitting at the tomb's entrance. All the Gospels mention the stone being rolled away and St. Mark speaks of the stone's unusual size. Consequently, Bruegel rejected the customary, door-like entrance in favour of a large cave-mouth with an enormous thick slab whose weight emphasizes the extent of the miracle. Dated 1562 by Grossmann, this is the only figure composition of upright format among Bruegel's drawings (except for *Artist and 'Critic'*). Otherwise the upright format is restricted to the paintings such as the *Adoration of the Magi* of 1564 in London. It is also distinguished by free use of brushwork, much more so than the *Temptation of St. Anthony* (page 20). In fact it evidently came to be regarded very soon after its execution as a grisaille-type painting, because it was mounted on wood and framed, and the engraving published by Cock reproduces the drawing with a frame. Grossmann draws attention to the intimate character of Bruegel's two other known grisailles, which were painted in oil on wood, and to the specifically private purposes for which they were used: the *Death of the Virgin* (page 100) was painted for a close friend, Ortelius, and *Christ and the Woman Taken in Adultery* (page 101) was kept in the family after Bruegel's death. So *The Resurrection* might perhaps have been meant as a present for his friend the merchant Hans Franckert. We can tell the drawing was not intended for engraving from the fact that in the engraving, because of the lateral inversion, Christ is giving his blessing with his left hand, an error Bruegel would have taken care to avoid. There can be no question of imputing alchemistic symbolism to *The Resurrection* as van Lennep tried to do in 1965. According to this theory, Christ, like the philosopher's stone, is leaving the darkness of the base material world to enter the realm of light. The sunrise represents the appearance of the philosophers' stone, and so on.

The drawing is in a poor state of preservation, and the paper, worn and flaking, bears traces of the engraver's transfer work. The signature below right has been renewed, probably by another hand.

As we have already said, Bruegel was fully occupied throughout the 1560s and right up to his death in 1569 with the great paintings, so that his graphic work received less attention. Nonetheless, various unusually fine compositions were produced which

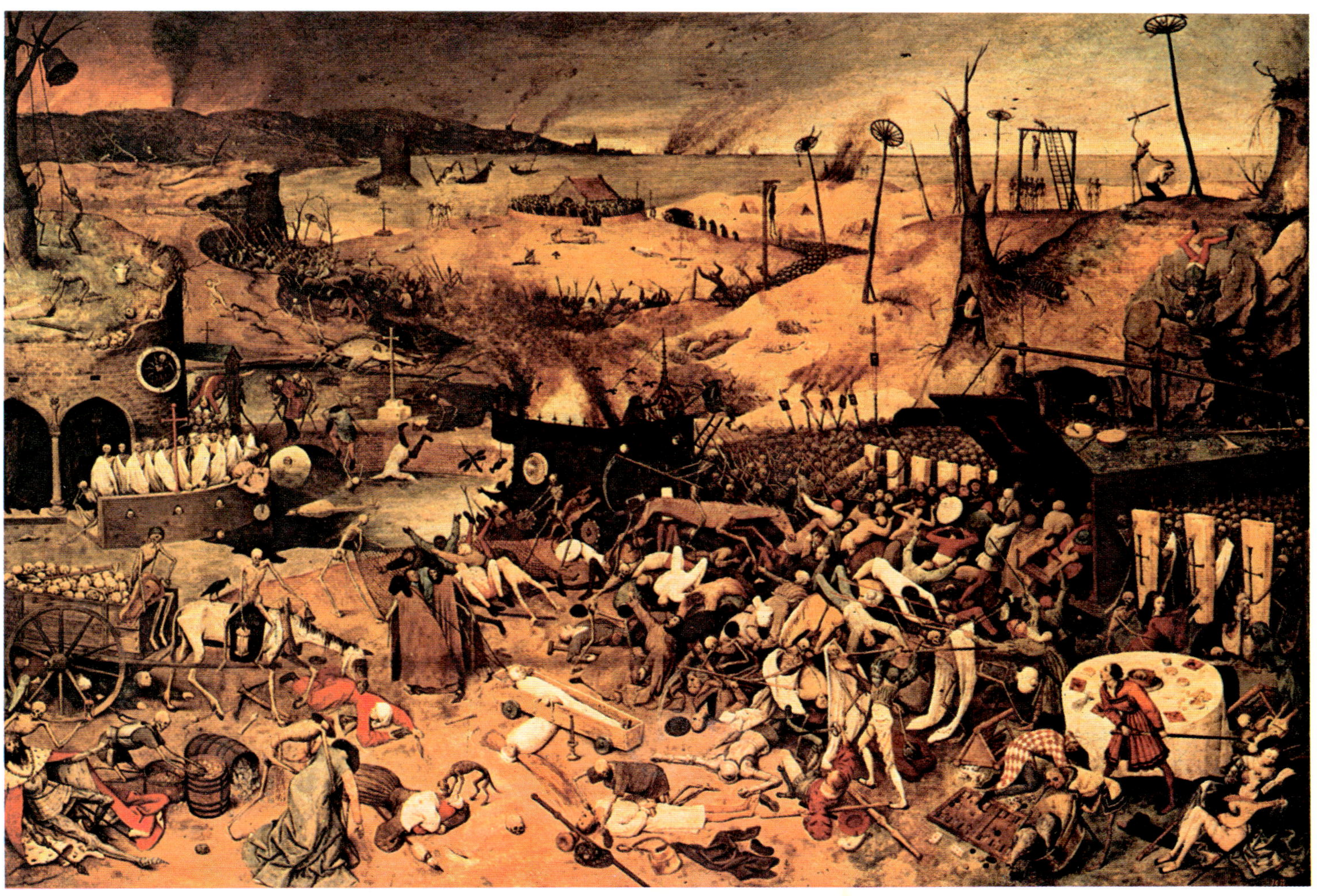

reflect the same changes of style as the late paintings: reduction of groups of figures to just a few splendidly emphasized individuals, and a merging of human figures and landscape. In 1563 two genre allegories appeared, *The Fat Kitchen* and *The Thin Kitchen* (page 54 and page 55), of which only engravings have survived, and the famous *Artist and 'Critic'* (page 127). *Spring* and the *Defamation of Apelles*, an allegorical work showing Italian influence, appeared in 1565, the woodcuts *Urson and Valentine* and *De vuyle Bruid* in 1566, *Summer* in 1568, and in the same year that crowning masterpiece of all graphic art *The Beekeepers* (page 153). No further religious themes appear in any of these drawings.

Although separated by three years, *Spring* (page 126) and *Summer* (page 152) are part of a planned series of four seasons whose completion was presumably prevented by Bruegel's death. Hieronymus Cock completed the series with *Autumn* and *Winter* by Hans Bol, which he published as engravings in 1570. In the drawings for these engravings, in contrast to the magnificent painted scenes of the months of 1565, Bruegel gave greater emphasis once again to the activities characteristic of the time of year – as traditionally depicted in calendar illustrations – whereas the basic theme of the painted series is nature herself as she passes through her various transformations. Here too, though, his treatment is thoroughly novel and individual. As the Flemish caption indicates, *Spring* in the Albertina Museum in Vienna combines the months of March, April and May. At bottom left are the words '*de lenten*' (the spring); at bottom right, in the little panel Bruegel liked to use for this purpose, the year M.D.LXV with his signature underneath.

The activities characterizing the three consecutive months are staggered spatially within the picture from front to back, the scheme being even more clearly emphasized in *Spring* than in *Summer*. Work in the garden is done in March, sheep are sheared and beehives set up in April, and the amorous amusements of the nobility (on the right in the background) have always by tradition taken place in May, the month of love. The various scenes appear to have been arranged quite casually, separated by no more than a balustrade and hedges. In contrast to the profound sense of restlessness in *Elck* we here

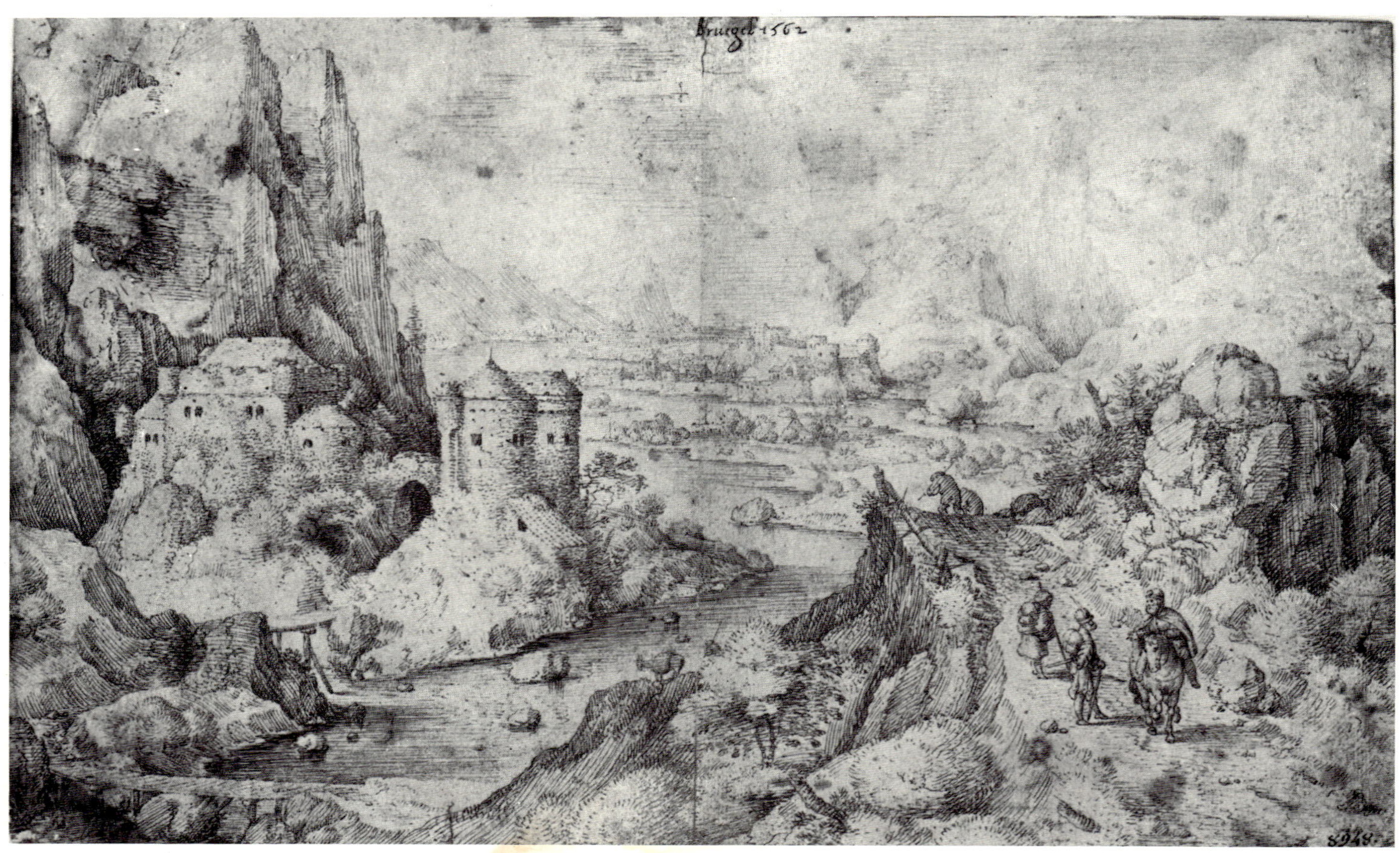

have perfect peace and quiet despite all the bustling activity. The silent, ordered application of the labourers is brought out in the repetition of similar gestures, an impression reinforced by the round hats shielding their faces, eyes turned downward intent on the job in hand. Where we do see a face, like that of the girl on the right, the gaze is lowered. This trick, also used in *Summer*, stresses our role as spectators: we observe from close by, but remain unseen.

Full use is made here of the dot technique, achieving an inimitable delicacy in the graduation of three-dimensional values which Pieter van der Heyden's lifeless engraving was unable to reproduce. Much has been made of the supposed drift of Bruegel's late work towards Italian models; but to take a specific instance, Tolnay's suggestion that the figure digging on the right was inspired by Michelangelo's portrayal of *Noah* in the Sistine Chapel seems to be going too far. The similarities are simply too few, and in any case, there is no reason to doubt that Bruegel was capable of drawing a labourer wielding a spade from life. An even greater degree of Italian influence, and even classical features too, have been found in *Summer* (page 152). The chief inspiration of these exaggerated claims has been the monumental figure of the drinking labourer. Tolnay speaks of the 'curious caricature of the Laöcoon motif', while Stridbeck suspects that the idea derives from the figure of a warrior on the shield of Athena Parthenos, possibly via Heemskerck and the *Rape of Europa*. The heaviness of the figures is quite justifiably seen as reminiscent of Michelangelo, but no direct model can be proved – which is hardly

ROCKY LANDSCAPE WITH CASTLE
Pen drawing in tones of light and dark maroon on white paper; 192 x 312 mm (7⅝ x 12¼ in)
Signed and dated at top centre: 'bruegel 1562'
Munich, Kupferstichkabinett
Bruegel here returns to the old theme of the panoramic landscape. With its wealth of precise detail and balanced structure this drawing anticipates the landscapes in the paintings, particularly the *Flight into Egypt* of 1563 (p. 82), and marks a step forward in relation to the preceding compositions.

VILLAGE
Pen drawing in maroon on white paper; 180
x 310 mm (7⅛ x 12¼ in)
Signed and dated at bottom centre; 'bruegel
1562'
Brunswick, Herzog Anton Ulrich Museum
The experimental nature of this interesting
and unusual work is emphasized by its extremely three-dimensional quality and the
picturesque effects achieved without shading
and simply by means of a sophisticated
graphic technique using small dots and brief
outlines.

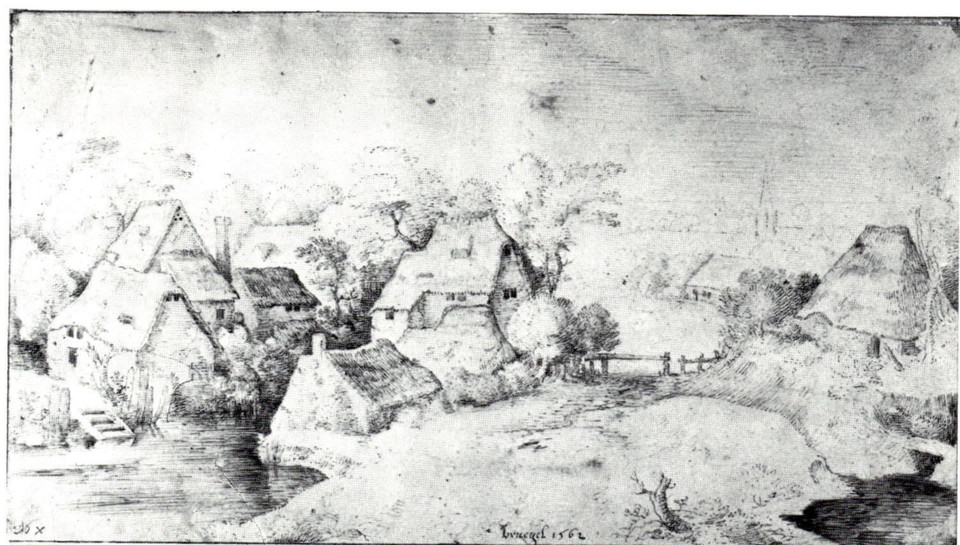

surprising when we remember that one of the achievements of genius is precisely to
disguise influences beyond recognition. Nor shall we have any luck if we look for direct
borrowings in Bruegel: he simply does not repeat either the work of other artists or his
own. For example, although this drawing and the *Corn Harvest* (pages 112–113) of 1565
share the same theme, not a single common detail can be found. We can only say once
again in quite general terms that the *contrapposto* in the positions of the main figures
relative to each other and in individual figures, the ease with which foreshortening
effects are achieved, the monumentality of the figures and their relation to the spatial
context can indeed be explained by Italian influence, which also goes for the illusionistic
way in which the foot and scythe project over the frame. But any such stimuli have been
entirely absorbed by an art that is quite unmistakably Bruegel's own and they are far less
discernible than in Dürer, for example, a fact due to the different nature of the artists'
interests.

Summer, too, combines three months, although the corn harvest (July or August)
dominates. The gathering of fruit in baskets stands for July (or August), while in the
background hay is being mown, which generally takes place in June or July. The whole
scene is bathed in the shimmering heat of summer. Bruegel has no need to use shadow
to represent light; and it is obviously not just a bright day but a hot one too. The bodies
are heavy, and so is the work in the August sunshine. This is suggested first and
foremost by the figure of the drinking labourer, whose head held far back as he drains
the jug expresses all the impatient satisfaction of quenching a burning thirst. Having
collapsed on to a sheaf of corn and flung his scythe to one side, he is emptying an
enormous vessel the shape and size of which play an important part in the overall effect.
The way his heel and scythe extend over the lower edge of the picture intensifies the

GATES AND TOWERS OF
AMSTERDAM
Pen drawing in yellow and maroon on white
paper; 183 x 304 mm (7¼ x 11⅞ in)
Signed and dated at bottom right: 'bruegel
1562'
Besançon, Musée des Beaux-Arts
C. P. van Eeghen suggested in 1935 that this
drawing shows part of the fortifications of
Amsterdam. The work belongs to a group of
three similar drawings, all of the same year,
which indicate that Bruegel made a trip to
Amsterdam at that time. The characteristic
pointillist technique is fully developed here,
recalling the texture of a greatly enlarged
photograph.

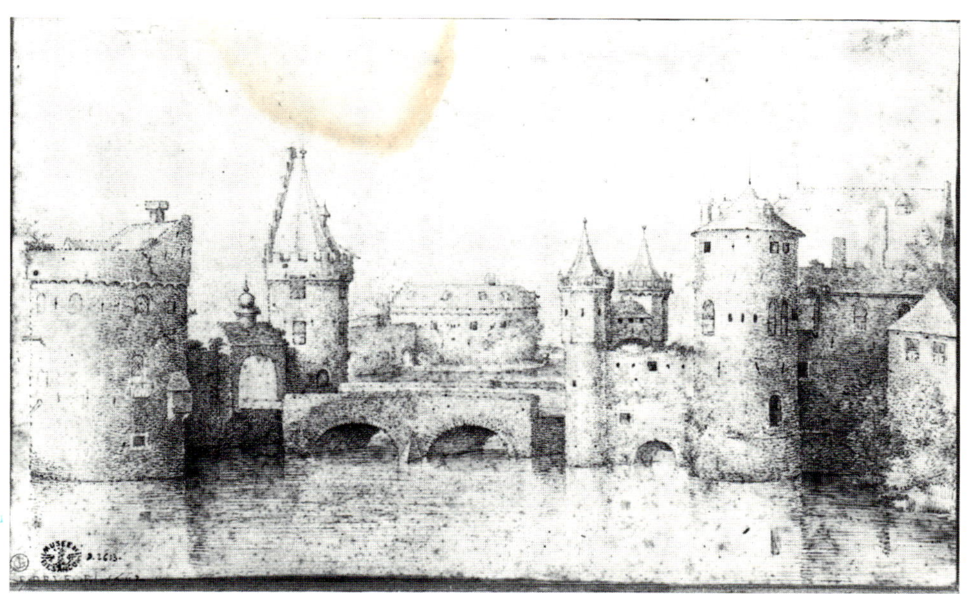

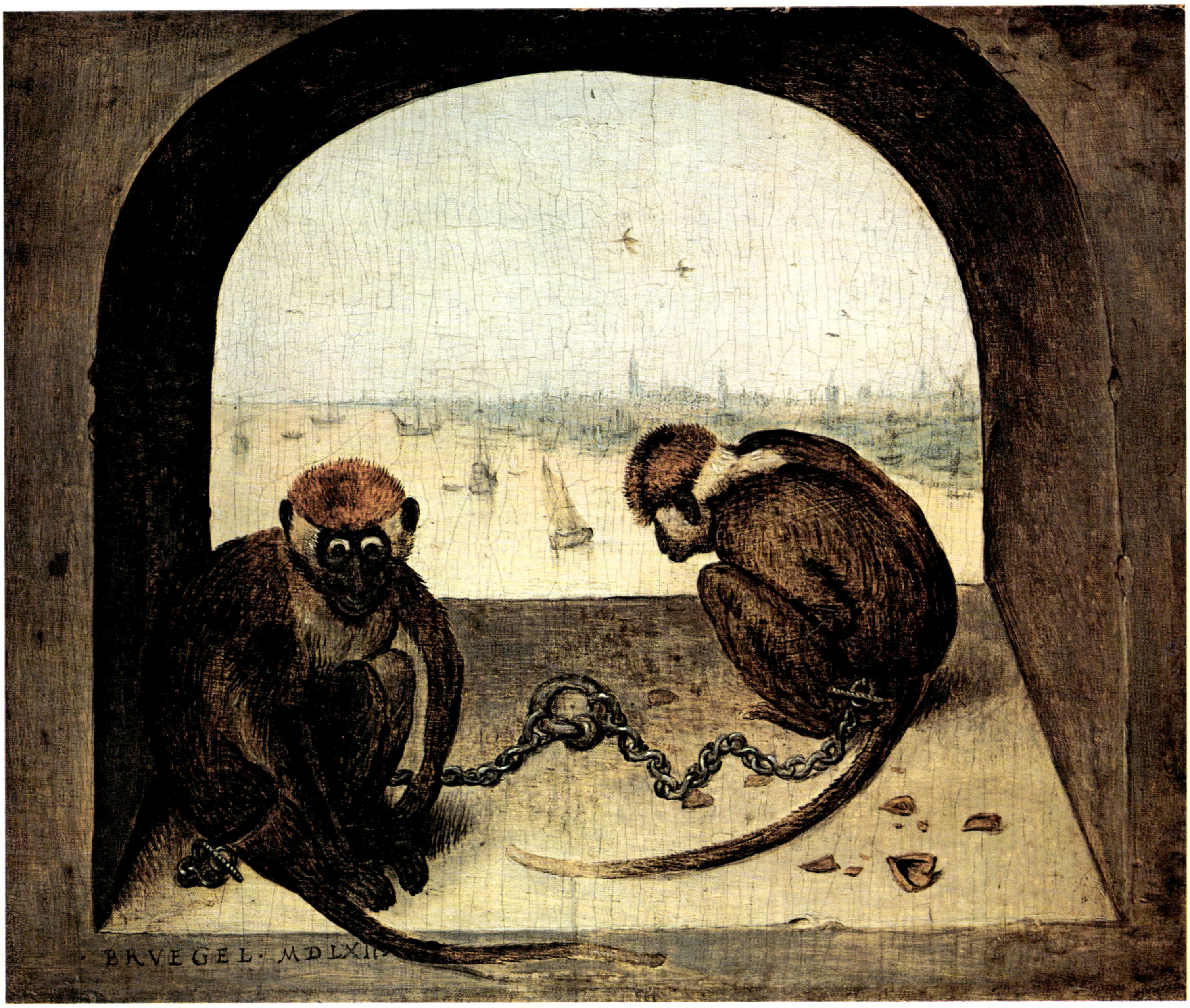

TWO MONKEYS
Oil on panel; 20 x 23 cm (7⅞ x 9 in)
Signed and dated: 'BRVEGEL MDLXII'
Berlin, Staatliche Museen, Preussischer Kulturbesitz
First mentioned in the inventory of the Antwerp collector Peter Stevens in 1668, acquired by the Museum in 1930. The apparently simple but in fact very sophisticated composition was painted in 1562 and anticipates later works featuring a small number of large figures. The realism with which the two chained monkeys are depicted, and the sadness of their expressions, have given rise to a variety of interpretations. Some have seen allusions to certain proverbs in the work and others have even suggested it refers to the submission of the Netherlandish provinces. However, there is no conclusive evidence for any of these theories.

three-dimensional impression. This drawing, too, makes allowances for later engraving:
the man wielding a scythe is shown left-handed to make him right-handed in the
laterally inverted engraving. The faces of the workers are even less in evidence here than
in *Spring*, a phenomenon on which the artist has expended his virtuosity by turning
most of the figures away. This technique is exploited to the full in the *Beekeepers* and
may be associated with Sedlmayr's theory of Bruegel's 'macchia' and alienation from a
familiar world. It is unlikely, but not impossible, that the peasant woman with a flat
basket of marrows and other vegetables on her head is meant as an allusion to the
proverb: 'It's hard to tell a marrow and a woman apart just by looking'. Finally, the
drawing is an enormous fount of information on contemporary costume and country
life. We can be certain that Bruegel copied every detail – belt buckles, garters, hats,
tools, etc. – with unerring accuracy from life.

De vuile Bruid (page 141) (*The Unclean Bride*) is the title of a farce much in favour with
wandering players during carnival time. The drawing has a companion piece called
Orson and Valentine, a woodcut dated 1566. Both scenes also appear, on a smaller scale
and inverted, in the *Battle Between Carnival and Lent* in Vienna (pages 50–51). No
drawing exists of *Orson and Valentine* as Bruegel probably drew it direct on the wood
block himself. The same is thought to apply to the *Unclean Bride*, the actual wood block
for which luckily still survives although damaged, in an American collection. A start has
been made on cutting at top left, the rest of the wooden surface being primed in white
with pen drawing on top. It is not now known for certain whether this really is Bruegel's
original drawing or merely an impression from the original, which Bruegel then in-
tensified by pen. But this is a secondary matter bearing more relation to the history of
woodcut techniques. The fact that the wood block has been preserved is sensational
enough in itself. The unfinished woodcut was clearly used for Pieter van der Heyden's
copper engraving published by Hieronymus Cock in 1570. The caption on this
engraving is a verse from Virgil (*Bucolica* VIII, 26): '*Mopso Nisa datur, quid non
speremus, amantes*'. In the light of this the picture always used to be called the *Marriage
of Mopsus and Nisa*. But the popular carnival farce has nothing to do with Virgil, except
that at the end a country wedding takes place, namely that of Mopsus and Nisa, so that
Cock's addition of the Latin text must be seen as an ironically learned quotation. Instead
of a bridal crown, the tattered, shabby bride wears a kind of sieve on her unkempt mop
of hair. Her house is a ragged tent and she dances with her groom to the 'music' of
improvised instruments of the kind used at carnivals, an example of which can be seen
in the *Battle Between Carnival and Lent* where one player is using a metal shovel and a
knife. On the right we see the money collector with a savings-pot (Bruegel uses the same
type of pot in the engraving entitled *Battle of the Money-Chests and Savings-pots*).

The Beekeepers (page 153), now in Berlin, is undoubtedly one of Bruegel's late
drawings. The date MDLXV at bottom right has been cut and ends with the figure V,
but the unanimous view is that it was executed in 1568 as indicated clearly by the
similarity of style and technique to *Summer*. Perhaps it was Bruegel's very last drawing;
at any rate it is certainly one of the finest and at the same time the most mysterious. The
fundamental question – the one that constantly recurs with Bruegel – is whether this is a
purely genre scene or an allegory, or possibly a mixture of both. Was Bruegel 'saying'
something, or just showing beekeepers at work? At first glance the answer seems easy:
the proverb in the blank space at bottom left will surely tell us all we want to know. But
this proverb has itself thrown up a further riddle which still remains unsolved. It says:
'He who knows where the nest is, knows it; he who has the nest, has it'. This common
Netherlandish proverb, which also has suggestive sexual undertones, was found by
Grauls in F. Goedthals' collection of proverbs published in 1568, the year the drawing
was probably executed. This text has 'bird' instead of 'nest', again an unequivocal
allusion. Bird's-nests feature as symbols of unchastity, twice in association with fishes
(symbols of male sexuality), in the drawing entitled *Christ in Limbo* (page 65) and in
the paintings *Dulle Griet* (page 69) and the *Fall of the Rebel Angels* (page 67). The
proverb could mean that anyone who doesn't know how to make use of this knowledge
will be superseded by someone else. From the moral point of view, however, that says
nothing at all, but simply raises the further question of which of the two is cleverer or
better. What, indeed, does the proverb signify and how is it related to the *Beekeepers*?

The drawing shows three men with beekeepers' masks in a village landscape, two of
them busy with beehives while the third moves between them. The third has put what
seems to be his own hive down in the meadow and a fourth hive is set against a wall in
the background. In the fork of a tree is a chubby boy holding on with his right hand. It
is impossible to see what he is doing with the other hand, but he could be taking out a
nest as hinted in the proverb. What in that case would be the significance of the

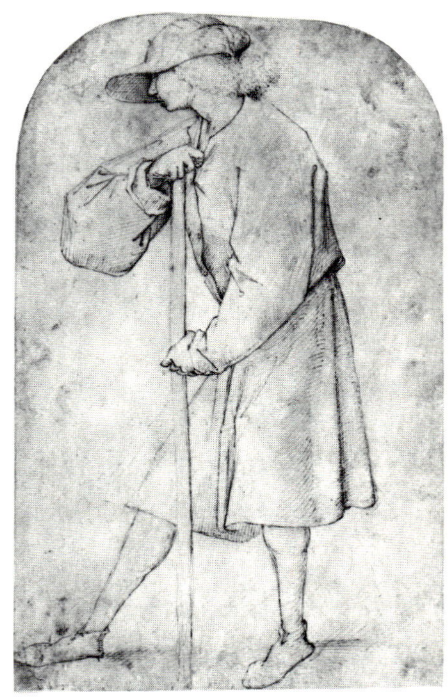

THE SHEPHERD
Pen drawing in light maroon on paper; 246 x
148 mm (9¾ x 5¾ in)
c. 1560–1563
Dresden, Kupferstichkabinett
This important drawing, of which a faithful
copy exists in the Albertina in Vienna, is to
be regarded as a finished drawing rather than
a sketch from life in spite of various *pentimenti*, a conclusion suggested by the
shepherd's graceful and studied posture.
Bruegel's son Jan inserted this figure into
several of his works.

beekeepers? According to one theory the boy is catching a swarm of bees in the tree, perhaps with his hat. He would therefore be a thief robbing the owners – the beekeepers – of their rightful property. Why in that case does the proverb expressly talk about a 'nest' when beekeepers are the subject of the drawing? If Bruegel had wanted to illustrate the proverb about the bird's nest he might perhaps have depicted bird-catchers, but certainly not beekeepers. However, Bruegel did actually paint a bird-nester: the famous painting of 1568 in Vienna called *The Peasant and the Nest Robber* (page 177) shows a boy in a similar situation as he plunders a bird's-nest, with a young peasant close at hand playing a somewhat obscure role. Apart from all the other confusion, this has resulted in the *Beekeepers* and the *Peasant and the Nest Robber* generally being discussed together ever since Hulin de Loo first drew attention to the connection in 1907. Constant attempts have been made to explain the *Nest Robber* by reference to the proverb which appears on the *Beekeepers* and also to establish a link between the latter and the proverb. The most detailed interpretation was undertaken by K. Boström in 1949. For him the proverb referred not only to the opposite concepts of passivity (knowledge) and activity (action) but also to modified versions of them: prudence and audacity. 'The man of action represents evil, the heavy plodder stands for good … The peasant's misfortune belongs to the here and now, but the idea expressed in the painting (the *Nest Robbers*) is beyond space and time. It encapsulates a problem without a solution, a question without an answer: why is the good man stupid and the wicked man clever?' Boström goes on to point out that the beekeepers are protected by their special clothing, while the thief is not, and he sees in this a kind of threat: the audacious thief will end up suffering. The plant shown in the foreground, according to Boström is a mandrake: to possess one brought unfailing happiness. It grew beneath the gallows, begotten by the seed of the wrong-doer, and could only be taken out of the ground at great risk and with the aid of magic rites. In the end it brought unhappiness and death to its owner, who fell victim to the snares of hell. The plant in the drawing was an allusion to the 'antisocial type of person who enjoys the "luck of the devil" in his daring exploits, but finally hangs on the gallows'. This extravagant hypothesis is hardly helped by the fact that the plant in question is not a mandrake.

K. Renger, writing in the 1975 Berlin catalogue, gives another twist to the proverb's meaning in the light of a text on an etching by M. Gheraerts in which a boy without any protective clothing is plundering three beehives. The text says we are obliged to put up with evil in order to enjoy good. More or less the same thing is expressed in a Netherlandish proverb: 'If you want to get the honey you must suffer the bees' stings'. Thus the boy, although stung by the bees, gets away with his plunder, while the beekeepers risk nothing at all in their protective garments but end up empty-handed. In other words daring is contrasted with timidity. But if this unsubtle message is really what Bruegel was driving at, why did he not put the proverb about the honey beneath the drawing instead of the one about the bird-nester? Another question concerns who wrote the proverb on the *Beekeepers*. The drawing is very carefully executed and was in all probability intended for engraving. Everyone agrees that all the inscriptions under Bruegel's drawings were done by someone else in another ink. The only exception is the one on the *Beekeepers*, which is assumed to be by Bruegel himself because the ink is the same as that used in the drawing. This would be the only surviving example of Bruegel's handwriting. However, opinions differ about this: Glück, for example, maintains the inscription was added in the seventeenth century, while the Berlin catalogue, on the other hand, regards the handwriting as Bruegel's.

To sum up, no-one has yet succeeded in establishing a satisfactory link between the *Beekeepers* and the proverb inscribed on it. And what would be gained if they did? This extremely weird picture surely produces its whole mysterious effect on its own, quite unaided. What could possibly be added by a rational exposition, even if Bruegel himself could provide one?

The same applies to the *Peasant and the Nest Robber*. The proverb about the bird's nest does relate to this picture quite specifically, as we can see from an etching of 1606 by David Vinckboon showing a similar scene with a similar text. And yet, how very much more is conveyed by the picture itself with its unfathomable sense of mystery! Pictures like this bring home to us the incommutability, the incompatibility of language and visual image. As soon as verbal definitions are devised, the picture dies.

THE RESURRECTION
Pen and brush drawing on paper applied to panel; 431 x 307 mm (17 x 11 in)
The name 'BRVEVGEL' appears in a later hand below right, probably superimposed on a signature which is no longer legible.
Rotterdam, Museum Boymans-van Beuningen
The authenticity of this grisaille, which tends to provoke a marked emotional response, has been put in doubt by the technique used, for it is not characteristic of Bruegel. However, Grossmann's convincing analysis has dissipated any doubts. Conceived as a present for a friend, the composition was not meant to be engraved; in fact it was eventually engraved, possibly by Philip Galle. But the engraver failed to notice that, when the picture is inverted, Christ gives the blessing with his left hand.

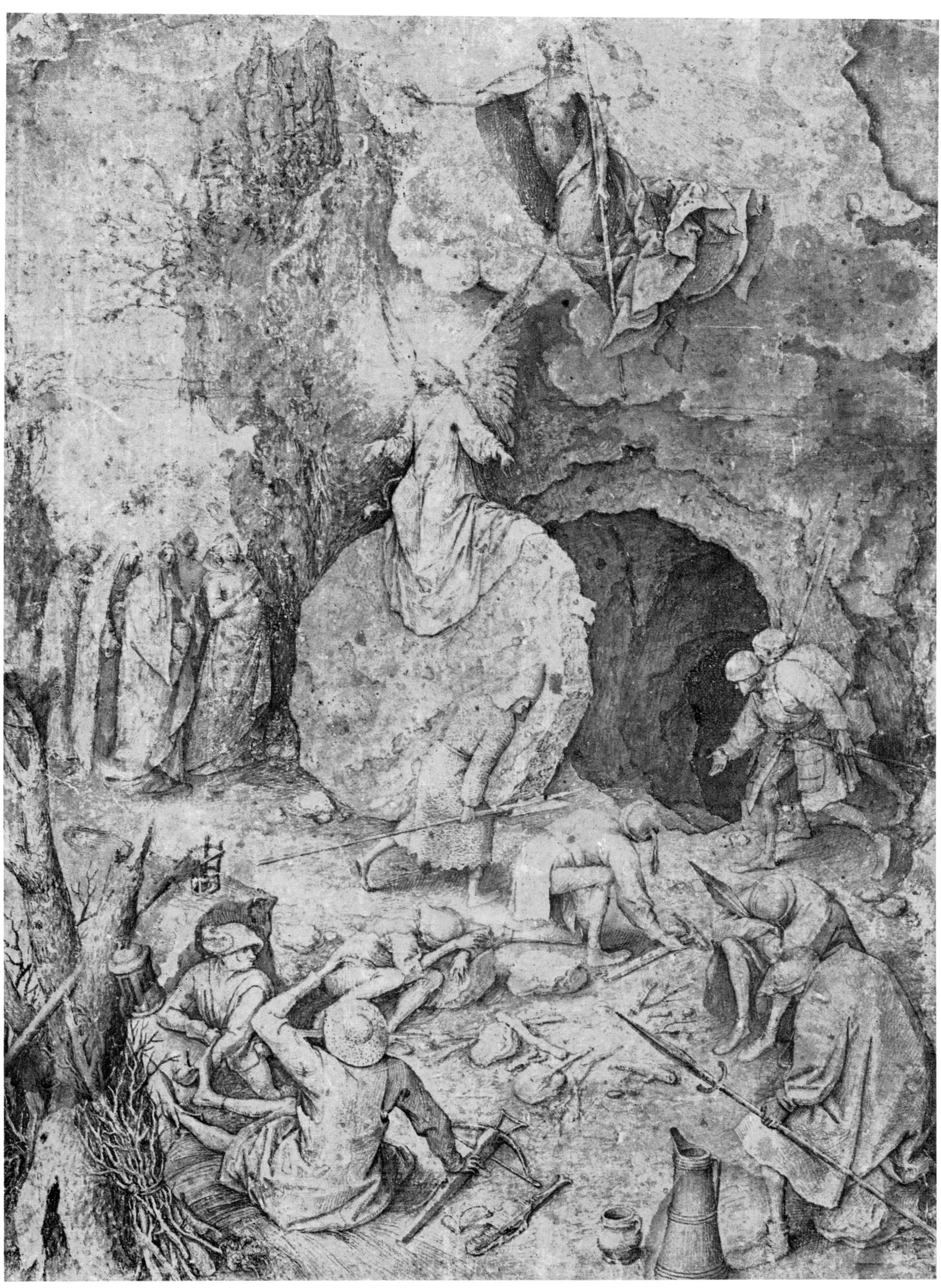

The Paintings

Two main thematic motifs can be identified in Bruegel's paintings right from the start: the human figure and landscape. In the early work these were treated separately, but in the later work they blend into a unified whole. Considerable influence can be attributed to the treatment of the human figure by Hieronymus Bosch, and, going back still further, to the Burgundian Books of Hours, the brothers van Eyck, and the landscapes of Patinir and his followers. At the same time Bruegel's landscapes also owe something to Italian influences and particularly to his own drawings of nature, which provided a basis for his unique landscape paintings. The oldest approach to Bruegel's art, which is to trace its development from Bosch, calls for certain modifications. For his contemporaries such as Guicciardini and Lampsonius, and immediate posterity, notably van Mander, he was the 'second Bosch', above all because of his graphic work and especially the demonic quality, which tended to be over-stressed. Of the paintings, only two works can be considered as parallels to the demon-infested world of Bosch: the *Fall of the Rebel Angels* (page 67) and *Dulle Griet* (page 69). Yet right from the outset the two artists can be distinguished by their starkly different intellectual attitudes: Bruegel is Bosch but in secular form. Bosch, the last of the Primitives, belongs to the very end of the Middle Ages; Bruegel, the first of the modern generation, to the beginning of the post-medieval age. Bosch's pandemonium hovers in a bottomless pit of religious fear and apprehension, full of trap-doors leading down to Hell. Bruegel's spirits and hobgoblins may rant and rave, but on the solid ground of humanist reason. In the former case they are beings whose existence is physically credible, whereas in the latter they appear merely as quotations. The *Fall of Hermogenes* (page 98) represents Bruegel's final farewell to them, and this may in fact be the essential significance of the drawing. Bosch's art has been called the ultimate 'ramification of what had gone before' while Bruegel's exemplifies ascetic confinement. Both artists are 'old-fashioned', but so far as Bosch is concerned, this quality is to some extent compatible with his own age. Bruegel's art, on the other hand, 'developed against the grain of the times', according to Jedlicka, 'being an important element in an artistic scenario which was contrary to the spirit of the Renaissance'.

The main achievements of the early period of Bruegel's art, say from 1553/6–1560, are the landscapes drawings and compositions for engraving (including the series of *Seven Vices* and *Seven Virtues*), various landscape paintings of the 'panoramic' type, and the first three great works – *Netherlandish Proverbs*, the *Battle Between Carnival and Lent* and *Children's Games* – in which a large number of small figures are distributed over a wide area in a way that is both novel and subtle. In the second period, from 1560 to 1565 Bruegel makes his final use of the demonic elements derived from Bosch, in the *Fall of the Rebel Angels* and *Dulle Griet*. He creates the *Tower of Babel*, perfects the type of picture featuring a multiplicity of small figures, such as *Christ Carrying the Cross*, and experiments with a variety of compositions on religious subjects. The most important and best remembered phase was the last one. The four final years of his life saw the fusion of all Bruegel's artistic experience in the great landscapes, figure studies and studio compositions. In 1565 he produced the magnificent scenes of the months, those paragons of landscape art; a series of winter landscapes incorporating religious themes; the *Sermon of St. John the Baptist*; a peasant dance, and a number of works, most of which illustrate themes from peasant life. These are figure compositions with large figures in the foreground (the *Peasant Kermis* and the *Peasant Wedding Feast* now in Vienna) and compositions with just a few, monumental figures (the *Land of Cockaigne*, the *Beggars*, the *Parable of the Blind*, the *Ambush*) and even a depiction of a single figure, the *Unfaithful Shepherd*. Here Bruegel got away from the whole Renaissance problem by modifying Italian compositional ideas for his own purposes. In short, he relinquished the temporal to gain the absolute. It was he who more than any other artist personified the reaction against Italian art in the 16th century, as did Rembrandt in the 17th. Bruegel withstood the temptations of his Italian journey, whereas Rembrandt resisted from the outset. Dvořák called Bruegel the greatest exponent of Mannerism in Northern European painting. But this does only partial justice to the last of his works; like El Greco, Bruegel transcends such definitions.

Bruegel is quite uninterested in the nude: the idea of voluptuous nakedness seems quite incompatible with his art. The movements of his round, heavy figures are draped about with thick materials. Bruegel, as Tolnay says, 'arouses an impression of grotesque comedy by transforming the heroically pathetic, magnificent gestures of Michelangelo's characters to uncouth peasants … thereby deliberately renouncing any kind of claim to pictorial grandiloquence'.

THE SUICIDE OF SAUL
Oil on panel; 33.5 x 55 cm (13¼ x 21 in)
(4 cm (1½ in) at top and 1 cm (⅜ in) at bottom added later)
Signed and dated by the artist: 'SAVL. XXXI. CAP. BRVEGEL.M.CCCCC.LXII'
Vienna, Kunsthistorisches Museum
First mentioned in 1783 as belonging to the Imperial Collection in Vienna. The text at bottom left reveals that the painting is of the suicide of Saul after his unexpected defeat at the hands of the Philistines on Mount Gilboa, as described in Samuel, (1:31). The work was depicted one year before the *Tower of Babel* (p. 85) and is therefore the first of Bruegel's Biblical subjects, of which there are very few. In the *Divina Commedia*, Saul appears as an example of punished pride, together with Lucifer and Nimrod. The battle scene has similarities with German pictures of the first half of the 16th century, particularly with Altdorfer's famous *Battle of Issus* (1529); however, the painting seems to have been directly inspired by a battle scene of Patinir's, now lost.
Details on *pages 80–81*

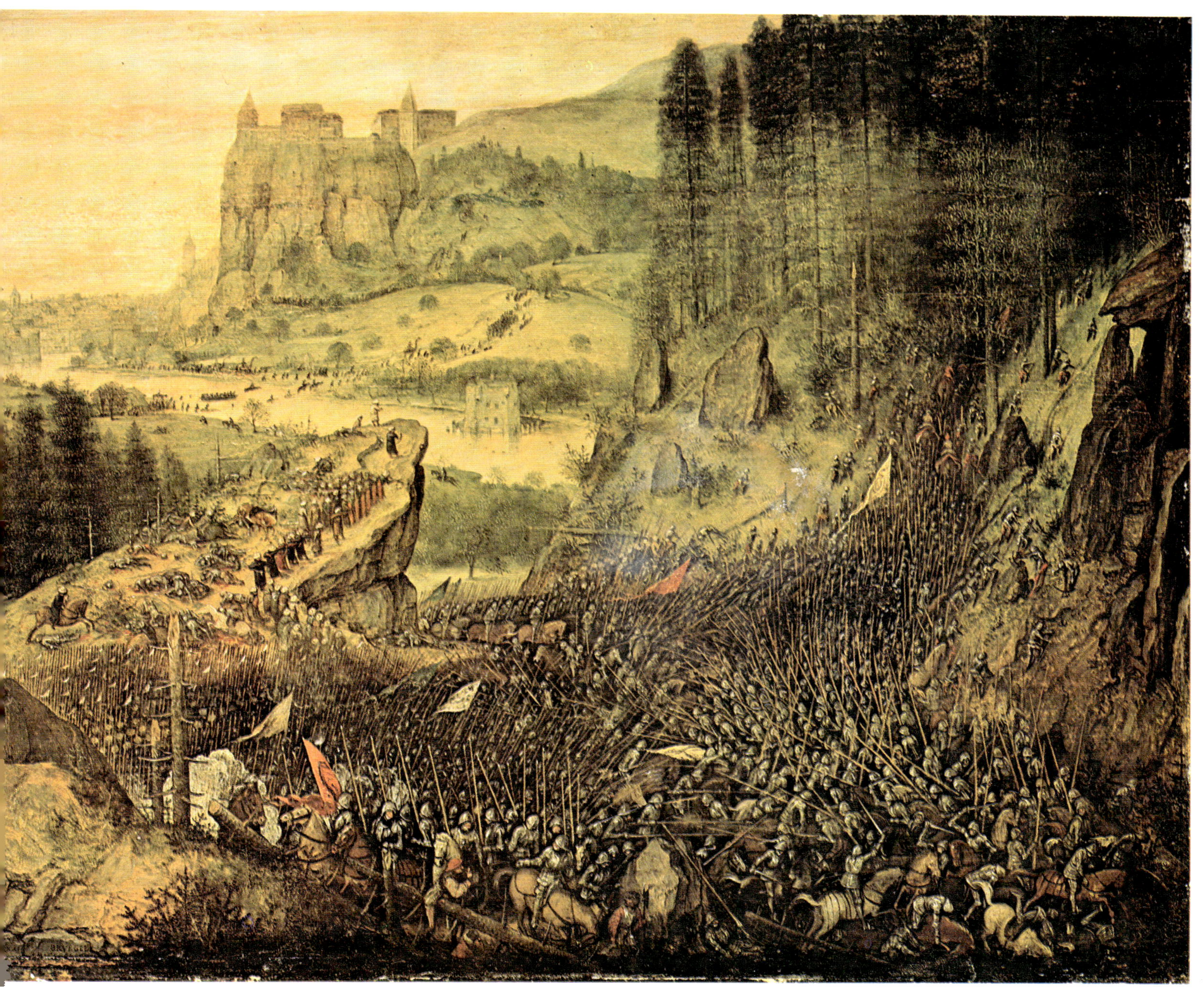

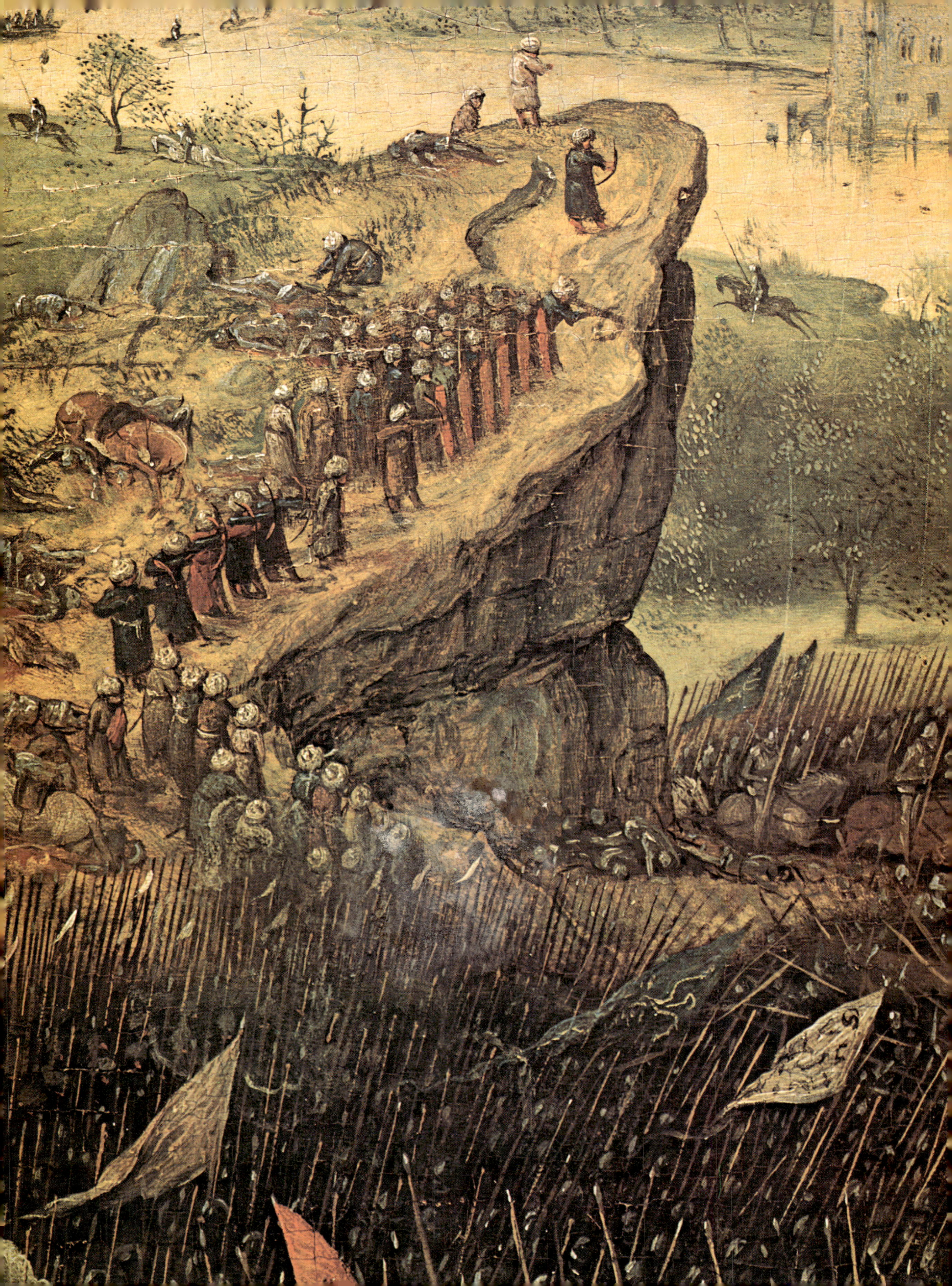

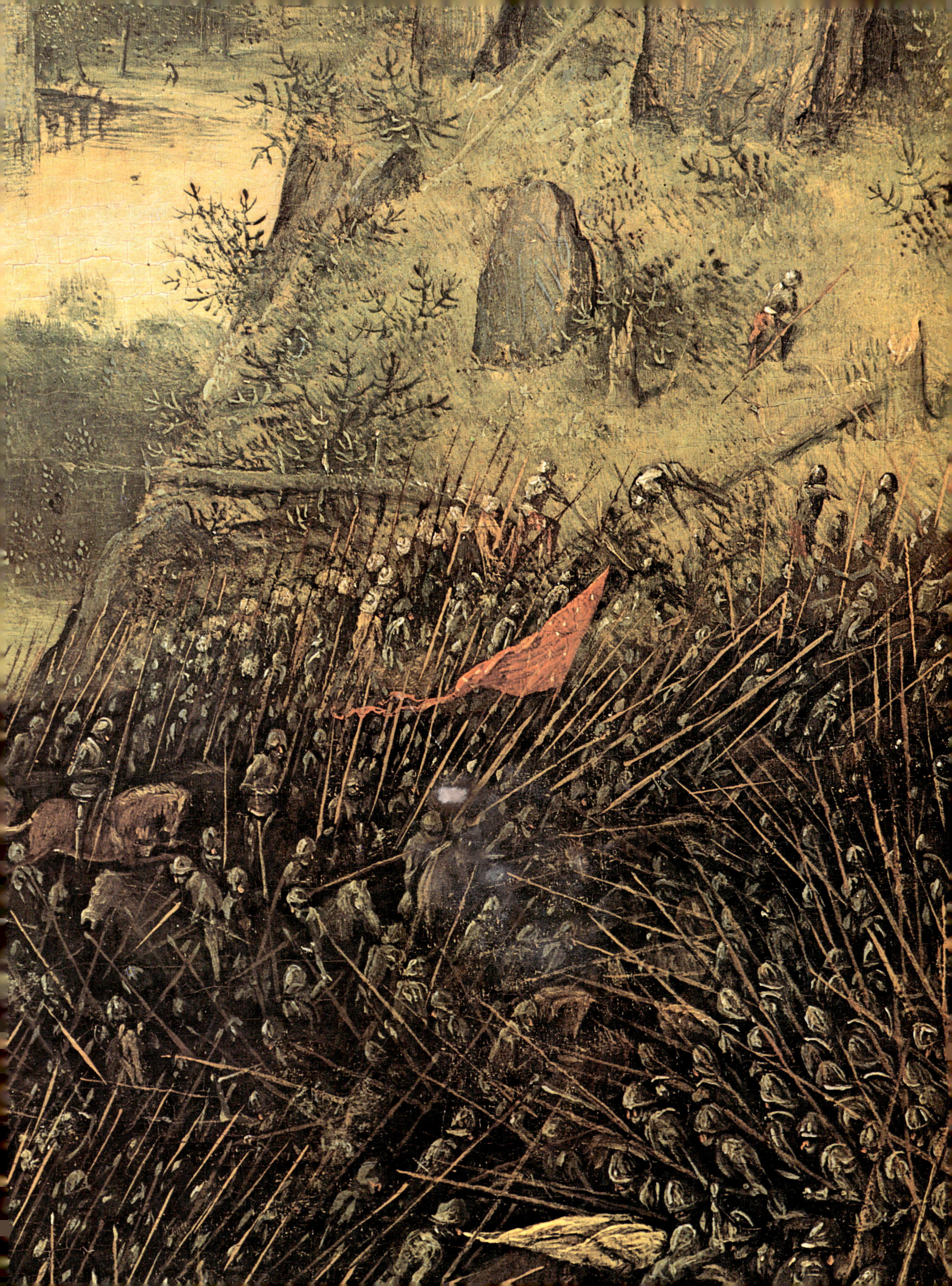

He shows equally little interest in the portrait, though he would probably have succeeded better at the genre than most others. Was it out of a harsh disregard for in-
dividuality as such (reflected in the faces in his pictures) or just from exaggerated
modesty that, apart from the small self-portrait in the crowd in *Christ Carrying the Cross*
he never made a likeness of himself? What a contrast to Dürer!

The early works (1553–1560)

Bruegel's earliest surviving paintings, all of them landscapes, reveal his genius for
turning visual impressions into something new and special while at the same time confidently covering up all traces of his own artistry.
The earliest surviving painting by Bruegel is generally accepted to be the *Landscape with
Sailing Ships and Burning Town* (page 9) in the Becker collection in Dortmund. This

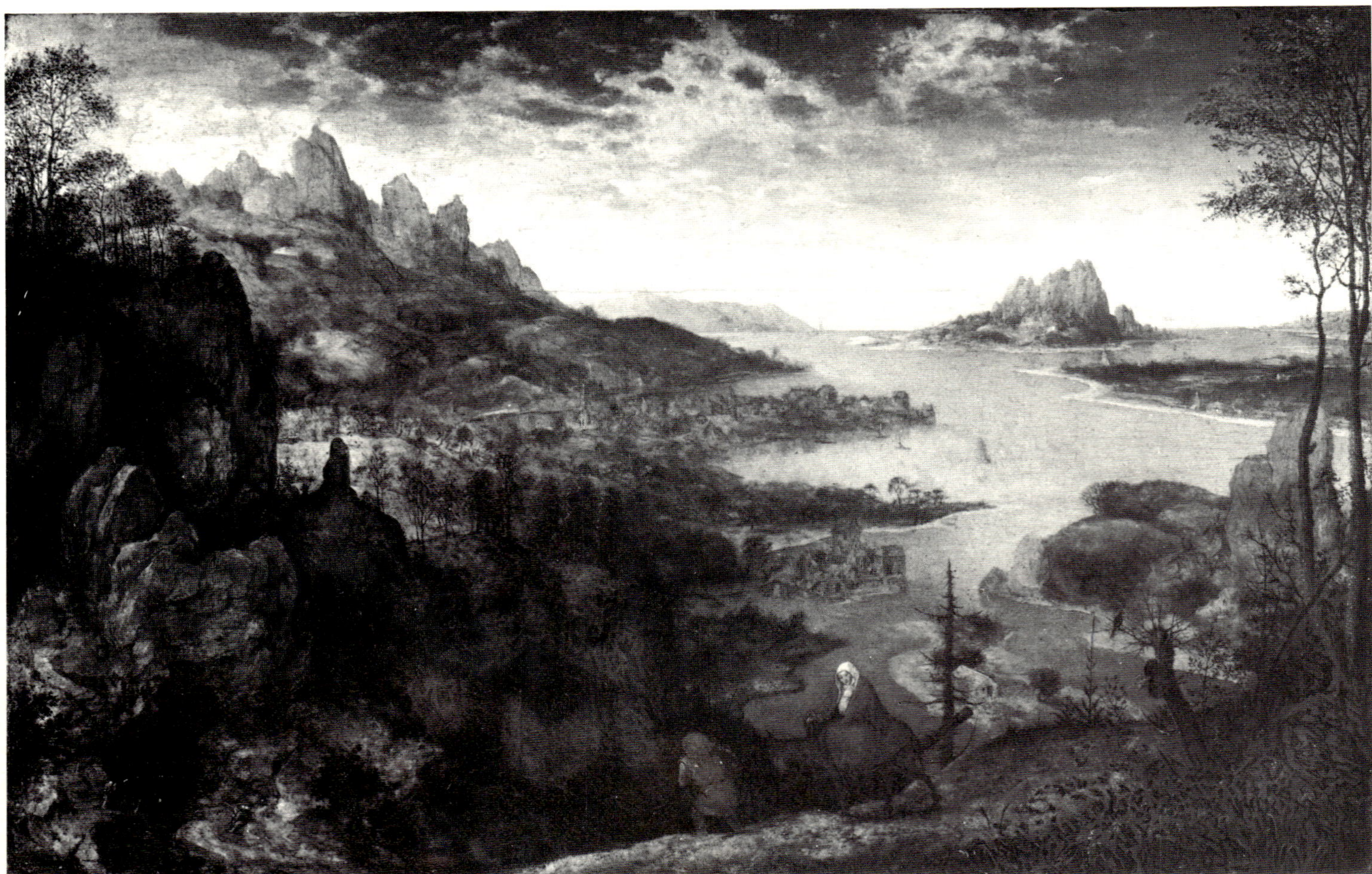

was first recognized as an early work of Bruegel's by Grossmann in 1955. In his later
writing Grossmann added a second version of the same composition and this once again
raised the question of authenticity, but no further work has yet been done on this
picture. However, numerous thematic links make it very likely that the painting is one
of the master's early works, probably executed in Italy in 1552 or 1553. The same can be
said of *Christ on the Sea of Tiberias*, which is signed and dated 1553 (page 11). Both
these works, with their strange cliffs and stretch of water in the centre, have more in
common with Patinir and his followers than any of Bruegel's later work. The theme of
the burning town could have been suggested by pictures such as the *Downfall of Sodom*
by Herri met de Bles, which also shows a burning town behind steep cliffs. Bruegel
always showed an interest in sailing ships, which he could study at his leisure in Antwerp
harbour. They also appear in the *View of the Bay of Naples* (page 26), the *Fall of Icarus*
(page 36), in a drawing in the Courtauld Institute, London and in the *Storm at Sea*
(page 183). The subject of sailing ships formed a series of engravings executed after
Bruegel in 1564 or 1565.
Christ on the Sea of Tiberias (page 11) is the earliest known painting with full signature
and date: Pieter Bruegel 1553. Now in a private collection in New York, it was originally
owned by a noble German family and it was there that Friedländer identified it as one of

Bruegel's works. Tolnay first published it in the *Burlington Magazine* in 1955. The scene is taken from Chapter 21 of St. John's Gospel. The figures, reduced in size, look very unnatural and it has therefore been justifiably supposed that they could have been executed by Maerten de Vos, who is thought to have accompanied Bruegel on some of his travels in Italy.

At this juncture we should also mention the interesting *River Landscape with Two Artists Drawing* in the National Gallery in London (page 12), as it is relevant to the early works of Bruegel. Painted on oak, the picture shows a bend in a river with the rocky bank reflected in the water. Two artists are drawing in the foreground. At one time it was thought to be Italian, having belonged to the family of Count Lechi in Milan, and has also been ascribed without success to various Netherlandish artists including Bruegel. But it would seem to be the work of an artist rather earlier than Bruegel. On the other hand it is known for certain that Bruegel was acquainted with London's river as we can see from the landscape engraving with Mercury and Psyche (page 19), in which these two figures are in fact a later addition by Hoefnagel. Particularly striking is the similarity between the two pictures of the artists at work and the reflection of the rocks in the water. Bruegel's drawing for the etching has been lost, but a drawing exists in Besançon, with the same motif and dated 1553, which is probably a copy of a drawing by Bruegel. There can be no doubt then, that Bruegel came across this motif on his Italian journey, even though it is probably not a view of the Tiber. At any rate, the picture in London is a rarity for the period – featuring as it does a pure landscape without mythological or Biblical subject – and reveals despite the fact that both left and right hand sides have been trimmed the sort of inspiration to which Bruegel was prone. The *Landscape with St. Catherine Being Beheaded* (page 20) is of similar style, but although Glück attributed it to Bruegel this has been rejected. These are just a few of the examples of conjecture about Bruegel's early work before the discovery of *Christ on the Sea of Tiberias* which is dated 1553.

However, at the same time as Bruegel developed his landscape art, he was also starting to work on subjects involving human figures. Although neither signed nor dated, the *Adoration of the Magi* in Brussels (pages 24–25) is regarded by most scholars as an early work influenced by Bosch. Grossmann assumes it was executed in 1556. The picture is painted in tempera on canvas, a method particularly favoured in Malines and which Bruegel also used in late works like the *Parable of the Blind*. This not very durable technique accounts for the painting's regrettably poor condition, many details having been lost. The central panel of Bosch's *Adoration* triptych in the Prado (page 24) is frequently quoted as the inspiration for Bruegel's early *Adoration*, but, in fact, similarities are not very easy to find. The dilapidated stall evidently struck Bruegel more than anything else: he uses it as the central item in his crowded scene with its mass of figures spread out on either side, already betraying a tendency towards epic treatment. The central group under the roof is set apart from the throng in a classic triangular composition consisting of the kneeling kings, Mary and Joseph, with the kneeling black king unashamedly depicted half-hidden behind a post. The group resembles that in the London *Adoration* of 1564 (page 99). Here, crowds of inquisitive soldiers, people on foot and horseback, and the kings' retinues are pressing round from either side, and the contrast between the dense mass of people on the left and the looser grouping on the right must certainly be deliberate. Bruegel's genius is already evident in the masterly treatment of gesture, while the different expressions – even the face at the back of the crowd – reflect the momentous nature of the event. There is a wealth of secondary detail: the ass braying in the stall, the huge dog on the left and – a more exotic touch – the camels and elephant on the right in the background. To give a comprehensive view of the large throng of people, Bruegel uses a trick of perspective employed equally as effectively here as in the later works and reminiscent of the old technique adopted in Gobelin tapestries: the ground below the figures rises very steeply like the steps of a theatre, the landscape background being much more level. But although the overall arrangement makes use of a plan view, the figures are seen not from above but from the side. Despite the wealth of detail, Bruegel shows his ability not only to infuse life into detail but equally to fuse a complex of disparate material into a carefully constructed picture.

Bruegel's treatment of the crowd as a compositional problem is similar in the *Feast of St. Martin*, which only survives in copies (eg. the fragment in Vienna, page 24), and in the *Sermon of St. John the Baptist* (pages 134–135).

The works whose dates are beyond any doubt are generally held to include the famous *Fall of Icarus*, of which two versions exist, one in the Musées Royaux des Beaux-Arts, Brussels, the other in the van Buuren collection (pages 36 and 37). Opinions differ

THE FLIGHT INTO EGYPT
Oil on panel; 35.2 x 55.5 cm (14⅝ x 27⅞ in)
Signed and dated: 'BRVEGEL MDLXIII'
London, Courtauld Institute
(formerly in the Collection of Count A. Seilern)
The only work by Bruegel known for certain to have belonged to Cardinal Granvella's collection at Besançon (listed in the inventory of 1607). The subject is fairly common in early landscape painting and was first treated by Bruegel in a copper engraving (Bastelaer 15) and in a drawing now in Berlin (Münz 25). This pleasant spacious panorama is a skilful fusion of elements drawn from the rich patrimony of drawings on this subject. The red of Mary's robe is the only clear hint at the religious theme.

about the authenticity of these two works, the most extreme standpoints being those of Glück and Jedlicka. Glück thinks both paintings are originals, giving preference to the one in the van Buuren collection; Jedlicka, on the other hand, considers both to be copies after a lost early work of Bruegel's, but he also prefers the van Buuren version which he finds closer to the putative original. Unfortunately it looks as though Jedlicka is right. However, any assessment of the Brussels version is made very difficult by its poor state of preservation, due to its having been transformed from wood to canvas (probably in the 19th century). Certainly there is no trace of Daedalus, who features in the van Buuren version. Apart from other defects, Jedlicka suspects that the sun's disc was added by a copyist who failed to grasp the significance of the golden halo of light shed by the unseen sun above, as in the van Buuren version. After all, the wings would only have melted if the sun had been somewhere near its zenith. The assertion once put forward that the low position of the sun shows how long it must have taken Icarus to fall seems to me absurd.

Whether or not, as in fact appears very probable, these really are two copies cannot be decided here. But there can be no doubt about the splendid originality of Bruegel's picture, the only mythological subject he ever painted. He stuck very closely to the relevant passage in Ovid's *Metamorphoses* (VIII, 217–222): '… some fisher, perhaps, plying his quivering rod, some shepherd leaning on his staff, or a peasant bent over his plough handle caught sight of them as they flew past and stood stock still in astonishment, believing that these creatures who could fly through the air must be gods …'. Bruegel modified the passage by making only the shepherd look up, while the fisherman and the peasant at his plough pay no attention or perhaps don't even notice Daedalus and his son's misfortune. The ship, too, sails calmly on. One is reminded of the proverb which says that a plough doesn't stop for a dying man, which presumably applies all the more forcefully when someone falls to his death out of pride, excess of stupidity. 'Moderation in all things' might be coupled here with 'Pride comes before a fall'. Marijnissen adds a further interpretation: the peasant is the realist who doesn't recognize the enthusiastic visionary (Icarus). One inconspicuous but macabre detail has not yet been explained, namely the presence of an old man lying dead beneath the trees on the left. Tolnay sees this as a symbol of natural death, as opposed to the unnatural death of Icarus.

Clearly the most striking feature is that no one pays any attention to the very subject of the picture. This is one of Bruegel's most brilliantly original ideas. Icarus is not noticed when he falls into the sea, nor is Christ when he falls beneath the weight of the cross, nor Saul when he is thrown from his horse. Everywhere the main event is reduced and hidden, wrapped up within a much larger scene with a quite incompatible atmosphere. The central feature of the *Fall of Icarus* is the peasant ploughing: our attention is drawn to him immediately by his scarlet shirt, if by nothing else. What could better express the unbridgeable gulf between a Flemish peasant and the poetry of the imperial Roman court than his quiet concentration as he ploughs steadily behind the brown croup of his docile horse? The picture radiates that blissful feeling of having the safe soil of home beneath one's feet, the reassuring, idyllic effect produced in us today at the sight of a farm-hand ploughing with horses. A sweet sense of security is induced by the contrast between the freshly-turned earth and the uncertain element of the water, in which Icarus is sinking. Even the sailing ship, potentially another symbol of insecurity, heads in leisurely fashion for the harbour, as will the horse for the stable. The painting's poetic effect on 20th-century man is expressed in two poems by W. H. Auden and Gottfried Benn. Its profound, enigmatic charm is probably one of the reasons for a number of writers having given it a later date: Friedländer, for example ('… the *Fall of Icarus* … may well be the last word to reach us from the master'), and Vanbeselaere. The composition exerted a very strong influence and was adopted and modified by followers of Bruegel including Hans Bol and Joos de Momper.

While the only question-mark hanging over the *Fall of Icarus* concerns the identify of the actual painter – there being no doubt that Bruegel was the originator – nothing is known for certain in either respect about the *Temptation of St. Anthony* in Washington (page 39). The apparently peaceful, lush green forest landscape with the shelter of the holy recluse under a hollow tree opens out on the left into a broad view of a distant river and town. But both forest and sky are full of all sorts of weird, ghostly forms. Despite its obvious qualities, scholars are not unanimous in ascribing the picture to Bruegel. Friedländer, Glück, Delevoy and Puyvelde regard it as an authentic, early work of about 1557 and the catalogue of the 1969 Bruegel exhibition in Brussels tends to endorse this view, while duly recording the doubts expressed in 1935 by Tolnay who thought it was an early work by Jan Brueghel the Elder. Jedlicka seconded Tolnay's theory in 1938, but

THE TOWER OF BABEL
Oil on panel; 114 x 115 cm (44⅞ x 61 in)
Signed and dated: 'BRVEGEL FE. M.CCCCC. LXIII'
Vienna, Kunsthistorisches Museum
This version of the Biblical subject was probably in the hand of Niclaes Jonghelinck at Antwerp in 1566. Van Mander mentions the work as belonging to the Emperor Rudolph II. The tower's monumental architecture was inspired by Roman ruins, and in particular the Colosseum, which Bruegel will have known either through engravings or by having seen it during his journey in Italy. The work in progress on the tower and all the machinery are represented with extreme precision and realism. In the foreground is King Nimrod, who had the tower built and is traditionally seen as an example of punished pride.
Detail on *pages 86–87*

Grossmann does not mention the work at all. It certainly does give an impression of
artificial compilation: the hollow tree, realistically depicted forest, castle or church,
unrealistic '*arco naturale*' (an artificial rock motif already out of date in Bruegel's time),
and on top of all that the spectral beings which, like the conical figure on the left, seem
rooted in the landscape. All this makes the composition look rather overladen, and with
borrowed material at that. If the picture were by Bruegel it would be the only one which
uses Bosch-style spectres as staffage. Even more suspicious are the proportions of the
figures relative to the space around them. Those in the foreground are much smaller
than usual with Bruegel; and the line of the horizon runs much lower – below the centre
of the picture – than in any other of Bruegel's works except for the *Tower of Babel* in
Rotterdam (pages 88–89), and in that case there are totally different compositional
reasons for it. The distance foreground and low horizon, in particular, indicate that the
picture was painted around 1600. Compared to the expansive, quiet, unified character

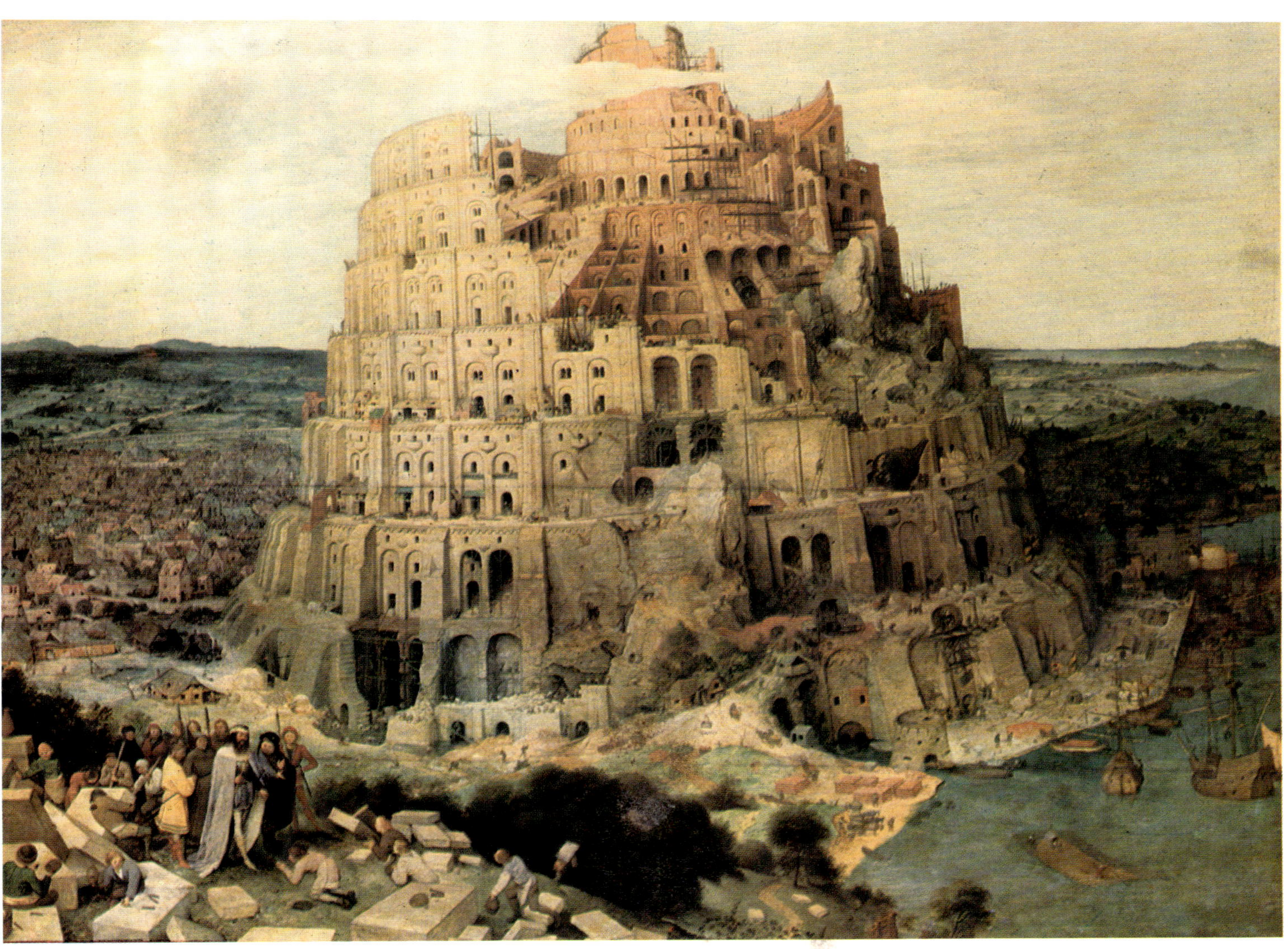

of the *Parable of the Sower* (pages 40–41) of 1557 in San Diego, California, the
Temptation seems heterogeneous in its composition, but that may be due to its
thematic content. It is not impossible that a later artist familiar with all the
achievements of the great master – perhaps Bruegel's younger son Jan Brueghel the
Elder – produced a Bruegelesque work using older details like the *arco naturale* and
Bosch-type gremlins.
Apart from *Christ on the Sea of Tiberias*, dating from 1553 (pages 10–11), the *Parable
of the Sower* (pages 40–41) is the earliest dated painting by Bruegel with an in-
contestable signature. It was executed in 1557 while he was working on the 'Large
Landscape' drawings, of which it contains echoes, and it was not until 1965 that the
Timken Art Gallery of San Diego acquired it from a private owner in Antwerp. The
painstakingly elaborate structure of the 'Large Landscapes' is here translated effortlessly
and naturally into paint. While following the pattern of the 'panoramic landscape',

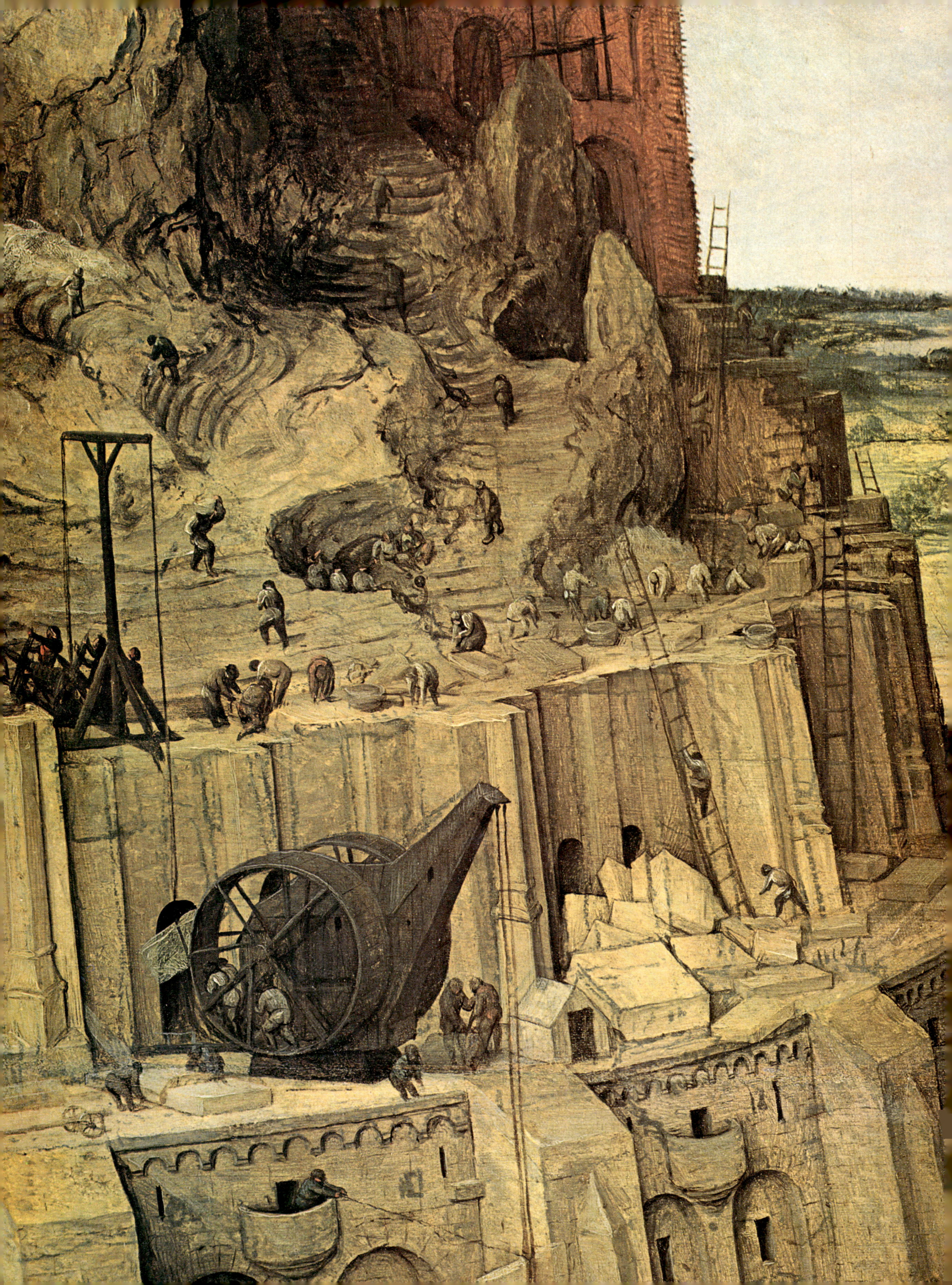

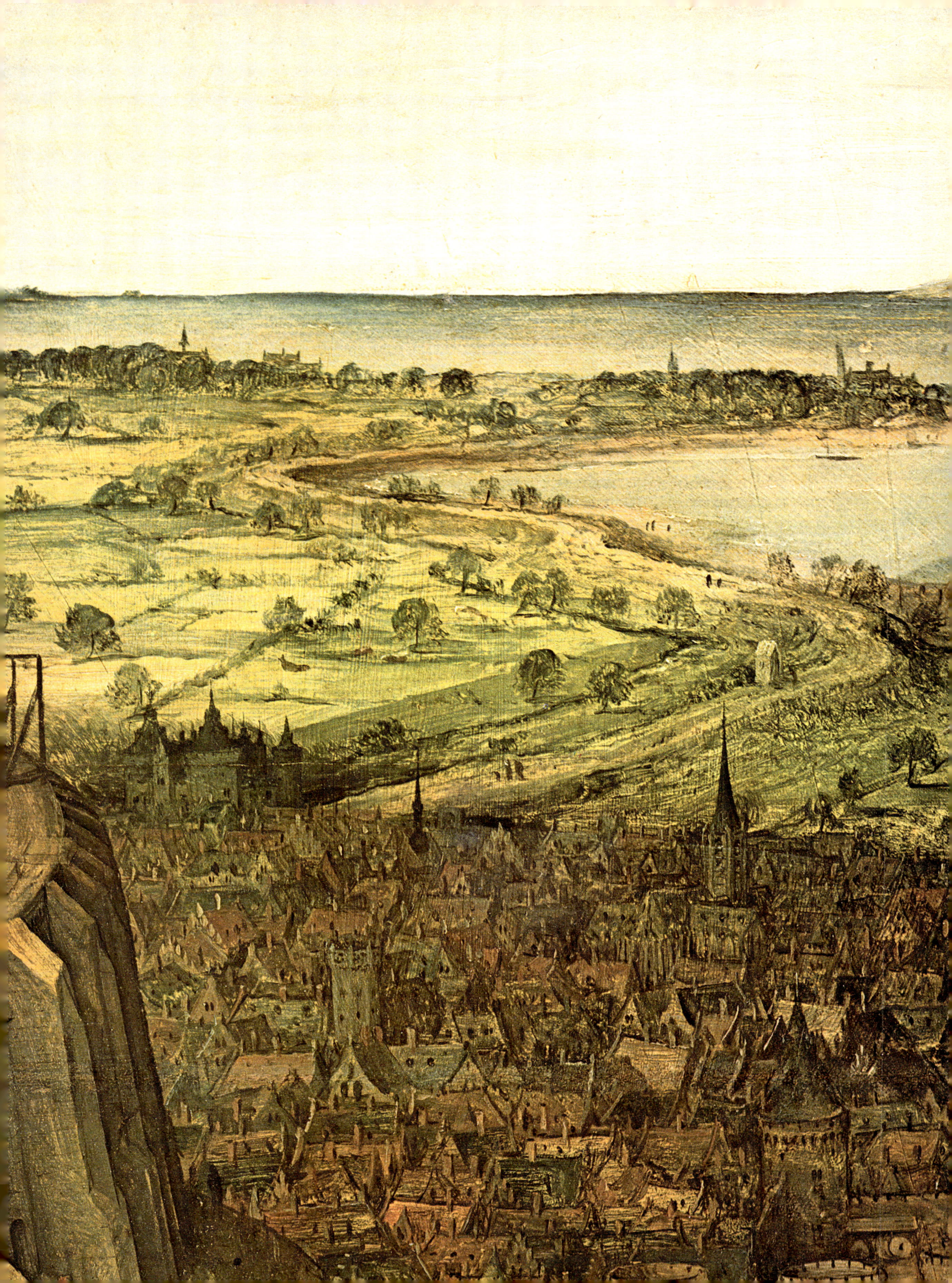

THE TOWER OF BABEL
Oil on panel; 60 x 74.5 cm (23⅝ x 29⅜ in)
Neither signed nor dated
c. 1563
Rotterdam,   Museum   Boymans-van
Beuningen
According to van Mander (1604) the painting
belonged, like the Vienna version, to the
Emperor Rudolph II, and was kept in his
collection at Prague. The Museum acquired it
in 1958. Here, the tower is seen at closer
quarters than in the painting in Vienna and
has a particularly sombre appearance due to
its dark closed facade and the clouds hanging
around it; the scene with Nimrod is absent.
Menzel has detected a number of strange in-
accuracies in the building which he interprets
as reflecting the legendary confusions of
tongues. Opinions differ widely about the
dating of the Rotterdam version, but 1563 is
certainly the most probable year.

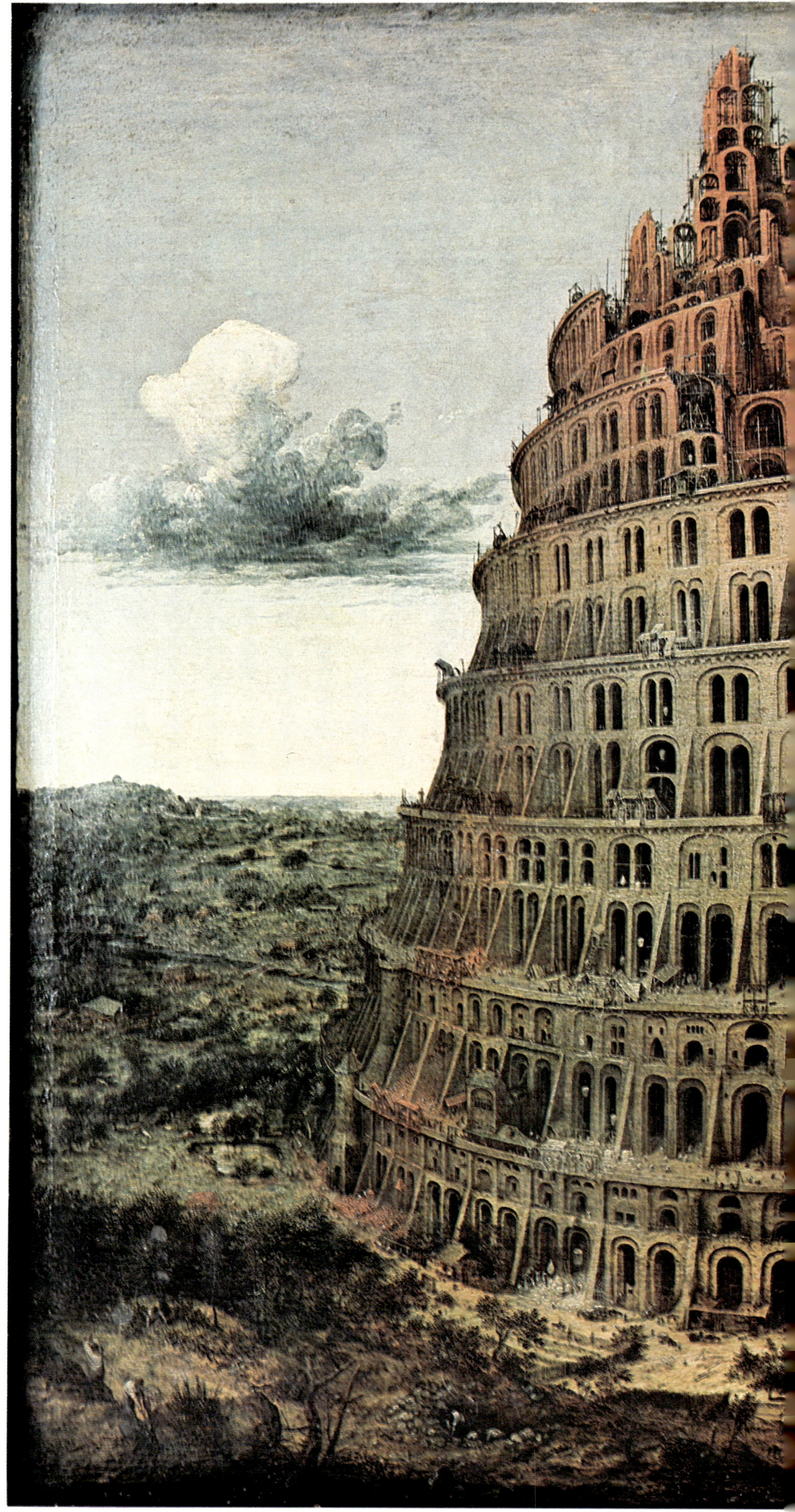

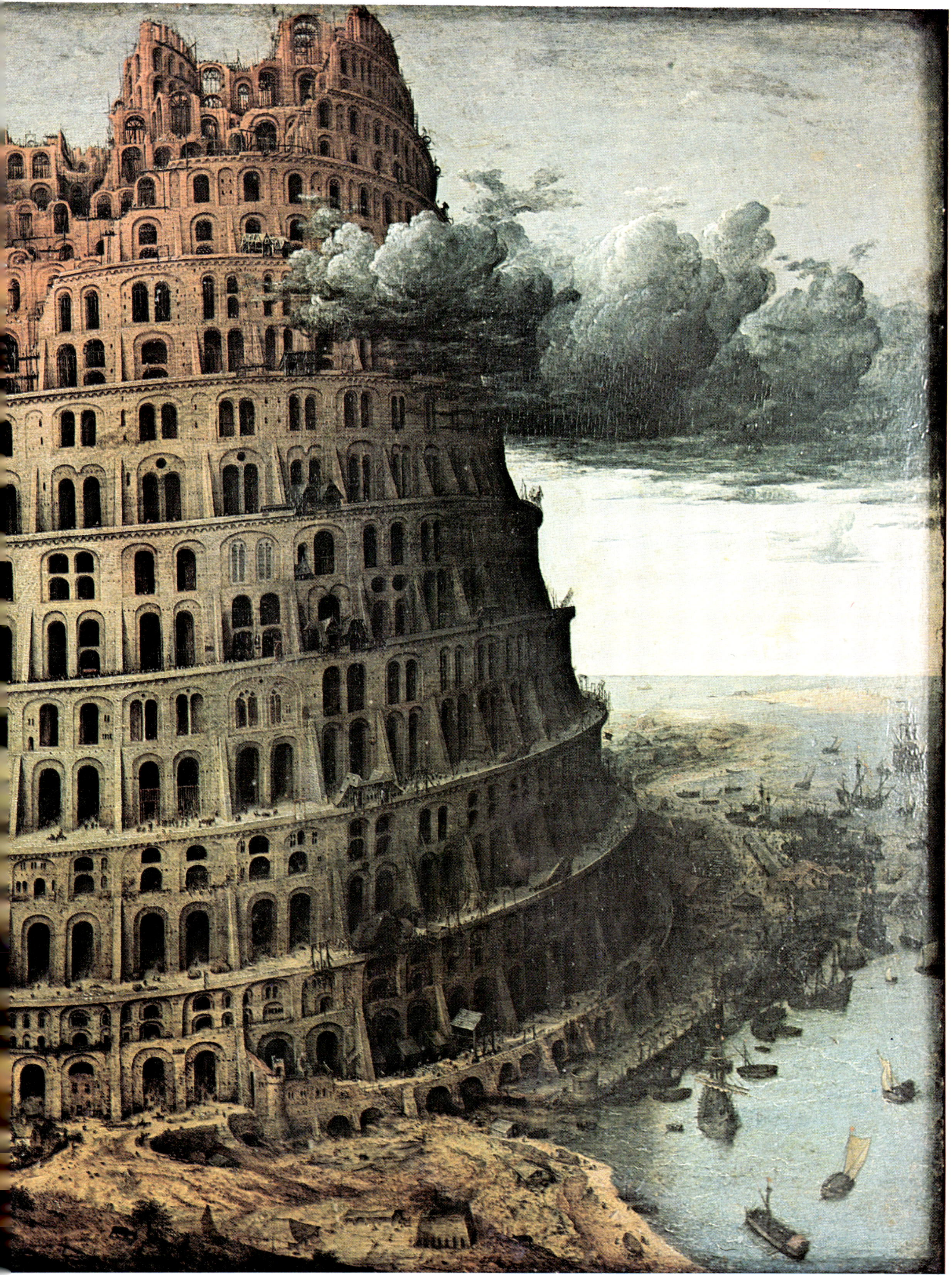

where the gaze is lost in the fathomless depths of the horizon, Bruegel already treats the different components in this early work with a greater sense of cohesion, making the overall impression more natural than at any time before. The sower fits into the landscape as easily as do the trees, meadows, farmhouses, church, cliffs, castles, distant mountains and ships. His presence and his labours do not need to be explained by reference to Matthew 13: 3–8, which relates Christ's parable of the sower. Nor are we obliged to decide whether the little crowd on the riverbank alludes to a sermon of Christ's or some other gathering. As so often, we are confronted with an unmistakable ambivalence in figures or episodes, which can be seen either in purely genre terms or with some special significance attached to them. In either case the central theme of this particular painting is nature: not a faithful representation of some specific landscape but an ideal summation of several possible landscapes.

The only surviving exception to this rule is the *View of the Bay of Naples* in the Galleria

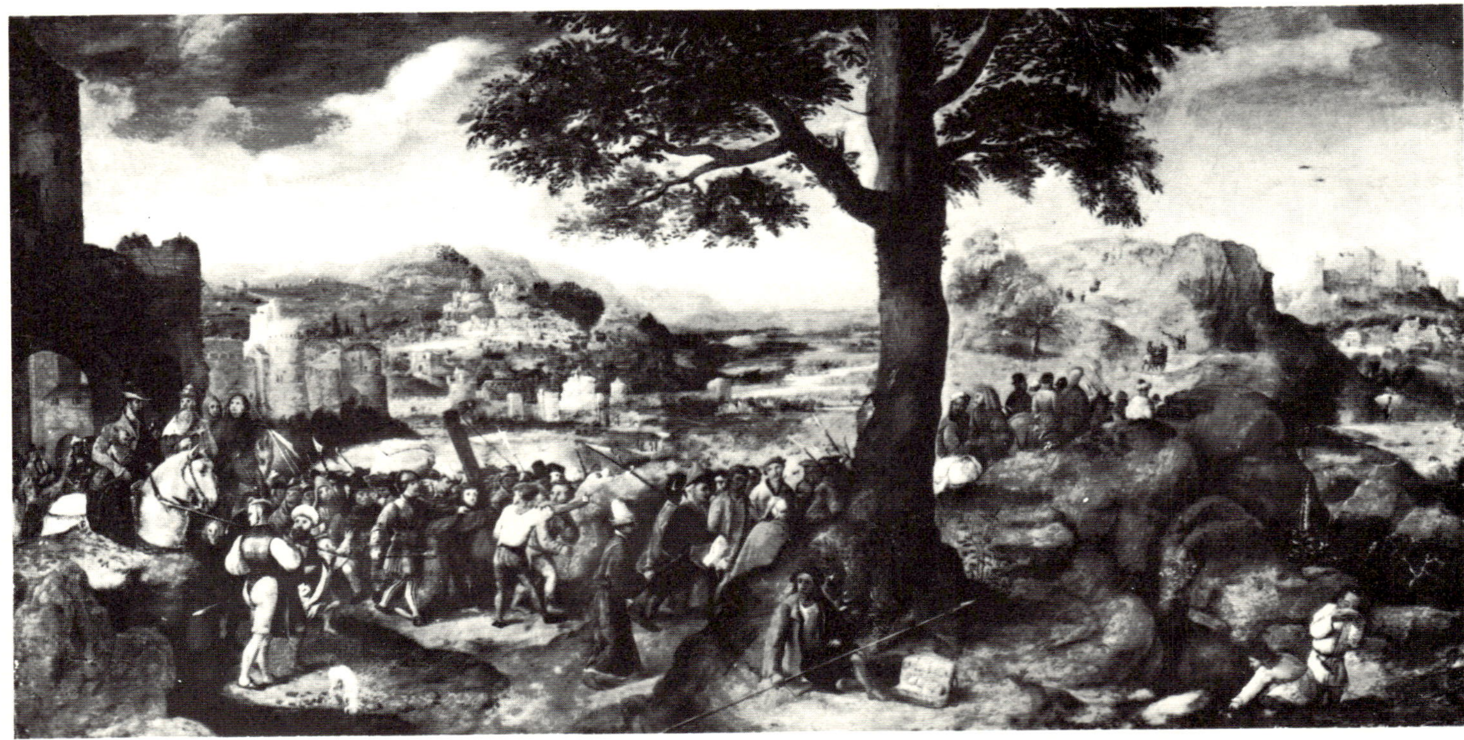

Doria Pamphili in Rome (page 26) in which Bruegel recorded a view of a city visited on his Italian journey between 1551 and 1553. Certain buildings can be identified beyond any doubt: from left to right, the Castel dell' Ovo, the Torre San Vincenzo (since demolished), the Castel Nuovo and, perched on a hill, the Castel Sant' Elmo. On the other hand a number of topographical details have been severely altered, particularly the harbour breakwater which was in fact square but which for artistic reasons has been shown round. Other views of specific places have been lost: the view of Lyons (mentioned in G. Clovio's will) and that of the St. Gotthard (in the Rubens inventory). Naples is seen from an elevated viewpoint out at sea, and Vesuvius can be made out on the far right. Ships are sailing in front of the entrance to the harbour, with smaller galleys – some manned by oarsmen, some under sail – moving amongst them. We cannot say for certain whether this represents a naval battle or just a fleet returning home with a salute being fired. According to F. Smekens, writing in the 1961 yearbook of the Royal Museum of Fine Arts in Antwerp, the subject is the defence of Naples against a Turkish attack in the war between Charles V and the Turks. The picture was painted from memory, but undoubtedly on the basis of travel sketches. The same method is found in the *Naval Battle in the Straits of Messina* engraved by Frans Huys after Bruegel in 1561, for which a sketch of Reggio still survives and which is almost identical in structure. The engraving shows a bird's-eye view of a fleet of vessels, with Etna on the right in the same position. Bruegel's love of ships is particularly evident here: attention has been drawn to the warship on the left, which appears again, laterally inverted but almost identical, in the series of engravings of ships dating from 1560–1565. Huizinga speaks of the unbelievably splendid decoration of Burgundian ships in the 14th and 15th centuries, striving to outdo all others in their finery. The chronicler Froissart, enchanted with their beauty, claims that many had their masts gilded entirely with gold leaf, and, in fact, leading artists were called in to do this kind of work. In 1387, for example, Melchior Broederlam was engaged in decorating Philip the Bold's personal vessel at Sluis, which was completely covered in blue and gold. 'The pennants, richly adorned with coats of arms, which fluttered from the mast-tops were sometimes so long they touched the water. Pieter Bruegel's depictions of ships still show these unusually long, wide pennants.' Increasing wear and tear from ever more frequent battles, however, must gradually have reduced the extent to which ships were decorated.

The *View of the Bay of Naples* is neither signed nor dated, but an early date of around 1555–1558 has been assumed in view of the subject itself and a certain undeniable awkwardness of execution. Grossmann, on the other hand, agrees with Winkler in plumping for 1562–1563.

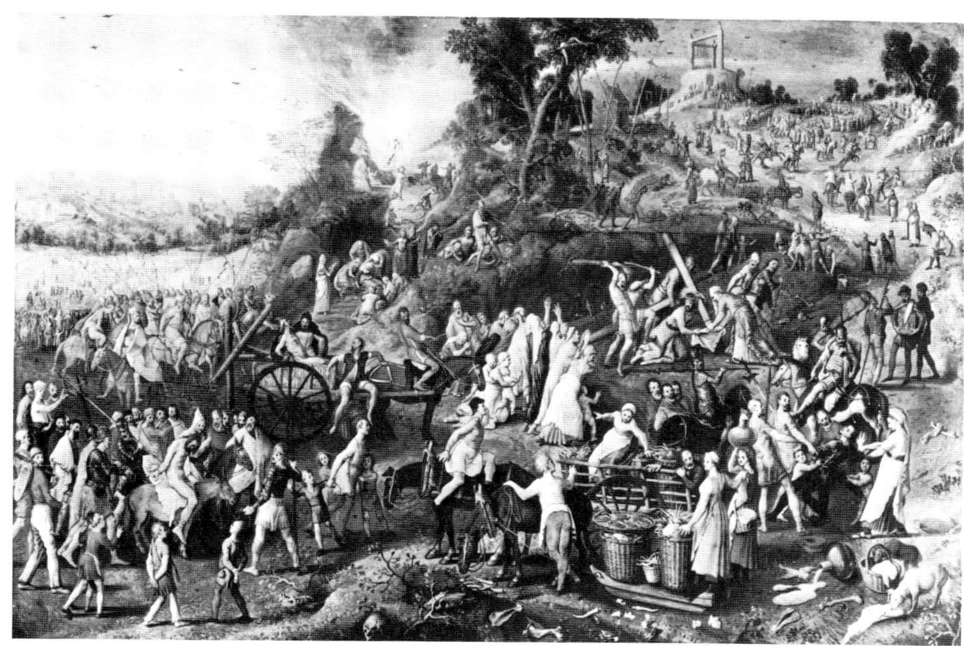

The *Netherlandish Proverbs* in Berlin (page 47) signed and dated 'BRUEGEL 1559' is the first painting which can be considered stylistically characteristic of Bruegel's art.

There is a close formal link with the *Battle Between Carnival and Lent* and *Children's Games*. All three works share a common compositional feature: the distribution of groups of small-scale figures over a large area. They were executed at roughly the same time, the first two in 1559 and the *Children's Games* in 1560. A certain clumsiness in the treatment of space suggests that the *Proverbs* are the first of this group.

Although proverbs had been represented pictorially before his day, Bruegel's conception is unique and without any direct precedent. It is now perhaps difficult to imagine how commonly proverbs were used at that time, but in an age when ordinary people could neither read nor write, proverbs played a living role—now entirely lost to us—in passing on and crystallizing folk humour and wisdom. As Huizinga rightly comments: 'We who habitually read newspapers can scarcely imagine the enormous impression made by the spoken word on an ingenuous and ignorant mind'. The year 1500 saw the publication of Erasmus of Rotterdam's *Adagium Collectanea*, a collection of 800 proverbs, and of the *Proverbia Communia* in Delft, followed in 1550 by the *Gemeene: Duytsche Spreekworden* in Campen. Erasmus in fact took most of his examples from classical authors. In 1541 Sebastian Franck published his *Proverbs, Clever Witticisms, Etc.*. Proverbs were well suited to the contemporary love of symbolism and pictorial puzzles. The immediate stimulus for Bruegel's work must have been Frans Hogenberg's engraving, published in 1558, depicting some twenty proverbs in clumsy juxtaposition with explanatory texts. Its title is taken from the central feature of the engraving, only half of which survives, the *'blauwe Huyck'* or blue cloak, which also occupies an important position in Bruegel's painting. The saying 'She's putting the blue cloak around him' refers to an unfaithful wife. All in all the picture contains over a hundred proverbs, of which the most comprehensive and convincing interpretations have come from Wilhelm Fraenger in 1923, Jan Grauls in 1938 and Gustav Glück (with Jan Borms) in 1951. G. Marlier counts sixteen copies of this painting, some with additional proverbs at top right in the background. In Marlier's book on Pieter Brueghel the Younger, published in 1969, Jacqueline Folie identifies a total of 132 proverbs, but we will here pick out simply the main ones, beginning at bottom left. Tying the devil to a cushion (cf. the Legend of St. Margaret, who overcame the devil, and also *Dulle Griet*, (page 69); the pillar-biter, a frequent but hypocritical church-goer; a woman carrying fire in one hand and water in the other; butting one's head against a brick wall; someone armed to the teeth tries to bell the cat; one man shears a sheep, another a piglet; one spins while the other weaves, in other words, they're gossiping; bringing light to the day in baskets. The picture's focal point is the blue cloak: blue being the colour of faithfulness in the colour symbolism of medieval courtly love, the lover testifying to his faithfulness by means of a blue garment. Huizinga notes that 'This is probably also the reason why the colour blue used hypocritically could mean un-faithfulness as well, and by a further leap of the imagination was attributed not only to the unfaithful party but also to the person deceived'. Later, blue acquired connotations of death and destruction, as in the notion of the *blauwe schuyt* (blue ship or ship of doom) which appears on an inn sign on the left in the *Battle Between Carnival and Lent* (pages 50–51). The idea of deception links up with the picture's central thematic feature, the man going to make his confession to the Devil (who sits in a blue porch-like structure) and lighting a candle to him. The scene in the crazy village symbolizes a topsy-turvy world in which the whole course of events has gone wrong: the blue (!) globe with its cross at the bottom speaks for the whole picture. Other scenes in the foreground include a man filling in a well after his calf has been drowned, casting roses before swine, 'bending to get on in the world', the nobleman making the world dance on his thumb, and 'he who spills his pudding cannot spoon it all up again'. Attaching a flaxen beard to the face of Christ refers to the godlessness of monks. A man on top of a tower hangs his coat out to see which way the wind is blowing, indicating that he is an op-portunist, while another casts feathers to the wind, symbolizing prodigality. On the horizon above right we can make out the blind leading the blind, an early reference to a subject dealt with in greater detail later on (page 161). A singular note is struck by the pancakes on the roof, which also appear in the *Land of Cockaigne* (page 147) and in-dicate a household of unusual luxury. To treat them, as Stridbeck does, as an allusion to Gula is as unnecessary as his other comparisons with the deadly sins.

As far as I am aware, no-one apart from Sedlmayr has drawn attention to the fact that the pancakes on the roof are shown in the wrong perspective, or construed them as a key to Bruegel's aesthetic method. All the pancakes are depicted as round, taking no ac-count of their positions on the roof. With a painter like Bruegel this sort of inaccuracy cannot be put down to ineptitude and must therefore have some secret purpose. Sedlmayr believes Bruegel was consciously asking us to look at the picture in a particular way, for which the Italian art historian Benedetto Croce (following in the footsteps of V. Imbriani) evolved the theory of the '*macchia*' or 'blob-of-paint' technique in the late 19th century. Sedlmayr maintains that 'In my view this strange detail only makes sense if we accept that Bruegel was inviting us to break the picture up and look at it in separate patches. This is no more than an exaggerated expression of what is happening less obtrusively in the rest of the picture'. The idea is fascinating, and we can certainly apply the most complete interpretation to the works of a painter of Bruegel's calibre. Perhaps Bruegel's intention in giving the bizarre front view of the pancakes, thereby making them stand out much more strikingly, was to underline the disparity between them and the tiles out of which they seem to be growing? Or are they his way of saying farewell, with one last pictorial quotation, to the outdated perspective of the Middle Ages? Dealing with the meaning of the picture as a whole, however, it seems that here, as with others of Bruegel's satires, the moral message has been overestimated. Bruegel is no preacher intent on improving the world, still less is he acquainted with *Weltschmerz*. We may come closer to divining Bruegel's intention if we apply Huizinga's apt com-ments on Netherlandish proverbs to the whole mood of this particular picture: 'The proverb played a decidedly living role in medieval thought. Hundreds were in everyday use, almost all of them pithy and apposite. The wisdom contained in a proverb is sometimes sober, sometimes gratifying and profound; the proverb's tone is often ironical, its flavour as a rule kindly and always resigned. The proverb preaches only surrender, never resistance. With a smile or a sigh it lets the selfish triumph, the hypocrites go on their way: big fish eat the little fish. The compassionate understanding of human nature implicit in this folk wisdom contrasts with the lamentations of the moralists bemoaning the sinfulness and corruption of man. A nation which makes plentiful use of proverbs leaves disputation to theologians and philosophers, preferring to settle its differences of opinion with some maxim which never fails to hit the nail on the head. It dispenses with empty chatter and abstruse reasoning: the apt proverb says all.' This does not mean that Bruegel was illiterate. He remains the cultivated humanist of the *Seven Virtues*, whose dry erudition he seasoned with his own brand of irony. How he must have welcomed the commissions for the proverb and carnival paintings which allowed him to get away from theology into the rough-and-tumble of everyday Flemish life.

The main attraction of the picture for us, however, surely lies not in the pleasure of recognizing the proverbs, as it would have for Bruegel's contemporaries, but rather in the overall impression of absurdity. Bruegel achieves this effect by translating the proverb's linguistic metaphor with seeming naïvety into a direct visual equivalent: the notion of the pillar-biter (hypocrite) is taken literally and we are shown a man actually biting into a stone pillar; one man shears a lamb while the other actually shears a piglet, and so on. This expedient alone enables Bruegel to create a dimension of absurdity, but he enhances the effect still further by locating the proverbial scenes in an imaginary but semi-realistic village landscape just as though everyone were going about his normal daily business. Yet all the various activities portrayed are utterly senseless. The resulting impression is of some kind of open-air lunatic asylum, a brilliantly innovative technique which Bruegel develops further in the *Children's Games*. The concept of the 'absurd' as propounded in Surrealism is, of course, an invention of the 20th century. But Bruegel makes ample use of another approach deriving from the idea of man's foolishness in a topsy-turvy world, an idea with which he would have been familiar from Erasmus' *Praise of Folly*. Penetrating the moral element, though, we come to the nucleus of Bruegel's art, to its new and most powerful weapon: humour.

A direct link exists between the *Netherlandish Proverbs* in Berlin and the *Twelve Proverbs* in the Museum Mayer van der Bergh in Antwerp (pages 44–45). This was put together in the 17th century, perhaps earlier, using individual medallions accompanied by the texts of proverbs. The script has been dated 1560–1580. In all probability these are preparatory studies by Bruegel for the full-size painting of 1559. The year '...8' next to the signature 'BRVEGHEL' on the twelfth proverb would have been 1558. The work's authenticity has been questioned by, amongst others, Tolnay and Glück, who regard it as a set of copies by Pieter Brueghel the Younger: Grossman, too, declines to attribute it to Bruegel. However, more recent laboratory tests conducted with a view to confirming the work's authenticity have shown that the tondi were never overpainted, as Jedlicka assumed. The medallions may in fact be identical with the '*Twelf afbeeldingen op teljooren gedaen by den Ouden Bruegel*' mentioned in the inventory of the estate of Nicclaes C. Cheeus drawn up in Antwerp in 1621. But I can see no reason to date the medallions *after*, instead of before, the painting in Berlin, as Friedländer and de Loo have suggested.

Finally, we should remember an important literary parallel often quoted in this connection: the twenty-second chapter of the fifth book of *Gargantua and Pantagruel* by François Rabelais (1494(?)–1553), in which Rabelais constructs a sequence of utterly nonsensical and paradoxical, not to say impossible, activities in which the queen's treasurers in the 'Kingdom of Quintessence' spend their time. No direct link exists between the two, however, as the fifth book of *Gargantua and Pantagruel* was not published until 1564, five years after Bruegel had produced his painting.

The subject of *The Battle Between Carnival and Lent* (pages 50–51) is an old one and can be found in Burgundy as early as the 13th century. In fact it was one of the favourite literary motifs of the Middle Ages in Italy, France and Spain. Amongst some Netherlandish paintings belonging to the Florentine collections of the Medici in the 15th century is one showing an allegorical representation of Lent being mocked by revellers, as Jedlicka has noted. Hieronymus Bosch also depicted this popular theme in a painting which now only survives in copies, one in the Rijksmuseum in Amsterdam and another, a grisaille, in the Galerie Cramer in the Hague. Both Bruegel and his client would have been directly inspired by the engraving by Frans Hogenberg, bearing the same title, which Hieronymus Cock had published in 1558 (page 50). This work is very much closer to Bruegel's than to Bosch's rather feeble composition. Its caption reads: 'Scrawny Lent Doing Battle with Portly Carnival And All His Guests'. Bruegel's treatment of the subject must have exceeded all his client's expectations: Hogenberg's engraving is utterly overshadowed by the wealth of fascinating detail. With masterly ease Bruegel has outdone all previous attempts at the subject, effortlessly controlling his medium within the large format (approximately 118 x 164 cm or $46\frac{1}{2}$ x $64\frac{1}{2}$ in) well known to him from the '*dobbel-doec*' compositions.

The picture shows a scene rather reminiscent of a tournament – and carnival processions in those days really were like that – with the allegorical figures of Carnival (male) and

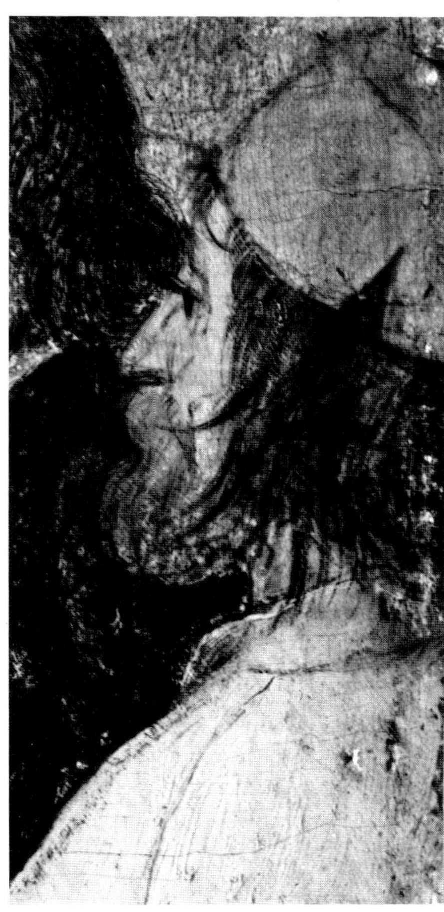

CHRIST CARRYING THE CROSS
Detail of the painting shown on the following pages.
It is thought that this figure (on the right in the picture), almost lost among the roughly two hundred others in this grandiose scene, is a small self-portrait of the master.

Lent (female) confronting each other. At an aristocratic marriage in front of the royal palace in Valencia in 1591, Lope de Vega appeared in the guise of Carnival, wearing a red doublet and crowned with sausages. But this painting is more than just a genre work: the detail is almost encyclopaedic, covering every possible figure and activity associated with the two protagonists. In its endeavour to include the maximum number of different aspects it resembles the *Proverbs* and *Children's Games*. This work, too, has been the subject of innumerable articles, several of which are referred to in the bibliography.

The exceedingly corpulent figure of Carnival, riding on a barrel, is being pushed from the left, while a monk and a nun pull a scraggy representation of Lent on a trolley. The whole picture is filled with the followers of one side or the other. Carnival holds a spit for a lance and has a pie on his head, the stirrups are pans and a leg of ham is stuck on one end of the barrel with a knife. Lent, by way of contrast, enters the fray with two fishes on a long bread-shovel, and on her trolley lie various attributes of Lent – loaves of bread, bretzels, a rush basket with figs and a bowl of mussels. Carnival's immediate retinue consists of three figures, two of them masked, playing improvised instruments: gridiron, cups and pot. Egg-shells and bones on the ground hint at immoderate eating, the cards at gambling. By the late Middle Ages these carnival festivals were already tending to lose their original religious content and degenerate into uninhibited orgies of eating and drinking.

The main group is followed by a darkly-attired figure carrying on his head a round table with bread and wafers, a common emblem of carnival-time. This is matched on the Lenten side by the children, an ash cross on their foreheads, bearing wooden Easter rattles, bretzels and Lenten bread. The contrast between the two main groups is developed throughout the two halves of the picture: to the left the inn (the 'Blue Ship'), to the right the church, to the left a carnival farce entitled 'The Unclean Bride', to the right distribution of alms. During carnival-time people's money ends up in the tavern; during Lent, in beggars' bowls and boxes in the church. Bruegel also drew the 'unclean bride' as an individual woodcut (page 141), and *Orson and Valentine*, which is being enacted in the background, in front of the 'Withered Bough' tavern, appeared as a woodcut in 1556.

Two men in the left foreground are playing dice for wafers, while on the right a beggarwoman with a sick child receives alms. A sick man lies beneath a beautifully depicted white sheet. He can actually be seen in a copy of the picture which used to exist in Cracow but now only survives in photographs: a naked figure with swollen belly (probably a hunger edema) and horribly distorted face. This harsh detail has been painted over in brown in the painting in Vienna and only the sheet is now visible. The corpse in the cart to the right of the well has also been painted over. The woman baking wafers on the left corresponds to the one selling fish on the Lenten side: the well means that water is now being drunk instead of wine. Almost every detail can be explained by references to local folklore, but there is disagreement with regard to the significance of the beggars and cripples on the carnival side and the children playing with whipping tops in front of the church. The cripples could be meant to show how the merrymakers remain oblivious to more unfortunate members of society, but might also refer to the customary processions of lepers. Tops are symbols of men's morality and faith, which flag if not kept up to the mark by constant practice and chastisement.

Bruegel treated the subject of cripples separately in the picture in the Louvre dated 1564 (page 155). Some of the cripples also resemble those in the drawing entitled *Cripples and Beggars* in the Albertina (page 154), which was always thought to be by Hieronymus Bosch but has more recently been attributed, by Grossman, to Bruegel. Further details are the doll representing the Count of Halvfasten (a character in a carnival play) hanging out of a window, and the straw doll, symbolizing winter, being burnt in the far background. The most detailed study of the folklore alluded to in the picture has been undertaken by C. Gaignebet (1972). Among other things he made out a semicircular arrangement of scenes connected with the main feasts from Christmas to Easter. The couple shown from the back with a fool holding a torch walking in front of them provided one of the knottier problems. Isolated as it is in the very centre of the composition, this group must have some significance fundamental to the picture. This raises the problem of how we are to interpret the painting as a whole, which has been seen as depicting the struggle between Lutheranism (Carnival) and the Catholic Church (Lent), a view held in particular by Stridbeck. The beehive on the head of the figure of Lent is interpreted by him as a symbol of the Church, but also of diligence in general. We can assume that Bruegel had no great sympathy for either group, which would be consistent with his anticlerical attitude. The Lutherans abolished Lent but retained the

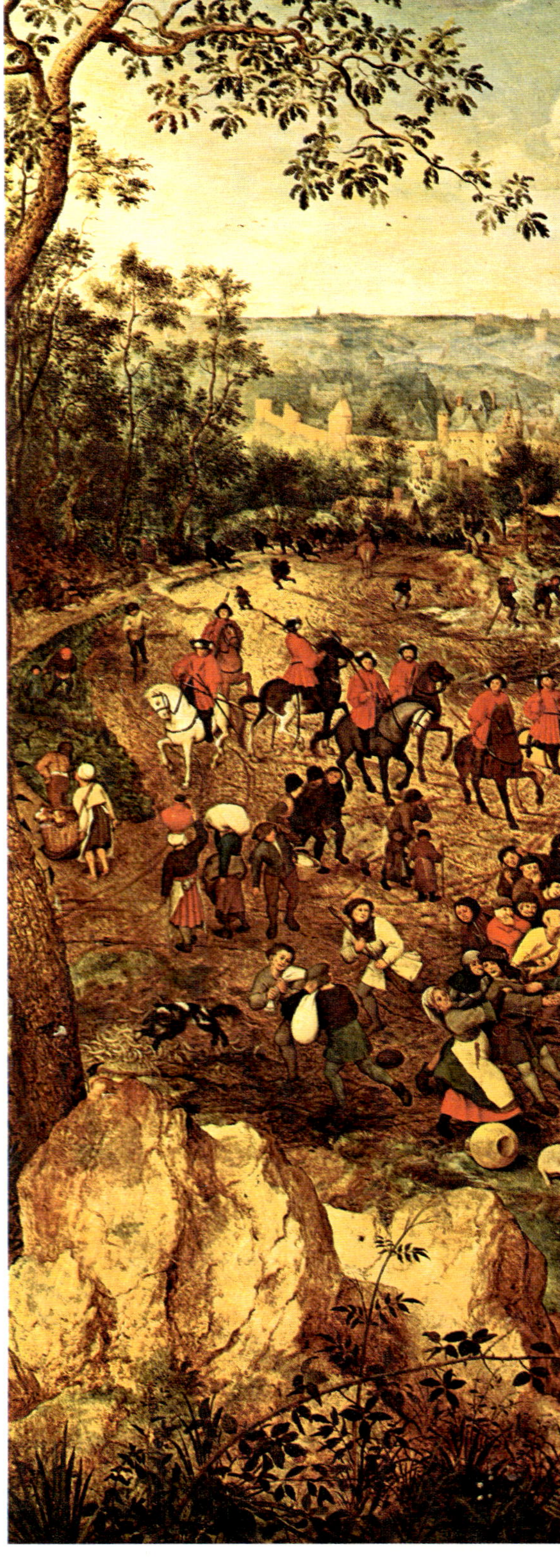

CHRIST CARRYING THE CROSS
Oil on board; 124 x 170 cm ($48\frac{3}{4}$ x $66\frac{7}{8}$ in)
Signed and dated: 'BRVEGEL MD.LXIIII.'
Vienna, Kunsthistorisches Museum
In 1566 this painting belonged to the collection of Niclaes Jonghelinck in Antwerp and is one of two paintings of this subject which van Mander quotes as belonging to the Emperor Rudolph II; it is not certain whether this is the *Christ Carrying the Cross* which appears in the Archduke Ernest's inventory of 1595. It is listed in the inventory of the Geistliche Schatzkammer in Vienna in 1748. The largest of all Bruegel's works, it contains

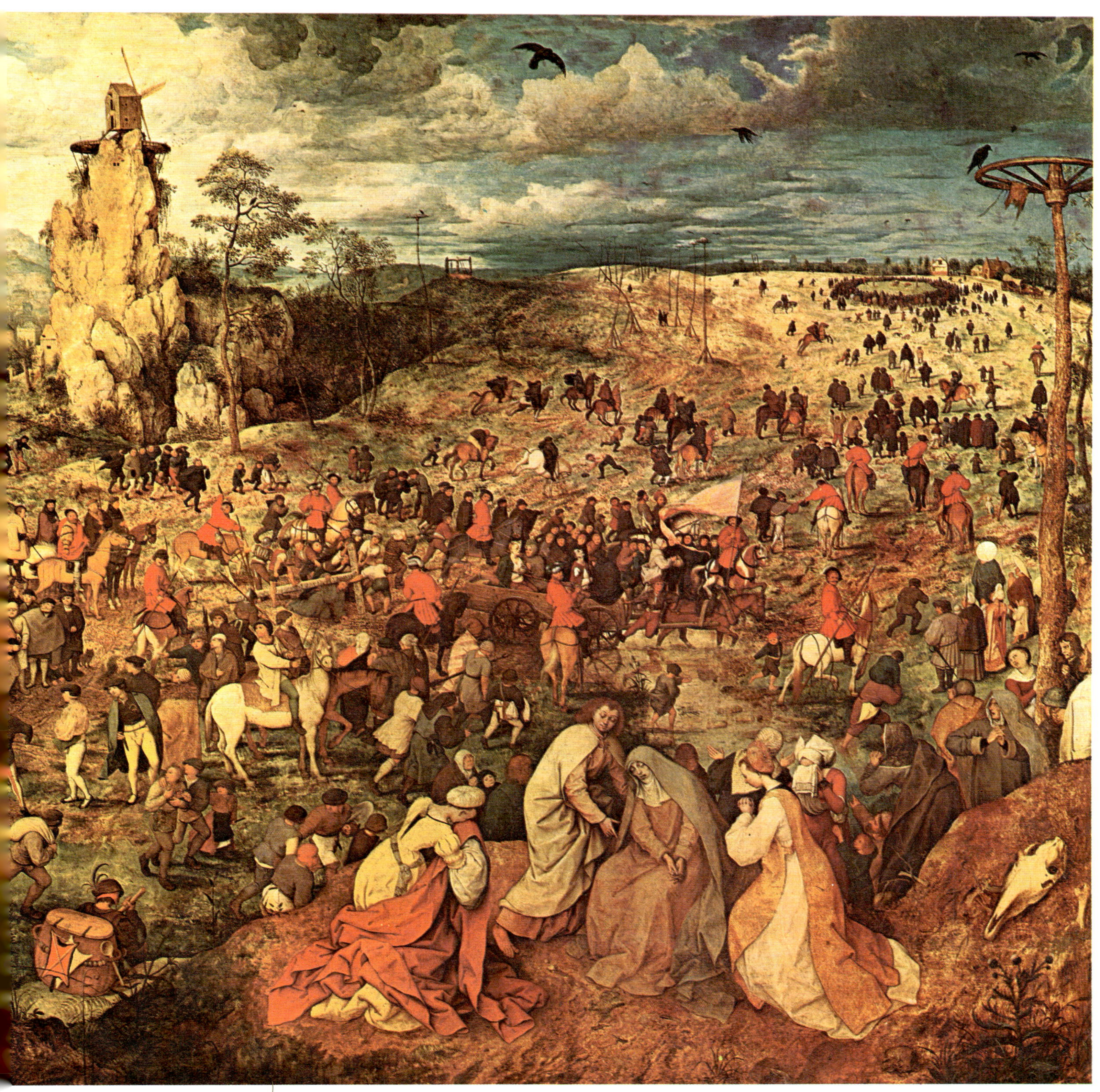

elements of a long Flemish tradition going back to van Eyck. Its direct forerunners are the depictions of the same subject by Jan van Amstel (p. 90) and Pieter Aertsen (p. 91): a comparison with these two works shows clearly how much further Bruegel had progressed. The wealth of detail in the two hundred or so figures reveals the artist's acute sense of observation.

Detail on *pages 96–97*

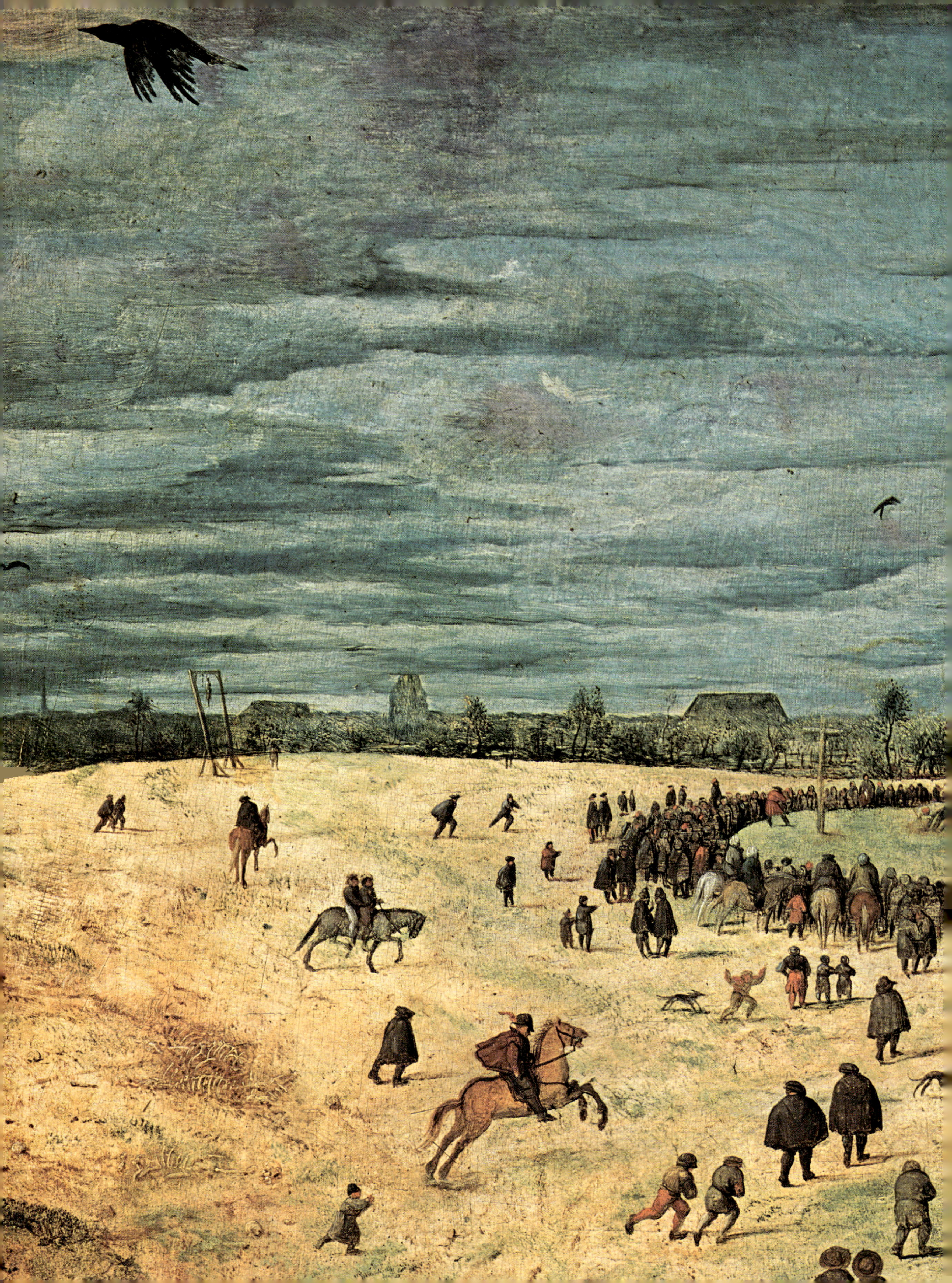

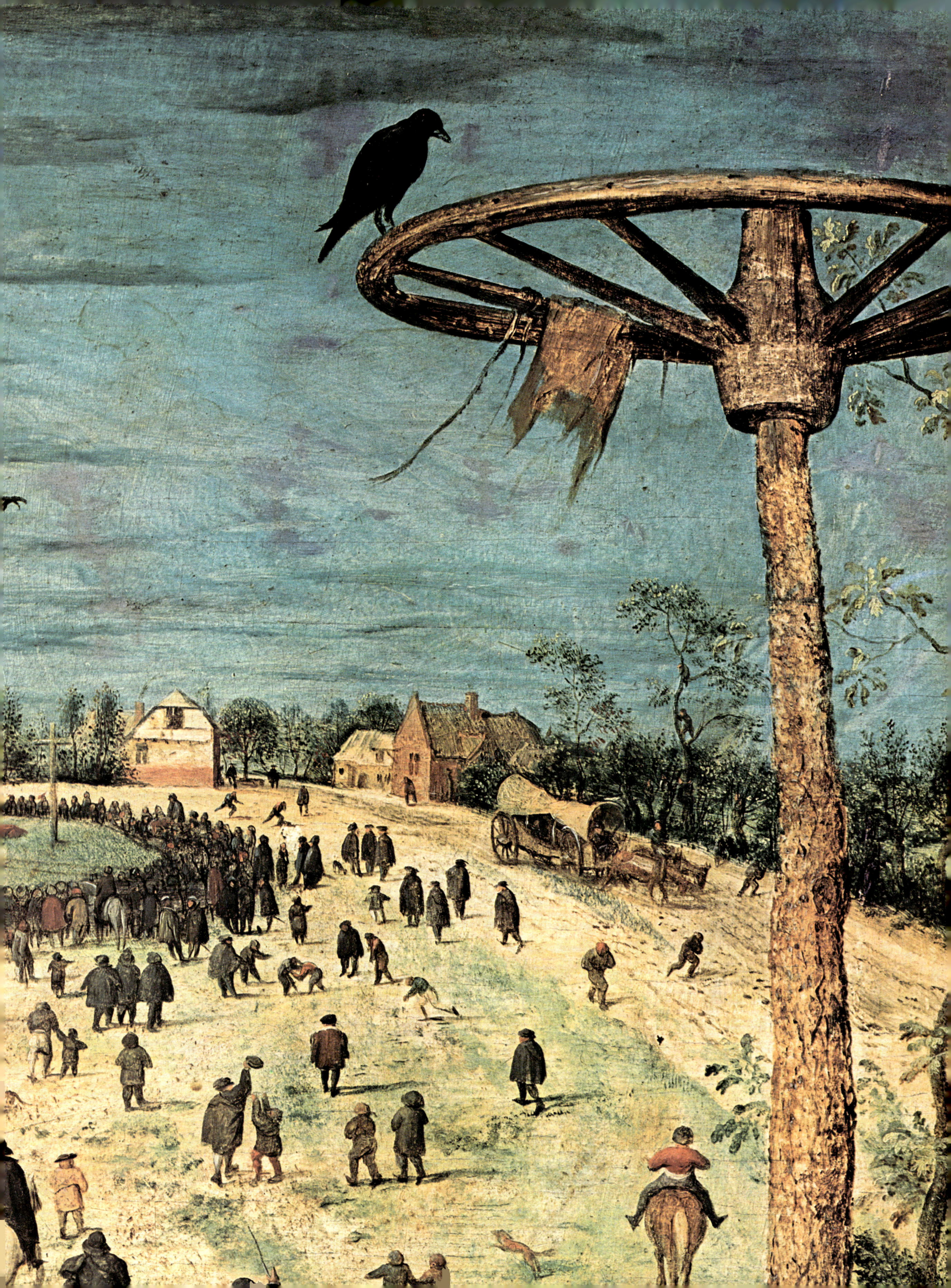

carnival celebrations. In contemporary religious polemics they were portrayed as
drunkards and gluttons. A revealing comment on anticlericalism in Bruegel's time is
quoted by Stridbeck from Coornhert: 'They [the Lutherans] make themselves out to be
true Christians, but they are not and are therefore guilty of terrible hypocrisy. The
Catholic doctrine is certainly deceptive too, but the deception practised by monks is so
obvious that no one is taken in'.

The couple have their backs to us and the woman carries the lantern unlit at her back,
while the fool lights their way home. That could mean that there is no real alternative in
this dispute because *all* are fools. But what then is the significance of the strange bulge
on the man's back? Once again, the explanation may rest on a purely genre interpretation, this being simply a couple going home with a small boy in fancy dress
carrying their torch before them. Jedlicka has observed that the fool's costume combines
all the main colours in the picture: blue, white, red, violet, brown. While the contrast

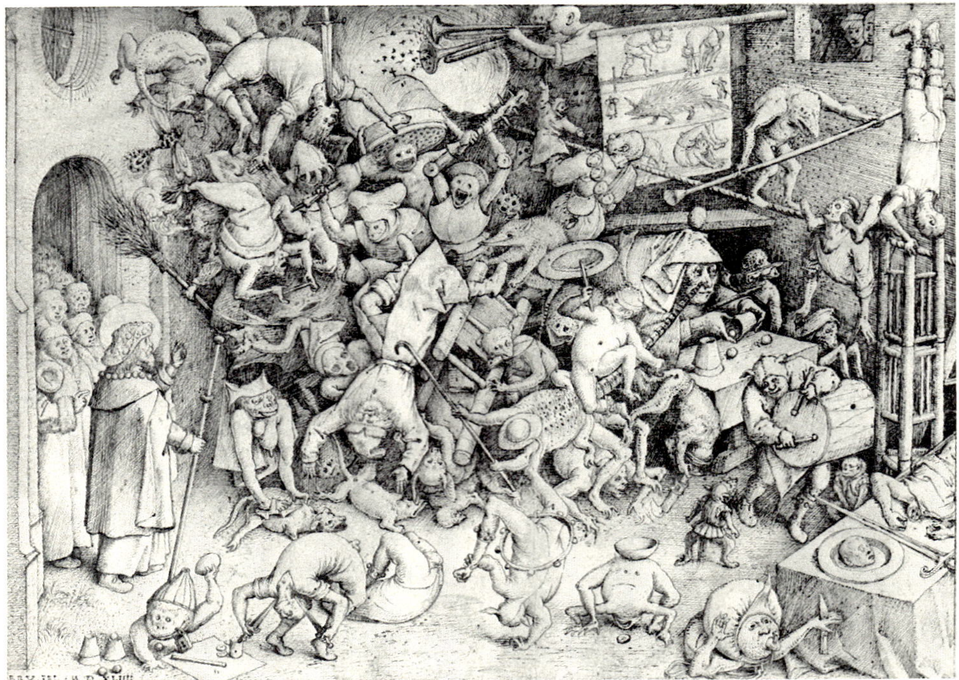

THE FALL OF HERMOGENES
Pen drawing in maroon on paper; 222 x
292 mm (8 x 11½ in)
Signed and dated at bottom left: 'BRVEGEL
MDXLIIII';
(the X and L in the year are transposed by
mistake)
Amsterdam, Rijksmuseum, Rijksprenten-
kabinett
This work, together with its counterpart
entitled *St. James and the Magician Hermogenes*, was published as an engraving by
H. Cock in 1565 (Bastelaer 117 and 118).
The preparatory drawing for the second engraving has been lost. The subject is taken
from the *Golden Legend* of Jacobus de
Voragine and is also used by Bosch. The
numerous details in the scene have been the
subject of a variety of conflicting interpretations.

between Lutheranism and Catholicism may possibly be a secondary feature it certainly is
not crucial. An age-old theme like this – the ever-recurring contrast of fish and meat,
fasting and feasting, acted out a thousand times on the stage, treated in literature and
encountered every year in real life – really needs no further explanation.

Finally, we should draw attention to the painting's brilliant composition. The bird's-eye
view enables the large number of people to be fitted in comfortably, hardly any of the
figures overlapping. At the same time the perspective is not mathematically true, the
rise in the terrain diminishing towards the back to suit Bruegel's requirements. Novotny
calls this expedient 'stretched perspective'. The composition of the groups of figures
runs on the one hand from the two bottom corners, which are crowded with people,
diagonally to the centre of the picture, and on the other in a shallow arc to the two main
figures, whose 'weapons' meet in the very middle. The throng also sweeps in a wide
ellipse around the central point, with a smaller one around the house in the
background. The 'astronomic' forms emphasize the cyclic repetition of the calendar's
various feasts.

The theme of Carnival and Lent is closely related to that favourite pair of opposites, the
fat and the thin kitchen. These suggest the social contrast of rich and poor, and thus
imply a degree of social criticism: we recall Dives and Lazarus, and the deadly sin of
intemperance. Bruegel developed this theme in two characteristically vivid compositions
which only survive in various engravings based on them. Those reproduced here (pages
54 and 55) are by Pieter van der Heyden and were published by Hieronymus Cock in
1563. Not even the rough lines of the engravings are able to destroy the vividness and
expressive intensity Bruegel instilled into his figures. The *Fat Kitchen* shows the table
sagging under the weight of sausages, sucking pigs, turkey, pig's head, pies. Things are
cooking and seething everywhere. The pot-bellied gluttons are full to bursting: they
seem on the point of spilling out of the picture, cramming its space like tightly-filled

THE ADORATION OF THE MAGI
Oil on panel; 111 x 83.5 cm (43¾ x 32¾ in)
Signed and dated: 'BRVEGEL M.D.LXIIII.'
London, National Gallery
This painting is probably the one acquired in
1594 by the Archduke Ernest and mentioned
in an inventory of 1619 of the Imperial
Collection in Vienna. It came to the National
Gallery in 1920 from the G. Roth Collection
in Vienna. It is one of Bruegel's few works of
vertical format. The composition seems to
make use of Italian ideas, even if the
typology of the figures reveals the unquestionable influence of Netherlandish
tradition

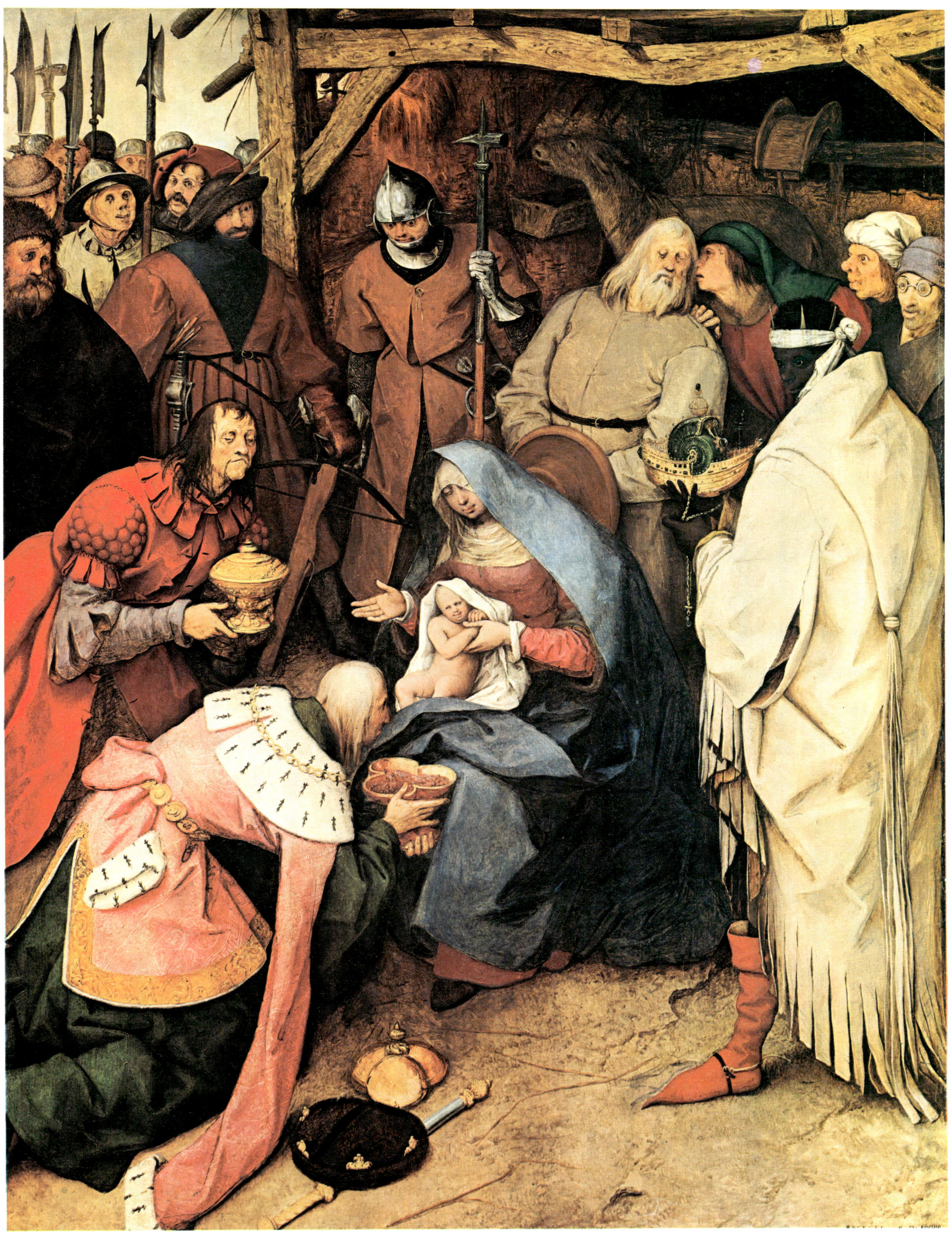

balloons or sacks, no longer consisting of anything other than big round bellies and little round heads. The smooth, round lines of the heavy bodies match the fat, generous shapes of the sausages and hams dotted around all over the room. Everything is bursting with luxuriance. In fact the feast is by no means over, for a mouth-watering piglet is just being basted on the spit. A corpulent monk is also included in the company. Bruegel has not forgotten anything: even the dogs and cats are fat, as are the overfed children, not to mention the baby – already a mini-Pantagruel – sucking at those enormous breasts. Everything in the gluttons' kitchen is fat, including the pots and pans; even the armchairs seem more massive, to take the weight of those enormous rumps. Every detail contributes to the overall impression of fatness. But the tattered, emaciated bagpipe player is leaving, spat out like a chewed bone by the band of rotund revellers. The way Bruegel conjures up the process of his ejection is a stroke of genius, the gesture of the outstretched hand leading the eye from the company seated at the table – note the

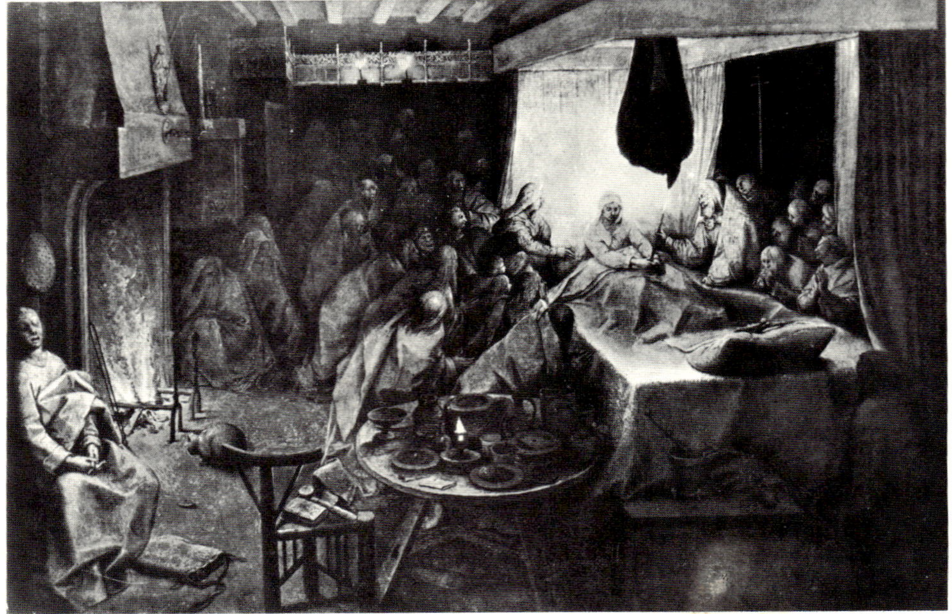

THE DEATH OF THE VIRGIN
Grisaille on panel; 36 x 55 cm (14½ x 22 in)
Signed: 'BRVEGEL'
Illegible traces of a date
c. 1564
Banbury, Upton House, National Trust
This work was painted around 1564 for Bruegel's friend Abraham Ortelius who had it engraved on copper by Philip Galle. Apart from this one there are two other grisailles which can be attributed to Bruegel with certainty, *Christ and the Woman Taken in Adultery* (p. 101), on panel, and *The Resurrection* (p. 77), on paper. The unusual iconographical character of this composition, which features a crowd of converts, goes back to the *Golden Legend*. It is possible that the death scene, set apart from the rest of the picture by means of a skilful play of light, is conceived as the dream of the evangelist John, shown sitting on the left.

monk's head – to the vagrant musician at the door. A cynical touch in the background is the glutton cutting himself a piece of ham while the one in front of him throws the starving musician out. The text below, in French and Flemish, says: 'Out with you, you sack of bones, you look so hungry. This is no place for you, this is the glutton's paradise'. Fraenger has shown that the German writer Johann Fischart (1546–1590) used Bruegel's engraving for his delightful description of a 'gluttons' kitchen' in the seventh chapter of his *Gorgelantua*, where it is followed by various socio-critical observations.

The thin kitchen (page 55) is a brilliant compositional counterpart. While everything in the fat kitchen swells to bursting-point, each feature here seems to be contracting inwards. The skinny hands of the emaciated figures stretch out concentrically into the mussel bowl, as though sucked in by the vacuum in the empty stomachs, by the constricting sensation of gnawing hunger. Their spindly limbs and shrivelled mouths seem to have had the very substance sucked out of them. Their cupboards are nearly bare, their fare the most miserable imaginable: mussels, bread, a radish. A single herring hangs over the fireplace, two more radishes or onions lie on a shelf with one precious egg. Mussels, of course, are also a Lenten dish. The withered breasts of the feeding mother give no milk: the underfed child has a drinking horn. The scrawny figure stirring the pot on the left recalls that other unfortunate character, the alchemist (page 43). The child puts the empty pot on its head, symbolizing utter destitution again, as in the *Alchemist*. A lean dog, all curled up and not unlike the one in Dürer's *Melancholy*, discontentedly licks the mussel-shells under the table. Every detail expresses thinness, constriction, emaciation and yawning emptiness. The shortnecked, potbellied figure at the door provides an absolute contrast, like a walrus among cackling geese. Eagerly and excitedly, the company try to get him to stay, but all in vain. As the caption points out: 'Where a lean man stirs the pot the meal is scanty, so as long as I live I shall go to the fat kitchen'. The rich man wants to know nothing of poverty, the fat man nothing of leanness and hunger.
The same theme is treated strikingly, though on a smaller scale, in a small oil painting

entitled *Three Heads* in Copenhagen (page 59) which has been attributed to Bruegel, although there is doubt as to whether he actually painted it. It shows a plump face reminiscent of a monk and an old, emaciated couple with wide-open, round eyes. As though in an effort to compensate for the blatant social injustice of it all, the starving man bites into the cheek of the fat one, while the open mouth of the old woman is on the point of doing the same.

The theme of *Children's Games*, too, crops up occasionally in calendar illustrations and tapestries before Bruegel. Countless games were known and mentioned in literature, as in the famous passage in Rabelais' *Gargantua and Pantagruel* (Book one, chapter 22). And long before that we find Froissart in an allegorical poem listing some sixty games he had played as a small boy. Bruegel's interpretation, though, has neither precedent nor successor. In his painting, children are playing their games in a townscape devoid of adults. Glück, de Meyere (1941) and J. Hills (1957) have noted and identified these

CHRIST AND THE WOMAN TAKEN IN ADULTERY
Grisaille on panel; 24.1 x 34 cm (9½ x 13 in)
Signed and dated: 'BRVEGEL. M.L.LXV.'
London, Courtauld Institute
(formerly in the collection of Count A. Seilern)
Like *The Death of the Virgin*, this grisaille was also meant for private use and in fact remained in the artist's family. It was engraved by P. Perret in 1579 (Bastelaer 111). Jan Brueghel the Elder, the painter's son, left it to the Archbishop of Milan, Cardinal Federico Borromeo, in 1625. Jan Brueghel the Younger later re-acquired it from the Cardinal. The subject is taken from St. John (8; 3–11). As an exclusively figure composition without any landscape it is a rarity among Bruegel's works. Grossmann has identified a cartoon by Raphael in the Victoria and Albert Museum in London as the inspiration for this work.

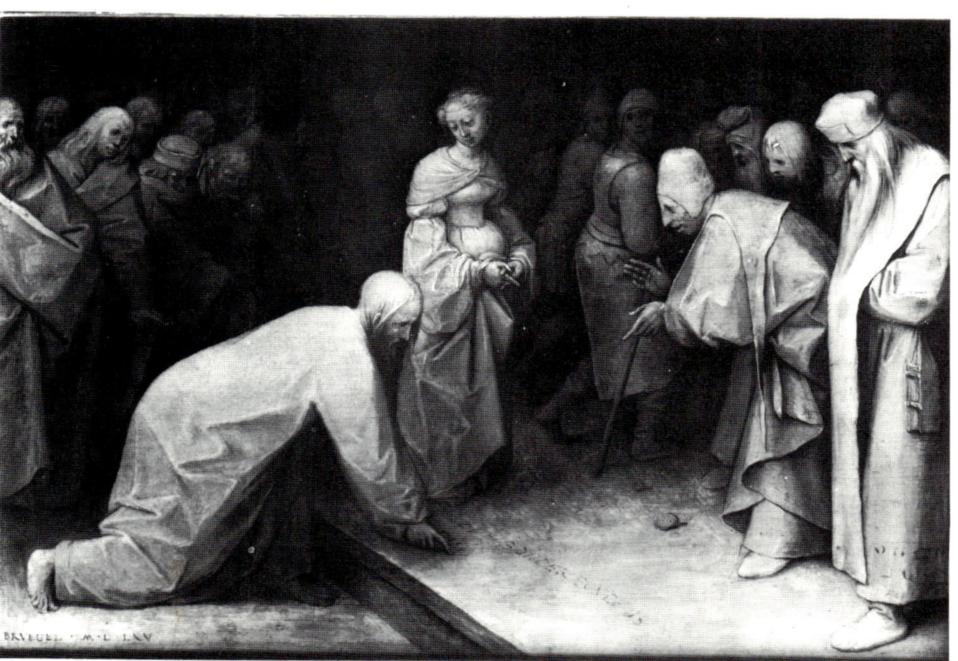

games precisely: there are almost ninety in all, possibly even more.

Below left two girls are playing fivestones, which involves completing a complicated series of movements with five small objects – in this case sheeps' ankle-bones – without making a mistake. Behind them two girls are playing with dolls, and further up is an improvised family altar: 'making altars' is generally regarded as a boys' game. To their right, a group is busy with a variety of different games: there is a *drilnoot* or spinning top, blowing bubbles, training a bird (this one not absolutely clear), and a whipping top held by the little girl with her back to us. The brick with a line attached to it could be an imaginary dog or horse. The children in front of it to the right are probably imitating a christening procession, and those behind them are playing a kind of blind man's buff. Riding the hobby-horse, beating hoops and riding a barrel are all clear enough. A little girl is shouting into the bung-hole of an upright barrel. Knights on horseback and leapfrog are immediately recognizable beyond the barrels, while to the right of the two hoops a girl is blowing up a pig's bladder. She wears the same kind of paper crown as the child on the far left in *Carnival and Lent* and in the *Gloomy Day* (page 71), a common article of headgear in Epiphany and Shrovetide processions. Two other children are wearing them in the *Children's Games*: the small girl with the long loaf of bread on the right in the middle distance, next to the insect-catcher by the tree-trunk, and one of the girls to the right of the group playing blind man's buff by the wall on the left. These two are guessing at 'rough or smooth'.

By the long, heavy beam on the right the two boys forming the 'horse' have to guess how many players are sitting on them. The girl to their right is playing shops with grated bricks. The game at the other end of the beam is a kind of punishment for anyone cheating in the other games, the culprit having his bottom banged on the beam by his friends. The hair-pulling ceremony on the far right is no doubt also a punishment. In front of this, two boys are throwing knives, and between these groups, four round caps on the ground represent a face, the three black ones making eyes and nose and the red one a mouth. 'The motif sums up the basic dual tendency in Bruegel's pictures: the disintegration of the pictorial and the face-pulling capacity of inanimate objects' as Sedlmayr points out. The expression on the 'cap face' is as blank as those of most of the 'children'.

A third level of physiognomy is represented by the human mask. A child in the first-floor window on the left has put on a grown-up's mask, no doubt to scare the children outside. It is a carnival mask, very similar to that worn by one of the 'musicians' in the *Battle Between Carnival and Lent.* A similar mask can also be found at the bottom right in the *Triumph of Death* (page 71), hiding a skull. In the very centre of the picture is a make-believe wedding procession with the 'bride' imitating the serious demeanour adopted by adults on such occasions. In the game to the right of this, the blindfolded player has to break a pot with a stick, originally a game for adults. The group sitting at the garden fence is playing at 'running through the lane', children in the garden are

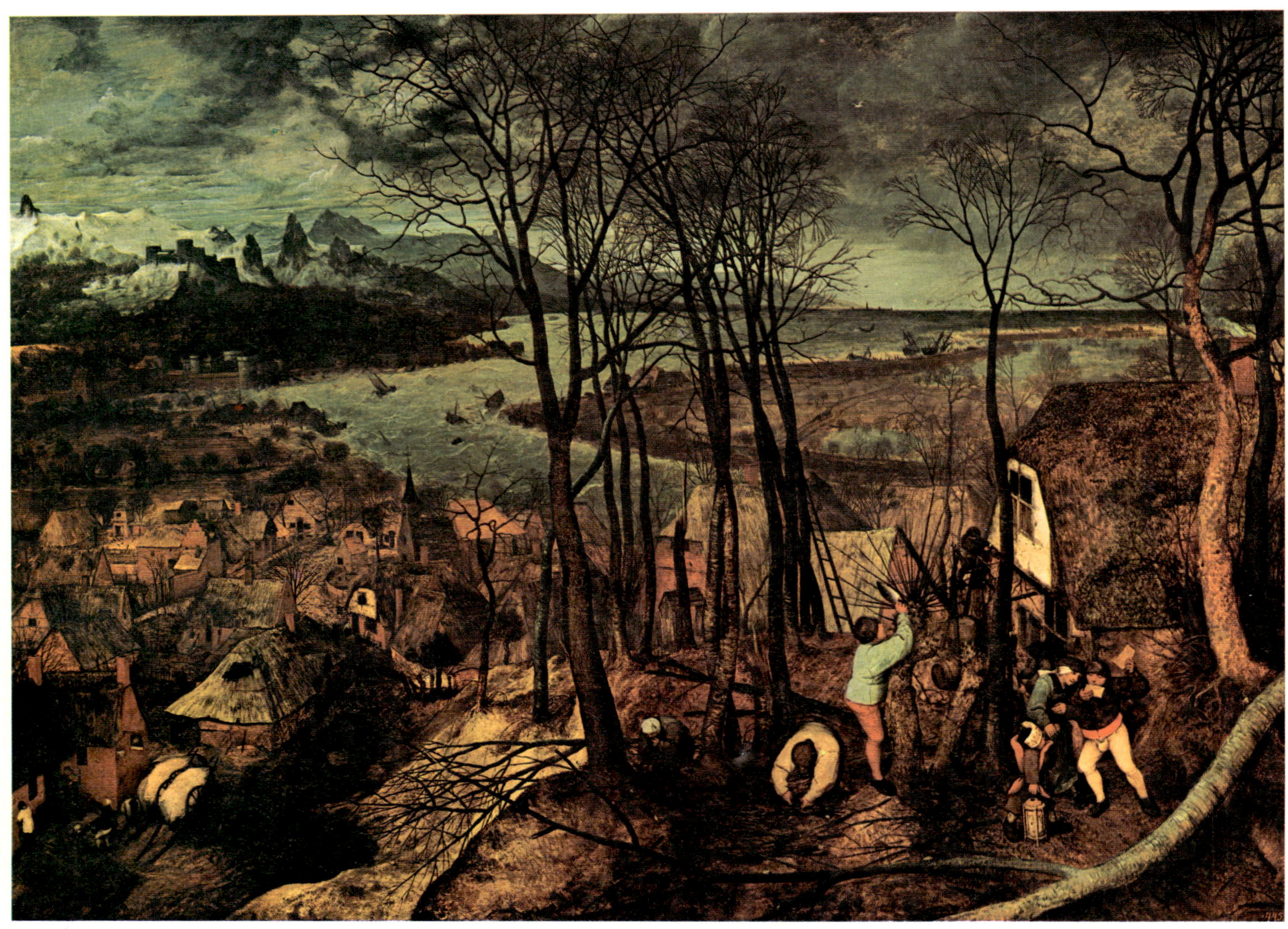

doing gymnastics, others on the fence are riding, and yet more beyond them spinning tops. A wide variety of throwing games can be made out, and some twenty further amusements are distinguishable all the way down the long street.

Despite the apparently arbitrary structure of the picture, Bruegel in fact follows a strict and very exact plan. Once again the horizon is extremely high, almost at the top. The ground rises steeply and the focal level is high to give a comprehensive view. All the lines of the edges of the buildings meet at the end of the seemingly endless street, the vanishing point being located at the foot of the church tower. The same is true of the brick wall on the left, the red fence and the darkened cornice of the late Romanesque building in the middle distance. A more eccentric vanishing point could hardly have been chosen. Bruegel was naturally familiar with the use of mathematical perspective, a discovery of the Quattrocento, but his painstakingly strict adherence to it and the dead straight, seemingly endless street for which there cannot have been any actual model, no streets of such length existing in those days, may be an ironical allusion to the

'Romanizing' architectural phantasies of his age. Its backward or upward sweep is in marked contrast to the horizontal stance of the stone building with moulded cornice, which enables the various scenes to spread out to the left with a degree of equilibrium. The horizontal element is reinforced by the red fence, located by no accident along the picture's central horizontal axis. To the left we see idyllic village scenery with children bathing in a stream flowing through a green meadow with trees. Beyond the houses the horizon becomes blurred in the remote distance, its line re-appearing briefly behind the church tower at the end of the long street.

The figures in the painting – approximately 250 of them – have been skilfully grouped. Individuals alternate with groups, and Jedlicka observes that the alternation of their postures and of the directions of their movement has been carefully thought out, like 'cogwheels whose individual teeth engage one another as the wheels move, only to move out again immediately'.

Although executed in 1560, only very shortly after the two previous ones, the painting contains clear signs of stylistic development. If we place it next to the *Proverbs* (page 47) the difference becomes clear straight away. Whereas in the *Proverbs* we have individual parcels of space linked separately to various figures and activities, the spatial treatment of the *Children's Games* gives an impression of complete unity. The different groups of children, on the other hand, are all the more isolated. Is this simply a depiction of delightful children at play, a genre painting full of childlike innocence and grace? Hymans noted in 1891 that the children in fact look like grown-ups: 'They are in no way genuinely childlike'. Their faces are expressionless, their features more reminiscent of old men and women than of children. To Jedlicka, their play seems 'externalized, a strangely alien activity'. Their movements have something almost distorted about them. Our impression is 'not so much one of seeing a crowd in motion as of hearing the monotonous humming of a huge clockwork mechanism made up of a multitude of small wheels'. Marijnissen observes that although engrossed in their games they do not appear to be enjoying them; they look more like adults hard at work: 'The whole atmosphere has nothing in common with a playground. One wishes the little things would fill the air with yells and cries of joy'. Grossmann concurs: 'The children ... are indeed absorbed in their games with the seriousness devoted by grown-ups to their own affairs, which – seen *sub specie aeternitatis* – have no greater importance. They can be compared to puppets which do not act from their own volition.'

Sedlmayr calls the *Children's Games* 'The first, classic example of alienation in art ... what the children are doing seems as absurd, eerie and suspect as the gesticulations of a crowd of lunatics or other beings we cannot understand. There are monsters with ten legs and three heads, the child beating a pot recalls an executioner, the one on stilts a cripple. The contortions the games involve remind us of the convulsions of epileptics, the bizarre toys of magical appliances, the whole thing having an air of mania about it'. We have here a large measure of agreement among writers whose views otherwise differ very widely. The *Children's Games* clearly have something common with the *Proverbs*. In the latter, the absurdity of human conduct is generally already suggested by the proverb itself; in the *Games* this absurdity is brought out by the fact that while children's games are indeed depicted, the people playing them appear to be adults. The whole picture in fact contains only one single grown-up: the woman in the street on the left pouring a bucket of water on a group of children. Thus, behind these apparently innocuous children's games Bruegel has concealed the world of adulthood: a world of senseless activity and useless motion, very earnest in its sense of its own importance.

Finally, E. Tietze-Conrat sees in the *Children's Games* an allegory of *Infantia* intended as the first work in a cycle depicting the ages of man. Writing in 1977, Dreyer rejected van Lennep's alchemistic interpretation of 1965 and summed up the picture's meaning in the formula: 'everyone does as he pleases'.

THE GLOOMY DAY
Oil on panel; 118 x 163 cm (46½ x 64⅛ in)
Signed and dated: 'BRVEGEL MDLXV'
Vienna, Kunsthistorisches Museum
One of the series of the *Months*, thought to have consisted of six paintings of which only five have survived. Originally owned by Niclaes Jonghelinck, the whole series was given in 1566 to the city of Antwerp, which presented it to the Archduke Ernest on 5 July 1594. This splendid picture, quite revolutionary in the field of landscape painting, uses preponderantly dark tones to depict the period of the year (around February, as indicated by various details associated with carnival time) which precedes the spring.
Detail on *pages 104–105*

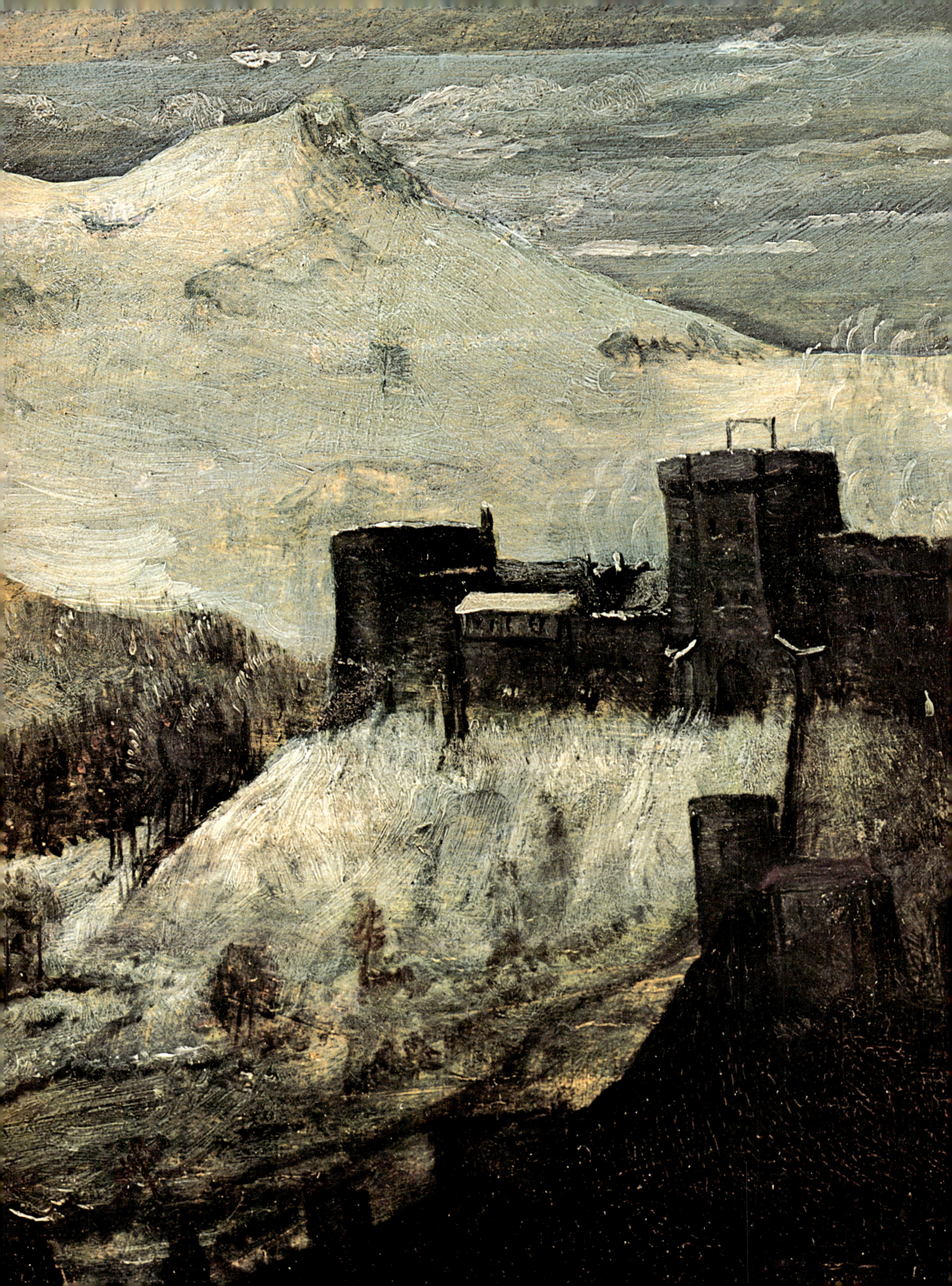

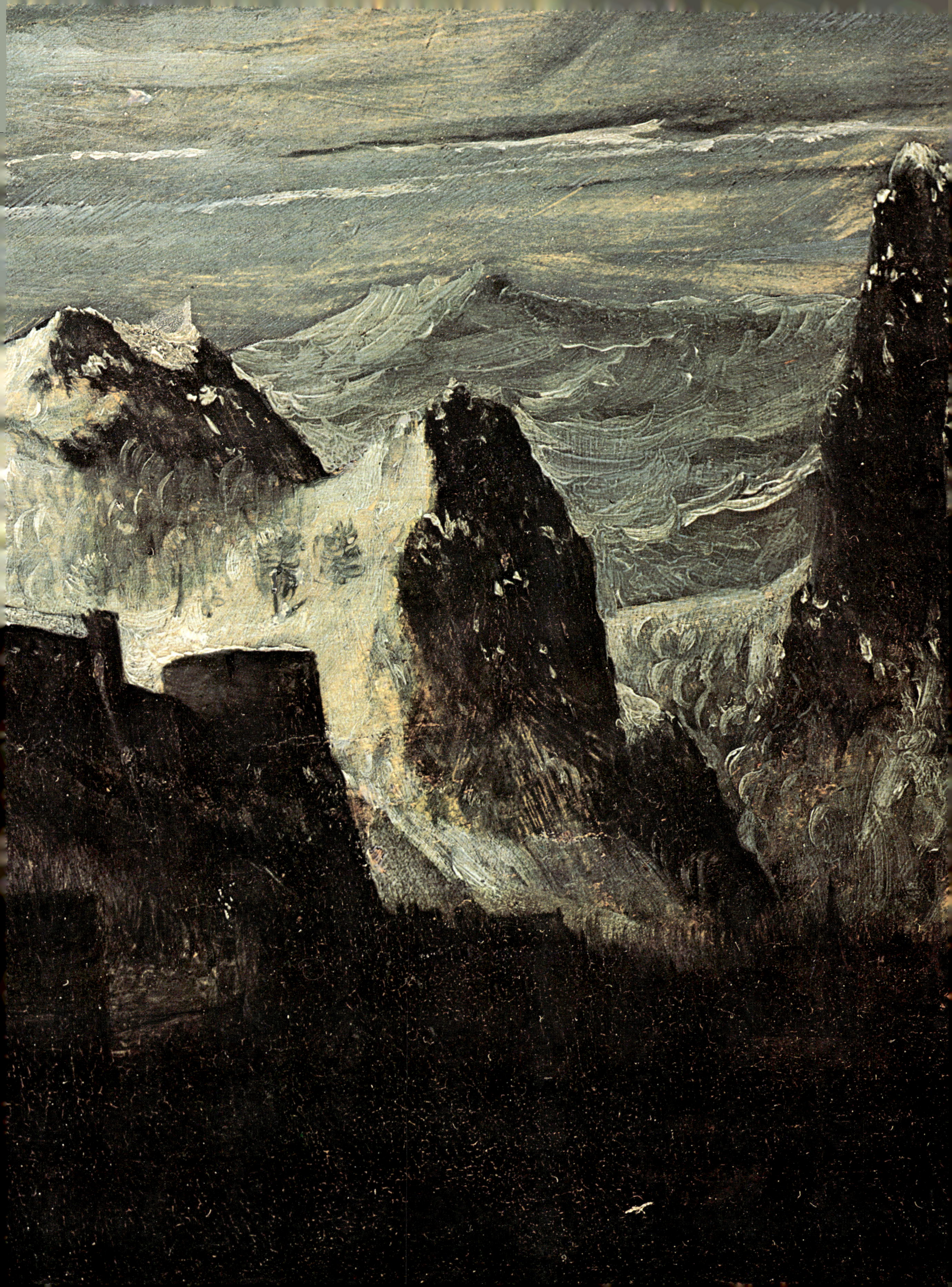

Remarkably, no dated painting exists from 1561. But the financially critical year 1562 saw the completion of five works, three of them major paintings of large dimensions: *The Fall of the Rebel Angels*, *Dulle Griet* and *The Triumph of Death*. The latter is undated but in view of its close links with the other two there can be no doubt that it was executed in the same year. Auner attributes all this to a long-standing debt which Bruegel supposedly had to settle shortly before moving to Brussels in 1563. These three pictures may have been painted for the same client, a collector wanting something in the spirit of Hieronymus Bosch. All three have the same format, so characteristic of Bruegel, and each in its different way is fundamentally visionary. In this respect they constitute a final climax in Bruegel's painted opus. He may already have begun working on one of these enormously demanding works in 1561. We assume the *Fall of the Rebel Angels* (pages 66–67) came first.

This work was acquired from F. Stappaert's collection by the Royal Museum in Brussels in 1846 and until the discovery of Bruegel's signature hidden under the frame was regarded first as the work of Pieter Brueghel the Younger, then of Hieronymus Bosch. Nowhere is the link with Bosch as evident as here. Indeed Bosch depicted the subject as the panel devoted to Paradise in his *Last Judgement* triptych in the Academy in Vienna, and there is a similar representation of it, equally small and insect-like, in the left-hand panel of the *Haywain* triptych in the Prado. Bosch shows the downfall of the apostate angels whom God expelled from Heaven at the beginning of the world's creation and who were transformed into infernal beings. Bruegel, however obviously worked on other sources of inspiration.

Critics have often drawn attention to the picture's affinities with the *Last Judgement*, whose mass of figures belong to the rich Netherlandish tradition after van Eyck and which Bruegel himself treated in the drawing for the engraving of 1558. He undoubtedly knew the St. Michael altar executed by Frans Floris in 1554 for Antwerp cathedral, with the archangel beating the throng of grimacing, naked figures towards Hell, and he probably also knew Dürer's woodcut of the *Apocalypse* (1498). Bruegel dispensed with the naked figures but retained and extended Floris' chaotic tumult, enlarging on the hybrid monsters with a wealth of explicit detail equally as grotesque as anything from Bosch's imagination. However, Bruegel's overall treatment is totally new and revolutionary in every respect. The stream of fallen angels, turning into monsters as they descend, come tumbling out of an enormous, abstract circle of light derived from Bosch's divine aureole. Although watching the cosmic event partially from below, we are at the same time presented with a second spatial reference system which turns the headlong flight towards us in a downward direction into the depths of Hell, as though the falling throng were sliding over an invisible surface formed by the picture screen. Angels and helpers of the archangel Michael are grouped around the centre of light, while the middle of the composition is dominated by the delicate-looking figure of the archangel himself in golden armour, trampling under foot the seven-headed crowned dragon. The spatial turning-point occurs where the blue of the firmament is cut off horizontally by the impenetrable chaos of the infernal rabble, behind which no spatially definable background can be discerned. Only at the very bottom can we perhaps detect the blackness of the nether regions or a whiff of hellish vapour rising from below. In the work by Bosch, the whole scene is set in Heaven itself as an extension of the earthly paradise, the angels with their insects' wings being cast out of the firmament without any recognizable goal. Bruegel, though, converts the secondary scene of action into the main one, linking Heaven and Hell and making his fallen angels descend directly from the centre of light into an imagined Hell in the chaos of their defeat. Here Bruegel handles spatial complications as difficult as any that could have been invented by the greatest fresco artist of the Baroque.

St. Michael, the 'paragon of chivalry and representative of an over-refined courtly culture', to quote Auner, wears the array of a knightly order. Harmony wins its victory with elegant ease and confident superiority over chaos, light vanquishes darkness, the holy white of the victorious angels overcomes the 'evil' hues of their fallen brethren. These colours also contain allusions to the animal symbolism of the seven deadly sins, particularly lust; thorough interpretation of the details was made by Knipping in 1949. Auner notes that, unlike Bosch, Bruegel is not depicting the fall of the angels at the beginning of the world's creation but the archangel's battle with the hordes of Satan on the Day of Judgement, as indicated by the trumpets. Bruegel's intention was clearly to combine the two events. The apocalyptic angels sounding their trumpets in the sky – recalling those in the drawing of 1558 – are caricatured in the two creatures madly

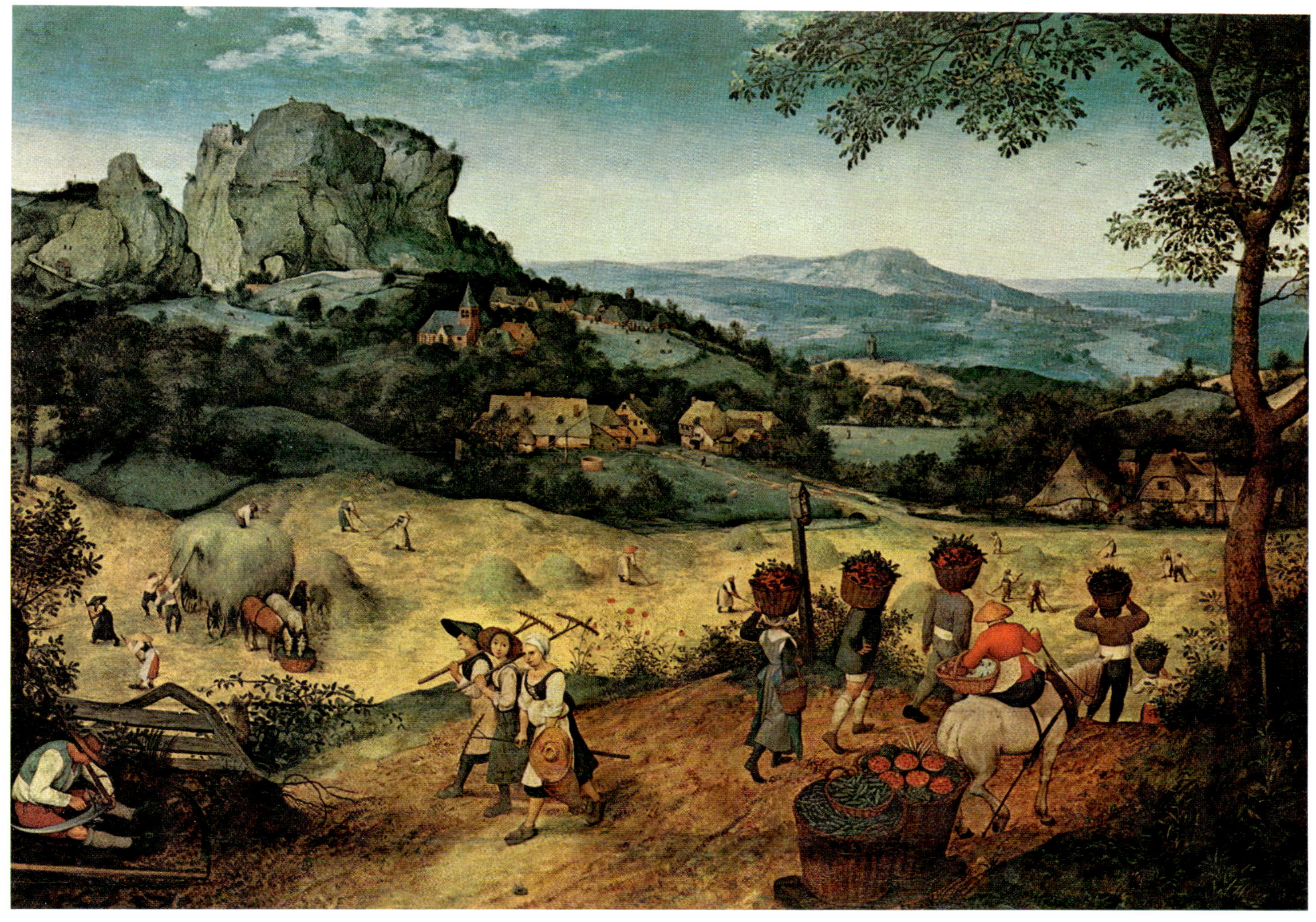

HAYMAKING
Oil on panel; 117 x 161 cm (46 x 63⅜ in)
Neither signed nor dated
1565
Prague, Národní Galerie
Also one of the series of the *Months*. It shows
haymaking, an activity traditionally as-
sociated with pictures of the months of June
or July. It was probably in the Imperial
Collections from 1659 and certainly up to the
18th century; after that it disappears from
view until turning up in the collection of
Princess Grassalkovich, who left it in 1864 to
Duke Ferdinand Lobkowitz of Raudnitz
Castle in Bohemia.
Detail on *pages 108–109*

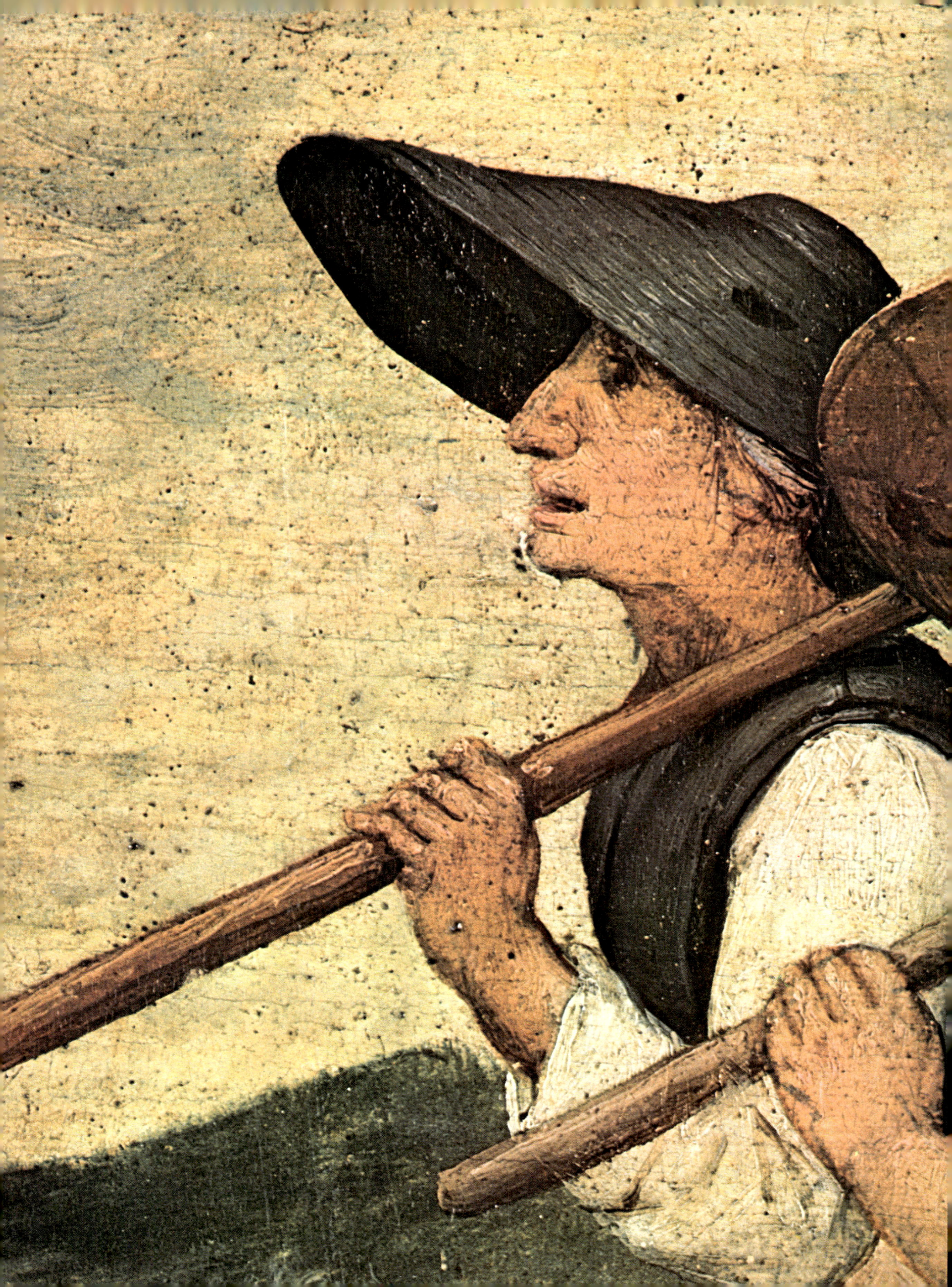

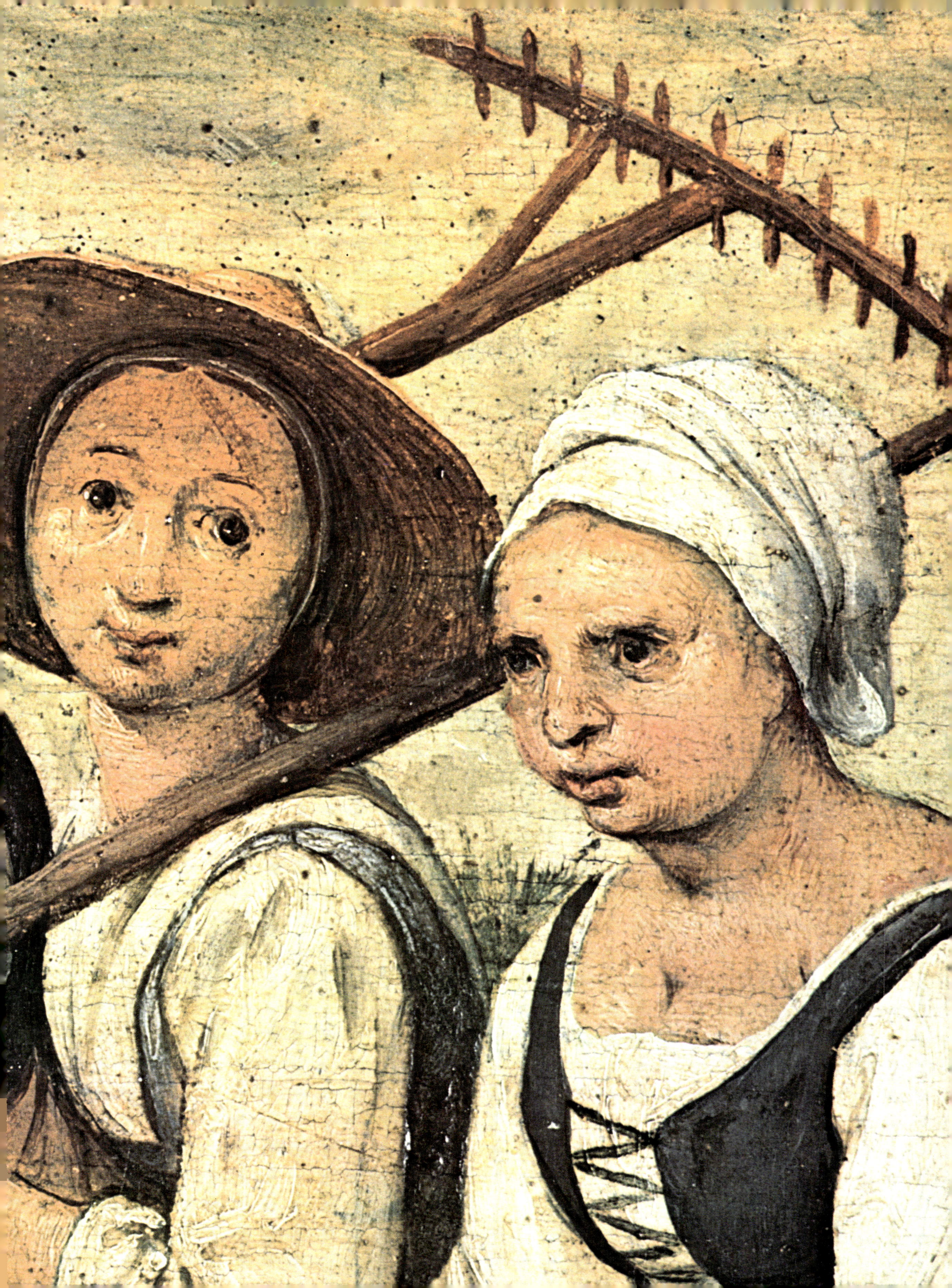

blowing their instruments down in Hell.
This painting must surely be one of the most colourful of all Bruegel's works, and the treatment of colour here deserves special attention. Jedlicka in particular has pointed to the sophisticated alternation of yellows, reds, greens and blues, and their different tones. Yellow, above all, appears in the most spiritual as well as the most material roles. On the highest plane it begins as light at the top of the picture, becoming more tangible in the robes of some of the angels and in the trumpets, acquiring sumptuous materiality in the glittering gold of the archangel's armour at the centre of the picture and finally being broken up into the sickly, gruesome and ghostly hues of the 'amorphous yet controlled mass of infernal monsters' in the words of Jedlicka. The same can be said of the other colours, which vary from ethereal purity to poisonous opalescence. The way the fighting figures are contrasted is equally masterly – above, the inviolable purity of the different materials; below, the slimy, hairy, prickly nakedness of animals' bodies. The butterfly wings are an invention of Bosch's: Auner maintains that '… the butterfly is not only a manifestation of soul but also an "evil thing" resulting from the Devil's intercourse with witches'.
Commenting on the archangel's golden armour, Menzel notes that St. Michael was the patron saint of Brussels. In Bruegel's time a gilt statue of him over 4 metres (13 ft) high topped the tower of the city's gothic town hall. Bruegel would probably have been familiar with this figure from earlier visits before he actually moved to Brussels in 1563 so may have drawn his inspiration from it, the painting dating from 1562.
The problematic work entitled *Dulle Griet* (page 69) takes us away from the apocalyptic preoccupations of the Book of Revelations and back to Netherlandish notions of hell and sin. Van Mander mentions it as being in the possession of the Emperor Rudolph II, and it probably also belonged to Queen Christina of Sweden before finally being bought in 1894 by the Museum Mayer van der Bergh in Antwerp. Both signature and date are in poor condition, but the figures MDLXI are still legible. Grossmann believes Glück was right to read this as 1562, an interpretation more or less confirmed by photographic enlargement. Its wealth of complicated detail makes this composition unusually baffling at first sight and it has duly received very widely differing interpretations. The most straightforward has come from Grossman, who regards *Dulle Griet* as a personification of the deadly sin of covetousness, driven by her greed to the very jaws of Hell. Seen in this light, the picture would be a monumentally enlarged and enhanced version of the drawings of 1558 representing the deadly sins. But let us begin with the central figure.
Griet is an abbreviated form of *Margriet*, i.e. Margaret. 'Dul' means stupid, but with the additional secondary sense of spiteful, cross and vicious. The name has been used on various occasions and in different forms for large guns: a cannon in Ghent dating from the time of Philip the Good is called *Dulle Griet*, for example. The character can still be met with in the country between Dunkirk and Kiel, and in France she is known as 'Margot-la-Folle'. In Schleswig they call her 'Black Margaret', while in Cologne, according to Jedlicka, she appears as a ghoul who eats children. There is a Netherlandish proverb which also occurs in the bottom left-hand corner of the *Proverbs* in Berlin: *De beste Griet, die man ter werelt vand, was die den Duyvel op 't Kussen bant* ('The best Meg in the world was the one who tied the Devil to the cushion'). Dulle Griet's retinue in the painting includes a number of small scale 'Griets' tying devils to cushions. It may be that the figure of Mad Meg is derived from St. Margaret, who, according to legend, overcame the devil but was transformed by folk literature into a witch-like shrew who was a match even for the Devil, as the proverb stresses. In everyday usage she was just a bad housewife, a malevolent jade capable of making Satan tremble.
Dulle Griet – described by Jedlicka as a mixture of 'witch and mad housewife, haridan and amazon, warrior and old maid', with the features of a 'fallen angel and a dogged bourgeoise' – has undertaken a raid all the way to the jaws of Hell, gaping wide on the left of the picture. The arbitrary nature of her greed is manifest: apart from jewellery, golden goblets and a money-chest, she has also grabbed worthless household equipment including an iron frying-pan. In one hand she has a dagger, on her head a round helmet with a soft veil over it – perhaps a symbol of virginity – and over her clothes, from which we can almost smell the musty vapours rising, is a breastplate. The way she moves seems to imply attack and retreat at the same time; her attitude as she advances is striking and strangely memorable. The scene is set in an infernal landscape characterized by a methodical interweaving of organic and inorganic forms, with menacing brown tones everywhere and fires raging in the background. It would be impossible even to describe here the inexhaustible wealth of detail in the picture, let alone explain it. Only Tolnay (1935), Jedlicka (1938) and Graziani (1973) have given complete interpretations of the picture based on detailed iconographic analysis. A battle is evidently in progress in a

kind of ante-region to Hell between the plundering women and Satan's mercenaries. The defenders do not seem to be standing up to the women's assault, for the drawbridge leading to the chasm of Hell is being hastily raised as a precaution. Jedlicka has drawn attention to the other figure in the picture which is of the same size as the main one: the giant sitting on the roof with a ship on his back, the counterpart to Dulle Griet. While she gathers up whatever she can lay her hands on, he discharges gold coins from his posterior on to the crowd below with the aid of a large spoon. This reflects the Netherlandish proverb '*Hy heeft Geld als dreck*' (He is stinking rich' – an allusion to excrement). Another view is that the figure on the roof is an accomplice of Satan, scattering gold to divert the attacking women from the battle. Jedlicka interprets the ship on the giant's back as the Ship of Doom, the '*blauwe schuyt*', although the ship is not blue but greyish black. The glass ball in the ship represents the world and a naked figure with a trunklike face is trying to roll a smaller ball overboard. According to Jedlicka, this is meant to represent the cause of the world's end, but Grauls takes it to be an attack on the prodigality of revellers and drinkers, and also cites the '*blauwe schuyt*'. Grossmann calls the giant a 'tempter', the one who gives occasion for greed in the first place. In the foreground we find a series of allusions to other deadly sins: *Gula* (intemperance), for example, in the wine cask and the wandering head eating gruel, its front orifice coinciding with its rear one. There is also the globular head, with its wide mouth and the pastry pan like the one in the drawing entitled *Christ in Limbo* (page 65, above right). The head has a fish (male sexual symbol) dangling on the end of a line above a bird's-nest (female sexual symbol), thereby establishing a link with *Luxuria* (lust), which may well also be referred to in the glass sphere at top left. The bird's-nest appears again in the *Fall of the Rebel Angels* (pages 66–67, far left) and in *Christ in Limbo*, where it is being carried on the back of a large fish. The storm bell on the tree and the wheel of Hell also occur in this drawing. These associations reinforce the notion that the scene is set in some kind of ante-region to Hell, the entrance to Hell itself being formed by the gaping jaws on the left. The composition of the head, consisting chiefly of inorganic components, has elements of the Mannerist picture-puzzle of the type developed in its purest form by Archimboldi. The eyebrows have recently been identified as starling pots, used by those who robbed the nests of starlings, thus adding a further allusion to theft and robbery. The numerous other containers and pots in the picture might be construed as symbols of the thirst engendered by the heat of Hell. Jedlicka believes that the contrasted activities of amassing gold and shovelling it out 'are a grotesquely exaggerated way of portraying the eternal struggle for survival', their uselessness demonstrated by the fact that they cancel each other out. To indicate the wide variety of interpretations put upon the main figure, a few have been chosen from the 1978 museum catalogue. She has been seen as a personification of *Ira* (van Gelder/Borms, 1938), of heresy, and of *Avaritia* (Grossmann). Many writers have construed her as a shrew or scold, others as a second devil complementing the triumphant Satan, a kind of Don Quixote (Tolnay), or the goddess Gridr from *Edda*. An alchemistic interpretation sees her surrounded by hermetic symbols as she seeks the philosopher's stone. For Graziani (1973) she is Fortuna taking back her gifts, inspired by Dante's *Inferno*; for Guldan (1969) the assault on the gates of Hell is modelled on Christ's descent into the regions of darkness, the picture representing the topsy-turvy world of a secularized Hell. Roseman has pointed out that Dulle Griet is in fact going *past* the entrance to Hell. Sedlmayr regards the picture as a vision of madness, of utter chaos: 'No modern work of art has come anywhere near to capturing what Bruegel with his peculiar "macchia" has succeeded in portraying in this picture – not just mad creatures and their antics, but the whole structure of a mad world'. He does, however, allow that Surrealism may in some cases have achieved the same thing. Other commentators have claimed that the picture represents oppression and the use of violence; anarchy; the ravaging of Jerusalem as envisaged by the Anabaptists; that it is part of a trilogy including the *Fall of the Rebel Angels* and the *Triumph of Death*; a mockery of the common fear of witches; a caricature of the zealous housewife; a purely ironical and humorous composition. Bastelaer and de Loo (1907), among others, think the work's significance has to be sought in proverbs and folklore, and attempts have been made to explain it in this way. Grossmann's interpretation of it as an allegory of covetousness seems to me the most convincing, though with one rider: the very complex, folkloristic figure of Griet herself creates a more solid dimension than would have existed with mere allegory. References to other sins recall the series of drawings representing the deadly vices. The giant in female attire scattering gold could thus most plausibly be explained as the tempter carrying on his back the illusory pleasures of sin symbolized in the glass sphere, which stands for transience. 'Women in whose hearts this sin ('*avaritia*') lives are

THE CORN HAR-
VEST
Oil on panel; 118 x
160.7 cm (46½ x 63¼ in)
Signed and dated:
'BRVEGEL ... LXV'
1565
New York, Metro-
politan Museum of Art
This third painting in
the *Months* series shows
harvest time, usually
associated with the
months of July or
August. Given to the
Archduke Ernest by the
city of Antwerp in 1594,
this wonderful com-
position went to Paris in
1809 with the rest of the
series of the *Months* and
other pictures of
Bruegel's (Novotny
1948). Unlike most of
the other works, it did
not return to Vienna in
1815, an indication of
the high esteem in
which Bruegel's art was
held. It went to New
York in 1912 by way of
the art market.
Detail on *pages
114–115*

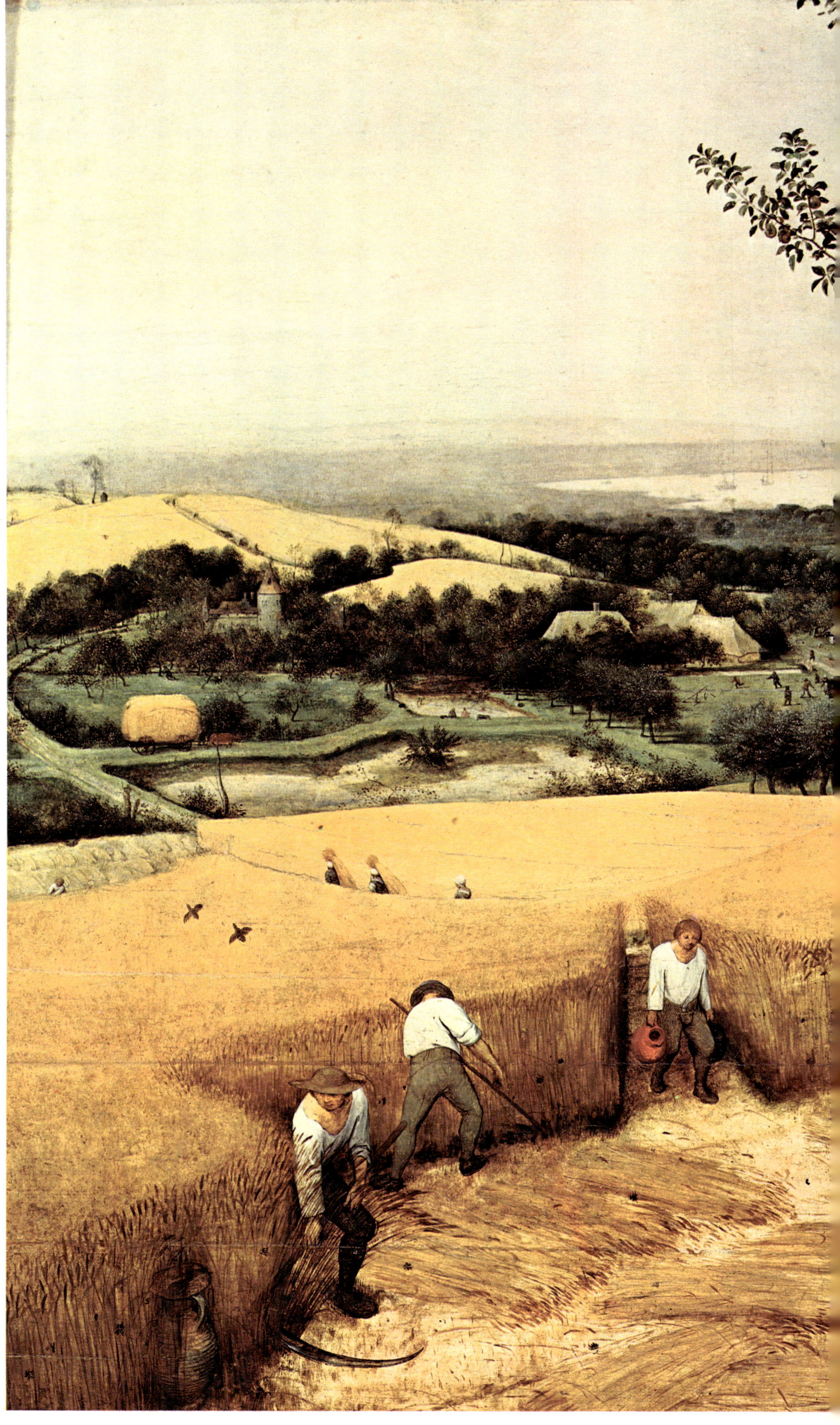

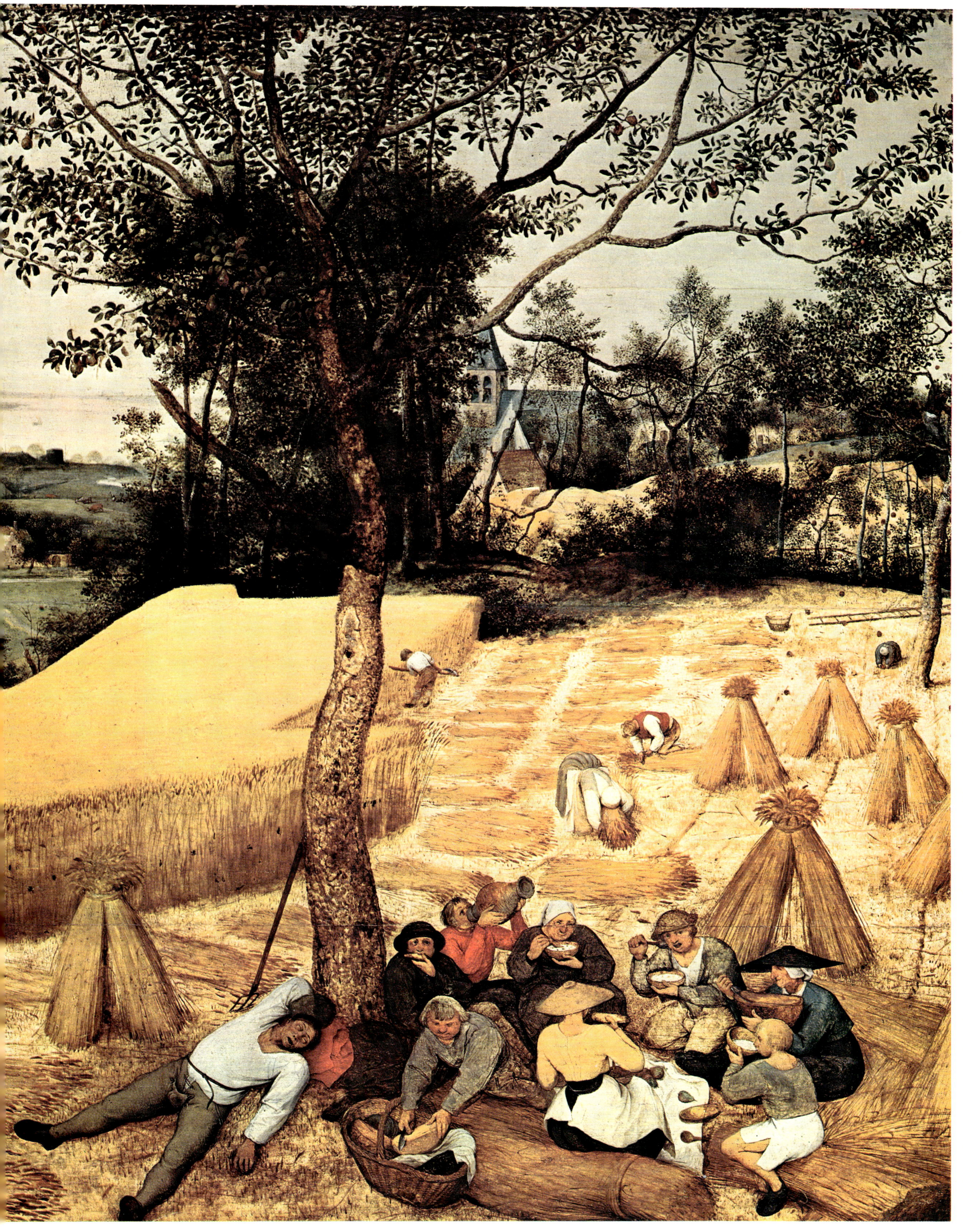

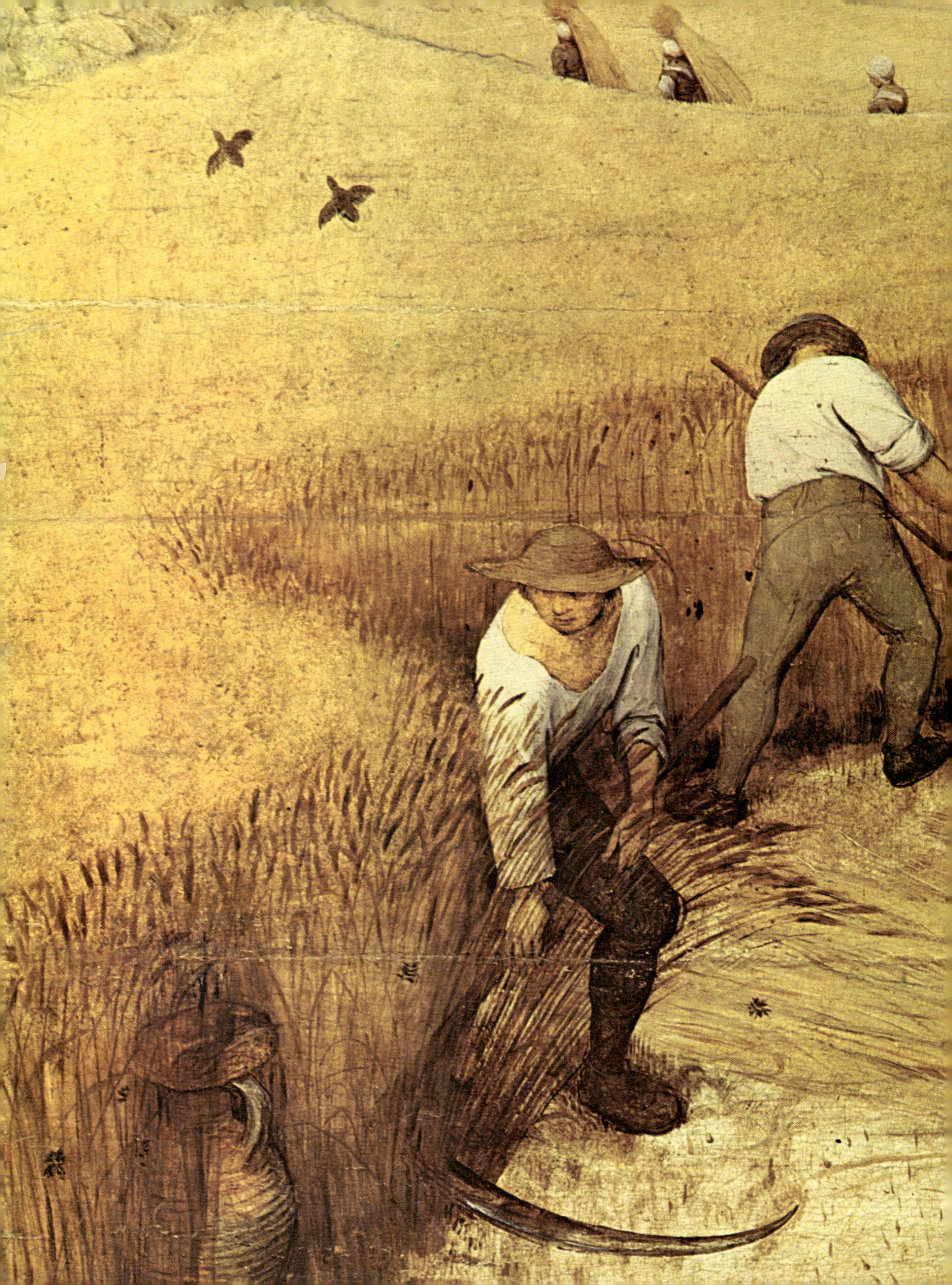

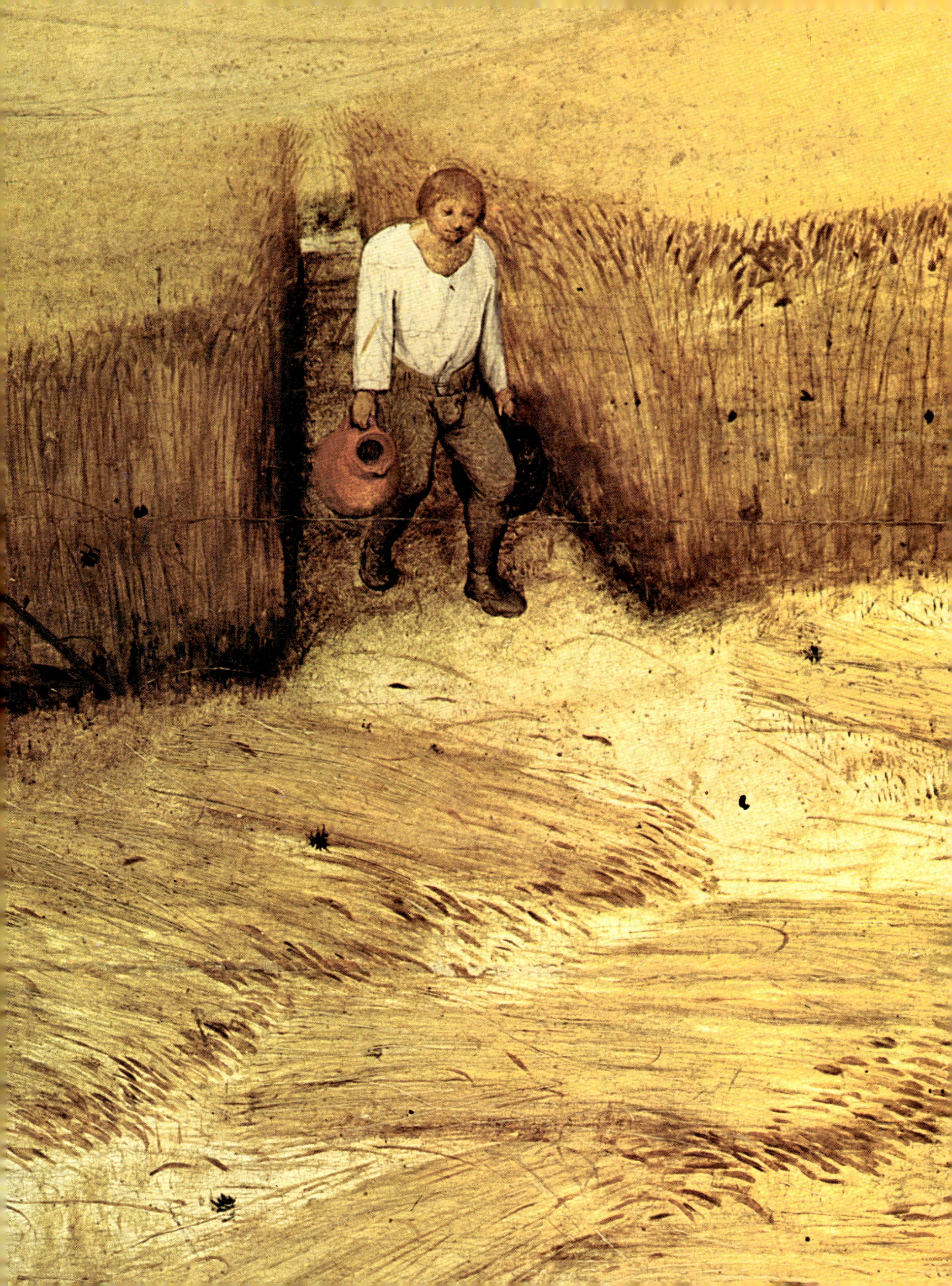

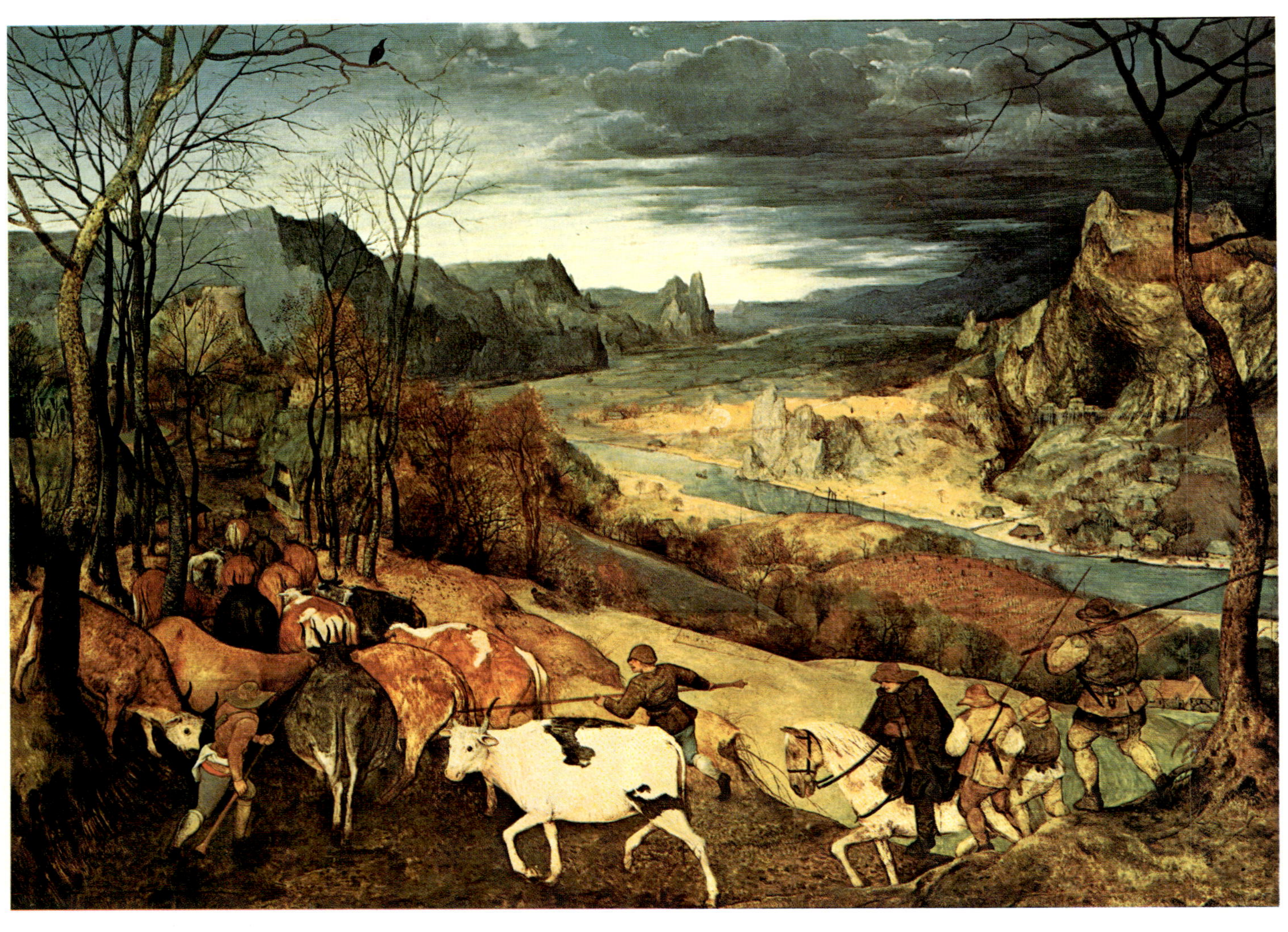

THE RETURN OF THE HERD
Oil on panel; 117 x 159 cm (46 x 62 in)
Signed and dated: 'BRVEGEL MDLXV.'
Vienna, Kunsthistorisches Museum
Iconographically, this is the most innovative
and unusual of the pictures in the *Months*
series. The return of the herd also appears in
a picture, obviously inspired by Bruegel, by
Maerten van Valchenborch (Vienna, Kunsthistorisches Museum): an inscription indicates that the picture, which belongs to a
series dedicated to the months, illustrates
November. Bruegel's painting features some
vineyards, which could point to October, the
month of the grape harvest. This grandiose
landscape has associations with an earlier
drawing (c. 1553–1555) entitled *Landscape
with Three Pilgrims* which is in a private
German collection (catalogue of the Berlin
Exhibition of 1975. no. 37).

certainly not afraid of fighting the devils' (Grossmann). The drawings of the seven deadly vices are unmistakably at the root of this great painting. In line with its large format, Bruegel has produced a complex composition and evolved an abundance of scenes allowing a variety of interpretations. We can only guess how many intended levels of meaning remain unrevealed.

The Triumph of Death (page 71) is perhaps the most richly detailed of all Bruegel's paintings dominated by a mass of small figures. Unlike the fantastic, infernal creatures of the two foregoing works – the *Fall of the Rebel Angels* and *Dulle Griet* – the various individual episodes of which it consists are taken straight from actual life. The overall composition can be more easily taken in, its different scenes more readily understood, its meaning and structure are more obvious. One is therefore tempted to assume it to be the last of this great trio of compositions executed in 1562. It was acquired by the Prado in 1827 and is neither signed nor dated, but there is little doubt that it belongs to the year 1562. The 'Manneristic' figures are even more elongated than in other pictures of the same period. The spidery skeletons are long and thin, and those of the people who still remain alive already resemble them with their strange forms extended like shadows. They reinforce the weird impression of an enormous *danse macabre*.

Van Mander tells us that the picture contains 'every possible contrivance against death', and it is almost certainly identical with the *Triumph of Death* in the inventory of Philip van Valckenisse, drawn up in Antwerp in 1614.

Tolnay realized that Bruegel has combined two iconographical traditions in this work: the Italian one of the triumph of death, as depicted in 15th-century frescoes in the Campo Santo at Pisa and even more strikingly in the Palazzo Sclafani in Palermo (page 70), and the northern tradition of the Dance of Death (seen in woodcuts by Hans Holbein the Younger and others). As already mentioned, it has been assumed that in the course of his Italian journey Bruegel went as far as Palermo, where he could have seen the fresco in the Palazzo Sclafani. In the *Triumph of Death*, Death appears as a skeleton on horseback with a scythe, dealing out death all indiscriminately around; in the *Dance of Death* he represents the individual death of a member of each social class – emperor, nobleman, bourgeois, peasant, cardinal, etc. In this case he features as a decrepit figure who, in accordance with the dictum '*mors certa, hora incerta*', eventually comes for everyone, whether king or beggar, pope or monk. Bruegel further enriches this novel combination by incorporating the motif of the 'battalions of death', in Tolnay's phrase, in combat with the living. Like *Dulle Griet*, this horribly gruesome scene is set in an infernal landscape of particular barrenness, with dead trees and numerous fires raging. Similar landscapes are found in the works of Bosch and later artists. Death, Hell and damnation are closely related concepts to which this depressing landscape is entirely appropriate; physical death derives its terror from the prospect of the Last Judgement, which is why the centre of the picture features a furnace manned by devils.

With accustomed thoroughness and inexhaustible imagination, Bruegel enumerates the various ways in which man is overtaken by death. People try to escape, but none suc- ceeds. On the right the way is barred by an army of skeletons, the 'battalions of death', holding coffin lids as shields. From the left the people are cut off and prevented from fleeing by armed skeletons and the figure of Death, the Great Reaper, riding on an old mare, itself hardly more than a skeleton. A little group thinking to slip off unnoticed in the opposite direction have been caught in a net of a kind formerly used for hunting. Meanwhile, two skeletons are clearly taking impish delight in raising a flap-like door to let through a panic-stricken mass of people who think they are going to escape. But the whole device is itself a death-trap on top of which a deathly figure swings his drum-sticks with fiendish enjoyment. On the left of the picture, Death rides on a horse (note the ghastly expression on its face) which is pulling a cart full of skulls. In his hand he holds a funeral bell and a lantern, while the skeleton on the cart plays the hurdy-gurdy, an instrument often found in Bosch's works. They have just run over three peasants without showing any great concern. In the background a group of skeletal clerics are drowning a heretic with the aid of a millstone tied round his neck. This is a brilliant excursion by Bruegel into contemporary polemic: with a sarcastic sense of mischief he uses the cross, symbol of salvation and redemption, as an emblem of death below which the clerical skeleton attends a drowning akin to that of St. Florian.

Bruegel illustrates the theme of the dance of death with five striking examples in the foreground. The emperor (on the far left, apparently wearing the Order of the Golden Fleece) has sunk down on the ground while death mocks him with an hour-glass to show him that his time is up. Another skeleton in chain-mail and armour plays joyfully with his money. Here particularly, but also throughout the picture, the maliciousness of death is emphasized. We have the impression that Death enjoys his work: There is nobody so remote or unimportant that Death will not willingly help him on his way. It may be someone falling into the water (left) or off a cliff (right), it may be an accident, execution or suicide: whatever the circumstances, Death is ready at hand, whether as executioner (right) or grave-digger (left), to carry men off to their ultimate fate in battle, shipwreck or fire. Moreover, he kills off what may still remain of living nature, for example by felling trees as seen in the left background. In the foreground, to the right of the emperor, a cardinal's skeleton looks after a collapsing cardinal. Although it appears to be supporting the falling figure it is in fact causing his death, whilst imitating the dying man's posture for good measure. Unusually, the cardinal's cloak is blue and Stechow suspects in this an allusion to the theme of deception or hypocrisy. A young mother has died prematurely, and the hound of death is already sniffing at her still-living child. The cap, staff and scrip reveal the man lying in the mid-foreground to be a pilgrim, and he, too, is at death's door as a result of a brutal assault. According to Grossmann, the purse carried at the pilgrim's neck implies an attack by the artist on merely outward piety. Like most writers he assumes that, since Christian doctrine defines death as the wages of sin, the picture is not just a representation of the different social classes in a *danse macabre*, meaning that all are equal in death, but that it represents certain specific sins as well. The gravest of these would apparently be greed signified by money chests, lasciviousness and clinging to earthly values, which result in God and the soul's salvation being forgotten. Thus various sins are being punished below right: anger seen in the mercenaries, intemperance, shown by the playing-board and wine and lewdness personified in the lovers. A few reservations need to be recorded about this theory, however. There seems to be no evidence of sinfulness, for example, on the part of the pilgrim. The fact that he is wearing a purse round his neck is neither unusual nor reprehensible; after all, it was scarcely feasible to go on a pilgrimage without any money at all. Moreover, the figure of Death is not cutting off the pilgrim's purse, as Jedlicka states, but simply cutting his throat. Death is not interested in purses. In other words, Death strikes down the innocent and the guilty alike, without distinction. It is also questionable whether Bruegel was so narrow-minded as to see the deadly sin of fornication in the pair of lovers listening to their music in the bottom right-hand corner. The only ones in the picture taking no notice of Death who is so close at hand, playing the violin behind them, they are the lovers' memento mori in the tradition of late medieval love poetry. Mercenaries and knights – experienced in battle, intoxicated and full of daring – revolt against death in one last senseless passage at arms, a hopeless attempt at opposition. The fool, by contrast, creeps under the table in the hope of escaping, while a skeleton wearing a carnival mask overturns a cooler with bottles of wine. Similar masks will be remembered in the *Battle Between Carnival and Lent* and the *Children's Games*. The two ladies at the table flee in horror at the approach, not of the waiter, but of Death in a fool's costume, bringing a skull and two bones instead of food. Certain details in the background recall the drawings of the *Deadly Sins*, for instance the clock with the human arm for a hand, which appears on the left above the gothic arcade and recalls *Desidia*, and the bells in the hollow tree-trunk at top left recalling *Ira, Desidia* and *Christ in Limbo*.

A brief look at the composition once again shows Bruegel's superior skill in organizing mass scenes on a large scale, with regard to both form and content. As so often in Bruegel's work, the right-hand side of the picture is structured differently from the left, the one intensifying the other. Both halves are unified by the foreground, where five different scenes are set out at equal intervals from left to right: emperor, cardinal, pilgrim, soldiers, lovers. These are arranged with classic Renaissance symmetry, which Bruegel artfully conceals: power and love feature as extreme opposites in the corners, while between them at the centre lies the man who has renounced both power and love, the pilgrim in the white garb of the penitent. All four corners are marked by striking details: emperor and lovers are deliberately rounded in composition to fit into their corners, while the eye is drawn up to top left by the huge funeral bells and to top right by the wheel.

Menzel sees criticism of the contemporary world as the main purpose of the painting rather than a moralizing Christian message. For him the emperor wearing the Habsburg Order of the Golden Fleece is, on the evidence of the ermine he wears, in fact a king with an imperial crown; in other words a king who has not attained the dignity of emperor. Understandably, the portrait bears no obvious similarity to Philip II. The cardinal would be Granvella; the pilgrim a symbol of intolerant Catholicism and of its hypocrisy; Death, and more specifically, execution, the scourge imposed by the Spanish regime. Menzel draws attention to the interesting fact that this painting, like the engraving entitled *Justitia*, is neither signed nor dated: '... in view of the reiterated criticism of the appalling state of contemporary affairs, anonymity was not only a deliberate ruse by the painter but in fact indispensable to his safety'.

Auner has a different, and rather more political or sociological interpretation. 'The *Triumph of Death* tolls the knell of the chivalrous culture of the Burgundian court which was approaching its demise around the mid-16th century with the abdication of Charles V'. Melancholy, says Auner, was the fundamental mood of late Burgundian culture; 'titanic melancholy', according to Huizinga, was a characteristic trait in Bruegel. Three good copies of the work exist: one at Vaduz (Liechtenstein), another at Graz (Joanneum) and a third currently on the art market.

As Jedlicka rightly points out, the little picture *Two Monkeys* (page 74) in Berlin, measuring only 20 x 23 cm (7 x 9 in), represents a pause for breath after the exertions of the three great compositions. Yet despite its small format it is a first step towards Bruegel's later monumental figure style. It shows two chained monkeys in a window niche in a warehouse at the port of Antwerp. Monkeys had already been depicted by Pisanello and in northern prints by van Meckenem and Dürer. The silhouette of Antwerp can be made out through the window and the monkeys are zoologically identifiable as red-headed mangabeys. Even in the most miner work like this we find painstaking attention to detail: note the compositional balance of the two crouching creatures within the niche, the confidently executed curves of their tails, which form a spiral starting from the ring in the middle and continuing in the back of the right-hand monkey and the arch. The contrast of the front and profile views of the heads, the position of the chains and nutshells, and the notches at the angles of the window are vitally important to the composition. Animal character is penetratingly observed in the body language, almost human, varying from wide-awake alertness to gloomy brooding. We might recall here Robert Musil's brilliant description of the monkeys at the Villa Borghese in Rome, in *Nachlass zu Lebzeiten*. Bruegel may perhaps have been attracted mainly by the idea of recording the natural antics of monkeys and trying out his skill in reproducing characteristic postures with animal models. However, this apparently uncomplicated composition has also been the object of various allegorical interpretations – rightly, no doubt, but without any satisfactory result. Bruegel was probably detained in Antwerp in 1562 by debts, before his move to Brussels. Auner concludes, in the light of this assumption, that he was comparing himself with the chained monkeys. Glück suspects that the picture refers to Bruegel's fellow citizens in Antwerp – in the spirit of the monkey of Heidelberg which used to stand on the bridge over the Neckar as a landmark, adorned with the following lines:

'Was thust du mich hier angaffen?
hast du nicht geseben den alten Affen?
zu heidelberg sieh dich hin und her
da findest du wohl meines gleichen mehr.'

('Why are you gaping at me? Haven't you seen the old ape? Look around in Heidelberg and you'll find quite a few more like me.') Tolnay cites a proverb: 'What funny people there are in the world, said the peasant, and he saw a monkey sitting in the window'. Neither notion is very convincing, and Tolnay and Jedlicka are even less so when they speak of the 'dualism of man and nature', the tragedy of which this picture apparently expresses. Terlinden rejects the theory that it contains certain allusions, but Grossmann suspects it to be more than just an animal study. He emphasizes the difficulty of arriving at the right solution in view of the fact that the monkey served as a symbol of the most widely differing, even contradictory ideas (cf. H. W. Janson, *Apes and Ape Lore in the Middle Ages and the Renaissance*, London, 1952). Stechow also makes a vain attempt to interpret another Netherlandish proverb: 'To bring a lawsuit for a hazel nut' means to do something thoroughly stupid. Accordingly, these apes must have surrendered their freedom for a nut, which explains the nutshells in the painting. The fact that the monkeys are chained and look so sad has also inspired a political interpretation: the animals are supposed to represent the Netherlandish provinces oppressed by Spain, while the birds soaring above the Schelde express their hope of liberty.

For his first subject from the Old Testament, *The Suicide of Saul* (pages 78–79), Bruegel goes to the struggle between the Israelites and Philistines. His only other use of the Old Testament is in two paintings of the Tower of Babel (1563).

The suicide of Saul features often enough as a Bible illustration, but is highly unusual as a painting in its own right. The explanatory caption in the artist's own handwriting, a rarity with Bruegel, says 'SAVL. XXXI CAPIT. BRVEGEL M.CCCCC.LXII'. This refers to the episode described in I Samuel; 31, in which Saul kills himself during the battle on Mount Gilboa so as not to fall into the hands of the Philistines. As usual, Bruegel has shown the event as a contemporary or near-contemporary battle in a rocky northern landscape with pine trees. On the outcrop of rock to the left we see Saul, wearing a splendid suit of armour, lying in a pool of blood: he has fallen on his own sword, and his armour-bearer is doing the same as soldiers ascend through the rocks to take them. Down in the valley the battle still rages; in the middle distance Mount Gilboa juts out like a shark's nose, strewn with dead Israelites. Bruegel may have been inspired by German battle scenes of the Danube School like those of Jörg Breu the Younger or Altdorfer's famous *Battle of Issus* (1529); but Grossmann has drawn attention to a more immediate model, the lost battle-scene by Patinir mentioned by van Mander.

The deliberately depicted landscape dominated by browns and greens is a studio composition which does not yet approach the visionary brilliance of the later scenes of the months. Local yellows and reds in the army's flags accentuate the tranquil impression which the composition conveys despite the excitement of the episode portrayed and the dramatic rock formations. Grossmann explains the surprising choice of subject by stating that Saul's suicide was seen as a punishment for his pride. Dante's *Divine Comedy* (Purgatorio, XII, 25 ff.), for example, mentions Lucifer, Nimrod (who built the Tower of Babel) and Saul as examples of punished pride. Curiously enough, Bruegel did indeed depict all these three subjects, if we count the *Fall of the Rebel Angels* as the fall of Lucifer.

Stridbeck points in this connection to Franck's and Coornhert's allegorical view of the Bible derived from Erasmus' rejection of Biblical, ecclesiastical and papal authority. According to this theory, the stories of the Old Testament only possess any moral value if understood as allegories with a universal significance common to all men everywhere. In Franck's opinion the suicide of Saul illustrates how men bring about their own downfall by renouncing God's guidance: 'But if we reject Him, He lets us go until, unconsoled, we ourselves approach Him and finally break ourselves to pieces on Him. Then we say he has beaten and slain us, while all the time it is we who have ruined and killed ourselves on Him. The immutable, unmoving God overcomes us with patience ...' (Sebastian Franck in *Paradoxa*). Stridbeck comments that in the nationalistic moral philosophy of these humanists, disdaining God is a characteristic concomitant of pride, the deadly sin of 'Superbia'.

The same ideas obviously inspired the *Tower of Babel*. This Old Testament theme (Genesis 11; 1–9) has a long iconographical history. Helmut Minkowski's book *Aus dem Nebel der Vergangenheit steigt der Turm zu Babel* (Berlin, 1960) gives the best account of its occurrence in the visual arts. But all the depictions prior to Bruegel (various woodcuts in German Bibles, French and Netherlandish book illuminations, e.g. in the Brevianium Grimani) are pitiful efforts without any vivid impression of size or grandeur. The subject does not occur as a panel picture before Bruegel, except for the lost work on canvas by Patinir which was reportedly in Cardinal Grimani's palace in Venice. This is the only work which could have given us an idea of how totally innovative Bruegel's work actually was. Bruegel depicted the subject three times: first in the lost ivory miniature mentioned in G. Clovio's inventory, then in the two paintings of 1563 in Vienna and Rotterdam. The pictures must have hit the public like a bombshell, for a flood of similar works, some of them of inferior quality, immediately began to inundate the art market – only to die away almost equally rapidly towards the end of the century.

It may be worth while at this juncture to give an outline of the Tower's historical background. The Sumerians built 'mountain temples' or ziggurats to their gods in the hope that they would set foot upon them and thus descend to man's level. For centuries these ziggurats were a characteristic feature of Babylonian cities: Assur and Kish each boasted two of them. The only purpose of these structures was to serve as a base for the elevated temple built in honour of the city's supreme deity. The most magnificent of all would have been the one at Babylon, which the Jews, forced to settle there by Nebuchadnezzar II in 586 BC, considered the ultimate in presumption and blasphemy. This was the origin of the paradoxical Bible story that the Tower – in reality a sacred building – had been constructed out of human ambition, and was duly punished by God with the confusion of tongues.

Bruegel's interpretation of the Biblical tale also contains a comment on the vanity and transience of all human undertakings. Indeed, Stridbeck has established that contemporary writers often saw ancient ruins in that very light, as for example in the *Eternal City*. Practically nothing was known about Babylonian culture in Bruegel's day, so the Netherlander dreamed up a monumental structure which combined Romanesque forms and Roman engineering techniques. There can be no doubt that he was inspired by the imposing ruin of the Colosseum in Rome: not only had he seen it on his journey, but he could also study it at his leisure in engravings from Cock's publishing house. Interest in

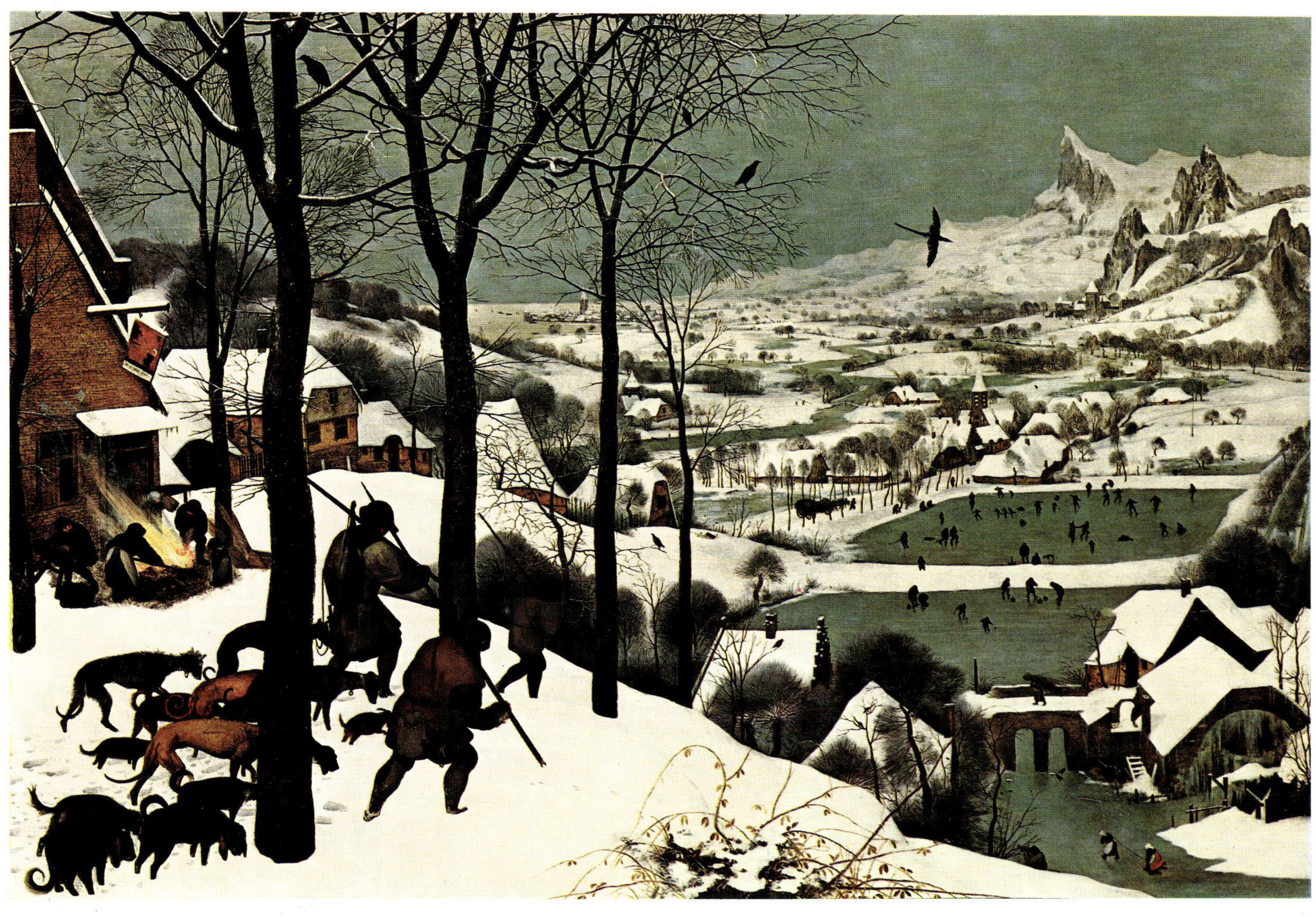

HUNTERS IN THE SNOW
Oil on panel; 117 x 162 cm (46 x 63 in)
Signed and dated: 'BRUEGEL M.D.LXV.'
Vienna, Kunsthistorisches Museum
Not only the most famous of the *Months* but
also the most celebrated depiction of winter
in existence. In an extraordinary synthesis the
colours of winter, the forms of the dogs and
the figures of the hunters are fused to pro-
duce an incomparable impression of cold, of
the livid light of winter. The killing of the
pig, to which the scene around the fire
alludes, is a motif traditionally associated
with December.
Detail on *122–123*

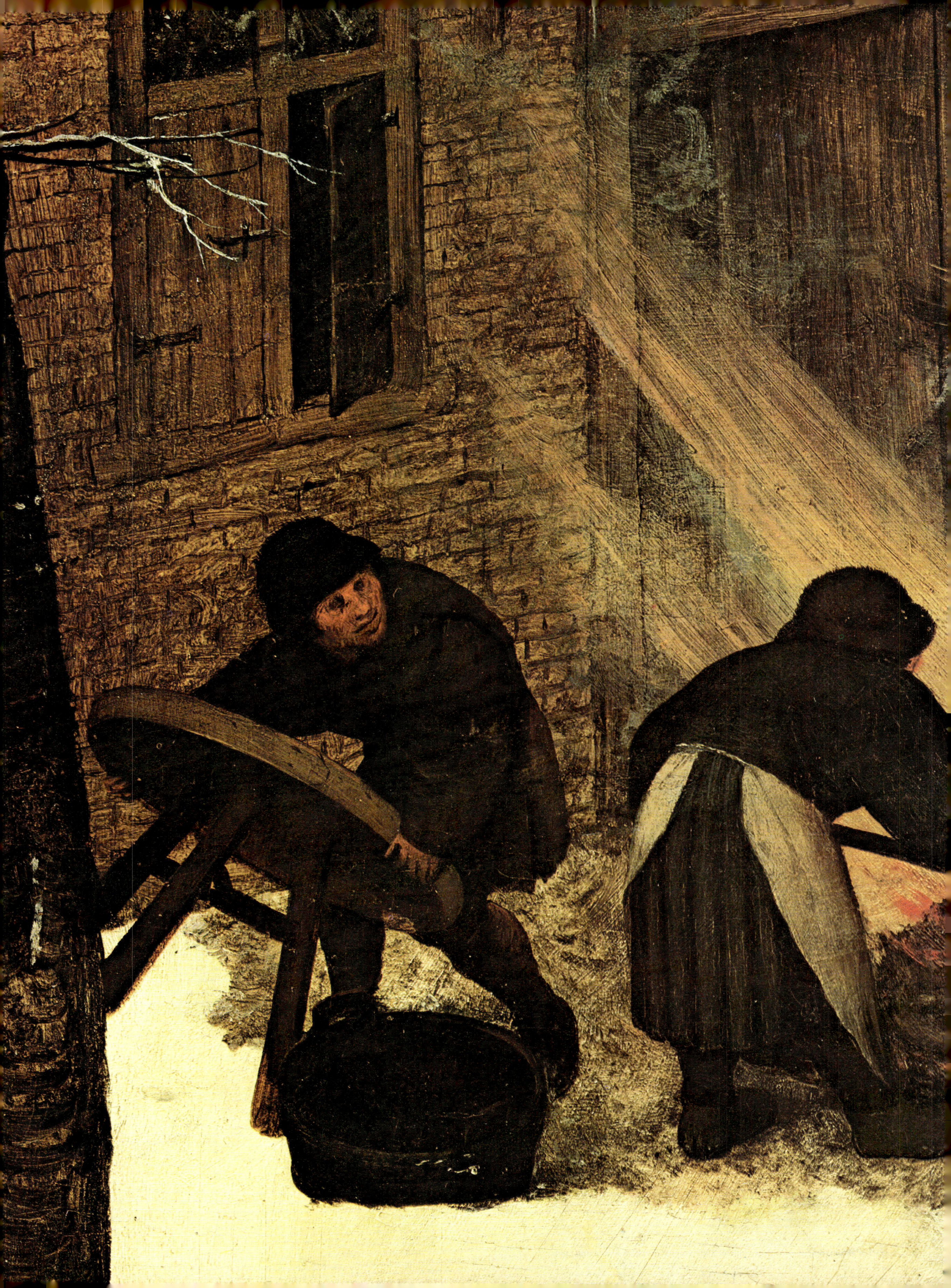

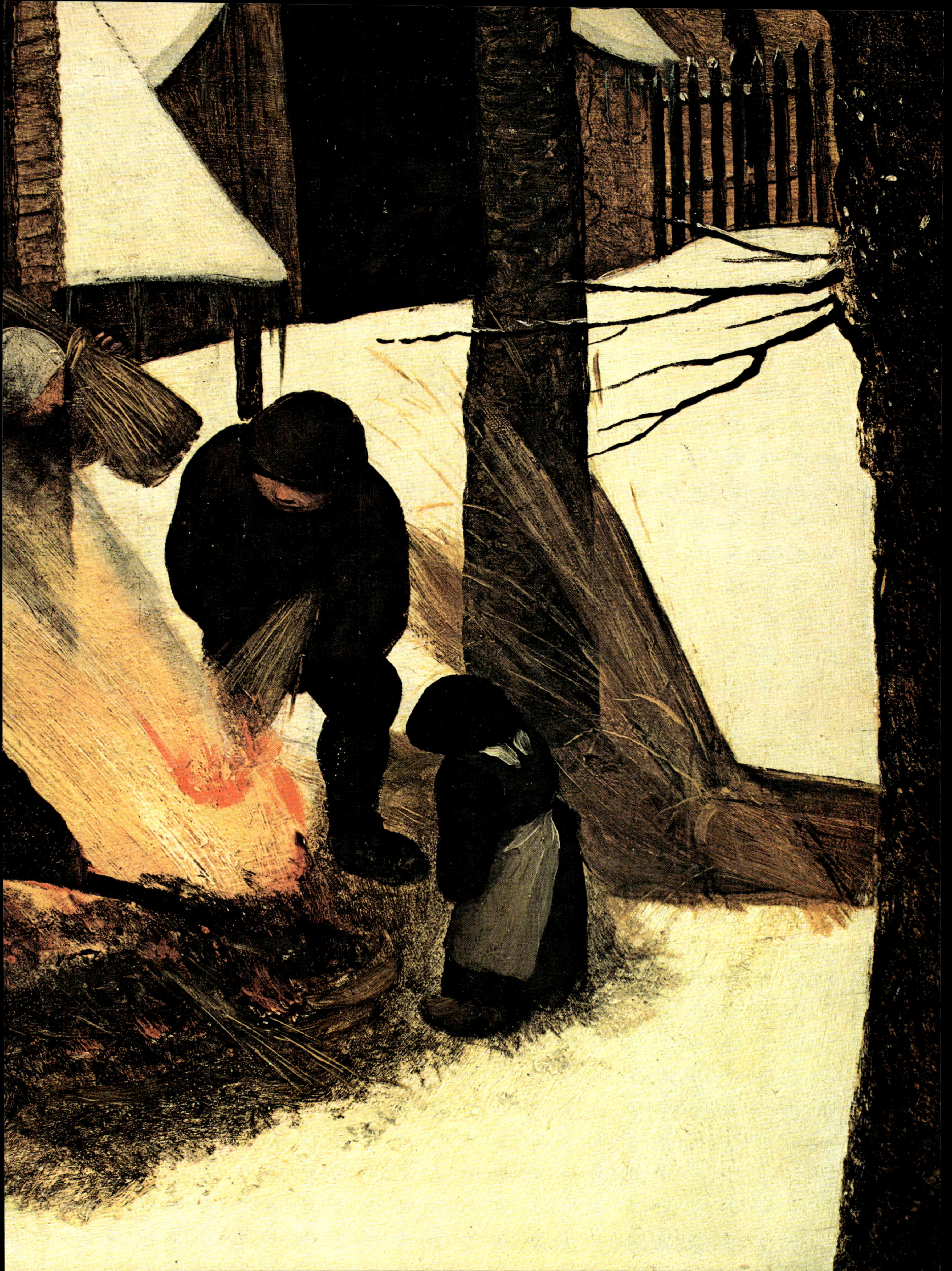

the ruin was enormous and Jan Gossart had already executed a drawing of it for Philip
the Fair in 1509. But most important of all for Bruegel was the impression of gigantic
size which he could only have obtained by seeing it himself – Goethe also, in the diary
describing his own Italian journey, speaks of the effect the sight had on him. Bruegel
thus evolved a vision of a Roman architectural monster, to which even the boldest of
today's urban planners and designers occasionally acknowledge a debt of gratitude and
whose terrifying scale dwarfs the megalomaniac inventors of all past cultures from the
pyramids through the Classicism of the French Revolution to the architecture of Fascism.
Some such consideration no doubt impelled Bruegel towards this brilliant visionary
achievement. The extraordinary structure expresses more than just transience: it speaks
of man's *hubris*, of the sheer wantonness of over-ambitious undertakings. The towers in
both pictures pass like mountains through the clouds and on towards the heavens: 'Go
to, let us build us a city and a tower, whose top may reach unto heaven; and let us make
us a name, lest we be scattered abroad upon the face of the whole earth.' There is a
sinister atmosphere in both pictures, which achieve their effect in different ways. The
larger version, now in Vienna, is executed in lighter ochre tones and unlike the one in
Rotterdam is fully signed and dated: it seems more massive and complex, impressing us
by the view into the very entrails of the tower and the amorphous surging of the bare
rock inside it. The Rotterdam version achieves a more menacing effect through its
proximity and height, the dramatic presence of the clouds and the disturbing darkness
of the facade itself, whose weather-worn lower storeys tell of its already considerable age.
Menzel offers an interesting interpretation of the striking architectural irregularities in
the Rotterdam tower. Owing to the confusion of tongues the builders were no longer
able to agree about the shape and size of the windows. As a result, some are entirely
open, others divided up by arches, small ones stand immediately next to quite big ones,
or gothic next to romanesque, indicating that even neighbours were no longer able to
understand one another. At the very top '… chaos reigns'.
There is disagreement as to which of the pictures Bruegel painted first but most experts
assign both works to the year 1563. The undated Rotterdam version, which is without
the Nimrod scene, where architects show King Nimrod sketches and plans for his ex-
travaganza, can be regarded either as a preliminary stage or else as a simplified and
smaller second version.
The extreme vividness and accuracy of detail in the reproduction of building aids, tools
and machines, cranes and winches, arch centerings, and so on have always aroused
admiration. This precision, which points to exceedingly thorough research and an
almost professional knowledge of contemporary construction techniques, is almost
totally lacking in the majority of later imitations, as is the ability to achieve Bruegel's
illusion of gigantic size. It was not by accident, therefore, that the Brussels City Council
commissioned Bruegel to record the building of the Antwerp-Brussels Canal, in 1565, in
a number of individual works, after he had shown how brilliantly he could handle even
the most difficult of architectural subjects. Jedlicka's contention that the tower has
subsided slightly to the left and that this may be an allusion to Pisa, is surely not to be
taken seriously: if any such impression really is present, it is due to the upward spiral
movement of the ramps forming the different storeys. The picture seems to depict the
moment at which construction has become completely bogged down and is coming to a
halt: the tower appears to be the millstone round the neck of the adjacent town, whose
resources it swallows up like an enormous sponge. Certain features of Antwerp have
been identified in the town, whose comparative scale emphasizes the proportions of the
tower. Auner saw a topical allusion in this, claiming that the tower was Bruegel's way of
saying farewell to Antwerp, the 'Babel of the contemporary world', whose financial
chaos was seen by pious souls as a tangible sign of higher powers taking a hand in the
sinful affairs of presumptuous man. Marijnissen quotes Marcus van Vaernewijck, who
compared the disputes among the Protestants (Lutherans, Calvinists, Anabaptists) with
the confusion of tongues accompanying the construction of the Tower of Babel. This has
led to the erroneous conclusion that Bruegel was using the tower to mock the Reformation. There has even been an optimistic, if somewhat grotesque, interpretation of the
tower as a glorification of the rise of Antwerp and of human achievement generally. In
the end, however, there can be no denying that the moral message of the work is about
the punishment of pride.
An enlarged copy of the Vienna version by Pieter Brueghel the Younger can be seen in
the Giuseppe Nehmad Collection in Milan.
The Flight into Egypt (page 83) came to the notice of scholars relatively late, only after
its acquisition by Count Seilern in 1939, and may perhaps represent a pause for breath
in Bruegel's creative effort. After his Herculean achievements of 1563, the artist now

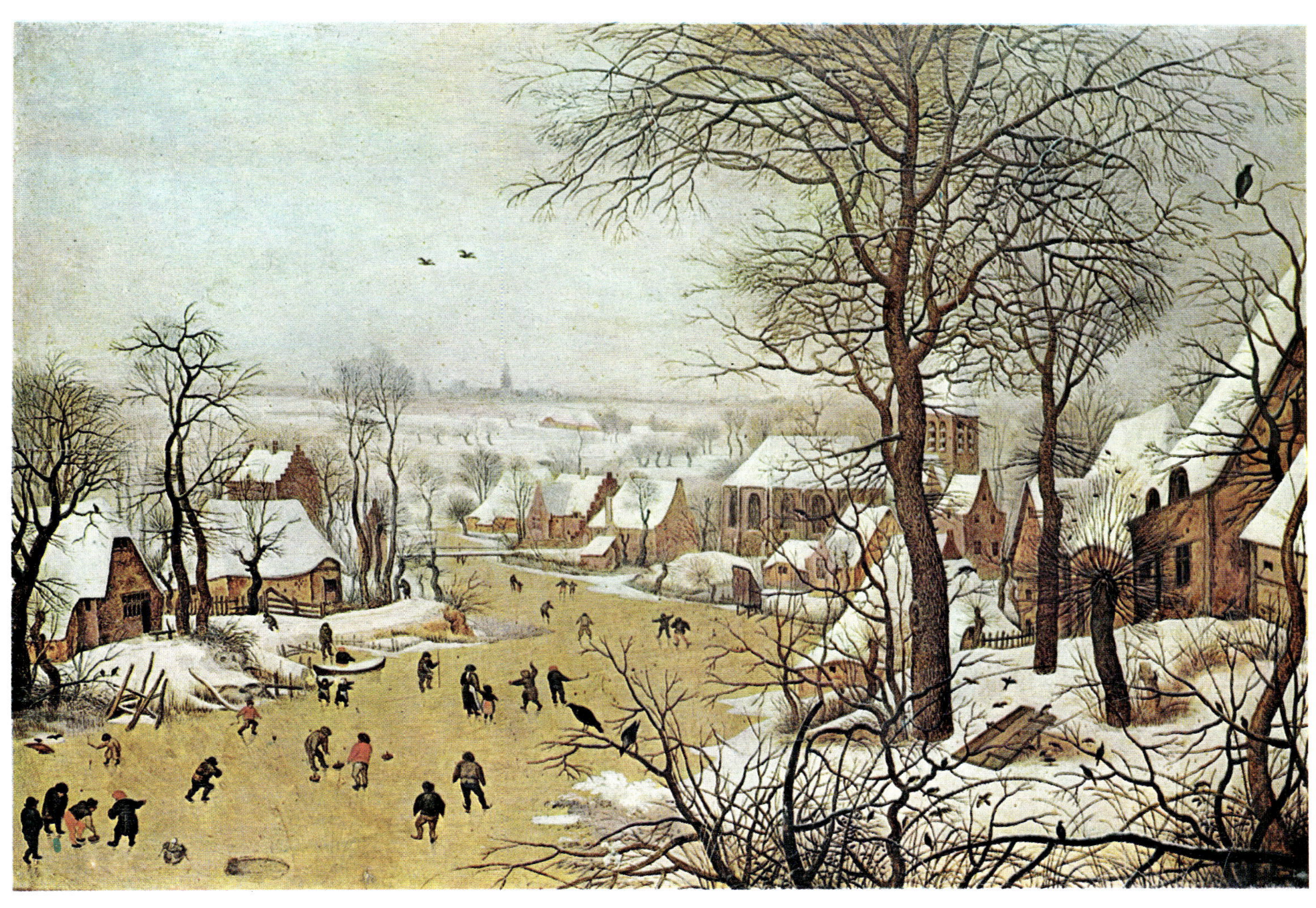

WINTER LANDSCAPE WITH SKATERS
AND A BIRD-TRAP
Oil on panel; 38 x 56 cm (15 x 22 in)
Signed and dated: 'BRVEGEL. M.D.LXV.'
Brussels, F. Delporte Collection
One of Bruegel's most copied works.
Executed in the same year as *Hunters in the
Snow*, this winter landscape has a quite
different atmosphere from the other; its
small size and 'natural' perspective made it
the prototype for 17th-century winter landscapes. The bird-trap on the right has been
interpreted as an analogy with the headless-
ness of the skaters, but no convincing
evidence for this theory has been produced.

returned to his beloved landscape art, and this landscape of 1563 is one of his most delightful. In format it is far more modest than the scenes of the months begun two years later, while its subject and composition still reveal a link with Netherlandish tradition. The theme of the flight into Egypt had been particularly popular since Patinir because it provided an ideal opportunity for the new school of landscape painters. Bruegel himself used it first for engraving (Bastelaer no. 15) and then in a drawing, now in Berlin, in which he gave preference to the more common treatment with the Holy Family shown at rest instead of travelling. Finally, in the present painting, he shows the family moving on their way. This is emphasized, as Grossman points out, by the fact that St. Joseph is shown with his back towards us, and, indeed, by his whole posture, which is echoed in the leaning willow-trunk on the right. On this trunk is an idol that has fallen forwards, a traditional emblem of the flight into Egypt. Derived from the *Apocrypha*, it symbolizes Christ's victory over heathendom.

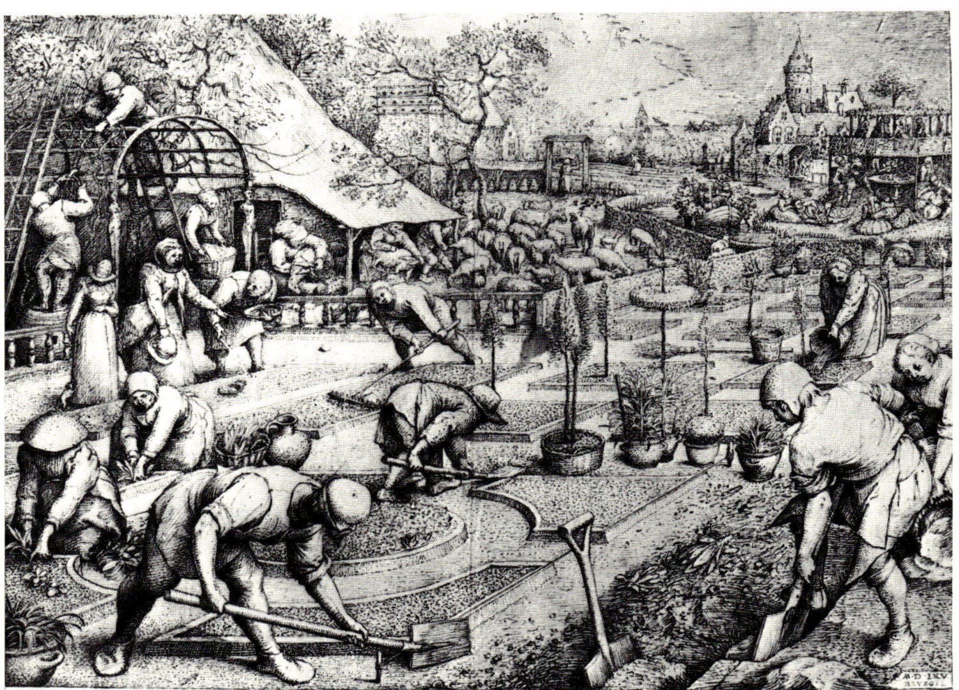

SPRING
Pen drawing in maroon on paper; 223 x 289 mm (8 x 11 in)
Signed and dated at bottom right: '.M.D.LXV. / BREVGEL'
The band at the bottom has the words: 'de lenten Mert April Meij'
Vienna, Graphische Sammlung Albertina
Preparatory drawing for the engraving by P. van der Heyden (Bastelaer 200). This drawing was the first of the series which Bruegel intended to dedicate to the seasons. The second drawing, *Summer* (p. 152), was executed in 1568. After the master's death the series was completed by Hans Bol. Bruegel here brings together the activities traditionally associated with the springtime months (sowing in March, sheep-shearing in April and gallant adventures in May).

To some extent Bruegel has produced a 'panoramic landscape' along the lines of his 1557 *Landscape with the Parable of the Sower* (pages 40–41) and he also freely uses Alpine motifs from the 'Large Landscape' series of engravings, but the individual elements are here more naturally and more skilfully interlinked. The masses of rock in both foreground and background are located well over to the left, this heavy emphasis on the picture's left-hand side contrasting with the loose structure of the right with the broad expanse of sea. Here we find the Holy Family, with Joseph advancing exactly through the central axis. This half of the composition is enlivened by various individual features like the dead pine, the willow stump and the mysterious rocky island in the sea, and rounded off by the two thin trees at the edge.

Christ Carrying the Cross (pages 94–95) is the most ambitious in scale of all Bruegel's works, and is the last and most accomplished of the small-figure compositions which began with the *Proverbs* and *Children's Games.* At the same time it takes a long Netherlandish tradition to a final peak of perfection which was never surpassed. It had been customary since Jan van Eyck to depict the procession to Calvary with a multitude of figures in contemporary costumes in a familiar European landscape. A much-discussed work in the Albertina and a painting in the Suermondt Museum in Aachen are copies of a lost picture depicting this theme which in its turn goes back to a composition from the circle of van Eyck known only through a copy in Budapest. The work in the Albertina, probably copied from a painting by Jean Fouquet, was long thought to be by Bruegel; but this view has recently been questioned. Martin Schongauer's famous engraving and the work by Hieronymus Bosch should also be taken into consideration. But Bruegel's painting is much closer to several more recent works such as the versions of *Christ Carrying the Cross* by the Brunswick Monogrammist Jan van Amstel (page 90), Pieter Aertsen (1552, page 91), Herri met de Bles, Joachim Bueckelaer (1563), and others. These painters depicted the theme several times and Bruegel himself made two versions, one of which has been lost. Whether the latter is preserved in the copies executed by Romdahl and Marlier is more than doubtful. The works by van Amstel and Pieter Aertsen – whose artistic and family links with Bruegel have already been discussed – clearly reveal Bruegel's debt to them, while at the same time illustrating the immense artistic gulf dividing them from the great master.

A further dimension was added to the Biblical event as it became increasingly coloured with the subject-matter of a contemporary execution. Bruegel reduced the main figure of Christ even further in size, but set Him at the very centre of the picture. Although this is a common expedient adopted by the Mannerists, there is a greater significance in Bruegel's composition. By making Christ so inconspicuous, the artist stresses the indifference of the crowd to what is happening, its blindness to the unique importance of the event. The mass of people fail to recognize the significance of this crucifixion and if Christ were crucified again they would fail to recognize it a second time, taking it for a popular entertainment as they do in the picture here. The windmill on the outcrop of rock is perhaps intended as a symbol of eternal change, of the recurrence of historical events, as in the proverb '*Dat gaat zoo wast als een omloopende Windmolen*' ('It turns like the sails of a windmill'): one also appears in van Amstel's work. However, Bruegel gives us an iconographical clue in the triangular group comprising Mary, John and two holy women in the foreground. These are distinguished from the mass of contemporary figures by their idealized apparel and the old-fashioned, 15th century style in which they are composed, as well as by the difference of scale. The group confirms the basic theme of the whole picture, underlining the completion of events which still lie in the future. Bruegel achieves dramatic effect by showing the lead-up to the crucifixion, as in earlier versions of the same theme. We have to overcome a variety of optical obstacles before arriving at Christ himself, whose fall beneath the weight of the cross is the only scene without spectators. Thus Jesus finds himself abandoned on the way to Golgotha just as previously on the Mount of Olives and later on the cross.

The riders clad in red, one of them carrying an imperial flag, have been seen as a political allusion to the hated Walloon horsemen – the so-called *roode rocx* or red-coats – who were in the service of the Spaniards. They also appear in the *Massacre of the Innocents*. But the allusion, if any such was intended, does not seem to have diminished the Emperor Rudolph II's love of Bruegel's art. The painter has carefully incorporated the red of the riders as a slightly undulating line along the picture's horizontal axis, accompanied further down by a less accentuated ripple of blue garments. The technical expertise, and the wealth of observation which have gone into this composition, so brimming with life are stunning. Only a profound depth of feeling and grasp of characterization could have enabled Bruegel, despite the tiny scale, to depict so tellingly the deathly pale faces of the two thieves as they are driven in a cart to the place of execution, accompanied by their confessors, a Franciscan and a Dominican. Another brilliant detail is the group on the left with the recalcitrant Simon of Cyrene, whom the soldiers are compelling to help Christ carry the cross and whose wife is doing everything she can to prevent it. The rosary at her side symbolizes the hypocrisy of those whose faith fails them when put to the slightest test. It has been said that the postures are reminiscent of Bruegel's lost drawing entitled *The Epileptic Woman of Meulebeecke*. No detail has been forgotten in this work: the mud dripping from the cart's wheel-spokes and the boy on the shaft adroitly pulling in his feet as they go through the ford are two striking examples of the artist's consummate thoroughness, and there is enormous variety in the attitudes of those accompanying the procession of condemned men; some hurrying to secure a good vantage point for the coming spectacle, some staring stolidly or rushing past unconcernedly, others showing anxiety or overcome with emotion, like the group on the right behind Mary. Despite this abundance of detail, however, no sketches for the picture have survived. The *Two Spectators* on the back of one of the *naer het leven* drawings in Rotterdam was always thought to be one of Bruegel's very rare studies. But since the elimination of the *naer het leven* group from Bruegel's oeuvre it has been regarded as a copy by R. Savery after Bruegel. The same applies to the second drawing, now in Uppsala, and considered to be an authentic Bruegel study for one of the hunters in *Winter*. Strangely enough it seems there is not one single known surviving figure study for a painting by Bruegel.

Jedlicka, whose studies published in 1936 are still unequalled, was the first to recognize the profundity of the composition, which rests partly on the contrast between the left-hand and right-hand halves of the picture. On the left lies Jerusalem in the midst of a sunny landscape; on the right is Golgotha, the Place of the Skull. On the left, the green tree rises as an emblem of life: on the right is a dead tree-trunk surmounted by a wheel of torture. To the left the sky has the brightness of summer; to the right it is clouding

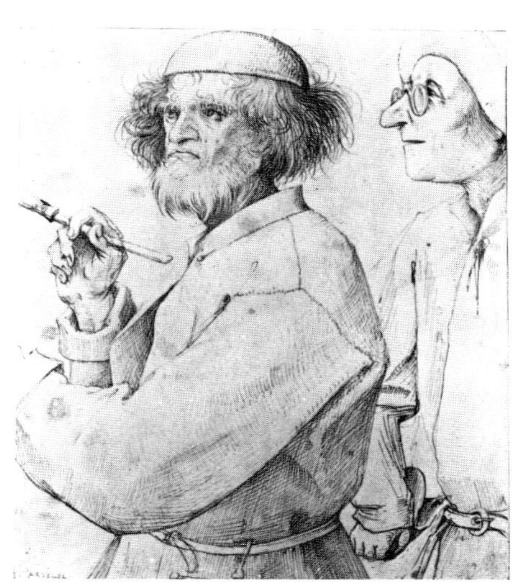

ARTIST AND 'CRITIC'
Pen drawing in maroon on paper; 250 x 216 mm (9 x 8½ in)
c. 1565
Signed at bottom left in lighter ink: 'BRVEGEL' (the authenticity of the signature is in doubt)
Vienna, Graphische Sammlung Albertina
This undated composition is regarded as a mature work and has been variously interpreted. It certainly expresses an entirely unsatisfactory relation between artist and layman (for this reason the word 'critic' in the title is put in inverted commas to emphasise the irony of the term). The painter has also been interpreted as a self-portrait of Bruegel or as an ideal portrait of H. Bosch, but both hypotheses are probably mistaken. Almost certainly conceived as a work for its own sake and not for engraving, this drawing was much appreciated by Bruegel's contemporaries, as demonstrated by the four copies which exist (London, Korda Collection and British Museum; Berne, Kornfeld Collection; Vienna, Christian Nebehay).

over, already providing a sinister suggestion of the approaching eclipse of the sun described in the Bible. The procession moves from life to death, from light to darkness, and between life and death lie all the possibilities of human existence.

Brief mention may also be made of Auner's interpretation of this work as a confession of Anabaptism. Auner bases his contention that Bruegel was an Anabaptist chiefly on the *Sermon of St. John the Baptist* (pages 134–135), but he also saw evidence for his theory in *Christ Carrying the Cross*, where the pedlar resting in the left foreground, who also features on the left in Aertsen's treatment of the same theme (page 91), is the disseminator of forbidden writings. These wandering chapmen actually did carry assorted forbidden material at the bottom of their bags. Auner sees the Anabaptist doctrine of suffering along with Christ embodied in the onlookers by the tree-trunk on the right – with Bruegel himself apparently among them. The crucial aspect of this, according to the theory, is the act of self-debasement: contact with executioners, gallows and everything to do with them made a man 'impure', 'dishonest'. The young woman is Bruegel's wife, the man next to her an Anabaptist preacher. The composition as a whole is the most brilliant expression of the Anabaptist *humilitas Christi*, the doctrine of Christ's human nature. Auner does not fail to realize that this treatment of the theme has also appeared before Bruegel, and concludes that all the painters involved – Jan van Amstel, Herri met de Bles, Pieter Aertsen and others – were Anabaptists. Even if one rejects Auner's theory that Bruegel was an Anabaptist, his comments on the group at the tree-trunk are valuable and convincing. It can be assumed that the bearded man with the cap really is a very small but authentic self-portrait of Bruegel.

The Adoration of the Magi (page 92) now in London, returns to the theme treated by Bruegel in the early canvas painting, with its multitude of figures, which is in Brussels (pages 24–25). The development is manifest, and the picture in London is remarkable in a number of ways. It is the only vertical-format painting by Bruegel and the first of his works to feature large-scale figures which take up almost the whole of the picture. Since Hulin de Loo, it has also been repeatedly cited as an example of the artist making use of Italian influences. Michelangelo, Parmigianino and Correggio have been adduced, one conjecture being that the Child was influenced by the one in Michelangelo's *Madonna of Bruges* (1503–1504). But this is surely unfounded, for the Child in the *Madonna of Bruges* is standing, whereas Bruegel's is sitting. The only similarity consists in the position of the hands and head, but the same motif occurs frequently in all contemporary Italian art. Stridbeck refers to an early *Adoration of the Magi* of 1503 by Raphael, in the Vatican, which he claims has many details in common with Bruegel's work. But a direct link cannot be established. Stridbeck's other example, that of the Antwerp Master of 1518, is much more convincing from the point of view of compositional similarity. The London *Adoration* seems to have been influenced at least as strongly, if not more so, by the Netherlandish tradition of the 15th century as exemplified, for instance, by Hugo van Goes. Moreover, the subject is so common in painting from the 15th century onwards that inspiration would certainly have been derived from the totality of works rather than from any single one alone. Obviously, Bruegel was experimenting with a fusion or synthesis. And indeed, despite its magnificence, the picture contains some awkward features, a confusion of northern and southern compositional principles, which mark it as a transitional work. The spatial treatment is unusual: the (unseen) ground-level at the back can hardly be a continuation of the foreground, as we can see from the positions of the figures. Jedlicka refers to the traditional arrangement of the colour scheme, as in the group with Mary and John in *Christ Carrying the Cross*, to Bruegel's inability to breathe new religious life into this traditional scene, and to the clash between life and art. Peasant faces surmount royal robes, and Mary combines the features of a peasant girl with the characteristics of the classic Italian Madonna. The figures are grouped in a circle around the unnaturally small Baby in the centre of the picture, arranged not 'in relation to a presumed ground-level but to the space all around them ... He lies, helpless and closed like a bud, in the Madonna's lap, the future hope of mankind – the painting's poetic focus, from which an awesome sense of humility goes out, holding all present in its spell,' to quote Dvořák. Contrast this with the blank stare of the soldier with the halberd, whom Menzel describes as 'unable to grasp this total reversal of the world order – a king kneeling before a child'. The other figures, too, are beautifully characterized: the burly, peasant form of St. Joseph leaning over slightly to catch a whisper, the magic in the facial expression of Balthasar, the Moorish king (an echo of Bosch in the Prado). Stechow thinks the words being whispered in Joseph's ear are to do with the gossip surrounding doubts about Mary's chastity. For Jedlicka this detail is an expedient designed to bring St. Joseph – always a difficult figure to incorporate in the scene – into closer association with

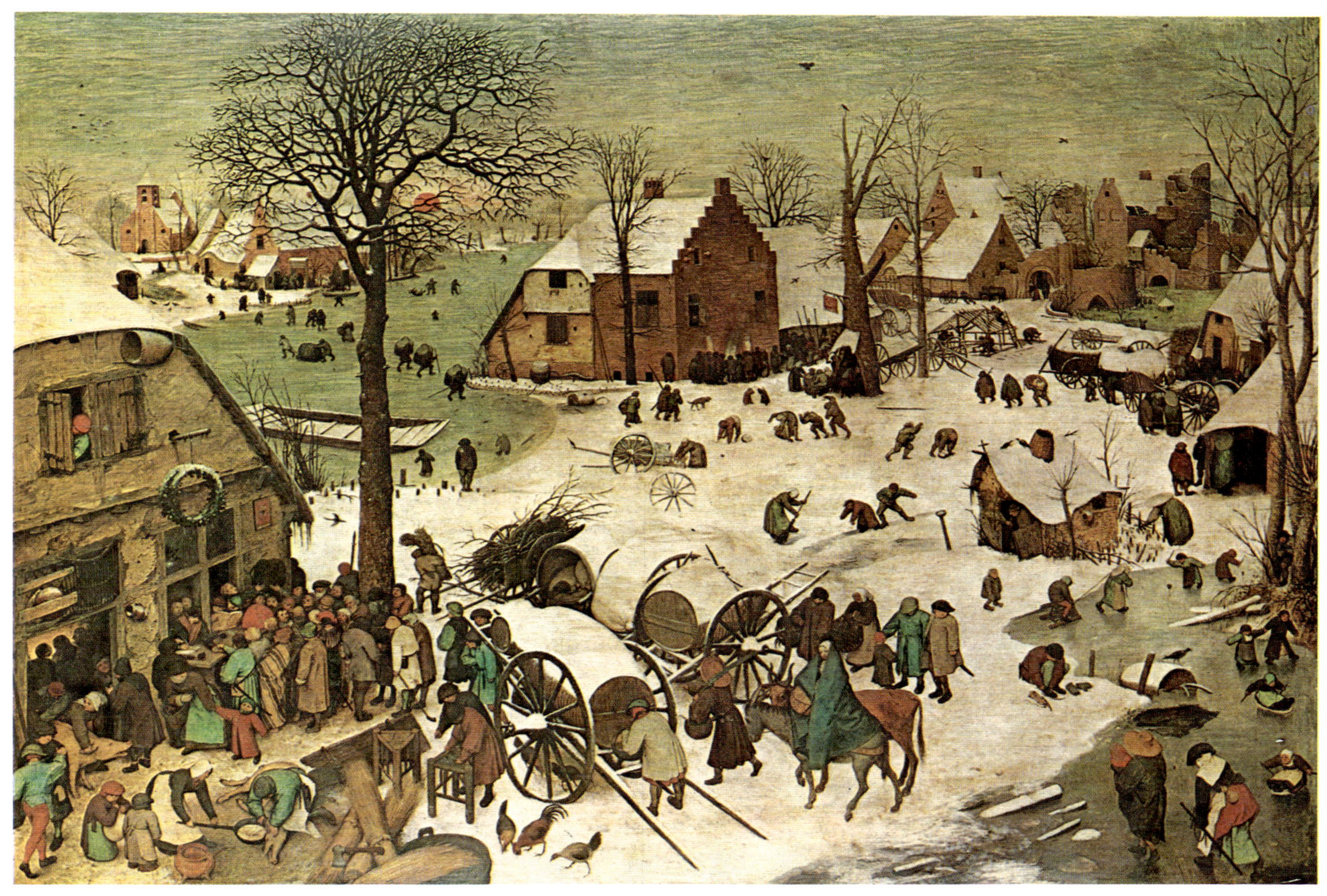

THE CENSUS AT BETHLEHEM
Oil on panel; 115.5 x 163.5 cm (45½ x 64 in)
Signed and dated: 'BRVEGEL 1566'
Brussels, Musées Royaux des Beaux-Arts
The painting came to the Museum in 1902
from a private collection in Antwerp (sale of
the E. Huysbrechts Collection). The subject
is taken from the Gospel according to St.
Luke (2; 1–5). Depictions of this event – the
payment of tithes – was unusual in Bruegel's
day; this and the fact that the people are
shown in contemporary dress – a method dear
to Bruegel – suggest that the artist wished to
allude to the political events of the day. The
winter landscape, quite different from the
preceding ones, contains a wealth of detail
which reveals Bruegel's minute observation
of nature.
Detail on *pages 130–131*

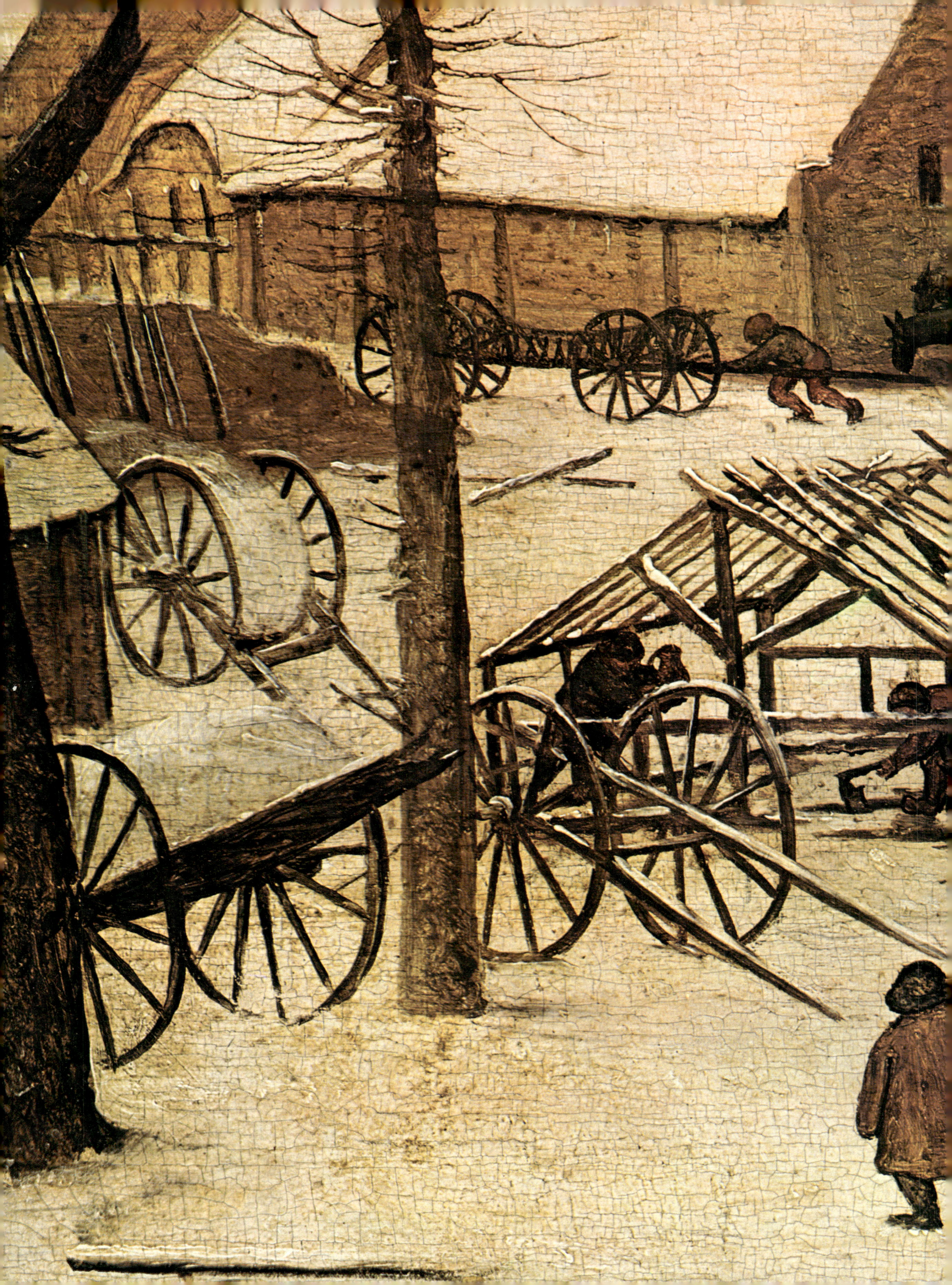

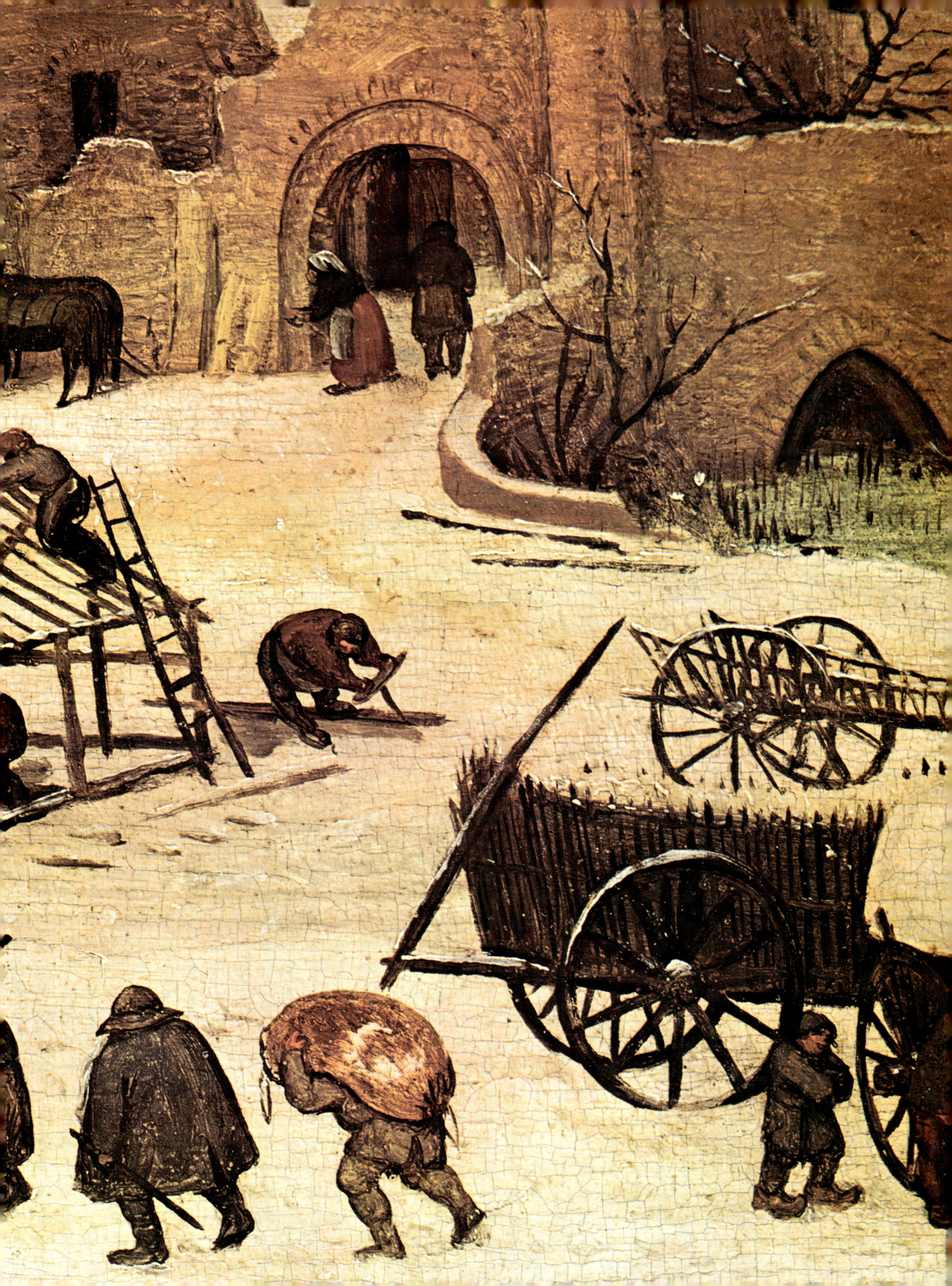

the crowd around him. Auner interprets the man on the far left as the humanist who commissioned the picture, 'whose profound devotion – in contrast to the blank gaping of the others – establishes his inward affinity with the holy event'. The man on the far right, surely also a portrait from life, he sees as the very opposite, an intellectual sceptic. Jedlicka speaks of the 'stolid yet violent world' reflected on the faces of the onlookers: the whole event, he says, is like a mystery play in which the people participate not only as spectators but as actors, where every individual recognizes every other – through whatever mask – as his like.

Again, great care has gone into every detail: the grain of the wooden beams; the gift proffered by the Moorish king, a golden ship with a paper nautilus of the type common in contemporary Mannerist applied art; the hem on the robe of the king kneeling on the left, depicting the four elements. There is a copy of the picture by Pieter Brueghel the Younger, and Jan Brueghel the Elder re-used some of the figures for three of his own works, including the *Adoration* in Vienna.

After this experiment Bruegel soon abandoned religious group compositions with large figures, and there are only two small grisailles with religious subjects: the *Death of the Virgin* (page 100) and *Christ and the Woman Taken in Adultery* (page 101), which belong to the same period. Bruegel had used grisaille in his very first work, the altar for the Glovers' Guild in Malines, undertaken in 1551, now lost and known only through surviving documents. He probably painted the *Death of the Virgin* for Abraham Ortelius, who had it engraved by Philip Galle in 1574 for distribution to his friends. In

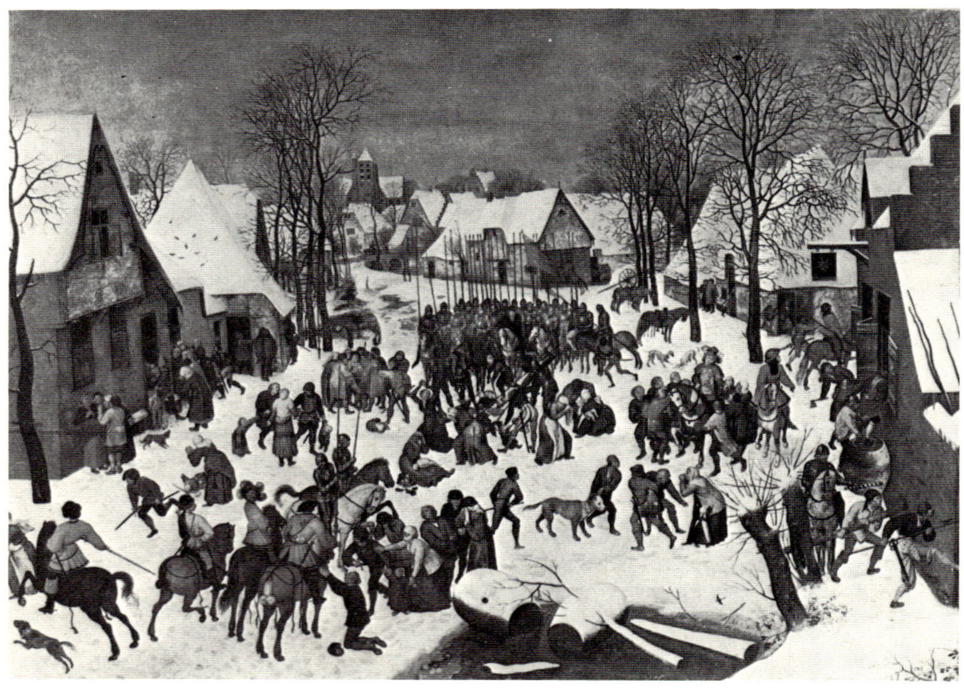

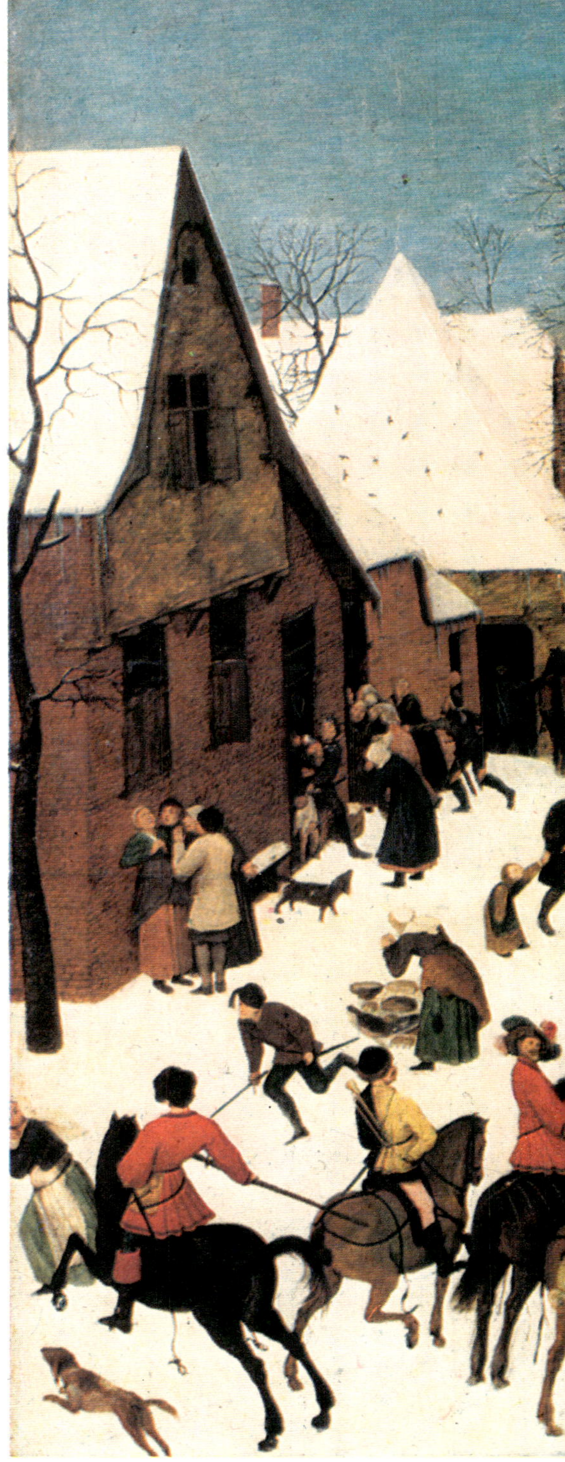

THE MASSACRE OF THE INNOCENTS
Oil on panel; 116 x 160 cm (45 x 63 in)
Signed: 'BRVEG.'; not dated
c. 1564(?)
Vienna, Kunsthistorisches Museum
Both versions of this painting are in a bad state of preservation and both have been regarded at various times as originals or studio works retouched by the master. Once again Bruegel represents a biblical episode in contemporary guise: as a punitive expedition into a Flemish village. Like the other version, this one has been taken to refer to actual events and particularly to acts of repression by the Duke of Alba.

1640 it was in the possession of Rubens. Discovered by scholars at a relatively late date, its authenticity has been called into question several times since 1931, but with no good reason. An unusual feature is the large throng of mourners. Bruegel here follows the *Golden Legend* of Jacobus de Voragine, who speaks of the patriarchs, martyrs, confessors and holy virgins present when the Mother of God was re-united with her Son. Bruegel is unusually bold in his treatment of light, long before Caravaggio, Georges de la Tour or Rembrandt. Natural sources of light like the open fire and candles – the one on the table illuminating a still-life, those on the wall the beamed ceiling – contrast with the supernatural glow around Mary's head. But the figure sleeping on the left is also illuminated by an invisible light, and has been interpreted as St. John the Evangelist. In view of his isolated position it has been suggested that the whole death-bed scene is being dreamt by the sleeping figure, who sees it as though he were actually there. The error of perspective in the chair-back in the foreground can no more be regarded as a mistake by Bruegel (it was corrected in the engraving) than the pancakes on the roof in the *Children's Games*. This chair-back has been explained as a compositional link between the main group and the sleeping figure, but it may have an entirely different significance. A coloured copy exists of the *Death of the Virgin*.

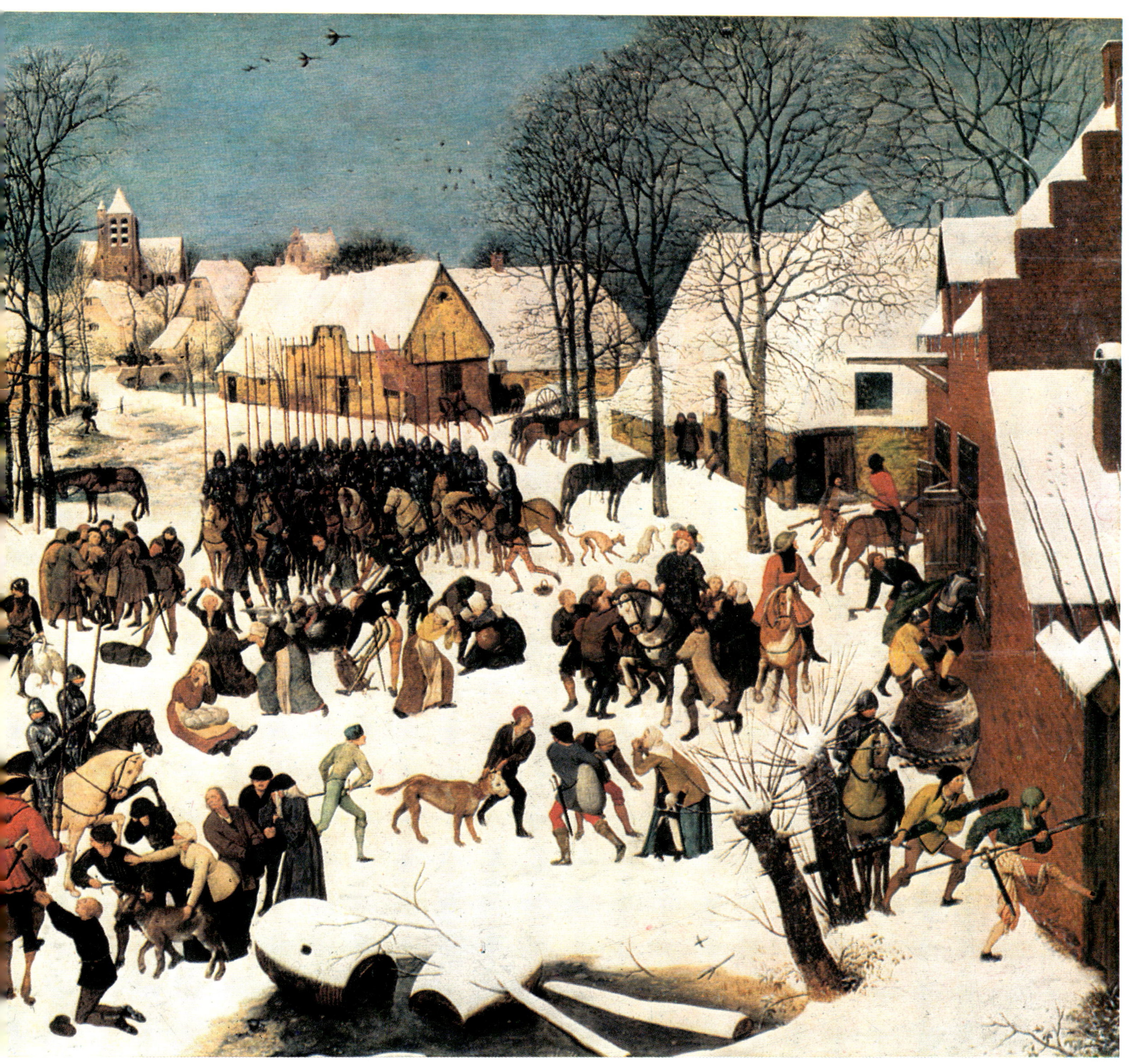

THE MASSACRE OF THE INNOCENTS
Oil on panel; 109.2 x 154.9 cm (43 x 61 in)
Neither signed nor dated
Hampton Court, Royal Collection
X-ray analyses carried out on Grossmann's
initiative have shown that this work, always
regarded as one of the various copies in existence, is in fact authentic; it is in a poor
state of preservation owing to early res-
toration and overpainting, and very little of
the original now remains. The overpainting
of the children and certain other obvious
modifications suggest deliberate concealment
of over-obvious allusions.

THE SERMON OF ST. JOHN THE
BAPTIST
Oil on panel; 95 x 160.5 cm (37 x 63½ in)
Signed and dated: 'BRVEGEL.M.D.LXVI'
Budapest, Szépmüvészeti Múzeum
The picture was formerly owned by Count
Batthyány and came to the Museum in 1951.
It has proved difficult to establish whether
this is the version which was in the collection
of the Regent Isabella in Brussels, as
Grossmann assumes; and uncertainty also
attaches to Auner's theory that Batthyany

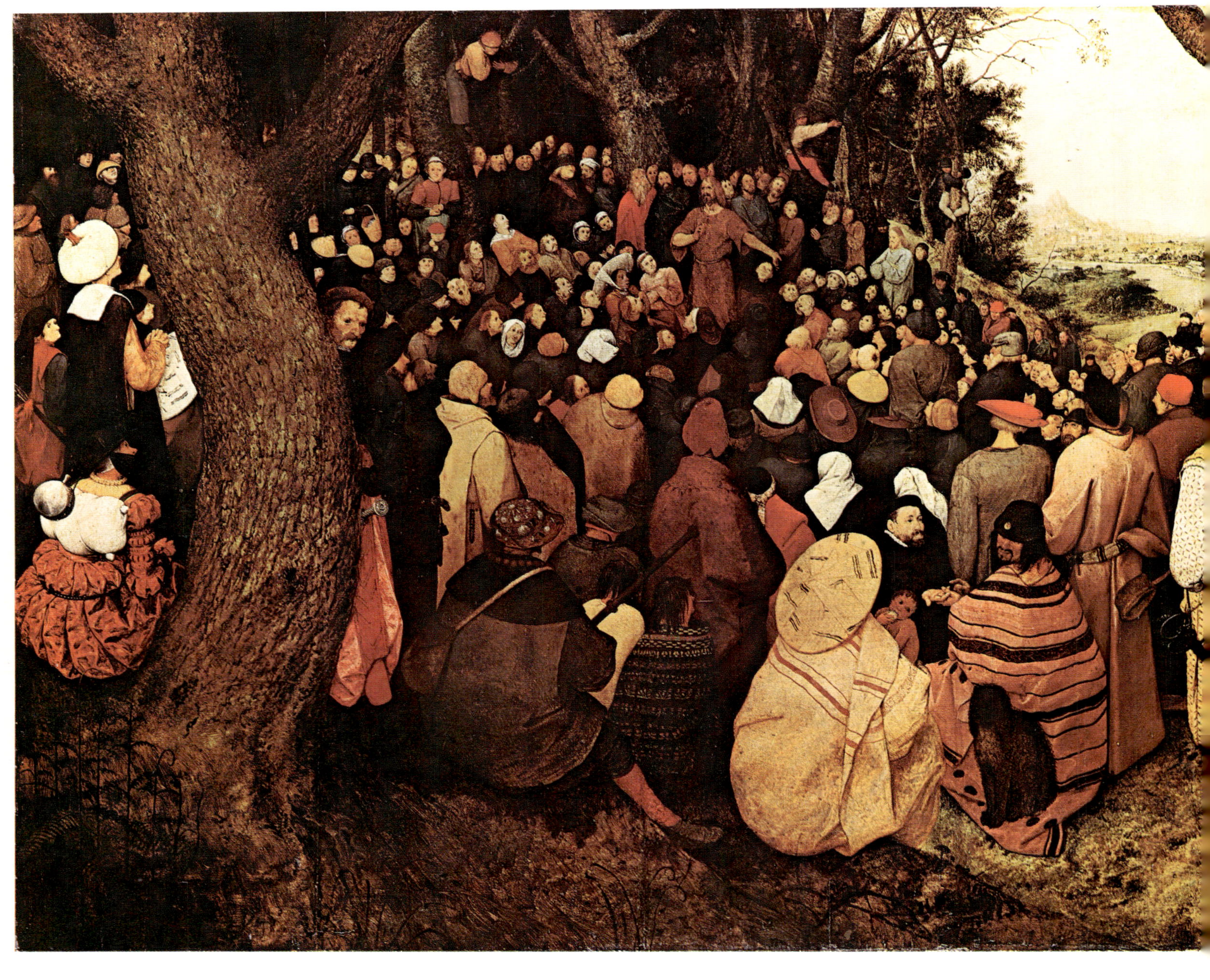

commissioned a painting with an Anabaptist theme from Bruegel direct. However, it is probable that this peaceful assembly in the open air is meant to represent an Anabaptist gathering. The scene with the man having his hand read by a gypsy must have had some profound significance as it is left out of almost all the copies.

Detail on *pages 136–137*

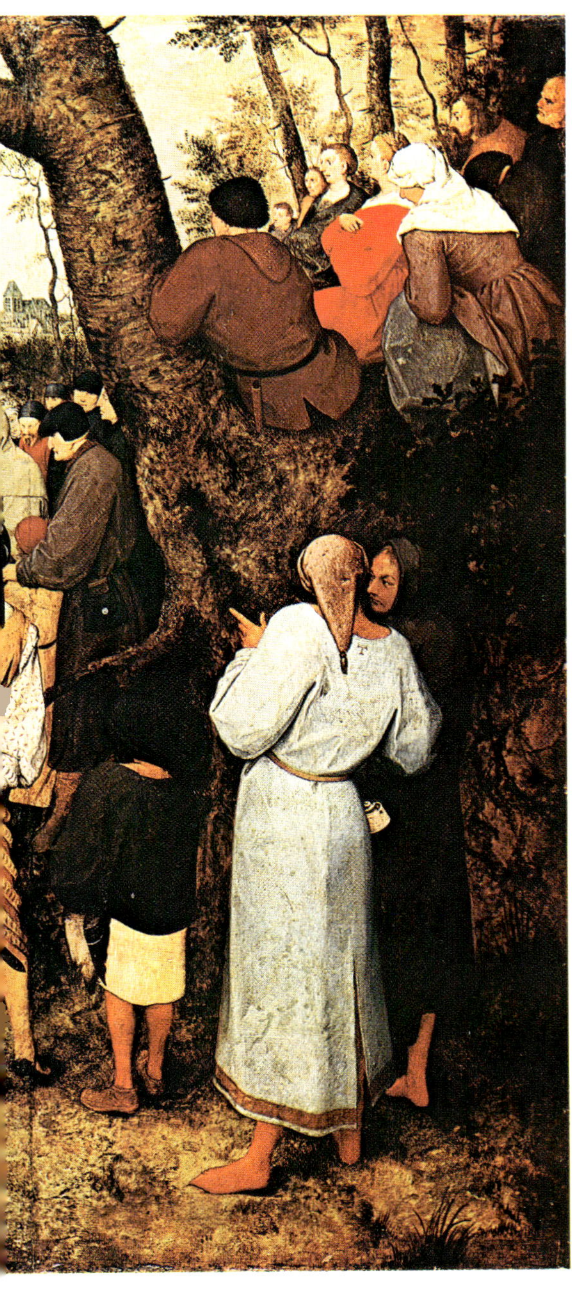

The second grisaille, *Christ and the Woman Taken in Adultery* (page 101), is dated 1565 and has a deliberate moral content. Bruegel left it to his family, in whose possession it remained for a while after his death, until his son Jan Brueghel left it in his will to the Archbishop of Milan, Cardinal Federigo Borromeo. Jan Brueghel the Elder wrote to the Cardinal in 1609 to say he had not succeeded in finding a painting by his father anywhere in the art market because the Emperor Rudolph II had spent large sums of money buying up every work of Bruegel's he could find. This was the only picture by his father which Jan possessed and he left it to the Cardinal in a will dated 12 January 1625. Jan Brueghel the Younger re-acquired it from the Cardinal. Then in the 18th century it disappeared from view in England until Count Seilern bought it in London in 1952. The painting appears to have been held in very high esteem: in 1579 Pierre Perret executed an engraving straight from the original, as we can tell from the small punctures along the edge of the painting where the tracing paper was attached. Thirteen painted copies also exist, seven in grisaille and six in colour. These two grisailles are a rarity among Bruegel's works, having no hint of landscape whatever. The question of Italian influence has been raised, particularly in the case of *Christ and the Woman Taken in Adultery*: Stridbeck cites a weak composition on the same subject attributed to Pieter Coecke in Ghent Museum. More convincing, perhaps, is Grossmann's reference to Raphael's tapestry cartoons, now in the Victoria and Albert Museum, London, which in Bruegel's day were in Brussels and 'among which the *Healing of the Lame Man* seems to have been the direct prototype' of Bruegel's composition. On the other hand the Pharisee's forward-leaning posture, if laterally inverted, recalls the spectator in Hieronymus Bosch's *Magician*. The figure of the Pharisee on the right is reminiscent of Bruegel's drawing *Four Men in Conversation*, in the Louvre.

A remarkably skilful combination of light and dark sets off the protagonists against the onlookers – the Apostles on the left, the Pharisees on the right. The woman taken in adultery, standing in the midline of the composition, looks down at Christ as he writes the famous sentence from Chapter 8 of St. John's Gospel on the temple floor: 'He that is without sin among you, let him first cast a stone at her.' Stridbeck calls attention to a picture on the same subject by Lambert Lombard (?) in which the Biblical text is replaced by the famous oracular saying written up in the temple of Delphi: *Nosse te ipsum* (Know thyself). He sees this as an example of religious universalism, where classical philosophy and Christine doctrine are regarded as equally credib e, parallel approaches, an attitude which Bruegel himself could well have held. And Grossmann has concluded from letters written by Ortelius that this grisaille was intended as an urgent call for tolerance in the violent religious conflicts of the time.

We might at this juncture mention two other grisailles occasionally attributed to Bruegel: *The Visit to the Tenant Farm* in the museum at Antwerp and the *Three Soldiers* in the Frick Collection, New York, signed and dated 1568. A coloured copy of the first of these by Jan Brueghel the Elder exists in the Kunsthistorisches Museum, Vienna, as well as other copies. The one in Antwerp is probably, like the one in Vienna, by Jan Brueghel the Elder. The *Three Soldiers* almost certainly dates from the early 17th century, but the signature is doubtful and the year has been retouched.

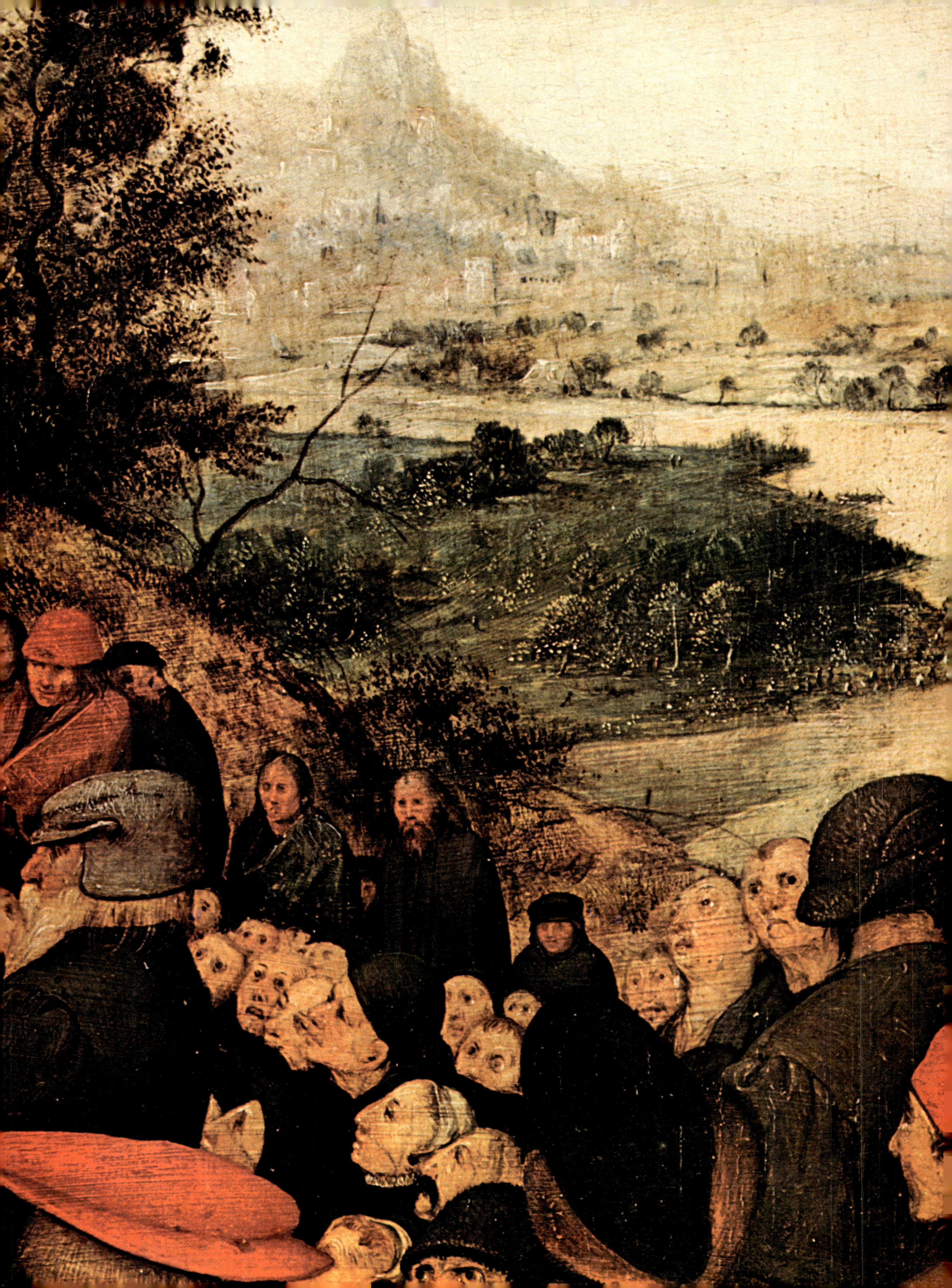

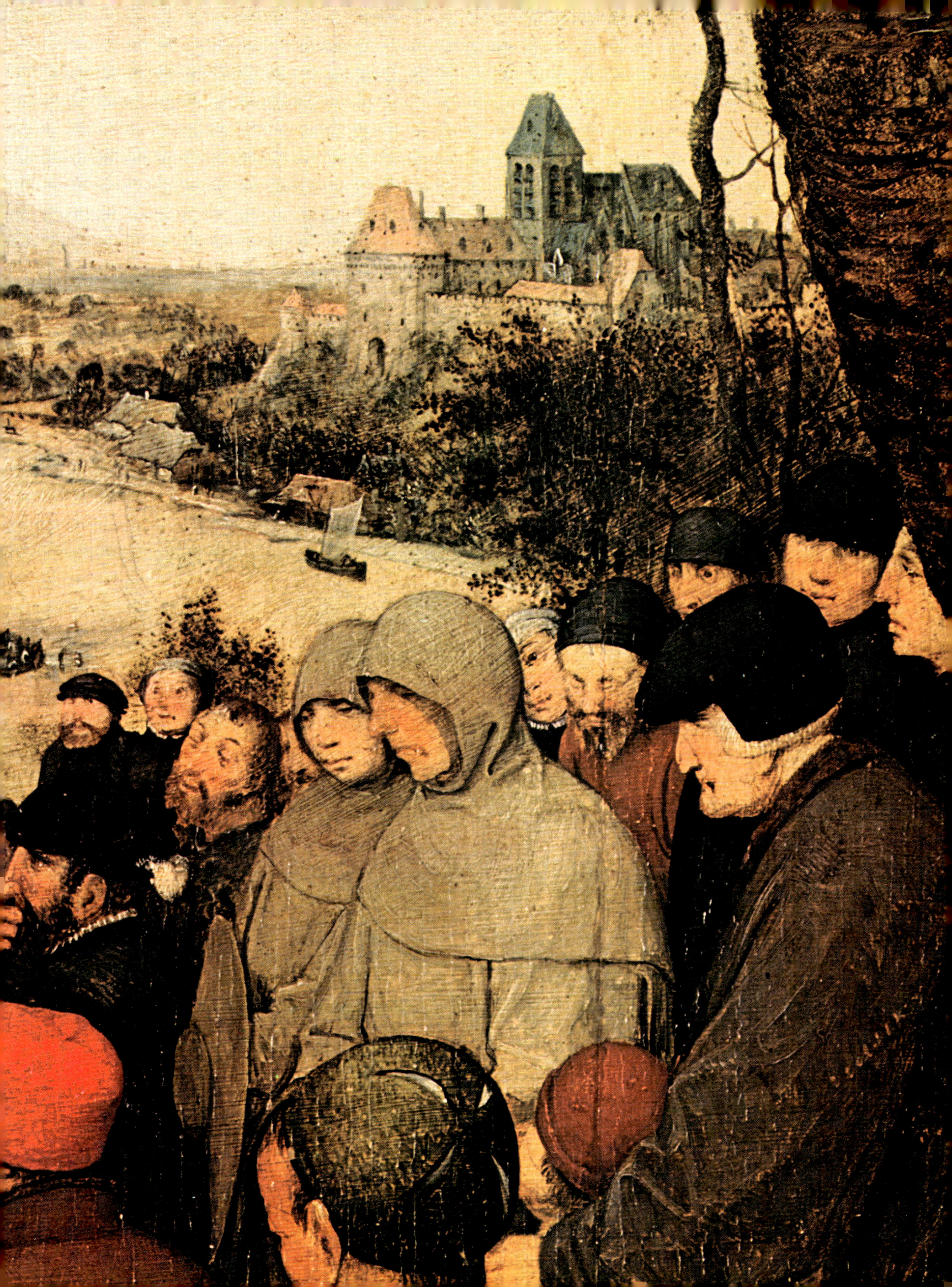

The so-called *Months* series – and more will be said about the need to correct this title – brings us to the unrivalled peak of 16th-century landscape art. Nothing comparable exists either before or after Bruegel. It represents a happy, if rare, combination of vision and faithfulness to nature, concept and reality, freedom and severity, general and particular, all fused together in the harmony of a natural world which includes man – and the peasant *par excellence* – as an integral part of its unending cycle. Compared with the universality of Bruegel's treatment all later landscapes seem parochial, contrived to satisfy some particular interest of the artist's: mood, light, pantheism, exotica, faithfulness to nature, impressionism, and so on. As Jedlicka points out: 'Later generations of landscape painters in the 17th century were less acute than Bruegel in their perception of nature. His own profound, first-hand experience invested him with a different feeling for the natural environment, a different degree of flexibility in the reproduction of organic life and the atmospheric mood of the landscape. It's as though he had worked not in the studio but in the landscape itself, not just drawing but painting there too, only putting the finishing touches to his work in the studio. But of course it wasn't like that at all. His landscape painting reveals him as a man of the modern age, for he seems to possess other sensitivities than his contemporaries. His landscapes are more than just manifestations of an unusually intense experience of nature, of an almost uncanny vision of space which must have been totally incomprehensible to his own age ...'. Much of 17th and 18th-century landscape painting was not simply anticipated by Bruegel but actually dictated by him, the exceptions being Rubens and Rembrandt. The story of how the *Months* came to be painted is a complex one. In the first place, it is not certain how many works the cycle originally comprised. Five survive, so there may have been a total of either six or twelve. A large amount of research by Novotny, Grossmann and others has produced the following thesis. There seems no doubt that the series was commissioned by the Antwerp collector Nicolaes Jonghelinck, brother of the sculptor Jacques Jonghelinck whose patron was Granvella. It is also highly likely that the series originally consisted not of twelve paintings, as Auner and Grossmann insist, but of only six. The combination of two consecutive months to give a total cycle of six may be unusual, but is not unheard of. We know that Jonghelinck pledged sixteen works by Bruegel, twenty-two by Frans Floris and one by Dürer as surety for a debt of 10,000 guilders owed by Daniel de Bruyne to the city of Antwerp. The pictures duly went to the city in the same year and were later presented as a gift to the Archduke Ernst. Bruegel's pictures formed part of an ambitious decor for Jonghelinck's palatial house in Antwerp, possibly in the form of a frieze-like band running round below the ceiling in one of the rooms. A document dated 21 February 1565 and published by J. Denucé in 1932 mentions 'the Twelve Months' among Bruegel's pictures, but as Tolnay rightly pointed out, the words *Twaelf maenden* (twelve months) could apply only to the title of the series, not to the number of pictures. Grossmann thinks it unlikely that, assuming the *Months* to consist of six pictures, six other pictures were mentioned without their titles, whereas the titles of all twenty-one pictures by Floris are given. This is one of his main reasons for concluding, as Jedlicka did before him, that there must have been twelve *Months*. Another important point here is that in those days in the Netherlands, the year began at Easter, and according to our current method of calculating time, the document mentioned above has to be dated 21 February 1566. Only on 1 January 1557 was the year deemed to start on 1 January. Otherwise we should also be faced with chronological difficulties, since all the *Months* except one are dated 1565.

The final solution to the problem seems to be provided by an entry made in the Archduke's Ernst's cash register by his secretary on 5 July 1594: 'six pictures of the twelve months'. And a later inventory item, quoted by M. de Maeyer, specifies the number six categorically: 'each picture two months with their figures'. As far as Marijnissen is concerned 'that settles the matter'. But not so, for various 17th-century inventories introduced a degree of confusion which nobody has yet succeeded in clearing up. The Archduke Leopold Wilhelm's inventory of 1659 in Vienna mentions five paintings from the *Months* series – no doubt the five works still surviving today, only three of them in Vienna. But M. de Maeyer discovered a later inventory of the Brussels Court dated between 1665 and 1692 which once again specifies six pictures by Bruegel depicting the twelve months ... The enigma of this duplication has not yet been solved, but the circumstance does lend new substance to the twelve-picture theory. Were the seven missing pictures perhaps burnt? And how could Bruegel have produced such an enormous quantity of work in one year, particularly as other pictures were also executed

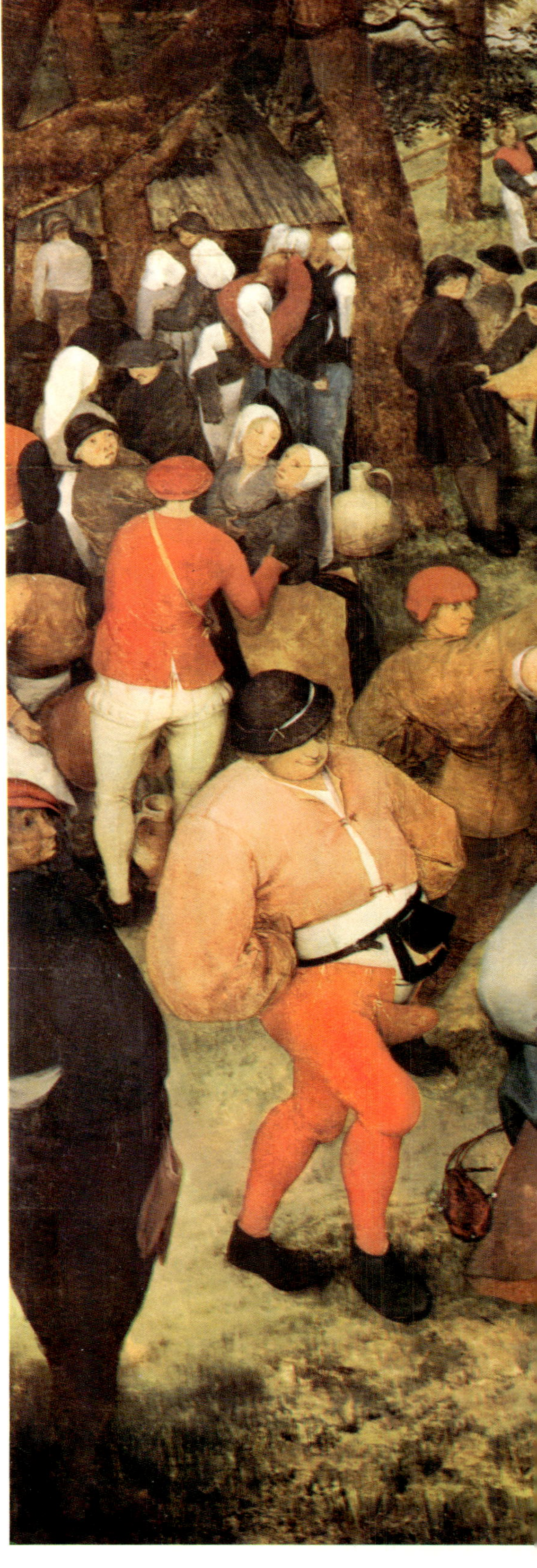

THE PEASANT WEDDING DANCE
Oil on panel; 119 x 157 cm (47 x 62 in)
Not signed; dated: 'M.D.LXVI.'
Detroit, Institute of Arts
Acquired in 1930 on the English art market. After it had been cleaned in 1941 all doubts about its authenticity were banished. Presumably this earliest representation of a peasant scene to have come down to us was

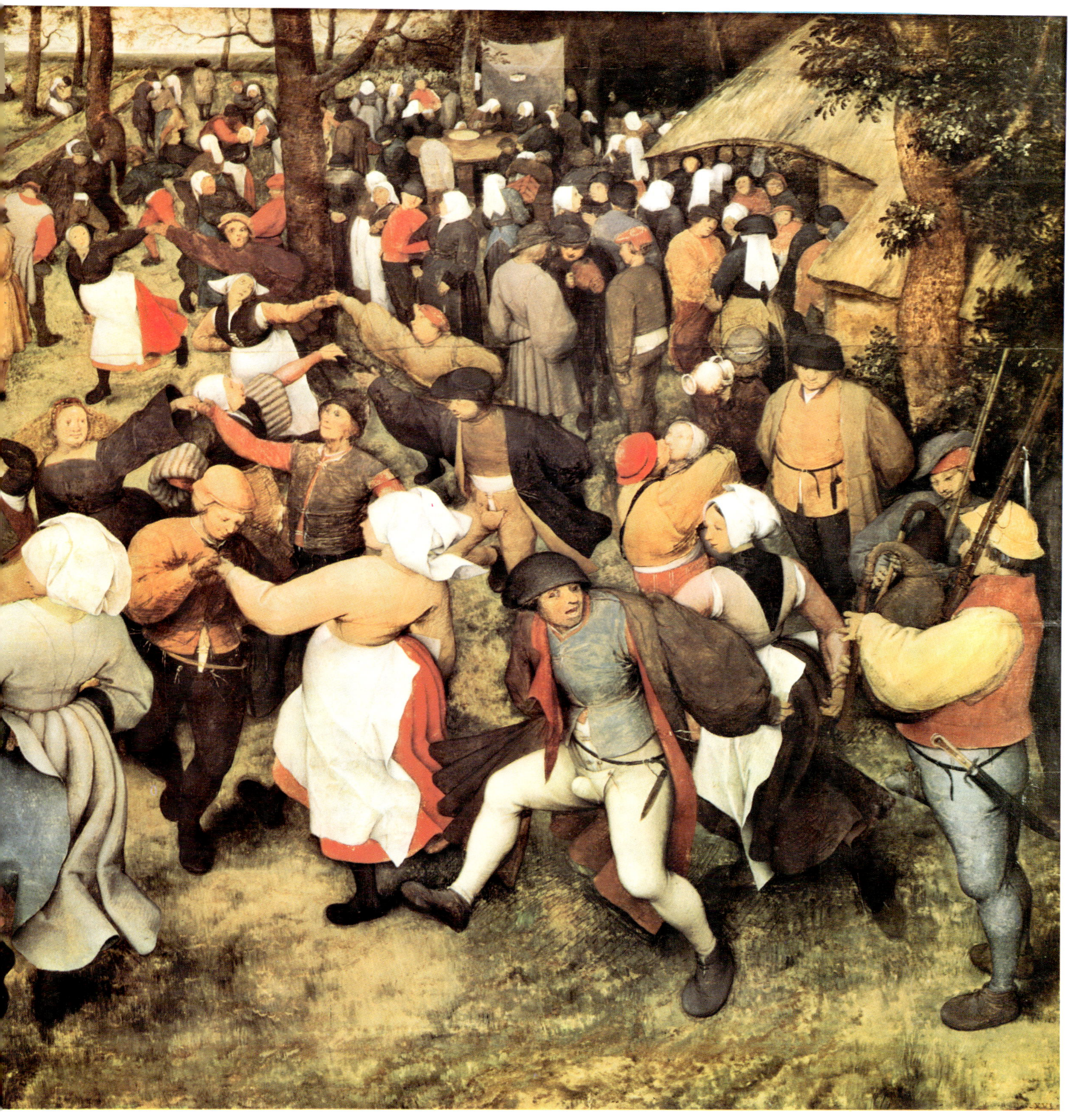

preceded by others, perhaps along the lines
of the *Kermis at Hoboken* (p. 49) and the
Feast of St. George. The large number of
figures differentiates it sharply from the later
Peasant Kermis in Vienna (pp. 168–169).
The picture is said to have a moralizing
significance as a condemnation of intemperance, which debases the sacrament of
marriage.

in 1565? Grossmann believes that an artist fully in control of his technical resources would have been capable of it. Moreover, he might have begun the series earlier and signed all the pictures together in 1565 when they were handed over. Not until Mechel's catalogue of the new arrangements of the Imperial Gallery in the Belvedere Palace at Vienna in 1783 do we find two of the *Months* mentioned again: the *Return of the Herd* and the *Corn Harvest* (autumn and summer) being somewhat curiously, and of course wrongly, combined with the *Children's Games* (as spring) and the *Massacre of the Innocents* (as winter) to make up the four seasons, while *Hunters in the Snow* and the *Gloomy Day* were ignored in the storeroom. The *Corn Harvest* was brought to Paris with other pictures in 1809, but failed to return in 1809 – unlike most of the rest – and was thus lost to the Imperial Collections. It finally ended up in the Metropolitan Museum in 1919 by way of the art market. It is not known for certain when *Haymaking* left the Imperial Collection on being acquired by a member of the Bohemian aristocracy, but it

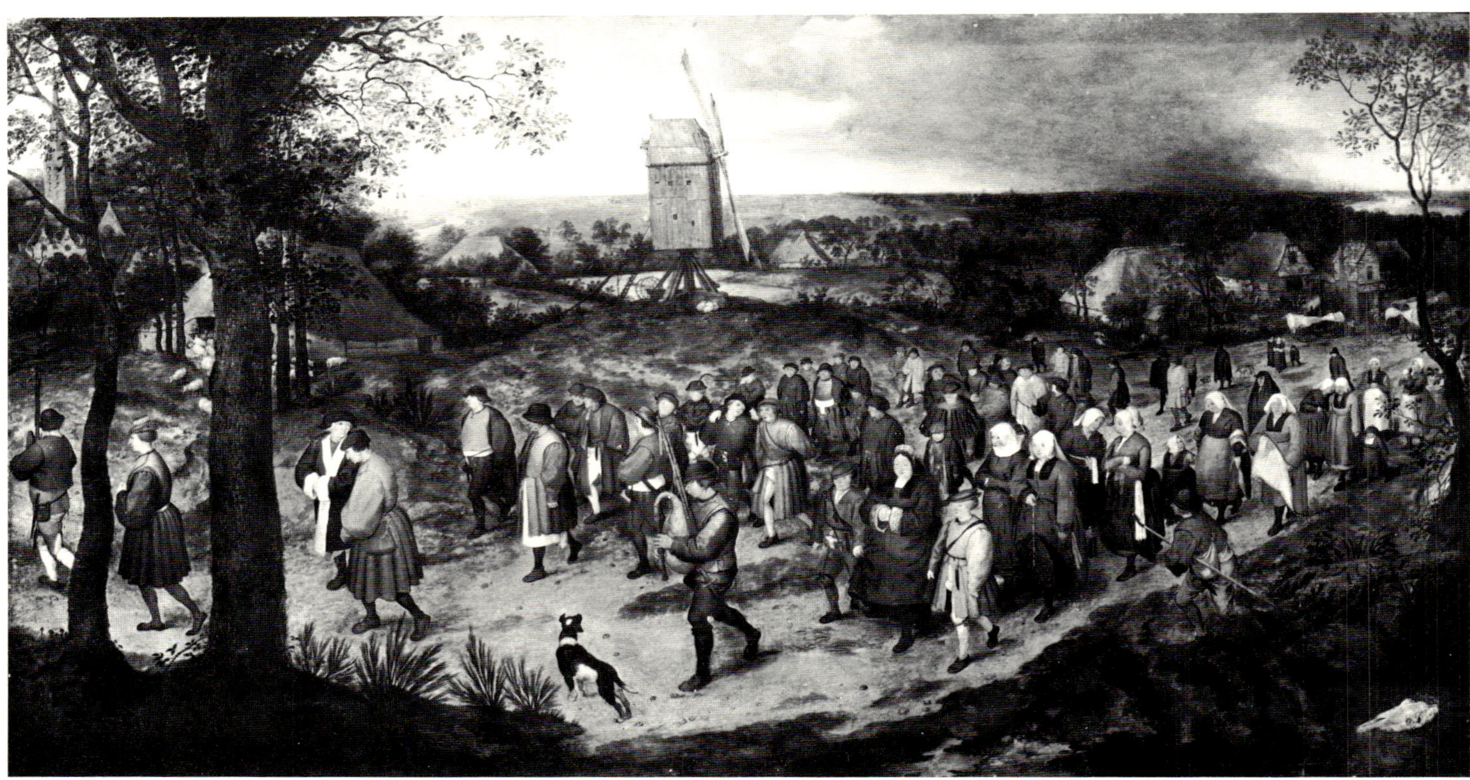

can now be seen in Prague. The sixth picture was already missing in the inventory of 1659.

The scheme of the *Months* conforms with the long tradition of medieval calendar illustration all the way through to the Breviarium Grimani, with typical occupations or types of country labour being shown for the various months. This involved certain minor differences, partly because traditional agricultural activities vary in time from country to country, partly because the subject-matter of Bruegel's paintings cannot be divided up unequivocally according to specific months.

Tolnay, who originated the six-picture theory, allocates them as follows: *Hunters in the Snow* to December/January, the *Gloomy Day* to February/March, *Haymaking* to June/July, the *Corn Harvest* to August/September and the *Return of the Herd* to October/November. April/May would then be the missing picture. Grossmann has shown that it is not necessary to assign two months to the motifs of a given picture. For him the *Hunters in the Snow* represents January, the *Gloomy Day* February, *Haymaking* July, the *Corn Harvest* August, and the *Return of the Herd* November or October. Marijnissen upholds the six-picture cycle and proposes the following tentative reconstruction, taking account of the year's beginning at Easter: March/April missing; *Haymaking*, May/June; *Corn Harvest* July/August; *Return of the Herd* September/October; *Hunters in the Snow* November/December; *Gloomy Day* January/February. A doubtful point here is whether early spring (the *Gloomy Day*) can be put at the end of the cycle instead of the traditional winter. Perhaps, though, we might usefully get away from preconceptions based on the calendar and credit Bruegel with an entirely original approach: it may be, after all, that instead of the customary four seasons he freely

THE WEDDING PROCESSION
Oil on panel; 61.5 x 114.5 cm (24¼ x 45 in)
Neither signed nor dated
Brussels, Municipal Museum
In Lord Northwick's Collection at Northwick Park in 1830; acquired by the Brussels Museum in 1960. Winkler, Friedländer, Glück, Genaille, Denis and Marlier considered it to be authentic; Michel thought it was by Pieter Brueghel the Younger; Tolnay regarded it as a work by Jan Brueghel the Elder; Jedlicka also rejected its authenticity. The catalogue of the Brussels Exhibition lists it among Bruegel's late works after the *Peasant Wedding Dance* of 1566 in Detroit (pp. 138–139): again suggesting it to be the probable original. However, it is rather doubtful whether this somewhat weak composition can be ascribed to the master.

selected six different faces of nature from the year's round without fixing on any specific calendar periods.

Much more important than this chronological classification, however, is the enormous innovation which consists in embodying the seasonal changes not in particular activities appropriate to the months, as in earlier calendar pictures, but in the landscape itself. For the first time in European art, the painter depicts a specific seasonal state of nature in each picture: as Grossmann says, 'In each the scenes are closely knit together in complete unity of time, place and action'. He regards the five pictures as the remains of a frieze, the continuous landscape background connecting each picture with its neighbour, but attempts to group them on this basis are fraught with difficulty. Mössner, a German art historian, put forward the view in 1975 that the series is based on a sequence of six ground shades, which is undoubtedly correct. Bruegel's amazing achievement is that the mere choice of particular colours enables him to strike a clearly different overall note

THE UNCLEAN BRIDE
Pen drawing in maroon on wood; 266 x 416 mm (10¼ x 16 in)
c. 1566
New York, Metropolitan Museum of Art
This block of wood from the Figdor Collection in Vienna is valued particularly highly by the Metropolitan Museum. The drawing was executed directly on the block of wood for subsequent engraving, which has been started in the top left-hand corner. *The Unclean Bride* is the title of a farce which was put on during carnivals. Previously also known as *The Marriage of Mopsus and Nisa*, the drawing has a counterpart in another wood-cut by Bruegel entitled *Orson and Valentine* (1566), which also depicts a popular farce. The two subjects are present as secondary motifs in the *Battle Between Carnival and Lent* (pp. 50–51). P. van der Heyden's engraving of the *Unclean Bride* was published by H. Cock in 1570 (Bastelaer 216).

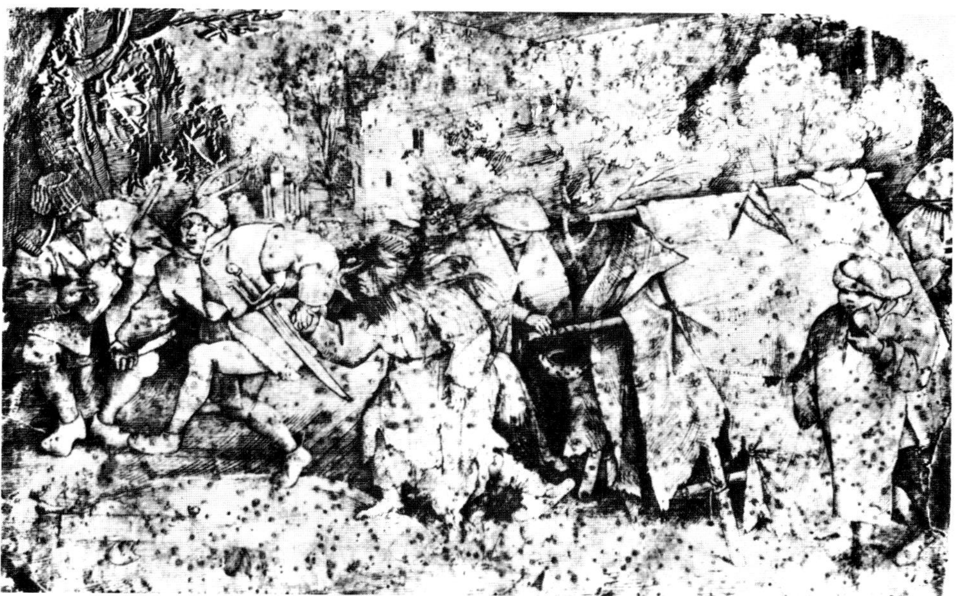

from picture to picture, corresponding to the season and its characteristic atmosphere. In the *Gloomy Day*, his darkest and perhaps most brilliantly conceived landscape, he typifies the short days of winter. It has been raining, so that even in the dwindling light the colours retain a deep intensity. In fact, a storm has just passed over, as we can tell from the rough sea with sinking ships; the cloud-covered sky holds the last light of late afternoon. The child's costume and paper crown, the peasant eating a wafer and the broom with a candle stuck in it at the back of the group indicate carnival time (see the *Battle Between Carnival and Lent*, pages 50–51), although Marijnissen cites folkloristic sources to establish a link between the child's fancy dress (a cushion strapped on to represent a liturgical garment, plus bell and lantern) and Twelfth Night (6 January). Hulin de Loo also sees a connection between the paper crown and Twelfth Night, particularly the so-called Feast of the Bean King.

Haymaking (page 107), which is in Prague, needs no special explanation. Its luxuriant abundance of rich greenish-yellow and green merges softly into a blue chain of hills with a meandering river in the distance. Besides hay, wild fruits including cherries and strawberries – fruits which ripen in June – are being gathered into baskets. Stridbeck sees in the group of three girls in the foreground the influences of Italian or Romanist art, and in particular of a drawing by Heemskerck in the Uffizi.

The *Corn Harvest* (pages 112–113) beams replendently with all the golden-yellow wealth of summer. Even the water in the background tells of the heat. The harvesting process is illustrated with brilliant simplicity. Jedlicka, who analyses in depth the flawless composition of each of the *Months*, notices how in this picture the far line of the corn plays about the horizontal axis. The zigzag curve on this side where the standing corn meets the stubble does the same with the diagonal. This linear scheme is bound up with the contrast between the left-hand and right-hand halves of the picture, between simplicity and animation, activity being found where the colours are quiet and stillness where they are more vivid. There are no accidents in Bruegel's work. Subject-matter, graphic technique and colour scheme are united in perfect harmony.

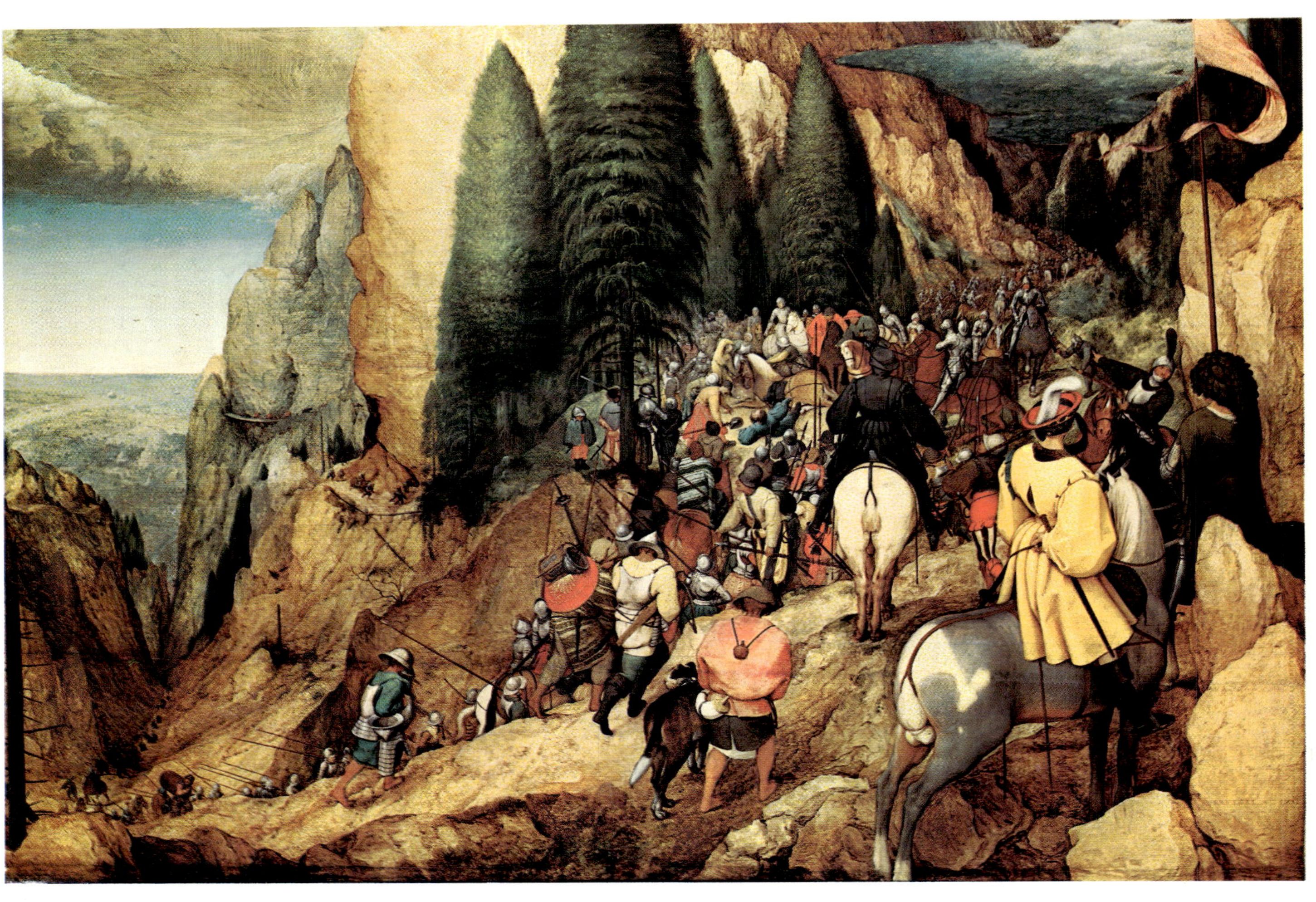

The recumbent figure looks forward to the *Land of Cockaigne* (page 147). Certain scholars have claimed to recognize Geneva in the background, but it is doubtful whether Bruegel passed through this city on his way from Lyons to Turin via Mont Ceris. Hofstede de Groot (1927) also sees a specific landscape in the *Return of the Herd* (page 116) and locates it in the Rhine Valley above the point where the river flows into the Lake of Constance near Ragaz and Vilters. Notwithstanding certain similarities, however, there is no question of a landscape portrait as we know it today. On the other hand this magnificent composition undoubtedly grew out of Bruegel's early drawing entitled *Landscape with Three Pilgrims* (1553–1555), now owned privately in Germany. Discovered by Arndt, this preparatory drawing for Cock's engraving *Euntes in Emmaus* reproduces some of Bruegel's travel impressions with stunning originality. The crystal-clear air has the atmosphere of late autumn. The figures of the shepherds and the peasant on horseback conjure up an impression of haste and cold. And how brilliantly Bruegel catches the typical, plodding movements of the cattle.

This painting reveals more clearly than any other Bruegel's technique of applying thin speckles of paint with an almost dry bush, the brown priming coat occasionally being left visible as part of the picture – for example in the clothing of the shepherds on the right. Traces of preparatory charcoal sketching also remain, in the white cow, for instance, apparently to Bruegel's entire satisfaction.

The winter scene (page 121) is certainly the most famous of all the *Months* and the best example of these landscapes' universal character. This is not just any winter landscape, but the very essence of winter itself – every time we see a winter landscape we see a 'Bruegel'. Snow-covered landscapes occur in Flemish books of hours from the early 15th century, but there white is used simply as an attribute of winter. Here all the colours are the purest expression of cold: white, icy grey, greyish-green, brownish-black. Writers have described often enough how the impression of cold is repeated in every beautifully observed detail: the muffled hunters trudging silently home, the freezing dogs, the dark forms of the branches and the black ravens amid all the whiteness (pages 2–3). Once again we can only marvel at the vividness of every detail, even the tiniest ones in the very background. A straw fire is being made below the inn sign of St. Hubert hanging half off its pole on the left (pages 122–123). This is associated with the singeing of the slaughtered pig, which, although it is not in the picture, is indicated by the wooden tub used whenever pigs are slaughtered, a happening common of December. The feeling of depth suggested by the diminishing size of the trees continues through to the sea in the far distance. With its typical Netherlandish villages and lakes, the winter amusements and precipitous mountains, this landscape is a visionary combination whose compositional balance rests on the intersection of the white wedge of foreground and the green wedge of lakes running counter to it. The mountains on the right seem to round off the gently curving sweep of three-dimensional space, re-directing the eye towards the left into the depths of the background and the frozen sea-shore.

Any attempt to identify the landscape with the Rhône valley at the Lake of Geneva (Conway, quoted by Novotny in 1948) is as unrealistic as similar attempts with the foregoing paintings.

Oddly, there are no copies of the *Months*. They were evidently kept under lock and key in Antwerp before disappearing into the Habsburg collections in 1594.

THE CONVERSION OF SAUL
Oil on panel; 108 x 156 cm (42½ x 61 in)
Signed and dated: 'BRVEGEL M.D.LXVII.'
Vienna, Kunsthistorisches Museum
Acquired on 13 October 1594 by the Archduke Ernest, Governor of the Low Countries, and mentioned by van Mander in 1604 as being in the collection of the Emperor Rudolph II. The subject (Acts of the Apostles 9; 3) occurs frequently in Italian art, particularly after Michelangelo's frescoes of 1542 for the Cappella Paolina in the Vatican. As so often, however, Bruegel has reduced the main event, concealing it in the background, to the extent of making it look like an insignificant incident at the centre of a grand deployment of soldiers in contemporary costume. The imposing and seemingly boundless mountain landscape must have been suggested by the artist's journey across the Alps. It has been claimed that the horseman in black and the figure of Saul are an allusion to the Duke of Alba's crossing of the Alps in 1567, but no evidence exists to support this hypothesis.

Besides the magnificent series of *Months*, the year 1565 also produced the small, more intimate *Winter Landscape with Bird-trap* (page 125), set in a village, which differs from the universal character of the *Months* both in its more modest perspective and in its general atmosphere. Instead of the crystal-clear, frosty mood of the *Hunters* we have a misty winter's day with yellowish sky reflected in the ice below. With its lower focal level and staffage-like skaters it became the prototype of 17th-century Dutch winter landscapes such as those by Avercamp. Surprisingly, perhaps, the bird-trap on the right in the foreground has suggested to certain critics that the picture may have a hidden moral message to the effect that the skaters are as regardless of what happens around them as are the birds under the trap. However, no really convincing interpretation has yet been put forward. The three big crows are certainly very striking; the perspective makes two of them look as large as the skaters, which is perhaps significant. The village is apparently Sint-Anna-Pede near Brussels.

The picture enjoyed enormous popularity and has been copied roughly fifty times, more than any other painting by Bruegel. Despite occasional doubts, the version in the Delporte Collection is unanimously recognized by scholars as the original. Stechow (1977) mentions a copy which, remarkably enough, is dated 1564.

As always, in *The Census at Bethlehem* (page 129) Bruegel depicts a Biblical scene (Luke 2, 1–5) as a contemporary event, in this case integrated into the everyday life of a Flemish village in winter. Both focal level and horizon are higher than in the *Winter Landscape with Bird-trap* (page 125). The main spatial effect follows the diagonal from bottom left to top right, and the other diagonal is also stressed, though much less strongly. The spatial layout is closest to that of the *Children's Games*, where the vanishing point also lies near the top right-hand corner, but the figures are grouped quite differently.

Once again the wealth of accurate detail is an invaluable source of information. On the left in front of the inn, the 'Green Wreath', the people are queueing up to be counted and assessed for tax. A striking feature is the striped yellow pattern of the overcoat worn by one of the people waiting. Similarly striped materials otherwise occur only in the *Sermon of St. John the Baptist* (pages 134–135) and the *Conversion of Saul* (page 142). Almost identical ones are still made today in Morocco and elsewhere in North Africa. A scribe at a table records payments while a higher official with a fur-lined coat collar takes the money. A sign with the imperial double eagle on the inn wall confirms the official nature of the tax collection, a message reinforced by a gendarme with a spear. Joseph and Mary have just arrived to be registered and are placed in the foreground, slightly right of centre – Mary, pregnant, is riding on an ass and already accompanied by an ox. Joseph the carpenter leads the way, identified by a saw carried over his shoulder. On top of the tumbledown little hut on the right in the mid-distance stands a small cross: perhaps, as Stechow suggests, indicating the place where Jesus will be born in a few days' time. In front of the inn we see the sticking of a pig, a frequent winter-time occurrence, and straw prepared for the singeing (cf. *Hunters in the Snow*, page 121). A girl catches the blood in a pan with sizzling fat, a meal still popular today in many regions. A beehive hanging under the eaves serves as a bird's nest (cf. the *Peasant Wedding Feast* pages 164–165); the children on the ice in small sledges made of jaw-bones are a recurrent motif in Bruegel's works. Marijnissen has drawn attention to the touching scene on the ice with the two elder children setting off across the ice with a three-legged stool for a sledge while the younger brother stands on the edge shivering with cold.

Here again Menzel produces a topical political explanation. 1566, the year in which Bruegel painted the picture, was a year of uncertainty. Granvella had gone, iconoclasm was breaking out, nobody knew what would happen next. Menzel quotes Brecht: 'It seems dangerous for people to let themselves be counted – far better not to be found at all'. And he himself states: 'The discovery by certain scholars that the census at Bethlehem has never been painted by any artist before Bruegel indicates that he was adopting the conventional expedient of taking an appropriate Biblical parallel with which to disguise his real intention. The subject is a cover for what he has to say about the dangers besetting people in contemporary society … The crumbling castle with its moat – a symbol of the past – may be Bruegel's way of giving his opinion of the changing times.'

The Brussels exhibition catalogue of 1969 interprets the picture quite differently. It sees the dilapidated building in the background as a symbol of heathendom, the wooden shell of a shed just in front of it standing for the coming of Christianity (pages 130–131).

THE ADORATION OF THE MAGI IN THE SNOW
Oil on panel; 35 x 55 cm (13 x 21 in)
Signed and dated: 'M.D.LXVII / BRVEGEL'
Winterthur, O. Reinhart Collection

The figures in the date are not well preserved, but the most convincing reading is 1567. The picture is first mentioned in 1696 as belonging to the E. Jabach Collection in Paris. This is the fifth winter painting executed by Bruegel within a very short time and once again it differs markedly from the others: similar snowy scenes had certainly already been depicted in Flemish calendars prior to Bruegel, but without the same atmosphere and realism. At the same time the master has shown the theme of the Adoration, located in an almost obscure corner of the painting, in an entirely new and original light, transferring the universal significance of the Biblical scene into an ordinary Flemish village on an ordinary winter's day.

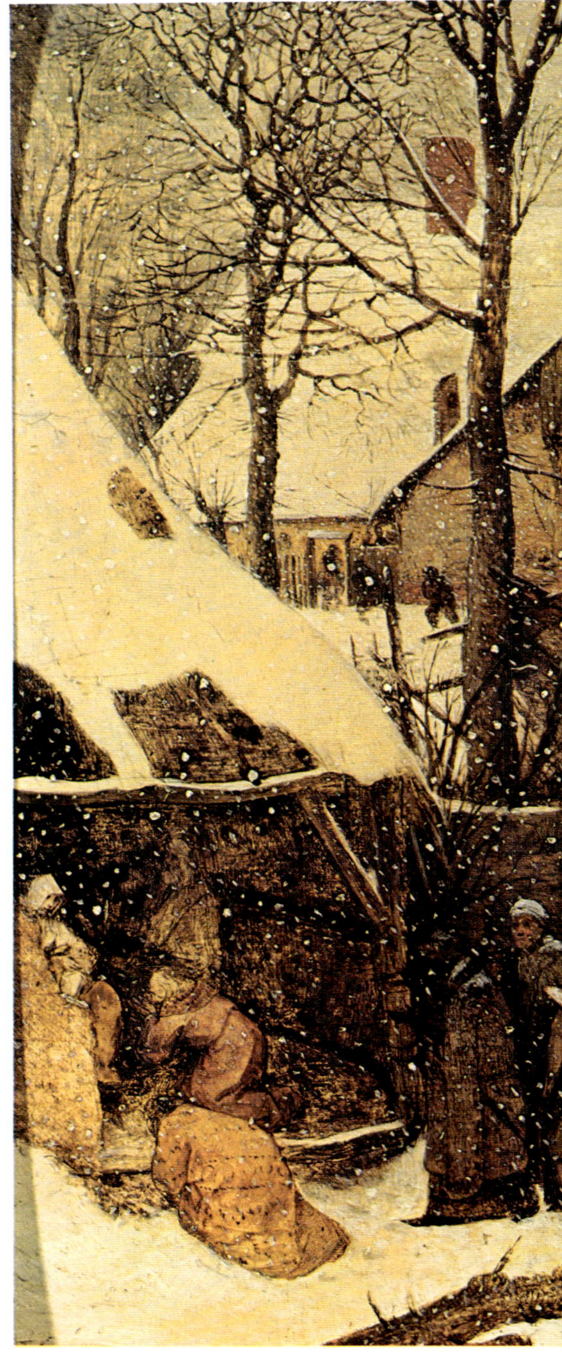

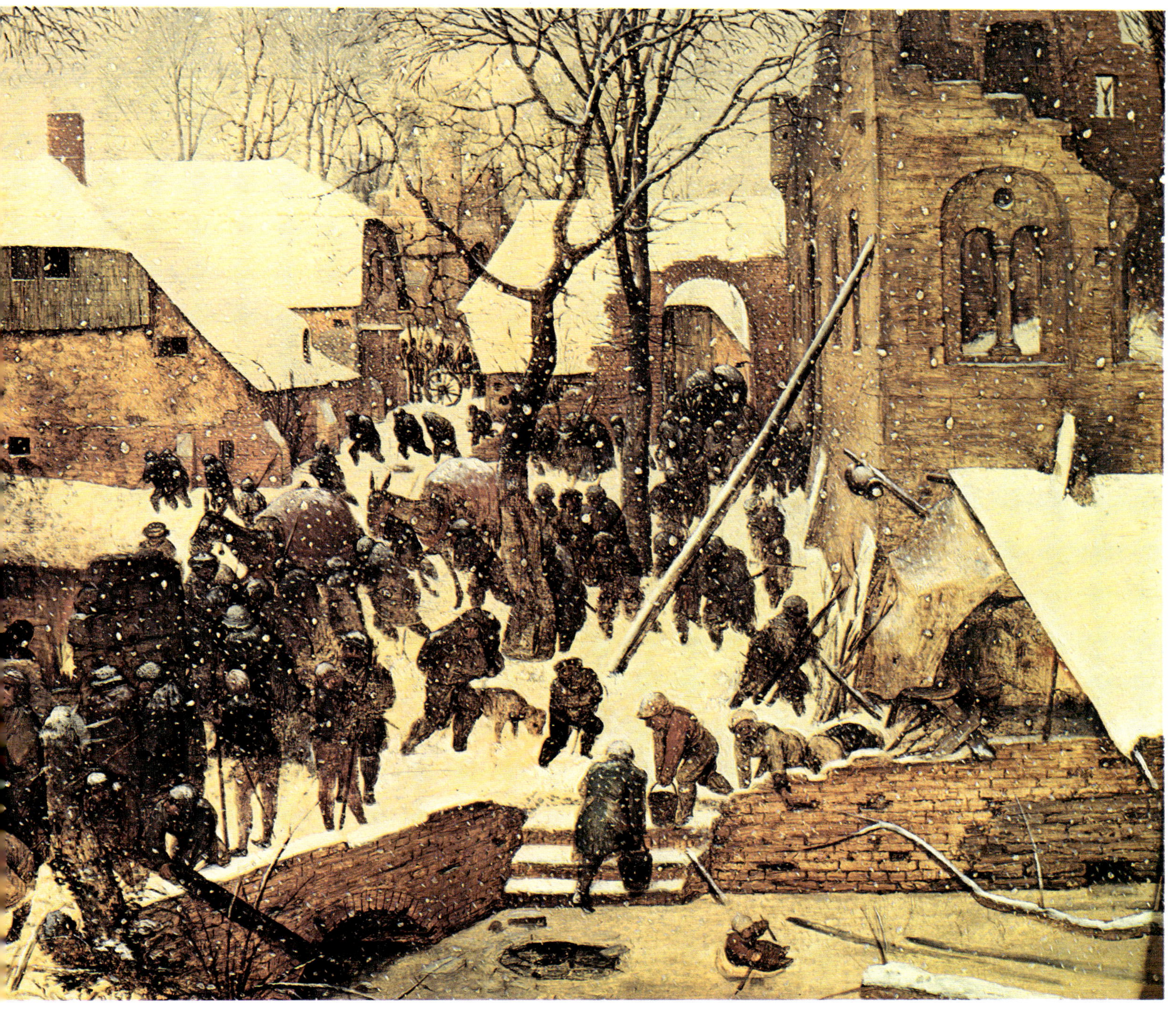

The tumbledown hut with the cross on the right is the home of someone suffering from the plague, while the church opposite in the background stresses the common faith. The stout, healthy tree by the inn the 'Green Wreath' contrasts with the inn in the hollowed-out dead tree where disreputable characters gather – hollow trees traditionally symbolize inferiority. Marlier has counted thirteen copies of this painting.

Apart from a number of copies (the best one in the Descamps Collection, Brussels; auctioned by Ader Picard Tajan of Paris in March 1979), there are two versions of *The Massacre of the Innocents* which merit serious consideration as originals: the signed one in Vienna (page 132) and the one at Hampton Court (pages 132–133). Both versions can be dated with a fair degree of certainty between 1565 and 1567 in view of similarities with the other winter pictures of this period, particularly the *Census* of 1566. Marijnissen mentions two replicas by Pieter Brueghel the Younger dated 1564, which cannot be correct since Pieter Brueghel the Younger was born in 1564.

The most thorough examination of the works' authenticity has been undertaken by Grossmann, who reached the following conclusions. Both versions can be traced back to the Imperial Collections and are in bad condition. The one in Vienna bears the partial but probably authentic signature BRVEG. However, X-rays have shown that 'Bruegel can have had no great share in the execution, though certain parts, especially those showing *pentimenti*, permit the conclusion that the picture was painted in Bruegel's workshop and partly retouched by him'. The version at Hampton Court, previously regarded as a copy, has been shown by X-rays to be authentic, though marred by 17th-century overpaintings which covered up the children in order to turn the picture into a plundering scene; in many places, too, the original paint has disappeared entirely and been clumsily replaced by early restorers. Only a few parts are in fact original: for instance certain details of the scene around the herald on horseback, with the circular eyes so typical of Bruegel. All this suggests that both pictures were executed in Bruegel's studio and under his supervision; but further research would be needed to establish whether Bruegel's share in the Vienna version, which does after all bear the artist's signature, was really as small as Grossmann assumes. In the light of consistent flaws and discontinuities in the application of the colours and in the smaller details, the present author has recently come to the conclusion (upheld by Dr. K. Demus) that the Vienna version is a copy and the one at Hampton Court the original, with overpaintings.

This was the fourth winter picture that Bruegel painted within an extremely short time. Whether there is a connection with the severe winter of 1564–1565, in which many poor people died of cold and hunger, is questionable. But the Biblical theme has been seen – and this is not the case with any other picture of Bruegel's – as a direct political allusion to the plundering and murdering by undisciplined Spanish soldiers. Looked at more closely this is a dubious assumption, since there were no foreign troops stationed in the Netherlands from 1560 up to the arrival of the Duke of Alba in August 1567, a fact clearly relevant to the dating of both pictures. At any rate the Redcoats, possibly Walloon horsemen in Spanish service, are present in this painting as well as in *Christ Carrying the Cross* of 1564.

The crux of the theory of a topical, political reference is the notion that the leader of the horsemen is the Duke of Alba. In the Hampton Court version this character has his visor closed, so cannot be recognized, whereas in the Vienna painting it is open; since the flowing grey beard indicates Alba, so the theory goes, the conclusion must be that the Vienna version was painted after Alba's arrival in Brussels. It has even been claimed that the commander is Herod himself, represented by Alba. Apart from the fact that the smallness of the detail makes any certain identification impossible, the identity is perhaps not really all that important. The mere cruelty of the scene is enough to indicate the artist's subject, namely a punitive expedition into a Flemish village. Van Mander recognized the psychological acuteness of Bruegel's observation: '... the mothers are fainting in their grief, and there are other scenes all rendered convincingly'. The overpaintings in the Hampton Court version and the differences between it and the one in Vienna indicate clearly that allusions were indeed recognized, since the whole point was to eliminate them – the overpainting of the children, the commander's closed visor, the Imperial double eagle of the breast of the mounted herald made unrecognizable by transforming it into a grotesque ornament, the obscuring of the cross on the commander's standard (identical with the cross on the death-trap in the *Triumph of Death*, page 71). If the work showing a village being plundered which is in Rudolph II's inventory in Prague is the same as the Hampton Court picture it would mean that the overpainting which turned the massacre into a mere plundering episode was done as early as 1621.

THE LAND OF COCKAIGNE
Oil on panel; 52 x 78 cm (20½ x 30 in)
Signed and dated: 'M.DLXVII. BRVEGEL'
Munich, Alte Pinakothek
First mentioned in 1621 in the inventory of the Imperial Collection in Prague, it may have been stolen from a private owner when the city was sacked by the Swedes, and was acquired by the Museum in 1917. The subject had been used by the German poet Hans Sachs in one of his poems and subsequently also became known in a prose version in the Low Countries. Bruegel's picture gave it its most popular and durable expression. Apart from the wealth of comic detail it alludes basically to the vices of sloth and intemperance. But the artist may also have wanted to underline ironically the contrast between the country of earthly delights and the actual situation in the Low Countries under the Duke of Alba.
Detail on *pages 148–149*

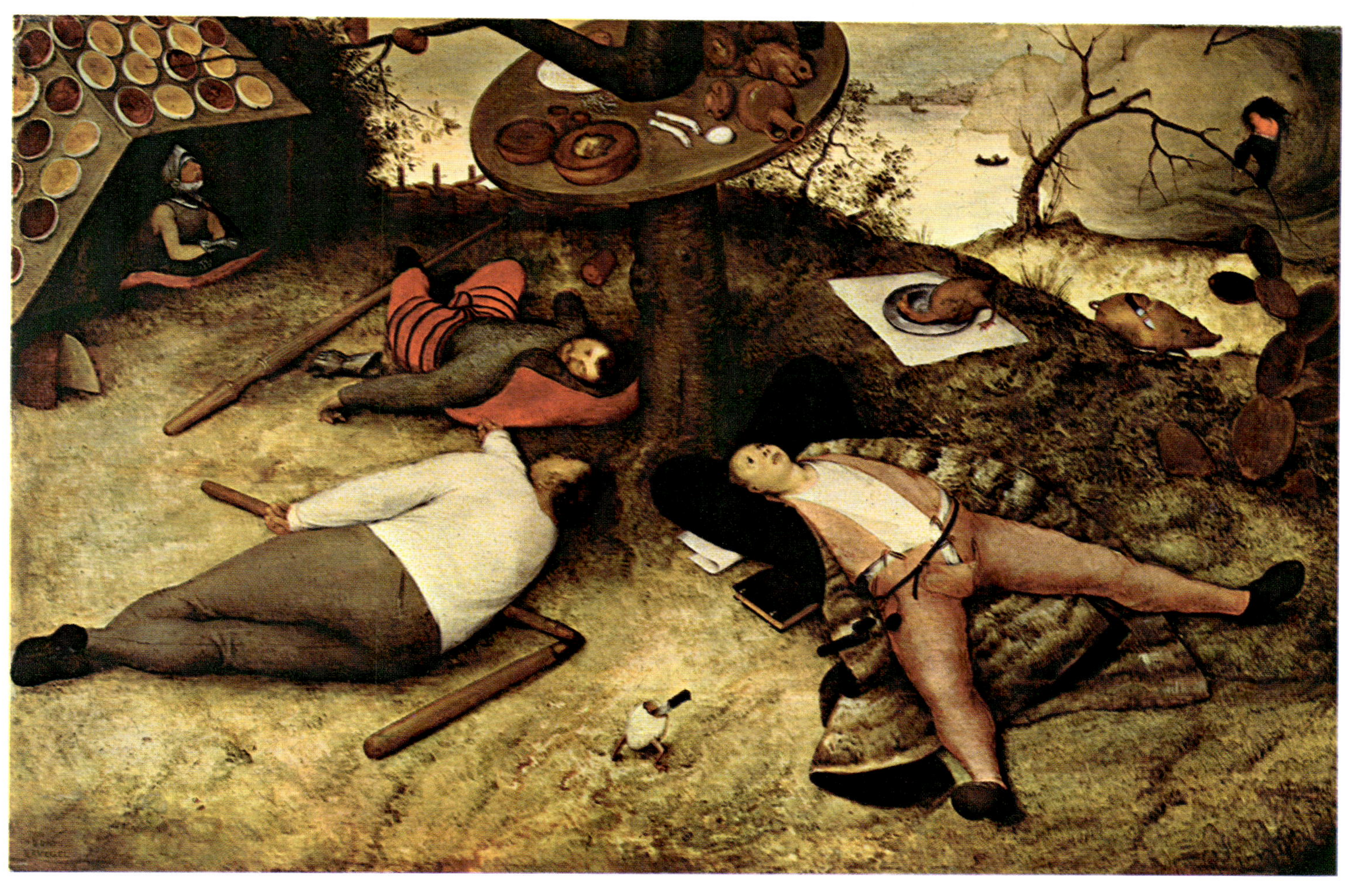

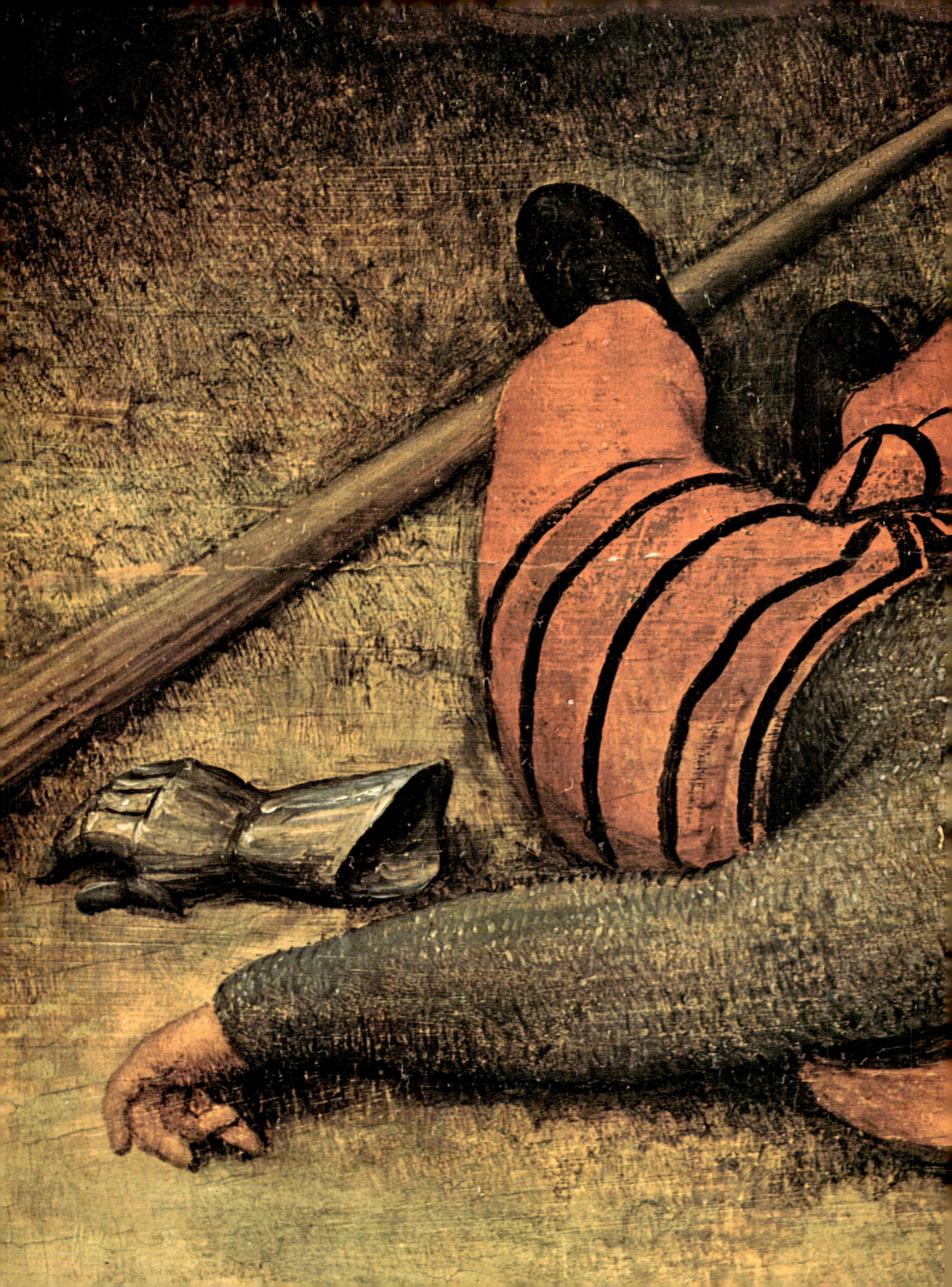

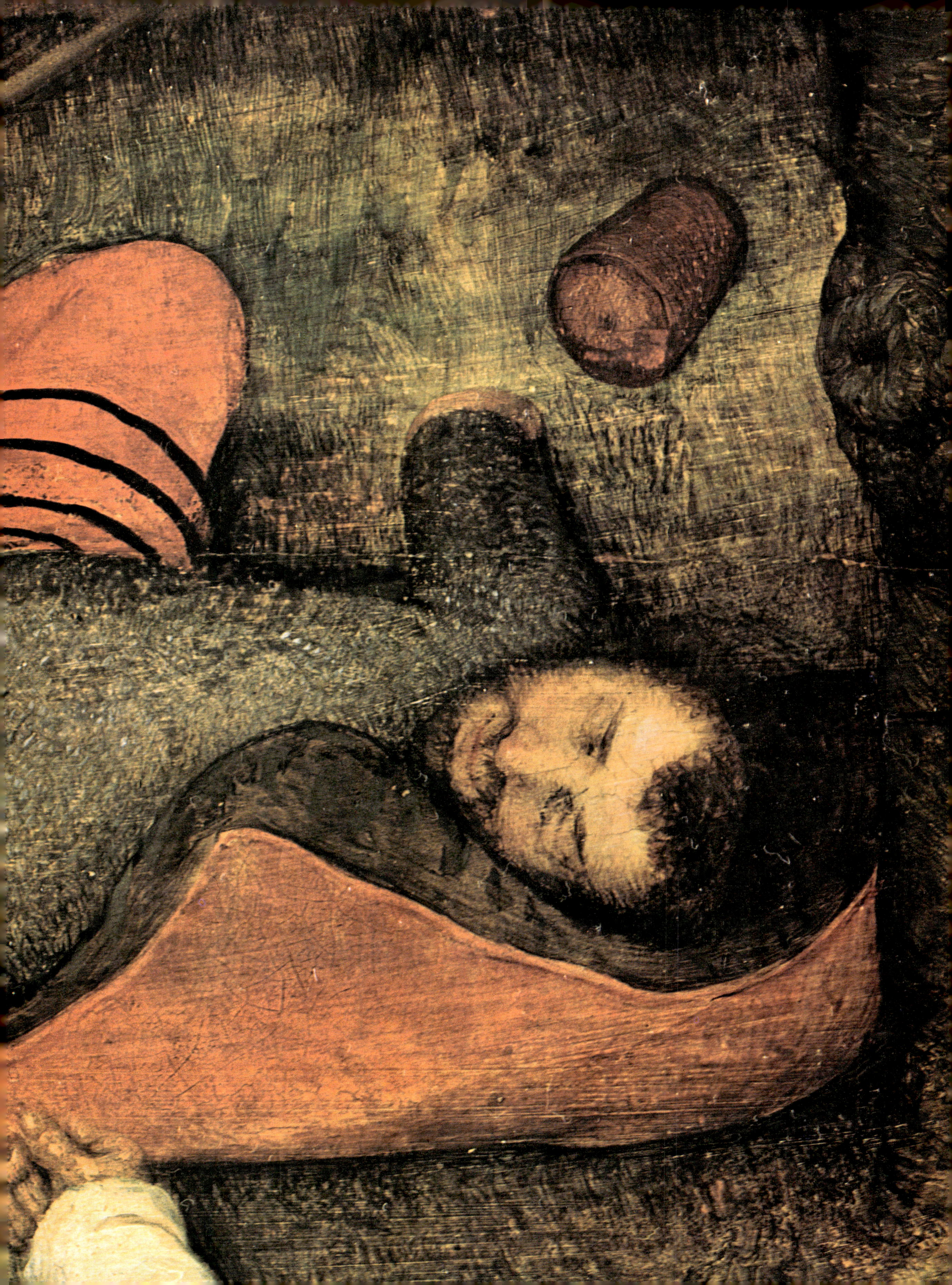

The Sermon of St. John the Baptist (pages 134–135) is perhaps the most charming of Bruegel's large paintings, with its cosy, peaceful forest, the delightful view out across the valley, and the colourful crowd of people tucked away amongst the trees. Yet the apparently idyllic mood and the depth of feeling emanating from the listening crowd may perhaps be deceptive. The subject had been popular before Bruegel's time; but there is still disagreement about the particular religious significance with which Bruegel may have wanted to imbue the work, which is full of innovative details. For example, Christ is present at the sermon – the red-haired figure standing somewhat apart, whom the Baptist is pointing out as the greater one who will come after him.

Clearly Bruegel was familiar with the wandering Protestant preachers who frequently delivered sermons in the open air despite the bans imposed on them. Indeed, every detail of this painting accords with the description of such gatherings given by Marcus van Vaernewijck. Once again Bruegel has clothed a Biblical event in contemporary dress, displaying before us a richly varied multitude whose mood ranges from spell-bound attention through sympathy to scepticism and plain indifference. 'The Baptist's spoken word and the willingness of the faithful to receive it form an invisible link which unites a gathering of unimportant, run-of-the-mill petit bourgeois into a spiritual community', according to Auner. Attention has been drawn time and again to the face of the blind man in the crowd, to the right of the man dressed in Turkish clothes, taking in the message open-mouthed. Auner regards this grimace as the sign of an epileptic fit under the influence of conversion and the picture itself as the one which according to van Mander showed 'truth breaking through' and which Bruegel apparently considered his best work.

By way of contrast the rows of backs are broken at several points in the foreground – most strikingly by the distinguished-looking man having his palm read by a gypsy. Allowing gypsies to tell one's fortune was punishable by excommunication during the Middle Ages as Huizinga tells us, and also earned unequivocal condemnation from Calvin, who saw it as superstition and expressly forbad his followers to indulge in it. Grossmann, who thinks the gentleman is a portrait, concludes from his behaviour that he is hostile to such meetings, but does not pursue that further with regard to Bruegel's own religious attitude.

Interestingly, the distinguished-looking man is absent from several of the copies of this picture, of which twenty-six exist, the best in the Vittorio Duca Collection in Milan, which van Puyvelde mistakenly regarded as an original. The absence of that figure renders the gypsy's gesture pointless and completely neutralizes the eye-catching effect of the striped materials worn by the gypsy pair. The man must therefore have been exceptionally important and Bruegel's sons would undoubtedly have been aware of it. So it seems unlikely that the master was jokingly passing on a portrait of one of his friends, such as Hans Franckert. But Menzel certainly oversteps the mark in equating him with a Pharisee about to be struck down by a curse – in other words Philip II himself. Auner interprets him as one of the hated Italian favourites of the governess Margaret of Parma. From his point of view the 'penitential sermon' provides the cornerstone of the theory that Bruegel belonged to the Anabaptist movement. He thinks the Lutheran Balthasar Battyany (1530–1590), who knew the Humanists of Antwerp, commissioned the painting direct from the artist and took it to his castle at Güssing. Auner claims that the artist's client is portrayed in the man with a walrus moustache wearing Turkish costume and looking out from behind the tree on the left. This piece of speculation is effectively dealt with by Grossmann, who demonstrates that the picture features in the inventory of 1633–1650 of the collection owned by the Infanta Isabella in Brussels, although this is not a matter of absolute certainty either, as the picture in question could be another version of the work. While rejecting Auner's Anabaptist theory, a number of writers agree that Bruegel portrayed himself in profile in the bearded figure at top right, rather as in *Christ Carrying the Cross* (page 93); and that the woman in red may possibly be his wife, with his mother-in-law Mayken Verhulst next to her. At the same time Auner is right in drawing attention to the markedly peaceful mood of this gathering, which offers a stark contrast to the noisy, aggressive Calvinist sermons immediately preceding the outbreak of iconoclasm. As he points out, the Anabaptists of the 60s were no longer the followers of plundering fanatics like Thomas Münzer and Johann von Leyden who had been active during the 20s and 30s, but a gentle minority purged by bloodthirsty persecution. Their preachers, undaunted by the prospect of death, prepared the faithful in secret places – in woods and forest glades – for the approaching end of the world and the return of Christ. The nucleus of John's sermon is the admonition: 'Repent ye, for the kingdom of heaven is at hand' (Matthew

THE AMBUSH
Oil on panel; 94 x 125 cm (37 x 49¼ in)
Signed and dated: 'M.D.LXVII / BRVEGEL.'
Stockholm, University Collection
Until very recently this important painting was regarded as a copy of the lost original; it was only after it had been cleaned in 1971 that the authentic date and signature of Bruegel the Elder came to light beneath the false signature of Pieter Brueghel the Younger. However, the last three figures of the year are doubtful and difficult to read. The composition with its few monumental figures corresponds to Bruegel's late style and has analogies with the *Peasant Brawl*, a mature work which has been lost and come down to us in numerous poor copies. The flat, desolate landscape recalls the backgrounds in the *Unfaithful Shepherd* (p. 157) and the *Misanthrope* (p. 159).

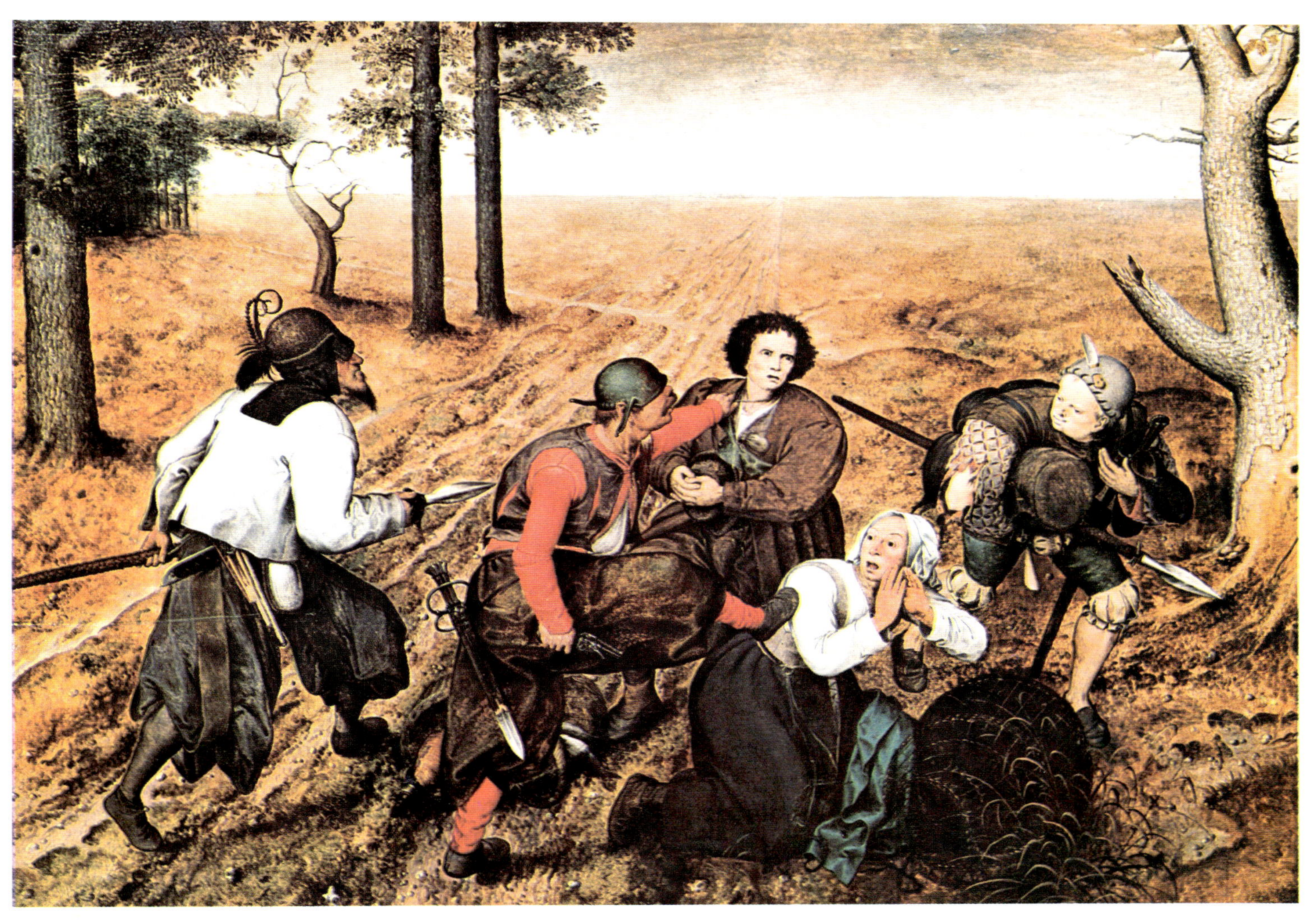

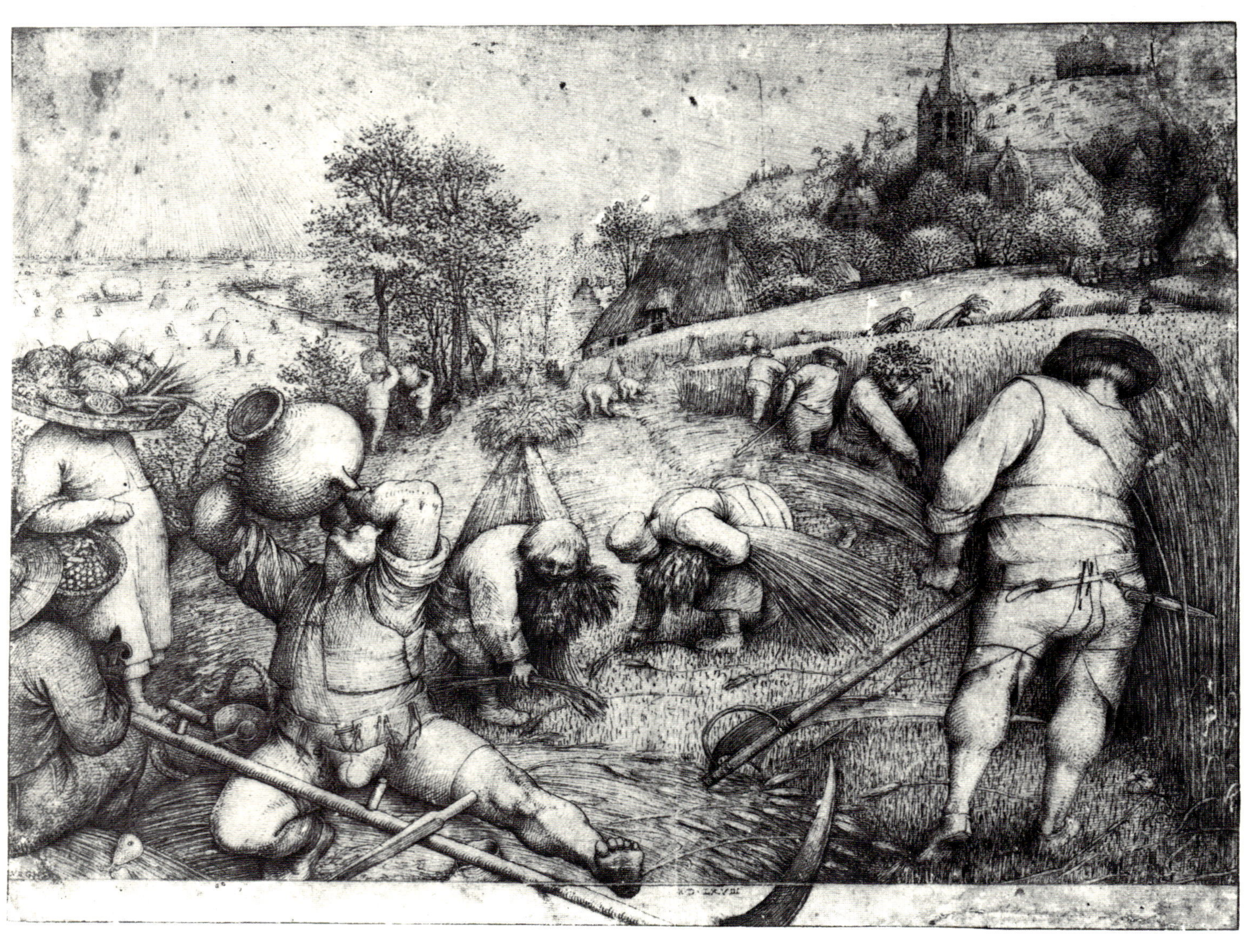

3; 2). The mathematician and orientalist Wilhelm Postell, a friend of Ortelius and Plantin, had forecast the end of the world for 1566, the year in which the *Sermon of St. John the Baptist* was executed. These and other arguments of Auner's certainly suggest a gathering of Anabaptists. Yet however sympathetic Bruegel may have been towards the movement, one is loath to impute to him a merely sectarian mentality.

The *Peasant Wedding Dance* (pages 138–139), also dated 1566, and now in Detroit, contains a wealth of motifs which preoccupied Bruegel's contemporaries and the following generation too. About thirty copies and partial copies exist of it, some substantially modified, others inverted in the manner of Pieter van der Heyden's engraving. The version in Detroit was also regarded as a copy of the lost original, but since it was cleaned in 1941 no-one has disputed its authenticity. This is upheld in particular by the *pentimenti* in the preparatory charcoal drawing, which show through the paint. In the *Neue Zürcher Zeitung* of 13 July 1969 Tolnay maintains, no doubt mistakenly, that the

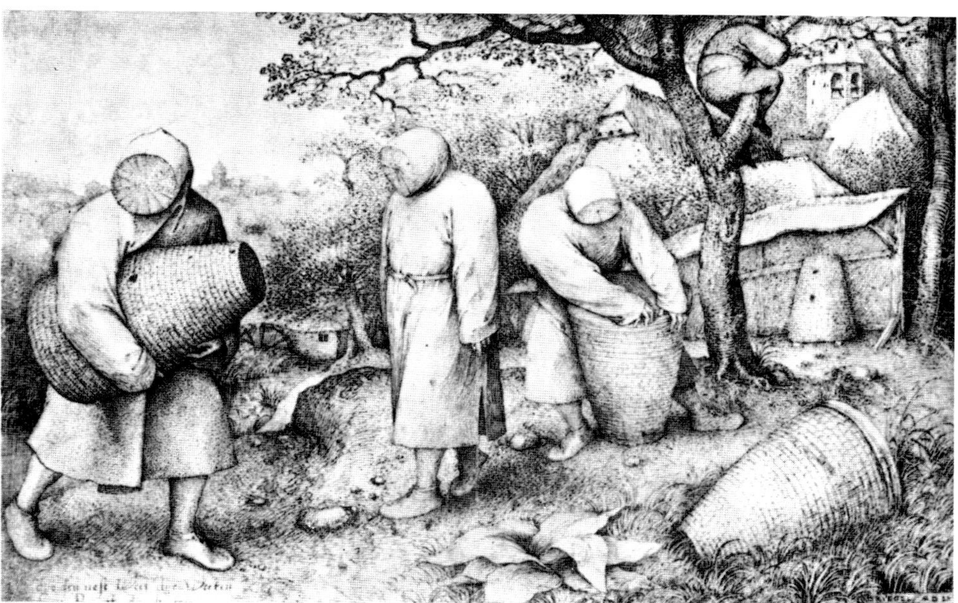

original is a miniature on parchment in the Uffizi, signed B.I.L.F.

Although it is the artist's first depiction of this subject, it was probably preceded by other, preliminary studies which are now lost. Bruegel had already tackled the theme of the peasant *kermis* in two earlier drawings, one of which is still extant (page 49). He was not the first artist to portray dancing peasants: they also appear in earlier engravings by Dürer and Hans Sebald Beham, but only in pairs, never in a crowd. It was the graphic artist Pieter van der Borcht who apparently initiated the new departure, either at the same time as or shortly in advance of Bruegel. We shall look more closely later on at contemporary attitudes towards the peasantry.

It can be assumed that Bruegel meant to inject a moralizing undertone into these harmless popular amusements. Bagpipe music seems to have sinful connotations in Bruegel's works, for example in the engraving of the unwise virgins. Moreover, bagpipes were seen as an allusion to male sexuality, not least because of their shape. The cleaning of the picture made this abundantly clear, as we can see in the bagpipe player and the three men dancing in the foreground. The ambiguity of all this comes out most plainly in the saying 'If the bagpipe isn't full it won't do its job', which features in a collection of proverbs produced by Sebastian Franck in 1528. But we should not let the moral message diminish our appreciation of the 16th century's propensity for crude criticism: It might be apposite here to recall the eighth chapter of Book III of Rabelais' *Gargantua*, which has the heading 'Why the fly is the most important part of a soldier's armour'. The bride can be seen to left of centre with a garland in her loose, wavy hair, dancing with an obviously much older man and surrounded by the dissolute throng of guests. This wedding dance can thus be interpreted as an allusion to the sin of unchastity which defiles the sacrament of marriage. Instead of representing sin explicitly as, for instance, in the series of engravings of 1556–1557, Bruegel here clothes it in the trappings of a genre scene. This view meets with the approval of scholars like Grossmann and Stridbeck; but it should be added at the same time that in this type of work the genre approach is still in the process of developing out of allegory. When we realize this we can understand the cases for and against regarding Bruegel's peasant compositions as simple

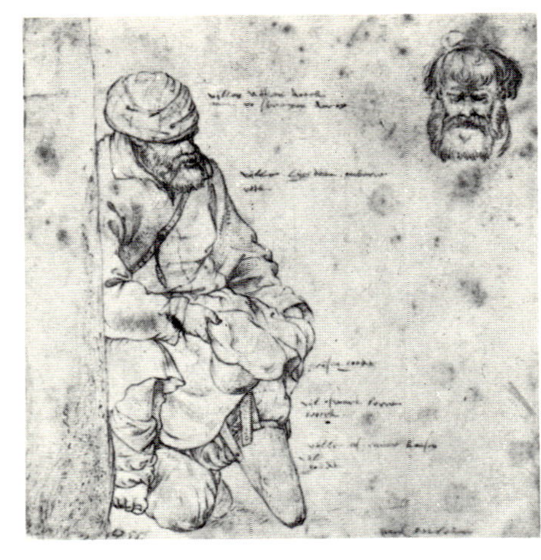

Roelant Savery (?)
CRIPPLE BEGGING AND STUDY OF
HEAD
Pen drawing in maroon on preparatory study
in sanguine on paper; 147 x 137 mm (5 x
5 in)
c. 1600
Amsterdam, Rijksmuseum, Rijkstren
penkabinett
One of the *naer het leven* series, now no
longer attributed to Bruegel but to Roelant
Savery (1576–1639). A comparison of this
work with the *Cripples* in the Louvre (opposite page) is interesting because the cripple
shown here is obviously feigning.

Pieter Bruegel the Elder (?)
CRIPPLES AND BEGGARS
Pen drawing on paper; 285 x 206 mm (11¼ x
8 in)
Vienna, Graphische Sammlung Albertina
This interesting drawing was published as an
engraving by Cock, giving Bosch as the
original author; it belongs to that group of
works which are sometimes attributed to
Bruegel and sometimes to Bosch. Recently,
Grossmann and others have expressed an
inclination to attribute the drawing in
Vienna and another very similar one in
Brussels to Pieter Bruegel. Bruegel's interest
in this subject was expressed most vividly in
the painting entitled *The Cripples* (opposite
page).

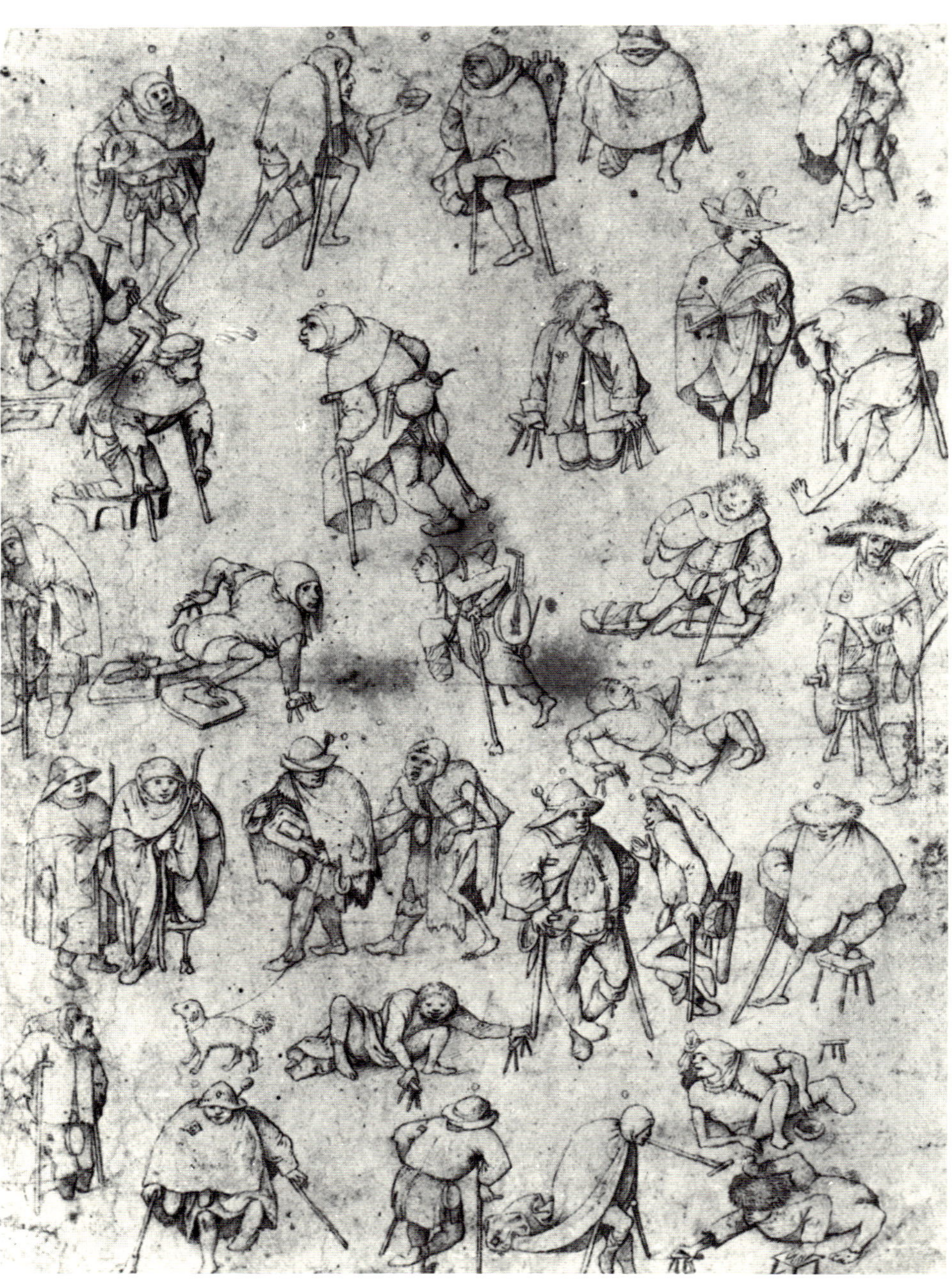

THE CRIPPLES
Oil on panel; 18 x 21.5 cm (7 x 8½ in)
Signed and dated: 'BRVEGEL M.D.LXVIII.'
Paris, Louvre
The work cannot be identified for certain
amongst the various mentions in old inventories, including that of the Imperial
Collection in Prague and that of the
collection of Queen Christina of Sweden.
Paul Mantz gave it to the Louvre in 1892.
The painting's literal significance is folkloristic and was identified by Gudlaugsson in
1947: *The Cripples* bizarre clothing is
associated with the processions of lepers
which took place during carnival time. The
compassion which we feel for such people

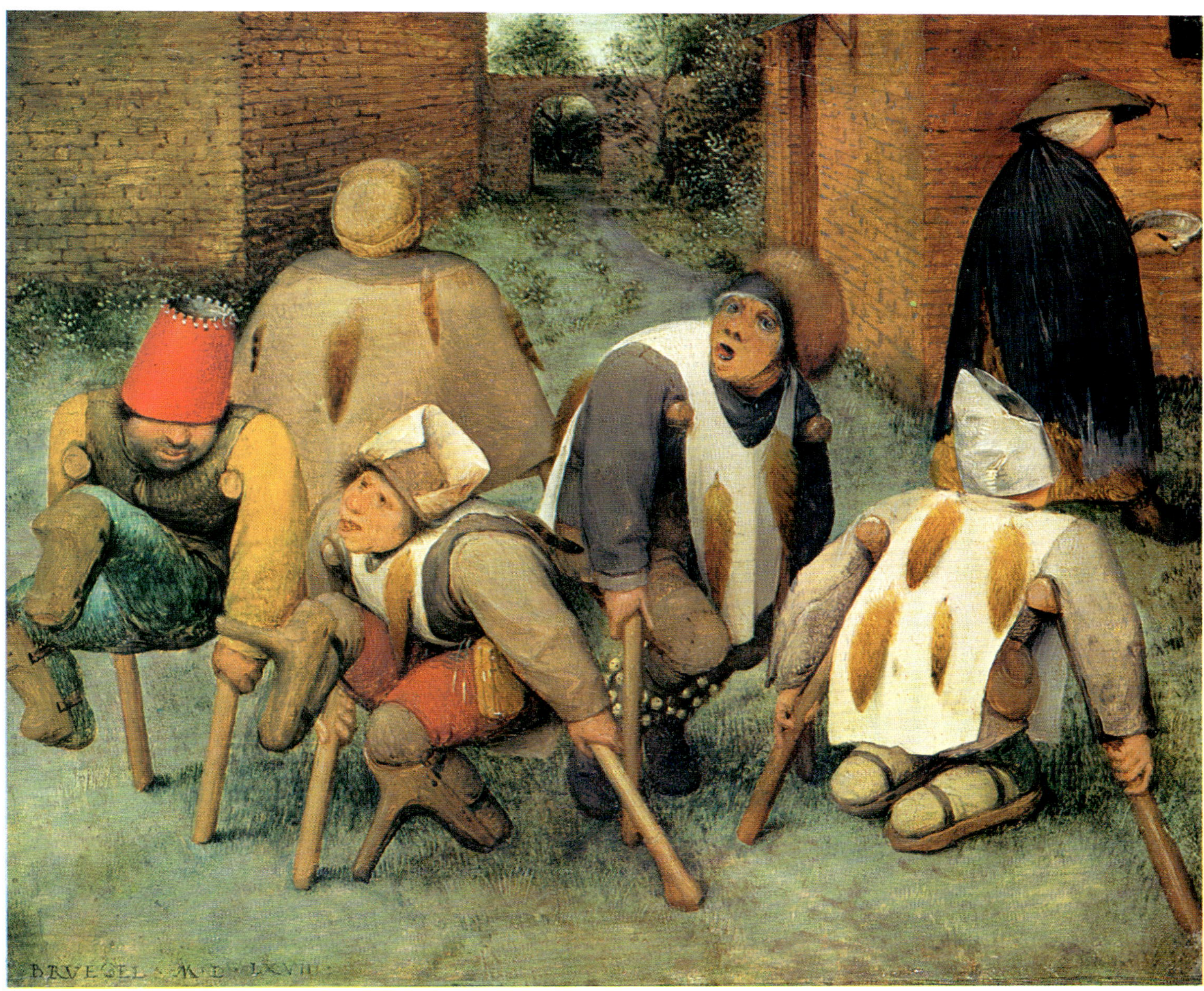

today would have been out of place in
Bruegel's day. The engraving in the
Albertina, taken from the drawing recently
attributed to bruegel (opposite page), bears
an inscription stigmatizing begging as a con-
sequence of poverty which the victims
brought on themselves. However, this in no
way detracts from the misery and desperation
betrayed on the faces on these unfortunate
beings abandoned by the world.

genre works without any deeper significance.

The uncouth movements, the rhythm of the dance and the almost uncanny interlinking of the dancers are all imbued with equal intensity. The main group seemingly rotating between the two men – onlooker and bagpipe player – standing post-like in the foreground is skilfully woven into a unified whole with the quieter crowd in the background. Thus, in spite of all its exuberant movement, the composition possesses a certain quiet stability.

The subject of *The Conversion of Saul* (page 142) Acts of the Apostles 9: 3, appears frequently in Italian painting after Michelangelo's fresco of 1542 in the Cappella Paolina, and also occurs in the Netherlands before Bruegel, for example in an engraving by Lucas van Leyden. Quite apart from the magnificent mountainous landscape, Bruegel once again makes iconographical innovations, reducing the scale of the principal scene and concealing it, rather as if it were an accident, within a larger scene. Troops are pouring up through a deep gully in the rocks, behind which we can glimpse a far-reaching plain. Roughly in the centre of the picture the path turns sharply and the troops move away steeply up towards the clouds, up the seemingly summitless mountain. In this latter respect the picture may reflect Bruegel's own travels through the Alps. Somewhere in the middle of the multitude of soldiers, Saul – later to become Paul – has fallen from his horse. The sound of Christ's voice ('Saul, Saul, why persecutest thou me?'), which caused him to fall, is suggested by two rays of sunlight directed towards the convert. Bruegel brilliantly catches the viewpoint of an eyewitness on the periphery of the event. The mighty croups of two horses dominate the foreground. All the figures are seen from the back except a man on horseback on the right who is telling the horseman in the extrordinary green costume about the incident, and at the same time diverting our eye towards the central scene. The composition plays around a group of strange-looking cypresses or spruces, the one nearest us dividing the picture exactly into two quite dissimilar halves whose dramatic focal points are nonetheless held in balance by their interplay of opposite effects. This is one of the most exciting and, by virtue of the impenetrable heights to which it seems to ascend, one of the most mysterious of Bruegel's landscapes.

Here again contemporary allusions have been sought. The horseman in black, the favourite colour of the Spanish court, and even Saul himself have been seen as the Duke of Alba crossing the Alps from Lombardy with his troops in 1567. But what could be the significance of such an interpretation? Nobody could seriously hope that Alba would be converted and if so, to what faith? To Calvinism; a sudden change of heart; a love of humanity? Stridbeck sees here the laborious path of virtue, a condition of man's redemption while Tolnay, on the other hand, regards it as the path of folly. In Grossmann's view, Saul's fall represents an admonition to follow God, which may be linked to the medieval tradition that Saul's conversion was associated with the deadly sin of pride. A copy of the painting exists in a private collection in Brussels.

A comparison with the two earlier versions of *The Adoration of the Magi in the Snow* (pages 144–145) in Brussels (pages 24–25) and London (page 99) reveals how far Bruegel had progressed, in this little work of 1567, in the secularization of Biblical themes. Even more than in the preceding work the holy event has been assimilated into a depiction of contemporary life, in this case a winter's day in a Flemish village. At the same time it represents a new type of winter landscape. The subject itself is located in an unexpected spot: the episode can just be made out in a dilapidated shed in the left foreground. The diagonal movement of the people tends to lead the eye away from the main event, though our gaze as it searches gets held up again by the figures standing off at a respectful distance. The veil of falling snow which covers the whole picture stresses the anonymity of everyone present, their utterly impersonal assimilation into the divine scheme. Although used as an attribute of winter in 15th-century calendar illustrations, falling snow had not previously been depicted for its own sake as a natural phenomenon in panel paintings. The idea was quickly imitated, for example in van Valckenborch's winter scene now in Vienna and in works of later artists.

Interest is added to the foreground with unobtrusive elegance in the willow trunk lying to the left, echoed onthe right by the branches in the frozen canal. A small child in a kind of sledge pushes itself unwittingly towards a hole in the ice and its mother has just become aware of the danger. A fire may possibly be on the point of getting out of control in the tent-like shack on the right. But who can tell whether any symbolic significance attaches to this odd-looking shelter with a jug sticking out ostentatiously at one corner. Located as it is directly opposite the stall where the birth has taken place. Or to the ruined, crudely propped-up Romanesque palace (not a church, as Stechow states)

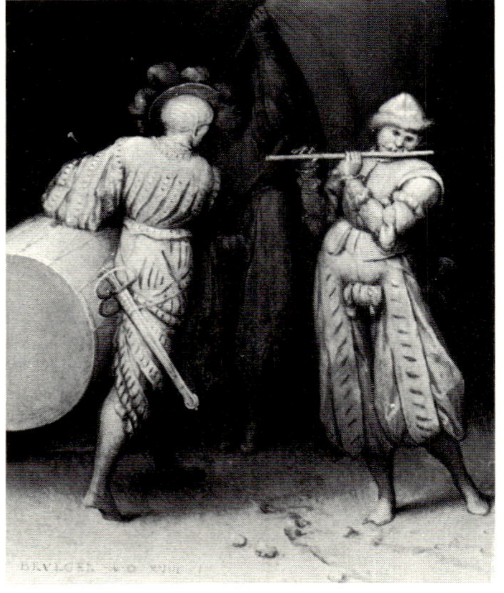

THE THREE SOLDIERS
Grisaille on panel; 20.3 x 17.8 cm (7 x 6 in)
Signed and dated: 'BRVEGEL. M.D. XVIII'
New York, Frick Collection
Mentioned in the inventory of King Charles I of England in 1639, it must already have belonged to him before he ascended the throne in 1625, as revealed by an acknowledgement of delivery on the back. The subject is unusual for Bruegel and stylistically the work would seem to belong to the period after him. The third figure in the date is not preserved and the 'VIII' has been retouched. The authenticity of the signature is doubtful and the work may possibly be by Jan Brueghel the Elder.

THE GOOD SHEPHERD
Oil on panel; 40 x 54 cm (15 x 21 in)
Neither signed nor dated
Antwerp, Kronacker Collection
Thematically this could be the companion
piece to the *Unfaithful Shepherd* in Philadelphia (below), but its different, weaker
composition makes this theory unaccepta-
ble. Grossmann recently attributed this
picture to Bruegel, though it has always been
known through the numerous copies by
Pieter Brueghel the Younger; however, this is
questionable in view of the work's lack of
pictorial and compositional strength.

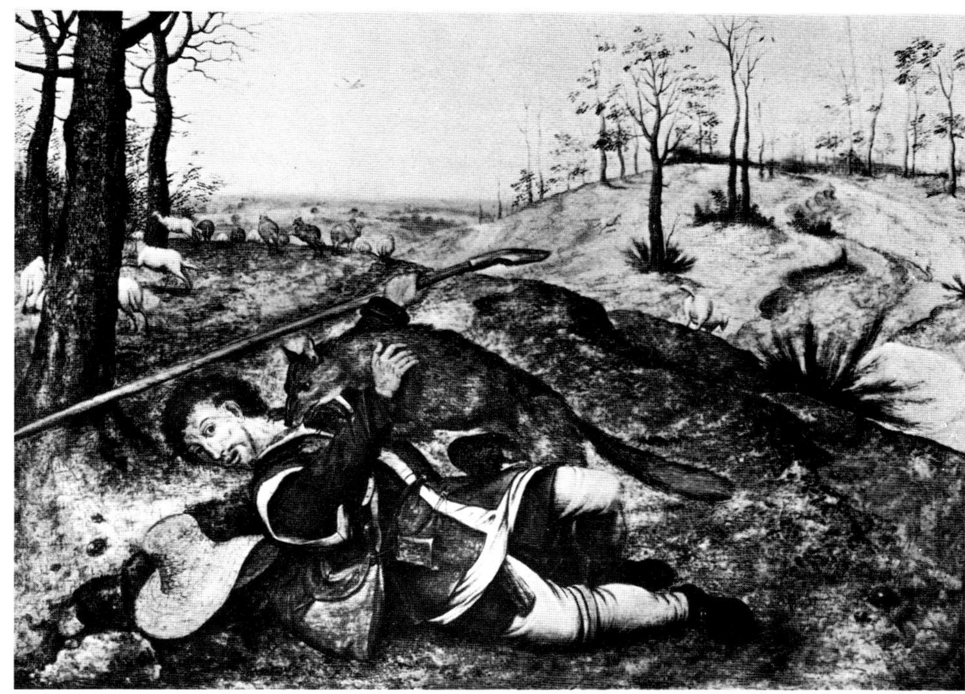

and the remains of an archway. The warm tones of the brick walls provide a deliberate
contrast to the figures wrapped up against the cold. The picture has always been extremely popular and twenty-nine copies exist, thirteen by Pieter Brueghel the Younger.
My own recollection of *The Land of Cockaigne* (page 142) goes back to earliest
childhood, the clearest proof possible of its almost magical power to imprint itself on the
mind thanks to those few unsurpassably expressive figures. Having stuffed themselves
full, they are stretched out on the ground like bursting sacks. According to the caption
on Peter van der Heyden's engraving after this picture, the idler on the right has difficulty even in moving the hands round from behind his neck to his mouth.
In an age of harsh drudgery and privation a stomach full of good things meant in-
comparably more than today, especially if coupled with the idea of permanent
dispensation from the slavery of daily work. In the *Land of Cockaigne* the idea of being
able to guzzle to bursting point runs riot with the extravagance of unbridled excess. The
reasonable desire to satisfy hunger after a hard day's work is transformed into a
positively indecent craving for a paradise dominated by the deadly sins of *Gula* (intemperance) and *Desidia* (sloth).
The 'Land of Cockaigne' corresponds to the Dutch '*Luilekkerland*' (*lui* meaning slow,
idle; *lekker* means tasty, pleasant; *lekkerbeck*, therefore, a sweet tooth). The idea goes

THE UNFAITHFUL SHEPHERD
Oil on panel; 61.6 x 86 cm (24¼ x 33 in)
Neither signed nor dated
Philadelphia, John G. Johnson Collection
This brilliant composition with its single
figure is one of the greatest large-figure
achievements of Bruegel's late period. The
originality of the composition could not be
attributed to any artist other than Bruegel
and the work can be dated to the last few
years of the artist's life. The rigorous
economy of its composition makes it far
superior to any of the various copies and
suggests that it is in fact the master's original,
perhaps retouched (a view shared by de Loo,
Michel, Glück).

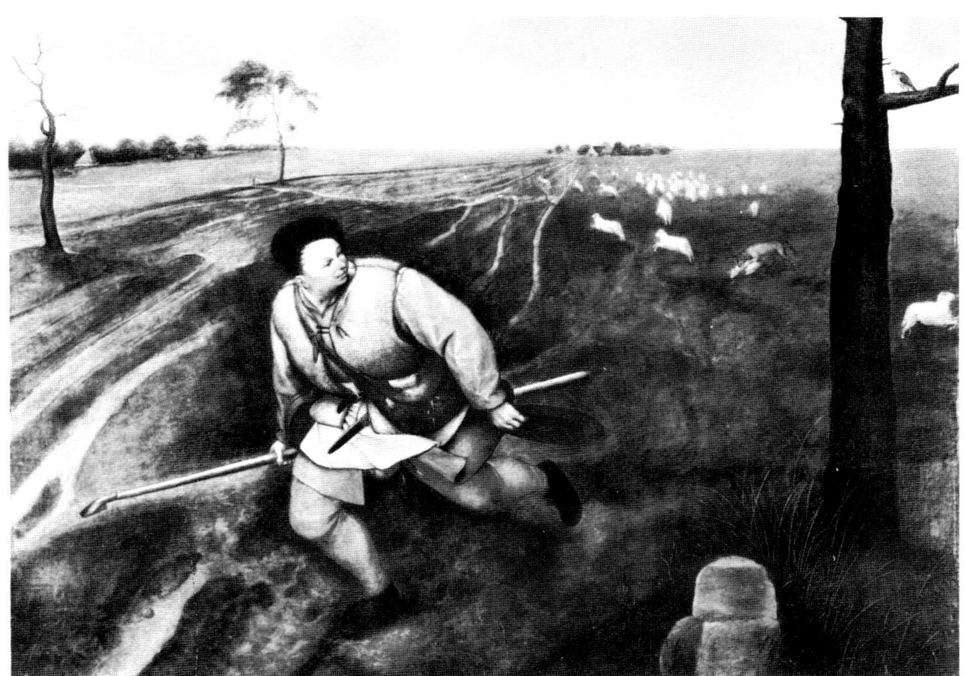

back to a poem on that subject by the German poet Hans Sachs, published in Nuremberg in 1536. This probably served as the model for an anonymous prose description of 'Luyleckerlandt' which appeared in print at Antwerp in 1546 and to which Bruegel referred. This was incorporated in a work entitled *Veelderhande Geneuchlycke Dichten, Tafelspelen ende Refereynen* which was published in 1600. This satire gives an exact description of every detail: the mountain of semolina which the new arrival has to eat his way through to get into the Land of Cockaigne in the first place, the roofs covered with cakes and pies, the fence of sausages, the river of milk (Bruegel has a sea of milk), roasted birds, and so on. The cactus made of bread is a characteristic invention of Bruegel's. The *Land of Cockaigne* is overrun with villains; the decent, well-behaved people are thrown out.

Bruegel has succeeded brilliantly in expressing the satiety of the three gluttons not just as the result of one single act of self-indulgence but as a permanent state. It is the uninterrupted succession of eating and sleeping which is sinful, with eating only turning into *Gula* and rest into *Desidia* when they become an obsessive habit. It looks as though the scholar (?) lying on his fur coat is just becoming aware of his contrary situation, of the transformation of happiness into misery. His expression is that of an unhappy man whose reflections on his misfortune keep him awake, so that he stares with open eyes into the void while his talents, represented by book and paper, go to waste. His sin itself is beginning to punish him, for his sloth will not allow him to alter his own situation. But the two other figures, whose stumpy forms are a bold experiment on Bruegel's part (pages 148–149), have surrendered themselves utterly and with a total abnegation of will to the sweet indolence of slumber. And yet, is the one on the left not blinking slightly, rather like a dazed pig? The 'scholar's' expression, too, can be seen as a sign either of mental despair or of impending physical collapse. In the soldier's case there is a certain professional link between sleep and death. The trio's enjoyment has certainly reached its climax. It is as though their very bliss contains the seeds of their destruction, as though in the hour of their greatest happiness these sinners are already being overtaken by the last great punishment which is death. Thus the dream turns into a nightmare.

Three social classes are represented: soldier, peasant and the figure who seems to be a scholar. A fourth figure, the knight, lies like a dog in the hut, thereby no doubt symbolizing the decline of his class. The 'scholar' has also been seen as clerk and priest. The contrast between his luxurious fur coat and the rustic simplicity of the rest of his attire has not been satisfactorily explained. Does it mean that *Gula* has turned him back into nothing better than a peasant? Certainly there is a similarity with the resting lad in the *Corn Harvest* (pages 112–113).

The round construction on the tree has associations with the Wheel of Fortune: the figures sprawled below are as if broken upon the wheel. An interesting comparison can be made with an engraving by Pieter Balten in which a garland of sausages is wound around the tree in the centre, a pointedly sarcastic allusion to the serpent Lucifer and the Tree of Knowledge in the story of the Fall.

The *Ambush* (page 151), now in Stockholm, was until recently regarded as a very good copy – there are six others – of a lost work of Bruegel's. The cleaning in 1971 revealed Bruegel's original signature 'M.D.LXVII BRVEGEL' under the later one 'P. BREVGHEL/1630'. This and the high technical quality of the painting down to the minutest detail make it very probable that the Stockholm version is not a copy but the original, which was thought to have been lost. The date has the drawback that the last three figures are unclear. The Roman V should in all probability be a Roman X and the final II doesn't seem entirely original. It is not impossible that Bruegel made a mistake with the date: the *Fall of Hermogenes*, for example, is wrongly dated 1544.

Originally in the Imperial Collection in Prague, the picture went to Stockholm in 1648 as booty. In 1654 Queen Christina let it go back to Antwerp to be sold and it was presumably on that occasion that the false signature was appended. This would have been done in 1668 or shortly before by the art dealer Forchoudt, the reason being that in the second half of the 17th century the works of Pieter Brueghel the Younger were fetching higher prices than those of his father. After various detours it ended up in the collections of Stockholm University in 1884.

Three heavily-armed soldiers have ambushed a peasant couple at the edge of a wood in flat, brown heath-like countryside. We look out from the clearing on to a broad plain which draws the eye along countless wheel tracks into the far distance, rather as in the *Unfaithful Shepherd* (page 157). At the centre stands the most active and aggressive of the robbers: holding a pistol in his right hand, he is tearing a purse from the peasant's

THE MISANTHROPE
(THE FAITHLESSNESS OF THE WORLD)
Tempera on canvas; 86 x 85 cm (33 x 33½ in)
Signed and dated on the painted frame: 'BRVEGEL 1568.'
Naples, Museo di Capodimonte
Painted in tempera like the preceding one, this work also arrived in Naples in 1734 in the same way as the *Parable of the Blind*, via the Masi and Farnese collections. The inscription reads in translation: 'Because the world it is so faithless I am going into mourning'. The perfidious world, where hypocrisy and deceit reign supreme, is symbolized in the thief inside the glass globe intent on stealing the old man's purse. The composition has been reproduced in six copies and, with a few variations, in the series of engravings on proverbs by Jan Wierix.

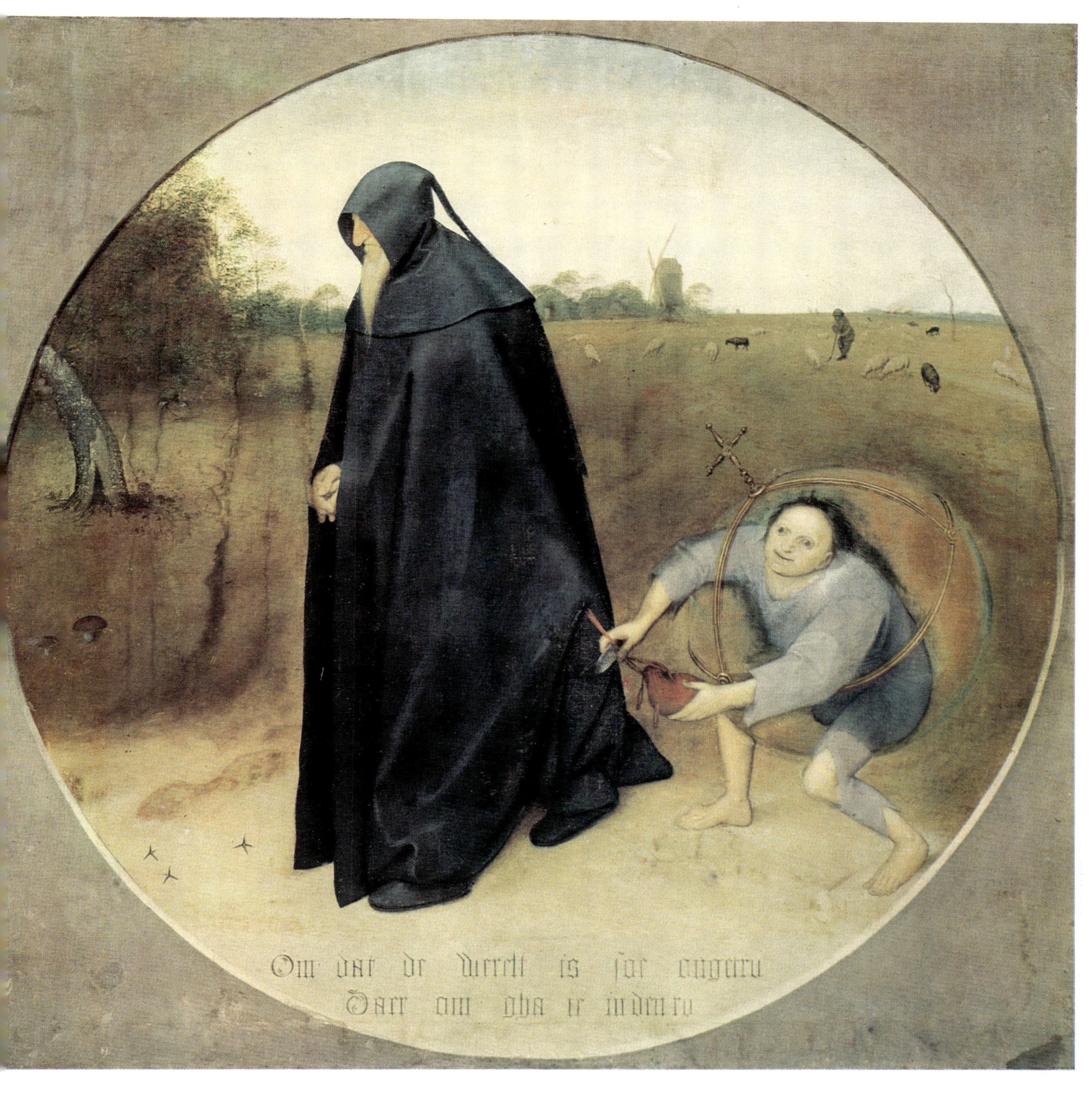

Om dat de werelt is soe ongetru
Daer om gha ic in den ru

neck and at the same time kicking his wife as she kneels with an imploring Niobean gesture of her arms. The robber on the left underlines the violence of the scene as he holds his spear at the ready, while the one on the right makes off with a leather sack. The powder horn hanging at the waist of the robber on the left bears a crucifix, a bitter allusion to the discrepancy between its significance and the actions of its owner. The fine doublet worn by the one on the right, no doubt stolen at some stage, is torn at the elbow. Mercenaries whose hire is presumably insufficient go out and plunder. Leaving aside the problematic figures in the date, the painting belongs stylistically to the latter years of Bruegel's life and is no doubt based on the artist's experience of encounters with marauding soldiers. It may be that Alba's troops are meant, but the overall message is still clearly a generalized one. The bizarre diversity of the mercenaries' stolen dress is itself an indication of something being wrong. And help is far away, there is nothing to deter the robbers from their aim. One has to look hard to find any sign of life in this

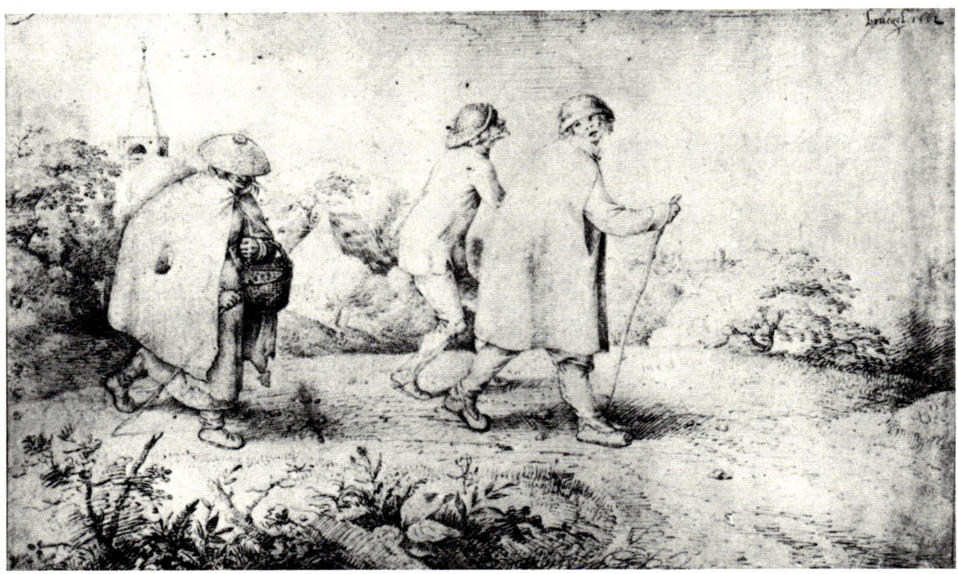

THE BLIND MEN
Pen drawing in maroon on paper; 192 x 310 mm (7½ x 12 in)
Signed and dated above right: 'bruegel 1562'
Berlin, Kupferstichkabinett
From the compositional point of view this drawing has nothing in common with the great painting entitled *The Parable of the Blind* in Naples (opposite page), but it does reveal Bruegel's interest in this subject. Its significance is not entirely clear. A beggar, perhaps not blind, is walking behind the two blind men, who, unusually, are not in the act of stumbling against some obstacle and falling to the ground. The work was apparently a preparatory drawing for a lost engraving illustrating a proverb, but this theory has not been confirmed. From a stylistic point of view the drawing has acquired considerable importance as an example of popular figures since the exclusion of the *naer het leven* series from Bruegel's work, even if these figures are not taken directly from real life. The drawing must in fact be regarded as a studio composition.

apparently God-forsaken place, although a village can just be made out on the horizon: to the right of it, almost invisible, a rider with a cart, and on the far right a gallows. A little nearer, but also clearly out of earshot, stands a shepherd with his flock; to the left, on the edge of the wood, an accomplice keeps a lookout. For Bruegel these criminals are anonymous representatives of violence: expressionless, eyeless, with their headgear pulled down low over their faces. Touched by the remnants of a bad conscience, the third one casts his eyes to the ground. All the more striking, then, is the contrast afforded by the unconcealed emotion on the faces of the victims – a rare effect in Bruegel's works. The couple acquire the stature of heroes: ennobled by their suffering, they are patient in the moment of affliction, raised above their own class. The horrified, despairing expression of the man, just off centre, forms the focal point of numerous converging lines which seem to suggest a halo: lance shaft, wheel tracks, and a path cutting across from the left and carried on to the right of his head in a hump in the ground.
Italian influence has been detected in the composition, particularly by Stridbeck, who quotes examples from works of the Romanist Barendt von Orley, but no specific and convincing evidence has ever been adduced. The robber in the act of kicking has a parallel in the figure on the right in the *Massacre of the Innocents* (pages 132–133). This type of composition, with a few large figures engaged in some violent action, also includes the *Peasant Brawl*, a work of Bruegel's of which numerous copies exist, one of them from Rubens' studio, and which was engraved by Lucas Vorsterman.

Interpretation of the *Cripples*, (Page 155), as of other late works, is made particularly difficult by the absence of any personal testimony. One is liable to be misled into attributing to Bruegel the same sort of sympathy for such people as we tend to feel today, or to assume he had a similar artistic interest in physical deformity to that of modern artists. Works of art do not have an absolute value, they are to some extent shaped by interpretation. The feelings aroused in us today by this masterly representation of human misery can no longer by discounted in any exposition of it. K. Renger, in 1971–1972, listed the most important attempts to explain the picture's significance. Tolnay, it seems, suspected in it a satire on human hypocrisy, the different types of head-gear representing different classes: priest, prince, soldier, bourgeois and peasant. Unlike these, woman suffers from real poverty. Stidbeck thinks the cripples symbolize

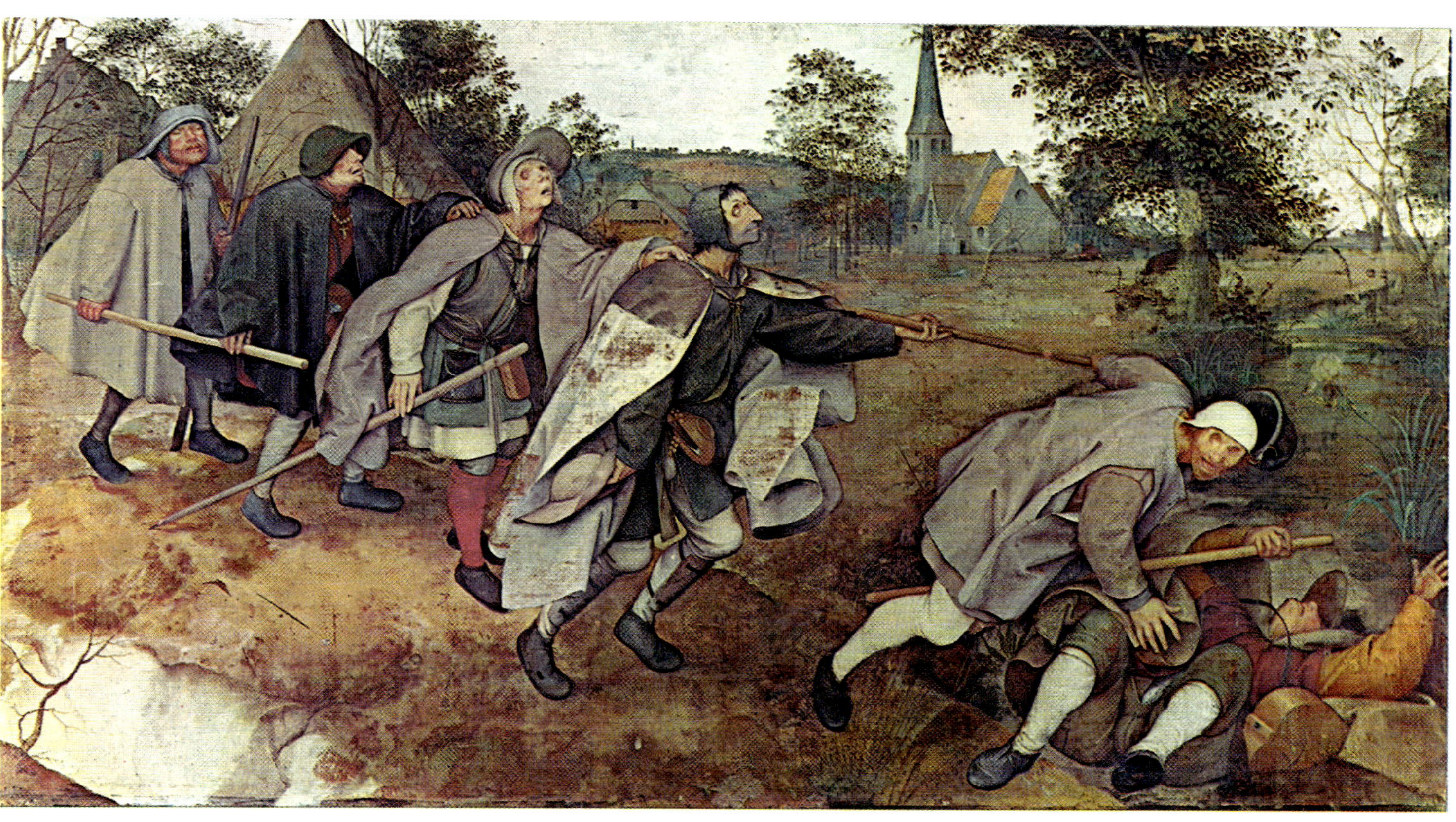

THE PARABLE OF THE BLIND
Tempera on canvas; 86 x 154 cm (33 x 60 in)
Signed and dated: 'BRVEGEL. M.D.LX.VIII.'
Naples, Museo di Capodimonte
Like the *Misanthrope*, this famous painting belonged to the collection of Count G. B. Masi of Parma; it was confiscated by the Farneses in 1611 and went to Naples with the Farnese collections in 1734. The phenomenon of blindness, which interested Bruegel all through his life (see also the drawing in Berlin, opposite page), found its fullest expression in this painting, where the essential significance seems transferred from the tragic infirmity of physical blindness to the human condition of spiritual blindness. It is not known why Bruegel chose the most perishable technique – tempera – for one of the finest pictures ever painted. However, it may be that he intended to keep the *Parable of the Blind* and the *Misanthrope* for himself or his family and therefore chose the least expensive technique. Detail on *pages 162–163*

'stupidity, lying, deceit and hypocrisy, the characteristics of sinful man'. A decisive clue was provided in 1947 by Gudlaugsson, who detected certain practices adopted by lepers during processions on the second Monday after Twelfth Night. This was the day on which lepers organized processions for begging. The foxes' tails in the painting were to advertise the fact that they were lepers, while the woman behind them was a hospital nurse collecting money. All this provided enough clues to make a historically correct interpretation possible. The important engraving showing beggars and cripples, published by H. Cock and now in the Albertina (page 154), has an inscription saying that those who waste their money in a life of debauchery go to the 'cripples' Bishop' – in other words, end up in the beggars' guild, where they hope to get a good income by feigning various infirmities. Peachum in Brecht's *Threepenny Opera* gives instructions on this very subject. The *Book of Vagabonds* published in Antwerp in 1563 lists forty distinct types of begging, and one can compare the false cripple in one of the *naer het leven* studies, (page 154). The 1691 inventory of Jan Baptiste Anthonie mentions a watercolour, now lost, *Cruepelen Busschop van der ouden Bruegel*. This ties up very nicely with Gudlaugsson's point. The 'bishop' is associated, amongst other things, with *Het Leenhof der Ghilden* by the rhetorician Jan van den Berghe in the first half of the 16th century, in which fiefs are granted to all social classes. Those who receive them are members of the fools', drinkers' and carnival guild. In the clerical class the Pope is followed by the 'Cripples' Bishop'. Van den Berghe's bishop is the same as the one to whom the beggars in the engraving after the drawing in the Albertina are making their pilgrimage after squandering their wordly possessions. The head-gear worn by Bruegel's

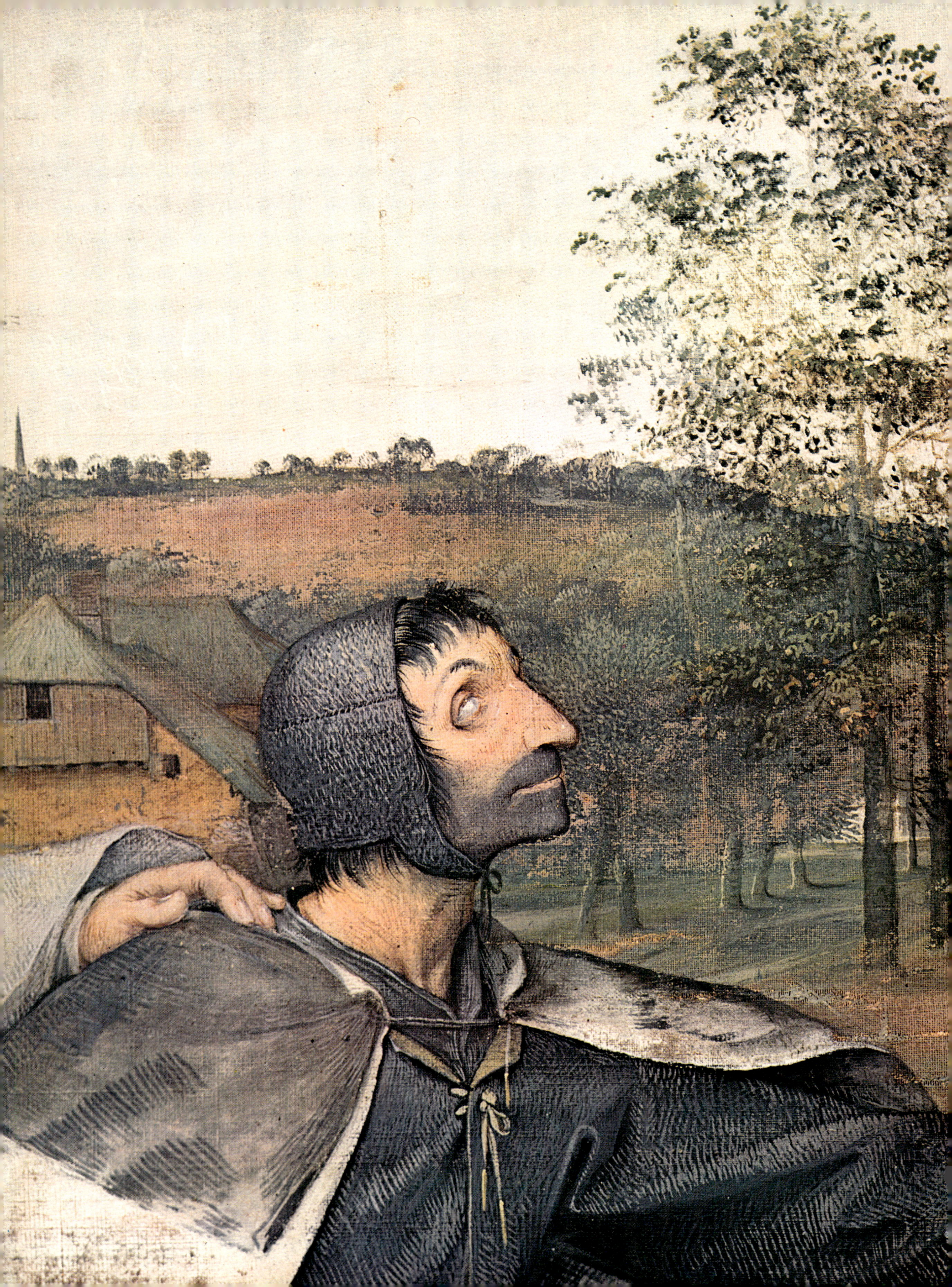

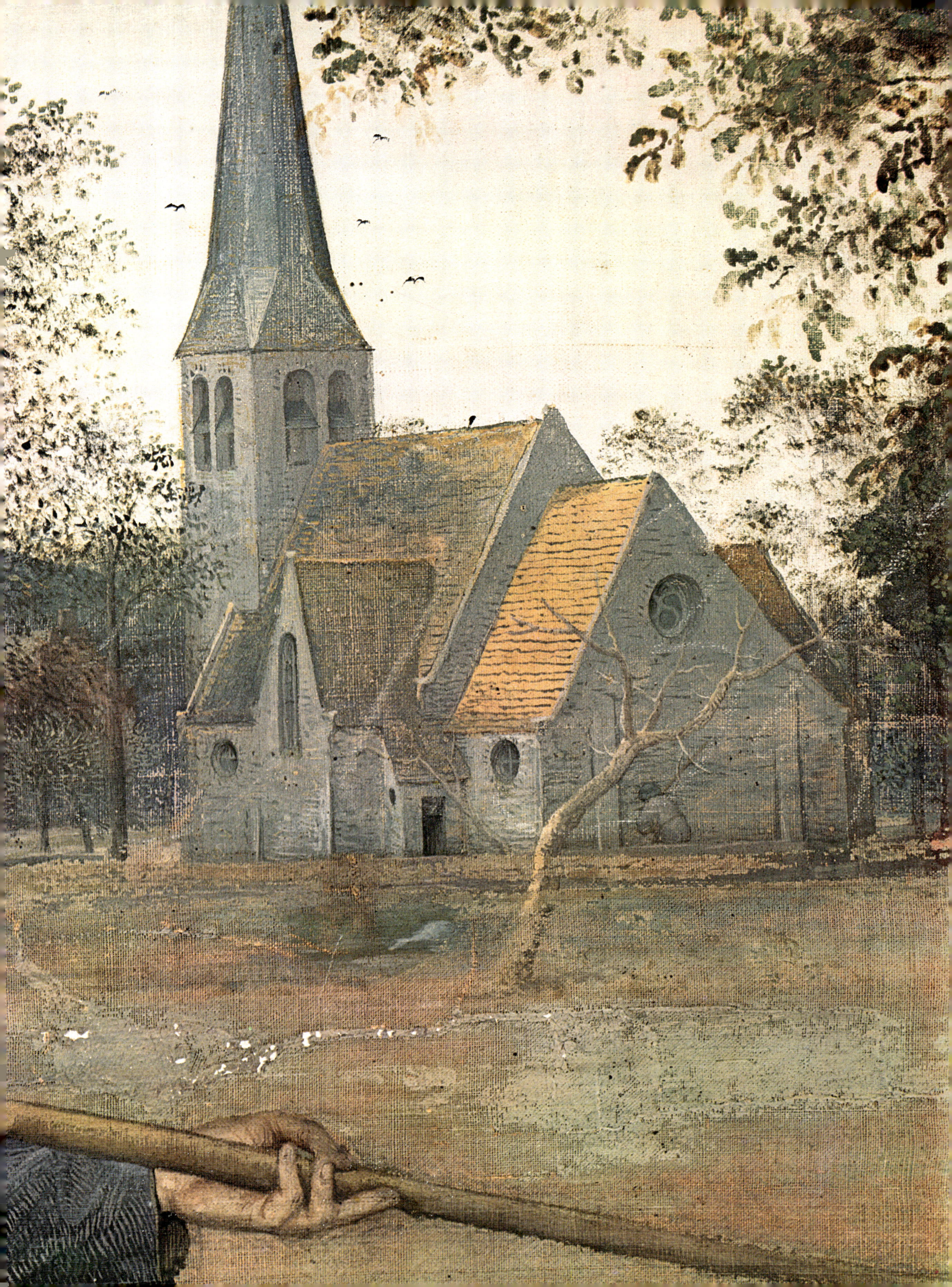

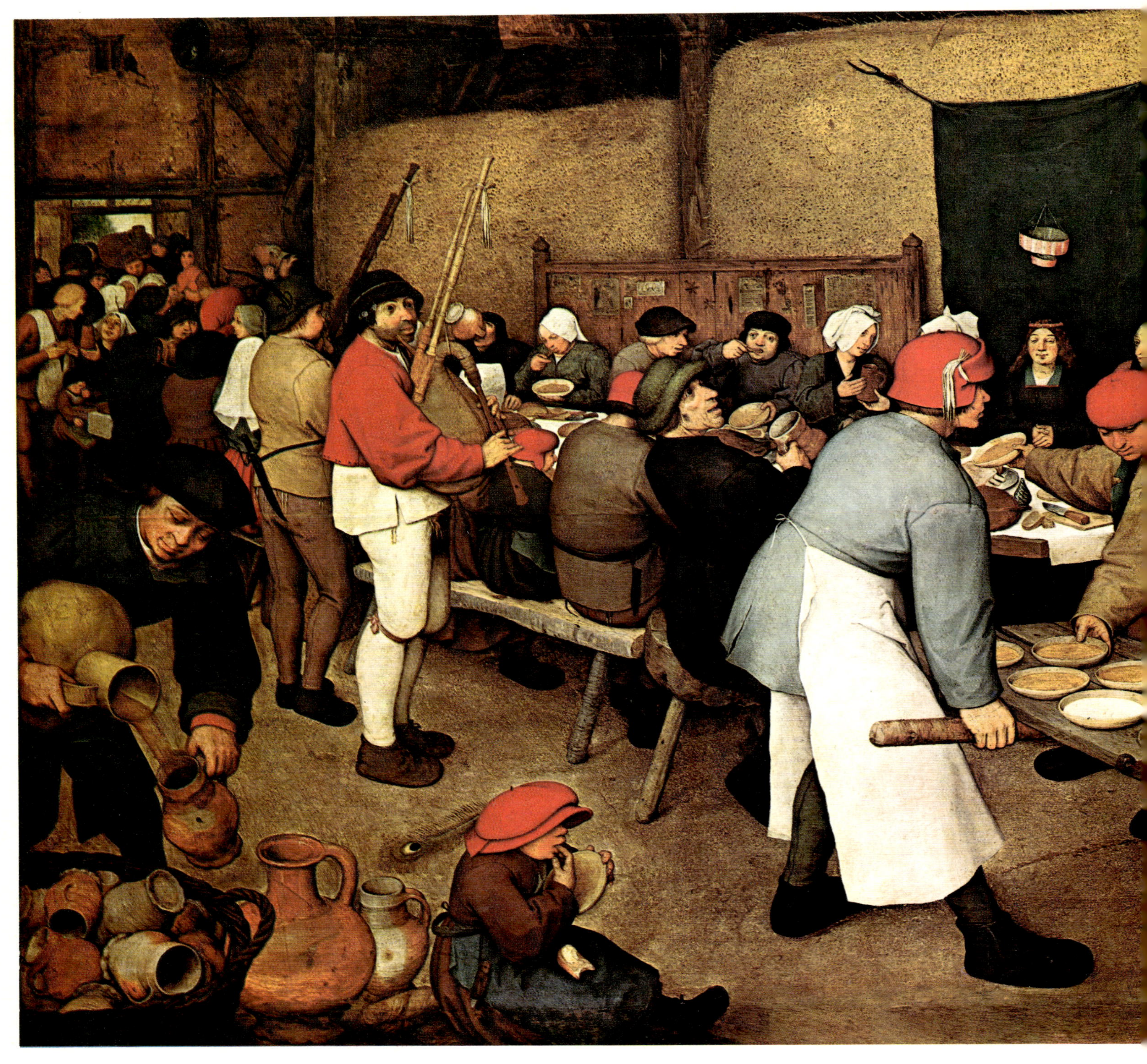

PEASANT WEDDING FEAST
Oil on panel; 114 x 163 cm (44 x 64 in)
Neither signed nor dated
c. 1568
Vienna, Kunsthistorisches Museum
This is the picture acquired by the Archduke
Ernest on 16 June 1594. A painting with the
same subject is mentioned by van Mander in
1604 as being in the possession of Herman
Pilgrims in Amsterdam. A strip 5.5 cm wide
has been added to the lower edge to replace

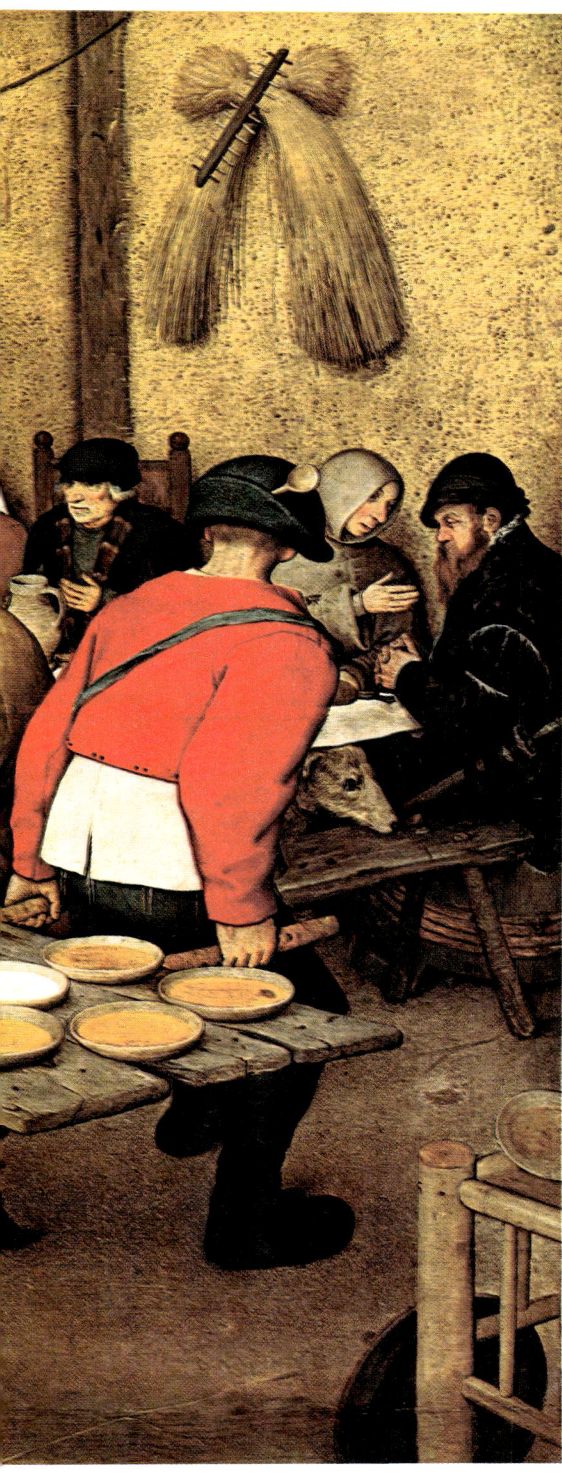

cripples can thus be explained as emblems of the guild, part and parcel of the carnival revelries. Van den Berghe includes in the guild the Count of Halfvasten, a carnival figure. This also reveals the significance of the cripples in the *Battle Between Carnival and Lent*. Thus the bishop's mitre worn by the cripple on the right is not meant to mock the clergy but alludes to the 'Cripples' Bishop'. Contrary to Glück's assumption the nurse does not represent Margaret of Parma disenchanted with the *gueuk* (beggars), but is one of the worn-out prostitutes who used to hire themselves out to look after lepers.

The foxes' tails were the most difficult detail to interpret because of their constantly shifting topical significance. In this connection it is interesting to recall the masquerade arranged on 19 June 1564 by Count Mansfeldt, in which Granvella is whipped with foxes' tails by the Devil. According to Martinissen, the farce referred to the intrigues of the ambassador Simon Renard ('fox'), an opponent of the Cardinal. However, there is no connection with Bruegel since the cripples in the carnival scene of 1559 are already wearing foxes' tails. Calvinist horsemen made an appearance with foxes' tails in Brussels in February 1567 as a challenge to the clergy, who had been mocking the reformers, and would now have to hide in their 'fox-holes'. Other, smaller animals' tails, for instance badgers' tails (see the picture in the Louvre), were also used at carnivals to designate lepers. But despite these perfectly acceptable explanations of the folklore behind the various details, the actual reason for Bruegel's painting the picture remains a mystery. Its extremely small format, the smallest of any of his oil paintings, means it was probably meant for a good friend, so its significance was most likely of a private nature. It has on the reverse an inscription consisting of a few words in Netherlandish, only partially legible, and two Latin distichs: '*Cruepelen ... hooch ... dat u nering bete en moeg*' ('Cripples ... up ... that your affairs may improve'). The distichs, written in capitals, read as follows: NATURAE DEERAT NOSTRAE QUOD DEFUIT ARTI / HAEC DATA PICTORI GRATIA TANTA (FUIT). / ALIUD / HIO NATURA STUPET PICTISEXPRESSA FIGURIS / VISA SUIS CLAUDIS HUNC BRUEGEL ESSE PAREM. (Nature did not possess whatever was wanting in our art, so great was the favour bestowed upon the painter; expressed in paintings and seen through cripples, Nature is amazed to find Bruegel her equal.)

In view of their similarity to Abraham Ortelius' *Epitaph* on Bruegel's art, Stechow thinks these texts are written either by Ortelius himself or by a friend of his for whom the picture was intended as a present. Both distichs speak of something quite different from the condemnatory caption on the engraving of the cripples, namely the artistic achievement, the picture's closeness to reality. This serves to remind us that Bruegel is first and foremost a painter, only in the second instance a moralist.

The group's uncertain, aimless scrambling, which Dvořák compared to a 'family of poisonous mushrooms growing out of the soft, wet earth in some lonely corner', produces a most powerful impression despite the small format. The truth of the situation is oppressively obvious: these cripples are feigning nothing, their misery is perfectly genuine. Perhaps they have just come home from a procession and are crawling around in their asylum. The one at the back seems to be gazing spellbound towards the gate, towards freedom and the world of healthy men and women from which he has just returned and which will never be his: we are confronted with unmitigated misery and despair. Again we query Bruegel's intention. In those days, sympathy certainly wasn't an emotion which could be expected – was Bruegel an exception? The picture's inscription and format indicate that it was not meant for the public. Nor do any copies exist. If it was a secret message to a friend, what was the purpose of its all-pervading cheerlessness, with those bleak brick walls which foreshadow van Gogh's prison yard?

Like the *Parable of the Blind* which also dates from 1568, the *Misanthrope* or *The Faithlessness of the World* (page 159) as it is also called, belongs to the treasures of the Museo Nazionale in Naples. Both are painted in tempera on canvas, the technique much used at Malines to which Bruegel evidently kept on returning until the end of his life. Both were confiscated in 1611 from the collection of Count G. B. Masi at Parma, passed into the possession of the Farneses and remained in the Palazzo del Giardino at Parma until 1680, coming to Naples in 1734. Auner points out that in 1596 a certain Cosimo Masi was governor of Cologne, which was where Bruegel's daughter moved to on her marriage.

An old man with a white beard is walking with folded hands and bowed head through a broad tract of flat countryside not dissimilar to that in the *Ambush* (page 157), or the *Unfaithful Shepherd* (page 154). His hooded cloak recalls monastic attire. Mantraps are scattered in his path and behind him is the symbol of the world, a tattered cutpurse who is cutting the old man's purse off. The blue tones of his clothing provide a deliberate contrast with the dark blue of the hooded cloak. This could be an allusion to mutual

the original piece which was destroyed and probably bore the date and signature. But there can be no doubt that the painting belongs to Bruegel's late style with large figures, like the *Peasant Kermis* in Vienna (pp. 168–169). Grossmann and Stridbeck saw in both works allegories of various deadly sins, particularly gluttony and lust. But the moralizing implications of this are somewhat forced.

Detail on *pages 166–167*

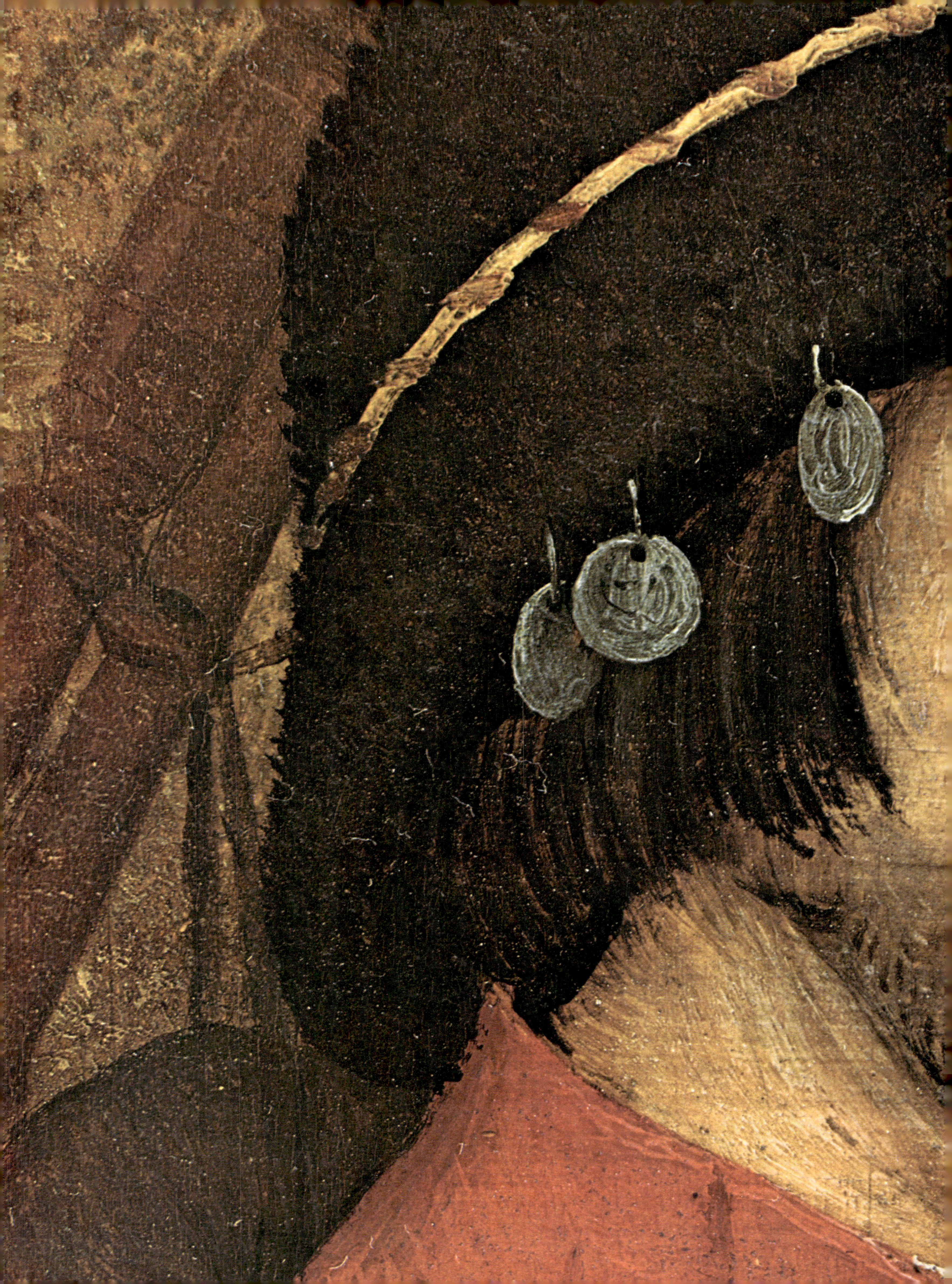

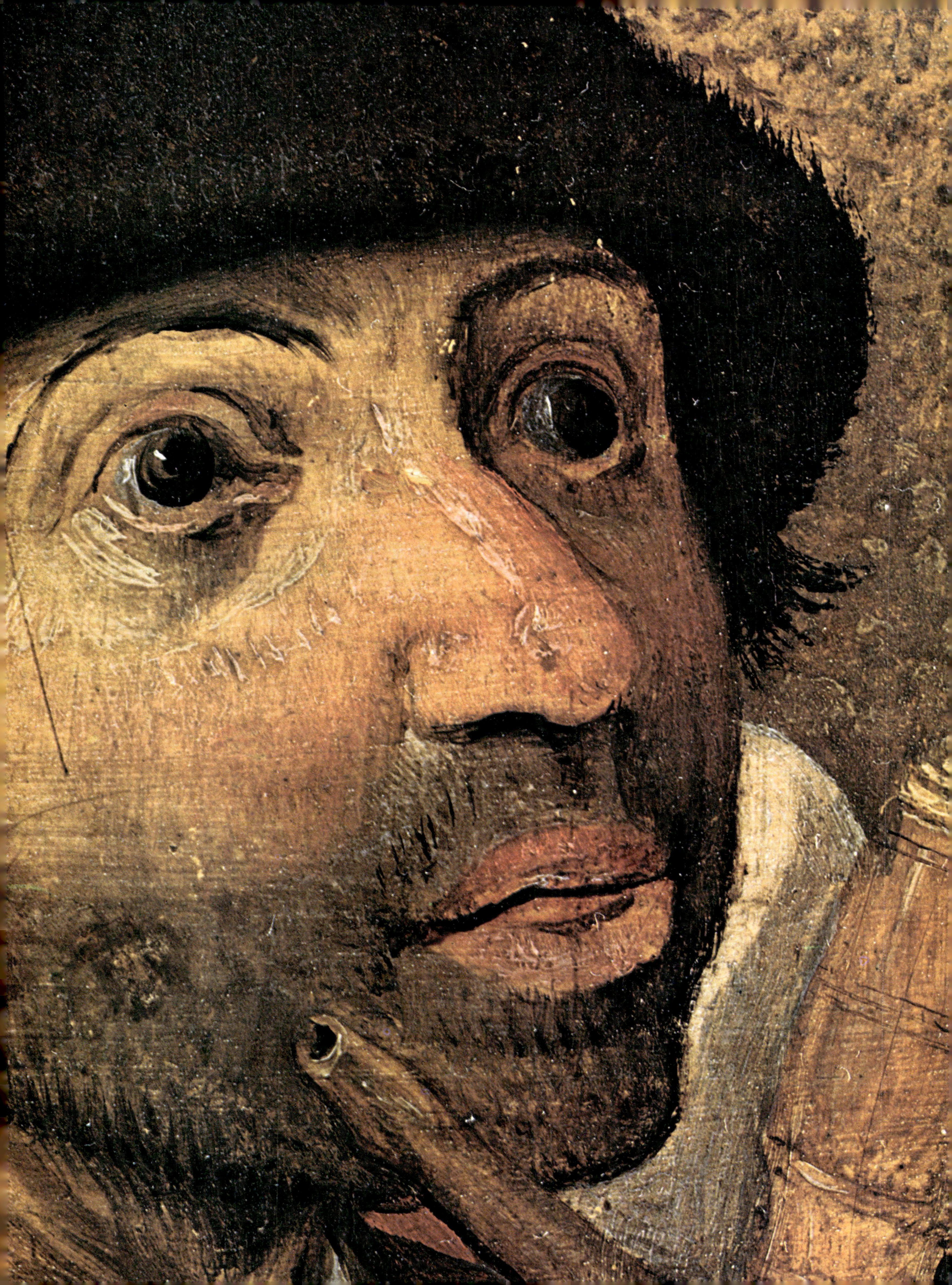

PEASANT KERMIS
Oil on panel; 114 x 164 cm (44 x 64 in)
Signed: 'BRVEGEL'
Vienna, Kunsthistorisches Museum
Listed in inventory G in Vienna (1612–1618)
as *'pauernmusica vom Altenbriegl'* and
mentioned again in 1748 in the Weltliche
Schatzkammer in Vienna. In its style and
composition this large painting has affinities
with the *Peasant Wedding Feast*; the two
paintings have therefore been regarded as
companion pieces or even as part of a series
on peasant life. The representation of bodies
in movement, at which Bruegel always excelled, is achieved with an unsurpassed
degree of skill. The spaces between the
groups of large-scale figures, the 'natural'
focal point and the consequent overlapping
of the figures reveal the gulf between this
picture and the *Peasant Wedding Dance* of
1556 in Detroit (pp. 138–139). Unconvincing attempts have also been made to detect
allegorical meanings in this work.

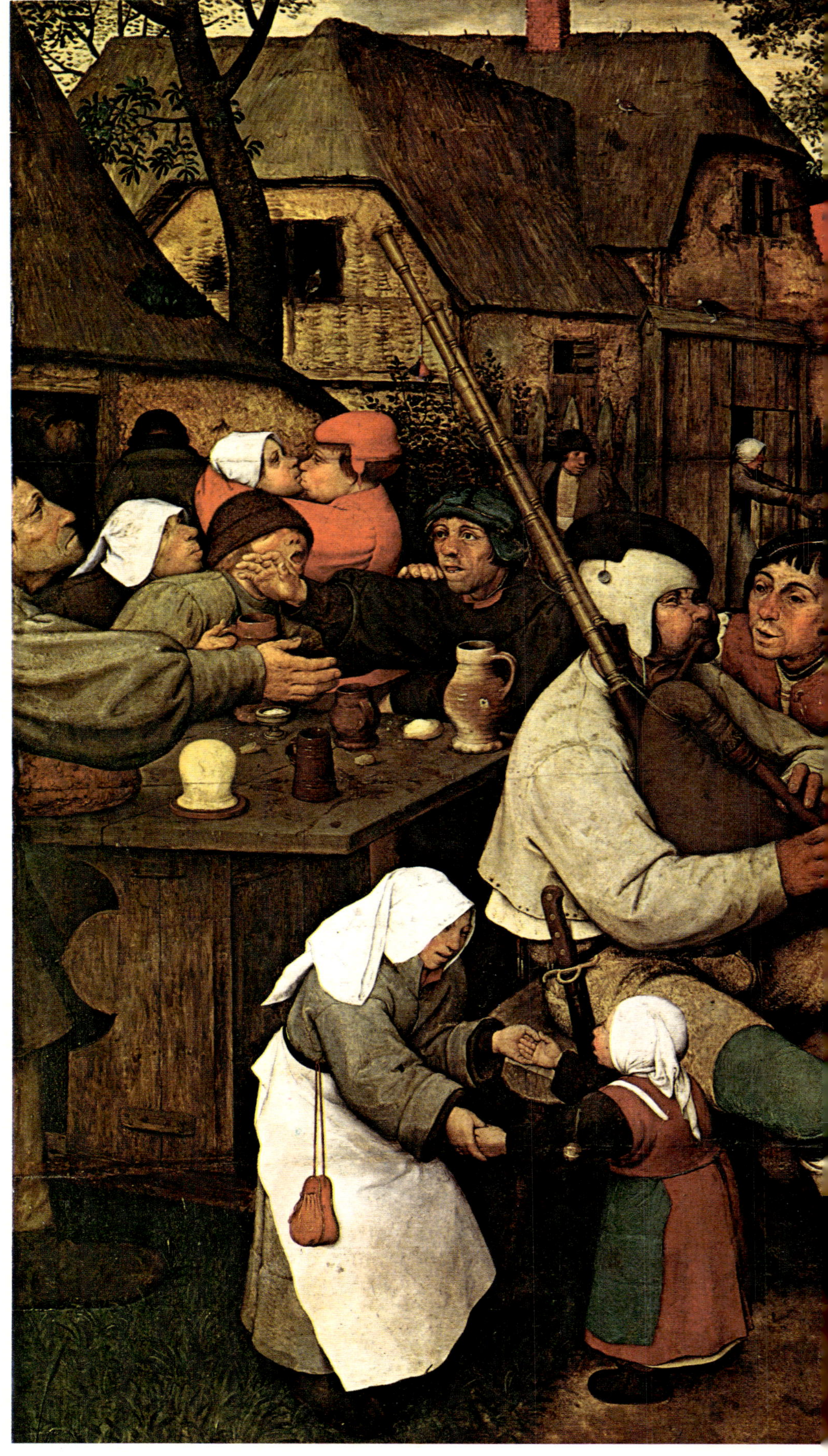

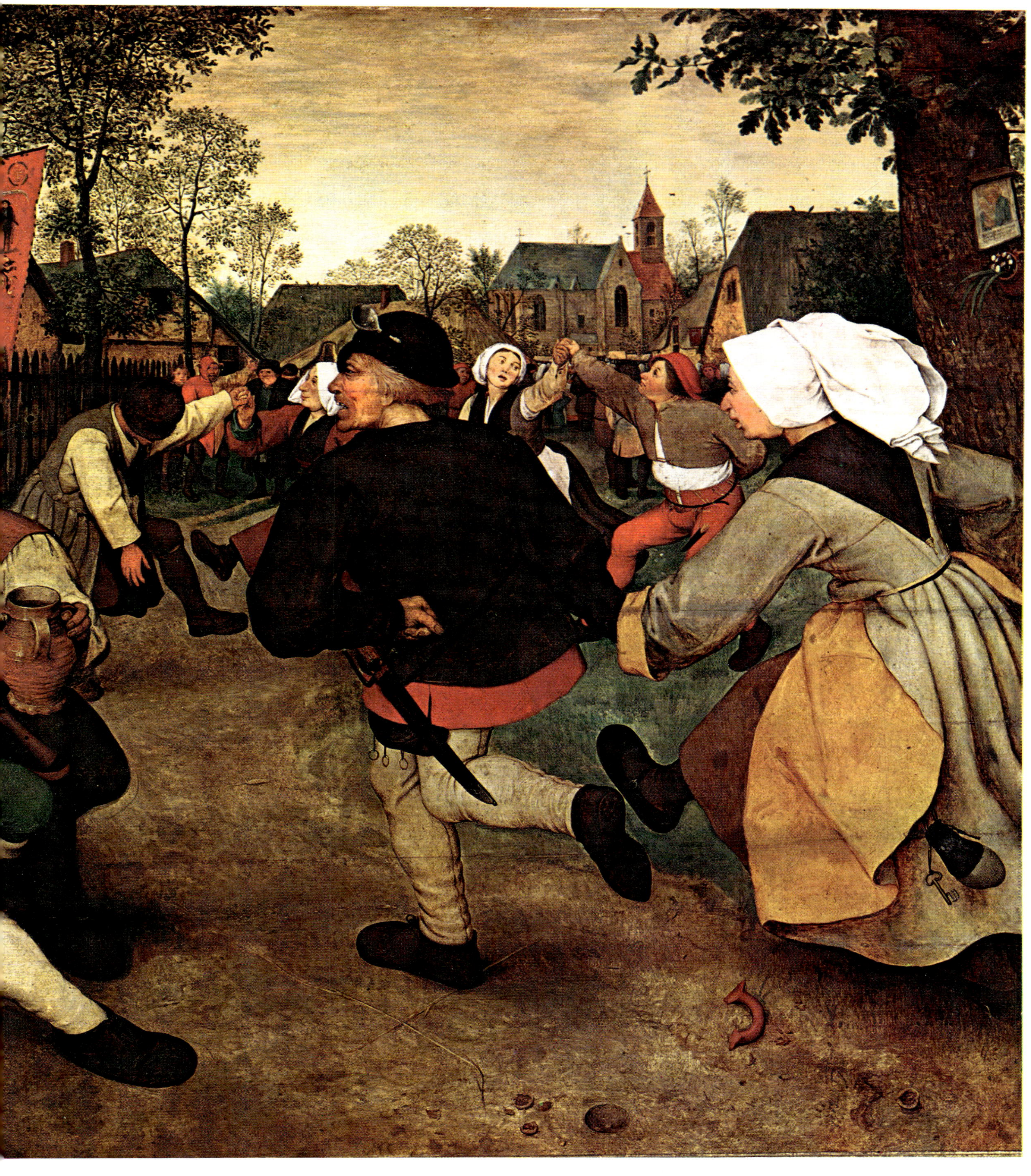

deception, while the red of the purse possibly refers to sin. In the background we can see a shepherd and a windmill, on the horizon a fire. The inscription in late gothic script at the bottom reads in translation: 'Because the world is so faithless I am going into mourning'. De Loo observed in 1907 that 'although Bruegel himself wrote the proverb he describes on the picture, the significance is almost impossible to fathom'. However, the caption is undoubtedly unauthentic, dating probably from about 1580, and as the difference in colour reveals, must have been written on a later overpainting. The verses may possibly have been taken from an unknown farce (D. Roggen, quoted by Marijnissen).

The first attempt at interpretation was made by Romdahl in 1904, who saw the picture as a critique of hypocritical monasticism. Bruegel, he thought, was attacking the monks for their meanness and the world for its rapaciousness. Monks flee the world because of its falsehood, but cannot themselves renounce sin. And at the time when the Protestants were stripping the churches, the world was simply dipping its hand into the purse of the clergy. Little has since been added to this interpretation, although the allusion to Church and politics is surely misguided. The significance of the two figures is universal: the old man is not a monk but simply someone in mourning. The only remaining question is whether Bruegel's attitude towards the misanthropic individual intent on abandoning the world is totally serious or whether he is drawing attention to the misanthrope's hypocrisy (symbolized by the concealment of the purse). Stechow regards the tondo form as a conscious repetition of the globe to emphasize that the misanthrope cannot in fact escape from the perfidious world. On the other hand, it has to be remembered that the circular form was commonly used for representations of proverbs, for example by Bruegel himself (page 45). But the shepherd in the background seems quite detached from the subject. In the context of perfidy, we are reminded of the *Unfaithful Shepherd* (page 151) and the *Good Shepherd* (page 151).

Six copies of the *Misanthrope* exist, as well as other copies after the engraving in the series of proverbs by J. Wierix.

One of the world's great paintings, *The Parable of the Blind* (page 161) passed through the same hands as the much less important *Misanthrope*. It was executed in the same year (1568) and shares the same technique – tempera on canvas.

The Parable of the Blind comes from St. Matthew (15: 14) and refers to the Pharisees: 'If the blind lead the blind, both shall fall into the ditch'. But the picture can readily be understood without any knowledge of Christ's words, its message being quite explicit. It meaning is clearly more profound and mysterious than the prophecy quoted by the Evangelist, or than the unsubtle moral pointed by the various engravings dedicated to the same theme.

Bruegel was not the first artist to be attracted by the parable: there is a small engraving of about 1545 by Cornelis Massys showing four blind men and an engraving by P. van der Heyden after Bosch (or more probably a follower of his) which H. Cock published sometime between 1560 and 1565 and which has only two blind men. Before painting this picture Bruegel himself touched on the theme of blindness, which in his day was such a common fact of everyday life, first in a background detail in the *Proverbs* of 1559 in Berlin (page 47), then in a blind beggar in the Vienna carnival scene followed by the Berlin drawing of 1562 (page 162), the blind 'epileptic' in the *Sermon of St. John the Baptist*, (pages 134–135). As Grossman says, '… If we see old age with the eyes of Rembrandt, we owe our image of blindness to Bruegel'. Bruegel's achievement was followed by the insipid pair of blind men in the series of engravings illustrating proverbs by Jan Wierix, after a picture formerly attributed to Bruegel, with its oft-quoted inscription: 'Go always with the greatest caution, be faithful and trust in none other than God for all things: for when one blind man leads another they both fall in the ditch'.

The monumental power of Bruegel's brilliant composition, the complexity of the interrelation between its different levels of meaning and the supreme confidence with which all its elements are organized have been analysed in the greatest detail by Sedlmayr (*Epochen und Werke I*, 1959, p. 319 ff.). Sedlmayr discovered three fundamental elements in the composition: an allusion to the Wheel of Fortune in its evocation of Fate, to the Dance of Death in its grotesque and uncanny quality, and to Eternal Damnation in the impression of hopeless confusion, particularly in the face of the second figure. Romdahl, who drew attention to Maurice Maeterlinck's *Les Aveugles*, characterized the picture as profound, ingenuous and ruthless.

The impressions it immediately suggests are eeriness, instability, softness, the sense of falling, and ghostliness. We become aware that the falling men are blind, and that they are falling because their leader, who has already fallen, is blind. The fallen leader is just sinking together with his hurdy-gurdy into a marshy pond, with the next man following

PEASANT KERMIS
Detail
The general atmosphere of merriment, movement and excitement throughout the scene finds a contrast in the quiet and almost controlled postures of these two children dancing on one side.
For complete painting see pp. 168–169

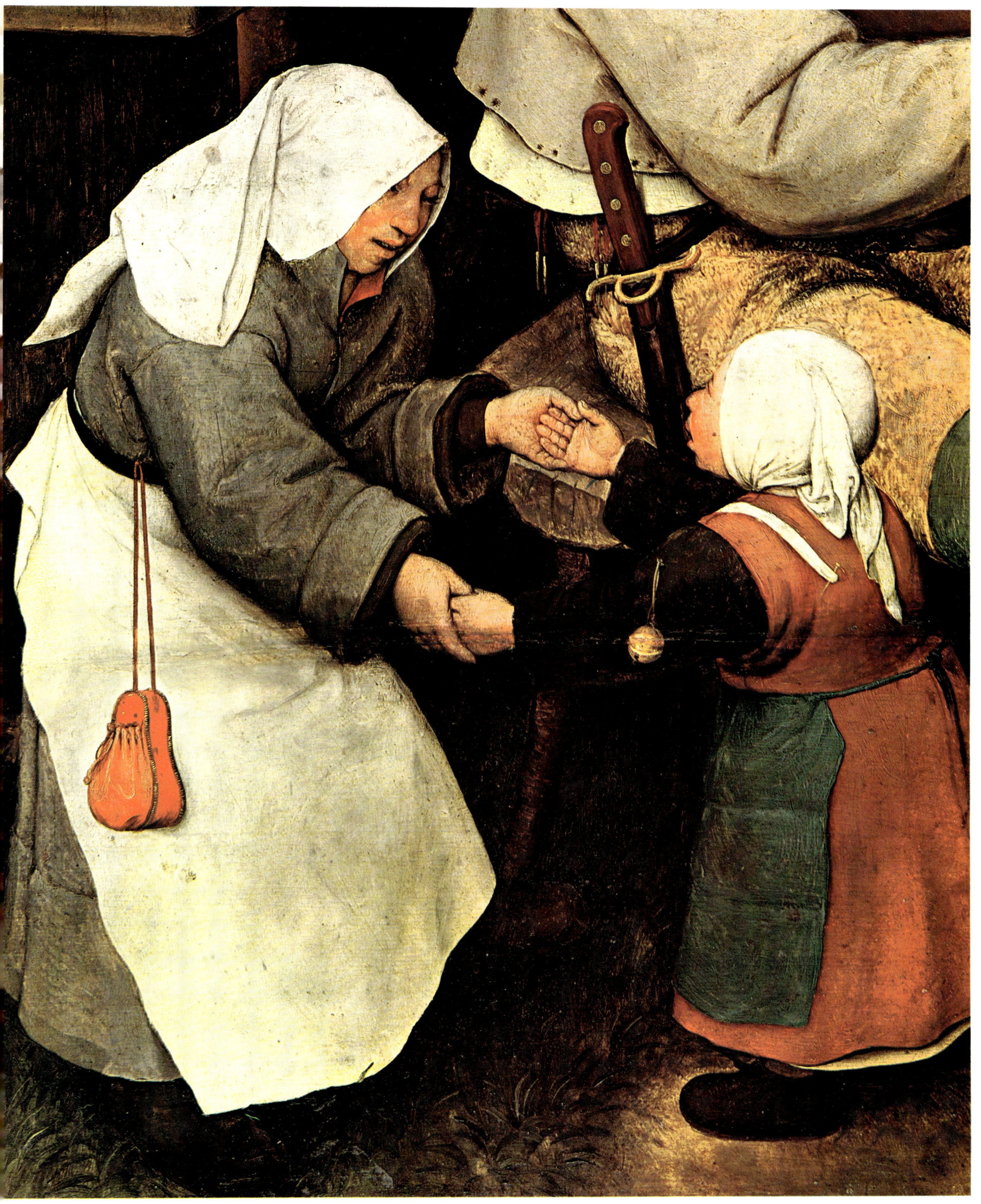

as he stumbles over his stick. As he goes down his face expresses his horrified realization
of what has happened; while the third figure is only just beginning to suspect from the
changed movement of the stick that something is amiss. His blind gaze is like a
caricature of holy ecstasy (pages 162–163), seemingly intent upon the church. The
others follow unaware, hanging on blindly to one another. The impression of helpless
falling (like a 'pack of cards slipping out of someone's hand') is lent emphasis by the
downward curve of the six figures, the way their sticks are pointing, and the sloping
terrain. The soft, uncanny quality lies in the folds of their garments, the gestures of their
arms as they tentatively feel their way and the grey tones of their clothing. But there is
also an unmistakably comic element in the 16th-century way of looking at the blind
and, indeed, at cripples. The harshness with which physical infirmities are mocked has
its associations with the laughter of modern children about things of the same kind. One
recalls Huizinga's description of the cruel popular amusement in which blind people
were given clubs or flails and had to chase a pig: whoever killed it could keep it. Their
clumsy movements and the blows they gave each other were apparently a source of
enormous merriment. Jan Verbeeck, a contemporary of Brugel's, recorded this 'game'
in a drawing (G. T. Faggin, *Critica d'Arte*, 108, Florence, 1970). But as Sedlmayr points
out, Bruegel's painting captures more of the terrible than of the comic in the plight of
blindness. Tolnay speaks of a 'degree of objectivity which goes beyond the human
sphere'. A Belgian doctor writing a medical dissertation once came to the conclusion
that Bruegel must have been a doctor. Only a doctor, he said, could have depicted the
different types of blindness with such medical accuracy that they could be diagnosed
from the picture.
Another interesting point is the contrast between the monumental character of the
composition with its large figures and the lowness of the surrounding features, as in
several of Bruegel's late works: the *Cripples*, for example, and the peasant scenes. In this
way the picture acquires a touch of parody, but without lapsing into comedy. The actual
physical episode is accompanied by various allegorical shades of meaning: the idiocy of a
situation in which the blind lead the blind had been current as an illustration of the
topsy-turvy world since the 13th century. Almost everyone accepts that the church in the
picture has an allegorical significance. There it stands, secure and peaceful on level
ground, while the blind men stumble over sloping ground because they have deviated
from the path of faith. The drawing of 1562 in Berlin (page 161) also features a church
tower. However, it is impossible to tell whether the tower behind the blind men in the
Proverbs is that of a church tower.
The apparently tragi-comic genre representation of stumbling beggars leads on to the
idea of mental blindness – of the blindness of blind people who stumble because they
have no leader who can see. It is a picture of collective misery, for the blind men are
victims of their utter abandonment by the world. Romdahl pointed out that we all feel a
measure of involvement in the episode: 'We all sense that we are links in an ominous
chain of blind men leading one another to their doom with the merciless inevitability of
fate'. And Stridbeck sees – apart from an allusion to the blindness of stupidity, of
heresy, of the world in general – a direct appeal to us outside the picture, an appeal
made by the second, stumbling figure turning his horribly distorted face straight
towards us. We cannot at this point go into the controversy between Auner and
Sedlmayr, which revolves around the fundamental question of whether modern interpretations are compatible with an artist's original intentions. For Auner the blind
figures do not possess a universal, tragic significance but are simply symbols of stupidity
intended as a warning to others, the whole episode having a rather comic, genre
character. This is true of the less severe versions which followed, for instance the one by
Hans Bol in which the leader is getting to his feet on the other side of the ditch, but
cannot be true of Bruegel's unique invention. When dealing with an entirely original
artist like Bruegel it is not necessarily correct to interpret a particular work in the light of
the 'spirit of the age', since these artists are, of course, precisely the innovators who can
be expected to transcend that spirit.
Opinions also differ about the painting's original format. There can be no doubt that it
has been slightly trimmed on the right: the hand of the fallen leader is entirely visible in
all the extant copies in the Louvre, the Liechtenstein Collection at Vaduz, the Galleria
Nazionale in Parma, and on the art market. The upper edge is more problematic.
Sedlmayr, who deals with this question in some detail, disagrees with Auner in
regarding it as genuine for compositional reasons, rejecting the additional portion in the
Louvre and Liechtenstein copies as unhelpful interference by copyists. To support his
argument he adduces the copy on the art market (in the Galerie St. Lukas, Vienna, in
1935), possibly by Pieter Brueghel the Younger, which has the same low top edge as the

Naples original. In other words, the original would have to have been trimmed prior to 1611 and copied thereafter. The view that the picture actually was trimmed is prompted mainly by the fact that the copies (e.g. the one in the Louvre measuring 118.1 x 167.7 cm or $46\frac{1}{2}$ x $65\frac{3}{4}$ in) have the customary 'Bruegel format', one of the standard formats for tapestry painting, whereas the painting in Naples (measuring 86 x 154 cm or $33\frac{7}{8}$ x $60\frac{5}{8}$ in) has just the right amount missing to uphold the theory of trimming. However, other paintings exist which have non-standard formats and are not trimmed – for example the *Sermon of St. John the Baptist* in Budapest.

Apart from *Hunters in the Snow* in Vienna, hardly any other work of Bruegel's has become so well-known as the *Peasant Wedding Feast* (pages 164–165). Frequently reproduced and generally very popular, this painting is often mistakenly assumed to be representative of Bruegel's art in general. This is probably the *Peasant Wedding Feast* acquired by the Archduke Ernest in Brussels on 16 June 1594. From 1659, according to the inventory of the Archduke Leopold Wilhelm it was certainly in the Imperial Collection in Vienna. After that date it was trimmed along the bottom edge, unfortunately losing the signature and also the date which was presumably there. A strip measuring 5.5 cm (or $2\frac{1}{8}$ in) in width was later added to restore it to the same format as the *Peasant Kermis* (pages 168–169). The two works are often regarded as companion pieces or even as the beginning of a series. In view of two wood cuts on the same subject by Erhard Schön which appeared as a pair we may suppose that from an iconographical standpoint a traditional link existed between *Peasant Wedding Feast* and *Peasant Kermis* as Renger maintains. They are certainly thematically akin and were clearly executed during the same period. The only important question is whether this was before or after the *Parable of the Blind*, and before or after the *Cripples*. This point will be taken up later. Strange though it may seem, the actual meaning of the picture has been a much more violent source of controversy. There can be no doubt that we are witnessing a wedding banquet following a peasant wedding. The scene is a barn specially arranged for the ceremony. The guests have sat down at a long table and two men are carrying in plates of yellow and white gruel placed on a door borrowed for the purpose. These two figures seen from the back, their positions, the red helmet, and the white and yellow of the plates all constitute the unforgettable central motif of the composition. The posture of the figure in front, who seems to have three feet, has aroused some humorous comment, but in fact this is an optical allusion which Bruegel probably included intentionally. The 'third foot' quite obviously belongs to the man sitting askew on the bench and passing on plates, although the reproductions do not generally show this. The man with the plates directs the eye straight to the bride who sits with folded hands in front of the green wall-hanging, her face expressing an enigmatic mixture of shyness and stupidity. Her parents are on the left. Two bagpipe players have arrived: the feast can begin. The other figures have been commented on most illuminatingly of all by Auner: 'The distinguished gentleman dressed in black velvet is the local aristocrat who has accepted his elderly tenant's invitation and listens with patience and boredom to the story of the marriage from the monk who has just conducted the ceremony. As still often happens today the bridegroom doesn't sit down but has to look after the drinks. He's the neatly dressed lad on the left, the former head farmhand who will now take over responsibility for the farm.' The man in black has also been seen as a judge, in the light of the description in the inventory of 1659, and as a self-portrait of Bruegel, but Auner's explanation carries a good deal of weight. Speculations as to why the bridegroom is not shown are groundless; whether or not he is one of the other men present is irrelevant.

Certain scholars, particularly Stridbeck and Grossmann, have interpreted both pictures as allegories of the deadly sins in genre disguise, and in fact, such an apparently extravagant theory shouldn't be rejected out of hand. A relevant factor here is the view taken of the peasant in the 16th century. In 14th-century Netherlandish literature he comes in for a measure of praise, though already in the *Kerelslied* (c. 1320–1330), written during the Flemish peasants war, we find him exposed to mockery. In the refrain, the poem makes out that the peasant is so stupid because his daily diet consists of curds, wine, bread and cheese. By the 15th century, the established popular image of the peasant was of a blockhead. Carnival games in the first half of the 16th century usually mocked him as a figure of fun whose vices were immoderate eating and drinking. Certainly, earlier engravings such as *Beggars Drinking* by Cornelis Massys and especially the *Peasant Kermis* and *Peasant Wedding* by Pieter van der Borcht contain a moralizing element apparently prompted by the unbridled debauchery they had observed. This applies only to a limited extent to the *Peasant Wedding Dance* in Detroit and not at all to the two late works in Vienna. The *Wedding Feast* in Vienna is anything but a portrayal of gluttony; on the contrary, it is doubtful whether things could possibly be more modest and well-behaved at a peasant wedding, where the bride's father traditionally lashes out a little. Unlike Stridbeck and Grossmann, the present writer tends to feel that Bruegel could even have been trying to counteract contemporary prejudice. How can the positively ritual simplicity of this solid, peaceful banquet – which without blasphemous intent contains subdued references to the Marriage at Cana and the Last Supper – be reconciled with the deadly sin of gluttony? What grounds are there for regarding the little titbit which the docile child in the foreground has managed to get hold of as a symbol of voracity, or the peacock feather in its cap – the joy of any child – as an attribute of *Superbia*? Why should the cooking-spoon in the man's hat be seen as an emblem of *Gula* or the bagpipes as a reference to *Luxuria*? However correct these observations may be from an iconographical point of view, there seems no adequate reason for insisting on their relevance. The same applies to the *Peasant Kermis*, in which the knife has been claimed to represent *Ira*, the purse *Avaritia*, and so on. The ultimate refinement in exaggeration is to interpret the crossed pieces of straw in the foreground as a sign of the Cross over which the sinful peasant tramples on the day of the *kermis*. All this must be treated with scepticism. Bruegel was not a clergyman but a painter. In these two pictures at least, the wedding feast and the dancing are no more sinful than the action in the *Parable of the Blind* is funny. It must be remembered that genius being in the vanguard of artistic achievement, there are things which have to be articulated for the first time, and are thus not explicable simply in terms of tradition. In this case the subject is the peasants depicted by Bruegel in his very last years. The are not yet humorously stereotyped as in the 17th century, nor utterly transfigured as in the bucolic poetry which followed, nor embellished and visualized through rose-tinted spectacles as in the 19th century; and most certainly they are not worshipped as aristocrats in the manner of Millet, or heroized as by Egger-Lienz and later by the Fascists. For the first time, and also for the last time for many years to come, they are seen as human beings with all their pardonable weaknesses and sensitivities, and they are portrayed not without a feeling for the charm of theiry heavy movements, for which Bruegel has a deep understanding. In common with Marijnissen, the present writer is inclined to go back to the old-fasioned view held by earlier scholars, who contemplated the two peasant compositions in Vienna without thoughts of allegorical undertones. Bruegel's overriding interest was clearly pictorial. It is conceivable, though, that he appropriated the moralizing tendency contained in his predecessors' peasant compositions and modified it by showing the peasants in a more human light, toning down their debaucheries, and extending the old moralizing attitude toward peasant merry-making to include all men everywhere. These paintings sum up the totality of artistic and human experience without any trace of accusation, bitterness or moral judgement.

Compositionally they constitute a new and singular development in Bruegel's oeuvre. The three-dimensional diagonal arrangement of the table and seated guests gives sustenance to a seed sown by Jan van Amstel's *Feeding of the Poor* in Brunswick and anticipates Tintoretto's *Last Supper* of 1592–94 in San Giorgio Maggiore, Venice. The master here unites compact, monumental groups of just a few large figures in the foreground with medium-sized groups containing numerous figures in the middle distance and background, attaching prime importance to the interplay of people and empty spaces. This is what distinguishes the two works compositionally from all earlier ones. The focal level, set lower than usual, gives a 'natural' perspective with isocephaly and overlapping figures. In this lies the picture's' formal and also thematic differentiation from the *Peasant Wedding Dance* of 1566 in Detroit (pages 138–139). In view of this we disagree with the early datings of 1565–1566, proposed by Jedlicka, and around 1567, proposed by Grossmann and go along with the majority of scholars who have cautiously suggested 'around 1568'. At the same time we tend to put these two paintings after the *Parable of the Blind*. Only Vanbeselaere goes for 1569.

What we have said with regard to the *Peasant Wedding Feast* also applies to the *Peasant Kermis* (pages 168–169), although this contains obvious references to vices such as drunkenness. The coarseness of the dance and the movements seems to have an element of finality about it, rather like the posture of the men carrying the food in the *Peasant Wedding Feast*.

A few further details are also worth mentioning. The two sisters dancing in the foreground have been linked with the proverb 'The young twitter as the old sing'. The red flag is Burgundian, but that is all we can say. The odd yellowish-white object on the table on the left is a so-called *drinkuit* or *stortebeker*, a drinking-vessel without a base which can only be placed upside down and therefore prompts its holder to drink up. J. Weyns has given a thorough account of the costumes worn.

HEAD OF AN OLD PEASANT WOMAN
Oil on panel; 22 x 18 cm (8 x 7 in)
Neither signed nor dated
c. 1568
Munich, Alte Pinakothek
Moved in 1868 from the castle of Neuburg on the Danube to Schleissheim. This is the only example in Bruegel's opus of a single head depicted as a character study (apart from the three heads in Copenhagen – p. 59 – whose authenticity is uncertain). But old inventories indicate that the artist painted numerous similar heads.

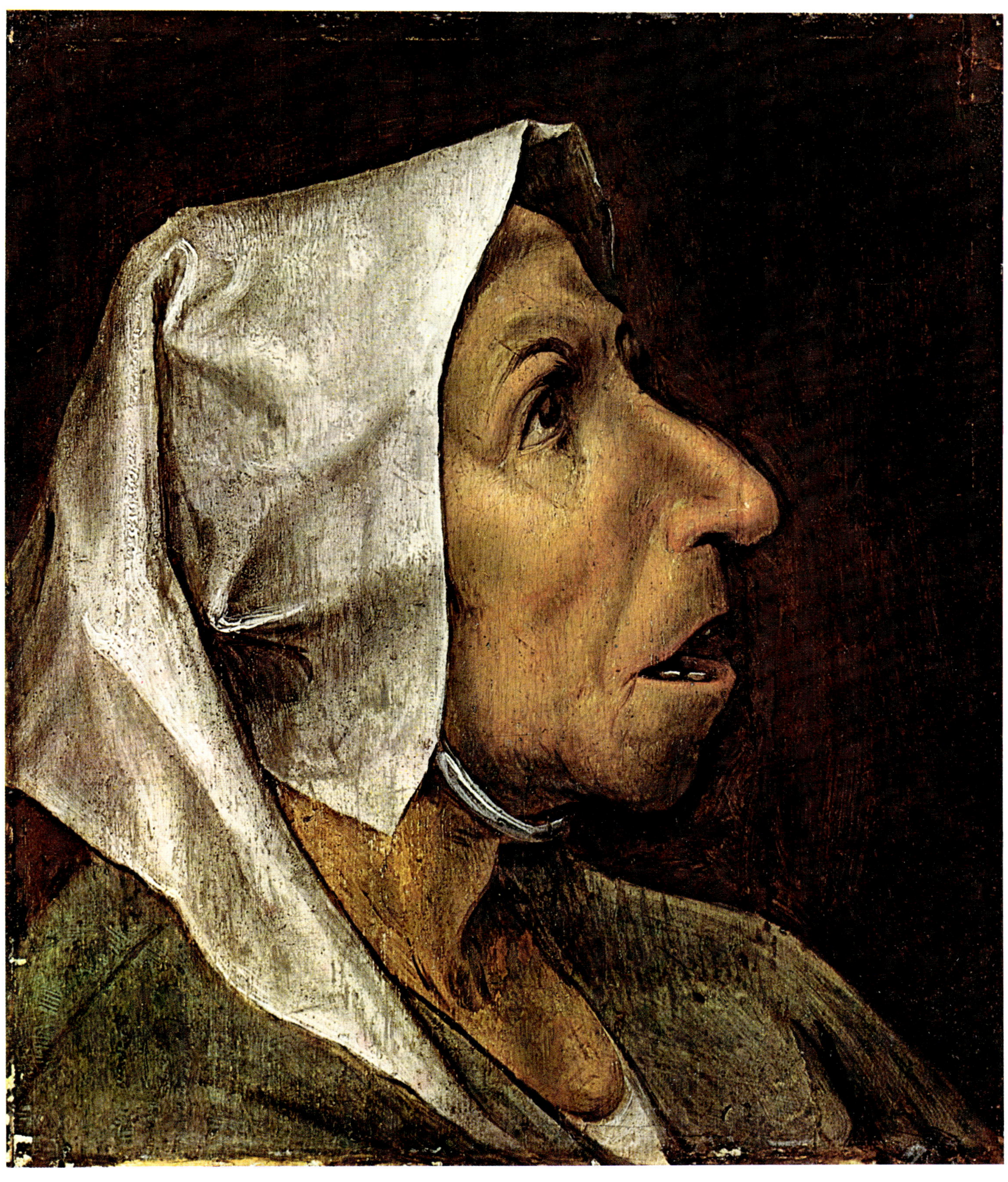

Generally speaking, of those works which were kept shut away more or less from the outset in the exclusive Habsburg collections, there exist only very few copies or none at all. Marlier found four copies of the *Peasant Wedding Feast*, one of them in the museum at Ghent. There are none at all of the *Peasant Kermis* although a version of it which has been modified by the addition of a group of figures was discovered in the Brussels art market in 1955.

As an isolated character study, the *Head of an Old Peasant Woman* (page 175) is unique among Bruegel's surviving works, although old inventories show that he in fact painted quite a large number of such heads. It was recorded for the first time in the castle of Neuburg on the Danube in 1804 and acquired by the Alte Pinakothek, Munich, in 1912, this small painting is neither signed nor dated but is generally recognized as an authentic work, except by Tolnay. While it used to be regarded as belonging to Bruegel's middle or early period, the general view today is that it was executed towards the very end of his life. The mouth and nose have reminded certain observers of the 'critic' in the drawing entitled *Artist and 'Critic'* (page 127). An unquestionable link exists with the series of etched peasants' heads which feature Bruegel's name as inventor.

The modest, late painting of 1568 *The Peasant and the Nest Robber* (page 177), which has only one monumental main figure in an idyllic flat landscape bathed in the brightness of summer, is at the same time one of Bruegel's most enigmatic works, although the proverb attached to it might at first be expected to supply the key to the mystery. The proverb reads 'Those who know the nest, know it; those who steal it, have it'. The same proverb appears as a caption beneath Bruegel's drawing *The Beekeepers* (page 53), which he probably also executed in 1568. The comments on the meaning of the proverb offered in that context will not be repeated here but are of course relevant. There are three copies on a reduced scale in tondo form, and a weak drawing showing a larger view in the Uffizi which Puyvelde mistakenly published as Bruegel's original in 1962.

The young peasant points with his left hand towards a boy robbing a bird's-nest, Stridbeck considers his three-dimensional striding motion to be derived from Michelangelo's *putti* on the Sistine Chapel ceiling, whilst Tolnay and others compare it to the *Conversion of Saul* in the Cappella Paolina. In his right hand he carries a stick, at his hip a cow's horn and knife. Behind him lies a sack, which could belong to him or to the nest robber. With an enigmatic expression which Romdahl has called melancholy and abstracted, others simply stupid, he points towards the thief in obvious unawareness that he himself is about to fall into the dark water running along the bottom of the picture. Unconvincing attempts have been made to interpret this as the parable of the person who beholds the mote in his brother's eye but fails to consider the beam in his own eye, (Matthew 7; 3 and Luke 6; 41). In the 1977 yearbook of the Berlin Museums, Dreyer associates the picture with a chapter in Sebastian Brant's *Ship of Fools* which criticizes obstinacy as a form of self-conceit.

Grauls, on the other hand, thinks the only acceptable interpretation of the proverb is the contemporary one, namely that the suitor with initiative wins the day over the one who is shy. This explanation, he claims, accords fully with the fact that the peasant has lost his bag, a sexual allusion, and is on the point of falling into the water. Those who make a mess of things get laughed at to boot. However, the strange indifference on the face of the young peasant leaves us in doubt about Bruegel's own interpretation of the proverb and the reason why it was used. If we accept the explanation offered by the theory of plant symbolism, the shy person would at any rate be the 'good one'. The blackberries on the left in the foreground allude to the Burning Bush, which burned but was not consumed, and therefore refers to someone who overcomes temptation. The nearby iris (pages 178–179), a kind of lily, symbolizes purity and virtue according to Grauls. But is the proverb in fact the only message of the picture. Why then the extravagance of that enchantingly beautiful landscape, why the peasant's mysterious expression which seems to say everything and nothing? What is the relation of the painting's lyrical mood to its thematic substance? The proverb in fact seems to create the enigma it promised to solve. Probably, however, this puzzle was part of Bruegel's plan too. At any rate the meaning of the painting was no longer understood in 1659 when an inventory of the Archduke Leopold Wilhelm's collection in Vienna was drawn up. Here it says: 'A landscape in oil on wood, in which a peasant with a cane in his left hand is threatening a boy stealing birds in a tree ...'.

The Magpie on the Gallows (page 181), a late work of 1568, is also ambiguous as far as its title is concerned and even less easy to elucidate than the *Peasant and the Nest Robber*. A gallows stands on an eminence in the foreground above a broad sunlit river valley, one of the loveliest landscapes Bruegel ever painted. A company of dancers has

THE PEASANT AND THE NEST ROBBER
Oil on panel; 59 x 68 cm (23¼ x 26 in)
Signed and dated: 'BRVEGEL MD.LXVIII.'
Signature and date, written in gold, have been renewed
Vienna, Kunsthistorisches Museum
This painting recalls the Flemish proverb 'He who knows where the nest is, knows it; he who robs it, has it', meaning that the person who shows initiative gets what he wants before those who are more reticent. The same proverb is inscribed on the drawing of the same period entitled *The Beekeepers* (p. 153) and is also illustrated in an etching by David Vinckeboons. The poetic mood of the beautiful landscape and the young peasant's enigmatic indifference raise doubts as to whether the only key to an interpretation is that provided by the proverb. The monumentality of the composition concentrated in a single large figure has suggested the influence of Michelangelo (Tolnay and Stridbeck).
Detail on *pages 178–179*

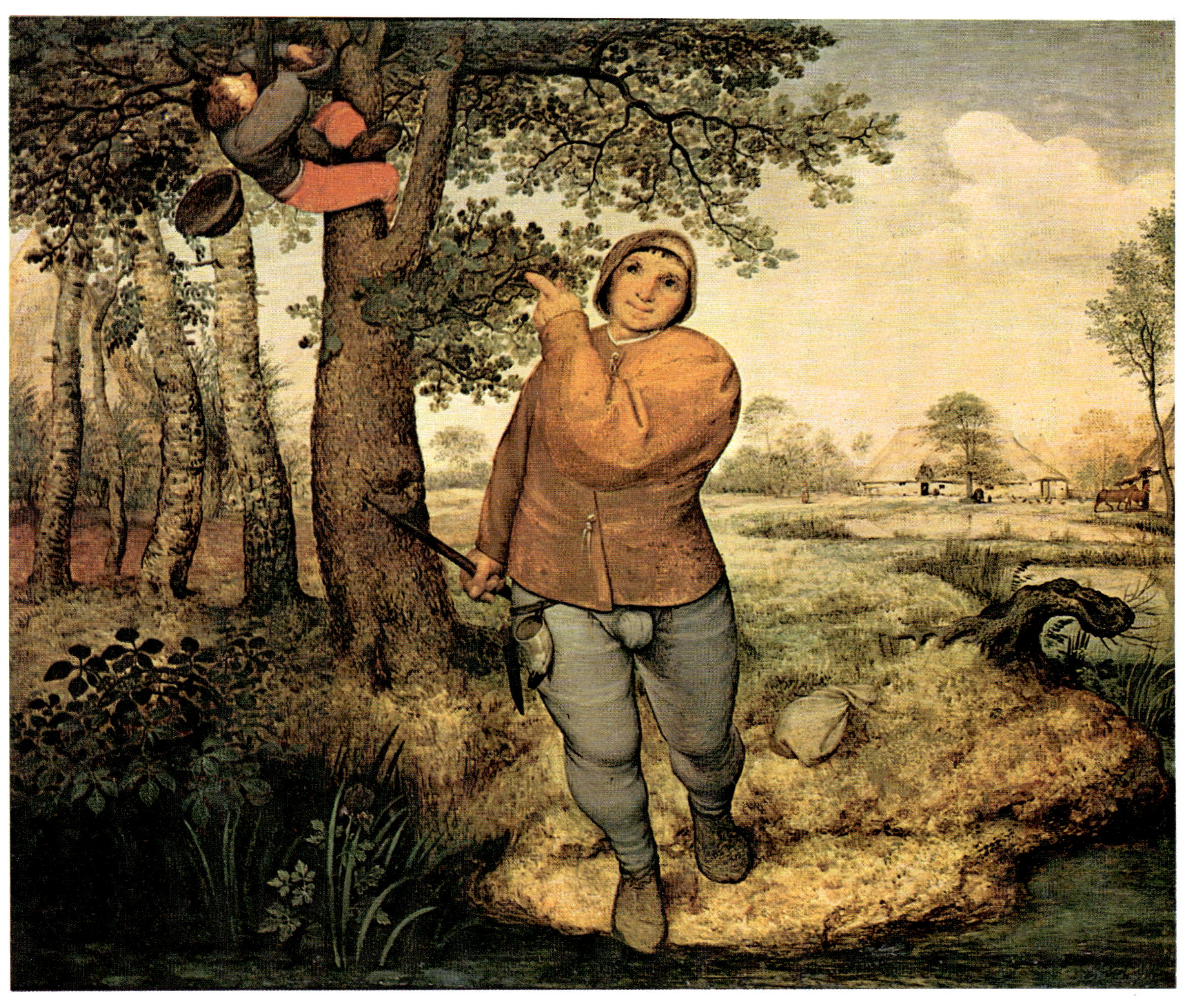

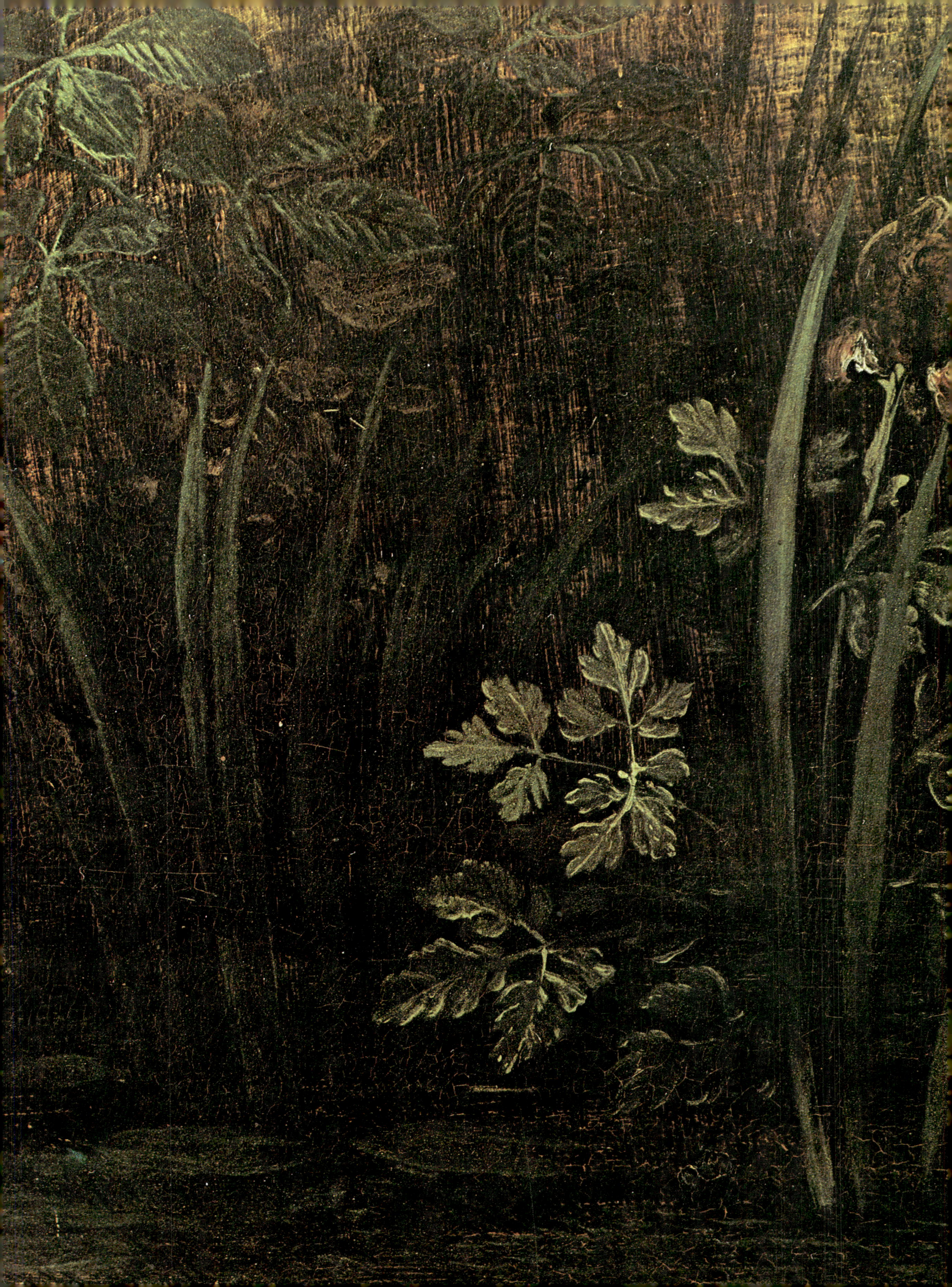

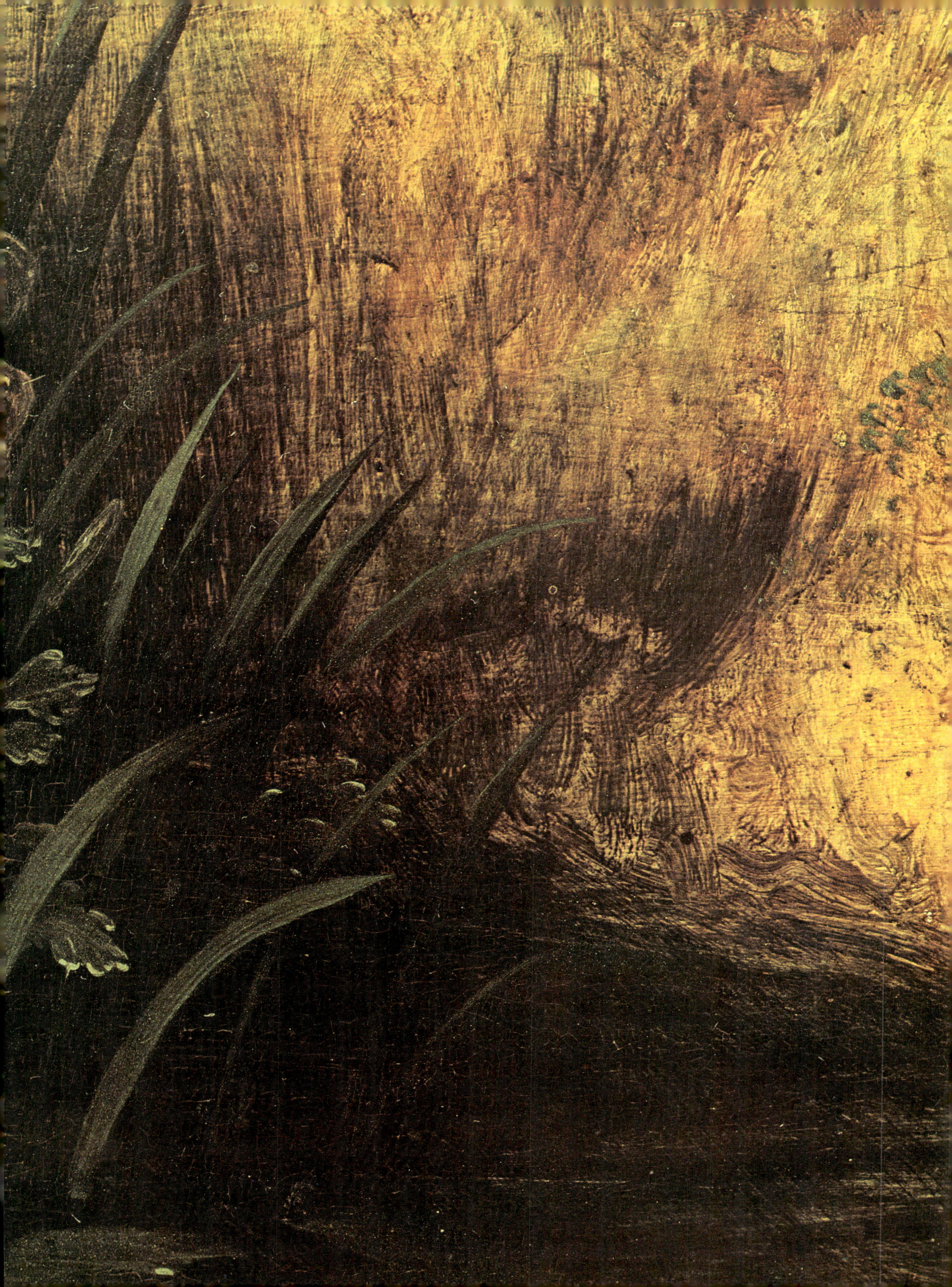

THE MAGPIE ON THE GALLOWS

Oil on panel; 45.9 x 50.8 cm (8½ x 20 in)
Signed and dated: 'BRVEGEL 1568'
Darmstadt, Hessisches Landesmuseum

This is one of Bruegel's last works and its
meaning is shrouded in mystery. According
to van Mander, Bruegel left it in his will to
his wife. The scholar gives this explanation of
the painting: 'The magpie is meant to refer
to the evil tongues who are worthy of the
gallows'. There is also a Flemish saying that
gossip can lead to the gallows. A number of
points remain obscure; it is particularly
difficult to explain the strange contrast
between the smiling, sunlit landscape and
the lugubrious presence of the gallows.

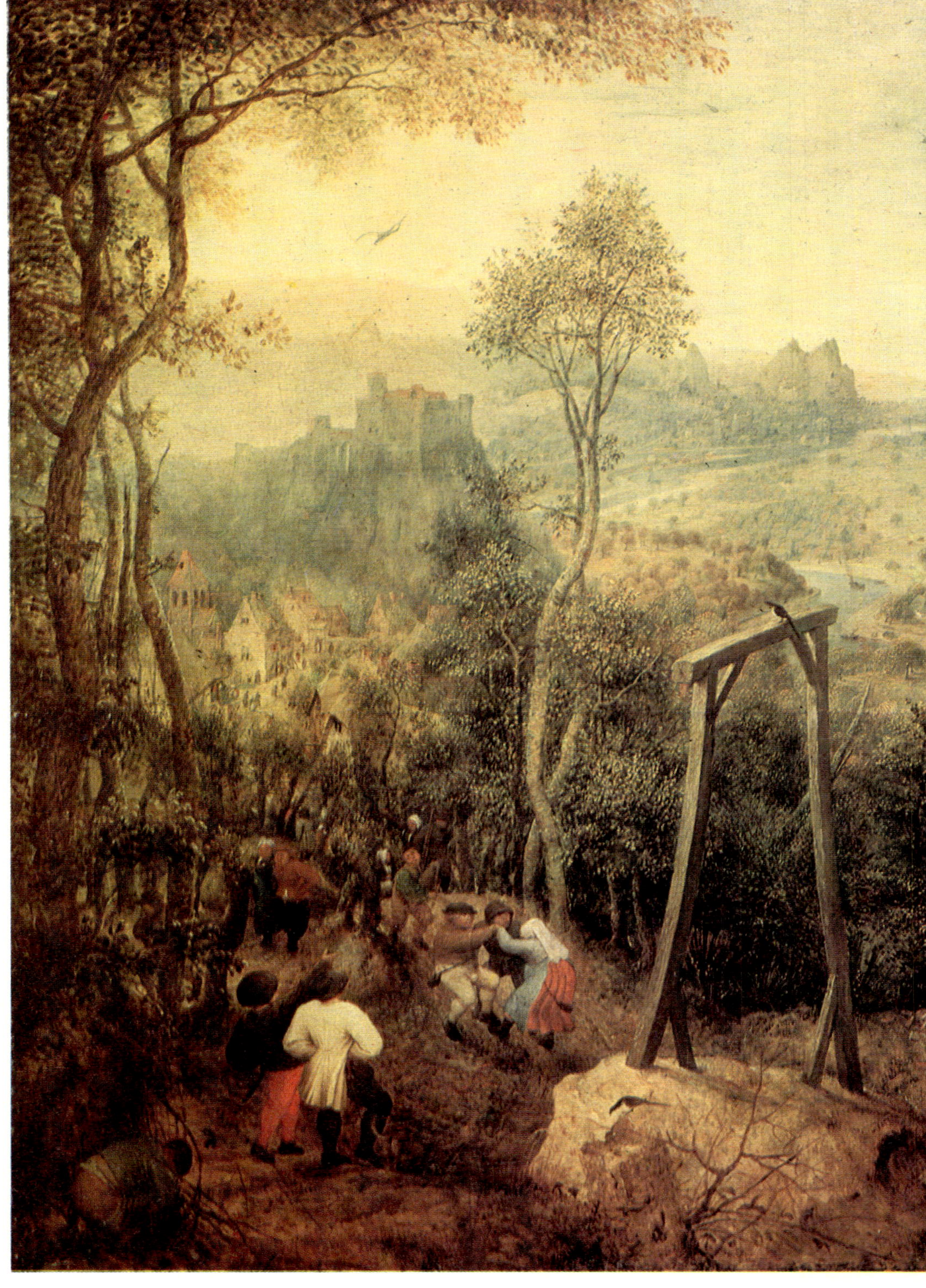

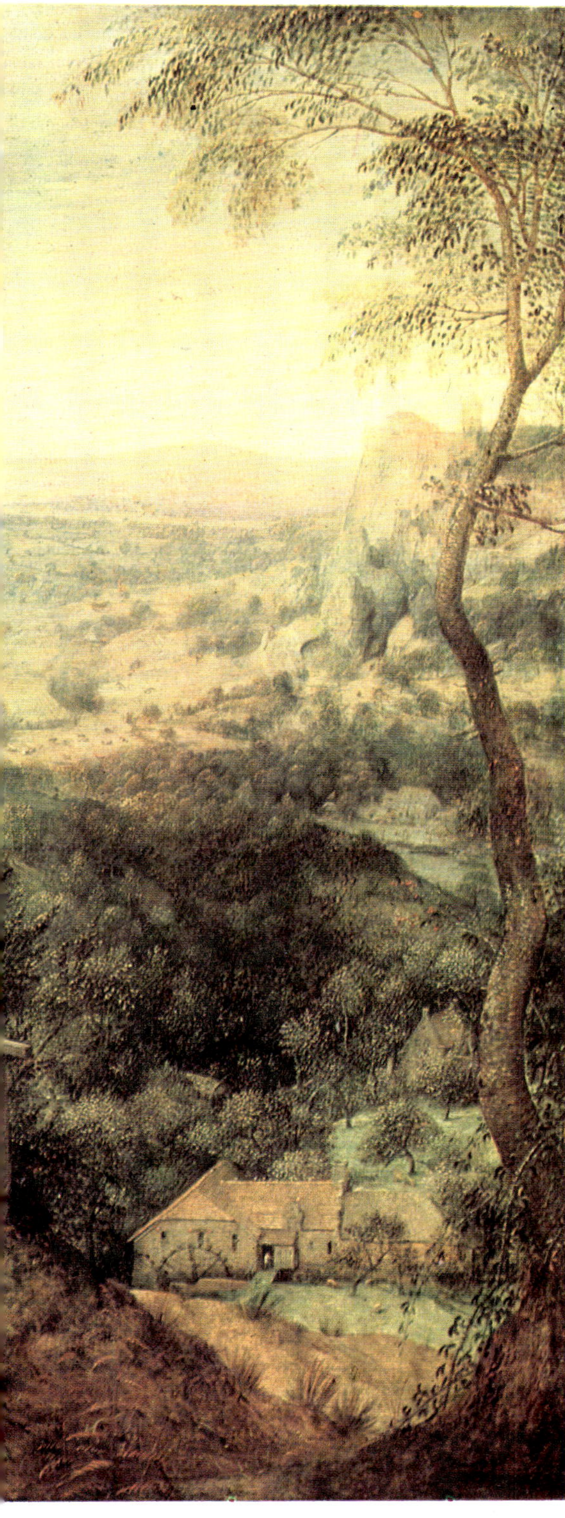

approached the gallows with a bagpipe player, clearly from the village below where a *kermis* is in progress. Two men are looking at the gallows, one of them indicating it with his hand. In the left-hand corner we can see a man relieving himself. On the gallows sits a magpie, while a second one perches on the tree-trunk in the foreground. Down the hill from the gallows stands a wooden cross and below right a mill-wheel turns.

According to van Mander, Bruegel left this picture to his wife: 'The magpie referred to the gossips, whom he consigned to the gallows'. 'To chatter like a magpie' is indeed a common Flemish expression. Van Mander's explanation is at the very least incomplete, for it fails to take account of a number of other motifs. D. Bax (1962) thinks Bruegel was saying that treacherous tittle-tattle sends people to the gallows, a particularly topical subject in the dangerous period following Alba's arrival. On his deathbed Bruegel asked his wife to destroy certain drawings because they could have caused her trouble. 'To talk someone to the gallows' and to be 'as garrulous as a magpie' are expressions which the artist may well have had in mind when he combined the motif of the magpie with that of the gallows at the very point where the picture's diagonals intersect. The Netherlandish word for a tree-stump, as Stechow points out, can also mean the pillory, another place where gossips could end up. Water-mills can also be seen as symbols of gossip. The people dancing may represent sinfulness or, like the gesture of the man in the left-hand corner, defiance in the face of the gallows: we should bear in mind the saying: 'He shits on – i.e. cheats – the gallows' in the background of the *Proverbs*. Fraenger also calls attention to the German proverb 'The way to the gallows can pass through pleasant pastures'. Glück interprets the Netherlandish saying '*aan de galg danzen*' (to dance to the gallows) as referring to those who have got themselves into the shadow of the gallows through stupidity, without noticing it. The gallows in the picture stands on a rock, the cross nearby on soft, sloping ground. At first glance this could seem perverse, for Peter was the rock on which Christ intended to build his Church. But it could equally mean that everything is now dominated by the gallows: either the gallows is oppressing Christian freedom or, vice versa, the Church is helping to uphold worldly justice. Another theory is that the gallows with the magpie, the Bird of Satan, dominates the cross of a condemned man. A contrast with human weakness and stupidity and the gloomy gallows motif is provided by the radiant, glistering landscape. It takes up much more space than any landscape in the foregoing works and the scale of the human figures is reduced to less than in the *Months*. With its synthesis of minute detail, all-pervading atmosphere and infinitely subtle composition it represents a new and final stage in the development of Bruegel's landscape painting. The picture's absolute signficance – springing out of the fusion of landscape, gallows and dance – hovers between a premonition of danger and the overcoming of fear and uncertainty.

The *Storm at Sea* in Vienna (page 183), unsigned and undated, is generally regarded as Bruegel's last painting, quite apart from the question of whether it is finished or not. In the late 19th century its authenticity was put in doubt and for a while Joos de Momper was believed to have executed it, a view revived in 1954 by K. Boström. F. Smekens likewise questioned Bruegel's authorship, one of his reasons being that the ships were not delineated with the precision normally expected from Bruegel. A much more striking feature is that the ships are sailing against the waves, that is, in the opposite direction to the storm. It hardly ever happens that Bruegel sacrifices correctness of detail to artistic necessity. But despite a certain similarity to works by Momper, Grossman believes that 'the greatness of the invention seems to be beyond Momper's powers and, moreover, there is a theatrical element in Momper's landscapes which is lacking in our picture'.

The wild turbulence of the tossing sea comes out in the broad strokes of brown underpainting, and it is clear that the picture was never finished, perhaps due to Bruegel's death. The vivid green wedge-shaped patch in the sea, the bright patch of sky and the blue shimmer on the horizon have been begun; the rain driven diagonally by the wind and a few plumes of spray on the crests of the waves are beautifully executed. The ship in the patch of bright water, which has been wrongly interpreted as castoreum to frighten the whale, is partly covered with blue-green paint and also clearly includes some *pentimenti*. This part in particular shows that the picture is unfinished and that the artist intended to do more work on the sea, and no doubt on the sky as well. The pictorial splendour of this vision was not enough for certain scholars, who insisted on loading the picture with allegorical ballast that has been a part of the critical tradition ever since L. Burchard (who discovered the passage in Zedler's Universal-Lexikon of 1732–1750). This reads as follows: 'If the whale plays with the barrel that has been thrown to him and gives the ship time to escape, then he represents the man who misses the true good for the sake of futile trifles'. But if Bruegel was concerned about anything, it was certainly not about the salvation of the innocent whale but about that of the sailors, who have put into practice the age-old wisdom of the seas – for which they had little need of an 18th-century encyclopaedia – by throwing some cargo overboard to divert the whale's attention and thereby save the ship and themselves. This would be the sort of yarn that Bruegel could have heard, or read in Claus Magnus (1539), as Stechow tells us, and used to give an added touch of interest to his picture. There may be more justification in Stridbeck's interpretation of ship and voyage as symbols of human life with all its dangers, from which the church on the horizon promises a haven of safety, but the church is far away and the ships are sailing past it. Auner saw the ships as a symbol of the Church and claimed to recognize Christ the Redeemer on the stern of the leading ship on the far left, creating a trail of light in the water. Another moot point is whether there is any significance in the fact that, despite the hurricane, the ship in the middle is very nearly under full sail, while the others have managed to take in all except a single sail. Friedländer found the picture satisfying enough on its own without any proverbial significance tacked on to it. In its pictorial breadth it looks forward to Rubens, in its reflection of the life of the spirit to Rembrandt's landscapes, in its evocation of the absolute which transcends all knowledge to van Gogh's *Cornfield with Cross*.

Doubtful Works or Copies

Of the doubtful works, of which we can only consider one or two examples, the most important is certainly the *Unfaithful Shepherd* (page 157), and I believe this is unquestionably by Bruegel. The reduction of the composition to a single figure clearly indicates a late work. Doubt still exists as to whether the version in Philadelphia is the original which has suffered from overpaintings, or a good copy. H. de Loo, Michel and Glück accept it as the original. One copy used to belong to the Robert Werner collection in Antwerp. With his unique skill Bruegel has succeeded in capturing the whole significance of the episode in a few details, imbuing the posture and facial expression of the shepherd as he steals away with all the baseness and cowardice of his despicable defection. This is how a man can behave when there is nobody to see. The brilliant stroke of having the wheel-tracks disappearing into the endless plain with the escaping sheep brings about the intensely three-dimensional allusion of the shepherd, almost coming out of the picture as he runs towards us. The landscape represents the final culmination of what Bruegel had been working on in the *Ambush* (page 157) and the *Misanthrope* (page 159).
The theme already appears in Philip Galle's engraving of 1565 entitled *Christ the Good Shepherd*, in which the good and the bad shepherd are compared. Bruegel treated the two individually in separate, monumental compositions. However, the *Faithful Shepherd* in the Kronacker Collection in Antwerp (page 157) is less original in its composition than the *Unfaithful Shepherd*, making it questionable whether they were intended as companion pieces. The picture was only recently attributed to Bruegel by Grossmann, but both its technique and composition make its authenticity look doubtful.
A small work of doubtful authorship is the so-called *Yawning Man* (page 46) in Brussels. Most modern scholars either ignore this oval miniature or regard it as a copy by Pieter Brueghel the Younger, but the catalogue of the 1969 Brussels exhibition raised the question once again. Clearly executed as a study of facial expression, it shows a man yawning with closed eyes. If, as is claimed, it belongs to a series of the seven deadly sins, the yawn would be intended to represent *Desidia*. It could have associations with another doubtful work, the *Head of a Mercenary* (*Ira*, or anger) in the Musée Fabre in Montpellier, and with a *Study of a Head* (*Invidia* or envy) in the museum at Bordeaux. In the 17th century the *Yawning Man* was engraved by Lucas Vorstermann as a study of temperament.
A large number of scholars such as Winkler, Friedländer, Glück, Genaille, Denis and Marlier consider the *Wedding Procession* (page 140) in the Brussels City Museum to be authentic. Tolnay and Jedlicka think it is a copy, and others, including Grossman, fail to mention it. It shows two parallel wedding processions, the bridegroom's on the right and the bride's on the left, each led by a bagpipe player. The length of the procession is emphasized by the picture's extremely broad format. A windmill and a horse's skull are in strikingly similar positions to those in *Christ Carrying the Cross* in Vienna. In view of

THE STORM AT SEA
Oil on panel; 70.3 x 97 cm (27 x 38¼ in)
Neither signed nor dated
Vienna, Kunsthistorisches Museum
This painting may have been in the collection of P. Stevens in Antwerp in 1668. On being taken from the depot of the Belvedere Imperial Gallery for the first time in 1880 it was attributed to Bruegel; subsequently it was ascribed to Joos de Momper, a view also held in certain quarters more recently. Today, however, it is generally thought that the magnificence of the painting's composition completely rules out the possibility of Momper have executed it and that only Bruegel could have achieved such equilibrium with a theme of such violence.

certain weaknesses in composition and technique it has to be doubted whether the work can be by Bruegel, but it seems to have been highly thought of as ten copies still exist.

The Feast of St. Martin (page 22) is no longer regarded as original, but as the surviving remains of a copy after a lost original of Bruegel's. Although painted in tempera on canvas, it had varnish applied at an early stage and this makes it look like an oil painting. The 1659 inventory of the Archduke Leopold Wilhelm mentions it as still untrimmed. The complete composition is known through an engraving by N. Guerard, about 1648–1719, with a dedication by Abraham Brueghel (1631–1690), who wrongly attributed the painted model to his grandfather Jan Brueghel the Elder. As a result Tolnay concluded the composition to be a youthful work by Jan Brueghel the Elder. It is also known through a lost copy which H. de Loo says was in the Paris art market in 1905. The original was undoubtedly one of the largest and most important works of Bruegel's early period, having links with the *Adoration of the Magi* in Brussels (pages 24–25). St

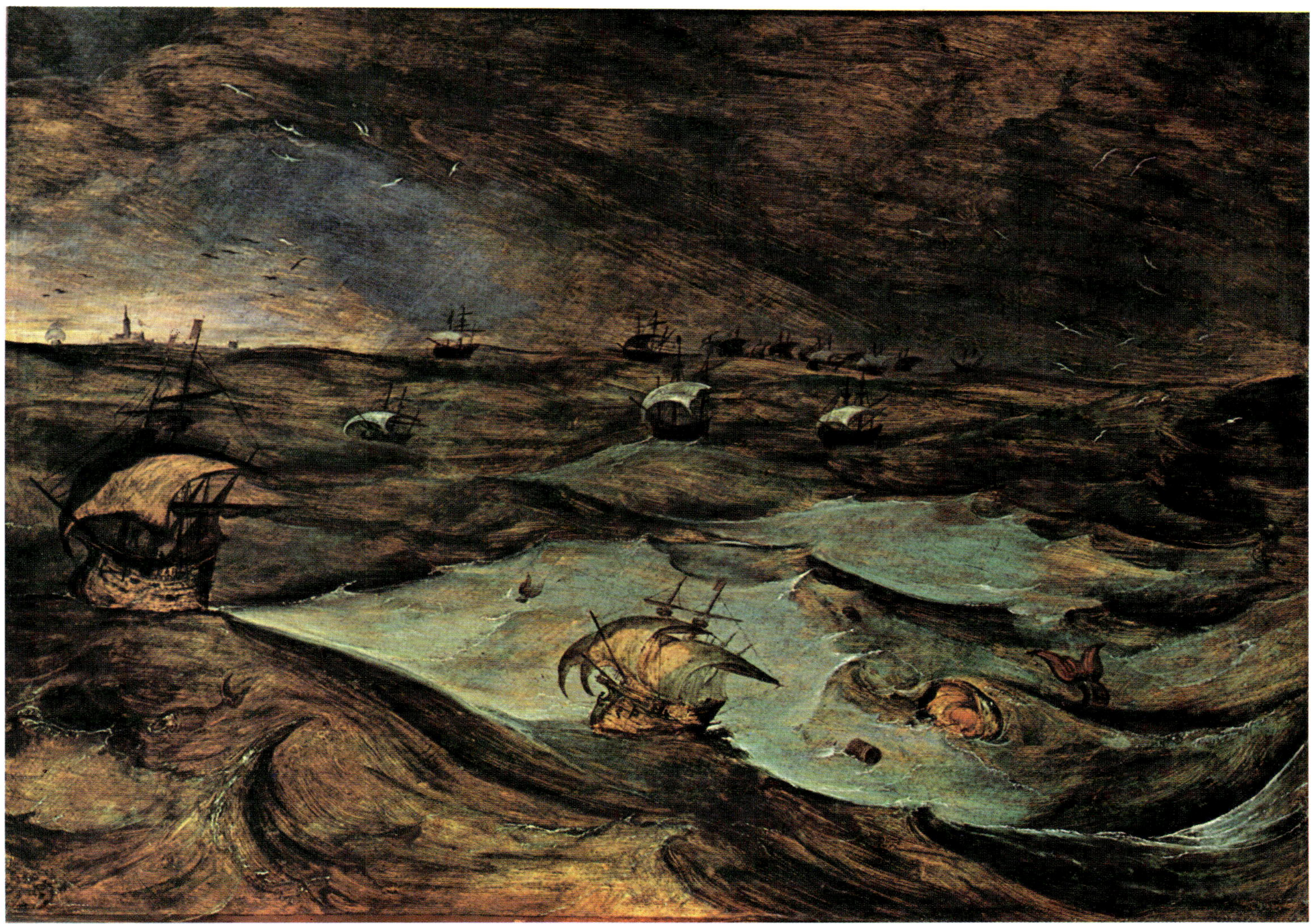

Martin is giving a cask of wine to the poor, but is repaid with ingratitude, brawling and drunkenness. Bruegel ironically uses a classic triangular composition for the wretched crowd surging round the cask of wine set up above them on a platform, while the saint, no longer involved in the episode, divides his cloak for two cripples and rides away. Two free replicas of the lost picture by Pieter Balten also exist in the Royal Museum in Antwerp and the Rijksmuseum in Amsterdam (discussed by Marlier, Pieter Balten, Copiste ou Créateur? in the *Bulletin des Musées Royaux des Beaux Arts de Belgique*, 1965, p. 127 ff.). Bruegel may also have been the author of, or had a hand in, another composition with St. Martin published as an engraving by H. Cock as the work of H. Bosch. Here the saint sits on horseback in a boat, surrounded by quarrelling, crippled beggars.

Catalogue of paintings

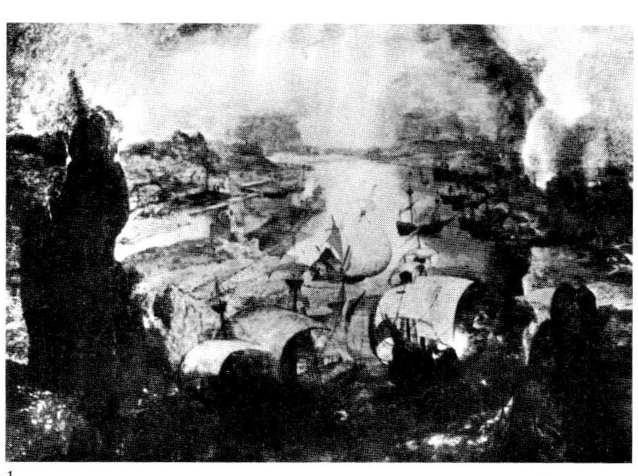

1

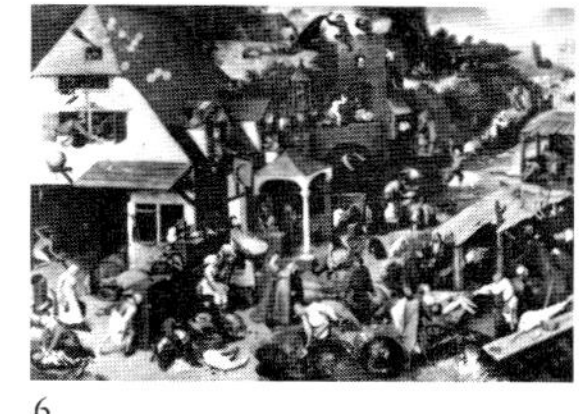

6

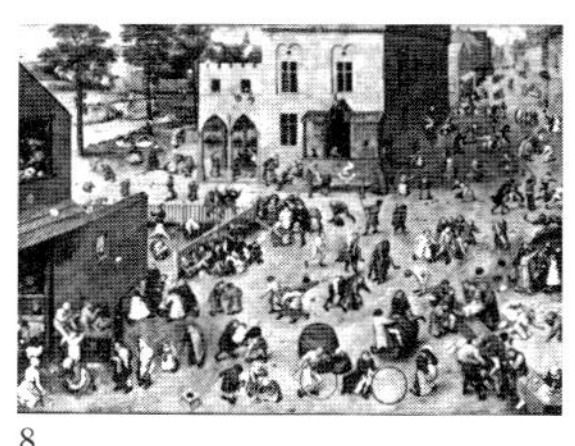

8

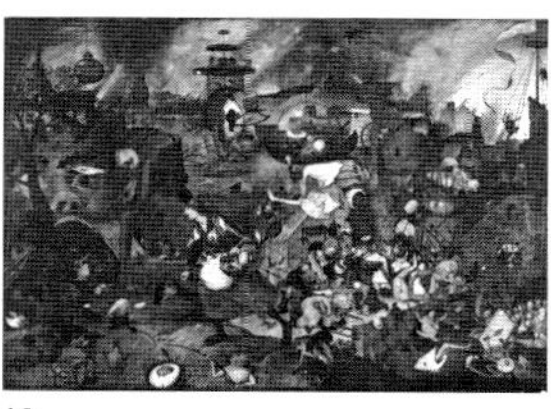

10

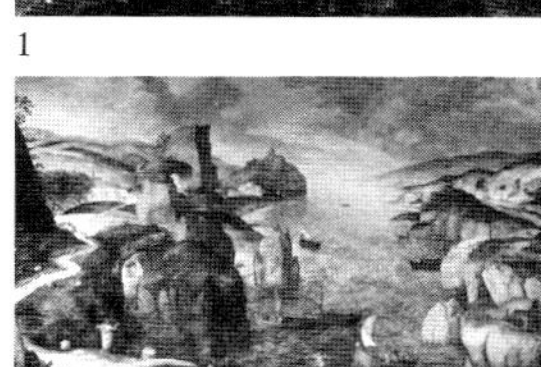

2

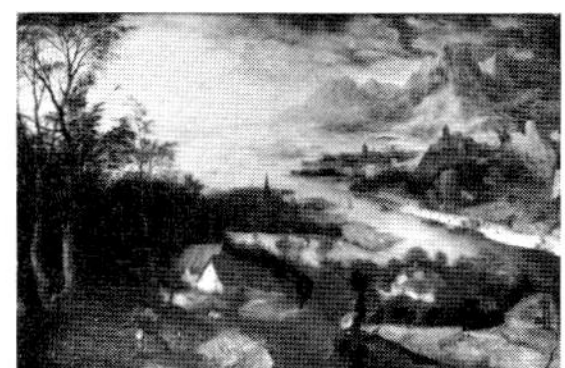

4

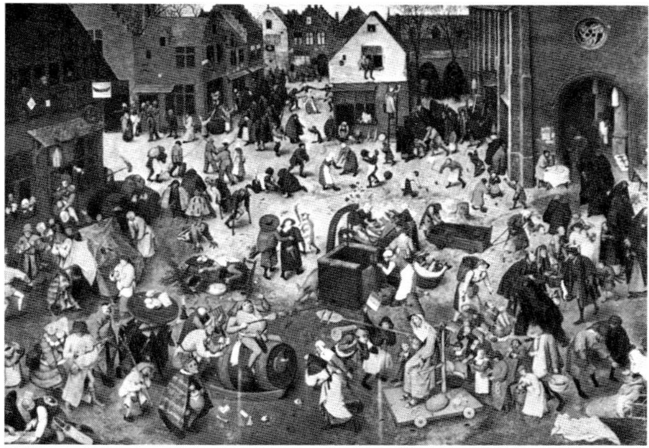

7

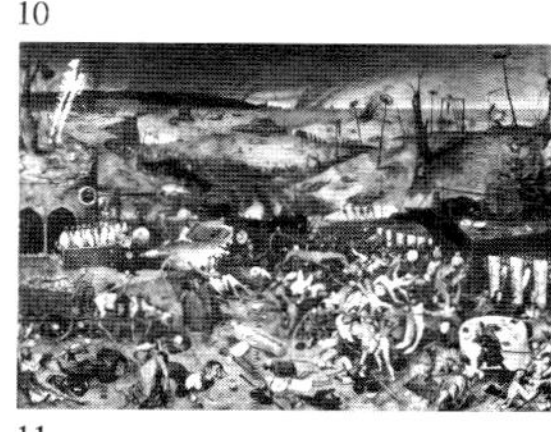

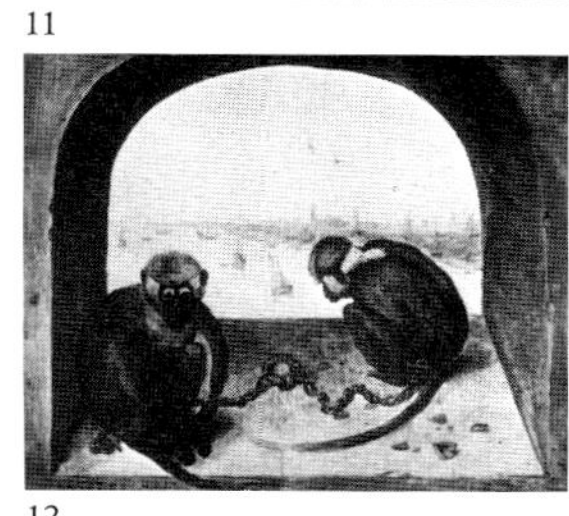

11

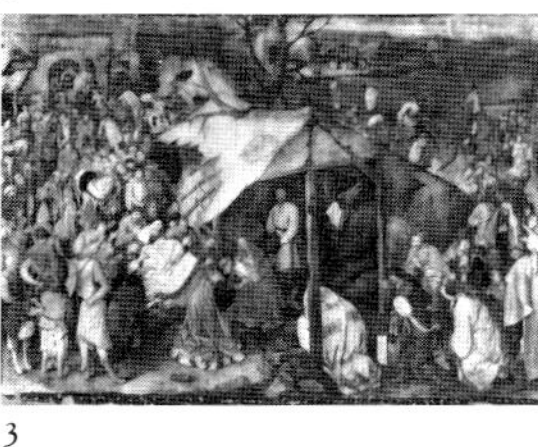

3

5

9

12

1. Landscape with sailing ships and a burning town
Oil on panel;
24.4 x 34.8 cm (9⅗ x 13¾ in)
c. 1552–1553
Dortmund, Becker Collection

2. Landscape with Christ appearing to the Apostles at the Sea of Tiberias
Oil on panel;
67 x 100 cm (26⅖ x 39½ in)
Signed and dated:
P. BRVEGHEL 1553
New York, private collection

3. The adoration of the Magi
Tempera on canvas;
115.5 x 163 cm (45¼ x 64⅖ in)
c. 1556
Brussels, Musées Royaux des Beaux-Arts

4. Landscape with the Parable of the Sower
Oil on panel;
74 x 102 cm (29⅛ x 40⅛ in)
Signed and dated: . . VEGHEL 1557
San Diego (California), Timken Art Gallery

5. View of the Bay of Naples
Oil on panel;
39.8 x 69.5 cm (15⅗ x 27⅜ in)
c. 1556
Rome, Galleria Doria Pamphili

6. Netherlandish proverbs
Oil on panel;
117 x 163 cm (46 x 64⅛ in)
Signed and dated: BRVEGEL 1559
Berlin, Staatliche Museum, Preussischer Kulturbesitz

7. Battle between Carnival and Lent
Oil on panel;
118 x 164.5 cm (46⅛ x 64¾ in)
Signed and dated: BRVEGEL 1559
Vienna, Kunsthistorisches Museum

8. Children's games
Oil on panel;
118 x 161 cm (46⅛ x 63⅜ in)
Signed and dated: BRVEGEL 1560
Vienna, Kunsthistorisches Museum

9. The fall of the rebel angels
Oil on panel;
117 x 162 cm (46 x 63¾ in)
Signed and dated:
M.D. LXII BRVEGEL
Brussels, Musées Royaux des Beaux-Arts

10. Dulle Griet (Mad Meg)
Oil on panel;
115 x 161 cm (45¼ x 63⅜ in)
The signature and part of the date are missing: ...MDLXI 1562
Antwerp, Museum Mayer van der Bergh

11. The triumph of death
Oil on panel;
117 x 162 cm (46 x 63¾ in)
c. 1562
Madrid, Prado

12. Two monkeys
Oil on panel;
20 x 23 cm (7⅞ x 9 in)
Signed and dated: BRVEGEL MDLXII
Berlin, Staatliche Museen, Preussischer Kulturbesitz

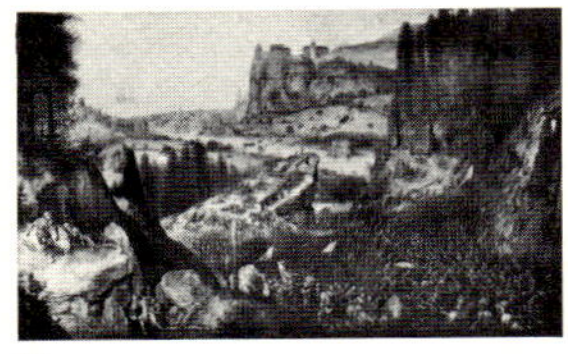

13

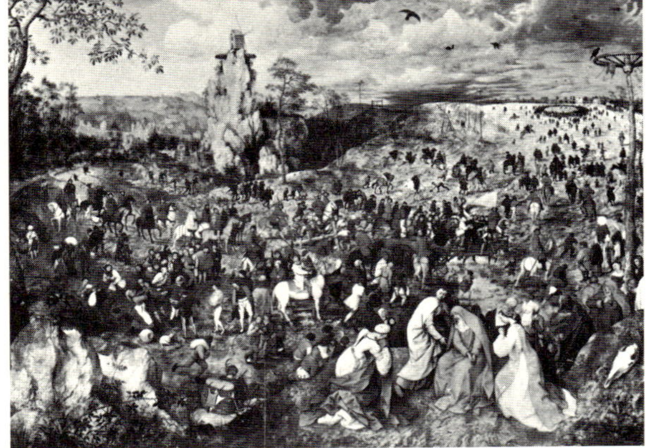

17

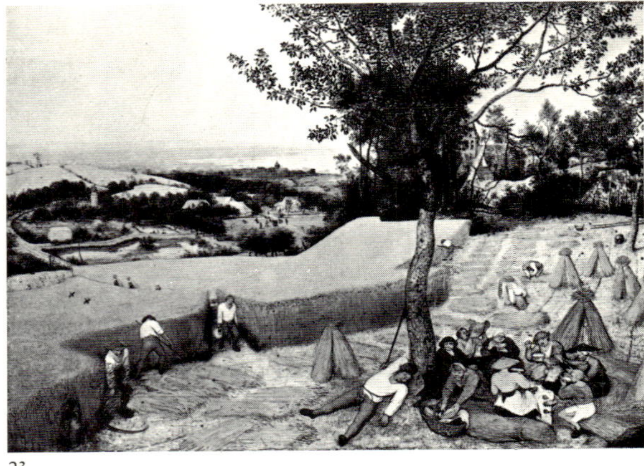

23

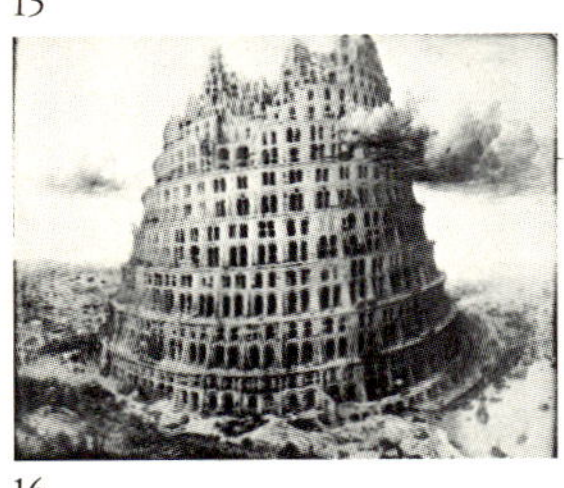

14

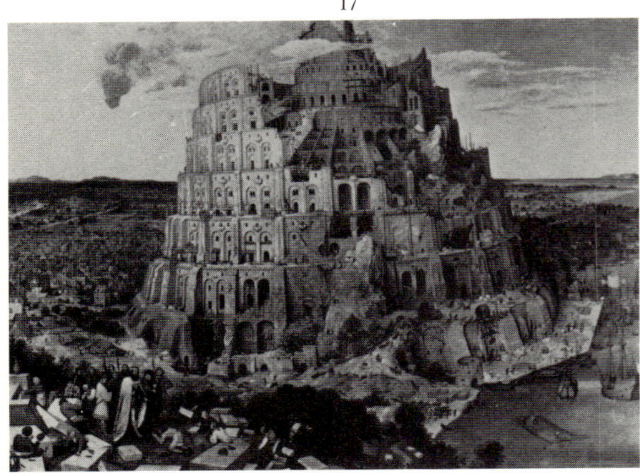

15

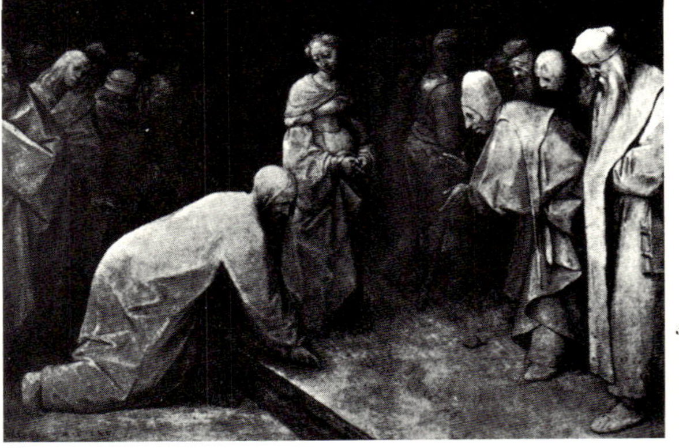

20

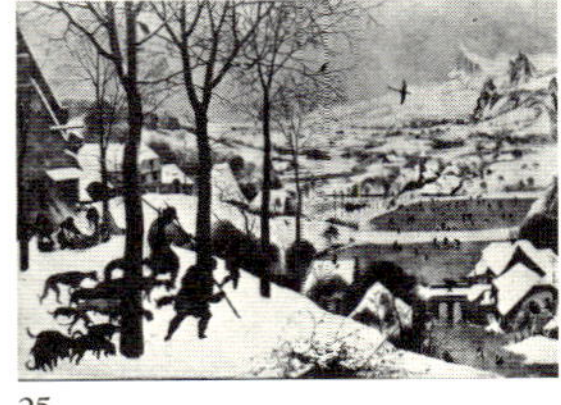

25

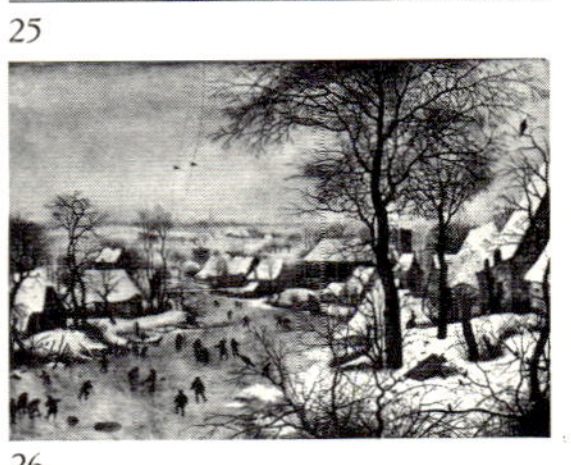

26

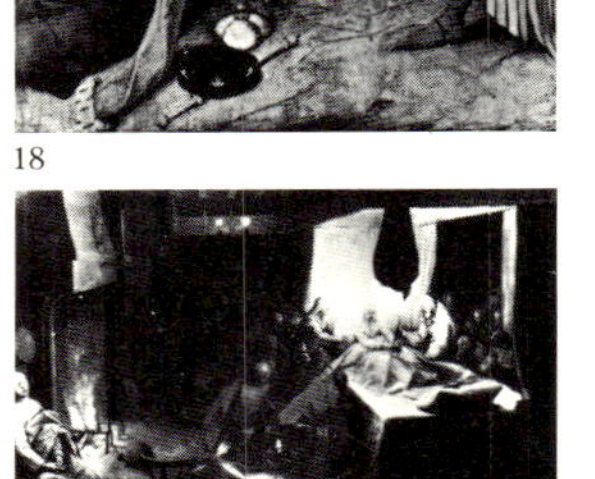

16

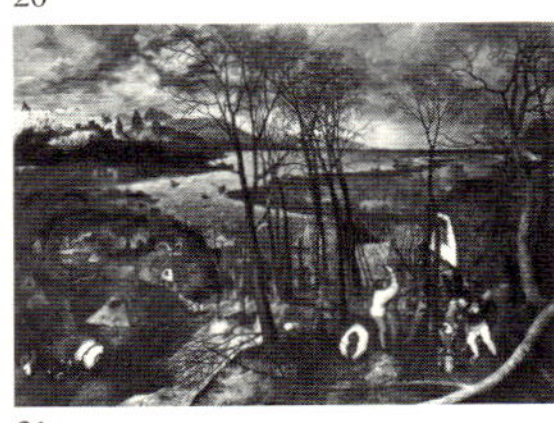

21

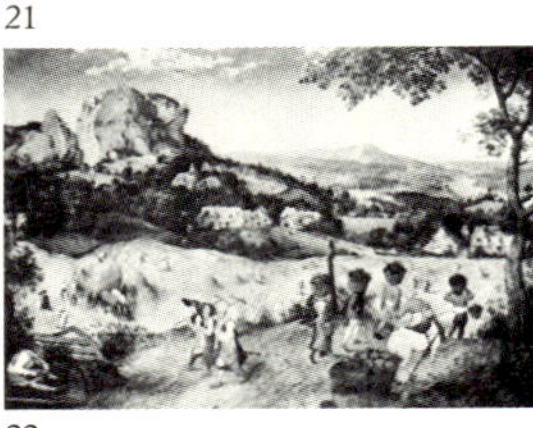

22

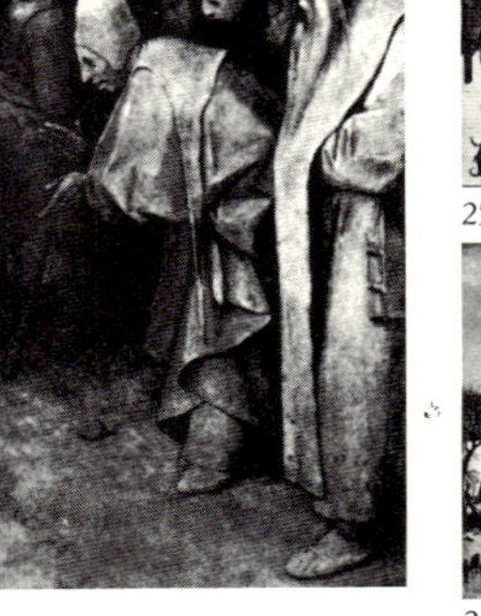

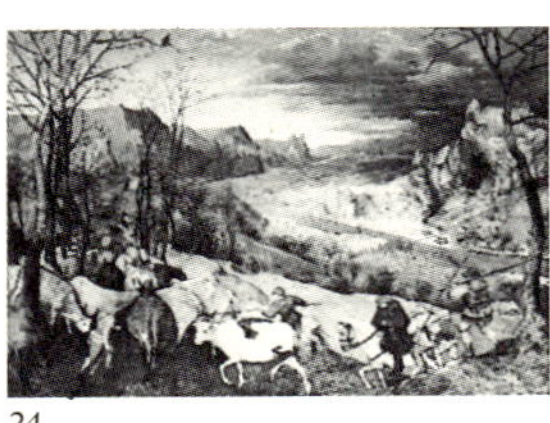

24

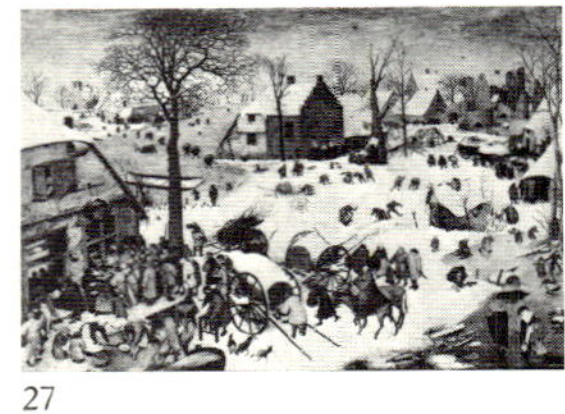

27

13. The suicide of Saul
Oil on panel;
33.5 x 55 cm ($13\frac{1}{4}$ x $21\frac{5}{8}$ in)
(4 cm at top and 1 cm at
bottom added later)
Autographic signature and
date:
SAVL XXXI. CAP. BRVEGEL.
M.CCCCC. LXII
Vienna, Kunsthistorisches
Museum

14. The flight into Egypt
Oil on panel;
37.2 x 55.5 cm ($14\frac{5}{8}$ x $27\frac{7}{8}$ in)
Signed and dated: BRVEGEL
MDLXIII
London, Courtauld Institute
(formerly in the collection of
Count A. Seilern)

15. The Tower of Babel
Oil on panel;
114 x 155 cm ($44\frac{7}{8}$ x 61 in)
Signed and dated: BRVEGEL FE.
M. CCCCC. LXIII
Vienna, Kunsthistorisches
Museum

16. The Tower of Babel
Oil on panel; 60 x 74.5 cm
($23\frac{5}{8}$ x $29\frac{3}{8}$ in)
Neither signed nor dated
c. 1563
Rotterdam, Museum Boymans
– van Beuningen

17. Christ carrying the cross
Oil on panel;
124 x 170 cm ($48\frac{3}{4}$ x $66\frac{7}{8}$ in)
Signed and dated: BRVEGEL
MD.LXIIII.
Vienna, Kunsthistorisches
Museum

**18. The adoration of the
Magi**
Oil on panel;
111 x 83.5 cm ($43\frac{3}{4}$ x $32\frac{3}{4}$ cm)
Signed and dated: BRVEGEL
M.D.LXIIII.
London, National Gallery

19. The death of the Virgin
Grisaille on panel;
36 x 55 cm ($14\frac{1}{2}$ x 22 in)
Signed: BRVEGEL
Illegible traces of a date
c. 1564
Banbury, Upton House,
National Trust

**20. Christ and the woman
taken in adultery**
Grisaille on panel;
24.1 x 34 cm ($9\frac{1}{2}$ x $13\frac{3}{8}$ in)
Signed and dated: BRVEGEL.
M.L. LXV.
London Courtauld Institute
(formerly in the collection of
Count A. Seilern)

21. The gloomy day
Oil on panel;
118 x 163 cm ($46\frac{1}{2}$ x $64\frac{1}{8}$ in)
Signed and dated: BRVEGEL
MDLXV
Vienna, Kunsthistorisches
Museum

22. Haymaking
Oil on panel;
117 x 161 cm (46 x $63\frac{3}{8}$ in)
Neither signed nor dated
1565
Prague, Narod ni Galerie

23. The corn harvest
Oil on panel;
118 x 160.7 cm ($46\frac{1}{2}$ x
$63\frac{1}{4}$ in)
Signed and dated:
BRVEGEL......LXV
1565
New York, Metropolitan
Museum of Art

24. The return of the herd
Oil on panel;
117 x 159 cm (46 x $62\frac{5}{8}$ in)
Signed and dated: BRVEGEL
MDLXV.
Vienna, Kunsthistorisches
Museum

25. Hunters in the snow
Oil on panel;
117 x 162 cm (46 x $63\frac{3}{4}$ in)
Signed and dated: BRVEGEL
M.D.LXV.
Vienna, Kunsthistorisches
Museum

**26. Winter landscape with
skaters and a bird-trap**
Oil on panel;
38 x 56 cm (15 x 22 in)
Signed and dated: BRVEGEL.
M.D.LXV
Brussels, F. Delporte
Collection

27. The census at Bethlehem
Oil on panel; 115.5 x
163.5 cm ($45\frac{1}{2}$ x $64\frac{1}{8}$ in)
Signed and dated: BRVEGEL
1566
Brussels, Musées Royaux des
Beaux-Arts

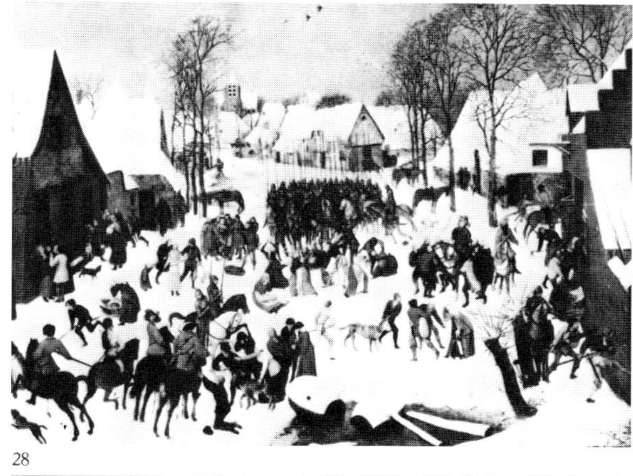

28

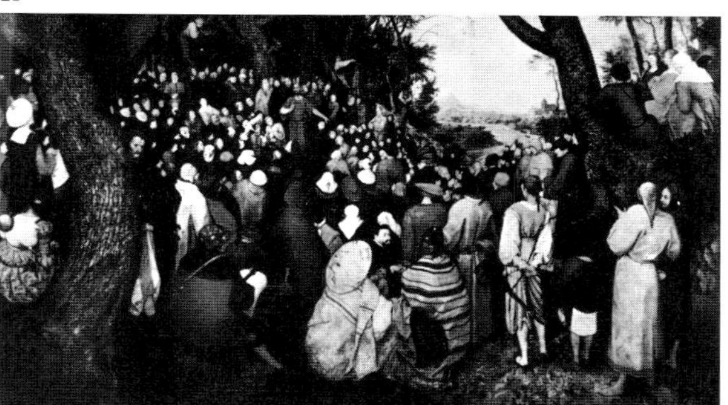

29

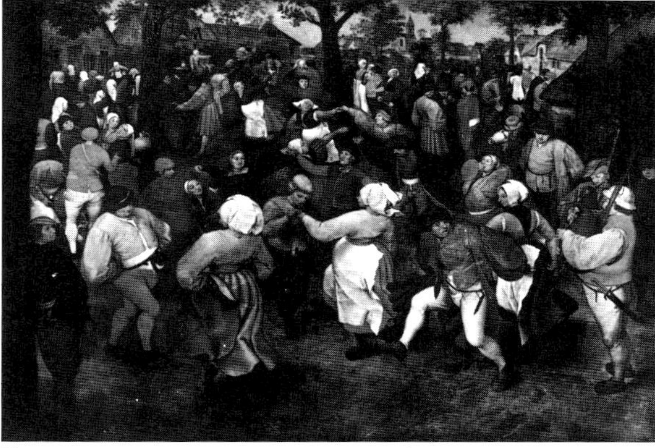

30

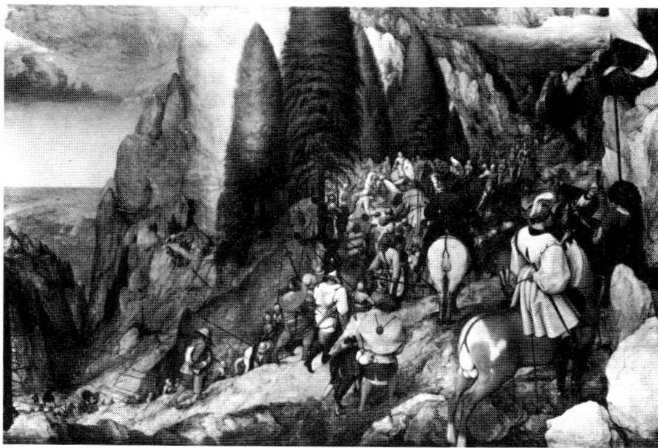

31

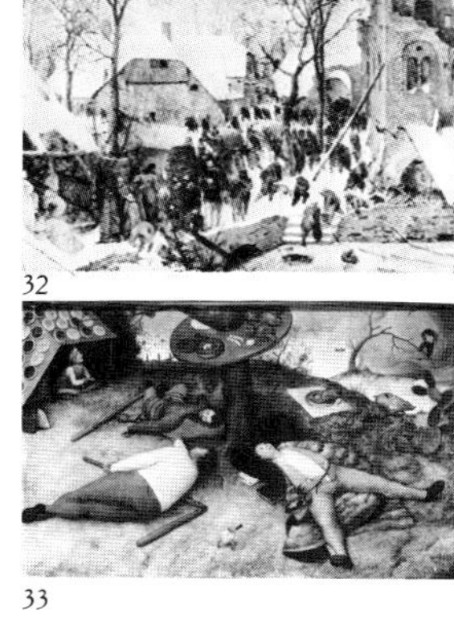

32

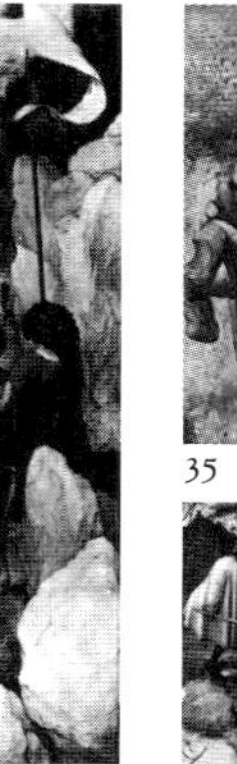

33

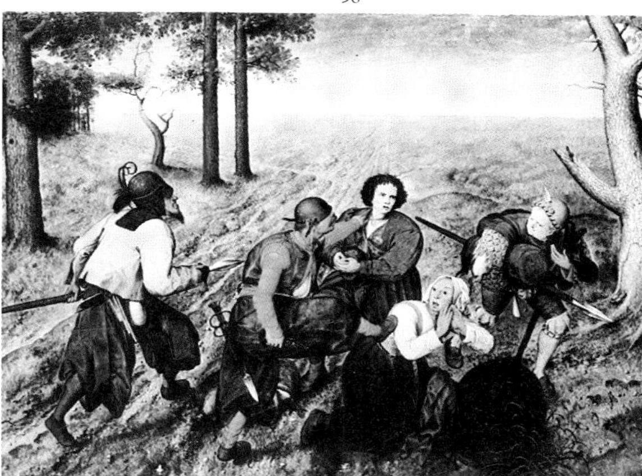

34

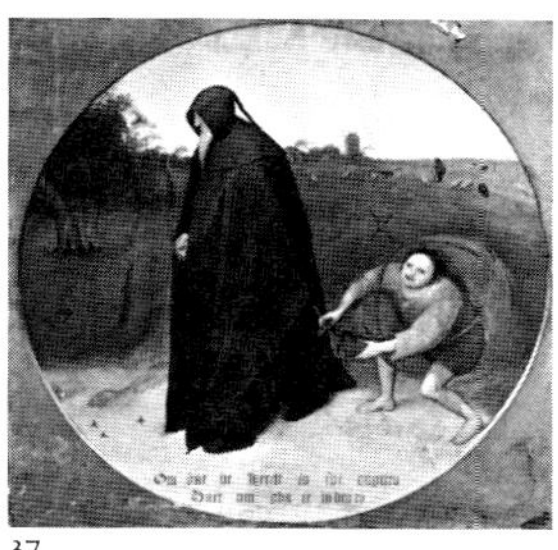

35

36

37

28. The massacre of the innocents
Oil on panel;
109.2 x 154.9 cm (43 x 61 in)
Neither signed nor dated
Hampton Court Palace, Royal Collection

29. The sermon of St. John the Baptist
Oil on panel;
95 x 160.5 cm (37⅜ x 63½ in)
Signed and dated: BRVEGEL. M.D.LXVI.
Budapest, Szépmüvészeti Múzeum

30. The peasant wedding dance
Oil on panel;
119 x 157 cm (47 x 62 in)
Not signed; dated:
M.D.LXVI
Detroit, Institute of Arts

31. The conversion of Saul
Oil on panel; 108 x 156 cm (42½ x 61⅜ in)
Signed and dated: BRVEGEL M.D. LXVII.
Vienna, Kunsthistorisches Museum

32. The adoration of the Magi in the snow
Oil on panel; 35 x 55 cm (13¾ x 21⅝ in)
Signed and dated: M.D.LXVII / BRVEGEL
Winterthur, O. Reinhart Collection

33. The Land of Cockaigne
Oil on panel;
52 x 78 cm (20½ x 30¾ in)
Signed and dated: M. DLXVII BRVEGEL.
Munich, Alte Pinakothek

34. The ambush
Oil on panel;
94 x 125 cm (37 x 49¼ in)
Signed and dated: M.D. LXVII / BRVEGEL.
Stockholm, University Collection

35. The cripples
Oil on panel;
18 x 21.5 cm (7⅛ x 8½ in)
Signed and dated: BRVEGEL M.D.LXVIII.
Paris, Louvre

36. The parable of the blind
Tempera on canvas;
86 x 154 cm (33⅞ x 60⅝ in)
Signed and dated: BRVEGEL. M.D.LX.VIII.
Naples, Museo di Capodimonte

37. The misanthrope (The faithlessness of the world)
Tempera on canvas;
86 x 85 cm (33⅞ x 33½ in)
Signed and dated on the painted frame: BRVEGEL 1568
Naples, Museo di Capodimonte

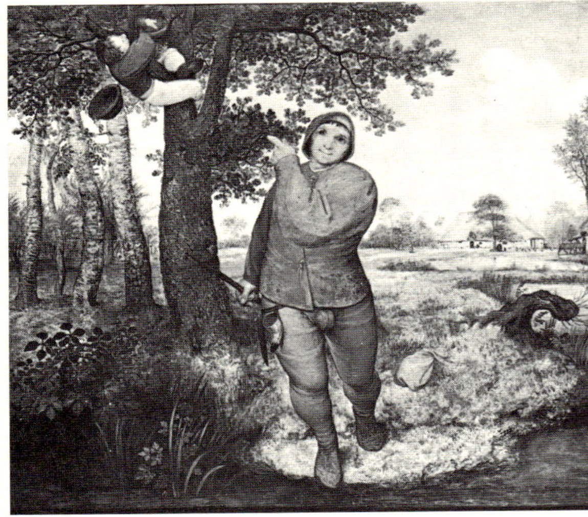

38

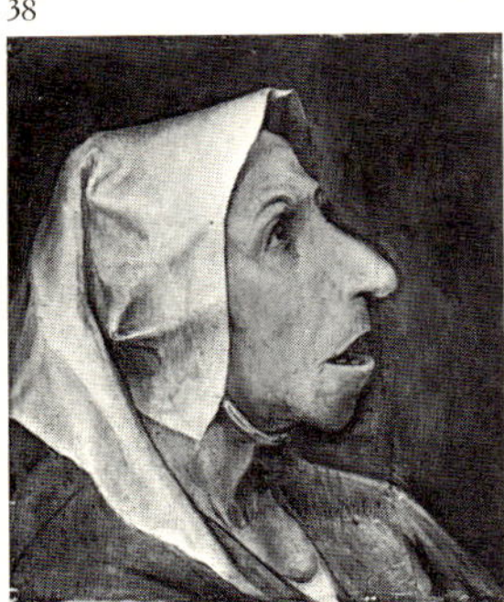

39

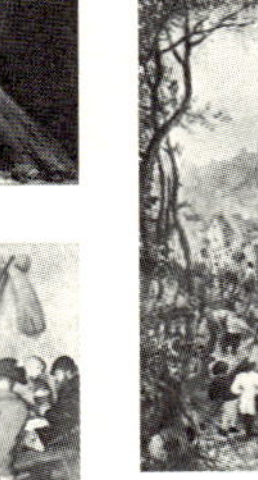
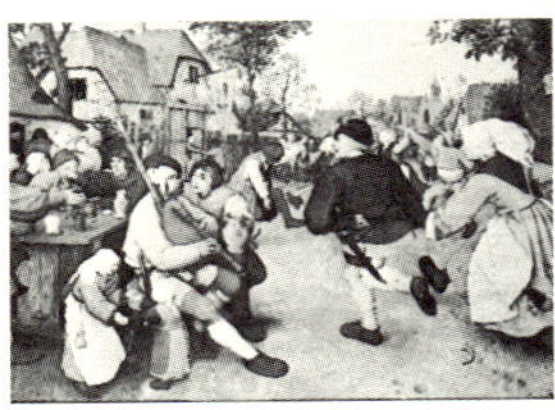

41

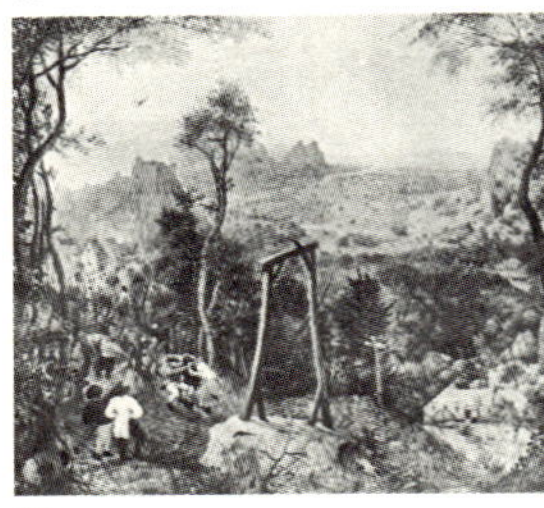

42

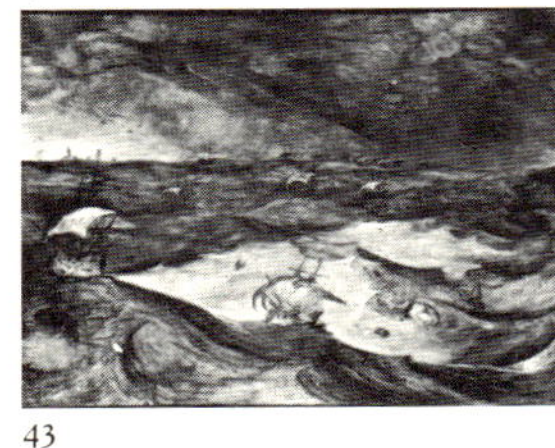

40

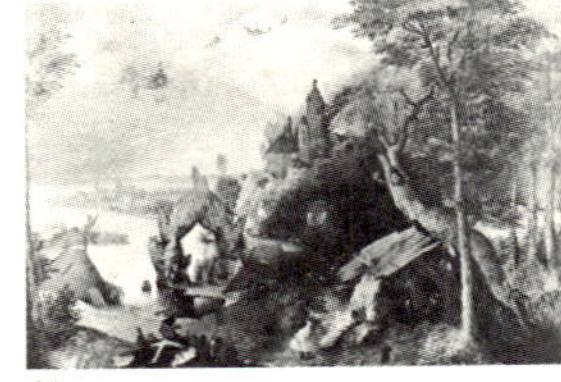

44

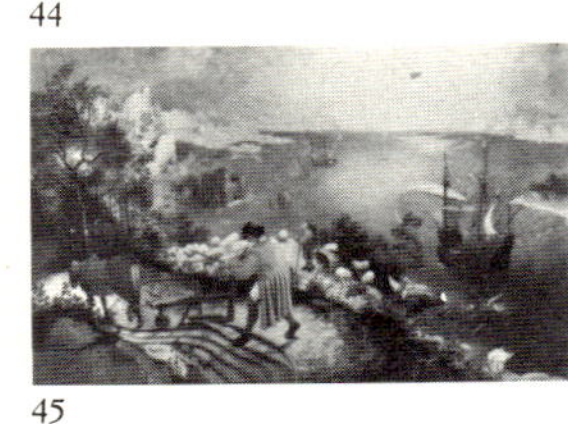

45

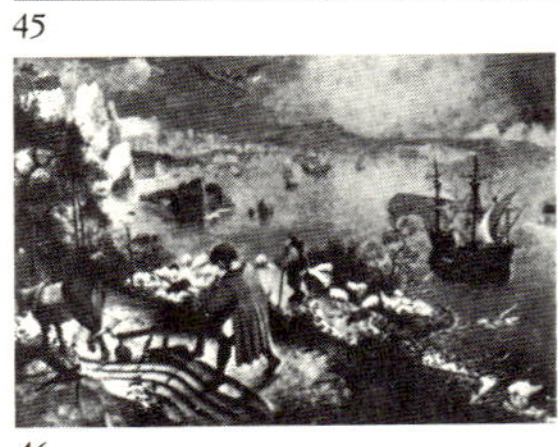

46

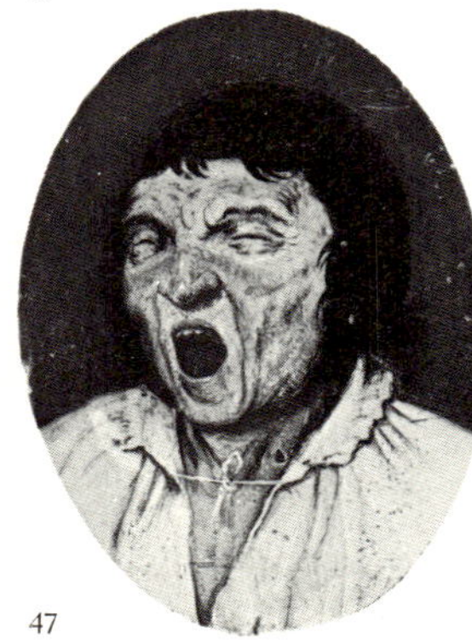

47

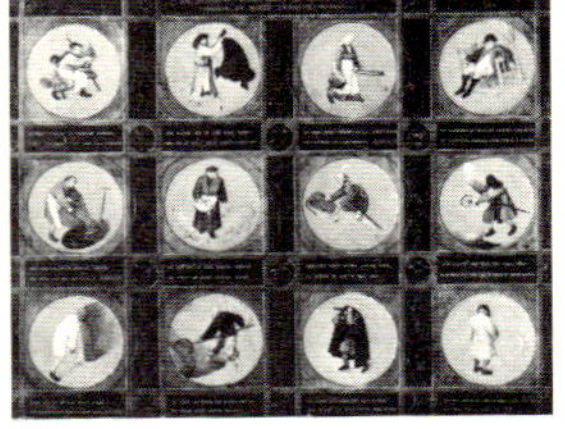

48

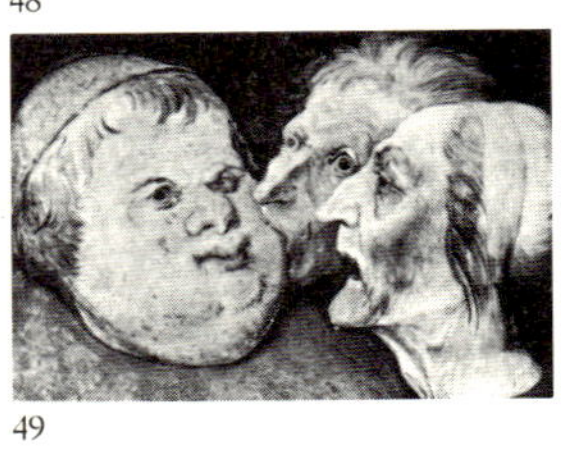

49

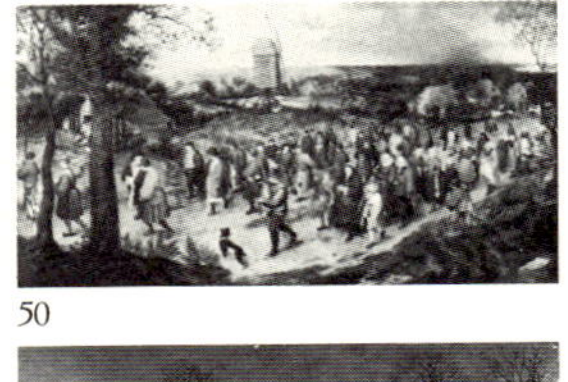

50

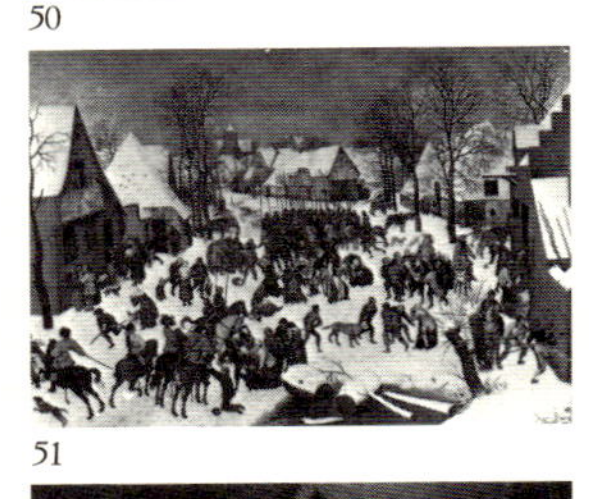

51

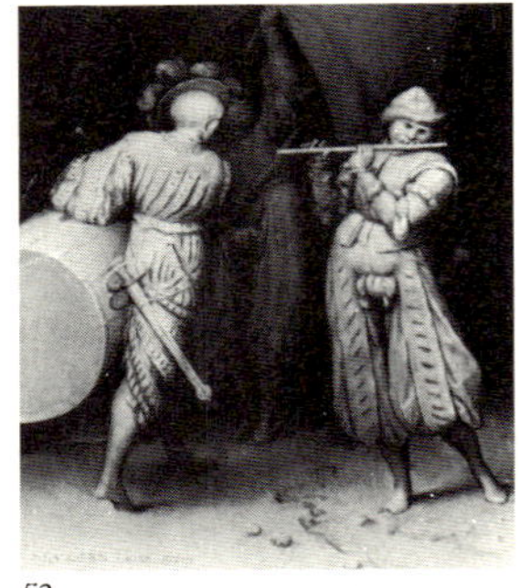

52

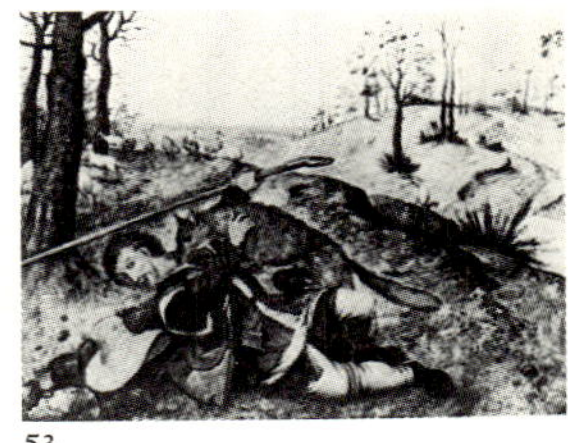

53

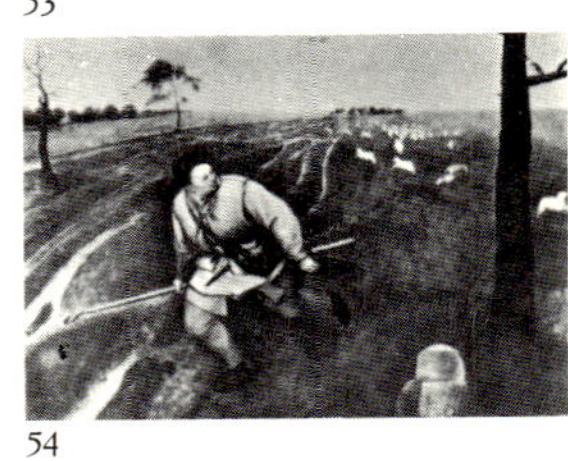

54

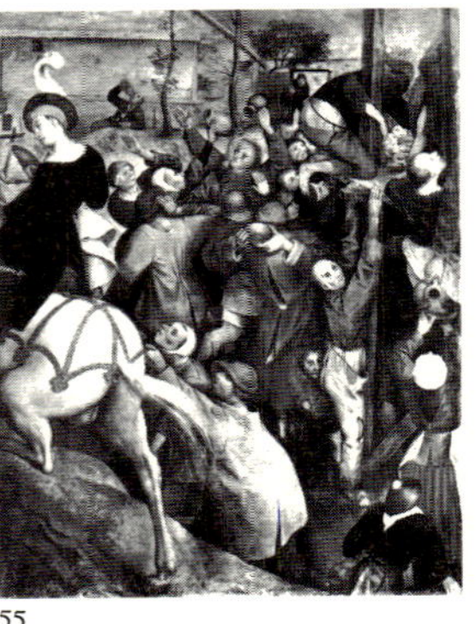

55

43

38. The peasant and the nest robber
Oil on panel; 59 x 68 cm
(23¼ x 26¾ in)
Signed and dated: BRVEGEL
MD.LXVIII
Signature and date in gold,
retouched
Vienna, Kunsthistorisches
Museum

39. Head of an old peasant woman
Oil on panel; 22 x 18 cm (8⅝
x 7⅛ in)
Neither signed nor dated
c. 1568
Munich, Alte Pinakothek

40. Peasant wedding feast
Oil on panel; 114 x 163 cm
(44⅞ x 64⅛ in)
Neither signed nor dated
c. 1568
Vienna, Kunsthistorisches
Museum

41. Peasant kermis
Oil on panel; 114 x 164 cm
(44⅞ x 64⅝ in)
Signed: BRVEGEL
Vienna, Kunsthistorisches
Museum

42. The magpie on the gallows
Oil on panel;
45.9 x 50.8 cm (8½ x 20 in)
Signed and dated: BRVEGEL
1568
Darmstadt, Hessisches
Landesmuseum

43. The storm at sea
Oil on panel;
70.3 x 97 cm (27⅞ x 38¼ in)
Neither signed nor dated
Vienna, Kunsthistorisches
Museum

44. Landscape with the temptation of St. Anthony
Oil on panel; 58.4 x 85.7 cm
(23 x 33¾ in)
Neither signed nor dated
Washington, National
Gallery, Kress Collection

45. The fall of Icarus
Oil transferred from panel to
canvas;
73.5 x 112 cm (29 x 44¼ in)
Neither signed nor dated
Brussels, Musées Royaux des
Beaux-Arts

46. The fall of Icarus
Oil on panel;
63 x 90 cm (24¼ x 35½ in)
Neither signed nor dated
New York and Brussels
D. M. van Buuven Collection

47. Yawning man
Oil on oval panel;
12.6 x 9.2 cm (4¼ x 3⅝ in)
Monogrammed: P.
Brussels, Musées Royaux des
Beaux-Arts

48. Twelve proverbs
Oil on panel;
74.5 x 98.4 cm (29⅜ x 38¾ in)
Each medallion 21 cm diam.;
signature and remains of date
on twelfth proverb:
BRVEGEL... 8.
Antwerp, Museum Mayer van
dan Bergh

49. Three heads
Oil on panel; 24.7 x 33.6 cm
(9¾ x 12¼ in)
Neither signed nor dated
c. 1560?
Copenhagen, Statans Museum
for Kunst

50. Wedding procession
Oil on panel;
61.5 x 114.5 cm (24¼ x
45¼ in)
Neither signed nor dated
Brussels, City Museum

51. The massacre of the innocents
Oil on panel; 116 x 160 cm
(45⅝ x 63 in)
Signed: BRVEG.; not dated
c. 1564?
Vienna, Kunsthistorisches
Museum

52. The three soldiers
Oil (grisaille) on panel;
20.3 x 17.8 cm (7⅞ x 6⅞ in)
Signed and dated: BRVEGEL
M.D.XVIII
New York, Frick Collection

53. The good shepherd
Oil on panel; 40 x 54.5 cm
(15¾ x 21⅜ in)
Neither signed nor dated
Antwerp, Kronacker
Collection

54. The unfaithful shepherd
oil on panel; 61.6 x 86 cm
(24¼ x 33⅞ in)
Neither signed nor dated
Philadelphia, John J. Johnson
Collection

55. The feast of St. Martin
Tempera and oil on canvas;
92.5 x 73.5 cm (36½ x 28⅞ in)
(fragment)
Neither signed nor dated
Vienna, Kunsthistorisches
Museum

Bibliographical note

To give a complete compendium of the enormous amount of literature on Bruegel would be almost impossible. This literature is no longer confined to Europe: books on the work of the great Netherlandish master are now available even in Japanese, and the number of studies of individual works is constantly increasing. The selection offered here calls for one or two preliminary comments. Grossmann provides an excellent bibliography under 'Bruegel' in the *Enciclopedia Universale dell'Arte*, (volume II, Venice/Rome, 1958). The bibliography given in Robert L. Delevoy's book *Pieter Brueghel*, (Geneva, 1959), is also exhaustive; finally, more recent and up-to-date bibliographies can be found in the monographs by W. Stechow (1969) and Marijnissen (1969). An essential contribution is the work by René van Bastelaer and Georges Hulin de Loo, *Pieter Bruegel l'Ancien, son oeuvre et son temps*, (Brussels 1907), in which Bastelaer covers the drawings and de Loo the paintings. It contains the first complete list of engravings taken from works by Bruegel. Particularly important, in my view, are the monographs by G. Jedlicka (1936 and 1947) and F Grossmann (last edition 1966; a second volume is to be published, containing a catalogue of Bruegel's works). Grossmann also gives a detailed account of sources and a history of critical works on Bruegel since the 16th century. Indispensable to any study of the graphic works are the complete edition of the drawings by L. Münz (1961) and the catalogue of the 1975 Berlin exhibition entitled 'Pieter Bruegel d. A. als Zeichner'. A stimulating if controversial interpretation of Bruegel's oeuvre is offered in H. Sedlmayr's lengthy essay on Bruegel's 'Macchia' (1934). Finally, there are G. Stridbeck's studies of the Netherlandish master (Stockholm, 1956).

SOURCES:

L. Guicciardini, *Descrittione di tutti i Paesi Bassi*, Antwerp 1567

G. Vasari, *Le vite de' più eccellenti pittori, scultori e architettori*, 2nd edition, Florence 1568

D. Lampsonius, *Pictorum aliquot celebrium Germaniae inferioris effigies*, Antwerp 1572 (critical edition by J. Puraye, *Les effigies des Peintres célèbres des Pays-Bas*, Bruges, 1956)

A. Ortelius, *Album amicorum*, Antwerp 1574–1596 (unpublished manuscript at Pembroke College, Cambridge; translated by F. Grossmann, published by A. E. Popham in the *Burlington Magazine*, London, LIX, 1931, pp. 184ff. and in W. Stechow, *Northern Renaissance Art 1400-1600. Sources and Documents*, Englewood Cliffs, N.Y., Prentice Hall 1966, pp. 38 ff. French edition by J. Puraye in *The Gulden Passer*, Antwerp 1967–1968)

C. van Mander, *Het Schilder-Boeck*, Haarlem 1604

Ph. Rombouts and Th. van Lerius, *De Liggeren en andere historische Archieven der Antwerpsche Sint-Lucasgilde*, I, The Hague 1872

J. Denucé, *De Antwerpsche 'Konstkamers'. Inventarissen van Kurstverzamelingen ten Antwerpen in de 16e en 17e eeuwen*, Amsterdam 1932

HISTORY:

H. Pirenne, *Geschichte Belgiens*, Gotha 1899–1907

J. Huizinga, *L'autunno del Medio Evo*, transl. by B. Jasink, Florence 1966

BIOGRAPHY AND PAINTINGS:

A. Romdahl, *Pieter Brueghel der Ältere und sein Kunstschaffen, in Jahrbuch der Kunsthistorischen Sammlungen des Allerochsten Kaiserhauses*, XXV, 1904–1905, pp. 85 ff

R. van Bastelaer and G. Hulin de Loo, *Pieter Brugel l'Ancien, son oeuvre et son temps*, Brussels 1907

F. Winkler, *Die altniederländische Malerei*, Berlin 1924

E. Michel, *Bruegel*, Paris 1931

Ch. de Tolnay, *Pierre Bruegel l'Ancien*, Brussels 1935

M. J. Friedländer, *Die altniederländische Malerei*, vol. XIV, Leyden

G. Jedlicka, *Pieter Bruegel, der Maler in seiner Zeit*, Erlenbach-Zurich 1938, 2nd edition 1957

M. Dvoràk, *Die Gemälde Pieter Bruegel des Älteren*, Vienna 1941

V. Denis, *Tutta la pittura di Pieter Bruegel*, Milan 1952

G. Faggin, *Brueghel*, Verona 1953

G. Glück, *Peter Brueghel the Elder*, New York 1955 (the latest of the many revised editions)

F. Grossman, *Bruegel: The Paintings*, London 1955, 2nd ed. in German, English and Dutch, London-Cologne-Amsterdam 1966

M. Auner, *Pieter Bruegel, Umrisse eines Lebensbildes, in Jahrbuch der Kunsthistorischen Sammlungen in Wien*, 52, XVI, 1956, pp. 51 ff

C. G. Stridbeck, *Bruegelstudien*, Stockholm 1956

R. L. Delevoy, *Pieter Brueghel*, Geneva 1959

F. Grossman, 'Bruegel', in *Enciclopedia Universale dell'Arte*, vol. II, Venice-Rome 1958

G. W. Menzel, *Pieter Bruegel der Ältere*, Leipzig 1966

G. Arpino and P. Bianconi, *L'opera completa di Bruegel*, Milan 1967

R. H. Marijnissen, *Brugel de Oude*, Brussels 1969; German transl., Stuttgart 1969

W. Stechow, *Pieter Bruegel*, New York 1969; Italian ed. Milan 1971; German ed. Cologne 1974, 1977

DRAWINGS:

Ch. de Tolnay, *Die Zeichnungen Pieter Bruegels*, Zurich 1952

L. Münz, *Bruegel, The Drawings*, London 1961, German transl. London-Cologne 1961

Catalogue of the exhibition 'Pieter Bruegel d.A. als Zeichner', Kupferstichkabinett, Berlin 1975

ENGRAVINGS:

R. van Bastelaer, *Les estampes de Peter Bruegel l'Ancien*, Brussels 1908

E. Feinblatt, *Prints and drawings of Pieter Bruegel the Elder*, catalogue of the exhibition of the Los Angeles Country Museum, Los Angeles 1961

H. A. Klein, *Graphic Worlds of Peter Bruegel the Elder*, New York 1963

J. Lavalleye, *Peter Bruegel the Elder and Lucas van Leyden, The complete Engravings, Etchings and Woodcuts*, New York 1967

L Leeber, *Bruegel, Le stampe*, Florence 1967

MISCELLANEOUS STUDIES:

W. Fraenger, *Der Bauern-Bruegel und das deutsche Sprichwort*, Erlenbach-Zurich 1923

F. Lugt, *Pieter Bruegel und Italien, in Festschrift für Max Friedländer*, Leipzig 1927, pp. 111 ff.

H. Sedlmayr, 'Die "macchia" Bruegels', in *Jahrbuch der Kunsthistorischen Sammlungen in Wien*, Neue Folge, 1934, pp. 237 ff.: reprinted in H. Sedlmayr, *Epochen und Werke*, I, Vienna-Munich 1959, pp. 274 ff

A. J. J. Delen, *Histoire de la gravure dans les anciens Pays-Bas et dans les Provinces Belges*, second part, *Le XVI siècle, I, Les graveurs-illustrateurs, II. Les graveurs d'estampes*, Paris 1934–1935

J. Grauls, *De Spreekworden van P. Bruegel den Oude verklaard*, Antwerp 1938

J. G. Gelder and J. Borms, *Brueghels Deugden en hoofdzonden*. Amsterdam 1939

L. Leeber, 'De blauwe buyck', in *Gentsche Bijdragen tot de Kunstgeschiedenis*, VI, Ghent 1939–1940, pp. 167 ff

Ch. Terlinden, 'Pierre Bruegel le Vieux et l'histoire' in *Revue belge d'archéologie et d'histoire de l'art* XII, Brussels 1942. pp. 229 ff

J. B. F. van Gils, 'Bruegel's Vasten-avond-gangers', in *Maandblad voor beeldende Kunsten*, XX, 1943, pp. 97 ff

W. Vanbeselaer, *Pieter Bruegel en het nederlandsche manierisme*, Tielt 1944

S. J. Gudlaugsson, 'Wat heeft Pieter Bruegel met zijn "Bedelaars" bedoeld?', in *Kunsthistorisches Medelingen* II, The Hague 1957, pp. 32 ff

F. Novotnu, *Die Monatsbilder Pieter Bruegels d.A.*, Vienna 1948

B. Knipping, *Pieter Bruegel de Oude: De Val der opstandige Engelen*, Leyden 1949

K. Boström, 'Das Sprichwort vom Vogelnest', in *Kunsthistorisk Tidskrift*, XVIII, Stockholm 1949, pp. 77 ff

H. Gerson, 'Overzicht van de Litteratuur betreffende Nederlandsch Kunst', in *Oud Holland*, LXIV, 1949, pp. 205 ff

Ch. de Tolnay, 'Bruegel et l'Italie', in *Les Arts Plastiques*, Brussels 1951, pp. 121 ff

E. van der Vossen, 'De "Maandenreeks" van Pieter Bruegel de Ouden' in *Oud Holland* LXVI, 1951, pp. 103 ff

H. Keller, 'Zur Deutung von Pieter Bruegels "Vogeldieb"', in *Neue Zürcher Zeitung* of 28/1/1971

F. Grossman, 'Bruegel's *Woman taken in Adultery* and Other Grisailles', in the *Burlington Magazine*, No. 593, vol. XCIV, 1952, pp. 218 ff

C. Bossus, 'Sur la date de naissance de Bruegel le Vieux', in *Gazette des Beux-Arts*, 6th period, vol. XLI, 95th annual, 1953, pp. 124 ff

O. Benesch, 'Besprechung von Ch. de Tolnay, The Drawings of Pieter Bruegel the Elder' (1952), in *Kunstchronik*, VI, 1953, pp. 76 ff

F. Grossmann, 'The Drawings of Pieter Bruegel the Elder in the Museum Boymans and Some Problems of Attribution', in *Bulletin Museum Boymans*, V, 1954, pp. 34 ff

C. G. Stridbeck, '"Stormen". Nagra synpunkter pa ett attributions problem', in *Kunsthistorisk Tidskrift*, XXIV, 1955, pp. 34 ff

L. Lebeer, 'Le pays de Cocagne', in *Bulletin Musées Royaux des Beaux-Arts*, IV, Erwin Panofsky, M.scellany, 1955, pp. 199 ff

I. Bergström, 'The Iconological Origin of "Spes" by Pieter Bruegel the Elder', in *Nederlands Kunsthistorisch Jaarboek*, VII, 1956, pp. 53 ff

J. Grauls, *Volkstaal en volksleven in het werk van Pieter Bruegel*, Antwerp-Amsterdam 1957

H. Sedlmayr, 'Pieter Bruegel: Der Sturz der Blinden', in *Hefte des Kunsthistorischen Seminars der Universität, München*, 2. 1957, pp. 1 ff; in H. Sedelmayr, Epochen und Werke, I, Vienna-Munich 1959, pp. 319 ff

O. Benesch, 'Zur Frage der Kopien nach Pieter Bruegel, in *Bulletin Musées Royaux des Beaux-Arts*', vol. 8, 1–2, 1959, pp. 35 ff

F. Grossmann, 'New Light on Bruegel: Documents and Additions to the Oeuvre; Problems of Form', in the *Burlington Magazine*, No. 678/9, vol. CI, 1959, pp. 341 ff

F. Grossmann, 'Bruegel Verhältnis zu Raffael und zur Raffael-Nachfolge', in *Festschrift für Kurt Badt*, Berlin 1961, pp. 135 ff

F. Smekens, 'Het schip bij Pieter Bruegel de Oude: een authenticit eits criterium?', in *Jaarboek Koniklijk Museum voor Schone Kunste*, Antwerp 1961, op. 5 ff

Index

Photographic References

a = above; b = below; c = centre; l = left; r = right

Archivio AME: pp. 8, 9l. Arte Fotografica: pp. 27, 28-29. Corvina Archivum: pp. 134-135, 136-137. DGM: pp. 56b, 57, 77, 88-89. Freunde der Kunsthalle E.V.: p. 152. Lichtbildwerkstatte Alpenland: pp. 6, 19, 21. 34, 42a, 49b, 50a, 54, 55, 63, 65, 126, 127, 154. Parisio: pp. 162-163. H. Petersen: p. 59. Photo Mayer, jacket, pp. 2-3, 52-53, 78-79, 80-81, 86-87, 93, 96-97, 102, 103-104, 122-123, 166-167, 178-189. Service de documentation photographique de la réunion des Musées Nationaux, pp. 9r, 14 Studio Meusy: p. 73b. Studio 7: p. 70.

All photographs not quoted have been kindly provided by the Museums and Collections in which the works are housed, whose names appear in the relevant captions.